EMPIRE BY DEFAULT

EMPIRE BY DEFAULT

THE SPANISH-AMERICAN WAR AND THE DAWN OF THE AMERICAN CENTURY

Ivan Musicant

A MARIAN WOOD BOOK
Henry Holt and Company
New York

Henry Holt and Company, Inc.
Publishers since 1866
115 West 18th Street
New York, New York 10011

Henry Holt® is a registered
trademark of Henry Holt and Company, Inc.

Published in Canada by Fitzhenry & Whiteside Ltd.,
195 Allstate Parkway, Markham, Ontario L3R 4T8.

LIBRARY OF CONGRESS CATALOGING-IN-PUBLICATION DATA
Musicant, Ivan, date.
Empire by default: the Spanish-American War and the dawn of the
American century / Ivan Musicant.—1st ed.
p.   cm.
Includes bibliographical references and index.
ISBN 0-8050-3500-1 (HB: acid-free paper)
1. Spanish-American War, 1898. I. Title.
E715.M97   1998   97-28238
973.8'9—dc21   CIP

Henry Holt books are available for special promotions and
premiums. For details contact: Director, Special Markets.

First Edition 1998

Designed by Kathryn Parise

Printed in the United States of America
All first editions are printed on acid-free paper. ∞

1 3 5 7 9 10 8 6 4 2

For Max

CONTENTS

ACKNOWLEDGMENTS

I express my appreciation to the University of Minnesota libraries, the Minnesota Historical Society, and the Linden Hills branch of the Minneapolis Public Library, whose assistance, as always, was vital for the completion of this work. Special gratitude goes to my editor, Marian Wood, at Henry Holt.

EMPIRE BY DEFAULT

CHAPTER 1

STATE OF THE UNION

Whether they will or no, Americans must now begin to look outward.

—*Captain Alfred Thayer Mahan, USN,*
December 1890

On the warm evening of July 12, in the exciting Chicago summer of 1893, Frederick Jackson Turner, a young history don at the University of Wisconsin, rose to speak before a stellar audience of international scholars. The setting was superb, the extravaganza of the World's Columbian Exposition, America's self-conscious debut commemorating four hundred years of progress since Christopher Columbus claimed the New World for the king and queen of Spain. Here on the shores of Lake Michigan, a gleaming white and gilt beaux arts temporary city rose to herald the remarkable achievements of the bursting new colossus of the Western Hemisphere. World-traveled tourists marveled at the breathtaking exhibits attesting to the social and technical advancement of the United States. Everything, from the giant Corliss electric dynamo, to George Washington Ferris's 250-foot wheel, to the hootchy-kootchy girls of the "Egyptian Village," brought wide eyes and gaping mouths to tens of thousands of parasoled and straw-hatted tourists. "We were all knocked silly," said the future secretary of state, John Hay. "It beats the brag so far out of sight that even Chicago is dumb." Historian Henry Adams, grandson and great-grandson of presidents, called the fair "the first great expression of American thought as a unity."[1]

3

Compared to these manufactured wonderments, it's no surprise that Professor Turner's learned address, "The Significance of the Frontier in American History," got so little attention in the public journals, or indeed, even among his fellow historians. Federal civil service commissioner Theodore Roosevelt, no mean historian himself and a man who understood before a good many others the significance of what became the "Turner thesis" of American history, sent a polite congratulatory note: "I think you have struck some first class ideas, and have put into definite shape a good deal of thought which has been floating around rather loosely."[2]

To present the "frontier" as a driving catalyst of American history, Turner lifted a virtually unnoticed passage of enormous significance from the U.S. Census Bureau's Bulletin No. 12, of April 1891. Until the national census of 1880, the social and political map of the United States stopped at a frontier line of settlement, a pale, beyond which its statutes and civilization did not cross. A decade later, the bureau declared this unwrought world "so broken into by isolated bodies of settlement that there can hardly be said to be a frontier line. . . . It cannot, therefore, any longer have a place in the census reports." The frontier had vanished in law as well as in fact.[3]

Turner grounded his thesis on American economic power generated by "free land." America's unique individualism, nationalism, political institutions, its very democracy, depended on it. "So long as free land exists," he told the assembly, "the opportunity for . . . competency exists, and economic power secures political power." For Turner, continental expansion, symbolized by the ever moving frontier creating more free land, was the driving, dynamic factor of American progress. It had been since Christopher Columbus, and remained so until the Census Bureau erased the frontier with the keystroke of a typewriter. Without the economic energy created by expanding the frontier, he warned, America's political and social institutions would stagnate. If one adhered to this way of thinking, America must expand or die.[4]

Even as he spoke, an imbroglio between President Cleveland and the U.S. Senate over the annexation of Hawaii was in high spate, making it an extraordinary time for such observations.[5] Would the United States halt at its saltwater margins? Must expansion be defined in terms of a terrestrial line across prairie or mountains, or might it include strategic and economic projection across a "free" ocean? Turner did not say. "And now," he concluded, "four centuries from the discovery of America . . . the frontier is gone, and with its going has closed the first period of American history."[6]

While Turner's lucid thesis created hardly an inch of newspaper copy or a poke of interest among contemporary national policymakers, the reverse was true with another equally obscure historian: Gauging the pulse of the time, Captain Alfred Thayer Mahan of the U.S. Navy had no qualms about moving the frontier beyond the coastline, and three years before Turner offered his thesis, he made his case.

Born in 1840 at West Point, the son of Mary and "Old Dennis" Hart Mahan, a highly regarded, puritanical Episcopalian professor of mathematics and engineering at the U.S. Military Academy, young Alfred eschewed the army life and graduated (number two of twenty) from the Naval Academy in 1859. For thirty years, his naval career was drudgingly undistinguished. During the Civil War his sole experience of gunfire occurred when his ship arrived late for his only battle. He was decidedly uncomfortable at sea, a poor sailor and indifferent ship handler—hardly the stuff of his hero, the great David Farragut. Though Mahan was an outstanding student and intellect, his first efforts at naval history, the vocation that shot his comet across the celebrity cosmos of the 1890s, was a mind-numbingly dull account of the Civil War, *The Gulf and Inland Waters,* published in 1883.[7]

It was both Mahan's and the navy's good fortune that he caught the notice of Commodore Stephen Bleecker Luce, a broad-whiskered educational reformer during the navy's sinkhole, post–Civil War dark age. Luce had already established the Naval Apprentice Training System for enlisted sailors, and duty at the Naval Academy provided experience in molding young midshipmen. But Luce chose as his special project the revolutionary conception of graduate study in naval warfare for junior officers. The modern naval officer, Luce believed, could richly profit by a study of naval history, examining wars, leaders, theory, and battles "with the cold eye of professional criticism." Seeking a distinctly separate institution from the undergraduate Naval Academy, Annapolis, Luce submitted a proposal for a postgraduate Naval War College to the Navy Department in 1876, and there it languished for eight years.[8]

Then, in October 1884, shortly after the general reform of the service had gotten under way with modest beginnings, Navy Secretary William E. Chandler, over protests from most of the barnacled, seignioral bureau chiefs, found temporary quarters for Luce's school in an abandoned almshouse on Coaster's Harbor Island, by the torpedo station at Newport, Rhode Island. Luce, nearing sixty years old, was appointed its first commandant. "Poor little poor house," said the commodore to the small group of officers with him. "Poor little poor house, I christen thee the United States Naval War College!"[9]

Luce had begun his own systematic study of naval history almost twenty years before, in the final months of the Civil War. During that conflict, steam-driven armored warships fought on both sides, heralding eight decades of the "battleship era" in naval history. In the years that followed that war, several ironclad battles had erupted on the world's oceans, from the Pacific coast of South America to the Black Sea. Yet there were no codified principles on which to forge a canon of the new naval warfare of iron (soon to be steel) and steam. Brainy Alfred Thayer Mahan, Luce thought, might be just the man to establish them, and he invited him to join the War College faculty.

Of the two subjects Luce proposed for Mahan's syllabus of instruction, naval tactics and naval history, it was the second that gave Mahan "more anxiety." But in the summer of 1884, he could not have been further removed from the intellectual ferment beginning to bubble up slowly within the service. Mahan commanded the *Wachusett,* a twenty-year-old Civil War wooden screw-sloop, on her last commission before being sent to the knacker's yard.

In the isolation of the far Pacific station, Mahan plumbed the well of naval history, "continuously seeking" the elusive thread that bound ancient and modern maritime empires, their admirals, galleons, ships of the line, and sea battles into a cohesive, encompassing historical theory. Aboard the tired *Wachusett* there came to him "from within, the suggestion that *the control of the sea* was an historic factor which had never been systematically appreciated and expounded." This was the nut, the kernel of Mahanian philosophy that would dominate the world's naval and foreign policy councils for decades into the next century.[10]

In October 1885, Mahan, newly promoted to captain, reported to Rear Admiral Luce at the War College. A year later, he succeeded to the presidency. Ignoring the sniping that constantly pinged around the college from the mossback element in the Navy Department, Mahan buried himself in research at the New York Public Library, trying to formulate basic principles governing the art and science of naval warfare. Eventually, his concept of the history of sea power was not a simple chronology of campaigns and battles, or even an examination of tactics; instead, it concentrated on the elements that combined to make a nation powerful at sea: trade, geography, natural resources, diplomacy and naval policy, the character of the people and their government. By the autumn of 1886, Mahan had synthesized his research into a series of lectures, which he delivered to an audience of twenty student officers at the War College. Occasional speakers from the civilian world complemented the classroom; one such, a recent Harvard graduate, had just written a well-accepted, creditable history, *The Naval War of 1812;* this was Theodore Roosevelt. Both men took an instant liking to each other.

In September 1887, at the beginning of Mahan's second year at the War College, he was convinced that his lectures might equally serve as naval history for a mainstream book publisher. Not only would theories on the development of modern naval warfare be presented to the public, but publication, said Admiral Luce, would "assist the college" in its continuing bureaucratic and financial struggle "for bare existence." The Boston house of Little, Brown, and Company was persuaded to undertake the project, offering Mahan an advance of $2,500. In May 1890, the lectures, bolstered with a hefty introduction, appeared under the title *The Influence of Sea Power upon History, 1660–1783.*[11]

As a work of historical prose, the book was an improvement on the pedantic yawner that had previously come from Mahan's pen. Yet it was not the four hundred–plus pages of straight-ahead naval history that captured the world's attention, but its introduction, "Elements of Sea Power," written as a marketing tool and designed, Mahan frankly admitted, to make the book "more popular," an "attractive subject to the public." Basing his introductory theme on the contemporary condition of the United States, an industrial complex manifestly capable of producing vast surpluses, Mahan held the mirror of history for his countrymen to see in their reflection England at the seventeenth-century beginnings of her maritime empire. Each capacity of the nation had grown too large for the strictly continental market to absorb. Further, having lost the landed frontier—a political line—it must turn to the sea, its ever present, strategic geographical frontier. Reversing the traditional American thought of the oceans as a barrier against European entanglements, Mahan compared them to "a great ocean highway; or better, of a wide common, over which men pass in all directions."[15]

Mahan charted America's imperial passage away from the mercantilism of European maritime empires such as Great Britain, the Netherlands, and Spain. Their colonies were mainly sources for raw materials, and markets and outlets for manufacturing and human surplus. These outposts of empire, be they at the mouth of the St. Lawrence River, the Cape of Good Hope, Havana, or Manila Bay, naturally assumed the roles of distant naval stations to service the colonial trade and, latterly, for local defense.

Mahan separated these functions and reversed their polarity. It is a given, he said, that colonies are markets, both outlets and nursery for home industry and commerce, but this is not their true value. That lies in what was formerly taken for granted, their role as strategic naval bases. Military conflict between nation-states will not end, and holding critical points in the strategic geography of the world is enormously important. Whatever the reason for the strife, Mahan stated, "when a question arises of control over distant regions . . . whether they be crumbling empires, anarchical republics, colonies, isolated military posts, or [small] islands, it must ultimately be decided by naval power." It was so in the British defense of Gibraltar, a strategic outpost purely, and it would be so when the United States acquired the way for its linchpin of empire, the Central American isthmian canal. Naval power, not the marching thousands of conscript armies, would decide these contests.[16]

Whereas Frederick Jackson Turner talked of closure, Mahan clearly understood the beginnings of an America dominant in a new, dangerously opportunistic world. Writing in 1890, Turner's benchmark year, Mahan, too, identified the disappearance of the frontier as a milestone of American history, with large implications for its economic and political future. In a companion piece to *The Influence of Sea Power*, he closed the circle of Turner's frontier thesis and charted America's new course: "Whether they will or no, Americans must now begin to look outward."[17]

The Influence of Sea Power upon History, translated into a dozen languages, exploded like a 12-inch shell on the naval and geopolitical world. Only the U.S. Navy Department turned a blind eye. "It is not the business of a naval officer to write books," said leading mossback Commodore Francis M. Ramsay, chief of the Bureau of Navigation, and he shipped Mahan off to sea in command of the new steel cruiser *Chicago.* But in Great Britain, Germany, and Japan, the book found wide audiences, and indeed, planted the poisonous seed of the Anglo-German naval rivalry that became a root cause of World War I. Kaiser Wilhelm ordered a copy placed aboard every ship of the growing Imperial German Navy.[18]

Certainly there were many midlevel and junior officers in the Navy Department who knew its significance. Those who sought reform came away impressed. Admiral Luce thought it "altogether exceptional." An enthusiastic Theodore Roosevelt wrote a splendid review in the *Atlantic Monthly,* calling it "by far the most interesting book on naval history which has been produced on either side of the water for many a long year." The *Chicago Times* assured its readers that Mahan was assuredly no "crank."[19]

And what of the America of Turner and Mahan, so ready to break its continental boundaries and burst on the international stage as a feature player in the great game of empire? These were peculiar and pregnant times. The Civil War had ended a quarter century before. Its history had been written, sectional and social passions had faded, the pain and gore of battlefields and gun decks had been forgotten; its great public figures passed into retirement or the grave. One of Mark Twain's minor works, *The Gilded Age,* contained the character of "Colonel" Beriah Sellers, an entrepreneurial braggart whose hollow standards and materialistic dreams painted, in broad strokes, the era between the Civil and Spanish-American Wars. The book's title was a very apt term, for gilding is a surface treatment only.

In November 1888, the nation elected the Fifty-first Congress—the "Billion-Dollar Congress," the first to ever spend a billion dollars during peacetime. When someone used the nickname to taunt the new Speaker of the House, Republican Thomas B. "Czar" Reed of Maine, he rejoined, "Yes, but this is a billion dollar country!"[20]

Reed was guilty of understatement. The national wealth in 1890 topped $65 billion, higher than Great Britain's, or Germany's and Russia's combined. The new America entering the decade craned its urban neck at the first iron-skeleton skyscrapers; incandescent light was no longer a novelty and, along with electric "trolleys," was rapidly replacing the gas lamp and horsecar on America's streets. The telephone was coming into use in the business world, and the navy installed an experimental system in the steel cruiser *Philadelphia*. On December 15, 1890, Sitting Bull died in a firefight with reservation police on the Grand River in South Dakota. Five days later came the Battle of Wounded Knee, the last major clash in four hundred years of Indian wars. Utah renounced polygamy as a preliminary to statehood. The navy, if any civilian noticed, was rising slowly from the status of the joke fleet into which it had degenerated since the Civil War. Two small battleships, the *Texas* and the *Maine,* were already under construction.[21]

The population stood at 75 million, a 50 percent increase in ten years, largely due to waves of immigrants, most from eastern and southern Europe and a fair number from Japan. "Wall Street" and its "interests" were established phenomena of American commercial growth, generating a boom of industrial jobs, along with financial "panics" almost on a programmed schedule. Great city slums were spawned, and in contrast, greedy monopoly trusts arose, hoarding and manipulating the wealth of railroads, mines, iron and steel, beef and sugar in the bank accounts of the new industrial plutocracy. Already in 1890 a groping public consciousness had aroused Congress to pass Ohio senator John Sherman's "anti-trust act," a still-toothless federal statute to quell rapacious capitalism. And at the opposite economic end of Wall Street came the contentious birth of industrial labor unions. To meet their threat, state National Guards and sometimes the regular army were called in to suppress them in the name of law and order.

The dry prairie states and the cotton-growing South suffered under the increasing burdens of erratic industrial prosperity. Economic growth since the Civil War had been wildly uneven. For the farmers, agricultural prices never seemed able to keep up with costs, and increasingly they turned to radical solutions to ease the down-spiraling plight. "In God we trusted, in Kansas we busted" read painted signs on wagons heading *east*. The "farm problem" became a chronic national agony. When farmers had a bumper crop, commodity prices sank to no-profit levels, and in drought or grasshopper years, farmers went broke anyway. By 1890 a significant proportion of the original homesteaders had sold out or quit. Class lines were drawn between the consuming, banking East and their dirt cousins of the plains and South.

The same election that created the Billion-Dollar Congress sent Benjamin Harrison, stalwart Republican lawyer of Indiana, to the White House. "A frigid little general" with a fine Civil War record, good brains, and an unshakable devotion to the Grand Old Party, he was described by a visitor as "the only man he ever knew who could carry a piece of ice in each pants pocket on a July afternoon and never lose a drop." While the candidate stayed home in Indianapolis, the campaign was dominated by the charge that Grover Cleveland's incumbent Democrats were out to kill the protectionist tariff and American industry with it. Manufacturers were "fried" by Republican fund-raisers for over $4 million in political "fat" that was lavishly spread in critical states. It worked, and Harrison squeaked through the electoral college with a sixty-five-vote majority.[22]

Benjamin Harrison and his first secretary of state, James G. Blaine, were frankly expansionist, though nothing directly would come of their efforts during their tenure in office. In the navy, however, important changes were occurring that would eventually position it to be, in Mahanian terms, the engine of U.S. expansion. Harrison's navy secretary, Benjamin Franklin Tracy of New York, a former Civil War brigadier and U.S. attorney in Brooklyn, continued the line of sound navy administrators begun when President Garfield had named William H. Hunt to the post in 1881, and it was due to the efforts of such men that the pattern of attrition and stagnation began to change.

At the end of the Civil War, the U.S. Navy ranked first in the world: seven hundred vessels mounting five thousand guns, with a modern, revolutionary fleet of ironclad monitors unmatched afloat. But within months of peacetime, the nation turned inward to settle the frontier and get on with Reconstruction. There followed sixteen years of the "dark ages" of the old navy. The service bottomed out to less than seventy steamers and a world ranking of twelfth, behind China and Chile. The monitors were laid up to rust in the navy yards, officer promotions stagnated, the number of enlisted sailors dropped to 7,500—the level during Andrew Jackson's presidency.

Technological experimentation did not exist. (When Captain Mahan reported as commanding officer to the *Wachusett,* he described her as an "old war-horse, not yet turned out to grass or slaughter, ship-rigged to the royals, and slow-steamed.") In part, the cause was endemic political corruption in the sleepy navy yards, usually attributable to the district congressman.[23]

In 1873, the navy had been utterly humiliated by Spain in the notorious *Virginius* affair. A small iron steamer, with an American captain and dubious American registry, the *Virginius* was illegally running guns and guerrillas to Cuba during the independence struggle known as the Ten Years' War. Captured by a Spanish gunboat, she was taken to Santiago de Cuba and declared a pirate. The American captain and 52 of her officers, crew, and "passengers" were put against a wall and summarily shot. The remainder, 155 men, would likely have met the same fate were it not for the arrival of a British warship whose commander vigorously protested the butchery.

The U.S. Navy, under Civil War hero Admiral David Dixon Porter, mobilized to meet the crisis, and all available ships assembled at Key West. Rear Admiral Robley Evans, then a lieutenant, remembered, "The force collected . . . was the best, and indeed about all we had . . . and if it had not been so serious it would have been laughable to see our condition. We remained several weeks, making faces at the Spaniards 90 miles away at Havana, while two modern vessels of war would have done us up in 30 minutes. We were dreadfully mortified over it all." Diplomatic intervention prevented a Spanish-American war. Spain, with ill grace, came up with an indemnity of eighty thousand dollars, allowing the United States to forget the incident.[24]

In 1881, however, the navy's condition started slowly to improve. During the short-lived Garfield administration, Congress refused to authorize ever more costly repairs for what had become floating museum pieces, and two years later, it authorized funds for the construction of the first ships of the "new navy," the small protected cruisers *Atlanta, Boston,* and *Chicago,* and the dispatch vessel *Dolphin*—the "ABCD" ships, the first U.S. naval vessels built of steel. In 1886, at the urging of Secretary of the Navy William C. Whitney, Congress wisely stipulated that all armor plate, structural steel, gunnery, and propulsion components be of domestic manufacture, guaranteeing a symbiotic relationship between the infant American heavy industries and the new navy, the birth of the modern military-industrial complex. In September 1888, just prior to the election of the Billion-Dollar Congress, Congress passed the largest naval appropriation since the Civil War. For around $16 million, the nation received an aggregate of 27,436 tons of new warships that included the armored cruiser *New York,* the protected cruiser *Olympia,* five smaller cruisers, and a Naval Academy practice gunboat.[25]

The Samoa crisis that unfolded in the winter of 1888–89 added further impetus to the development of the new navy. Relationships between Germany, Great Britain, and the United States neared the sparking point over proposed coaling stations in those South Pacific islands. Rumors of a clash between American and German ships brought a flurry of war talk and once more turned public and legislative attention to the navy's unreadiness. It was nature, in the form of a gigantic hurricane on March 16, 1889, that calmed the diplomatic waters. Of the three obsolete wooden American naval vessels in Apia Harbor, the *Trenton* and the *Vandalia* (ships similar to Mahan's creaking *Wachusett*) were a total loss. Fifty-one American sailors died. The United States was left, as the *New York Herald* reported, "with almost no . . . war vessels worthy of the name in the Pacific Ocean." The disaster provided an excellent argument for accelerating the naval construction program.[26]

Then came the Chilean war scare, a crisis of the first order. Through 1890 and 1891, Chile was enmeshed in a civil war between presidential and congressional factions, with the latter eventually gaining the upper hand. For slights true and imagined, it held decidedly anti-American sentiments. On the evening of October 16, 1891, there was a violent, premeditated incident in the harbor of Valparaiso. The new steel cruiser *Baltimore,* skippered by Captain Winfield Scott Schley, an officer of some note and ability, was at anchor there. Many of her crew were on shore, and, in one of the city's saloons, a fight erupted when a Chilean spat in the face of an American sailor. The brawl spread; police stood aside, except when they joined the mob. The locals dragged two sailors from a streetcar. One, after being stabbed, was shot and killed by police; the other died after receiving eighteen knife wounds in the back. Thirty-six sailors, eighteen seriously injured, were arrested and beaten at police stations. The episode was a national insult, and the American (and Chilean) press demanded war. Conflict was a real possibility, and President Harrison was all for it. But the Chileans yielded, tendering a grudging apology and seventy-five thousand dollars to the families of the two killed American sailors. Interest in American naval preparedness zoomed.

As Mahan's *Influence of Sea Power* neared completion, Navy Secretary Benjamin Tracy was similarly absorbed in writing his first annual report. Released by the department in December 1889, it is one of the most revolutionary documents in the history of American naval policy. Defense, he cautioned, not conquest, was the object; but it required a "fighting force," and the navy didn't have one. The ABCD ships and their immediate successors—and even the big armored cruisers *New York* and *Brooklyn,* then nearing completion—were simply scouts and commerce destroyers, unable to "prevent a fleet of [hostile] ironclads from shelling our cities." To raise a blockade of its coasts, or to "beat off the enemy's fleet on its approach," America required "armored battleships." Embracing the as yet unpublished Mahanian principles, Tracy concluded that naval war, "though defensive in principle, may be conducted most effectively by being offensive in its operations."[27]

On the theory that if he asked for everything, he would receive something, Tracy decided to risk all. He recommended building "two fleets of battleships," twelve for the Atlantic, eight for the Pacific, plus sixty fast cruisers. To stroke the ultraconservatives in the department and the handwringers from congressional coastal districts, he further requested twenty useless monitor-type coast-defense vessels.

To put real bone and sinew into the fleet, the navy's congressional partisans endorsed the portion of Tracy's report that established battleship fleets in both oceans, but nowhere near the secretary's inflated numbers. The bill for the "Increase of the Navy" that came out of the Billion-Dollar Congress provided funds for three "sea-going coast-line battle ships designed to carry the heaviest armor and most powerful ordnance," one commerce-raiding cruiser, and a torpedo boat. Following Tracy's dictum for a two-ocean fleet, the act stipulated that one battleship be constructed on the West Coast.[28]

The reason for the battleships' oxymoronic "sea-going coast-line" designation was basely political. The "coast-line" designation was plugged into the bill to placate those who feared the advent of a truly offense-minded navy, those who would vote funds only for a service whose duties were strictly confined to coast defense. Indeed, strong opposition to the battleships came from a wide range of the politically conscious population: Quaker pacifists, midwestern and southern "small navy" congressmen, commerce-raiding enthusiasts with their eyes glued to the War of 1812 and the need for coastal and merchant shipping defenses, and antiexpansionist Democrats who knew an offensive weapon when they saw one.

Very few of the national legislators who voted for passage understood what they had actually done. Advocates still spoke in terms of coast defense and commerce raiding as the true mission of the navy. Republican senator Henry Cabot Lodge of Massachusetts, a leading expansionist posing as a naval authority, asserted with palpable inaccuracy that the battleships were no deviation from tradition, were "merely the continuance" of American naval policy from the War of 1812 "and consistently followed since."[29]

Precisely the opposite: The naval appropriations act of 1890 irrevocably stamped congressional endorsement on a radical departure in America's philosophy of national security. No longer would the navy huddle in defense of seaports, nor dash out in cruisers to overhaul fat merchant prizes. The battleships were a giant stride, as Tracy and his allies frankly admitted, toward creating a fighting fleet to seize command offensively of the open sea and destroy the enemy in blue water.

When the Democratic administration of Grover Cleveland took office in March 1893, the critical post of navy secretary went to Congressman Hilary Herbert of Alabama, formerly chairman of the House Naval Affairs Committee. Hitherto a typically southern small-navy man, he had been turned around by Mahan's writings, and now endorsed the battleship theory at least as strongly as his Republican predecessor. Under the Tracy-Herbert regimes, Republican and Democratic, the navy transformed itself from a newly awakened agency for national defense into an instrument of diplomatic and military power extending American interests over a significant portion of the globe.

In November 1890, amid a groundswell of midwestern populism, the Billion-Dollar Congress was swept out of office, a victim of a swelling disgust at the economic power of the "interests." A primary cause could easily have been the so-called McKinley tariff.

William McKinley of Ohio, rising Republican star, chairman of the House Ways and Means Committee, called "Major" in memory of his Civil War rank, was given the job of shepherding the tariff through Congress by President Harrison. Early in his political career McKinley embraced the shrewd message that there are two sides to every question, something which later prompted Theodore Roosevelt to comment that McKinley possessed no more backbone than a chocolate éclair. With keen political sense, McKinley saw that the new economic forces of the nation needed a political voice, and he became that voice, a champion of protectionism and high tariffs. Very much like Ronald Reagan with his "voodoo economics" a century later, he instinctively understood that the politics of wealth, if presented boldly and without apology, could be transformed into a broad-based movement. Workers and farmers alike could be hypnotized into believing that what was good for the rapacious industrial trusts was also good for them.

"I do not prize the word cheap," McKinley speechified in his defense of the protective tariff. "It is not a word of hope. . . . It is the badge of poverty. . . . Cheap merchandize means cheap men and cheap men mean a cheap country." As such, the tariff sharply raised the rates on imported cotton cloth, linen, carpets, thread, tinware, tools, hides, and food. Raw sugar was the only commodity on which tariffs were removed, and this profited nobody but the sugar trust. The Democrats sent peddlers into the streets to hawk tin cups marked "A 5¢ cup for 25¢—the price raised by the McKinley tariff." In the 1890 election, William McKinley lost his congressional seat by three hundred votes, and the new House of Representatives counted 235 Democrats, 88 Republicans, and 9 populists.[30]

Two years later, in 1892, an unenthusiastic Republican Party, meeting in Minneapolis, renominated President Harrison. The Democrats convened in Chicago, and in fragile unity, amid shouts of "Grover, Grover, Four More Years," nominated ex-president Grover Cleveland to carry the banner on a platform of sound money and tariff reform. The People's Party, the "populists," a melding of farmers' alliances and elements of the infant labor movement, held their convention in Omaha, sending General James B. Weaver of Iowa out on a crusading platform against organized wealth. They demanded a graduated income tax, popular election of United States senators, postal savings banks to compete with private banks, government ownership of railroads, telegraphs, and telephone companies, laws guaranteeing the right to strike, protection of labor unions, and inflation of the currency to alleviate debt.

In the general election, Cleveland's margin of victory was substantial: 277 electoral votes to Harrison's 145. Significantly, Weaver pulled 22, and over a million popular votes, ballots that should have gone to the Democrats and were an ominous preview.[31]

Literally from the moment of his oath taking on March 4, 1893, Cleveland's presidency was beset with large problems and calamitous events. The issue of Hawaiian annexation—which Cleveland vehemently opposed—came immediately, and while he was dealing with that, the great panic and depression of 1893 burst on the national scene. Its causes were both foreign and homegrown. In London and Paris, the collapse of commercial investment houses combined with slush-funding government scandals to shake international stock markets, including those in the United States.

Gold, the standard that backed every nation's public debts, drained away to Europe, leaving the U.S. Treasury perilously short of reserves. On May 4, "Black Friday," the National Cordage Company went belly-up, and stock prices on Wall Street plummeted. Banks called in loans, credit disappeared, and fifteen thousand businesses failed in the ensuing grim weeks. There were runs on state and nationally chartered banks, six hundred of which, mostly in the West and South, locked their doors. Five major railroads went into federal receivership. Unemployment rose to 2.5 million workers, or 20 percent of the industrial labor force. It was the worst financial and social calamity to strike the country until the Great Depression of the 1930s.

All classes and sections were hurt, badly, but none so hard as the farmers of the wheat, corn, and cotton belts. Corn sold at ten cents a bushel, cotton at six cents a pound, and mortgage foreclosures reached record levels. Eastern newspapers and other distant authorities attributed the rural plight to glutted world markets, domestic overproduction, and inefficient farming methods. The afflicted farmers blamed it on tight money, squeezed by a conspiracy of Wall Streeters and their international cohorts. The conspiracy angle aside, the farmers had a point about the money. In 1865 the circulating currency in the United States was $2 billion. In 1890, with double the population and triple the business activity, the money supply had actually shrunk to less than $1.5 billion, a seesaw effect of raising the value of money and debts while lowering the prices of staple commodities. The farmers, caught in the crunching middle, saw the gold standard as the evil oppressor of their class and the coinage of "free silver," one silver dollar to every sixteen of gold, as the inflationary panacea for their problems.

To President Cleveland, who saw it exactly otherwise, the maintenance of gold as the nation's monetary standard was not just a question of monetary policy, but an issue of national morality. It was a case of honest value for honest work, and any "cheapening of the dollar" with silver meant cheating the consumer with debased currency. He was not naive; he understood that his position on sound money greatly benefited lenders over borrowers, but after four years as a Wall Street lawyer, he saw no intrinsic evil in that. Unfortunately, by trying to keep the issue above politics, he heightened the sinister class-conspiracy theories that always stuck to the currency question.

In June 1893, to stem the outflow of gold and preserve the government's credit, Cleveland called a special session of Congress to repeal the Silver Purchase Act, which enabled the issuance of silver-backed paper money (and which nearly everyone redeemed instead in gold). It was certain than the radical western and southern Democrats would follow silver out of the party rather than hew the gold line coming from the White House, and good riddance to them, thought Cleveland.

On August 8, Congress convened on a soggy, ninety-degree day. Congressman William Jennings Bryan of Nebraska, the banging new drum of the disenchanted silverites, delivered a three-hour speech excoriating the "goldbugs." He did not doubt the president's honesty on the question, Bryan said, but it was of a piece with "the Indian mothers who with misguided zeal threw their children into the Ganges." Cleveland countered the attack by ruthlessly turning off the federal pump until Congress voted for absolute repeal. "One thing may as well be distinctly understood by professing Democrats in Congress," he wrote to Treasury Secretary Carlisle. "They must not expect me to 'turn the other cheek' by rewarding their conduct with patronage." Unfortunately, Cleveland had a knack for equating any opposition, even that of honest principle, with an attack on himself, and he alienated many a Democrat who just needed a scrap of political cover from the White House, turning potential allies into enemies.[32]

"All men of virtue and intelligence know that all the ills of life— scarcity of money, baldness, the common bacillus, [Irish] Home Rule . . . and the potato bug—are due to the [Silver] Bill," wrote cynical Republican John Hay. Through the late summer and early fall, Cleveland, the eastern press, and the party's regular leadership wore the Senate silverites down, and on October 30, 1893, the Senate voted 48–37: the Silver Purchase Act disappeared into history. But it did not produce anything like instant recovery from the panic and depression; it just ended the government purchase of silver. Gold continued to drain out of the Treasury, eroding domestic and foreign confidence in the dollar.[33]

A great bitterness enveloped the Democratic Party as it slid ever deeper into the maw of internecine bloodletting. Grover Cleveland won a skirmish in what has been called "the battle of the standards," but he surely lost the war for the soul of the Democracy.

As the depression winter lifted its grinding boot on Easter Sunday, March 25, 1894, a bugle sounded on the outskirts of Massillon, Ohio, and the traveling circus of the "Commonweal of Christ," commonly known as "Coxey's Army," stepped out on its march to Washington. Its soldiers were Americans who had lost their jobs, and their shaggy movement to confront the government by direct action, one of several that had emerged out of the 1893 depression, was a phenomenon new to domestic politics.

A number of these depression "armies" (often referred to as the "tramp movement") had already staged marches on the national capital, receiving little support and inviting nervous ridicule. Anarchy, socialism, communism, and other foreign imports were seen behind every group of unemployed men. The press naturally overblew the story, feeding ignorant biases toward unassimilated immigrants with unpronounceable names. One New York paper recommended "the best meal to give a regular tramp is a leaden one."[34]

A black man, carrying the American flag, marched at the head of Coxey's column. The lead banner read, "Peace on Earth, Good Will Toward Men! But DEATH TO *INTEREST* ON BONDS!!" The parade's poetic "grand marshal," Carl Browne, decked out in a wide-brimmed cowboy sombrero, a white-lace cravat, and a buckskin vest with silver-dollar buttons, sat upon a white stallion, and called himself the "Cerebellum of Christ." The deputy commanders in the vanguard included an Oklahoma cowboy, a striking Pennsylvania steelworker, an astrologer, and a leather-lunged speechifier identified only as "the Great Unknown." Ahead of all moved a half-breed Indian, scouting the road, already lined with gawkers, for the next day's march.

In the main body, surrounded by long lines of ragged men, sacks of food and blankets around their shoulders, moved a carriage with "General" Jacob Coxey himself, a mild little round-shouldered citizen of Massillon, owner of a profitable quarry and horse farm. With him were his family and infant son, Legal Tender Coxey.

The army's legislative agenda had already been introduced in the U.S. Senate by the populist William Alfred Peffer of Kansas, and included government public construction programs that predated Franklin Roosevelt's Works Progress Administration by forty years. But next to such sane proposals as hiring the unemployed to build macadam roads across the country at wages of $1.50 a day were demands that states, cities, and even individual towns be allowed to issue their own paper money.

For over a month the lean, shabby companies of Coxey's Army walked (and hitched rides on canal boats) across Pennsylvania and Maryland, reaching Washington on April 26, 1894. Congress and President Cleveland refused to meet with their leaders, who in reality were something of a joke. On May 1, with a phalanx of police and thousands of sight-seers waiting along the route, Coxey's Army, now down to four hundred men and heavily infiltrated by the Secret Service, started up Pennsylvania Avenue toward the Capitol. At the entrance, Grand Marshal Browne jumped from his horse and dashed for the marble steps. Two policemen knocked him down and dragged him away. Unoffensive little Jacob Coxey kissed his wife, slipped through the crowd, and read his petition on the value of "Good Roads," whereupon he was arrested for walking on the grass.

The defeat of Coxey's Army and the tramp movement raised Cleveland's popularity, but for the populist movement no good came of it. They were all seen as cranks, weirdos, malcontents, the pathetic; anyone, it seemed, but real workers and farmers with real problems. Attorney General Richard Olney called the army "an eccentric and ephemeral demonstration." Yet he maintained legitimate fears that this was but the vanguard of far more serious social upheaval, to be carried out by aggrieved workers who were not crazy or led by starry-eyed prophets, and he was right.[35]

The historian Allan Nevins called the year 1894–95 the *"année terrible"* of American history between Reconstruction and World War I. The year marked the apogee of the robber barons, those whom Theodore Roosevelt later called "malefactors of great wealth." As Olney predicted, the Coxey parade proved a harbinger to class warfare in the nation. Nothing more symbolized that struggle than the Pullman strike, the gravest labor disturbance the country had yet experienced. No event of Cleveland's presidency provoked more controversy or was as badly handled.[36]

Just across the southern boundary line of Chicago was "a bright and radiant little island in the midst of the great tumultuous sea of Chicago's population; a restful oasis in the wearying brick-and-mortar waste of an enormous city." This was Pullman, a pretty village of lakes, parks, libraries, grass lawns, cemeteries, and redbrick cottages, lauded by newfangled sociologists as the triumph of worker-capital cooperation, the "model town" of the Pullman Palace Car Company. It was also America's version of a Potemkin village, a company town with higher rents and fees than in comparable Chicago neighborhoods—paternalistic capitalism perverted. "The town of Pullman is not American," wrote a friend to Secretary of State Walter Gresham. "In fact, a man at Pullman can neither keep a chicken nor a dog nor any living thing. It is more rigid than the laws of Russia." Model town? "Oh hell, model shit house!" sneered Ohio Republican and mega-industrialist Marcus Alonzo Hanna, a man with no apology for accumulating capital. "Go and live in Pullman and find out how much Pullman gets selling city water and gas ten percent higher to those poor fools."[37]

The long winter of 1893 hit the people of Pullman town as hard as anyone. Wages had been reduced by one-fourth, many men were dismissed, and many more were put on part time. The company whined this was necessary because of a decline in business. But the company was flush with profits, counting $25 million for the fiscal year, and had distributed dividends in excess of $2.5 million to its stockholders. Yet rents and utilities in Pullman town remained as before, and a typical family, after deductions, had about 76¢ a day for food and clothing. When company founder George Pullman, a true malefactor of great wealth, was later asked if it would not have been wiser and more just, in light of what happened, to divide some of the company's assets with the workers, he replied, "I do not. It would have amounted to a gift of money to these men; it was simply a matter of business."[38]

Early in May a deputation of workers called on Pullman, pleading that either wages be raised or rents reduced. He refused even to consider it, and three members of the deputation were summarily fired. This might have been coincidental, but Pullman was certainly capable of such vindictive behavior, and it was so construed by the workers. Virtually the entire shop floor walked out on strike. Pullman fired the cowed remainder and shut down the works. "A man who won't meet his men half-way is a God-damn fool!" said Marcus Alonzo Hanna, hardly a left-winger or anarchist.[39]

Some 4,000 Pullman workers were members of the American Railway Union, a radical body organized by the socialist Eugene V. Debs. In the summer of 1894, it mustered a national membership of 150,000 men in 465 locals. In June, their national convention had met in Chicago and pleaded for arbitration. "We have nothing to arbitrate," Pullman announced from his New Jersey shore vacation home. "The workers have nothing to do with the amount of wages they shall receive." On June 26 the union voted to boycott all trains carrying Pullman sleeping and dining cars, an action that brought it into direct conflict with the General Managers' Association, comprising the heads of twenty-four railroads that headquartered or terminated in Chicago. Hardly unexpectedly, the association sided with Pullman.[40]

Overnight the strike and boycott reached menacing proportions, extending into twenty-seven states and territories, becoming a struggle to the death between capital and labor. Federal investigators later affirmed that the General Managers' Association had "determined to crush the strike rather than accept any peaceable solution through conciliation, arbitration, or otherwise."[41]

President Cleveland, just returned from a fishing trip, learned of the action on June 28, by which time 20,000 railway workers had quit in Chicago alone, with perhaps 40,000 more striking at all points west. It was remarkably effective. Whenever a railroad tried to move or attach a Pullman car, the whole train crew quit in a body. The postmaster general reported mails completely stalled on the Southern Pacific lines. On June 30, freight traffic became paralyzed in and out of Chicago, the national rail hub. As yet, there was no violence; Debs had given strict orders against it. But the great Chicago Columbian fair had drawn to the city a mass of floating labor that the depression had stranded. There were perhaps 100,000 drifting, desperate, unemployed men roaming the streets, eating in soup kitchens and sleeping in hovels along the tracks, dry tinder awaiting a spark.

Fearing massive disturbances, the largely conservative press, led by the Chicago *Tribune,* headlined "Debs Is a Dictator"; "Mob in Control"; "Mobs Bent on Ruin." Illinois governor John Peter Altgeld cabled President Cleveland that these press accounts were grossly exaggerated. But the papers trumped him, declaring the strikers were no longer battling just Pullman, but the public itself.[42]

This placed the administration in a severe dilemma. Whatever the situation, be it extremely tense or not, Grover Cleveland, as President of the United States, was invested by clear constitutional and statutory authority to secure the uninterrupted delivery of the mails and to safeguard interstate commerce. But by what right did the federal government interfere with strikes? Action could be taken if strikers illegally obstructed mails or commerce; but what defined "illegal obstruction"? A liberal might claim that only actual violence or riot met the definition. A reactionary could argue the strike alone constituted obstruction. Attorney General Richard Olney, a man who honed tenacious belligerency into an art form, took the latter view and pressed Cleveland, strongly, to adopt it. This was no surprise, for Olney had spent his considerable legal career as counsel for any number of railroads, and as recently as 1889 was a director of the Chicago, Burlington & Quincy, a member line of the General Managers' Association.[43]

Olney, whose mustached face and close-cropped hair gave him the look of a bulldog, had for months been immersed in railroad problems brought on by Coxey's horde. The economic losses of the panic had left many of the western railroads in federal receivership. Lacking money for tickets, the tramps sometimes took over the trains. To protect the government's interest in bankrupt lines, Olney instructed the federal courts and marshals to apply to the Justice Department for direct help from the U.S. Army.

Olney's anger at the Coxeyites and their ilk, who *had* performed illegal acts, easily transferred to the railroad unionists, who had broken no laws and were engaged in a perfectly legal strike. He resolved to deal harshly with them, and left to his own devices, he would have ordered in the troops without any preliminaries. When Grover Cleveland recoiled from this summary execution of the statutes, Olney fell back on the methods he'd used against the Coxeyites. First he would coerce the federal district court in Chicago to issue an injunction against the strikers prohibiting interference with the mails. The judge and marshal would certify the injunction could not be enforced, and Olney would persuade the president to send the army to the rescue. If the strike were crushed in Chicago, it would fail everywhere. As special counsel to assist the U.S. attorney in framing the injunction, Olney hired Edwin Walker, counsel for the Chicago, Milwaukee & St. Paul Railroad, a member line of the General Managers' Association.

On July 2, with friendly federal judges providing suitable phrases, the district court enjoined Debs and the American Railway Union. In sweeping language, all persons were prohibited from any "interference" with the railroads in Chicago "engaged as common carriers." "Interference" was defined as a host of acts including "persuasion" of workers to stop work. In other words, it forbade them to join a striking union. The general managers were satisfied, very; "a Gatling gun on paper," they called it. "A veritable dragnet," said the *New York Times*.[44]

Olney had created a formidable weapon, but putting it into effect was inflammatory. By impeding trains carrying the mails, demonstrating workers could now be arrested in wholesale batches and sentenced without trial. For the General Managers' Association, it could not have come soon enough. The railroads were losing millions, to say nothing of the disruption of commerce and the economy. Freight traffic had stalled all over the Northwest. The grain trade had ceased functioning; meatpacking houses were closed, with livestock unloaded at junctions up and down the Mississippi Valley. Hospitals ran out of ice. Factories closed for want of coal. Governor Altgeld ordered the Illinois National Guard to liberate trains blocked downstate. West of the Mississippi, however, hundreds of federal marshals and thousands of National Guardsmen had little effect. Unlike the tramp movement, the striking railroad workers, real men with real jobs, collected widespread public sympathy. When civil authorities proved incapable of handling the situation, regular army troops in California, Colorado, Montana, and New Mexico were called on to move the trains.

July 2 saw the first outbreaks of violence in the Chicago area. A sizable mob of strikers and camp followers gathered on the tracks at Blue Island, near Joliet. When Federal Marshal J. W. Arnold, backed by over one hundred deputies recruited by the General Managers' Association, read aloud the injunction, he was openly defied. The mob tipped over a number of boxcars, a deputy was stabbed, and Arnold was knocked down and rolled in the dirt. Immediately he telegraphed Olney: "Have read the order of the court to the rioters . . . and they simply hoot at it." Local factory and stockyard workers, he believed, were ready to quit their jobs and join the mob.[45]

For a time, beyond the roughing up at Blue Island, nothing more happened in Chicago. Police reinforcements and rumors of phantom troops kept the strikers peaceful. Olney, however, was not satisfied, and wired the U.S. attorney that any request for the army would be favorably received. The response was immediate. The entreaty was drafted and Arnold had it over the wire, endorsed by U.S. Attorney Milchrist, special counsel Walker, and Federal Judge Peter Grosscup: "emergency exists for the immediate presence of United States troops." Olney carried this sizzling bomb to the White House.[46]

President Cleveland, Secretary of State Gresham, and Secretary of War Daniel Lamont, along with generals John M. Schofield and Nelson Miles, respectively the army's commanding general and commander of the Department of the Missouri, were already there. Olney expertly agitated for the commitment of troops. All but Miles, who considered strikers simply anarchists, opposed it. But Olney, waving the marshal's telegram as if it were exhibit A in a courtroom, won the argument, and without waiting for an application from Governor Altgeld, Lamont crossed the street to the State, War, and Navy Building and wired the commanding officer at Fort

Sheridan to move his command—infantry, cavalry, and artillery—into Chicago.[47]

On July 4, General Miles reached the city, its streets and lakefront parks thronged with holiday crowds. The next day agents provocateurs of the General Managers' Association incited real violence: seventy-five cars and locomotives were wrecked, the central roundhouse was burned, forty-four trains were stoned or shot at, twenty men were killed or injured, and half a dozen buildings of the once lovely Columbian Exposition were burned to the ground. The mob was reported moving into the city center from Blue Island. Indian fighter Miles's inherent nativism was jolted by the large number of immigrant workers among the strikers, and he reversed his earlier reluctance to use the army to quell civil disorder. "Shall I give the order for troops to fire on mob obstructing trains?" he wired the War Department. "The riot will soon embrace all the criminals of the city and vicinity."[48]

Keeping their sanity, Olney, Schofield, and Cleveland recoiled from the thought—absolutely not, came the answer over the telegraph. Miles became nearly hysterical; succumbing to the General Managers' Association's propaganda and his own basic prejudices, he saw "anarchists and socialists" everywhere and predicted a French Revolution "reign of terror" by the union. The line was clearly drawn; it was either "anarchy, secret conclaves . . . and mob violence" or "peace [and] absolute security . . . under the shadow and folds of 'Old Glory.' " Debs was labeled by the general a "dictator."[49]

The ranks of the strikers, filled with riffraff petty criminals and the unemployed stranded in the city, collided with the army, and seven civilians were killed. On July 6, Governor Altgeld ordered the Illinois National Guard into Chicago. Two days later, President Cleveland issued a proclamation ordering all unlawful assemblages to disperse before noon the next day, warning, "There will be no vacillation in the decisive punishment of the guilty." On July 10, Eugene Debs and his lieutenants of the American Railway Union were arrested and indicted for obstructing the mails, and with that, the strike collapsed.[50]

From both sides of the aisle the U.S. Senate sounded a ringing endorsement of the administration's actions, with only the populist Peffer of Nebraska voicing an objection. Republican and Democratic newspapers alike applauded the use of federal troops. "If it takes the entire army and navy of the United States to deliver a postal card in Chicago," said President Cleveland, "that card will be delivered."[51]

As was so often the case, the off-year elections of 1894 hinged on the national economy, and the Democrats were poleaxed at the ballot boxes by the depression. Republicans whipsawed the administration for what it had and had not done. "We are on the eve of a very dark night," wrote New York Democratic lawyer Francis Stetson, one of the founders of U.S. Steel, to his friend the president. The former and now returning Speaker of the House, Thomas "Czar" Reed, as brilliant and upright a politician as ever walked the Capitol aisles, predicted, "The Democratic mortality will be so great . . . that their dead will be buried in trenches and marked 'unknown.' "[52]

The party of Jefferson and Jackson had hopelessly divided, and one after another, large constituencies turned against the president on their particular issue, the candidates wading into internecine slaughter instead of battling the Republicans. Western Democrats declared "free silver" a higher loyalty than any party. The president himself was becoming a liability. An Illinois congressman declared the party had carried many a heavy load, "but it cannot carry Cleveland and win this fall." Speaking at a banquet, Illinois governor John Peter Altgeld railed, "To laud [Grover Cleveland] on Jefferson's birthday is to sing a *Te Deum* of Judas Iscariot on a Christmas morning!"[53]

The day after the disastrous November election, Missouri Democrat and future House Speaker James "Champ" Clark echoed Reed's comments, calling the defeat the greatest slaughter of the innocents since the biblical Herod. Politically he was right, and the Democratic dead amounted to 113 lost seats in the House of Representatives and five in the Senate. What House seats remained came principally from the South. Across the wheat and corn prairies, silverite anti-Cleveland candidates killed the regular Democratic machines, resulting in twenty-four states electing not a single Democrat to national office. New England, Wisconsin, Illinois, New York, and the Far West returned Republicans.

The election marked a historic reestablishment of the Republican Party, with very significant trends for the future, as the party of national majority. Its platform and rising new leadership, symbolized by the smooth, moderate Governor William McKinley of Ohio, seemed infinitely more able to conduct national legislation than the discredited, disunited Democrats. The country, exhausted by the election, lay back to catch its breath, and as Captain Mahan lectured, began to look outward.

On February 28, 1895, in the winter of the *année terrible,* those Americans who read a morning newspaper saw a brief article accompanied by official assurances of its complete unimportance. Yet another revolt had broken out in Cuba. The Spanish minister in Washington declared the rebels nothing more than bandits already in flight from swift-moving authority. "The revolutionary movements . . . are wholly a matter of fiction," he said, and in any event, the insurrection, such as it was, had ignominiously and quickly collapsed. For a few months, people took the minister at his word. Cuba, at the moment, held little of the nation's interest. On the other hand, Richard Olney, seeking further beyond the southern horizon, flexed some newly developed national muscle to embroil the United States in a first-class foreign policy stew with Great Britain.[54]

Grover Cleveland's friend and personal physician, Dr. Joseph Bryant, remarked that the president "was temperate in all things unless unduly irritated by those who would annoy him persistently and selfishly—then appropriate and emphatic remarks were made." This is precisely what happened in 1895 when the obstreperous Richard Olney backed the nation into an obscure South American boundary dispute, and Cleveland shocked the English-speaking world with an onset of major attitude. As in his approach to the Hawaiian annexation question, he placed America on a perhaps too lofty moral plane and insisted Great Britain hew to the same severe standards of international ethics he himself espoused. Shouts and fears of war again smeared the headlines.[55]

The unsettled boundary between British Guiana and Venezuela had already brought on more than casual discussion and unease in the State Department. The line had been in dispute since Great Britain had wrested the territory from the Dutch in 1814, and American possessed characteristics that in Mahan's view were vital to the growth of a modern naval, indeed world, power.[12]

First, strategic geography. Unlike certain maritime states, France or the Netherlands, for instance, the United States need not worry about protecting a landed frontier that drained manpower and resources better suited for overseas expansion.

Second, physical geography. A nation embarking on a course for sea power needed extensive coastlines, deep, protected harbors, and a fertile agricultural interior. The United States held all in abundance.

Third, a well-distributed seafaring population having "an inborn love of the sea." Until the post–Civil War maritime doldrums, the United States had been a great seafaring nation, and it was time to rekindle the spirit.

Fourth, the establishment of a large merchant marine. America's carrying trade had once rivaled Great Britain's in tonnage and prestige. But that had ended for all time at the hands of Confederate sea raiders during the Civil War. (Mahan soon realized this as false doctrine. A nation no longer needed to ship products under her own flag to become commercially prosperous; it need only have a navy capable of protecting the goods and vessels.)[13]

Fifth, national character. The people of a maritime state must be materially acquisitive, with a knack and yearning for profitable overseas trade, and generally "love money." Americans held these traits—indeed, held them rather high. To Mahan, the full flowering of these national qualities was held in check by the "legislative hindrances" of those distinctly unwilling to expand into overseas possessions.

Last, character of the government. Mahan granted that the governments of several historically great maritime powers, Carthage and Spain for example, had been particularly despotic, and it was infinitely more desirable to have a participatory political structure. "In the matter of sea power, the most brilliant successes have followed where there has been intelligent direction by a government fully imbued with the spirit of the people. Such a government," he observed, "is most certainly secured when the will of the people . . . has some share in making it." England in the late seventeenth century contained the germ of this ideal. The United States in the late nineteenth had arguably progressed somewhat further.[14]

As Mahan reasoned, the theories of history and the reality of the present molded themselves in the America of 1890. The productive diplomats believed the British wished to keep it that way. For Britain, the ideal border touched the mouth of the Orinoco River, giving entrance and trade control into a fabulously wealthy hinterland. Every year, Venezuela tried to resolve the issue, but was always met by British obfuscation and delay. In December 1894, the president offered to bring the parties to the arbitration table. Britain, he noted, had in the past always favored arbitration in principle. He was completely snubbed.

The following spring, the British further annoyed the president, this time in Nicaragua. A bit closer to home than Venezuela, it was also where the United States had some definite ideas about the future building of an isthmian canal. In April 1895, three Royal Navy cruisers appeared off Corinto, on Nicaragua's Pacific coast, demanding damages of £75,000 for the arrest and expulsion of several British subjects. Nicaragua refused payment, and the British put ashore a landing force of four hundred sailors and marines, who seized the customhouse and extracted the indemnity. Riots ensued, Nicaragua formally protested the action and asked President Cleveland to intercede. Great Britain, however, was well within the wide boundaries of international law of the times. The United States engaged in similar actions in the region, and would do so time and again. Nicaragua, faced with a negative reply by the United States, paid the bill.

Because he was legally powerless in the situation, Cleveland vented his exasperation to former Postmaster General Don Dickenson. Within days, Dickenson delivered a jingoist speech in Detroit, sequined with Monroe Doctrine issues that the public could not ignore. The United States, he claimed, was not a disinterested party, not in Venezuela, not in Nicaragua. "We may indulge in a reciprocity of polite phrasing," Dickenson told his audience, "if our alert watchmen will meantime keep an eye upon our good friends across the Atlantic, especially when [they] . . . take an interest, not altogether born of curiosity . . . in this hemisphere."[56]

Grover Cleveland was always ready to suspect the "Powers"—big and small—of opportunistic readiness to exploit the defenseless. Africa was almost completely partitioned by the Europeans. And now, joined by an avaricious Japan, they were dismembering East and Southeast Asia as well. Monumentally angry at British arrogance in the Americas, Cleveland ordered Secretary of State Walter Gresham to compose a diplomatic note to the British government on the whole Venezuelan question. Gresham, however, took ill. A cold worsened into acute pleurisy and then pneumonia. On May 28, 1895, he died. Gresham had been a gentle friend to all. On June 10, Cleveland named his literal opposite, the pit bull Richard Olney, to succeed him at State.

Olney had begun working on the report during Gresham's illness, and in early July he took a draft to Cleveland at his Lakewood, New Jersey, summer home. The president loved it, saying, "It's the best thing of the kind I ever read." Here was an issue concerning the Monroe Doctrine, the United States' seminal hemispheric code, and Cleveland heartily endorsed it, "on better and more defensible ground than any of your predecessors—or *mine.*" The president suggested Olney read the draft to the rump cabinet still sweltering the summer away in Washington. Treasury, War, Navy, and Justice put no veto, and the note was sent off.[57]

It cut no corners, trimmed no sails, and was far more belligerent in tone than anything Gresham could have conceivably written. It was the work of an aggressive lawyer, chopping away the foundation from an adversary, rather than the position of a statesman seeking diplomatic solutions. Olney's interpretation of the Monroe Doctrine cut a broad swath. Its principle, he wrote, "has but a single purpose and object. It is that no European power . . . shall forcibly deprive an American state of the right and power of self-government." Great Britain's itinerary in Venezuela was just such an interference with those rights and powers.[58]

The boundary dispute had degenerated into a running hemispheric sore, the "honor" and "interests" of America were deeply involved, and it could no longer regard the issue with "indifference." So far this was within the bounds of diplomatic engagement, and something even Gresham might have done if he were particularly incensed. Whitehall might harrumph and sniff, but the United States had a point regarding legitimate spheres of strategic influence.

But the hyperbolic Olney had inserted certain eye-popping opinions completely unjustified by historical facts or contemporary international politics, and these transformed a "stiff note" into what the president called Olney's "twenty-inch gun." Distance, said Olney, especially three thousand miles of ocean, makes "any permanent political union between an European and an American state unnatural and inexpedient."

"Today," Olney said, going further on that theme, "the United States is practically sovereign on this continent, and its fiat is law upon the subjects to which it confines its interposition." America, the secretary continued, had been spared the need for "great warlike establishments"—a big army and navy to muscle its way around the Western Hemisphere. But, he warned, jerking the lanyard of the 20-incher, "with the powers of Europe permanently encamped on American soil," these "ideal conditions . . . cannot be expected to continue."[59]

Summer and then autumn passed with no answer from the British. Cleveland and Olney were on edge; they wanted Britain's decision on arbitration before the president's annual message in December. Not that the British government was being intentionally rude, though there was some of that. Much of the delay was the fault of the American minister to Great Britain, Thomas Bayard, and British Foreign Office underlings who did not communicate upward the seriousness with which the Cleveland administration held the matter.[60]

The text of the "twenty-inch gun" message had not yet been made public, but hints of its explosive nature were being leaked from the State Department to friendly, "large policy" expansionist senators. In an article for a popular magazine, Senator Henry Cabot Lodge, the genteel jingoist, had argued that the supremacy of the Monroe Doctrine must be established "peaceably if we can, forcibly if we must." Republican senator William E. Chandler of New Hampshire, a reforming navy secretary in the Garfield and Arthur administrations, insanely editorialized on "Our Coming War with England—A Prediction." He thought war over Venezuela inevitable, and if need be, the United States should precipitate the conflict. Cleveland, greatly perturbed at the leaky State Department, admonished, "It is very provoking to have such matters . . . prematurely and blunderingly discussed in the newspapers." It was in the administration's best interests to "discourage . . . news gatherers and news harvesters as to be free from their vexatious intermeddling."[61]

Still without a British response to the 20-inch gun, Cleveland's annual message, which contained several paragraphs admonishing the nation to remain neutral in the suddenly messy insurrection now ravaging Cuba, was delivered to Congress on December 2. The president left for a duck-hunting vacation, telling Olney that if something came in the meantime, to keep it secret and draft a suitably sober statement.

Five days later, Britain's counterbattery arrived. Her Majesty's Government took a strict constructionist's view of the Monroe Doctrine and denied its principles justified the United States' insistence on arbitration whenever a European nation was engaged in a territorial dispute in the Western Hemisphere. They did, however, agree to arbitrate all points not in critical dispute, but never anything "based on the extravagant pretensions of Spanish officials in the last century," nor the wholesale transfer of British subjects "to a nation of different race or language." Briefly put, Her Majesty's Government would put on the table nothing of value.[62]

The shell now in Cleveland's trench, he lobbed it back across the Atlantic in his special Venezuela message to Congress on December 17, 1895. Again Olney provided the draft and the president did the editing, until, as Cleveland admitted, he could not tell which sentences were his own and which were Olney's. He asked Congress to fund a commission to determine the true boundary and declared it the duty of the United States to "resist by every means in its power, as a willful aggression upon its rights and interests" any British grab at the disputed lands. It was received with lusty cheers. The Washington correspondent of the *Times* of London telegraphed home, "There could not be a more sinister indication of the sense in which the message is understood." Olney had an answer to that. His hostile language had been intentional, because "in English eyes the United States was then so completely a negligible quantity that it was believed only words the equivalent of blows would be really effective."[63]

But Grover Cleveland had not been blindly led by devious courtiers, and was certainly the equal of Olney at tweaking Albion's nose. As was his wont, the president impatiently equated opposition to his policy with political immorality, and he unleashed, said his biographer, "a primary wave of warlike enthusiasm, followed by a secondary wave of imperialist sentiment." For about a week the country rose in a unanimous wave of presidential support. Absurdist senators waved the bloody shirt. William Stewart, Democrat of Nevada, asserted, "War would be a good thing even if we get whipped, for it would rid us of English bank rule." The *Washington Post* screamed from its editorial page, "It is the call to arms; the jingoes were right after all." The Irish National Alliance offered the service of one hundred thousand soldiers to the colors. "This country needs a war," New York City police commissioner Theodore Roosevelt wrote enthusiastically to his friend Senator Lodge.[64]

Not everyone lined up in lockstep behind the president. The Democratic New York *World,* owned by Joseph Pulitzer, who despised Richard Olney above all men, denounced the special message as "a grave blunder . . . a colossal crime." Several journals accused Cleveland of pandering to the Irish Catholic vote for a third term. President Charles Eliot of Harvard dismissed alumni Roosevelt and Lodge as "degenerate sons" of that ancient institution.[65]

For all this, nothing happened. Not a shot was fired, not a broadside was trained, not a soldier marched. In Great Britain, influential parties headed by the Prince of Wales and Liberal ex–prime minister Lord Rosebery did much to mobilize official opinion to salve America's ruffled feathers. Britain faced problems of far greater seriousness in South Africa and could not allow a minor territorial dispute to shift her attention. Expressions of Anglo-American amity flooded across the Atlantic, actually improving relations between the countries. Eventually, in the fall of 1899, an arbitration commission meeting in Washington handed down a ruling largely upholding Britain's claims.

In the United States, the Venezuelan squabble heralded a broader interpretation by government, the press, and the informed public of the Monroe Doctrine, and national opinion suddenly awoke to the nation's importance in world affairs. There was a new thrust toward vigorous action in foreign relations, and with it, an acceptance of America's newfound overseas responsibilities. Oddly enough, it was a movement anathema to the fiercely "little America" philosophy of Grover Cleveland and a precursor to events three years in the future. America was looking outward.

The fight over the Venezuelan boundary question segued into the domestic political bloodletting of the "battle of the standards"—gold versus silver—and the American presidential elections of 1896. The Democrats had irrevocably split into the dying camp of Cleveland's eastern "goldbugs" and the cresting wave of southern and midwestern free silverites championed by Cleveland's populist arch-enemy, William Jennings Bryan of Nebraska, "the boy orator of the Platte."

The two men loathed each other with total mutuality. Cleveland, in Bryan's baroque rhetoric, had done absolutely nothing for the de-pressed small farmer, except increase his burden by repealing the Sil-ver Purchase Act, colluding with eastern bankers to save the hated gold standard. Cleveland had shown his enmity to the working class by cracking the Pullman strike, and Bryan accused the president of in-fecting the party with a "Republican virus." The farmer, to Bryan as to Thomas Jefferson, symbolized the mythical American common man, and the Quixotic orator easily donned the mantle of the myth's spokesman against the manufacturing, banking, and mercantile windmills.[66]

Cleveland struck back, but it was the death bellow of the old Democratic donkey. "He has not even the remotest notion of the prin-ciples of Democracy," the president told his intimates, and in a "Let-ter to the Democratic Voters," he urged the party to remain "the party of the people," to shun Bryan's dangerous notions "born of dis-content." Sound money, the gold standard, were bedrock institutions of national honor and must be preserved. Rendered to its basics, the battle of the standards for the soul of the Democratic Party drew the line between the declining agrarian producer and the growing urban consumer. For the Democrats, William Jennings Bryan was the more effective propagandist for his cause.[67]

With wonderful symbolism, on July 9, 1896, the party convened in Chicago, scene of so many of its past and future coronations and im-molations. Pure and simple, it was a free silver convention. The nom-ination, however, was still open. But when Bryan had his turn at the podium, in one of the great moments of American political theater, he swept all before him. He was but thirty-six years old, young for any time to seek the presidency, and the first politician of national promi-nence grown up after the Civil War.

"This is not a contest between persons," he began. "The humblest citizen in all the land, when clad in the armor of a righteous cause, is stronger than all the hosts of error." In layer upon layer of the richest tub-thumping rhetoric, he said he had come to speak in defense of a cause "as holy as the cause of liberty—the cause of humanity."

Theatrically pointing to the western end of the hall, Bryan dismissed all Democrats, save those of the newfound dogma, the "hardy pioneers who have braved all the dangers of the wilderness. It is for these that we speak." Opening unnecessary sectional wounds among the big-city Democratic clubhouse machines, whose resources and foot soldiers were absolutely vital to turning out the vote, he aimed the self-righteous finger of scorn: "We beg no longer; we entreat no more; we petition no more. We defy them." Then came the crescendo, the holy motto on the banner of the battle of the standards: "You shall not press down upon the brow of labor this crown of thorns; you shall not crucify mankind upon a cross of gold." The twenty thousand hypnotized delegates thundered forth a great sound of joy; they had found their man and would march over the cliff, their eyes on the shining guidon of free silver. As for the Democratic Party itself, the legacy of Jefferson and Jackson, "There was nothing left of the Democratic Party at Chicago but the name," crowed Nevada's senator William Stewart, silverite, populist, and champion of white supremacy politics.[68]

The confident Republicans gathered in a mammoth, electric-lit auditorium in St. Louis, nominating the easygoing, hand-shaking, ear-to-the-ground major from Canton, Ohio, the man who never saw a protective tariff he didn't like, Governor William McKinley. He was no match for the stem-winding oratorical Bryan, so McKinley's keepers ensconced the candidate on his front porch, where he intoned carefully rehearsed speeches to visitors whose railroad tickets were like as not paid for by the Republican National Committee.

The real street fight against Bryan and the Democrats was waged by McKinley's steam-engine campaign manager, Marcus Alonzo Hanna, the Lake Erie coal, iron, and newspaper magnate. After shelling out $100,000 from his own pockets to secure McKinley's nomination, he "fried the fat" from insurance companies, railroads, trusts, any corporation or industry that had benefited from Republican tariffs or politics. Demanding open ledgers, he assessed big banks 0.5 percent of their capital funds, until he amassed the staggering campaign chest of something like $3,350,000.

Bryan, however, conducted the most energetic, peripatetic campaign in presidential history, and had the election been held that summer, he might have won. The Democratic candidate traveled over eighteen thousand miles, addressed five million people, and spoke twenty times a day to real crowds. Relentlessly he attacked the gold standard, big business, the trusts. "One of the most important duties of government is to put rings in the noses of hogs" was a constant theme and brought great yelping cheers. Exhorting farmers from atop a manure spreader, he quipped, "This is the first time I have ever spoken from a Republican platform."[69]

Bryan's tracks were dogged by 1,400 Republican campaign workers, who refuted his message at every whistle-stop and crossroad. Hanna distributed 100 million pieces of campaign literature and tons of mock-gold elephants, gold bugs, and gold wheat sheaves. He organized a "sound money" parade of 150,000 somber-suited, bowler-hatted businessmen, bankers, clergymen, and lawyers, who marched serried rank upon rank up New York's Broadway. Who did America really want in the White House anyway, the candidate of cowshit, gone-bust, farmers, and Coxey Army crazies, or the major from Canton who symbolized the new, growing America in carefully phrased sentences from his white-painted porch?

William Jennings Bryan did not go down to overwhelming defeat. Lose though he did, he managed to collect the largest Democratic popular tally in the nation's history to date, 6.5 million. William McKinley, led by his master general, racked up 7.1 million and 271 in the electoral college. On November 10, celebrating with Hanna at a gargantuan victory lunch in New York, Police Commissioner Theodore Roosevelt felt a certain revulsion at it all. "He [Hanna] has advertised McKinley as if he were a patent medicine," Roosevelt penned in a prophetic letter.[70]

CHAPTER 2

EVER FAITHFUL ISLE

We must act. Cuba must be free from Spain and the United States.

—José Martí, January 1895

I am not a politician, I am Weyler.

—Lieutenant General Valeriano Weyler y Nicolau,
Marquis of Teneriffe, Governor and Captain
General of Cuba, February 1896

There is a Castilian proverb that God granted Spain warm skies, good grapes, and beautiful women. When asked also to provide good government, God refused, saying if Spain had that too, it would be heaven on earth. If this was true of the mother country, it counted doubly so for its once golden, truly global empire. When, after more than three hundred years, it collapsed in the early decades of the nineteenth century, Cuba and Puerto Rico, alone in America, and the Philippines and certain island groups in the Pacific—the Ladrones (Marianas), Carolines, and Palaus—were all that remained. To Cuba, pearl of the Antilles, a grateful metropolis awarded the self-delusional mantle of "Ever Faithful Isle."

In theory, the island was not a colony, but an overseas extension of Spain, electing its own representatives to the Spanish parliament, the Cortes. The island's Spanish-born population, *peninsulares,* mostly military officers, clergy, and civil bureaucrats, dominated Cuba's official life. Leagued with shipping and industrial cartels in Spain, they

38

dictated its commercial intercourse and selected most of Cuba's delegates to the Cortes. These pocket legislators, pretending to speak for
Cuba's welfare, actually spoke only for the entrenched privileges of
the *peninsulares* and their Iberian home allies. The parliamentary
program was simple: no reduction of the Spanish military or civil establishment in Cuba, reserved commercial privileges, and maintenance of historic opportunities for skimming and graft. Casting their
support to Conservative or Liberal, whoever offered the best deal,
they prevented the Spanish government from enacting any true
Cuban reforms, even if Spain were capable of it.

The *criollos,* Creoles, second element of Cuba's white society,
island-born descendants of Spanish colonials, constituted the middle,
professional, and intellectual classes, as well as the landowning farmers—sugar, tobacco, and coffee growers. The political and free-trade
aspirations of the Creoles naturally clashed head-on with the stifling
bureaucratic and ancient mercantilistic policies of Spain and the
peninsulares. Numbers of Creoles had traveled widely throughout the
Americas, including the United States, which had a sizable Cuban
population, and they increasingly rejected the corrupt, repressive
Spanish colonial reign.

The only thing the *peninsulares* and Creoles shared was a fear of
Cuba's blacks and of black revolts. Cuba's emergence in the early
nineteenth century as the world's leading sugar producer provided the
impetus to import tens of thousands of African slaves to work the
plantations. Despite Spain's acceptance in 1817 of an international
agreement to end the slave trade, though not slavery itself, the illegal,
inhuman flow of wretched cargo increased. By midcentury, of Cuba's
total population of just over one million people, 436,000 were slaves,
and another 153,000 were classified as "free colored." The nightmare
of a mass slave uprising, as had occurred in Haiti, bound the Cuban
planters to the Spanish government, particularly the Spanish army, as
their primary protector. It was this dread that, until rather late in the
game, kept the Creoles generally cool toward arguments for Cuban
independence. Before the American Civil War, when Spain actually
seemed ready to end African slavery, the Creoles had nurtured strong
annexationist sentiments toward the United States, but it was a flirtation that evaporated with the threat; the total abolition of Cuban
slavery would not occur until 1880.

In 1865, Spain, bleeding from dynastic struggle, civil wars, and economic collapse, apprehensive of independence movements in the rump empire, cast her paternal eye at the Ever Faithful Isle. Although a Colonial Reform Commission was established to discuss various modernizations, Spain, on the brink of revolution, instead imposed crushing new taxes.

Coming as they did at a time of economic depression, the taxes stoked major political and social discontent, especially in rebellion-prone Oriente Province, in eastern Cuba, where small planters were especially hard-pressed. The disenchanted and disenfranchised—black, white, and mulatto—gathered in Masonic lodges and planned rebellion. It burst out in October 1868, at Yara, in southeastern Oriente, when the Creole planter Carlos Manuel de Céspedes issued the *Pronunciamiento de Yara* and, at the head of 147 men, including his 30 freed slaves, launched the Ten Years' War for Cuban independence.

The rebels, hungry, tattered scarecrows, armed with only machetes for weapons, and never amounting to more than 20,000, spilled over the mountains of Oriente into neighboring Camagüey Province, dispelling at once the notion that the rebellion could be stifled in its cradle. For a mother country, no time is opportune for colonial revolt, but for Spain this came at a particularly bad moment. Only a month prior to the *pronunciamiento,* the corrupt reign of Queen Isabella II ended with her overthrow and exile. In the six years that followed, Spain suffered from shaky military rule, an unpopular foreign king, the Carlist dynastic civil war, and an ill-fated radical republic, before a constitutional monarchy was established in 1874, anointing the favored Alfonso XII, son of the deposed Isabella.

In Cuba, the Spanish troubles should have boded well for the insurgency. But the rebels were too deeply divided, especially over so root an issue as complete independence versus mere domestic autonomy. The revolt was also seriously hampered by the Creole leadership's failure to confront squarely the large numbers of black soldiers in their rebel ranks, perhaps a quarter of the fighters, and the entire question of African slavery. The rebel leaders were also torn by personal jealousy, and their forces were severely hampered by chronic shortages of ammunition as well as by the reluctance of their men to operate outside their home districts. There was almost no support in the rich western half of Cuba, and because the insurgency was confined to the eastern, poorest, blackest third of the island, the Spanish authorities and *peninsulares* successfully propagandized the rebellion as a black revolt rather than a movement for Cuban independence.

By 1876, Spain, having papered over its domestic problems, dispatched the man who had successfully ended the Carlist civil war, General Arsenio Martínez Campos, a seasoned veteran campaigner, with 14,000 regulars to join the 24,000-man garrison already in Cuba. Together with *peninsulare* volunteers, the new governor and captain general of Cuba commanded about 70,000 men. He divided the island into eight operational commands and, instead of large, heavily equipped columns, he ordered "flying forces" of light infantry and locally enlisted cavalry, *guerrilleros,* to search and root out the insurgent forces. To confine the rebels in the east, he also built a *trocha,* a vast fortified line in the jungle at the narrow point of the island near the western border of Camagüey where it joins Santa Clara Province. But no matter what his tactics, Martínez Campos was smart enough to know he could not defeat the rebels in sufficient numbers to end the war with a complete military victory. He would have to negotiate.[1]

In February 1878, the insurgent military and civil leadership convened with Martínez Campos at Zanjón in Camagüey. If peace there would be, it could only happen at the cost of wide-ranging, legitimate reforms. In return for the public surrender of the rebel forces, Martínez Campos conceded amnesty to all, freedom to slaves in rebel ranks, plots on the old royal lands, and government assistance to all who wished to emigrate to the United States or other Caribbean states from Cuba.[2]

The ensuing Pact of Zanjón ending the Ten Years' War pleased no one. Antonio Maceo, the brilliant, charismatic black rebel known as the "Bronze Titan," had refused to attend the Zanjón conference. After a private interview with Martínez Campos, he issued his own "Protest of Baraguá" and denounced the agreement for not abolishing slavery totally and immediately. In Spain, the manipulative Conservative premier, Antonio Cánovas del Castillo, faced what he considered bad choices on every hand. If he ignored Martínez Campos's demands for reform, he confronted the likelihood of a new Cuban insurrection, which would discredit his own civilian government. Moreover, Martínez Campos held a high profile both in Spain and in Cuba, and his influence posed a real threat to Cánovas's power. The premier could bring the general home as minister of war in the cabinet, but that might cause other cabinet resignations and the consequent fall of his ministry. The wily premier discovered an extremely devious way around all this. Ensuring his own domestic survival, and that of every other regime to follow, Cánovas laid the foundation that henceforth would drive Spain's Cuba policy: Say anything, pretend everything, do nothing.

Late in January 1879, Cánovas recalled Martínez Campos from Cuba and engineered his elevation to premier, giving the general enough rope to hang himself on Cuban reforms. Their undoubted unpopularity among the Spanish military and commercial classes would surely undercut the authority of Martínez Campos, paving the way for a return to power of Cánovas and the status quo Conservatives. The American minister to Madrid, James Russell Lowell, clearly recognized the shell game from the start. In a message to the State Department he warned of "the desire being to neutralize or rather to annihilate Martínez Campos with as little inconvenience . . . and with as much apparent undesignedness as possible." Good things, however, were expected of the new government. The reformist Madrid newspaper *El Imparcial* noted that Martínez Campos had comported himself in Cuba "not in words, but in deeds, not in promises, but in realities." In contrast to Cánovas, the general was "more liberal, more sympathetic to democratic tendencies."[3]

It soon became clear that opposition in the Cortes to any reform of consequence in Cuba was both wide and deep. Worse, the ministry of Martínez Campos was badly undercut in August 1879 when the *Guerra Chiquita,* the Little War, broke out in Cuba. No matter that it was entirely contained in Oriente, and that the Spanish army took rapid, effective action. That several leading rebels had been parties to the Pact of Zanjón weakened the foundations of Martínez Campos's ministry. Then on December 7, his government fell over the issue of the Cuban budget. Two days later, just as planned, Don Antonio Cánovas resumed the premiership. "The only firm conclusion I have been able to draw," noted Minister Lowell, "is that the gravity of the Cuban question is hardly yet understood in Spain."[4]

The collapse of the Martínez Campos government ended any hope that Spain could retain her Cuban colony over the long haul. Cuba's moderate Creole landowners and merchants were finally disgusted enough by Spanish bureaucratic corruption and the choking tariffs of an outdated Spanish colonial mercantilism that utterly stifled trade with any commercial partner save Spain. The Cuban middle classes loosely coalesced into political parties that demanded economic reforms and quasi independence from Spain, including a Canada-like dominion status from the crown. And there were other men, less patient, grown to political and military maturity during the Ten Years' War, who sought truly radical solutions leading to real independence.

The *apóstol* of the War for Cuban Independence was born in Cuba, in 1853, to *peninsulares* Leonor Pérez Martí and her husband, Mariano Martí y Navarro, a sergeant of the Spanish army turned policeman. The boy was named José. The elder Martí, profane, brutal, alcoholic, carried all the superior attitudes of the Spanish-born in Cuba, which did not take in his Creole son. "At first [Mariano] had tried to impress upon him," says Martí's biographer, "through sheer regard for tradition, a strict loyalty to Spain. But he soon learned that it was part of the fate of Spaniards in America . . . to be fathers of Creole rebels."[5]

At twelve, José met his political mentor, the teacher-poet Rafael María Mendive, principal of the Havana Municipal High School for Boys. Young Martí absorbed the lessons of "civic integrity" and the struggles of liberation heroes from classical Rome's Gracchi brothers to Simón Bolívar. The student body was divided. The smaller group, the "Sparrows," wrote Martí's biographer, were "robust and with hair close cropped, wore rough half-boots and spoke with a strong Spanish accent." They, like Martí, were sons of Spanish soldiers or *voluntarios,* local militia attached to the Spanish army in Cuba. José Martí, though certainly of that clan, instead aligned himself with the majority of Creole students, the dandified "Hummingbirds," budding intellectuals who mocked the swaggering Sparrows with "humorous disdain."[6]

In 1868, at the start of the Ten Years' War, Martí, heeding Mendive's lecture that anything other than real independence was just "ways of wasting time," organized a club of insurgent Hummingbirds and began to write revolutionary poetry. The moment of truth came on January 5, 1869. At a theater "benefit for the poor," really a rebel fund-raiser, shouts of "Long live the land of sugarcane!" and "*Viva Cuba!*" started a panic to the doors. *Voluntarios* opened fire from the streets. The disturbance spread. Mendive's house was searched, and in it was found one of Martí's seditious poems. Jailed for nine months before being charged, the boy was accused of "suspicion of disloy-alty"; the charge was later broadened to "insulting a pioneer squad of the First Battalion of Volunteers." The sixteen-year-old was sentenced to six years' hard labor. At Havana's *Presidio,* he was now "prisoner No. 113, first tier, Whites."[7]

Shackled in leg irons, Martí labored in a limestone quarry under the most extreme, inhuman conditions of Spanish colonialism. After six months, herniated and half blind, he was shipped off to the Isle of Pines and thence to exile in Spain. In Madrid, with the scars of the lash still on his body, Martí's life unexpectedly bloomed. Here, in the cultural vortex of the Hispanic world, Martí moved freely, a completely liber-atcd man, mingling with the large Cuban community, attending the the-ater, habituating cafés. He enrolled at the university to earn his degree in law. He was initiated into the Masons and socialized with high-ranking officers of the army. As an intelligent, cultured, and presentable young man, José Martí was welcomed at the homes and salons of influ-ential Madrileños, including members of the Spanish nobility, and par-took fully of the social and intellectual life of the wonderful, welcoming metropolis. In fact, he might easily have succumbed to its allure.

With effort, Martí did not. Casting a cold eye, he recoiled from what he saw was just a spectacle. Spain was divided by jealousies large and petty. All political life had been reduced to quarrelsome personal factions in constant discord, which frustrated attempts at domestic and colonial reform. Parasitism, inertia, and rhetoric were all that mattered. Now Martí clearly understood that Cuba's central problem was Spain herself and would be settled only when Spain's own deepest problems were confronted—if Cuba could wait that long.

In November 1871, Martí decided that Cuba could not wait. Nei-ther reform nor autonomy were meaningful. Only independence mat-tered. The root of his decision lay in Cuba, where eight medical students from the University of Havana, having "desecrated the tomb" of a recently assassinated *voluntario,* were executed, while thirty-five others were condemned to the rock quarry. The news changed Martí's life forever. Any vestiges of loyalty to Spain were lost, replaced by the fire of revolution for an independent Cuba. In 1880, after stays in Central America, Mexico, and Cuba, he arrived in New York. He was twenty-seven years old, slight of build, sharp featured, with a high, intelligent forehead and a large black mustache.[8]

Now began the years of organizing that were to culminate in his followers proclaiming on February 25, 1895, the prophetic *Grito de Baïre*, the "cry of Baïre," which heralded Cuba's last war of independence. Unlike so many revolutionary movements, Martí's, by self-effacing design, was neither his personal property nor a vehicle for self-aggrandizement; he sought instead "to obtain, with the united forces of all men of good will, the absolute independence of the island of Cuba." On January 5, 1892, he created *El Partido Revolucionario Cubano,* the Cuban Revolutionary Party. In New York City, he organized the Cuban Junta, the council, as the overall propaganda and coordinating body dealing with the practical matters of the coming revolution. Under the leadership of the lawyer Tomás Estrada Palma, late president of the "Cuban Republic in Arms" during the Ten Years' War (and independent Cuba's first president in 1902), it immediately garnered considerable support from American labor unions and a sympathetic press.[9]

The party concentrated on the organizations of the Cuban émigré communities in the United States, especially Florida, where sixty-one clubs flourished in Key West alone. This was no simple task, for the thousands of exiles had sharply divided into rival factions and held distinct opinions on the nature of the revolution and the republic to follow. Martí alone, by the force of his will and personality, achieved unity. He refused to yield to those who insisted blacks be subordinate in the organization, and he likewise rejected the demands of wealthy expatriates that socialist members be eliminated from leadership positions. To spread the message, he began the newspaper *Patria* (Fatherland), the expenses of the first issue being funded by New York cigar makers. Money was a constant problem, and here too Martí was helped by the tobacco workers, who donated a day's earnings each week, 25¢ to $2.50, to the cause. Wealthy Cuban exiles, by contrast, were cold to his appeal. Yet by the spring of 1892, a bare three months after the party's founding, it had become an established organization, with associated clubs in all centers of the émigré population, and through *Patria,* its message reached into Cuba as well.

Unlike organizers of previous Cuban revolutionary movements, Martí intentionally excluded the military leadership from any role until he had a sound organization in place. Then, without hesitation, he turned to Máximo Gómez, the wizened Dominican who had played a key role in leading the rebels during the Ten Years' War. In September 1892, Martí journeyed to Santo Domingo to offer Gómez the revolution's military command. "I have no other remuneration to offer you," he told the wispy, white-mustached ancient, "than the pleasure of sacrifice and the probable ingratitude of man." In January 1893, Gómez was formally named general in chief of Cuba's revolutionary forces under arms, a general as yet without an army.[10]

Everyone in the movement wondered about Antonio Maceo, the Bronze Titan, the astonishing black mule driver turned field commander who had rejected the Pact of Zanjón and now lived comfortably in a plantation colony he had established in Costa Rica. In June 1893, Martí traveled there as well. Maceo did not agree at once. Leery of conspiracies, he had seen too many revolts precipitously declared and just as many trampled underfoot by the Spanish army. He was, however, very impressed by Martí's groundwork—no one had ever planned so carefully before. When Maceo agreed to join the cause, Martí advised him to settle his affairs and await the order from Gómez to move into Cuba. Meanwhile, other important Cuban officers were recruited in the United States.

Martí continued his ceaseless activities. A large defect of the Ten Years' War and lesser Cuban revolts had been a distinct lack of political and military direction from within Cuba itself. The frequently exiled insurgent leadership had always attempted to dictate policy and strategy from abroad, weakening the authority of the fighting forces on the home ground. Martí, now a political operator of the first rank, made contact with shadow echelons in Cuba. Military commanders, generals of the phantom revolutionary army, were appointed for the island's six provinces and assorted districts. A military-civil commissar was named to coordinate activities between the army and rural population, on whom they would have to depend for intelligence and sustenance. Responsible men were chosen at local levels to begin stockpiling clothing, ammunition, and weapons. To a political educator like Martí, nobody would be left in the dark as to what it was ultimately all about. "Arm the decided," he instructed the commissar in

Cuba, "convince the undecided, supply information to all good Cubans, so that none will be ignorant of events."[11]

Early in 1894 Martí began actively putting the machinery in place for imminent revolution, not least because expansionist attitudes in the United States caused him to fear that somehow America would manage to absorb Cuba before the island could liberate itself from Spain. Alarmed at the growing mood of imperialism and the rush, albeit stalled, to annex Hawaii, Martí saw its portents for Cuba. "Cuba would make one of the finest states in the Union," said the Detroit *Free Press,* among many others. "We must act," Martí told a colleague. "Cuba must be free from Spain and the United States." Yet there was also the dilemma of moving too prematurely. If the rebellion drum banged before all was ready, it would break like every other. In balance, said Martí, we must "fall on the island before the [Spanish] Government [can] fall on the Revolution."[12]

Martí alerted the contingents in Cuba to prepare themselves for action by the end of February. But the time slipped away and nothing was ready. From his outlook in Santo Domingo, Máximo Gómez saw little support in Camagüey Province, where plantation owners pleaded for time to finish harvesting the sugar and grinding the cane. If the rebels would just delay a while longer, they promised substantial contributions. Gómez knew these were just obfuscating lies. He had no respect for the Cuban propertied classes. Disgusted, he ordered the revolt to begin on his command. "This situation will not change," he wrote to Maceo in September 1894; "the rich people will never enter the Revolution. We must force the situation—precipitate the events." After the middle of November—at the latest—the height of the dry, grinding season—"we must all be prepared to move immediately."[13]

To inject his key commanders and sufficient military stores into Cuba, Martí turned to "filibustering," and chartered three fast yachts, carrying General Serafín Sánchez and eight hundred men, from Fernandina, Florida. The convoy would stop at Costa Rica to embark Maceo and two hundred more, and finally to Santo Domingo for Gómez and his contingent. All members of the expedition were disguised as agricultural workers. In December 1894, with everything ready, one of Sánchez's men blabbed the plan. It spread to Spanish consular officials, and quickly enough, they lodged a protest with the

U.S. government. On January 14, 1895, federal officers seized the yachts at Fernandina, and with them, three years of work and fifty-eight thousand dollars in military stores were lost.[14]

The debacle had an unforeseen effect. Martí, grown despondent, saw the enthusiasm for his leadership wane not a bit; instead, it grew enthusiastically. The scope of his work had at last been revealed, and funds from the tobacco workers and a loan engineered by Gómez from the president of the Dominican Republic outfitted another expedition.

Just over two weeks later, Martí's representatives and commanders in Cuba signed the formal revolutionary declaration. When he determined there was sufficient support on the island, the mulatto ex-slave Juan Gualberto Gómez, military-civil commissar, chose February 25, 1895, to begin the war of liberation. In Oriente Province, at the eponymous village some fifty miles from the provincial capital, Santiago de Cuba, the rebels raised the *Grito de Baïre*.

The uprising was nearly stillborn, and the Spanish authorities were not boasting when they claimed to have the rebels on the run. The leadership of the western provinces were taken prisoner that very day, and with that, the insurrection in that wealthy end of the island collapsed. The exiled military commanders strained at their forced inaction. "The smoke of gunfire is visible in Cuba and the blood of our comrades is being shed on its soil," wrote Gómez to Maceo. "We have no other choice but to leave [for Cuba] from wherever and however we can." Maceo instantly agreed: "I do not think we can afford to wait any longer. . . . Once in Cuba, we can depend on the machete to open the breach."[15]

On March 25, Maceo, his brother Juan, and twenty men pushed off from Costa Rica in the American-flagged vessel *Adirondak,* officially bound for New York. Again the scheme leaked and Spanish gunboats shadowed them at sea. Scared off, the *Adirondak*'s skipper landed the party in the Bahamas, where the American consul rented Maceo his schooner and crew. On the thirty-first it ran up the beach near Baracoa, by the far eastern tip of Cuba. "Maceo is here!" went the word immediately throughout Oriente Province.

To avoid encirclement and capture by Spanish forces, Maceo kept to the jungle, living off wild green oranges. Near Guantánamo he skirmished with a Spanish patrol, losing several of his men. His force then split into smaller groups, and eventually Maceo and five follow-ers, exhausted and near starving, reached a main rebel camp. Of the original twenty-odd men who began the journey with him, thirteen were still alive. That night, April 20, Maceo issued a general order to the insurgents in Oriente Province announcing his command. The next day he directed all officers "to hang every emissary of the Span-ish government . . . who presents himself in our camps with proposi-tions of peace. . . . Our motto is to triumph or die." On the thirtieth, the Bronze Titan wrote to his wife that he had six thousand "well-armed" men under his orders.[16]

With even more frustrating adventure, Martí and Gómez landed in Cuba on April 11. When their original vessel's crew deserted in Santo Domingo, Martí, Gómez, and four men took passage on a German ba-nana freighter bound for Haiti. The captain, on payment of one thou-sand dollars, agreed to drop them in a small boat as they passed the Cuban coast. Martí's presence in the party was controversial. There were those who thought he should remain outside Cuba, directing rev-olutionary policy, raising recruits and money. Others sniped that he could talk a good rebellion but had no stomach for the real fight. Martí came back to Cuba because the country would not accept "without scorn . . . one who preached the need of dying without be-ginning by risking his own life. . . . I called up the war," he confided to a friend; "my responsibility begins rather than ends with it."[17]

On May 4, the rebel leadership joined at La Mejorana, near Santi-ago de Cuba, to formulate the overall politico-military strategy for the revolution. Martí and Gómez favored civil control, lest when in-dependence was achieved, there would be nothing in place but a mil-itary dictatorship. Maceo disagreed. Pointing to the incompetence of the civilian "government" during the Ten Years' War, he came out strongly for a military junta, at least until victory. The Martí-Gómez plan was generally accepted, with Gómez confirmed as general in chief of the army, Maceo as lieutenant general in the east and com-mander in Oriente, and Martí as the revolution's supreme leader abroad and in all civil matters in Cuba.

Gómez outlined his long-range strategy for the conduct of opera-tions. There were many reasons the rebellion had collapsed in the Ten Years' War, one of which was its confinement to eastern Cuba. Unable to match blows with the large, well-equipped Spanish army in the field, Gómez announced a scorched earth, slash-and-burn campaign along the length and breadth of the island, a brutal tactic aimed at the sugar industry primarily and the economy in general, intent on destroying every possible source of Spanish revenue. An exhausted Spain, he reasoned, must ultimately grant independence because the cost of maintaining control in the face of intransigent revolt far outpaced any revenues reaped from Cuba's devastated soil. It would bring massive suffering to the people of Cuba, but that was the very high price for independence. "The chains of Cuba have been forged by her own richness," said the ruthless little general, who had scant appreciation for war's higher arts and sciences, "and it is precisely this which I propose to do away with soon." Over the protest of Maceo, who proposed less draconian measures—for example, levying tribute on wealthy planters on pain of losing all if they did not pay—Gómez's plan was adopted.

On May 19 a Spanish column surprised Gómez at Dos Ríos, near the large town of Bayamo. Martí, ordered to remain in the rear, instead rode forward on a white horse to his first battle and was shot and killed. Attempts to retrieve his body failed. It was taken away by the Spanish and buried in Santiago de Cuba. He was forty-two years old, and until Fidel Castro, no Cuban political leader who followed came anywhere near his stature. But the revolution now had the stimulus of a hero and genuine martyr, the single figure of the movement around whom all Cubans could unite. The fighting and propaganda could now be left to the generals in Cuba and the émigré lawyers of the Junta in New York.

Spain was not completely oblivious of the need for reforms in her Ever Faithful Isle. Premier Práxedes Mateo Sagasta and his Liberals were now in power. With significant effort, all the time fighting the reactionary Cuban *peninsulares,* Sagasta presented the Cortes a small set of incremental reforms giving Cuba a bare increase in her own governance and trade. These "Abarzuza laws," so named for the colonial minister, were in the process of legislative enactment when the *Grito de Baïre* proclaimed the revolution and, with it, a whole new game.

For several weeks following the *grito,* Spanish official reaction in both Madrid and Havana was muted and not overly alarmed. The easy capture of the rebels' western provincial leadership had fostered the opinion that the revolution could be quelled without much difficulty. It was only with the news that Gómez and Maceo were involved that any real concern was raised. General Arsenio Martínez Campos, victor in the Ten Years' War, author of the Pact of Zanjón, and Spain's most eminent soldier, attributed "great importance to the fact that chieftain Maceo is embarking for Cuba, because I know the prestige he enjoys and the military skill he exhibited in the previous campaign." Premier Sagasta, who lived by the credo "Time and I against everybody," took the hard line, pledging "an energetic campaign of repression, persecution, and chastisement" of the Cuban rebels. He did, nonetheless, proceed with the Abarzuza laws, telling the Cortes their passage provided the most effective deterrent to the Cuban revolution, for it would pacify moderate Havana reformists, and thus might confine the uprising to Oriente Province.[18]

On March 14, with the rebellion in Cuba three weeks along, and nothing much besides a lot of noise coming from either the insurgents or the regime, the Madrid daily *El Resumen,* in an editorial that struck at the heart of one of Spain's most nationalistic and reactionary institutions, the army, sharply criticized the majority of junior officers over their laggard volunteering for service in Cuba. Much insulted, a mob of lieutenants broke into the paper's offices. When *El Resumen* and another journal protested, both were vandalized by several hundred young officers brazenly wearing their army uniforms.

Sagasta and his government were excoriated on the floor of the Cortes—not for failing to protect the newspaper offices from the military mob, but for cowardice in not hauling the editors in front of courts-martial for defaming the army! Why was there no punishment of the journalists? Why had it been necessary for the officers themselves to soil their hands? When Sagasta cravenly capitulated to the army by apologizing, offering the excuse that the law did not permit such action against the press, the Madrid area senior commanders insisted he do it anyway. Reportedly, the guardians of the state were so incensed that, if the government were "besieged," neither the army, the rural constabulary (*Guardia Civil*), nor the police would budge to protect it.

The government was in the sort of crisis that was to become endemic, eventually, in 1936, ripping the country apart. The queen regent, Doña María Cristina, mother of thirteen-year-old King Alfonso XIII, summoned General Arsenio Martínez Campos to pacify his more obstreperous comrades of the upper ranks. Meanwhile, Sagasta, aware that no government could resist the army and survive, resigned with the whole of his cabinet. A Conservative government, once again headed by Antonio Cánovas del Castillo, dean of Spanish political survivors, took the reins of office.

Juggling demands for true reform on the one hand and reactionary agendas pushed by Catholic and *peninsulare* factions on the other, and barely in control of his own party, Cánovas announced his intention to go forward with the Abarzuza laws and, in March 1895, a month after the *Grito de Baïre,* declared no effort would be spared to remedy Cuba's legitimate grievances. Even better, he arranged for the posting to Cuba of General Martínez Campos himself, with unlimited powers, credits, and every promise of support, as governor and captain general of the Ever Faithful Isle. Again, a brilliant stroke. Not only would a dangerous potential rival of tremendous prestige be shipped halfway across the world, but failure in Cuba would stick to the general, not the government. As for the Abarzuza laws, it was just as well to delay putting together their bureaucratic machinery. In brief, Cánovas's policy, according to U.S. minister Hannis Taylor, became one of promising everything while "conceding nothing in the way of real autonomy except a few empty forms."[19]

"War of the present day is another thing"—worse in every respect than any previous Cuban revolutionary crisis—Martínez Campos told the queen regent on his leave-taking; prophetically, he said, "My heart tells me that it will be the last that Spain has to endure in America."[20]

"When Spain sends its great general Martínez Campos to put down the uprising in Cuba," noted Joseph Pulitzer's New York *World,* "it means that the trouble is serious." On April 2, Madrid papers announced the departure of a battalion of marines, with 7,252 soldiers scheduled to leave within a fortnight to join the 13,000 Spanish regulars already on the island. By the end of the year, the Spanish army in Cuba would number close to 100,000 regular troops and over 60,000 marines, Spanish-officered *voluntarios,* Cuban *guerrilleros* (locally raised, irregular cavalry under their own officers), and *Guardia Civil* constabulary.[21]

Captain General Arsenio Martínez Campos arrived in Cuba on April 16, but instead of stepping ashore into the steamy pomp of the capital, he landed at Guantánamo, in faraway Oriente. From there he traveled by rail and coastal steamer to Havana, inspecting garrison towns and giving instructions along the way on military and civil affairs, even to the diet and medical services of his regiments.

At first, Premier Cánovas's window-dressing policy of all and nothing bore fruit, albeit small. As he cynically predicted, Cuban autonomists heatedly denounced the revolution and pledged their loyalty to Spain. But Martínez Campos saw the true situation, and it boded ill. "The few Spaniards who are on the island," he cabled the premier, "only dare to proclaim themselves in the cities; the rest of the inhabitants hate Spain." Nothing could regain their loyalty, not kindness, not cruelty, neither reform, nor repression. Going deep into the countryside, "there are no men to be seen, and women, on being asked after their husbands and sons, reply with terrible frankness: 'in the mountains, with So and So.' "[22]

Yet, if Spain only desired to keep Cuba groaning under the royal yoke and nothing more, Martínez Campos understood the methods: total ruthlessness, verging on barbarity. As had been done on a limited scale in Oriente during the Ten Years' War, Spanish forces, he advised, must "reconcentrate" the rural population into the garrison towns, depriving the rebels of any succor in the countryside; "the misery and hunger would be terrible." It might indeed come to this, but Martínez Campos was not the officer to carry out such practices: "I lack the qualities," he said. He knew who had them, however, and in abundance, telling the premier, "Among our present generals only Weyler has the necessary capacity for such a policy."[23]

Spain's original hopes to stifle the rebellion at birth proved an illusion. Still, an objective military analysis indicated an eventual, though bloody, Spanish victory. The Spanish regular army, the *Ejército de España,* was a standard Continental European conscript force of peasants and city boys: passably trained and equipped, well armed, patriotic, disciplined, though poorly officered, and nobody's pushover. Their rapid mobilization of nearly one hundred thousand men for Cuban service had been tolerably well done. They could increase their numbers at will, and by 1898, nearly a quarter of a million regulars, plus sixty thousand auxiliaries, outmanned the rebels in the field by perhaps eightfold. The Spanish navy, with sixty-seven vessels in Cuba, theoretically controlled the entire coastline and surrounding waters. Spain's leading political parties, at the outset, were united in their calls for suppressing the revolt. The national economy was in reasonably good shape, far better than during the Ten Years' War. Very importantly, Spain was at peace with herself.

Operationally, General Martínez Campos believed that a successful application of his methods in the Ten Years' War would equally serve in the present. To suppress the rebellion wherever it might explode, he deployed forces in all the major towns, many of the small ones, the ports, the sugar plantations, and along the whole of Cuba's railroads, most of which lay in the four western provinces. Every inch of land physically occupied by the army was suitably, not to say heavily, fortified with barbed wire, trench works, and blockhouses. The strategic reserve he placed in Camagüey, hemming the insurgents into the eastern tail of the island, trusting to overwhelming numbers to push the rebels into a corner of Oriente and crush them.

Along the narrow-gauge military railroad that bisected Cuba's thin waist in the jungles of western Camagüey, near its border with Santa Clara Province, stretched a fortified line athwart the entire island. Called simply the *trocha,* the railroad right-of-way, and built during the Ten Years' War, it had fallen into disrepair. To no small extent the line had kept rebellions from spilling westward in past conflicts, and of late there had been much feverish work on it.

Richard Harding Davis, an adventurous, experienced war correspondent for the Hearst papers, visited the area with permission of the Spanish army. A cleared swath 200 yards wide had been cut through "apparently impassable" jungle. Thousands of felled trees lay piled up on either side of the tracks in parallel rows, "forming a barrier of . . . trunks and roots and branches as wide as Broadway and higher than a man's head." At every half mile along fifty miles on the east side of the *trocha,* there was a substantial two-story stone or adobe fort and watchtower holding a dozen men. Between each of these lay a smaller blockhouse, and between each of *these* were three plank and mud brick fortlets surrounded by a trench, in hailing distance of the positions on either side. Fronting the entire system were multiple aprons of barbed wire, 450 yards of wire for every dozen yards of distance, trip mines at likely infiltration points, and another barrier of felled trees. According to the Spanish engineers to whom Davis spoke, they hoped eventually to have the *trocha* illuminated by calcium lights in the watchtowers.[24]

Much to the detriment of Spanish arms, Martínez Campos deviated from his original strategy. Instead of light marching columns tracking the rebels throughout the countryside, he divided Cuba into two great military camps, one inside the lines of forts and garrisoned areas, the other without. Inside, the Spanish had near complete control, but outside they had virtually none, and there the Spanish army was loath to march. Daily, columns of regulars, mostly infantry, with nowhere near enough of the mounted troops they should have deployed against the fast-moving rebels, marched out, and invariably by nightfall, they clumped back in. The Spanish gave battle quickly, bravely, and well enough, but they never pursued. Instead of camping on the battlefield and following on the enemy's heels at sunrise, they withdrew to their garrison towns as soon as the last shot of the skirmish died away. The excuse was always fear of rebel ambush, or of abandoning the wounded to the enemy. It was not uncommon for a column of a thousand men to conduct a textbook retreat after a handful were wounded.

For an army primarily composed of infantry, its marksmanship was appalling. The small-bore bolt-action Mauser magazine rifle that equipped most of the regular army was the best in the world, but the Spanish made little use of its qualities. It was not unusual for soldiers to break off the front sights because it tore their clothing, or so they said. Taking no time for aiming, the Spanish infantryman often fired his rifle with the stock in his armpit rather than at the shoulder, and he always fired high. When attacked, a Spanish column invariably formed an anachronistic hollow square and banged away with ineffective volleys. They knew little of open order or skirmishing, relying instead on ponderous movements by large formations. "If the Cubans were only a little better marksmen than their enemies," Richard Harding Davis observed, "they should, with such a target as a square furnishes them, kill about ten men where they now wound one."[25]

Davis watched the Spanish army in its multitudes, and "never saw one [soldier] drunk . . . which is more than you can say of his officers." Eager, alert, stoic, the Spanish soldier in rope-soled canvas shoes, white, light blue, or dun-colored cotton tropical uniform, with rifle, 150 rounds of ammunition, blanket, "and as many tin plates, and bottles and bananas and potatoes and loaves of white bread" as he could carry, trudged up to thirty miles a day "over the worst roads ever constructed by man." Discipline in the regular army was good "in spite of his officers, and not on account of them." In truth, the average Spanish officer cared little for his men, and showed almost no consideration for their dogged adherence to duty.[26]

Besides the insurgents, the Spanish army had to contend with a tropical climate and disease. "The summer is extremely hot and the royal troops are forced to fight not only against the insurgents but also against the yellow fever which plays havoc with the men," wrote Nicolas de Truffin, Russian consul in Havana, to his government. About ten Spanish soldiers died of disease or wounds to every one killed in battle. In the three-year course of the insurrection, thirteen thousand would die from yellow fever alone. At Manzanillo, a third of the eighteen-thousand-man garrison sweated it out in the fever wards. Thus the rebel commander Máximo Gómez, when asked to name his best generals, replied, "June, July and August."[27]

The negatives notwithstanding, the Spanish remained confident of eventual victory.

> *With the beard of Maceo*
> *We will make brooms*
> *To sweep the barracks*
> *Of the Spanish troops*

went the barracks song of the Spanish army.[28]

The rebels, loosely called the Liberation Army, wore no uniforms, ate little, had less ammunition, took no care of their weapons, horses, and equipment, and were likely to run away under fire. Captured Spanish Mausers counted for some of their rifles, but more common was the older Remington .43 caliber American export, numbers of which were smuggled in from the United States or taken on the field from dead *voluntarios*. There was no artillery except the odd gun at odd times. A member of Gómez's staff described "a cannon of the period of Christopher Columbus, which was buried no one knows where and found by no one knows whom." Rusted through, with no ammunition, it was nevertheless cleaned up and named *Trifulca*, the "Fighter." Some black powder was found, a carriage, rammer, and sponge were knocked together, and it was fired at a Spanish blockhouse. On the second shot the gun blew up, "and with this," recalled the officer, with grandiloquent nomenclature, "was finished the artillery of the Fourth Army Corps." The only weapon of any abundance, in fact all rebels carried one, was the wicked two-foot-long cane-cutting machete.[29]

Gómez had initially, and unrealistically, envisioned a rebel military organization extending from one end of Cuba to the other, all 750 miles, from Oriente to Pinar del Río. On paper, this force eventually contained two main "armies," east and west, comprising six corps of fourteen divisions, and subunits. "They are divided into groups, more or less numerous, to which they give the pompous names of regiments and brigades," said a Spanish officer in Havana. First to last, if all were mustered simultaneously on parade, they numbered, perhaps, fifty-four thousand men, with no more than thirty-five thousand at any given time.[30]

The big formation rose in the east, mainly in Oriente, and counted around twenty thousand fighters. They were mounted on badly used horses, and usually did not operate in units larger than a company of one hundred men. Commissary, quartermaster, engineering, and medical departments did not exist in a practical sense. Each formation had its own unarmed *impedimenta* of cooks, firewood gatherers, muleteers, and foragers, freeing the fighting men for single duty.

On July 1, 1895, as the drenching tropical heat of summer covered the whole island, Gómez ordered his economic warfare strategy into practice; Cuba would simply stop functioning, and if need be, would starve. Prohibited by rebel decree were the transport of leather, timber, wood, tobacco, coffee, wax, honey, and cattle into any town occupied by a Spanish garrison, no matter its size. "The sugar plantations will stop their labors," read his edict. "Sugar cannot be allowed, because to work means peace, and in Cuba we must not permit working." For the rebels, a positive side effect brought thousands of now unemployed workers into their ranks. In Havana, Gómez's pronouncements were derisively received, and the rebel commander was dubbed "Don Quixote de Camagüey" for having the foolish temerity to tilt at sugar mills.[31]

Two weeks later, on July 15, the Republic of Cuba formally declared itself. A shadowy organization of a president, vice president, and council established a phantom state in the mountains of northern Camagüey. American political satirists dubbed it a "government in the woods." Whatever it was, it performed no real executive duties and remained completely under the rebel military thumb. The actual work of the rebel government was done by the Junta in New York and Washington.[32]

Gómez or not, when the summer rainy season ended, preparations throughout Cuba went forward for the autumn grinding of the sugar crop. In November, Gómez upped the ante, ordering all plantations "totally destroyed"; all who worked were to be considered "traitors to their country" and shot. Every officer of the Liberation Army was ordered to carry out these measures, "determined," Gómez said, "to unfurl triumphantly, even on ruin and ashes, the flag of the Republic of Cuba." These decrees, he informed the Junta, would result in "the total paralyzation of all labor in Cuba."[33]

There were those in the Liberation Army, Antonio Maceo chief among them, who opposed this horrendous strategy, not only for the havoc it brought Cuba, but for the adverse reaction to the policy, especially in the United States. Maceo concluded a number of private agreements with planters and mill operators, and through them collected a decent share of revolutionary revenue. But whether the methods of Gómez or Maceo prevailed, the big picture was clearly seen by the Russian consul, de Truffin: "The very fact that such an important question as harvesting depends on the will of the insurgents gives a clear idea of the scale and strength of the uprising."[34]

In Madrid, on October 8, Premier Cánovas continued with ostrich-like blindness, or a gambler's desperation, telling a reporter from the paper *La Liberal* that once the war ended, "it is evident that there are great reforms to undertake. . . . Cuba needs full freedom from the central government." Finessing the whole point of the rebellion, keeping it a running sore that Spain could not heal, and making eventual conflict with the United States a certainty, Cánovas drew the proverbial line in the sand. "I am intransigent on only one point," he said, "intransigent against separatism." As for anything else, "I have an open mind." For the rebels, however, there was nothing else, it was the only point.[35]

In June 1895, when the rains began to fall, Gómez ordered forward preparations to carry the war into Cuba's fertile western provinces, the operation to coincide with the autumn sugar grinding. In the Ten Years' War, the sights and sounds of battle and burning had not come close to

Havana; this time things would be different. For the rebels it would constitute their one great general offensive, as Gómez stated, the "great military movement that insured the triumph of the revolution."[36]

The primary formation consisted of Antonio Maceo's "Invading Army" of less than 2,500 men, divided into two "corps." But even these paltry numbers were reduced when Gómez placed one of Maceo's formations under his own direct orders. As commander of all forces in Oriente, Maceo refused to countenance this. The matter was placed before the ineffective rebel government, and as Maceo expected, that body came to no decision. This seriously widened the rift between Gómez and Maceo, something Maceo knew would happen if civilians were given any authority over military operations or policy.

On October 22, Maceo, with 1,700 men, moved west from the rough terrain of Oriente toward the plains of Camagüey. Here it was not so easy to hide, and the rebels were vulnerable to the large, plodding columns of Spanish infantry. Yet through a good part of November there occurred only two small engagements. "I am on my way to the western province," Maceo informed the Junta in New York, "up to now without having faced any troubles." And to his wife, Maceo wrote, "In this Revolution there is hardly any fighting." In part this was because he was moving too fast to be caught. But as well, the Spanish were more concerned with the forces under Gómez, the "man of the torch," moving parallel, north of Maceo. Plantation owners, mill operators, and ranchers insisted their property be defended. In response, Martínez Campos, who had already dribbled away sizable numbers of his troops in penny packets along the length of the island, concentrated his strategic reserve to block the Gómez advance, leaving Maceo a clear path in the south.[37]

November 29 found Maceo only three miles from the town of Ciego de Avila on the *trocha,* guarded by 16,000 Spanish troops. Using some local Camagüey rebels to create a diversion, he began his crossing in a heavy early-morning fog and took 1,500 men over in less than an hour; he was so fast that the Spanish, even with the ability to move by rail, were too late in bringing reinforcements to the critical point. As for Gómez, "if he wants to pass, he will pass," said Martínez Campos. Both "the fox and the lion," as the Spanish called the insurgent leaders, were now across the *trocha* with 2,600 fighters and nearly into Santa Clara Province. The barrier with which the Spanish had hoped to confine the rebellion had been breached with ridiculous ease. The rebel generals temporarily joined forces. Maceo was confirmed in command of the entire Invading Army, healing the schism, and he predicted that, when the campaign ended, General Martínez Campos, whom he personally respected as a chivalrous enemy, would be totally discredited as a military commander.[38]

For the rebels, the problem was how to traverse Santa Clara—rich, populous, cultivated, the central province of the island—without scattering their forces in the process. Here the Spanish *had* to make a stand and destroy the Invading Army, or at least turn the rebels around before they entered the western provinces. Anything less would be a political as well as a military disaster. Martínez Campos brought forward another 25,000 men.

Gómez and Maceo divided the Invading Army into two wings. While the main body continued westward through the center of the province, a diversionary force of 1,000 infantry would penetrate the south coastal mountains along the Caribbean Sea, creating as much destruction and confusion as was possible. Once across Santa Clara, the wings would rendezvous in either Matanzas or Havana Province. Gómez warned they must constantly remain mobile, avoiding large Spanish formations. Reluctantly, Maceo agreed. He always wanted to fight one set-piece action, a European-style pitched battle, and defeat the Spanish army in the open field. If he could do that, the Spanish would never recover their morale.

At this time two young British cavalry officers, barely out of their teens and on leave from their regiment—having "searched the world for some scene of adventure or excitement," wrote Lieutenant Winston Churchill of the 4th Hussars—arrived in Cuba to observe the Spanish army. From Havana they took the train southeast to Cienfuegos: "The journey was quite practicable; the trains were armored; escorts traveled in special wagons at either end; the sides of the carriages were protected by strong plating; when firing broke out, as was usual," Churchill wrote, "you only had to lie down on the floor of the carriage to arrive safely."

From Cienfuegos, they traveled by coaster east to Las Tunas, thence overland to Sancti Spiritus, joining the column of General Suárez Valdés as supernumerary members of his staff. The force of four battalions of infantry, two squadrons of cavalry, and a mule battery numbered over 3,500 men. Churchill noted that "the troops looked fit and sturdy and none the worse for their marches." The column set out at dawn, hiked eight miles in five hours, halted for breakfast of bread and sardines, then continued until 1:00 P.M., when it spread hammocks for a three-hour midday *siesta*. Another eleven miles were covered in four hours when the column camped for the night after marching through twenty miles of rough country, entirely acceptable by military standards. "The infantry," Churchill said, "did not seem in the least fatigued. These tough Spanish peasants . . . could jog along with heavy loads over mere tracks with an admirable persistence. The prolonged midday halt was like a second night's rest to them."

On the following day they were hit by Invading Army rebels. The leading Spanish battalion cleared the broken ground, threw a company forward on each flank, and smartly deployed from column into line. The cavalry maneuvered to the right, the mule battery trotted forward to the center, while the second battalion followed the guns in columns of companies. Rebel fire was continuous across the entire front. The Spanish infantry replied with enthusiasm and advanced. Churchill, along with General Suaréz Valdés and the staff, remained mounted with no cover whatever from the enemy fire and observed the infantry's rushes. "The Spanish were on their mettle. . . . It really seemed very dangerous, and I was astonished to see how few people were hit amid all this clatter." When the Spanish volleys wore the rebels down, the final infantry rush took their ground. But pursuit, he noted, was impossible, "owing to the impenetrable jungle."

Writing other thoughts, Churchill, a keen historian, likened the Spanish forces to the armies of Napoleon trudging their way across the length and breadth of Spain eighty-odd years before, "league after league, day after day, through a world of impalpable hostility, slashed here and there by fierce onslaught." Spain was not a rich country, and the cost of supporting a huge occupying army across five thousand miles of ocean he compared to "a dumb-bell held at arm's length. . . . We did not think the Spaniards were likely to bring their war in Cuba to a speedy end."[39]

On December 3 the Invading Army had its first significant encounter. Learning from local peasants of a nearby Spanish column escorting a supply-laden mule train, Gómez, with only cavalry at hand, deployed for an ambush. Discovered, he opted to fight, and the Spanish, instead of pressing their advantage, withdrew into the local fort at Iguará. The skirmish was costly for both sides. Against rebel losses of thirteen killed, the Spanish lost eighteen men, fifty-four Mauser rifles, eight hundred rounds of ammunition, and twenty fully packed mules.

After burying his dead, Gómez, with 1,600 horsemen, moved forward, intending to halt and re-form inland of the big Caribbean port of Cienfuegos. On his heels was a Spanish brigade of infantry, cavalry, and mountain artillery. While Maceo fought a rearguard action, Gómez marched west. On the morning of December 13, the Spanish guns bombarded the rebel positions. Again Gómez slipped away, leaving Maceo to cover his back with delaying actions. True to form, the Spanish ceased the pursuit, broke off, and returned to base.

With rebel ammunition now exhausted, Gómez seriously questioned if the invasion could proceed, especially in the face of the heavier concentrations of Spanish forces they were certain to encounter the farther west they advanced. But Maceo refused to consider retreat; he would go all the way to Cape San Antonio with only a machete if that was all he had. Bravado notwithstanding, the rebels desperately needed ammunition, and the only way to get it was from the Spanish. They would have to engage a sizable detachment, no simple task, suicidal in fact.

Martínez Campos had moved his headquarters by sea to Cienfuegos, endeavoring once again to "rat-trap" the westward-moving swarm of rebels along the cross-island commercial railroad. Armored trains loaded with well-equipped soldiers steamed up and down the line. The countryside teemed with marching columns. The rebels came on, along the main road, right into the Spanish concentrations. On the morning of December 15, near the aptly named village of Mal Tiempo (Bad Time), Maceo's scouts discovered a strong Spanish force deployed under groves of guava trees and extending outward from both sides of the road as far as the eye could see. In naval parlance, the enemy had "crossed his T." The rebel force straggled behind for miles, and unless Maceo acted instantly, the whole Invading Army faced annihilation.

Maceo and Gómez brought their men into line and sent in their machete-wielding cavalry. The Spanish responded with an orthodox, textbook defense, forming a hollow square that should have shattered the rebel horse completely under disciplined volleys. But the Spanish infantry flinched and went to pieces. Bravely their officers re-formed the square a second and yet a third time. In the hand-to-hand combat that ensued, the Spanish broke, escaping into thickets of sugarcane, where they were safe from the slashing cane knives. Their dead and wounded were counted at 210, and the rebel booty came to 240 rifles, 10,000 rounds of ammunition, plus horses, mules, the medical supplies, and the colors of the Canarias Regiment. The rebels also salvaged an interesting directive from Martínez Campos, castigating his senior officers for concealing losses, inflating their reports, and boasting of "repeated victories over the Insurgents, tales I have never seen verified."[40]

The Battle of Mal Tiempo was probably the most important of the campaign, because if the rebels had not restocked their ammunition, no matter what Maceo said, they could not have progressed in any significant strength. What they captured was not enough to support the whole invasion, but it did enable them—"escorted in the rear by 8,000 Spaniards," as a rebel wit put it—to keep moving westward. In the second half of December, they crossed the Río Hanabanilla into Matanzas Province. Here was the heart of Cuba's sugar industry, where cultivation literally stretched from the edge of one town to another, broken only by the odd pasture where fat cattle grazed for the taking. It was a true vision of tropical paradise, and in it, Martínez Campos had stationed eighty thousand men, with more than enough field artillery to blast the rebels back to Oriente.[41]

Just after crossing into Matanzas, the Invading Army accidently divided into halves. Maceo and Gómez had feared being isolated and destroyed piecemeal; it nearly happened. On December 23 at Caliseo, just as the wings were beginning to reunite, a Spanish column under the personal command of Martínez Campos attacked in "unusual fury," with deadly, concentrated rifle fire. Several members of Maceo's personal bodyguard were killed, and the Bronze Titan's horse was shot from under him. Mounting another, he led a cavalry charge against the Spanish line. But this was not Mal Tiempo, and the rebels were stopped dead in their tracks. Gómez ordered a retreat, but Martínez Campos, who finally had the insurgents beaten in the field and on the run, misread the rout for a flanking movement and did not follow. For the rebels it had been expensive. Their ranks were thinned by casualties, among them numbers of the better officers, and many of the wounded were left behind.

Captain General Martínez Campos and his senior commanders expected the Invading Army to continue its march north and west into the lushness of Havana Province, and they concentrated their forces accordingly. Instead, Gómez and Maceo faced about and temporarily headed in the opposite direction, deceiving the Spanish general staff about their true intentions. On January 1, 1896, Havana newspapers announced the threat to the west at an end. It was a big mistake, for on that day the Invading Army faced front again and poured into Havana Province. In its wake and flanks, the way was marked by cloud-reaching towers of black and reeking smoke from destroyed cane fields and sugar mills. In the first week of the new year, the rebels covered over one hundred miles, devastating the most valuable property in Cuba.

The town of Güra de Melena, just off the main east-west highway, surrendered after a stiff fight by its garrison of three hundred *voluntarios*. Gómez addressed the prisoners, whose reputation for atrocity was well founded: "If things were the opposite way and you were the victors, not a single one of us would remain alive to tell the tale." He was correct. The despised *voluntarios* and *guerrilleros,* not the Spanish regulars, performed the diverse, inhuman acts of butchery now being reported in daily news dispatches. But hardly an American correspondent would ever make that distinction.[42]

In Alquízar, all arms and supplies were given up without a fight. At Ceiba de Agua, the rebels were welcomed by the town band. Completely outgeneraled, Martínez Campos sent a frantic cable to the minister of war in Madrid: "The enemy keeps advancing through the lines North and South . . . destroying all. They burn the railroad stations. Numerous families reach Havana fleeing from nearby villages. The panic is extraordinary." Town after town fell, and at every one the rebels increased their ranks.[43]

In Havana city the war had seemed too far away for anyone to care. Shops and cafés were stocked and crowded as before; there seemed no concern. After all, Martínez Campos commanded upwards of two hundred thousand men, and he was Spain's greatest general. What could a half-naked mob of scruffs and *negros* accomplish against that? The complacent attitude now changed. It was possible to hear gunfire at night from the outskirts of the city. "What's happening is really inconceivable," said the *Heraldo de Madrid,* Spain's most popular evening daily. "The government should know that this situation cannot be prolonged."[44]

Under increasing criticism from Spain, Martínez Campos declared a formal state of war in Havana and Pinar del Río provinces. Sending eight fresh columns totaling twenty-five thousand men to chase the elusive rebels around the capital province, he bolstered the city's defenses. Nothing worked. The slow Spanish infantry had no chance of catching the Invading Army, and because the rebels kept tearing up the railroads and telegraph lines, it became nearly impossible to shift troops rapidly across the front. "A sad fiasco," Nicolas de Truffin informed the Russian ambassador in Madrid; "Marshal Campos's prestige has been considerably shaken."[45]

On January 7, 1896, Gómez and Maceo met in the northwest corner of Havana Province to sketch operations for the immediate future. A witness to the meeting described the two insurgent generals, now at the height of their prestige. Maceo came "carefully groomed, neat, impeccably dressed in course linen . . . and mounted on a superior sorrel-colored horse of large build." Gómez, by contrast, presented the picture of "a gloomy little old man, dried up, thin . . . seated on a little white mule." It was decided that Maceo would take fifteen hundred men and carry the war into the westernmost reaches of Pinar del Río, while Gómez, with the main body, would remain in Havana keeping up the carnage and guarding Maceo's rear from any Spanish attempt at bottling him up in the western finger of the island. Other units were sent back to Santa Clara to carry on the war of destruction there, and reinforcements were ordered westward from Camagüey.[46]

Maceo conducted a reconnaissance of the far corner of Havana Province, first to scout the half-built western *trocha* at Mariel, then to determine if he could actually enter the Havana city suburbs, a truly audacious move. There would be enormous international repercussions, a major military demonstration literally in sight of the capital of the Ever Faithful Isle. It was, however, too much of a task, and Maceo was nearly trapped with his back to the sea. After a running rearguard battle, he and his men came to rest at a sugar mill whose friendly owner relayed the aphorism making the rounds of the Havana cafés: "If you pass the *trocha* of Mariel you will be greater than Hannibal." The Bronze Titan was not a self-effacing man. "Give me tomorrow," he said, "and I will be situated in Pinar del Río."[47]

True to his word, on the following day, January 8, 1896, Maceo crossed the *trocha* and debouched into Pinar del Río, center of Cuba's tobacco industry, where the world's finest cigar leaf was grown. There the rebels torched 75 percent of the crop. The Spanish were not overly concerned; they had multiple thousands of troops able to cork Maceo into the narrowest confines of the island. They also launched a new propaganda offensive, depicting Maceo as a crude, barbaric *caudillo de negros* who delighted in practices forbidden by the rules of civilized warfare and sought only a black republic of Cuba, headed by himself.

Maceo ignored it, countering the Spanish charges by exercising extreme discipline among his men, even to executing three fighters for pillaging. At Guane, he ordered the municipal treasury opened to pay the back salaries of primary-school teachers. People poured out to see the man who had outwitted Spain's best generals, men trained in the classic European military tradition. Only those towns strongly fortified and garrisoned stayed immune. On January 22, Maceo entered Mantua, the westernmost town of Cuba, to be greeted by the mayor and church bells. Two mountain howitzers, fifty rifles, and four thousand rounds of ammunition were taken from the *voluntario* garrison.

It had been a truly remarkable achievement, rightly compared to the campaigns of Hannibal in Italy, San Martín in Chile, and Sherman's march through Georgia. In ninety days, the Invading Army had marched 1,051 miles, from Baraguá to Mantua, fought twenty-seven actions, and captured twenty-two major towns. This against a foe who numbered 183,571 soldiers of the regular army and, said a Spanish report, "a system of defenses and *trochas* thought up by expert military engineers."

This was the high-water mark of the Cuban Revolution. Fables in the American press to the contrary, the insurgents would never achieve anywhere near this sort of battlefield success again. The situation in Cuba and for her people was about to undergo a massive, brutal change for the worse.

In Spain, public opinion among the influentials swung to a more energetic military approach. Questions arose in the Cortes as to whether

Martínez Campos had been showing too great a degree of tolerance toward the rebels. Rumors spread that he had even punished the officer who killed José Martí. By the close of 1895, the archly patriotic Madrid papers and army journals began a campaign to dump the governor and captain general of Cuba. Persuaded of Martínez Campos's failing health and memory loss, the queen regent and Premier Cánovas reluctantly agreed. He resigned his post on January 17, 1896, saying, "In my own bosom I feel that I have permitted severer measures than meet with my approval." That would not be a problem with his replacement, dark, brooding, stunted Lieutenant General Valeriano Weyler y Nicolau, Marquis of Teneriffe, Captain General of Catalonia.[48]

Weyler, a military technocrat, embodiment of the army's ideal of "salutary rigor," held very definite and public views regarding Martínez Campos's less than draconian response. "I believe that with regard to the rebels," he told a Madrid paper, "a policy should be followed diametrically opposite to the one being followed." On getting the appointment, he promised zealous performance in prosecuting the war. He would meet all expectations, receive the sobriquet "Butcher" from the Hearst papers, and create a public-relations disaster for Spain. Even before arriving in Cuba, he had been tagged by the *Chicago Times-Herald* as "the most brutal and heartless soldier to be found in a supposedly civilized country." "I am not a politician," the general told an American reporter in one of his rare interviews, "I am Weyler."[49]

Weyler was born in Cádiz in 1839, son of a Spanish mother and German father. At eighteen, he graduated from the infantry school at Toledo and received his first posting to Cuba. With his natural, intrinsic feel for the army and colonial service, promotion came quickly, as did success in 1861 during Spain's brief reoccupation of Santo Domingo, where he and Gómez fought on the same side. Weyler's duty brought him to Washington as Spain's military attaché during the American Civil War, where he became a great admirer of General William Tecumseh Sherman. In the Ten Years' War, he commanded the army in Oriente Province, establishing a take-no-prisoners reputation; he was rewarded with promotion to Captain General of the Canary Islands and was created Marquis of Teneriffe. His successful administration was followed by service in Spain's Carlist civil war and promotion to Captain General of the Philippines. He proved a good administrator and returned to Spain in 1889 for the Catalonian command, where he remained until the rebellion in Cuba. Puritanical, anticlerical, a role model for ambitious junior officers (later including the young Francisco Franco), sloppy in appearance, he slept in a soldier's hammock in the field and shared their rations of bread, sardines, and rough red wine.

The war would now be total on both sides: Spaniard and Cuban all suffering equally.

In the interim between the departure of Martínez Campos and the arrival of Weyler, the home government prodded the army to more vigorous conduct. In Pinar del Río, Antonio Maceo suffered casualties he could ill afford in several actions. In February 1896, he moved toward Candelaria on the east-west railroad. The Spanish, he knew, must defend it, and he might provoke his yet elusive big battle in the field. Maceo's determination increased when he learned the town's garrison consisted of many black *guerrilleros* among its defenders, and nothing was more guaranteed to drive him to savagery than those of his own race fighting for the oppressor. He gave the order that once the town fell, all blacks were to be killed with the machete. The garrison knew this—it had happened before—and they fought all the harder in a ferocious defense. Just as the town was about to succumb, a relief column arrived, and Maceo was forced to retreat after twenty-six hours of fighting.

Maceo ambushed the relief column on its march back to base and was again on the verge of victory when Spanish reinforcements entered the fray. Against rising odds and high losses Maceo refused to leave the field. Another horse was shot from under him and he sustained a gunshot wound in the leg. Mounting anew, the Bronze Titan carried successive machete charges into the enemy lines. At nightfall both sides ceased firing. These battles had been extremely costly to the rebels; they could not prevail in this sort of attrition combat against a large European army.

On February 10, 1896, Weyler arrived in Havana and changed the face of the war. Almost immediately he reorganized the army's higher echelons, improved its intelligence service, and generally tightened discipline at all levels. Self-sufficient march columns of a thousand men were mobilized for given areas. Posts in the countryside were reduced to the minimum, and defense of small towns was turned over to the *voluntarios*. He did not, however, abandon the basically defensive strategy carried out by his predecessor. The army was still too clumsily big, having far too much infantry for the debilitating hot climate, and too little cavalry and light artillery. With fast-moving mounted columns the Spanish could have hunted the insurgents everywhere, pursued them when flushed, attacked them when cornered, routed them in the field, and, said a U.S. Army officer, "driven them into the sea." Given their superiority of numbers, anyone, Martínez Campos, Weyler, their predecessors and successors, should have done it and wiped out the rebellion inside of a year. But intelligent command was not the Spanish army's strong suit.[50]

Weyler aimed to compress Maceo into an ever smaller area within Pinar del Río and Havana and smash him against the "anvil of the *trocha*." He planned to repeat this procedure in the central provinces, and finally, when the rebels were crowded into a corner of Oriente, the whole Spanish army would fall on them, inflicting a final defeat by sheer weight of numbers.

During these operations Weyler launched a parallel scorched-earth strategy in the countryside among the Cuban rural *pacificos*, the "neutral" people, to deprive the insurrection of any succor from the land. The only problem was the Spanish army had neither the organization nor the deployment for the mobile campaign Weyler envisioned, and his civilian policy did more to bring on the Spanish-American War than anything else the Spanish could have done.

Virtually the moment he settled in his headquarters, Weyler proclaimed the first of his infamous *reconcentración* decrees. Implemented first in Oriente, Camagüey, and Santa Clara, then in Pinar del Río, these would stretch out until the entire rural population of Cuba became subject to their awful effects. Eight days were given for all *pacificos* living outside fortified areas and garrisoned towns to move inside with all their cattle and goods. Their houses and plots were systematically destroyed, and those crops they could not carry were burned or dug up to rot. Transport of food from one town to another was expressly forbidden. Instead, to feed the rural people Weyler ordered special "zones of cultivation." All *pacificos* gathered inside a "dead line" drawn 150 yards beyond every garrison town, plantation, or fortified area, including bridges, and railroad and highway junctions. "Wherever there are forts there are *pacificos*," wrote Richard Harding Davis.[51]

Food and housing were scarce in most of the towns even before the arrival of the *reconcentrados,* and the original inhabitants did not welcome the internal refugees with open arms. Old warehouses, abandoned buildings, and temporary shelters were the best facilities that could be provided. Old men, women, and children slept in doorways and courtyards. "Sickness among these families increases every day," wrote an American in the Havana area. "Spanish troops occupy so many buildings that no suitable lodging is left for excess people. The living quarters of the *reconcentrados* are little more than pigsties. . . . This, along with the scarcity of food, is resulting in hundreds of deaths." Hideous bands of starving people moved ghostlike through the streets, scavenging like animals for the merest crust or orange peel, begging from soldiers for mess scraps. Women offered their bodies for bread.[52]

The *pacíficos* suffered equally from both sides. The rebels made a habit of tearing up the cultivated zones. If they came upon a field of potatoes, or a goat, scrawny chicken, or donkey, it was fair game; they took away as much as they could, burning the rest—house, crops, goods. Cattle were slaughtered wherever they roamed. Frederick Funston, Gómez's volunteer artillery commander, and later a general in the U.S. Army, remembered, "Pack-trains scoured the country, taking from the miserable people the last sweet potato, ear of corn, or banana that could be found." The *pacíficos* of Cuba perished in the thousands. Of the four hundred thousand souls ensnared by the *bando de reconcentración,* about ninety-five thousand died as a direct result. It turned public opinion enormously in the United States. At the feet of Weyler was rightly laid the onus of misery and death, but little enough was said or written of the blood on the hands of the Liberation Army. "The country was wrapped in the stillness of death and the silence of desolation," reported a U.S. consular official. Weyler saw it differently. "How do they want me to wage war?" he asked rhetorically. "With bishops' pastorals and presents of sweets and money?"[53]

On February 19, 1896, two days after Weyler issued his orders, Gómez and Maceo conferred and agreed that events had turned very serious. The Cuban "plain people" now understood the lengths to which the Spanish would go to retain the island. For the insurgents, any concentration of Spanish troops near Havana was to be absolutely avoided, because Weyler was just waiting for this. It was agreed that both wings of the invasion would withdraw east, into Matanzas Province, with Maceo at the sharp end, operating directly against Weyler.

Later in the month, a confident Weyler publicly predicted the complete pacification of Pinar del Río and assured the sugar mill owners they could grind cane without fear of retribution. Maceo instantly reacted. He refused to allow "Weyler's dreams to come true," and ordered the entire sugar crop of Pinar del Río and Havana provinces destroyed to "spread the necessary terror." Retreating eastward into Matanzas, the Liberation Army left its spore of sweet-stinking fires to mark its progress. "On the whole," observed Nicolas de Truffin, "it looks as if the two sides, equally aloof from the desire to make concessions, have sworn to lay waste to this unfortunate country."[54]

At El Galeón on March 10, Maceo and Gómez held their last meeting. Both men concluded the tempo of destruction must increase to make the burden on Spain unbearable. Maceo, who had been complaining of a lack of supplies, would finally get his fair share from the stockpiles in the east. "Due to the fact that many landowners were inclined to trust Weyler," he reported, it was also decided to return to Pinar del Río with a new plague of torching destruction.[55]

Maceo announced his presence in Pinar del Río with a proclamation designed to make Weyler appear a fool. Then for the next five weeks, he wrecked the sugar industry in western Cuba, though not without cost. Never having more than five hundred men, Maceo was forced to fight a series of costly skirmishes that whittled his strength almost in half.

Weyler considered it the prime moment to deal with Maceo for good. West of Havana, at Cuba's thinnest neck, from Mariel twenty miles south to Majana, he added electric lights to the western *trocha* and stationed fourteen thousand troops to seal Maceo inside the western finger. A column of three thousand seasoned campaigners under General Suárez Inclán, commander of Pinar del Río Province, was especially charged to search and destroy. Again Weyler predicted publicly that Maceo would be finished in May. Nearly out of ammunition, Maceo withdrew into the coastal Tapia Mountains above the east-west railroad. Inclán's soldiers doggedly pursued, attacking Maceo repeatedly.

At the end of April, Maceo learned of the *Competitor,* a filibustering schooner that had landed seventy miles west of Havana. She had been captured by a Spanish armed launch, but not before her arms had already gone ashore. Maceo evacuated his defensive position with 170 men and attempted a rendezvous. In the hills not far from the coast, Suárez Inclán flushed him into the open. With success nearly in hand, however, night fell, and as their practice dictated, the Spanish column withdrew, leaving the ground to the rebels. The *Competitor* party arrived on the battlefield, together with local reinforcements, rifles, and ten thousand rounds of ammunition.

Maceo took his provisioned command, grown again to 500 men, back into the Tapias. Through May he fought a series of actions, culminating in a Spanish defeat and the severe wounding of General Suárez Inclán himself. Weyler's latest *bando* announcing the rebels' demise had proven premature at the least. When news of Maceo's latest escapade reached Havana, de Truffin wired the Russian minister in Madrid: "The attitude of the [Spanish] Government, whose forces and resources do not, alas, in any way correspond to its implacable stand, give grounds to assume that Spain's cause in Cuba is a lost one."[56]

The only way for Weyler to retrieve his now battered reputation was by taking the field himself. A force of 1,200 men and a dozen guns was mobilized to strike directly at Maceo and the 500 men under his immediate command. On June 19 a portion of Weyler's column struck at San Gabriel de Lombello. In a five-day seesaw battle, Maceo fought desperately to keep from being pinned down. On the fifth day he received his twenty-fourth wound when a rifle bullet broke one of his legs. Again, he retreated to the Tapias.

The problem of supplies continued to dog the Invading Army, bringing out old sores. During his convalescence, Maceo complained to the New York Junta's Tomás Estrada Palma and Gómez that, in large measure, his recent actions had been fought with captured arms. Here he was, fighting the cream of the Spanish army, Weyler himself. There was not a man left whom he had brought across the *trocha* from Oriente who was not dead or wounded. He was certain the useless insurgent civilian government in Cuba, "the gentlemen," were allocating munitions on the basis of favoritism, and he demanded his rightful share. "Is this the way a government fulfills itself? Or patriots? Or soldiers?" he asked. Or was it all because he was *negro?*[57]

In September, a filibustering expedition brought Maceo a thousand rifles, half a million rounds of ammunition, two thousand pounds of dynamite, a small artillery piece with one hundred shells, and three American gunners to serve it. He also received news of the death of his brother José, killed two months back in Oriente. No one in the movement had bothered to inform him, and getting the information from a rebel newspaper was further evidence, if any were needed, of the undercurrent of racism that percolated under the revolutionary bombast. On October 29, with only two hundred men fit for duty, he received an order from Gómez to break off operations in the west, cut through Weyler's new electric-lit *trocha,* and return to Camagüey.

In Spain, the voters returned a comfortable Conservative majority, allowing Premier Cánovas to hedge from strength instead of weakness. On May 11, 1896, the queen regent addressed the new Cortes, promising Cuba an ambiguous program of "exclusively local" administrative and economic reforms, at the same time declaring the "rights" of Spanish sovereignty and the "indispensable conditions for its substance." The long since shelved Abarzuza laws had not touched economics. Could this statement, fuzzy as it was, actually be a crack in the mullioned window of archaic Spanish mercantilism? And did it matter anymore?[58]

For Premier Cánovas, all that mattered was holding Spain together. While not directly contradicting the hard-liners on Cuba, he admitted the "necessity" of "great" reforms in all spheres, ending in "complete freedom from the central government . . . what the English call 'self-government.' " A few days later, Cánovas went further, claiming it was no longer necessary to pacify all Cuba before the new laws were initiated. "It will be enough if the insurrection is broken" and the major population centers "free from the menace of the enemy." Once that happened, "we will not delay for a minute." But typical of Cánovas, he would delay his promises to keep everyone happy while doing nothing for as long as he drew breath.[59]

By October Weyler's failure to achieve victory over the ragged rebel forces had disillusioned even his army partisans in Madrid. The military journals began to suggest his ouster, and General Martínez Campos urged Weyler's replacement upon the queen regent. For Premier

Cánovas this was politically impossible because there were no generals with enough seniority and strong enough Conservative credentials to fill Weyler's place. Cánovas also had to walk a very fine line himself, lest Weyler's critics presume the only way to sack the Governor and Captain General of Cuba was to dump the national government first. Since Weyler's reactionary views were well circulated, Cánovas had to take only the smallest step toward reform to prove he and the general maintained widely differing opinions.

On December 8, 1896, *El Imparcial*'s Cuba correspondent reported that Maceo and his band had crossed east over Weyler's allegedly impenetrable *trocha* and Havana itself might possibly be endangered. A day later the Madrid papers were full of rumors more than hinting of the queen regent's desire to dismiss Cánovas and appoint a new Conservative cabinet, or even a coalition government headed by General Martínez Campos. What saved the premier's political life and indeed transformed the whole public mood in Spain from frustration to jubilation was the first confirmations of rumors announcing the death of Antonio Maceo. This monumental event in the revolution permitted Cánovas to promote a semblance of reform from a position of military success.

Maceo had received, and ignored, orders to return east before, but this time, he turned about and marched toward the Mariel *trocha*. It had become a truly formidable defense, electric lit with well-sited artillery and forts, and a garrison of 14,000 men. Weyler, observing Maceo's reverse, ordered 10,000 additional troops to move on his rear, pinning the rebels against the fortified line from both sides. On November 9, Maceo encountered the hammer and anvil of Weyler's crushing weight in the valley of the Tapias; with great effort, he extracted himself, losing 77 of his remaining 230 men. Next day he was surrounded almost completely by the main Spanish field force of eighteen battalions of infantry and thirty-six guns—over 6,000 men— under Weyler's personal command. Against this, Maceo had 153 scarecrows, but again he just managed the infuriating slip.

Maceo planned to cross the *trocha* on November 11, meeting a rebel party with fresh horses on the far side. On reconnoitering possible crossing points, Maceo became very uneasy, surprised at the elaborate

Spanish defense. A second reconnaissance two weeks later confirmed his fears. Weyler had done it: the line was impregnable; the rebels were sealed into Pinar del Río with the *trocha* to their front and a confident Spanish army commanded by the captain general at their back.

Weyler, like most Continental soldiers, paid little heed to the watery margins of his command. The northern end of the *trocha* ended at the port of Mariel. Maceo, with a common sense no one else seems to have possessed, decided to flank the defenses by sea. Recruiting a local civil servant with rebel sympathies to get a boat and act as guide, Maceo picked seventeen men to make the dangerous crossing with him. On the night of December 4, within sight of the Spanish barracks, they rounded the northern tip of the *trocha,* landing safely on the far side.

In the first hours of December 7, Maceo and his seventeen men joined the rebel force awaiting his arrival. At San Pedro de Hernández, near the border of Havana and Pinar del Río provinces, they were surprised by the Spanish, a shock, as the enemy never attacked at night. Maceo, weak and ill from a multitude of old wounds, lay asleep in a hammock. He had to be helped onto a horse, but was soon in the thick of the action. Turning to an aide, he shouted what were probably his last words, *"Esto va bien!"*—This is going well!—and took a bullet in the face and another in the chest. The rebels, overwhelmed by fire and numbers, ran from the field, leaving the bodies of Maceo and young Lieutenant Francisco Gómez Toro, son of the old general, to the enemy, but not before all clothing and identification had been taken off. After the action the rebels returned and carried the corpses to an abandoned house, where they were buried.[60]

If Cuba could now have been removed from the headlines of the American press, Weyler, whom William Randolph Hearst's *New York Journal* called "a fiendish despot . . . a brute, the devastator . . . pitiless, cold, an exterminator of men," might have succeeded in putting down the rebellion in the western third of Cuba. The death of Maceo brought the war to a standoff. The Spanish army controlled the ports, cities, and large towns, the *trochas,* and the *reconcentración* centers. The rebels virtually roamed the countryside at will, wreaking their own havoc on the plots of the *pacíficos,* adding immeasurably to the woe of the island. "The whole island is not what you might say occupied," wrote the observant Nicolas de Truffin, "but rather infiltrated by the insurgents, and never a week passes without their making their presence known by some bold sortie, be it a derailed train, a blown-up bridge, a sacked village. . . . Such is the present situation in the country."[61]

Despite the death of Maceo and Weyler's reports of light at the end of the tunnel, the war was bleeding Spain white. Factories in Catalonia shut their gates as the Cuban market disappeared, and unemployment grew in the large cities. The Spanish treasury found it ever more difficult to raise money to prosecute the war. As if this were not enough, a revolt in the Philippines began to drain military resources slated for Cuba, further tearing at Spain's fragile economy. More troops were shipped off from metropolitan Spain into the endless sinkhole of the insurgency. "It makes one sad to see the quality of the expeditions packed off in heartless shoals to Cuba," wrote a British attaché, "boys, to look at, fifteen or sixteen, who have never held a rifle till this moment, and now are almost ignorant which end it fires, good lads—too good to go to such uneven butchery—with cheerful, patriotic faces, but the very antithesis of a soldier." A far cry from the stolid route marchers seen by Winston Churchill only two years before. Spain was at the end of her rope.[62]

From France and the Vatican came diplomatic urgings for Spain to get its Cuban house in order by initiating some reform. Spanish republicans loudly united on the issue, protesting the government's procrastination, demanding autonomy for Cuba, now. In the United States, the Cleveland administration tendered its good offices to mediate and was rebuffed by Cánovas with dangerous arrogance. The American president had taken a strong stand against the interventionist crazies in Congress and the press, but in his last annual message of December 1896, he warned Spain that its time was fast running out.

Cánovas was being hit from all sides, the left and the right each clamoring that he was giving too little and too much on Cuba. Martial law was declared in Barcelona and Valencia. Shouting for no compromises with Cuba, ever, fifteen thousand young men swarmed Barcelona's Ramblas and stoned the American consulate after Congress introduced resolutions to recognize Cuban belligerency. In January 1897, the Spanish government finally published the Cuban reform decrees, and Cánovas, ever stalling, declared them in effect "when the majority of provinces are cleared of rebels." In April 1897, a month before the Cortes was to reconvene for its spring session, he announced the decrees' promulgation "before or after" the delegates took their seats.[63]

Just then, he received a report from Weyler giving an exaggerated summary of the army's success during the latest dry season. The Madrid papers sarcastically noted that the captain general had only twenty-eight battalions in the rebellious provinces, but eighty-three in areas he reported as "tranquil." Taking Weyler at his word, Cánovas declared in late April that reforms could now begin in Cuba's newly pacified provinces.

To keep Spain from tearing itself apart, Cánovas knew, there must be a significant solution to the Cuban problem. There were some optimistic noises coming from the new Republican administration of William McKinley, and these must be cultivated. The United States, though not a critical problem for now, certainly had dangerous potential. Friends recalled Cánovas saying, "If over and above what exists, we were to add thirty or forty thousand Americans landed on the island, the great fleet, and all the power of that republic, what would be our fate?" He would never know. On August 8, 1897, at the queen regent's summer court in San Sebastián, Premier Cánovas was assassinated by a young anarchist. After a short interim Conservative government, the queen regent and the revolving door of Spanish politics admitted Liberal ex-premier Práxedes Sagasta to head the government.[64]

As the year 1897 neared its close, the war ground into a nightmare of aimless, uselessly destructive marches by both sides across the devastated Cuban countryside. On November 1, Weyler, having failed on both the public-relations and military fronts, was replaced by General Ramón Blanco, a man of more humane impulses. He came too late to affect the course of history. Spain's sun had set; America's was beginning its climb.

CHAPTER 3

MAINE TO HAVANA

I do not like the suggestion of a man-of-war [to Havana]. . . .
I do not want now *anything of that kind made a convenient*
excuse for trouble with Spain.
—Grover Cleveland, July 1896

American popular reaction to the Cuban insurrection instinctively backed the rebels and cast Spain in the role of brutal oppressor, her boot on the neck of a ragged people struggling against a European tyranny. It was no stretch for public and press to link the *Grito de Baïre* of 1895 to the "shot heard round the world" at Lexington 120 years before.

Cuba, astride the approaches to the Central American isthmus, could not but vitally concern U.S. interests, and had done so since the early nineteenth century. Almost from the founding moment of the American republic, its statesmen considered the island part and parcel of the national polity. Cuba's European ties were considered an accident of history. So Thomas Jefferson wrote, "I have ever looked on Cuba as the most interesting addition which could ever be made to our system of States." In 1823, the year the Monroe Doctrine was formulated, Secretary of State John Quincy Adams, having acquired Florida from Spain and recognizing the independence of the revolting Spanish colonies in the hemisphere, found it "scarcely possible to resist the conviction that the annexation of Cuba . . . will be indispensable to the continuance and integrity of the Union itself."[1]

In the decades before the American Civil War, southern politicians cast envious eyes at Cuba, seeing it as prime slaveholding territory. In 1854, when Spanish authorities in Havana improperly boarded and seized the American steamer *Black Warrior* on the suspicion that it was smuggling cotton, President Franklin Pierce, a man heavily in debt to southern slave interests for his office, was urged to hostilities by his secretary of war, Jefferson Davis of Mississippi. It was, both men thought, the perfect opportunity to absorb Cuba as a flourishing slave state. A stiff note was sent to Madrid demanding an indemnity of three hundred thousand dollars for cargo and ship and an apology for "the insult offered to the dignity of the nation whose colors it bore."[2]

Spain delayed. With war fever climbing in the United States, its envoys to Spain, France, and Great Britain met at the Belgian resort of Ostend to seek a solution. The result, dubbed the "Ostend Manifesto" by the *New York Herald,* is one of the flakiest documents to grace American diplomatic history. The time had come, said the gentlemen, to buy the island of Cuba, for "the Union can never enjoy repose, nor possess reliable security" without it. If Spain refused the generous offer, she would lose Cuba by revolution, forfeiting both the island and the price the United States was willing to offer. And if neither of these pertained, the United States would take the island, justified "by every law, human and divine." Spain eventually apologized for the incident and paid an indemnity. The American Civil War then silenced for more than a generation any talk of absorbing Cuba into the United States. Republican reformer and antiexpansionist Carl Schurz was correct when he declared that for America, "one South was enough."[3]

During Cuba's Ten Years' War, the *Virginius* episode of 1873 pounded the drums anew, and the rust-bucket U.S. Navy put to sea. President Grant wisely turned America away. Thus when the *Grito de Baïre* proclaimed the latest revolution, the Cleveland administration cast an extremely wary eye at the tar pit of the Ever Faithful Isle. Official neutrality was to be the strictly enforced order of the day. But within a fortnight of the opening shots, the United States was deeply embroiled.

Aided by skillful propaganda churned out by the Cuban Junta in New York and Washington, the insurrection gained wide public sympathy, which the administration could not ignore. Cleveland was also confronted with the perplexing question of American security. From a strictly parochial standpoint, continued Spanish sovereignty, in whatever form, was a much better option for the United States than a weak independent Cuba constantly at war with itself and prey to European imperial interests, especially German ones. Cleveland and Secretary of State Richard Olney, however, could not directly articulate their anti-independence bias. It ran counter to American public opinion and to the nation's historic ideals of liberty. But neither could they look approvingly on the Cuban rebels. This ambivalence formed the basis of the administration's neutrality policy, and it was met with stunning public disapproval. A Kansas City letter writer summed up the common mood, telling the president: "I believe it is not the fear of a war with impotent Spain that stays your hand from the execution of justice. It is your sympathy with tyranny."[4]

From the beginning, Congress excoriated the president and State Department for adopting neutrality. This schism between the executive and legislative branches stymied any effective national strategy. Eventually Cleveland and Olney pinned their faith on diplomacy as a way of solving the Cuban dilemma. Through it, Spain might agree to a truly diminished level of sovereign control over the Ever Faithful Isle, and the Cuban revolutionary leaders might perhaps accept something less than complete independence. Elephants might also learn to fly. Only the Spanish-American War would bring an end to Cuba's colonial status.

The Republicans, seeing a "wedge" issue, to use a late-twentieth-century term, forcibly inserted Cuba as a divisive force into American domestic politics. In seeking to discredit Cleveland's neutralist position, they effectively widened the gap between the dying philosophy of Democratic isolationism and the emerging dogma of Republican expansionism. In this battle for American foreign policy (though, ironically, the parties would reverse their positions), the Cuban question formed the critical mass that determined an interventionist trend well into the next century.

For the Republicans, Cuba was a heaven-sent opportunity. The large number of blacks on the island and in the Liberation Army was hugely appealing as a domestic issue, and Cuban independence was far easier and safer to espouse than the gold standard, high tariffs, or the social benefit of trusts. Such Republican organizations as the Civil War veterans of the Grand Army of the Republic, the Civil Service Reform Association, and the Union League Club, assisted by an ever eager to please Junta, sponsored pro-Cuban mass meetings across the nation. Significant support for the revolution came from mainline Protestant churches, who saw an opportunity in the Cuban issue to unite the American upper and working classes, and who joined in a general anti-Catholic bias against "Pope-ridden Spain."

The first diplomatic clash happened at sea. On March 8, 1895, two weeks after the *Grito de Baïre,* the Spanish gunboat *Conde de Venadito* fired on the American merchantman *Alliança,* which was six miles off the eastern tip of Cuba, homeward bound from Panama to New York. First came a blank shot, then two live shells. The *Alliança* continued on, gaining headway until she passed out of range. Though a common vessel in these waters, not even touching at a Cuban port, she had through the doltishness of a Spanish naval officer been identified as a possible filibuster running arms to the rebels. In fact, her cargo consisted of nothing more lethal than wine, bananas, rubber, and mustard seeds.

Grover Cleveland considered the affair a regrettable accident. But Secretary of State Walter Q. Gresham, in his last months of office and life, argued that conduct of this sort "under no circumstances can be tolerated when no state of war exists." Gresham demanded a "prompt disavowal [and] due expression of regret" from the Spanish government for the inexcusable action.[5]

From every section of the country the press lavished rivers of headline ink on the incident, heralding a campaign of Spanish vilification that continued almost unabated for more than three years. "Our Flag Fired On," announced Joseph Pulitzer's Democratic, interventionist New York *World.* The nation had been insulted and the lives and property of American citizens endangered by the reckless conduct of "a stupid commander" of the Spanish navy. The independent New York *Sun* argued that Spain, whose "arrogance and brutality" had sparked the Cuban insurrection, needed "a sharp and stinging lesson at the hands of the United States"; the next Spanish vessel that tried such a thing "ought to be pursued and blown out of the water." This was hardly the first of the "outrages" committed on the United States by "hot-blooded Spaniards," said the pro-rebel Chicago *Tribune,* and it "is high time they should be stopped." A "hostile and insolent act," noted the Milwaukee *Sentinel.* Spanish naval officers, said the usually nonpartisan *New York Times,* were a lot of "haughty and irresponsible beings." Of the New York press, only the antiexpansionist, antijingo *Evening Post* refused to join the editorial lynching, and claimed, "We should treat it as a private gentleman would a private insult—not do anything until the committing party acknowledged it as intentional."[6]

Spain acceded to the demand for an apology, though they took their maddening time about it. The Madrid press stoutly defended the naval officer and castigated the Conservative government for not immediately telling the United States where to get off. *El Heraldo de Madrid,* the leading evening paper (whose proprietor happened to be Captain Emilio Díaz Moreu of the Spanish navy), charged that Premier Cánovas would have given a very different answer "if he had not been profoundly deceived . . . as to the effective power of the republic of Washington" and the "decadence" of Spain herself. *El Imparcial* thought an "injustice" had been committed against the vigilant commander of the *Conde de Venadito* and quite wrongly claimed Spanish rights to "scrutinize and detain" all suspicious vessels.[7]

On June 12, 1895, Grover Cleveland, issuing the first of two neutrality proclamations, declared a state of insurgency (though not of war) existed in Cuba, and that it had gone beyond Spain's ability to quash it. With a stern eye on the Cuban Junta's propensity for outfitting filibustering expeditions and the romantic inclinations of Americans for taking commissions with the Liberation Army, both of which involved the United States in diplomatic controversies with "a friendly power," the president promised vigorous prosecution for all violators.

The U.S. Navy and the Revenue Cutter Service (precursor to the Coast Guard) expanded the naval facilities at Key West and geared up to patrol coastal waters. And despite Spain's complaints to the contrary, the American sea services did more to hinder the resupply of Cuban rebels than the Spanish navy ever did. In three years of the revolution, seventy-one filibustering vessels sailed for Cuba from American ports. Thirty-three were intercepted by American warships; two were stopped by the British; four were turned back by storms; five were chased off the Cuban coast by Spanish patrols; and one, the *Competitor,* was captured by a Spanish armed cutter. What really infuriated the Spanish authorities was the general leniency shown by the U.S. federal courts to the captured miscreants brought to justice for violating the neutrality statutes. It infuriated Grover Cleveland as well, but there was nothing he or they could do about it.

When Richard Olney became secretary of state, he initially bought into the Spanish view of the struggle, if for no other reason than to preserve the status quo in the region. The rebels, he was told by Spanish Minister Enrique Dupuy de Lôme, belonged to the lowest social orders. A rebel victory, he warned, would devastate the island; independence would presage only anarchy, and black anarchy at that. Olney conceded that if this were so, then all right-thinking Americans should pray for Spanish success.

But with the remarkable invasion of Gómez and Maceo into western Cuba, Olney began to view things differently. One agent of change turning him was Paul Brooks, owner of a sizable sugar plantation near Guantánamo in Oriente Province. In September 1895, Brooks called on Olney at the State Department. The rebels, he said, were no "nigger rabble," but a real movement that crossed the entire spectrum of Creole society, with every prominent family represented in the ranks. Only fear of Spanish confiscation prevented most of the property owners from publicly supporting the insurrection. Brooks claimed that the Cuban people overwhelmingly favored independence, and no vacuous promises of reform were going to convince the rebels to lay down their arms. Spain, he prophesied, will drench Cuba in blood, then pull back exhausted, offering the island to the highest bidder.[8]

To Olney, the thought had nightmarish implications. Spain, as a toothless guardian of Cuba, posed no threat to the United States. Cuba under German control would, and Germany had been mucking around the Caribbean, in Haiti especially, looking for a convenient coaling station for her rapidly expanding navy and colonies. Olney had no qualms about flying the Monroe Doctrine from the mastheads of American battleships. But it was far better to cauterize the Cuban crisis with sane diplomacy.

Olney's temporary sympathy with the rebels waned with the onset of autumn, and a dose of realpolitik, and he moved even further away when Congress returned for its year-end session. Fueled by the Junta's sophisticated public-relations campaign, the violent and sanctimonious congressional floor debates over recognition of Cuban belligerency canceled the administration's brief flirtation with the insurgent cause. Olney was now convinced by antirebel American planters that the Liberation Army was torching American property to precipitate U.S. intervention. When Tomás Estrada Palma, general legate of the Junta, called at the State Department, Olney leveled the question: Were the rebels burning American property to push an armed response? Estrada Palma evaded the issue. There had been no specific order, but he knew and approved of the destruction as a necessary war measure. "Well, gentlemen," Olney replied, "there is but one term for such action. We call it arson." With that he concluded the interview.[9]

The Junta operated on many fronts. If Richard Olney was not impressed with their brief, countless others were, especially the American press, most of whose papers could not afford reporters outside their circulation areas, much less send correspondents to Washington or Cuba. To these and anyone else with an empty in-basket, the Junta supplied an endless stream of news releases from its New York and Washington offices, splashing lurid Spanish atrocities, real and imagined. Paid agents were situated on the editorial and reporting staffs of the New Orleans *Times-Picayune* and *Washington Evening Star.* "Sympathy meetings," carnivals, theater performances, and countless speeches were organized to canvas money for filibustering expeditions and other material assistance. The War for Cuban Independence, stoked by the Junta, drove American public opinion and politics, but it did not drive American policy. That, until February 15, 1898, no matter the Capitol Hill cacophony or self-important vitriol of the editorial pages, would stay firmly in the White House.

Receptive to electoral moods, Congress increased the pressure for a more active legislative role in the Cuban morass and an agenda that aided the rebels rather than the Spaniards. Grover Cleveland resisted. In his December 1895 annual message, the president reaffirmed the national course, calling on the people to remain impartial in the Cuban conflict. The "traditional sympathy" of Americans toward a people "who seem to be struggling for larger autonomy and greater freedom" must not lead to public lawbreaking, or make the government's task more difficult in its relations with "friendly sovereign states." The somber phrases fell on deaf ears. The next day, a House resolution demanded the president initiate steps to "civilize" the rebellion in Cuba.[10] Two more resolutions were submitted in Congress proposing the independence of Cuba and the purchase of additional islands in the region. To bring some order, the Senate Foreign Relations Committee moved to examine the whole Cuban situation and submit a formal report. But it soon became clear that a number of Republican senators were not really moved by the plight of the Cuban people or by any genuine support for Cuba's freedom. For them, Cuba became a convenient stick with which to beat the Cleveland administration.

Olney cooperated with the committee. But its report, released in January 1896, put the administration in a no-win situation. Yes, the president could deal with the Cuban matter, but "within the principles of our Constitution"; it was for Congress to define the "final attitude" of the government. This emasculating statement was pure nonsense, but to add to the confusion, the report also resolved that Cuba be afforded full belligerent rights. Even this was not enough for the Republican fire-eaters.

From almost the first day of the insurrection, U.S. recognition of Cuban belligerency and of an independent Cuban republic had been debated nonstop in Congress. Numberless resolutions were introduced in one chamber or the other, even to the extent of declaring that a state of war existed between the United States and Spain. For the first year of the rebellion none of these went much beyond committee rhetoric. But on February 28, 1896, the first anniversary of the *Grito de Baïre*, a belligerency resolution was approved by the full Senate. Cleveland ignored it. Olney knew that domestic politics was the real intent. The Republicans, he wrote to the president, were "setting their sails . . . to catch the popular pro-Cuban breeze."[11]

For those who cared to investigate international law on the matter, there was absolutely no advantage to be gained for the rebels from America granting recognition; in fact, it would be highly detrimental. Bestowing the status of a belligerent power on the rebels *would* have given Spain the uncontested right to search neutral merchant ships on the high seas for contraband of war *and* it would have relieved her of any responsibility to protect foreign lives and property in territory under insurgent control. Also, once recognized as a warring "power," the Cuban rebels would be prohibited by American neutrality laws from purchasing arms and military stores in the United States, nor could they enter and leave the country as they pleased. The only way the Cuban rebels could have materially benefited from official

belligerent status was if they possessed a navy able capable of harassing ocean traffic with Spain. But to the Republican congressional
screamers, none of this mattered.[12]

At the end of February, Cleveland assembled his cabinet to ponder
the administration's stand on Cuba. Olney dusted off and read
aloud the policy drafted for President Ulysses Grant twenty years before, in the wake of the *Virginius* affair, by his Republican predecessor, Hamilton Fish. If the United States truly desired war with Spain,
Fish wrote, it should enter the fray "straightforwardly" and not on
"discreditable" grounds. To recognize a Cuban government during
the Ten Years' War would have been, Fish thought, legally and
morally indefensible. But he also warned Spain that unless the island
were "pacified," the United States might be forced to intervene if only
to safeguard its citizens and economic interests. Cleveland and the
cabinet, according to Postmaster General William Wilson, considered
this policy "as pertinent to the present situation as it was to that crisis," and adopted it anew.[13]

In Spain, greeting the Senate resolution, Barcelona students once
again stoned the American consulate, an act interpreted by the normally sober Republican *New York Tribune* as exceedingly antagonistic.
"If Spain insists on fighting the United States," noted the editorialist,
"the feeling here is that it can be accommodated." The paper urged
Congress to pass a $10 million national defense bill, arguing for "mil-
lions to make the United States the equal if not the peer of any nation
on earth . . . if millions will not do, let us take billions."[14]

On April 6, the House of Representatives voted 287–27 to pass a
concurrent resolution authorizing the president to accord belligerent
rights to the Cuban rebels and, if necessary, forcibly intervene on the
island to protect American interests. Moderate Republicans of New
England invited President Cleveland to offer his views. The president
remained ponderously silent. There was no sound from the White
House, and the first session of the Fifty-fourth Congress declared itself adjourned.

With Congress out of town, Cleveland and Olney grabbed the initiative. Since the February cabinet meeting, Olney had drafted a comprehensive communication to the Spanish government, one of the

most interesting papers of U.S. diplomatic history. For the first time, a presidential administration abjured America's traditional record of supporting a colonial people struggling for independence in the Western Hemisphere. Henceforth on the Cuban issue in particular, and in the Caribbean as a whole and Central America in large, the national security of the United States dictated America's course of action.

Olney went through the motions of uttering the proper humanitarian noises, saying that Spain must conclude the war in order to end human suffering and, with a nod to U.S. economic interests, noting the damage wrought on $35 million of American property. But he never believed these reasons justified U.S. intervention; quite the contrary. Olney for his several faults was never a hypocrite. American capitalists had invested in Cuba of their own free will. The fact that those ventures had soured was too bad. He deemed the rebellion a natural hazard of business in an unstable region, telling Cleveland he could not understand "how this Government can protect them from the inevitable consequences" of war. Olney's bias in favor of Spain was evident, and he did not criticize its strictly military measures. The mother country, he noted, "wisely undertook to make its struggle with the present insurrection short, sharp, and decisive." His large complaint was that the Spanish army could not do the job.[15]

To the Spanish foreign ministry, Olney laid it on the line. Despite massive Spanish efforts at a military solution, rebel successes in the field convinced him that pacification of Cuba was impossible and Spain must eventually be driven to abandon the Ever Faithful Isle "to the heterogeneous combination of elements and of races now in arms against her." He compared the probable future of an independent Cuba to the division of Hispaniola into the black and Hispanic states of Haiti and the Dominican Republic, and no one needed another of those perpetual hemispheric curses. Spain thus far had faced the rebellion "sword in hand," and even if victorious, something Olney seriously doubted, she promised nothing but a return "to the old order of things." That, the secretary warned, was a dangerously naive position. Spain must face reality; she could no longer orchestrate Cuba's future, and when conditions inevitably worsened, America would intervene, be sure of it: "That the United States can not contemplate with complacency another ten years of Cuban insurrection . . . may certainly be taken for granted." In essence, listen to us now or fight us later.[16]

Olney offered President Cleveland as an honest broker to mediate the end of the rebellion and the institution of true autonomy to Cuba, "leaving Spain her rights of sovereignty," but also granting to the Cuban people "all such rights and powers" of self-government "as they can reasonably ask." As to what was "reasonable," the president would decide, and Spain could trust him on that score. The rebels could too, because if the agreement was anathema to the Cubans, "it would arouse the indignation of our whole people."[17]

If, on the other hand, Cleveland negotiated an honest peace and the Cubans rejected it, the rebellion, in Olney's opinion, stood a chance to "lose largely, if not altogether, the moral countenance and support" of the American public. It was a subtle warning to the rebel leadership against intractability, and moreover a warning of possible United States military intervention to pacify *them,* something the vast majority of Americans would not have tolerated for a second. Olney truly believed the bombast of his 20-inch gun that "today the United States is practically sovereign on this continent, and its fiat is law upon the subjects to which it confines its interposition." The sentiments of the nation and Congress had absolutely no impact on his thinking.[18]

In the months before Spain replied to Olney's note, a second diplomatic flap over filibustering further strained relations, leading the Chicago *Times-Herald* to warn the administration, "The ghosts of the *Virginius'* crew arise to torture American statesmen, who venture to treat with the Spanish as with a highly civilized nation."[19]

The affair involved the schooner *Competitor,* the same vessel whose munitions resupplied the empty bandoliers of Antonio Maceo. The vessel cleared Key West on April 20, 1896, carrying twenty-four passengers and a crew of five, ostensibly bound for Port Lemon, Florida. According to probably false testimony, the passengers mutinied and captured the craft. Twenty-five more "passengers" came aboard, plus large amounts of arms and ammunition. On April 25, she reached Punta Berracos, west of Havana, safely landing her human and military cargo. Spotted by a Spanish armed launch, the *Competitor* was captured with five men still aboard, the sole filibustering vessel taken by the Spanish navy during the entire conflict.

The prisoners, one claiming American citizenship, one British, and three Cuban, were taken to Havana, where the U.S. consul general demanded they be tried under long-standing treaties and protocols.

These, dating from 1795 and 1877, the latter stemming from the *Virginius* flap, stated that American citizens, and those sailing in American-flagged vessels, charged with treasonous acts to the Spanish crown be tried in open court, unless they were actually caught "with arms in hand." The case came under the jurisdiction of the commander in chief of the Spanish navy's West Indian Station, whose judge advocate brushed the precedents aside and moved ahead with a summary court-martial. On May 8, he handed down the death sentence on four of the five men. Richard Olney dispatched a hot note to Madrid, demanding a full review of the case. In Havana and Madrid the public demanded the prisoners be shot as pirates, while in the United States the men were seized upon as martyrs to the cause.[20]

"Weyler's drumhead tribunal. . . . Uncle Sam has been defied," screamed the New York *World,* which flogged the story for all it was worth. Its editorial columns equated the death sentences to an act of war equal to a Spanish naval bombardment of Washington, D.C. "It might be well to send a few [ships of the North Atlantic Squadron] down to Cuba and add the weight of cannon," said the Chicago *Tribune,* which urged a fleet and army be sent to Cuba to "sink every Spanish vessel there, knock Morro Castle to flinders, and march in and hold the city." There had been altogether too much "trifling and dillydallying."[21]

Ignored in the entire blowup, or conveniently fabricated otherwise, was the fact that the *Competitor* had been seized inside Cuban waters after unloading several tons of military stores. Six months later, the prisoners were released, Spain seeing discretion as the best policy in the matter. Although the Spanish succumbed to American pressure, this was one situation that might have given them some positive international press had they handled it with anything other than their usual heavy-handed bumptiousness.

The congressional resolution for Cuban belligerency and the *Competitor* business, coming so hard on each other, caused Spain for the first time to begin taking American reactions to its Cuban policy more seriously. Although a war was still unthinkable, Premier Cánovas directed his foreign minister, the Duke of Tetuán, to assemble a formal brief against American interference in Cuba. Cánovas hoped for an endorsement by the European powers, which, by extension, might diplomatically align them with Spain in any future conflict with the

United States. The white paper was finished by the summer of 1896, and unofficially circulated to the Spanish embassies in Europe. In no time it came to the attention in Madrid of U.S. Minister Hannis Taylor, who bluntly explained to Tetuán that formal delivery of the document to any government would be interpreted by the United States as an "unfriendly" act. Tetuán, first ensuring that the contents were well leaked, was forced officially to disavow the initiative. The vague, noncommittal expressions of sympathy that barely whispered from European foreign ministries nonetheless convinced the duke that he had built a foundation for future alliances to deter American interference in Cuba.

In June, Richard Olney received Tetuán's reply to America's offer of presidential mediation. Spain turned it down flat; to accept would be "derogatory to Spanish sovereignty." If the United States envisioned ill consequences of a Spanish defeat in Cuba, Tetuán countered, then it could help Spain quash the revolt by restricting the activities of the Cuban Junta in the United States. Spain, he promised, would achieve military victory in Cuba and saw no reason why she must concede anything to anyone. The rebels, according to the Duke of Tetuán, did not possess qualifications "which entitle them to respect," much less recognition.[22]

The rebuff of Olney's note led Attorney General Judson Harmon to suggest granting immediate belligerency rights to the Cuban insurgents on the grounds that Spain herself regarded a state of war as existing in Cuba. It was folly to ignore it, and by not according belligerency status to the rebels, the United States was hampering its ability to deal with the arms-purchasing and filibustering issues that were driving a dangerous wedge between two historically friendly nations. Cleveland still refused. Citing a favorable Supreme Court decision that established grounds for prosecuting filibusters as an illegal "military expedition or enterprise," the president renewed America's official neutrality. Beyond that he would not go.[23]

Cleveland had recently appointed a conservative Democrat, General Fitzhugh Lee, an ex-Confederate cavalry officer, former governor of Virginia, and nephew of Robert E. Lee, to the very sensitive post of consul general in Havana. Dramatic, impulsive, unversed in Spanish, Lee had never before held a diplomatic post and seemed an awkward fit in the Havana powder keg. Lee was also not above using his office for personal enrichment, investing his own and political friends' money in Cuban ventures. He was never entirely trusted by the State Department, and much of what Lee reported over the next two years reflected basely annexationist opinions. But there was a fair degree of unpalatable truth to his dispatches, and when the crisis came he, unlike many, kept his wits.

In their final months, Cleveland and Olney concentrated on the discreet promotion of Cuban autonomy as the only solution possibly agreeable to all sides. For that, they required of Lee hard information regarding the inclinations of the Cuban people. The nature of the insurgent "government" was critical. Indeed, was there, asked Olney, "any such civil government *de facto?* Has it any fixed seat?" Were the rebel forces under its control? Did it collect taxes, provide schools and law courts? In short, Olney wanted to know, was there anything at all to the insurgency other than the Liberation Army, or were the Junta and its allies in the United States just blowing smoke; was there a "so-called Cuban Republic? . . . or a mere government on paper?"[24]

After two weeks in Havana, Lee's first reports shattered the administration's autonomist hopes. Yes, a written constitution existed and taxes were collected in areas controlled by the rebel army. There were some courts in the eastern provinces, and scattered schools and hospitals hidden in the mountains. But the insurgent government had no permanent seat, no one of consequence paid any attention to it, and it exercised no control over the Liberation Army. "Practically," Lee wrote, "General Máximo Gómez' views on all questions prevail." There was no political faction in Cuba, no one willing to accept reforms or autonomy, and no one who thought Spain was serious about granting them.

The great majority of Cubans desired independence or even annexation to the United States, Lee's fervent wish as well. The United States, he suggested, should buy it, turning the island into "its richest and most prosperous possession," or set up an independent republic in whose "splendid harbors" American naval vessels could "conveniently float . . . charged with defending American interests and promoting American commerce." Or to go another way, the United States might support Cuba, with American diplomatic recognition, in its declaration of independence. Events would then unfold very much as they had after President Andrew Jackson's recognition of the Texas Republic in 1836. A war with Spain would "almost certainly follow," as it had with Mexico over Texas. But the conflict would be "short and decisive," and the price of Cuba could be credited to the war.[25]

As for Spanish tenacity in holding Cuba, Lee estimated 240,000 troops on the island, "or nearly 90,000 more men than the combined armies of Wellington and Napoleon at Waterloo, or of Meade and Lee at Gettysburg." The Spanish army, he truthfully saw, had but two options: "an ignoble surrender to the demands of the insurgents," or war with the United States. Of those, they preferred to fight the Americans and "lose the Island with honor."[26]

On July 8, 1896, Lee wired Olney a confidential report urging preparations for U.S. intervention. Attitudes and conduct between Spaniards and Americans in Cuba were growing "intense" and might reach a flash point. It just might be wise to station a warship, under a "discreet" commanding officer, at Key West, ready, at the consul general's order, to steam to Havana with a marine landing force "to protect the consulate and the lives of Americans from mob violence."[27]

Olney was not impressed with these extraordinary proposals. Cleveland felt likewise: "I am a little surprised at Consul General Lee's dispatch. He seems to have fallen into the style of rolling intervention like a sweet morsel under his tongue." The reference to Jackson's recognition of Texas and its consequences was "unfortunate." And with the coming presidential elections, sending a warship to Havana was politically very dangerous. "I do not like the suggestion of a man-of-war. . . . I do not want *now* anything of that kind made a convenient excuse for trouble with Spain."[28]

The July Democratic convention in Chicago, dominated by southern and western delegates, dumped Cleveland and his eastern Wall Streeters in favor of "free silver" and William Jennings Bryan. In his dispatches to Olney, Fitzhugh Lee recommended that Cleveland call a second convention of conservative, gold standard Democrats, issue a call for Cuban independence and "if necessary American intervention." The president "would get . . . the credit of stopping the wholesale atrocities," give employment to thousands of young men signing up for the army, and acquire Cuba in the bargain. Olney made no reply to the ludicrous suggestion, and with that silence, Lee's outlandish statements from Havana for the most part ceased.[29]

Although domestic issues dominated the presidential campaign of 1896, Cuba inevitably drew a crowd. At their St. Louis convention, the Republicans inserted a plank for Cuban independence, though it steered well clear of demanding American intervention. At the Chicago Democratic convention, a rebel sympathizer who unfurled a Cuban flag was "promptly squelched." The Democrats' thin Cuban plank could just as easily have come from Cleveland as from the Bryanites, who said with the barest nod, "We extend our sympathy to the people of Cuba in their heroic struggle for liberty and independence."[30]

On William McKinley's Republican victory, Joseph Pulitzer's New York *World* carried an interview with Spanish Minister Enrique Dupuy de Lôme. "With Mr. Cleveland at the helm of the government," he said, Spain "had no fear of intervention in Cuba but the same comforting assurance does not come with the inauguration of the next President."[31]

Cleveland's lame-duck period was marked by feverish activity on Cuba. Congressional Republicans constantly urged immediate action, trying to stick Cleveland with the onerous duty of completely solving the problem in the next sixteen weeks. The president did not shy away, telling the cabinet, "I want to dispose as many of these difficulties as I can so as to clear the way for McKinley." While Olney attempted a last-ditch effort at secret diplomacy to get the Cuban insurgent leaders to accept autonomy, Cleveland vainly tried to convince Congress to shut up for five minutes to let him get on with the job. The constant rain of resolutions demanding Cuban independence could not but influence the rebels to reject autonomy for a better deal with the new, Republican administration. Fitzhugh Lee, on leave, confided to Olney that none of the Liberation Army commanders "in the hills would touch reforms." Olney didn't trust him, but the consul general's observations were correct.[32]

On December 7, 1896, Grover Cleveland delivered his last annual message to Congress. Disgusted, frustrated, he took everyone connected to the Cuban insurrection to task. In the last full year, the war had dragged on "with all its perplexities" and no progress toward any conclusion. Each side, Spanish and Cuban, remained inflexible, yet neither had secured its strategic goals. Spain had not crushed the rebellion or reestablished her authority much beyond the cities and railroads. Opposite that, the rebels, still bushwhacking in the field, had not "made good their title to be regarded as an independent state." The United States, he warned all, could no longer remain a disinterested spectator. It was being sucked into a conflict not of its making or to its benefit, and its "patient waiting for Spain to end the contest" had its limits. In a last, vain attempt at mediation, he offered that Spain could terminate the war "either alone and in her own way, or with our friendly cooperation."[33]

As to Cuba, "The spectacle of the utter ruin of an adjoining country . . . would engage the serious attention of the . . . United States in any circumstances." But we also had investments there, $35 million worth, second only to Spain, plus a prewar annual trade of $100 million. Both had plummeted, with dire consequences to the American and Cuban economies.

Cleveland castigated the Junta for fomenting enmity within the United States, which made for difficulty in foreign relations. Cubans who had no desire to remain American citizens were applying for naturalization papers "with a view to possible protection by this Government," and this resulted in constant demands on Spain for "explanations and apologies" for acts committed against American citizens in Cuba. He blasted the Junta for mongering the rebellion through a scandal-driven press, public meetings, and fund-raising, "which the spirit of our institutions and the tenor of our laws do not permit to be made the subject of criminal prosecution."[34]

If peace did not come, Cleveland warned, the insurrection would end with American intervention, "even at a cost of a war between the United States and Spain—a war [not] doubtful in its issue." The principals had been put on notice.[35]

Republican reaction to Cleveland's last annual message was predictably partisan, and they refused to allow the president to exit office with even the hint of Cuban progress. On December 9, Senator James Cameron of Pennsylvania introduced a resolution demanding immediate recognition of Cuban belligerency. Olney appeared before the Foreign Relations Committee, urging in the plainest language that the membership constrain itself; their actions could lead to war. Chairman John Sherman appeared to agree, but the seventy-four-year-old suffered from memory loss. The next day he shocked Olney, telling him the committee was going to adopt a joint resolution with the House requiring presidential action, and he would be grateful for the secretary's advice on the language. Cleveland was off duck hunting, and Olney explained to the Washington *Evening Star* that authority to recognize the "so-called Republic of Cuba" rested completely with "the Executive"—the president. As legislation, this frivolous resolution was "inoperative." Cleveland simply ignored it as he had so many others. Wall Street, however, did not. Stocks plummeted.[36]

In Havana, rumors of the death of Antonio Maceo swept the city. Lee cabled a warning of anti-American riots and requested a ship be sent to safeguard the consulate and American citizens. The cruiser *Newark,* on filibustering patrol at Key West, was ordered to prepare to steam. Navy Secretary Herbert was not comfortable with this at all. There was no telling what dangers lurked in Havana harbor, and he prevailed on the president to cancel the order.

What of William McKinley during the excruciatingly long lame-duck period? The very soul of moderation, the president-elect remained at Canton, and though he favored autonomy in principle, he had no precise Cuban agenda. So long as Spain rejected American mediation, he could not propose any terms. If, however, Spain were to entrust the matter to presidential good offices, he would give two assurances: The United States would not annex Cuba; and he would allow Spain sovereign rights that were acceptable to the Cuban leadership. For now, he could say no more.

In his heart, McKinley hoped it would all be taken care of by inauguration day. Senator Henry Cabot Lodge of Massachusetts, the leading intellectual expansionist, visited Canton several times. To his friend Theodore Roosevelt he wrote that Cuba "is much on his mind. He very naturally does not want to be obliged to go to war as soon as he comes in. . . . He would like the crisis to come this winter and be settled one way or the other before he takes the reins." The Cameron resolution, however, aimed exactly at bringing on that crisis. If it passed both houses, as soon as McKinley took the oath of office he would be at war, with either Spain or the Congress.[37]

Through his surrogates, McKinley leaked his desire to the congressional leadership to table the inflammatory piece, leaving him free to deal with Cuba in his own way. Publicly, the president-elect expressed his gratitude that Cleveland and Olney were hanging tough; he appreciated their "conservative" recommendations and knew they were "not disposed to do or say anything likely to create an immediate ugly situation for the new administration."[38]

A return to "good times," erasing the stubborn clouds of the depression of 1893, and a restoration of sound business and full employment were McKinley's dearest wishes. They were also the wishes of some of his biggest contributors, men he most admired: John D. Rockefeller, George Pullman, J. P. Morgan, and William Cramp of Philadelphia, builder of the new navy. For them, a war was the worst possible scenario—look what had happened to the stock exchange with the Cameron resolution. Like Cleveland, McKinley was being dragged in opposite directions. He would have to yield to the Republican jingoes in Congress or fight them, and he recoiled from either option. Cuba, now the most potentially explosive domestic issue, was impossible to ignore. Yet McKinley, politically and by nature, could not immediately plunge into bold initiatives. His national business constituency would spurn them. But he could not just stand by and do nothing. The whole Cuban mess was tearing apart the national fabric.

The foreign front could not be ignored either. Since the Cameron resolution, constant tremors shook the ministries of European states sympathetic to Spain. The French and Russians were reported to be ready for diplomatic intervention to prevent a Spanish-American war. *Novoye Vremya* (New Times), the leading St. Petersburg daily, fired an anti-American broadside, claiming "Europe has every reason to oppose the strengthening of the United States in the New World and must be ready to support Spain if she is threatened with the loss of Cuba." There were tales of a Spanish-Japanese alliance to keep the United States out of Cuba *and* Hawaii. All of it contributed to McKinley's unease, dictating a very cautious policy.[39]

On March 3, 1897, his last day in office, Grover Cleveland invited President-elect McKinley to dinner at the White House. Talk was of Cuba and the dangers of war with Spain. "Mr. President," said McKinley with solemn feeling, "if I can only go out of office at the end of my term, with the knowledge that I have done what lay in my power to avert this terrible calamity, with the success that has crowned your patience . . . , I shall be the happiest man in the world."[40]

William McKinley remains one of the most enigmatic men to occupy the presidency. He left no trove of private correspondence as a window to his soul, and the hundred volumes of personal papers in the Library of Congress contain almost nothing in his own hand; nor do they go beyond the mundaneness of office. His public addresses follow the inflated rhetoric of the times. He told people what they wanted to hear; he was "a bit of a jollier," said Theodore Roosevelt. A kind and gentle man who shied from conflict, a devoted husband and son, ever attentive to his invalid wife and mother—these were his hallmarks. But was there anything to elevate the speechifying master of the tariff to the executive mansion? With blunt truth, a historian has written that before the presidency, William McKinley of Canton, Ohio, exhibited no loftier ambition than to "climb the greasy pole. There are traces of virtue but few of character."[41]

McKinley had been cabinet building since the election. He sought solid, respected men, representative of the nation and its better classes; "brilliance was not necessarily required." Of the three most likely to be intimately concerned with any Spanish conflict, the most controversial appointment was for secretary of state: old, addled, antiexpansionist Senator John Sherman. Like as not, McKinley chose him in order to create an Ohio vacancy in the Senate for éminence grise Marcus Alonzo Hanna. To protect all involved in the game, McKinley wrote publisher Joseph Medill of the Chicago *Tribune*, "[T]he stories regarding Senator Sherman's 'mental decay' are without foundation and the cheap inventions of sensational writers or other evil-disposed people." In office, Sherman proved unable to perform official tasks beyond the daily humdrum. The real work of the State Department was accomplished by the two assistant secretaries: Judge William Rufus Day of Ohio, silent, capable friend of the president, and Alvey A. Adee, the department's expert, long-serving, deaf senior bureaucrat. This diplomatic triumvirate led a foreign envoy to remark, "The head of the Department knows nothing; the First Assistant says nothing; the Second Assistant hears nothing."[42]

The War Department, traditionally a sleepy sinecure for loyal hackdom, went to Civil War old soldier, ex-governor of Michigan, lumber tycoon, and Republican stalwart Russell Alger. A wealthy, vain schmoozer, there was no quality to recommend him for the post save sectional politics and the vigorous support of old Union army veterans, the archly GOP Grand Army of the Republic. When McKinley announced Alger's appointment to the War Department, Mark Hanna jokingly cracked that it was the only cabinet seat for which a busy man could spare the time from his own affairs. Though at best a well-meaning mediocrity, Alger has gotten an inflatiedly bad rap for many of the administration's political cavings and War Department mistakes. In the end, he would be offered up as the sacrifice for the army's logistic nightmares in the coming war.[43]

The navy portfolio was also awarded for basely political motives, but turned out extremely well. New England always had a prior call on the department, and McKinley chose John Davis Long, former governor of Massachusetts. A "comfortable old Yankee," mildly hypochondriac, fond of restful vacations, and author of little books of poetry with charming titles such as *At the Fireside* and *Bites of a Cherry,* Long was a respected conservative, a likable, pleasant man. He didn't know much about his new job and was the first to admit it, confessing, "I have no special aptitude for the Navy Department—no more than any well-informed man who is interested in public affairs." But Long knew who did, and he surrounded himself with a set of first-class professional and civilian advisers.[44]

If the secretary-designate had no "special aptitude" for the Navy Department, another politician, still too young, too loud, too ready to fight to be considered for a cabinet seat, certainly did—the toothy, frustrated, thirty-eight-year-old police commissioner of New York City, Theodore Roosevelt. From the moment of McKinley's election, Roosevelt lobbied hard for the post of assistant secretary, and he was eminently qualified. When his friend and mentor Henry Cabot Lodge journeyed to Canton to speak with the president-elect, he wrote Roosevelt of McKinley's "great regard" for his character, and how much he would like to see Roosevelt in Washington. But there was a hitch. "I only hope," said the man from Canton, "he has no preconceived plans which he would wish to drive through the moment he got in." With a straight face, Lodge promised McKinley he need not have "the slightest uneasiness"; Roosevelt had no agenda at all.[45]

Bellamy Storer, a wealthy Ohio congressman, and his influential lobbyist wife, Maria, pushed the Roosevelt cause. "I want peace," replied McKinley, "and am told that your friend Theodore . . . is always getting into rows with everybody. I am afraid he is too pugnacious."

"Give him a chance to prove he can be peaceful," asked Maria.[46]

Roosevelt stubbornly refused to plead his own case, unless McKinley sent for him. "I don't wish to appear as a supplicant," he told Mrs. Storer, "for I am not a supplicant. I feel I could do good work as Assistant Secretary."[47]

Came March 1897, the inauguration, and still silence from McKinley. Lodge mobilized a group of high-powered friends, among them Czar Reed, Speaker of the House; John Hay, ambassador-designate to Great Britain; Judge William Howard Taft; and Vice President Garret Hobart, to convince the president to name Roosevelt. Lodge was frankly stumped. "The only, absolutely the only thing I can hear adverse is that there is a fear that you will want to fight somebody at once."[48]

Through Lodge, Roosevelt sought to assure John D. Long that he would faithfully hew to the administration's peaceful policies, and with exquisite tact added, "I shall stay in Washington, hot weather or any other weather, whenever he wants me to stay there." For Long, who enjoyed his summer vacations in New England, nothing could appeal more. He would be happy, he informed Lodge, to have Roosevelt on board.[49]

There was one final barrier, Senator "Easy Boss" Tom Platt of New York. Platt and Roosevelt were political enemies, and Roosevelt as assistant secretary of the navy could interfere with patronage at the Brooklyn Navy Yard, "Mr. Platt's yard," as it was sometimes called. Yet, from Platt's view, Roosevelt in Washington was much less of a political headache for the machine than having the galloping reformer stay on the New York Police Commission. He let McKinley know he could appoint Roosevelt to the Navy Department, so long as no one knew Platt had agreed to it. On April 6, 1897, Theodore Roosevelt was nominated by the president for the post of assistant secretary of the navy. Two days later, with Platt noticeably absent, the Senate voted to confirm the appointment at a salary of $4,500 per year. On April 9, John D. Long entered in his journal, "Roosevelt calls. Just appointed Assistant Secretary of the Navy. Best man for the place."[50]

The U.S. Navy, the country's first line of defense, entrusted the Naval War College with the study and preparation of war plans. In the summer of 1896, Rear Admiral Stephen Luce, seven years in retirement, wrote to Captain Henry Clay Taylor, president of the college, "To me it is utterly inconceivable that the government has not long ago matured plans for a joint military and naval campaign for the occupation of Cuba."[51]

"What you say about Cuba and Spain interests me very much," Taylor responded, "and will . . . produce greater results than you fancy." Unknown to Luce, the college had been drafting its Cuban-Spanish war plans for a year.[52]

In July 1895, less than six months after the first shots of the Cuban insurrection, Taylor had ordered his twenty-five student officers to chart a "special problem," concentrating on war with Spain. By January 1896, three options were presented for serious study: direct naval attack on the coast of Spain; attack on Spain's Pacific colonies of the Philippines and Guam; and attack on Spain's American colonies of Cuba and Puerto Rico. Attacking Spain was dismissed as too overreaching, expensive, and very risky. The Pacific operation was considered safe, though indecisive, and remote from the strategic cockpit of war, the Caribbean. The third option, Cuba and Puerto Rico, presented the opportunity of forcing Spain to fight at a place of the U.S. Navy's choosing, far from the Spanish logistic bases, but very close to America's, an extremely key advantage.[53]

The War College outline was given cogent form by the Office of Naval Intelligence, whose chief assigned the task to quite a sophisticated thinker, Lieutenant William Kimball. The resulting "Kimball Plan" underscored the national strategic and political objectives lacking in the War College draft. Given that war with Spain would erupt "upon the Cuban question," Kimball offered, America's strategic aims must be designed to "liberate Cuba from Spanish rule." Thus, the Caribbean must be the main theater of operations. Lacking political guidance from the Navy and State departments, Kimball postulated his own: "the establishment of a Cuban Republic through the efforts of its own citizens."[54]

Kimball invoked the "most economic means" of conducting the war as purely naval, a blockade of Cuba, starving the Spanish army into surrender in a matter of a few weeks. As for the United States Army, its employment was only necessary if naval operations alone did not succeed, or the war continued beyond what the U.S. government thought politically practical.[55]

Kimball, as was the common practice, spoke of charging Spain, the foreseeable loser, "a fair war indemnity for the cost of the war." To coerce that, he suggested the United States Asiatic Squadron, a modest force of cruisers and gunboats, "should capture and reduce Manila [capital of the Philippines] at the earliest possible date." It was a logical conclusion having the most profound consequences for the future of the United States and all Asia. In June 1896, Kimball's plan was submitted to Navy Secretary Hilary Herbert.[56]

The Kimball Plan, strategically sound but operationally short-sighted, did not meet with the approval of Captain Taylor of the War College, who strongly recommended "active aggressive work by navy and army." To coordinate war planning, or simply to control competing territory in a departmental turf war, Secretary Herbert appointed a "Senior Board." Membership consisted of the commander in chief of the North Atlantic Squadron, the chiefs of the bureaus of Navigation and Ordnance, the president of the Naval War College, and the head of the Office of Naval Intelligence.

In December 1896, during Cleveland's lame-duck period, the board produced its own war plan. Adhering to Kimball's political direction and retaining a minor role for the army, it dropped the Philippines from consideration, advocating instead a dangerous scheme that called for a rendezvous of the North Atlantic, Asiatic, and European squadrons in a joint assault on the Canary Islands, preparatory to an attack on Spain itself.

Captain Henry Clay Taylor refused to put his signature to the plan, choking on the "difficulties and dangers" of the Canary venture, in "a region 3,500 miles from our home bases." Instead, he submitted his own minority report to Secretary Herbert, recommending "all the naval forces at the disposal of the government be concentrated upon

Cuba." On March 2, 1897, two days before he left office, Hilary Herbert attached a note to the war plan for his successor to keep a weather eye on the international situation "with the most anxious care."[57]

John D. Long reconvened the Senior Board on June 6 with orders to examine all previous work and, if needed, come up with their own design. The membership offices were the same, but most of the people had changed. Significantly, the chair moved from the shore establishment bureaucracy to a seagoing officer, Rear Admiral Montgomery Sicard, commander in chief of the North Atlantic Squadron, a man of ability nearing the end of his active career. The Bureau of Navigation, the department's nominal senior office, was still headed by a very conservative officer, though younger and less archly pigheaded, Long's man, Captain Arent Schuyler Crowninshield. Commander Caspar Goodrich, a man trained in the Luce tradition, represented the Naval War College. Only the chief intelligence officer, Lieutenant Commander Richard Wainwright, remained of the old board.

Their revised war plan completely vindicated the War College's previous efforts, while keeping the best of Kimball's ideas. The war in Caribbean waters was not to be conducted solely by a naval blockade of Cuba, but as Captain Taylor had proposed, with the full cooperation of the army from the start. In addition, "for the purpose of further engaging the attention of the Spanish navy," the Asiatic Squadron, instead of steaming halfway around the world, would "go and show itself in the neighborhood of the Philippines," and in cooperation with Philippine insurgents, attack Manila. Should the capital of the Spanish empire in Asia fall, the United States "could probably have a controlling voice" regarding the archipelago's future at war's end. The Canary venture was tossed in the waste basket. This is how things stood with the U.S. Navy's strategic readiness in the last summer of peace.[58]

William McKinley's Cuba policy was held hostage to Republican politics and the preservation of party unity. The continuation of Republican executive and congressional dominance through a return of prosperity was the president's program. But Cuba, as always, threatened to upset the agenda. The president had an acute political nose.

"It is a watchful nose," wrote a columnist, "and it watches out for McKinley." McKinley knew if he did not take the lead on Cuba, the Senate would propel the nation at full tilt toward war. But now, with their own man in the White House, even some of the Republican leadership was becoming wary of the party's bomb throwers. "I think I see everywhere . . . a disposition to provoke hostilities," said Ohio Republican Congressman Charles Grosvenor, "and to bring about a condition that will ruin us all."[59]

McKinley was also at a disadvantage because he could not trust Secretary of State Sherman to develop a Cuban program, and the president was forced to borrow in large part from Olney and Cleveland. Like them, McKinley reserved the ultimate right of the United States to intervene, both to put an end to the sorry plight of the Cuban people and to terminate the war's direct effect on the United States' institutions and politics. McKinley, like Cleveland before him, believed Cuban autonomy, not independence, the best answer, and resolved to give Spain a reasonable time to bring order to its Cuban house. But here McKinley significantly broke with the previous administration's policy and veered sharply away.

His predecessors had spoken of Spain's "justified" military campaign against the rebels, refusing to permit the Cubans to get in the way of what Olney considered a purely Spanish-American agreement to reinstate peace and a measure of autonomy in Cuba. McKinley abandoned that. So far as principle was concerned, he inserted a Cuban perspective in the diplomatic equation, and refused to impose any solution repugnant to them. This was crucial because it made any settlement, even with American mediation, absolutely dependent on the rebel leadership. And they stood for nothing less than total independence, while Spain refused even to consider the point. The result was a complete impasse.[60]

The president needed firsthand information from the island. Like Cleveland, he did not entirely trust Consul General Lee, but to remove him, even though he was a Democrat, was politically dangerous, liable to excite the congressional and press jingoes. Instead, he sent Chicago attorney William J. Calhoun on a special fact-finding mission. Calhoun spent the spring of 1897 in Cuba, traveling in the fat agricultural region between Havana and Matanzas. Beyond the "military lines," the countryside, he reported, was "practically depopulated. . . . Every house had been burned, banana trees cut down, cane fields swept with fire, and everything in the shape of food destroyed." In as "fair" a landscape as he ever imagined, "I did not see a house, man, woman or child, a horse, mule, cow, nor even a dog. I did not see a sign of life, except an occasional vulture. . . . The country was wrapped in the stillness of death and the silence of desolation." Calhoun held no confidence that Spain could retain its hold, or that autonomy, or even independence, might rescue the island from its degradation.[61]

Assistant Secretary of State William Rufus Day put Minister Dupuy de Lôme on notice that the president would formally protest the *reconcentración* if Spain did not immediately remedy the appalling conditions. In a confidential letter to de Lôme, ostensibly from Sherman but crafted by Adee, and carefully leaked to certain senators, the McKinley administration struck at the "uncivilized and inhumane conduct" of the war, not only demanding that Spain pacify the island, but insisting that she do it "according to the military code of civilization." The letter condemned on behalf of the American people and "of common humanity" Weyler by name and the entire policy of *reconcentración*, with its "cruel employment of fire and famine to accomplish by uncertain indirection what the military arm seems powerless to directly accomplish." The Spanish foreign ministry, disdaining American diplomatic intervention in what they considered purely an internal problem, took its standard excruciating time to answer.[62]

But of what to do, no sane person in Washington knew. For a few days McKinley even toyed with the idea of giving Spain $150 million in bonds in return for Cuban independence. Annexation? No, McKinley was very opposed to that. It dawned on the president, as it had on Grover Cleveland, that only a negotiated settlement between Spain and the rebels would end the insurrection—an impossible hope since the principals were entirely intractable. Instead, the war, reported Fitzhugh Lee in an evenhanded dispatch, would "drag its weary length so long as the insurgents can dig sustenance from the ground upon one side or money [from landowners and sympathetic Americans] . . . by the other, with the continued suffering, loss of human life, the murder of innocent men, women, and children by both sides, and the frightful havoc which disease makes."[63]

. . .

Another reason to clean up the Cuban mess in America's front yard arose from the insistent noises coming from its back. Hawaii, whose annexation by the United States in 1893 had been rejected by Grover Cleveland, had again, with the uncomfortably close interest of Japan, stirred herself into the diplomatic mix. The 1896 Republican platform contained a Hawaiian plank advocating American control of the islands and preventing any foreign interference, a sort of Monroe Doctrine of the central Pacific. As candidate and president-elect, McKinley had typically waffled, telling envoys from the Hawaiian Republic, "Of course I have my ideas . . . but consider that it is best at the present time not to make known what my policy is."[64]

Inside two weeks of taking office, McKinley revealed his position: to annex Hawaii to the United States. The president and his cabinet were keenly sensitive to the hugely growing numbers of Japanese agricultural immigrants working the sugar and fruit plantations. It had reached twenty-five thousand people, about a quarter of the entire population and three times the number of whites. The Hawaiian government had refused to admit the latest coolie contingent, prompting an official protest from Japan. The Imperial Navy's cruiser *Naniwa* came to Honolulu in May 1897, and there was talk of further naval responses, increasing the diplomatic pressure.

In early June, McKinley sent a Hawaiian treaty of annexation to Congress, prompting a protest by the Japanese minister in Washington. The U.S. Navy, which had just completed its first war plan envisioning conflict with Japan, dispatched reinforcements to Hawaii. Assistant Navy Secretary Roosevelt advised the president that the battleship *Oregon* could reach Hawaii from the West coast in two weeks. Alfred Thayer Mahan urged that the United States take the islands *now* and explain later; the menace of a newly militaristic Japan was too dangerous to ignore. The Hawaiian government, fearing Japanese retaliation, offered to submit the Japanese immigration question to international arbitration. At the same time, the State and Navy departments telegraphed their Pacific and Asiatic station commanders "secret and confidential" instructions to prepare for a possible Japanese attack on the Hawaiian Islands. In Honolulu, Rear Admiral Lester Beardslee received orders that if Japan resorted to hostilities, he was to "land a suitable force" and officially announce an American protectorate. The administration was not really expecting armed action, and Beardslee and the U.S. Asiatic Station chief, Rear Admiral Frederick McNair, were to avoid any acts that might spark a conflict, being ordered to push the arbitration option discreetly to Japanese naval and diplomatic officers.[65]

The signing of the Hawaiian treaty of annexation—"not a change" in U.S. direction, said McKinley, but a "consummation"—took place at the White House on June 16 and was dispatched to the Senate for ratification. No action was taken. Japan, in the meantime, received enough diplomatic stroking to withdraw her protests of the treaty and the treatment of her nationals.

McKinley was still short of the two-thirds majority in the Senate to ratify the annexation. Southern Democrats, unhappy with the islands' racial mix, allied themselves with domestic sugar beet interests to stall yet again. McKinley, stymied, withdrew the treaty and instead moved for a joint congressional resolution, which required only a simple majority. But even that would have to wait until the troubles over Cuba were dealt with.

The issue of a new American ambassador to Madrid had dragged for months. McKinley needed more than just an official emissary; he wanted a personal representative in accord with his desire "to adopt every possible measure to bring about a change" in Spanish-American relations. If, in the end, nothing could be done, he had to show that America had gone the last mile for a settlement, "that we had spared no effort to avert trouble," as he said to Columbia University President Seth Low. McKinley offered the job to half a dozen eminent Republicans and men in public life, including Seth Low, and all demurred. Eventually he found Stewart L. Woodford, a journeyman Brooklyn lawyer with a résumé that included Civil War brigadier, lieutenant governor of New York, congressman, and U.S. attorney for the Southern District of New York.[66]

On July 16, 1897, Secretary of State Sherman handed Woodford his official instructions and the note he would present to the Spanish government. The sentences took a significantly threatening tone toward Spain, but made no firm demands and in most ways reiterated the phrases of the previous two years: The patience of the United States was limited; it was no longer content with a policy of "mere inaction." Where it diverged from previous warnings was in turning up the diplomatic heat to force Spain by incremental steps to sever irrevocably her four centuries' bond with Cuba. McKinley finally understood the rebels would accept nothing less.

If sincere, bedrock progress were not forthcoming, McKinley threatened, the United States would recognize Cuban belligerency and, if necessary, a "Cuban Republic." American "intervention" was also a possibility, though not with "unfriendly intent." The United States was now a player. It could no longer remain idle, "letting our vast interests suffer, our political elements [be] disturbed, and the country perpetually embroiled." Spain must face the truth that she could never regain her old sovereignty. Like Cleveland, McKinley offered to broker a lasting, honest agreement, giving "justice and self-respect" to Spain and Cuba, and being "equitable" to the United States. Spain, McKinley thought, *must* understand the wisdom of submission to the reality of the Cuban fiasco.[67]

Other instructions came in person from McKinley himself to Woodford. He was secretly to take the pulse of Europe, feeling for reactions should war threaten between the United States and Spain. In addition to regular communications with the State Department, he would send additional private letters, marked "To be handed unopened to the President by his direction." From the first he did so. Stopping in London and Paris, meeting with American and European diplomats, Woodford sent back assurances to the State Department. "I believe that most Englishmen, Frenchmen and Germans," he noted, "regard Cuba as within the legitimate zone of American influence." Great Britain was also not averse to the United States absorbing Cuba should it come as a natural result of "great events." Woodford put a damper on that, telling each minister that "the United States does not seek to annex Cuba nor to form a protectorate over her."[68]

On August 8, before Woodford put his first step in Spain, Premier Cánovas took the assassin's bullet at Miramar.

By summer 1897, the Cuban fault lines in Spanish politics ripped apart any tissue of national unity on solving the problem. Liberal ex-premier Práxedes Sagasta, leader of the opposition, condemned the Conservative government's colonial policy for bringing ruin to Spain in Cuba and, lately, in the jungles of the Philippines. The economy was a shambles, international credit was almost wiped out, and mobs were in the streets. The Liberals demonstrated their strength through all classes.

On June 24, Sagasta had published the Liberal manifesto displaying bitter truths that "all the efforts in the world are insufficient to maintain peace in Cuba by the bayonet alone." He denounced Weyler and his "policy of excessive severity and repression" as utterly, disastrously failed. It meant nothing. Sagasta and the Liberals, sincere in their quest for reform, were just as opposed to Cuban independence as their Conservative rivals, ensuring the war would go on forever.[69]

On Cánovas's death, an interim Conservative government headed by the minister of war announced its full confidence in Weyler and his conduct of things. The Duke of Tetuán remained as foreign minister and eventually deigned to reply to Secretary Sherman's letter of two months past. The President of the United States, averred the duke, was simply wrong in all his assertions, doubtlessly because of "incorrect" information. Spain's methods to end the insurrection, he said with selective logic, were no worse than those of "the invincible General Sherman" in his devastating march from Atlanta to the sea in the American Civil War.[70]

In September, Woodford arrived in Madrid to take up his post. On the twenty-fourth, at the hushed marble foreign ministry, he handed Tetuán McKinley's note, expressing America's hope that Spain do the right and honorable thing "to her Cuban colony and to mankind." It would be best all around, Woodford said, for the government's reply to come by November 1, before the president's annual message and the congressional adjournment. Woodford privately held little hope for success. Delay, endless delay, Woodford knew, was really the chief Spanish strategy. The Spanish, like Mr. Micawber, were simply waiting for something to turn up. "It is a hand to mouth policy," he reported.[71]

The new Liberal government, Sagasta at its head, Don Pío Gullón y Iglesias in the foreign ministry, and Don Segismundo Moret y Prendergast as minister of *ultramar* ("countries overseas"), took office on October 14. They at once moved to sack Weyler and offer Cuba some

form of autonomy. Appeasement of the *norteamericanos* and a negotiated peace with the rebels indicated the most promising method of
healing Spain's internal troubles. This plan was heralded by Gullón as
a complete, historic reversal of "immense scope," with "real self-
government" for the Cubans; the Liberals were prepared to grant
Cuba "all possible self-government . . . [and] every concession compatible with inflexible defense of Spanish rule and sovereignty." In effect, for the rebels, nothing.[72]

The queen regent signed the autonomy decrees for Cuba and
Puerto Rico on November 15. Every Cuban and Puerto Rican henceforth would exercise the same rights as Spaniards in Spain. Governed
by a crown-appointed governor general and elected insular parliament, Cuba would control her own domestic affairs, education, tariffs, charity, public works, agriculture, and industry. Spain kept
foreign relations, defense, law courts, and church-state relations. But
if one read the fine print, a different story appeared. The Cortes
would decide when the actual practice of autonomy commenced. The
governor general was to appoint a majority of the parliamentary
upper house. That royal officer could also veto any legislation, dissolve parliament, and revoke the constitution. Cuba, in return, was
saddled with the entire debt of the war of liberation.

Sagasta made it clear that military operations against the Cuban
rebels would continue, though more humanely. The queen regent appointed a new governor and captain general, "equipped with every
possible means of pacification": Lieutenant General Ramón Blanco y
Arenas, Marquis of Peña Plata, lately Captain General of the Philippines. Additional military reinforcements were planned for Cuba,
with the Spanish army to be maintained at a strength of 145,000 men
until the whole island had been pacified. Sagasta announced considerable monies to induce the rebel leaders to give up the fight.

In response, the Junta's Tomás Estrada Palma countered with
"nothing short of independence." In Cuba, Máximo Gómez promised death to any Spaniard offering the money.[73]

But there were signs even more ominous for the future of autonomy. *El Imparcial* recollected that since the start of the rebellion,
200,000 soldiers had left Spain, singing "the March of Cádiz" as they
boarded transports for Cuba. Of these, only 53,000 men were still in
the front lines. More than 26,000 lay in military hospitals, unfit for

duty; 35,000 others were deployed as railroad guards and constabulary. Where were the rest? The answer seemed to be, dead from disease. Every poor Spanish family unable to purchase a 1,500-pesatas
exemption from military service grieved for a dead son. Spanish manpower reserves had bottomed out. At the port of La Coruña, Captain
Tasker Bliss, the United States military attaché, saw long lines of ambulances and litter bearers awaiting the unloading of sick and
wounded soldiers, "who return by every steamer from Cuba. . . .
Wives mothers and sisters . . . were crying and some screaming at the
sight of the death-like forms being landed from the boats."[74] Cuba devoured Spain's blood and treasure.

In the United States, Weyler's dismissal and the publication of the
autonomy decrees represented a considerable success for President
McKinley. "Thus far Spain has surrendered everything asked of her,
and the policy of the administration has been completely vindicated,"
noted the Chicago *Tribune*. Not quite. McKinley understood autonomy's shortcomings, but trusted that conciliatory gestures coming
from the White House and State Department might compel Spain to
proceed even further.[75]

In the wonderful, bizarre pile of the State, War, and Navy Building
across the street from the White House, an efficiently obscure commodore, hardly known beyond the naval service, wrapped up his
work as president of the navy's Board of Inspection and Survey. The
commodore's friend, Senator Redfield Proctor, later said that fellow
members "at the [Metropolitan] club no more realized the fire in him
than neighbors saw a general in Ulysses S. Grant." He was Commodore George Dewey, just short of forty years in the navy, and for
good or ill, he would win America her empire.[76]

Dewey was of that group of the navy's senior officers who provided a link to an earlier service and an America fast disappearing
into history and myth. He entered the navy as a midshipman in 1858,
and in four years had been promoted to lieutenant, under his hero,
the great David Farragut. Dewey, with courage and intelligence, conducted himself extremely well at New Orleans and Port Hudson,
compiling an excellent combat record in the Civil War. In the humdrum sea and shore duties that came his way during the postwar dark

ages of the old navy, he took what came: admiral's flag lieutenant on the European Station, commanding sloops in the Pacific, a supply ship, torpedo-school duty at Newport, lighthouse inspector, a stint as skipper of the *Dolphin,* first steel ship of the new navy, commanding officer of the steam frigate *Pensacola,* chief of the Bureau of Equipment, and at age fifty-six, in what had seemed the end of his career, president of the Lighthouse Board in the Treasury Department. "I do not want war," he told a friend in 1894, "but without it there is little opportunity for a naval man to distinguish himself. There will be no war before I retire from the Navy, and I will simply join the great majority of naval men, and be known in history . . . as 'George Dewey who entered the Navy at a certain date and retired as Rear Admiral at the age limit!' "[77]

In November 1895, after two years on the Lighthouse Board, Dewey received the welcome and very responsible billet of president of the Board of Inspection and Survey, the navy's ship quality control office. Three months later, he was promoted to the rank of commodore.

Dewey was not one of the luminaries in the intellectual kingdom of the War College, or of the strategic expansionist group that clustered around Mahan and Roosevelt, or even the scientific and mechanical tinkerers in the bureaus. He was noteworthy only as a solid, dependable officer. A newspaper column truthfully informed, "He has never had the reputation of being a specially studious officer; indeed his reputation has been rather that of a society man." A socially popular widower, Dewey lived alone, fastidiously, in an apartment on H Street, near the Metropolitan Club, where he took lunch and dinner. In July 1896, around the time Lieutenant Kimball was perfecting his war plan one floor below Dewey's office in the State, War, and Navy Building, Dewey applied to the Bureau of Navigation for Pacific sea duty. Months passed and he heard nothing. "No orders for me yet," he wrote in a letter, "and probably none will come before Spring [1897] unless we have a brush with Spain, which is not likely." But that spring, the new assistant secretary of the navy, Theodore Roosevelt, joined the Metropolitan Club, and the two men often rode together through Rock Creek Park.[78]

The post of commander in chief of the Asiatic Squadron would soon come vacant at the retirement of Rear Admiral McNair. Dewey and his old 1858 Naval Academy classmate, Commodore John Adams

Howell, commandant of the Philadelphia Navy Yard, inventor of the Howell torpedo, the Howell disappearing gun carriage, and other devices, were the two candidates for the flag. In the Navy Register, Howell stood one number above Dewey in seniority and had notable departmental and congressional backers, chiefly Crowninshield of the Bureau of Navigation, and the former navy secretary, Senator William E. Chandler of New Hampshire. Dewey, not alone, thought Crowninshield "a pronounced bureaucrat, with whose temperament and methods I had little more sympathy than had the majority of officers at the time. He would hardly recommend me to any command."[79]

But Dewey had his champion as well, the unstoppable Theodore Roosevelt. The roots of TR's very serious string pulling and red tape cutting to get Dewey the Asiatic command are difficult to uncover. Roosevelt in later years invented a completely fictitious episode of the 1891 Chilean troubles, placing Dewey in the Argentine. In fact, Dewey was in Washington at the time, chief of the Bureau of Equipment.

TR knew all about Dewey's naval career, from having his ship burn under him at Port Hudson, to supervising the steaming trials of the battleship *Maine*. Politically Dewey was a cipher, with no interest in or even awareness of Roosevelt's grand expansionist ideas. That did not matter. What TR sought was someone he could trust "to act fearlessly and on his own responsibility when the emergency arose." What propelled the highly visible assistant secretary to gamble an awful lot of political capital on an agreeably ordinary naval officer to make the first lunge for American empire was that Commodore George Dewey was simply better than Commodore John Adams Howell for the job.[80]

Roosevelt didn't like Howell. He'd seen the man's work on the Armor Board, thought him no leader, and made sure Long knew it, too. Long was away in September, vacationing at Hingham Harbor. Roosevelt was doing such a good job at the department that the secretary saw no reason to cut his holiday short. "Theodore's enthusiasm and my conservatism make a good combination," he told dinner guests at the Massachusetts Club. "It is a liberal education to work with him." Long didn't know how liberal. On September 27, the day before Long's scheduled return, Roosevelt intercepted a letter from Senator Chandler to the secretary, recommending Howell's appointment to the Asiatic command.[81]

This was very bad. He swiftly sent a note by department messenger begging the senator not to commit himself before Roosevelt had a chance to show how things stood. Howell, he admitted, was "honorable" and had "great inventive capacity," but TR had yet to meet an officer "less fit" for important executive duty. "He is irresolute and . . . extremely afraid of responsibility." Roosevelt appealed to Chandler's like-minded expansionist "foreign policy" for the sort of man "with whom there is no chance of failure." The senator remained unconvinced.[82]

Frantic, TR called to an orderly, "Ask Commodore Dewey to come down."

"I want you to go," he told the commodore a few moments later, giving him a cigar and lighting it. "You are the man who will be equal to the emergency if one arises. Do you know any Senators?" Dewey admitted to an acquaintance with Senator Redfield Proctor, an old family friend, and an excellent choice. The millionaire "marble king of Vermont" was deeply wired into the administration as an investment partner of Vice President Hobart and Secretary of War Russell Alger, to whom he sometimes gave orders. As a stalwart, money-making Republican businessman, he naturally carried large influence with the president. Once Senator Proctor expressed himself "delighted" to help push the nomination on President McKinley, Commodore Howell hadn't a chance.[83]

Proctor duly called at the White House and the president cheerfully promised to act on Dewey's behalf "right away."

Not good enough, said Proctor. "Here, write it down, Mr. President," he suggested, pushing some notepaper across the desk.

McKinley scribbled in pencil, "Long, appoint Dewey command Asiatic squadron."

Proctor took the sheet. "You'll never regret this, Mr. President," he said on his way out. Reportedly, he went straight to the Navy Department across the street and handed the note to an astonishingly angry John D. Long.[84]

Without kicking up a public fuss to no good end, because Dewey *was* the best man for the job, Long "Respectfully" signed Dewey's orders on October 21, 1897. Effective November 30, he was detached from the Board of Inspection and Survey and ordered to San Francisco, and thence by steam liner to Yokohama to assume the post of "commander in chief of the Asiatic Station, aboard the [flagship] *Olympia*."

But there was one other thing. "*Commodore* Dewey," Long said slowly, "you won't go as a rear admiral. You'll go as a commodore. Perhaps," he paused, "you used too much political influence." This was serious punishment, publicly and diplomatically. The command rated a rear admiral, with the proper staff, emoluments, and a thirteen-gun salute; a commodore rated all things less, only eleven guns, and no personal flag, merely a broad pennant. He would be junior in protocol to almost every foreign flag officer on the station.

Dewey was taken aback at this. Yes, he said to Long, he had spoken to Senator Proctor, but others had used politics as well.

"You are in error, Commodore," said Long. "No influence has been brought to bear on behalf of anyone else." It was only hours later, when Roosevelt produced the letter from Senator Chandler, that Long understood. He wrote Dewey a note acknowledging the fact, but the man would still command in the rank of commodore. Dewey always felt that his bête noir, Crowninshield, instigated the "little pin-pricking slight."[85]

The desirability of sending a warship to Havana on a courtesy visit was often discussed in McKinley's cabinet. Cleveland had suspended the calls on the basis of neutrality and out of fear some incident might mushroom beyond control. McKinley felt otherwise. Acting on information that Havana was about to undergo what Long called "disturbances, anti-American in character," the president thought it prudent to station a warship forward. On October 8, Long detached the second-class battleship *Maine* from the North Atlantic Squadron, ordering her to Port Royal, South Carolina, near enough to Cuba to be available, yet far enough to be inconspicuous. "I had no instructions to take any measures whatever," Captain Charles Sigsbee remembered; "the *Maine* was simply awaiting further orders." On November 15, just over a month later, she steamed for Norfolk for dry-docking and minor repairs.[86]

In dock, an inspection showed the *Maine*'s antifouling paint in bad condition, her bottom crusted with barnacles, and a heavy growth of seaweed skirting the waterline. Over the side, on swaying ledges with

no safety devices whatever, the hands turned to with chipping hammers and paint. On December 3 came secret orders from Long to Sigsbee and the skipper of the cruiser *Detroit* at Key West. Should they
receive a coded message from Consul Lee, the letter *A*, the battleship
would steam to Havana and the cruiser to Matanzas.[87]

William McKinley's first annual message was read to Congress on December 6. The sentences reflected the president's fond desire to give
the Spanish reforms a chance to succeed. Spain, droned the House
clerk through the president's words, had embarked on "a course from
which recession with honor is impossible." To Spain's great relief, the
address halted well short of any recognition of Cuban belligerency.
The administration would see if "the new order of things" bore any
fruit, but McKinley also applied the screws. If nothing altered the
Cuban situation for the better, "further . . . action by the United
States will remain to be taken. When that time comes, that action will
be determined in the line of indisputable right and duty . . . to civilization and humanity, to intervene with force." Spain had heard all
of this before; there was no need for alarm.[88]

The message got mixed reviews. In Congress, the predictably strident Republican champions of Cuba, joined by nearly every partisan
Democrat in the Senate, condemned the wait-and-see attitude, construing it as weakness on the part of the administration. House
Democrats, closer to the electorate, "resolved" their own declaration
that war indeed existed in Cuba. The New York press split in its approval. "We have had enough of war, more than enough of jingoism";
now, perhaps, there would be "peace," summed the generally anti-
interventionist *Herald*. The thoroughly Republican *Tribune* praised
every word. "Eminently pacific," said the *Journal of Commerce*.
Hearst's *Journal* positively hated the president's statement, calling it
"lacking in virility, worse than mild . . . timid . . . cringing. . . . In regard to Cuba, Cleveland is still President."[89]

From Madrid, Captain Tasker Bliss, the military attaché, reported
most of Spain receiving the presidential message in "a spirit of intense
hostility." Only Sagasta and some of his cabinet were mollified. Official Spain combed the phrases, looking for duplicitous encouragement of the Cuban rebels, subtly veiled with threats of intervention;

"and against that," wrote Bliss, "all Spain is one." Lieutenant George L. Dyer, the naval attaché, sent a clipping from the *Nacional* suggesting "the burning of a little diplomatic wood . . . as we have done before"—to torch the national emblem fronting the U.S. legation.[90]

After the annual message the American government shut down for the year-end holidays. "There is absolute quiet and lack of news," cabled de Lôme to Foreign Minister Gullón. "The press scarcely concerns itself with the Cuban question." Congress, preoccupied with local matters and constituent politics, went home. Most of the administration was at Canton attending mother Nancy Allison McKinley's funeral.[91]

On December 15, the *Maine* navigated through the tricky coral reef at Key West and moored in the harbor. The imposing 6,682-ton, sixteen-knot ship was ideal for her coming mission. Planned and built as an armored cruiser in the early days of the American naval renaissance, the *Maine* had joined the fleet in 1895 as a second-class battleship, a designation more in keeping with her characteristics. It had been fully nine years since her funding authorization, and seven years from the day Navy Secretary Benjamin Tracy's granddaughter, Alice, broke the champagne bottle over her ram bow at the Brooklyn Navy Yard.

She was a queer duck of a ship. The *Maine* was intended as the first armored vessel of the new navy; her design came from the British-built Brazilian battleship *Riachuelo*—at the time, the most powerful warship in the Western Hemisphere. The decades 1870 to 1890 witnessed great flux and experimentation in naval architecture as it tried to conform to the new tactics inherent in steel ships, breech-loading guns, and locomotive torpedoes. It was not surprising that even the best naval architects should have been confused over the form and function of modern fighting vessels. The U.S. Navy, so recently a pile of antiquated junk and stepping hesitantly into the new era, was no exception.

The ram, both as weapon and as tactic, was a retrograde concept mistakenly reintroduced in the last third of the nineteenth century. It was what ultimately decided the design of the *Maine* and her close sisters in several of the world's navies. To ram the enemy, individual vessels and ships in squadron must close him bows on, in line abreast. It was thus highly desirable for the ship's main armament to bear forward, firing all the while during the advance to crushing contact. This concentration of heavy guns might leave up to half the ship's main armament useless in a traditional broadside-to-broadside battle. The solution was to balance the main armament en echelon, theoretically permitting the big guns to fire together: forward, aft, or on either beam. It made for ugly ships, and it didn't work. The strain of broadside, cross-deck firing stressed the hull, and there was topside damage caused by blast and concussion during fore and aft firing along the ship's long axis.

The principal battery of the *Maine*, four 10-inch guns in twin turrets, with barbettes prominently projecting outboard from the hull, were sited with the starboard set forward of the center superstructure and the port set aft. Her intermediate armament of six 6-inch guns were individually mounted in casemates, two each in the bow, stern, and amidships. Thirteen light, rapid-firing guns were distributed in the hull and superstructures. The ship's two fighting tops each held a 1-pounder cannon and .50-caliber Gatling gun. Four 18-inch torpedo tubes were carried in the underwater hull. The *Maine*'s complement of 343 enlisted men berthed forward, its 31 officers aft, the classic arrangement of the ages, which remained unchanged until the advent of the all-big-gun battleship in the early twentieth century. Her top speed was a fraction over sixteen knots. To extend cruising range, the *Maine* was also designed with a full set of sails, 7,135 square feet of canvas on three masts, but these were never delivered to the ship. Detaching the *Maine* from the North Atlantic Squadron for special service provided one of the classic roles of the armored cruiser, one for which she had been originally intended: sending an imposing ship of force to a distant station, without materially weakening the main fleet.

Captain Sigsbee's confidential orders in effect placed him at "the immediate judgment" of Consul General Lee. Once at Key West, Sigsbee promptly opened communications with the Havana consulate by regular mail and underwater cable. The correspondence was in innocuous code, and it was arranged that on receiving the signal "Two dollars," the *Maine* was to make all preparations to steam for Havana, departing on the coded message "One dollar." Sigsbee actually received the "Two dollars" message and the *Maine* prepared for sea. But the action-execute never came and the ship stood down.[92]

. . .

On December 20, President McKinley sent a long note to Woodford for the Spanish foreign minister. Presenting it as a follow-up to the Spanish reply note of the previous October, he encouraged the Liberal government to persevere with its intended reforms. Spain, he said, "has entered upon a pathway from which no backward step is possible."[93]

Autonomy in Cuba and Puerto Rico became legally effective on January 1, 1898. Save for a distinct minority, and some newspapers, it had almost no support, and there were no tangible changes in the daily life of the Cuban people. Starvation and *reconcentración* were still the order of the day. In many towns the supply of coffins had long been exhausted. Homeless rural vagrants begged in the Havana streets. The fortunate found sleeping space in the old city walls, lining up for a daily dole of lentil *rancho* soup. In Matanzas, women, desperate with hunger and need for their children, raided the market. U.S. Vice Consul Joseph Springer estimated that a third of the city's fifty thousand people were "absolutely without food and clothing, and 11,000 without homes or shelter." Appalled by the suffering, President McKinley made a special appeal for Red Cross donations, himself giving five thousand dollars anonymously.[94]

The Fifty-fifth Congress convened on January 5, 1898, and Minister Dupuy de Lôme optimistically noticed a "complete abstention from our matters. Our situation is bettering every day." Others were not so sanguine. On January 11, Navy Secretary John D. Long cabled the commander of the European Squadron to "retain" all sailors whose enlistments were about to expire.[95]

In Havana on January 12, a new pro-Spanish but antiarmy newspaper, named *El Reconcentrado,* published an article, "Flight of the Scoundrels," excoriating one of Weyler's key subordinates. Certain army officers and their *peninsulare* partisans took offense, and a group trashed *El Reconcentrado*'s editorial offices and those of two autonomist papers. Angry crowds of Spaniards and Cubans gathered in the streets, protesting each other, and they were joined in the demonstrations by pro- and antiarmy factions. Consul General Lee moved about the throngs of diverse demonstrators, trying to gauge their temper. Back at the consulate, he composed a short message to Judge Day in Washington: "Mobs, led by Spanish officers, attacked today the offices of the . . . newspapers here advocating autonomy. Rioting at this hour, 1 p.m., continues." Later in the day, he sent another: "Much excitement, which may develop into serious disturbances. No rioting at present." Shouts of "Death to [Captain General] Blanco!" and "Death to autonomy!" rang in the air; the cry "Viva Weyler!" was very popular. The palace of the captain general and the American consulate were heavily guarded by Spanish troops. The next morning, Lee sensed a quieting down; the army, discipline restored, was back in control of the city and of itself. Lee had heard a rumor of a mob "shouting a proposal" to march on the consulate, but there was nothing to that. "Presence of ships may be necessary later," he cabled Judge Day, "but not now."

Hours later, Lee was less confident. Listening to Spanish troops shouting, "Death to Blanco!" he was not at all certain the captain general remained fully in command of his forces. If Blanco could not maintain discipline in the army, or if it seemed that Americans were in actual danger, then "ships must be sent," he wired the State Department, "and to that end should be prepared to move promptly."[96]

The New York press had a wallowing field day. According to the *World,* "The riots in Havana mean revolution," and the paper hammered the message of acute danger to Americans. Hearst's *Journal* spread a full-page headline, "NEXT TO WAR WITH SPAIN," blatantly falsifying the riots as aimed against American citizens in Havana, rather than a brawl between rival Spanish and Cuban factions. The *Journal* declared, "The end is in sight," and predicted United States military intervention within forty-eight hours. The *Sun* reported four successive days of rioting. The public was unaware of Lee's cables sent on the fourteenth, "Noon. All quiet," and the fifteenth, "Quiet prevails." The consul general, though, was of many minds about the need for a warship. Yes, it might be necessary to protect American citizens, but now wasn't the right time; perhaps the last week of January would be better, so it could not be construed as conspicuously part of the riot response. Coaling, he thought, might be used as an excuse for a visit.[97]

On Thursday the thirteenth, a day after the riots, Assistant Secretary Roosevelt marched into his boss's office, shut the door, "and began in his usual emphatic and dead-in-earnest manner." As Long noted in his journal, after discussing "sensibly . . . two or three matters of business, he told me that, in case of war with Spain, he intends to abandon everything and go to the front." Long knew what was coming, and his eyes veritably glazed over when TR, completely in accord with Naval War College doctrine, proposed launching a full program of naval readiness, "and the necessity of having some scheme of attack arranged for instant execution in case of emergency." By tomorrow, he knew, his bellicose assistant would have conferred with the pertinent bureau chiefs and stayed up the night, "having spoiled twenty pages of good writing paper."[98]

Indeed that is what happened exactly. Signed "Very respectfully," the sheaf of papers reposed on the secretary's desk the next morning. More than recommendations, the blunt memorandum read like a set of curtly drawn orders for the rapid mobilization of the navy and the concentration "at once" of its "scattered" forces at critical points for the coming war. The attack, or as Roosevelt put it, the "demonstration against the Philippines," was plainly cast for the secretary's eyes. Long scratched his head when he read Roosevelt's call for an East Coast "flying squadron of powerful ships and great coal capacity" for instant dispatch to the Canary Islands, where it might attack Cádiz, or steam through the Strait of Gibraltar by night and bombard Barcelona. "When the war comes," TR concluded, "*it should come finally on our initiative,* and after we have had time to prepare." Though Long scoffed before and after reading this astounding instrument of foresight, he wrote in his journal: "The funny part of it all is that [Roosevelt] actually takes the thing seriously." And now, so did Long; he began dictating instructions for vessels in the South Atlantic to steam northward without attracting undue attention, and coal stocks, "the best that can be had," were ordered topped off throughout the fleet.[99]

Congress caught a dose of the panic bug. House Democrats shouted for recognition of Cuban belligerency and, an extreme measure, for the appointment of commissioners to negotiate a peace treaty "between the United States and the Republic of Cuba." Senate Republicans adopted without debate a resolution requesting that the president keep them informed of measures taken to protect American citizens in Cuba.[100]

Minister de Lôme reported Washington's reaction to Madrid. Lee's cables he considered "not alarming, and unless he requests it, no war vessel will be sent." But he also noted a new and ominously "abrupt" focus in American sentiment, dormant for many weeks, toward Cuba. De Lôme had been approached by the editor of the *New York Herald,* possibly an unofficial emissary of the State Department. What would be Spain's reaction, the journalist wanted to know, if President McKinley were to order a force of U.S. Marines to protect the consulate in Havana? "I told him," de Lôme informed Foreign Minister Gullón, "that it would mean fighting; that Spain would never submit." Gullón responded in kind. De Lôme must make very clear to Judge Day that the utterances of the *Herald* editor "lack even the pretext of reason." The *Heraldo de Madrid* echoed the sentiments: "If the government of the United States sends one warship to Cuba . . . Spain would act with energy and without vacillation."[101]

After a fortnight the Havana crisis ebbed away. So confident was the McKinley administration's perception of light at the end of the Cuban tunnel, the navy felt the time opportune for the North Atlantic Squadron to return, after two years away, to its traditional winter drill grounds in Florida's warm, inviting waters. Minister de Lôme expressed some concern about the move south, but was assured the exercise was "entirely peaceful."[102]

On January 24, what John D. Long called "an interesting day," the cabinet met to discuss "a slight change in its Cuban policy," the resumption of the courtesy visits by U.S. warships to Cuban ports, especially Havana. "Not only because our vessels ought to be going in and out of it like those of any other nation," Long wrote in his diary, but because of possible danger to Americans, "some means of protection should be on hand." True, the *Maine* had been standing by at Key West, and Lee could send for her "at any time." But to Long this was "a risky arrangement," a crisis trigger. He wanted to suggest to the Spanish government the "wisdom" of sending a ship "in a friendly way" to Havana, "to exchange courtesies and civilities," reflecting the positive changes and "improved conditions of things . . . from the new Spanish policy." McKinley and Day thought it a perfect idea.[103]

Across the street at the State, War, and Navy Building, Day met with Dupuy de Lôme. He began by hinting at new initiatives, including a commercial treaty with Spain, then went on to say it was a mistake to keep American warships from visiting Cuba, "because now what is fresh proof of international courtesy [by the United States in carrying on the calls] is looked upon as a hostile act." De Lôme answered positively, adding that naval visits should not have been canceled in the first place; had that been the case, there would be little, if any, problem now for the U.S. Navy to call at any Cuban port. Day returned to the White House, briefed the president, and telephoned the Spanish legation for an afternoon meeting.[104]

Day, Long, Justice Joseph McKenna of the Supreme Court, and General Nelson Miles, commanding general of the army, first met to discuss de Lôme's reaction to the resumption of naval visits. All concurred the proposal should go forward. "And I called on the President," Long wrote that evening, "and we arranged that the *Maine* should be ordered at once to Havana. . . . I hope with all my heart, that everything will turn out all right."[105]

Judge Rufus Day went to his second meeting with de Lôme immediately afterward. What had been talked about between them in principle in the morning was now fact. The president, the Spanish minister later cabled, "has determined to send the *Maine* to Havana as a mark of friendship." Day and Long had just released simultaneous statements to the press, and as soon as they received instructions, Lee and Woodford would do the same in Havana and Madrid. The Spanish could do nothing but smile stiffly at the fait accompli and pretend to be very pleased.[106]

Lee received the State Department cable within hours. The *Maine* would arrive in Havana "in a day or two," and he was to arrange "a friendly interchange" of calls with the local authorities. Lee thought it was very bad timing. General Blanco was out of the city inspecting garrisons and would not be back for two weeks. Could not State and Navy at least postpone the visit to allow any residual "excitement" from the riots "time to disappear." No, responded Day, "*Maine* has been ordered." Lee did not give up. He obtained an interview with Blanco's deputy and members of the staff, and they, too, were not overjoyed, fearing the *Maine*'s call might "produce excitement and most probably a demonstration." Please, they asked, don't send the ship until further direction from Madrid. If the visit was friendly, as the United States professed, there was no need for undue haste.[107]

On the twenty-fifth came the official Spanish response from Madrid. On behalf of the queen regent and the Spanish government, Dupuy de Lôme gladly accepted the visit "of cordiality and courtesy," and to reciprocate, the armored cruiser *Vizcaya* would call at American port cities while "passing to and from the island of Cuba."[108]

On Sunday, January 23, Rear Admiral Montgomery Sicard brought the North Atlantic Squadron to Key West, where it was joined by the *Maine* and the cruisers *Montgomery* and *Detroit* for maneuvers and drill. Monday, at two bells in the evening watch, 9:00 P.M., with the ships anchored during night signaling practice, the torpedo boat *Du Pont* came racing out from Key West, as Captain Sigsbee remembered, "making Very's [pyrotechnic] signals to attract attention." Obviously she had dispatches for the commander in chief, but Sigsbee intuited that his orders for Havana had come as well. "I ordered fires spread and preparations for getting the *Maine* under way." In half an hour a signal winked from the flagship *New York* for Sigsbee to report on board and the *Maine* to prepare for steaming. "All ready," the *Maine*'s signalmen replied.[109]

Admiral Sicard had received orders from the Navy Department to send "the *Maine* to Havana, Cuba, and make friendly call." Sigsbee, a sober, trusted, walrus-faced officer of thirty-five years' service, was to act according to his best judgment "in the usual way; . . . it was assumed that I would know how to act on my arrival in Havana." Sigsbee returned to the ship, and by 11:00 P.M. the *Maine* was under way, standing southward into the Gulf Stream. He intended to enter Havana at full light, "when the town was alive and on its feet." At daylight on January 25, the hands were roused and the ship scrubbed and burnished to present the spotless, orderly appearance standard to the U.S. Navy. The crew were required to dress in their winter service blue "with exceptional neatness," the officers in frock coats. When all was ready to Sigsbee's satisfaction, the *Maine,* ensign at the peak, jack at the foremast head, steamed at flank speed toward the harbor entrance, in full view of the city. A harbor pilot boarded to seaward of the Morro and took the battleship through the narrow cut with care and skill. The forts, shores, and wharves were crowded with Spanish soldiers and Cuban civilians. The ship eased way, and came handsomely to her mooring buoy, opposite the *machina* shears of the navy yard.[110]

"Ship quietly arrived 11 a.m. to-day. No demonstrations so far," cabled Lee to the State Department.[111]

CHAPTER 4

"FOR NATIONAL DEFENSE, FIFTY MILLION DOLLARS"

I must have money to get ready for war.
—*President William McKinley, March 6, 1898*

Statesmen might publicly claim the *Maine* had been ordered to Havana to signal the new era of a peacefully autonomous Cuba, but no one was fooled. The battleship was there to provide a refuge for American citizens should disturbances be rekindled. The Havana street riots had badly jolted William McKinley's misplaced faith in Spain's ability to pacify its colonial house, dashing hopes that she might, at last, grow beyond centuries of oppressive authority to initiate actual reform in Cuba. Real autonomy, a true dominion, not the Potemkin village so laboriously pried from the Spanish government, was still nothing more than a concept, and for stiff-backed Spain, a wholly unacceptable one.

McKinley was far from alone in his disappointment. In the weeks since the replacement of the disastrous Valeriano Weyler as governor and captain general by the relatively complaisant Ramón Blanco, the informed public and the less bellicose politicians and newspapers in the United States had taken a step back, adopting a cautious attitude toward the new Spanish scheme. But the Havana riots, led by ultrapatriotic army officers, convinced large segments of American society and its opinion makers of the futility of incremental transition for Cuba, honest or not. Witnessing the now ominous national mood, Minister Dupuy de Lôme cabled the foreign ministry in Madrid;

"[T]he change of sentiment has been so abrupt, and our enemies, influenced by it, so numerous, that any sensational occurrence might produce a change and disturb the situation."[1]

Once the *Maine* had secured to her moorings and set the in-port watch, those men on deck took in the panorama of the great Antillean port, chipped and fading in shabby grandeur, over which the crimson-and-gold Spanish flag had flown since the time of Christopher Columbus. The navy yard, with its loftily emblematic shears, the *machina,* an obsolete tripod derrick, lay five hundred yards west at the water's edge of the city. From the battleship it was easy to see clear up the cobbled, portico-shaded streets, right into the white and pastel heart of the metropolis. Astern, toward the harbor channel, rode the masted cruiser *Alfonso XII,* stationary flagship of Rear Admiral Vicente Manterola y Taxonera, commandant general of the naval station of Havana; nearby lay the German navy's square-rigged training ship *Gneisenau.* Northward, beyond, by the massive harbor fortifications of the Castillo de Cabaña, stretched the mercantile and fishing-boat piers. East lay the suburb of Regla with its municipal *plaza de toros,* the bull-ring. "In command of the *Maine* at Havana," Captain Sigsbee recalled, "I had but one wish . . . to be friendly to the Spanish authorities as required by my orders."[2]

The ship's first Spanish visitor was a naval lieutenant, representing the captain of the port. In bearing and deportment the officer conducted himself with polite dignity, a trait Sigsbee recognized as the invariable face of the Spanish navy. Behind the official facade, however, he detected embarrassment, even humiliation, in the faultlessly uniformed man having to carry out an odious duty. Sigsbee expressed himself delighted to have the Spaniard aboard his ship and warmly conducted him to his cabin for some refreshment. The man relaxed somewhat when they were joined by Admiral Manterola's flag lieutenant, who, Sigsbee noticed, "seemed to take matters more philosophically."

Captain Sigsbee, too, needed to observe the tenets of naval diplomatic etiquette, and he welcomed this official visit because it permitted him to gauge at least a segment of opinion in the skittish city. On that observation would rest Sigsbee's decision whether to allow his officers and crew liberty ashore. On his part, Sigsbee's first official call was to the senior Spanish naval officer in the port, Rear Admiral Manterola. He donned full dress, which included cocked hat, epaulets, and sword, was piped over the side into his gig, and rode the short distance to the admiral's residence at the *machina*. A fair-sized, sullen-faced crowd closed around him at the fleet landing, but it was more curious than threatening. Sigsbee paid particular attention to the bearing of the Spanish troops, where his trained eye might discover motivations and behavior invisible to a casual observer. "They saluted me, as a rule," he said, "but with so much expression of apathy that the salute really went for nothing"—an indicator of poor morale.

Sigsbee's official and social obligations with the Spanish navy went smoothly. He found their officers alert, intelligent, and up-to-date on the science of their profession, and "they all had their polished national manner." But it was clear from conversations and innuendo that the Spaniards did not regard the United States Navy as their equals in battle. Traditional pride caused them dangerously to overestimate their own fighting capability, while at the same time deprecating that of the United States. As to the Spanish warships Captain Sigsbee examined during his time in Havana, he found them "admirable . . . clean and well kept." But their crews, he noticed, did not measure up well, in physical stature or intelligence, to either the *Maine*'s enlisted men, or those of the U.S. Navy as a whole. So far as he could see, no Spanish warship ever conducted combat readiness or ship's safety drills. "In everything they did," Sigsbee later wrote, "except in respect to etiquette, the practiced nautical eye could not fail to note their inferiority . . . to the vessels of our own squadron at Key West."

Later, when the new armored cruisers *Vizcaya* and *Almirante Oquendo* arrived in port, Sigsbee noticed their captains' and officers' quarters "were one long stretch of beautiful woodwork, finer than is the rule on board our own vessels." He ominously reported these ships would be "all aflame" within ten minutes of going into "close action."

In Havana, the *Maine*'s in-port routine was unlike that in New York or even in a friendly foreign port. Outwardly reposed, the battleship assumed the hidden guise of a fortress besieged. Taking every precaution against "injury or treachery," so far as he was able, Sigsbee, through his able executive officer, Lieutenant Commander Richard

Wainwright, stationed the ship's marines for a ready guard force on the forecastle and poop decks. On the bridge and poop, the regular lookouts were augmented by a quartermaster and signal boy. At the port and starboard gangways, the officer of the deck, assisted by the quartermaster of the watch and marine corporal of the guard, received special instructions regarding the security of the accommodation ladders. At night, instead of the usual anchor watch, a full "quarter watch," one-fourth of the ship's company, manned their posts. Sentries went about armed, and a supply of ready-use ammunition for the rapid-fire guns was stowed in the pilothouse amidships and in the admiral's pantry aft. There were also ready shells at hand near the 6-inch guns. The hogging line and dip rope of the collision mat were rove and kept standing. And just in case the main battery needed to go into action, two boilers, instead of the usual in-port practice of one, were kept on-line to power the turrets' hydraulic machinery. "Extreme vigilance . . . by day and by night" became the standing order governing the entire ship. Captain Sigsbee would have liked to drag the harbor bottom around the ship, have his picket boats on patrol, and keep the searchlights in continual night use, but such extreme precautions could not be effected without deeply offending the Spanish. This was, after all, a friendly visit.

Rather, Sigsbee personally instructed the ship's master-at-arms and sergeant of marines that their men keep a weather eye on every visitor who came on board, to watch for packages seemingly put aside casually that might contain sticks of dynamite and to inspect the routes over which visitors passed. And there were many visitors, at times three hundred to four hundred in a day, invariably Cubans, "representatives," Sigsbee observed, "of the refined class in Havana . . . perhaps more than I could have wished, in view of the situation." Spaniards, military or civilian, stayed away, refusing to visit the battleship save on official business.

After two days in port, Sigsbee permitted the *Maine's* officers to go ashore freely when off watch, day or night. Regretfully, for the captain was, unlike many of his peers, a generous granter of liberty for his crew, he ordered the enlisted men to remain on board. Harking to the Chilean war scare of 1891, Sigsbee considered the opportunity for an ugly incident involving inebriated sailors too great a risk given the already tense atmosphere.

With Captain General Blanco away inspecting garrisons, Sigsbee, in the company of Consul General Fitzhugh Lee, paid an official call on his deputy, Major General Gonzalez Parrado. The Americans found a reception table bending under the weight of refreshments. The talk was polite and, to a degree, relaxed. General Parrado returned the call promptly and was received in the *Maine* with a seventeen-gun salute, eight side boys, the full marine guard, and the Spanish flag at the foremast. Sigsbee personally conducted a tour of the ship, and Parrado "seemed much pleased."

For several days in the local press, announcements had appeared of Mazzantini, the "famous gentleman bull-fighter of Spain," and his coming trials in the Havana bullring. Although the contest was to be held on Sunday, Sigsbee, a Sabbath observer, mentioned to General Parrado his desire to attend. He was not a devotee of blood sports, but Sigsbee understood "the common people were likely to be greatly excited" at the spectacle, and the response to his entrance would afford the best evidence of the true feelings of Havana toward the presence of the *Maine*. Parrado was delighted with the request. He at once offered a private box for the captain and several of the ship's officers, and ordered up a case of excellent sherry for the *Maine*'s wardroom. Sigsbee had nothing "distinctly American" of value to return, so he presented General Parrado with a signed copy of his book, *Deep-Sea Sounding and Dredging.*

For the outing at the bullring, Sigsbee donned a black civilian suit, bowler hat, and heavy watch chain and carried a rolled umbrella, making himself the very picture of comfortable bourgeois prosperity. Following a lunch hosted by Fitzhugh Lee at the Havana Yacht Club, Sigsbee was handed a crudely printed flyer, written in Spanish, violently critical of Cuban autonomy and the *Maine* visit, dotted with laudatory praises of "our brave and beloved Weyler," and condemning "these Yankee pigs who meddle in our affairs, humiliating us to the last degree, and . . . order to us a man-of-war of their rotten squadron." The screed concluded with "Death to the Americans! Death to autonomy! *Viva España! Viva Weyler!*" Sigsbee put the paper in his pocket, thinking it "the screaming appeal of some bigoted and impotent patriot." Forget it, Consul General Lee said; these things littered the whole city, and the consulate could paper its walls with the copies stuffed inside the gates.

The bullring was located at Regla, an eastern suburb across the harbor that required a short ferry ride. Sigsbee's box sat high up on the expensive shady side of the arena, very near that of General Parrado, attending with his staff. Armed Spanish troops were stationed at fixed intervals throughout the large crowd, and a full platoon occupied a bench directly in front of the Americans' box. As a favor to General Parrado, and to avoid the crowds, Sigsbee and his party departed after the fifth kill, not waiting for the finale. Once back in the *Maine*, Sigsbee watched a party of *voluntario* officers returning from the bullring and passing close aboard, making "derisive calls and whistles." He recalled it as the only hostile demonstration against the ship during the course of her stay.

The *Maine* was not the only United States warship in Cuba. Friendly visits to other ports were also conducted by the cruiser *Montgomery*. At Matanzas, sixty miles east of Havana, the American consul reported the ship's arrival to the State Department as a success, "hailed with delight by all classes." That was the good news. "The striking feature was: Poor people thought the vessel was bringing them food from the United States; their disappointment was great."[3]

On Wednesday evening, January 26, the day after the *Maine* tied up at Havana, President McKinley hosted the annual White House dinner for the diplomatic corps. Like most large formal affairs of the time, it was held in the main downstairs corridor. In the smaller state dining room, several little tables awaited the men when they retired for their coffee and cigars. Here McKinley, in plain formal black, pointedly invited the Spanish minister, Enrique Dupuy de Lôme, aglitter in gold-laced diplomatic coat, medals, and ceremonial sword, to sit with him. "I see that we have only good news," said the contented president, lighting a well-savored cigar. With the U.S. Senate exercising rare self-control, and Spain apparently ready to accept the administration's position on Cuba's future—pacified and reformed beyond pro forma autonomy—"you have no occasion to be other than satisfied and confident." Dupuy de Lôme reported the conversation to Madrid as a "sincere declaration" of the president's conservative approach toward ending the Cuban crisis.[4]

The Navy Department, though, believed it prudent to cable Commodore Dewey, who had just arrived to take up his Asiatic command at Yokohama, instructing him to "retain" sailors in the squadron whose enlistments "have expired." It was nearly the identical order Secretary Long had sent to the European Squadron just over a fortnight before. The president might be a little confident of the Cuban outcome, but for John D. Long, affairs on the island were still "very disturbed."[5]

On February 1, Spain responded to President McKinley's lengthy note of December 20, dashing the scenario the president had so optimistically depicted at the White House reception. In sentences that verged on insult, Foreign Minister Pío Gullón embedded the Spanish position regarding Cuba in diplomatic concrete. Merely because Cuba was ninety miles from the United States did not mean the great American Republic had any influence over what transpired there. If Spain took forever to put down the insurrection and pacify the island, that was her colonial problem, and too bad for the United States. Cuban autonomy had been proclaimed by the queen regent, and an autonomy council now existed in Havana. The United States had demanded this drastic measure for the last three years, and Spain was extremely nonplussed at the president's "hints of a change of conduct"; what more did America want? If its government was really serious about ending the insurrection, they could do so by aggressively prosecuting, indeed, dissolving the Cuban Junta, "which is sitting publicly in New York, and which is the active and permanent center of attacks upon the Spanish nation." Gullón declared Spain's "firm resolution" to maintain its traditional, legitimate sovereignty in Cuba "at every hazard."[6]

It was a clear shove to the McKinley administration to back off. Responding with uncharacteristic bluntness, Stewart Woodford in Madrid informed both the hard-lining Gullón and the ostensibly more compromising minister of *ultramar*, Segismundo Moret, that the note was a "serious mistake," and he would advise his government to take the longest possible time in framing its reply. As it happened, the State Department never did acknowledge its receipt, for any true answer would have been tantamount to the threat of war, and it had come nowhere near to that, yet.[7]

A week later, Gullón unburdened himself in a vexatious cable to Dupuy de Lôme over the "display and concentration" of U.S. naval forces near Havana, the move to the southern drill grounds. He also had evil premonitions regarding the "persistency" of the visits of the *Maine* and *Montgomery* in Cuba, like boorish houseguests who simply refused to leave. The longer they stayed, the higher the "anxiety" levels rose in Havana and Madrid. The ships' very presence in the Cuban hot spot, Gullón warned, might, "through some mischance, bring about a conflict." To offset that dire possibility, Spain was making "heroic efforts to maintain ourselves in the severest rectitude."[8]

That quality, above all others, should have been first nature in a Spanish diplomat. But even as this telegram found its path along the submarine cable beneath the Atlantic Ocean, Don Enrique Dupuy de Lôme, minister plenipotentiary and envoy extraordinary of His Catholic Majesty, was reporting back the gravest lapse in probity, and one that had flowed from his own pen. "To-morrow," Wednesday, February 9, he warned Gullón, William Randolph Hearst's scurrilously pro-Junta *New York Journal* would print a confidential letter Dupuy had written to a Spanish colleague, "which, in stating my opinion, I used expressions humiliating to the President." Once the paper hit the streets, and the corner newsboys began shouting the headlines, "my position here would be untenable."[9]

Though the letter was undated, Dupuy de Lôme had inscribed it two months previously, in mid-December 1897, following William McKinley's annual message to Congress, and he had sent it by regular mail, not the diplomatic pouch—to Havana. The intended recipient, José Canalejas, editor of Spain's daily *Heraldo de Madrid*, visiting in Cuba, never saw it stolen from his desk. The contents were truly damning.

The president's annual message, Dupuy wrote with impolitic venom, held no promise for Spain. In a word, it was "bad. . . . Besides the natural and inevitable coarseness with which he repeats all that the press and public opinion . . . have said of Weyler, it once more shows what McKinley is, weak and a bidder for the admiration of the crowd, besides being a would-be politician who tries to leave a door open behind himself while keeping on good terms with the jingoes of his party." Lèse-majesté it might be, but it was also mostly true, and William McKinley had been called much worse things in his political life, and by Americans. If this had been all of it, Dupuy de Lôme was only guilty of his own stupidity in putting private thoughts to purloined paper. The American yellow press would wave a bloody shirt of righteous indignation, Dupuy de Lôme would probably depart Washington in personal disgrace, but there would be no lasting harm, if that was all of it.[10]

But it wasn't. The real, critical damage to Spanish diplomacy lay in Dupuy de Lôme's mention of the seemingly innocuous issue of free trade. There had been talk in the U.S. Congress of a reciprocity treaty with Cuba, the exchange of goods without tariff. The minister set forth the disingenuous advantage of having "even if only for effect, the question of commercial relations, and to have a man of some prominence" sent to Washington, "in order that I may make use of him . . . to carry on a propaganda among the Senators and others in opposition to the *junta*." Spanish hypocrisy lay exposed.[11]

According to Horatio Rubens, a prominent Cuban American attorney and the Junta's Washington lobbyist, the letter was stolen by a certain Gustavo Escoto, a Cuban friend of Canalejas's private secretary. It lay among a stack of correspondence Canalejas intended to answer on his return to Spain. Spying the imprimatur of the Spanish embassy on the envelope, "with [its] careful injunction to personal privacy," Escoto, in a fit of Cuban patriotism, removed the letter, replacing it with blank paper, "hoping the extraction . . . would go unnoticed." Once Rubens received it, first making certain it was no forgery, he gave it to Hearst's *Journal*.[12]

On February 9, the *Journal*, no shrinking violet when it came to hurling hyperbole at the president, published a facsimile of the letter and charged Dupuy de Lôme with "the greatest offense of which a diplomatic officer can be accused." Distortions, even outright lies, were nothing new in the popular dailies. But when Assistant Secretary of State Rufus Day called at the Spanish embassy, demanding to know the veracity of the *Journal*'s report, Dupuy de Lôme, first claiming the right to express himself privately in any manner he chose, had to admit the letter's genuineness.[13]

The next morning, amid a firestorm of press invective, attorney Rubens carried the original letter to the State Department. Day wordlessly examined it. Alvey Adee thought it a forgery, then changed his mind; it was legitimate, he said. Day asked to keep the paper for a time, dismissed Rubens, and took the letter across Seventeenth Street to the White House. McKinley looked at the Spanish sentences without comment. But why, the president wanted to know, had it not been brought to him first? Why had the damn newspapers gotten it first? Judge Day could only repeat what Rubens had told him, that President McKinley would have forbidden its release as injurious to *American* diplomacy in the Cuban morass.

Despite the carnage, a number of senior administration officers were sorry to see the last of Dupuy de Lôme. A contemptuous, arrogant Spaniard he might be, but he knew his way around Washington. Navy Secretary John D. Long, who had to cancel a Thursday dinner with the envoy, thought him "a man of a good deal of ability. . . . So it is, that little things are obstacles that throw great movements off the track and sometimes lead to disaster."[14]

For William McKinley this was a transcendent moment to step into the breach and, like Abraham Lincoln, boldly lead the nation, and its adversaries, to the correct path. For the briefest time, days it turned out, he had the country solidly for him, defending him, looking to him for meaningful leadership. This major diplomatic flap—and no mistake, it was serious—could be turned to advantage. Right now, as William McKinley pulled the figurative dagger, with Spain's and the Junta's dirty handprints all over it, from his political back, he had the popular will and moral suasion to draw the hitherto impossible line between Cuban independence and Spanish sovereignty.

Grover Cleveland and Richard Olney had the aggressive personalities, but probably not the vision, to seize such a moment. Lincoln and his secretary of state, William Seward, possessed both qualities. William McKinley, with a senile secretary of state, had neither. In a word, he behaved correctly; he did nothing. Silent, a battered oak in the storm, for him to comment publicly on the affair was, he thought, utterly beneath any president's dignity. From Canton's Stark County Court House to Washington's White House, William McKinley had spent his entire political life deflecting this kind of offal, and personally he could handle it. But politically, no slur like this could go unanswered. Declaring Dupuy de Lôme persona non grata would not atone for the insult or cool the American public's anger, and public opinion was something the president could read like a tariff schedule. Spain must tender a formal apology. McKinley sat at his desk and wrote the outline on a scrap of notepaper to be parsed by Adee, signed by Judge Day, and cabled to Woodford in Madrid: "Expression of pained surprise and regret at the Minister's reprehensible allusions to the President and the American people, which it is needless to say the Govt. of His Majesty does not share, and promptly disavows."[15]

Everyone played along. No one saw the big picture. It didn't matter that the administration understood the false-faced diplomacy revealed in the letter to Canalejas had far more serious consequences than the personal insults, only that the president had been slurred, and that became the issue. The brief possible opportunity for an American-brokered peace died with the *Journal*'s banner headline: "WORST INSULT TO THE UNITED STATES IN ITS HISTORY." Resolutions were introduced calling for American intervention in Cuba, for recognizing Cuban belligerency, and, by Congressman "Uncle Joe" Cannon, chairman of the House Appropriations Committee, demanding an ultimatum be sent to Spain to end the war in a month.[16]

Spain had been in this game a few hundred years and knew the rules instinctively. The Spanish government accepted Dupuy de Lôme's resignation on February 10, effectively divorcing his departure from the American demand for the envoy's "immediate recall." Stewart Woodford lost no time in getting to the foreign ministry, where he received Gullón's bland assurances of Dupuy de Lôme's exit and the appointment of a new envoy. Woodford was flabbergasted by the nonchalance. Laying polite diplomacy aside, he brusquely told the foreign minister that an official apology from Spain was expected now, to assuage the screaming American press and the congressional jingoes. Something like this could lead to war; didn't Gullón, Premier Sagasta, or the queen regent understand that? Gullón shrugged. Spanish public opinion, he soothingly explained, might get overly excited if the ministry offered its regrets too hastily. Depressed, Woodford departed to his embassy.

On Monday the fourteenth, Woodford called at the foreign ministry to inform Gullón that unless an apology was forthcoming, he had no choice but to resign and return to the United States; he could not remain accredited to a government that tolerated slander against his president. Gullón, graciousness personified, touched Woodford's arm and, "with entire sympathy," explained how much he lamented the whole incident. Ambassador Woodford and America must understand, he purred, that Spain sincerely desired the reciprocity treaty between the United States and Cuba. Yes, Dupuy de Lôme had been exceedingly indelicate in his penned utterances, but as things like this went, it was relatively a long time ago. The Spanish written apology, a bare one, but couched in smothering diplomatic roses, was accepted by Woodford and cabled to the State Department on February 16. Some weeks later, Assistant Secretary Day closed the incident in a note to Woodford: "If a rupture between the countries must come, it should not be upon any such personal and comparatively unimportant matter." By then, the affair had been subsumed in a crisis of ultimately more monumental proportions.[17]

The presence of the *Maine* at Havana was troubling not only to the Spanish authorities, but in its own way to the United States as well. It was neither intended nor expected of her to remain as long as she did; Secretary Long thought it "not prudent" for "sanitary reasons"—yellow fever. Lee reassured him there was no danger to the crew's health until the start of the rainy season, April, or even May. But under no circumstances, he warned, must Havana be empty of at least one United States warship. "We should not relinquish position of peaceful control of the situation," he wired the secretary, "or conditions would be worse than if vessel had never been sent." But if the *Maine* was withdrawn, Lee thought, her replacement should be one of the navy's four first-class battleships "as object lesson" to counter Spanish low opinion of the U.S. service.[18]

Truthfully, there was no telling what might happen in the palpably agitated city. The secret telegraphic code Fitzhugh Lee had devised to bring the ship to Havana in an emergency was now altered to "Vessels might be employed elsewhere," meaning the *Maine* herself required assistance. Fear that the cable line to Key West might be cut, a fairly drastic scenario, prompted Lee and Captain Sigsbee to request another vessel in Havana to carry dispatches if necessary. Sigsbee suggested a torpedo boat begin a series of visits to Havana, staying a little longer each turnabout, giving the Spanish time to accept its presence. State and Navy approved. The torpedo boat *Cushing* was ordered from Key West to arrive at Havana on Wednesday, February 15, under the pretense of replenishing the *Maine*'s galley stores, and to return home immediately.[19]

When Long's order was deciphered at the Key West cable station, the *Cushing*'s sailing date was inadvertently omitted. Thus, Lieutenant Albert Gleaves, her commanding officer, started for Havana four days early, at 7:30 A.M. on February 11. The little turtle-decked craft smashed into a severe gale that washed the executive officer over the side. Recovering the body, the battered *Cushing* continued on, tying up alongside the *Maine* in late afternoon. The officer's sailcloth-wrapped corpse was returned to the United States by commercial steamer. "The first victim," said Lieutenant Gleaves, "of our trouble with Spain." The next day the *Cushing* returned to Key West.[20]

The evening flood tide had swung the *Maine* around the mooring buoy so her bow pointed northwest, toward the harbor mouth. The stationary *Alfonso XII* occupied her permanent berth about 150 yards ahead. A little further on, where the German school ship *Gneisenau* had lately been, rode the Spanish transport *Legazpi*. Off the *Maine*'s stern, passengers in the American steamer *City of Washington* took in the sultry Havana air on deck. The night was overcast, and the winter atmosphere was peculiarly heavy and uncomfortably hot. Except for watch standers and sentries, the *Maine*'s crew had turned in to their bunks. Several officers fond of the excellent local cigars congregated at their "smoking quarters," by the port-side turret.

Captain Sigsbee sat behind the dark, polished, damask-covered table in the admiral's cabin. After completing a report to Assistant Secretary Roosevelt advising against torpedo tubes on battleships and cruisers, he turned to writing a letter home. The captain was dressed in the blue winter service uniform, but because of the heat, his steward brought in a light civilian "office jacket," and Sigsbee put it on. It was unthinkable to be anything other than properly dressed. At ten minutes past nine o'clock, Newton, the marine bugler, began sounding taps, and Sigsbee laid down his pen and listened. During the pauses, he recalled, "the echoes floated back to the ship with singular distinctness." As the bugler finished, Sigsbee, putting his letter into an envelope, started at what sounded like a rifle shot. A second later, a tremendous "bursting, rending, and crashing" roar split open the Havana night.[21]

Sigsbee heard, indeed felt, "ominous, metallic sounds, as if the ship were rending itself in pieces. There was a trembling and lurching motion" as the battleship sloughed down by the head, listed badly to port, and did not right herself. The electric lights went out, and "there was intense blackness and smoke." He did not mistake the cataclysm for anything else. The *Maine* had blown up and was sinking away beneath him. From the *machina* and the ships in harbor, horrified watchers stared at the vast column of fire and gray smoke shooting 150 feet above the ship, spreading out into a rolling canopy of flame and burning debris that fell to earth half a mile away.[22]

Charles Sigsbee's initial fear that the ship would capsize and take him down with her, what he called, unashamedly, "the instinct of self-preservation," took hold for an instant. But that very human reaction became immediately dominated "by the habit of command." In total, suffocating blackness he made his way forward into the passageway and collided violently with the marine orderly. The man saluted, then apologized for the crash, and in strict adherence to orders, made a proper report that the ship had blown up and was sinking.[23]

The first explosion, the one sounding like a gunshot, had occurred well forward, port side, against the double bottom, near two 6-inch gun magazines, one holding some four and a half tons of gunpowder in copper tanks, the other, a reserve store of saluting powder, perhaps three hundred pounds. The second explosion had been a little farther aft and to starboard, in the immediate vicinity of the starboard 10-inch magazine. It contained between eight and nine tons of black powder, and in hot weather, the temperature of the compartment had been measured at 110 degrees. According to one officer, the second blast "was more violent than any explosion I had heard. . . . I could not liken it to anything, except possibly the explosion of a magazine."[24]

Seaman Reden, sleeping in the after turret, felt no shock, but woke to a blaze of fire and the rush of water coming up the ammunition hoist. For those closer to the bow, the shock effects multiplied horrifically. Marine Corporal Thompson, slinging his hammock outside the central superstructure, just twenty feet forward of Seaman Reden, was thrown through a canvas awning. Then it was all blackness, with escaping superhot steam and agonizing cries for help. He thought the Spaniards had opened fire on the ship. To Master-at-Arms Load and Landsman Kane, standing inside the aft end of the superstructure, the first jolt felt like a small boat had struck the ship. Then the deck beneath their feet trembled and yawned open, and they dropped into a flaming maw. Pinned under heavy weights, seawater crashing in, they were doomed, until the second explosion lifted the weights and enabled the two men to escape. Landsman Fox, sleeping in the lamp room by the fore funnel, awoke smelling burning cloth, and found his compartment upside down, back to front, the whole deck literally flipped over. From the forecastle, where the majority of the enlisted men had their quarters, fewer than half a dozen, all wounded, escaped. Only two men made it out alive from the berth deck. Boatswain Bergman had been well forward, near the mess lockers. Two men standing closest to him were killed outright. He heard "a terrible crash—an explosion. Something fell, and then . . . I got thrown somewhere in a hot place. I got burned on my legs and arms, and I got my mouth full of ashes. . . . Then the next thing I was in the water." Only one sailor, Fireman Gartrell, escaped from the compartments below the armored deck. On watch in the steering engine room, he saw a blue flash shoot by, followed by the prolonged trembling of the ship breaking apart in the holocaust of the second explosion; then "the whole earth opened up."[25]

Coming out onto the main deck, Captain Sigsbee saw nothing with any clarity; midships had turned into "an immense dark mass." On the poop, the only fragment of the ship relatively safe and above water, he found his executive officer, Lieutenant Commander Wainwright, with several officers and a few enlisted men. Amid the disaster Sigsbee discerned no apparent excitement, and "perfect discipline prevailed." Believing then, and ever after, that the *Maine* had been blown up by a mine, his first order was to post sentries topside. Then seeing the conflagration, he ordered the magazines flooded—a useless command, as the whole forward half of the ship was already under water. Coming from starkly lit cabins, eyes not yet adjusted to the night, hardly anyone on the poop deck yet comprehended the magnitude of the catastrophe, and the enormous loss of life. Only three of the ship's outfit of fifteen boats endured the explosion, and orders were given to lower away. Two were manned partly by officers, so few enlisted men seemed alive. No swarm of sailors scrambled up from below to take their posts for "fire and rescue." Wainwright, bearing a fire hose, climbed to the superstructure amidships, taking off all the men he could find, a lieutenant and two midshipmen.

The fire mains were gone; "everything had gone," Midshipman Wat T. Cluverious remembered. The superstructure had blown apart, and the fires consumed nearly everyone within and below; "the poor wretches, pinned down and drowning, mangled and torn, screamed in agony." The injured men, those that could be reached, were passed into boats, or just thrown into the water to keep them from roasting to death. The few unwounded survivors climbed onto floating debris. The fore funnel toppled over on the starboard side.

Dimly, now, Sigsbee saw large white objects bobbing on the water and heard "faint cries for help." The "white forms," he realized with a ghastly shock, "were our own men." The fire in the superstructure blazed brighter, cooking off the ready ammunition topside. Wainwright reported that all the wounded men who could be found had left the ship, and when he saw the poop deck nearly awash, he turned: "Captain, we had better leave her." Sigsbee nodded: "Get into the boats, gentlemen," he said. Wainwright and a lieutenant offered to hand him down. Sigsbee shook his head no: "I suggested the propriety of my being the last to leave, and requested them to precede me, which they did. . . . [I]t would have been improper otherwise." In quiet, awful sadness, Captain Sigsbee turned his grimy, spectacled eyes aft, to the flag, and saw the ragged cloth hanging over the stern.[26]

Boats from the *Alfonso XII*, *Legazpi*, *City of Washington*, and the navy yard, all heedless of danger, instantly made for the dying vessel, picking wounded men off the ship and out of the debris-choked water. Of the 355 officers, sailors, and marines on board at the time of the destruction, 252 were killed outright; 8 others would die of wounds in Havana hospitals. Many of the dead were never recovered, nor were their body parts identified. Asleep in the immediate area of the cataclysm, they were blown to atoms or ripped apart into bloody rags. Of the 96 survivors—Sigsbee, 24 officers, 60 sailors, and 11 marines—only 16 remained wholly unhurt.[27]

The majority of the wounded lay in the *City of Washington*'s dining salon. Sigsbee walked among them, offering a comforting word where he could. Constantly he jerked his eyes outboard, to the smoldering wreck, still in "fitful" exploding torment. He entered the steamer captain's stateroom, dipped a pen into an inkpot, and beneath the letterhead of the New York and Cuba Mail Steamship Company, wrote his report to the Navy Department.

How this dispatch was received by the nation—not by the administration, but by the press, Congress, and public—Sigsbee knew could well mean the difference between peace and war. "I found it necessary to repress my own suspicions" of a mine or other cause "initiated from outside the vessel," he said afterward, and intentionally gave his terse prose "an uncommonly strong advisory character."[28]

"*Maine* blown up in Havana harbor at nine forty to-night and destroyed. Many wounded and doubtless more killed or drowned. Wounded and others on board Spanish man-of-war and [Cuba Mail] Steamer. Send Light House Tenders from Key West for crew and the few pieces of equipment above water. No one has clothing other than that upon him." Sigsbee ended with a sentence noting that two young officers, Jenkins and Merritt, were not yet accounted for, then signed his name. Immediately he crossed it out; he had to make plain that no one knew anything beyond that the ship had blown up, and he needed to add some words to temper public feeling in the United States, "which I believed would be . . . irrepressibly antagonistic to the Spaniards. It was not fair to attach criminality short of evidence." Accordingly, Sigsbee penned, "Public opinion should be suspended until further report." He also noted that many Spanish officials, civilian and military, had come to the *City of Washington* "to express sympathy." In addition to his Navy Department report, Captain Sigsbee composed a similar message for Rear Admiral Sicard. Addressed to Key West for routing to the fleet, it ended significantly, "Send Light House Tenders. . . . Don't send war vessels if others available."[29]

Sigsbee returned to the deck to greet the Spanish emissaries. The military and naval officers "seemed especially desirous" of his theory of the explosion. Politely he told them he must wait for the official investigation before answering. General Salano declared unequivocally that Spanish authorities knew nothing whatsoever of the eruption. Sigsbee took him at his word, "as a man, an officer, and a Spaniard." He then entrusted the messages of the *Maine*'s destruction to *New York Herald* correspondent George Bronson Rea for transmission to the United States from the Havana cable office.[30]

Around 10 P.M. at Key West, before the official dispatches had even been sent out from Havana, much less received in the United States, Lieutenant Albert Gleaves, skipper of the torpedo boat *Cushing,* got word from his quartermaster that a certain "gentleman" had come on board who wished to see him on a matter of extreme importance.

Gleaves described the man as "our secret agent," who explained he had just read a telegram from his "representative" in Havana that "the *Maine* had been blown up by her powder magazine." Gleaves was inclined to doubt it. Rumors abounded every day at Key West predicting the destruction of the American consulate at Havana, the assassination of Fitzhugh Lee, and other dire happenings. The intelligence man, however, was completely convinced of the report's veracity. Gleaves conferred with his immediate superior, Lieutenant Commander Walter Cowles of the gunboat *Fern,* and the three men repaired to the Key West cable office to await further news. "Finally," Gleaves said, "about 11 o'clock, the instruments began to click." Midway through, the operator and the secret agent exchanged a quick glance. With a shock, Gleaves realized the report was true. The telegraph operator handed the form to the agent, who handed it to Commander Cowles. Gleaves was the last to see it. It was Captain Sigsbee's message to Secretary Long, "*Maine* blown up in Havana harbor. . . ."[31]

On the night of the catastrophe, John D. Long, accompanied by his daughter, Helen, dined at the White House with the president. Afterward, the secretary returned to his apartment at the Hotel Portland while Helen continued the evening at a ball. What happened next is somewhat muddled. Accounts depend on which participant or historian one wishes to believe, on the selective memory of the men who put their recollections to paper, often more than once and inconsistent to certain facts, and on what degree of drama the reader wishes to place on the events.

Sometime before 1 A.M., February 16, Captain Sigsbee's cable, relayed from Key West, was delivered to the Navy Department by Western Union messenger, and receipted for by Commander Francis Dickens, Assistant (and at the time, acting) Chief of the Bureau of Navigation. Dickens immediately sent it to the Hotel Portland. Perhaps half an hour later, Helen Long, returning from the dance, awakened her father with "the terrible news that the *Maine* had blown up . . . the cause unknown."[32]

In pencil, Long wrote orders for Dickens to send the gunboat *Fern* and other necessary vessels to Havana, the ships' sailing instructions to be telegraphed "in ordinary language, not using cipher." When Dickens arrived shortly after at the Portland, he found the entrance to the secretary's apartment crowded with "the bright representatives of the press," already privy to the disaster through correspondent Bronson Rea's cables to his newspaper. At this point, Long either telephoned William McKinley at the White House or sent Commander Dickens with the telegram to inform the president personally, something which seems more likely. The president, Dickens said, "came out in his dressing gown. I handed him the despatch which he read with great gravity. He seemed to be deeply impressed with the news, handed [it] back to me, and took it again, two or three times, expressing great regret that the event had happened, particularly at that time."[33]

Consul General Lee's cable to the State Department came in mid-morning. He reported the Spanish flags at General Blanco's palace and throughout the city, including on the naval and merchant ships in the harbor, flying at half-mast. All business in Havana had been suspended, the theaters closed. The captain general and the Spanish army and navy officers were rendering every assistance. "Hope our people will repress excitement and calmly await decision," he ended in an echo of Captain Sigsbee.[34]

Washington, official and otherwise, assumed a dark, foreboding mood of calamity, not experienced since the blackest days of the Civil War, nor again until December 7, 1941. All flags limped at half-mast. Public and government functions were canceled. People congregated in front of the White House, while across Seventeenth Street, other civilians officiously elbowed through the doors of the State, War, and Navy Building. Outside John D. Long's office, a knot of visitors stared at a builder's model of the *Maine* and watched a clerk open the glass case, remove the tiny flag from the gaff, and replace it with a half-masted one at the stern. The entire Spanish embassy called on the president. The chargé, Juan Du Bosc, wired the foreign ministry a morsel of premature news: "In all official circles the conviction is felt that the catastrophe on the *Maine* was purely accidental."[35]

The tragedy, coming after the Dupuy de Lôme affair had barely left the front pages, whipped the "filibustering press," as the Spanish called it, into a froth. Shameless pains were taken to gather or manufacture the smallest speck of "news." For a week, the *New York Journal* devoted an average of eight and a half pages of news, editorials, and pictures to the *Maine*. The editors mobilized a crack team of reporters and artists, including Frederic Remington, and dispatched them to Havana in the paper's own press boats. William Randolph Hearst offered a fifty-thousand-dollar reward "for the conviction of the criminals who sent 258 American sailors to their death."[36]

Hearst veritably wallowed in lying sensationalism. The *Journal* for February 17 had no doubt whatever: "THE WARSHIP *Maine* WAS SPLIT IN TWO BY AN ENEMY'S SECRET INFERNAL MACHINE"; and "Captain Sigsbee practically declares that his ship was blown up by a mine or torpedo." An accompanying illustration, highlighted with a Maltese cross below the ship's waterline, "shows where the mine may have been fired." "THE WHOLE COUNTRY THRILLS WITH WAR FEVER," screamed the headline on February 18; "REMEMBER THE *Maine!* TO HELL WITH SPAIN!"[37]

Joseph Pulitzer's *World,* though not adopting the lurid shrill of its New York rival, nevertheless mucked about in the same story lines: "THE *Maine* EXPLOSION WAS CAUSED BY A BOMB—SUSPICION OF A TORPEDO." Five days after the ship had blown up, Pulitzer informed his readers, "*World*'s discoveries prove the mine theory," and the following day, "Government accepts mine theory of the *World.*" Pulitzer admitted, however, that "nobody outside of a lunatic asylum" believed Spain had officially sanctioned the dastardly act. Nevertheless, she stood guilty of "treachery, willingness, or laxness" for not ensuring the safety of the harbor. The only acceptable "atonement" Spain could offer for the loss of the *Maine,* the *World* editorialized, was the granting of complete Cuban independence.[38]

The New York *Sun* stood in opposition to the mass. It asserted "no lynch law for Spain," attacked Hearst and Pulitzer as "purely professional shriekers of sensations," and lamented the dearth of legal remedies to prevent their brew of "freak journalism." The New York *Evening Post,* anti-interventionist to the core, devoted as much editorial ink to denouncing the war hawks as to the story of the *Maine* tragedy itself: "A thousand different explanations have been offered by editors and reporters who were not there, and a thousand different pictorial illustrations of the scene have been given by persons who did not see it." It utterly condemned all talk of war, and quoted General Miles that the United States Army was in no way ready for one.[39]

Protestant religious organizations, previously hot for intervention, took a step back, allying with business and financial interests in counseling patience and self-restraint. The French ambassador informed his government, "In nearly all the churches pastors have given pacific sermons; this is especially noteworthy because there is in the passions aroused against Spain something of the old Huguenot and Puritan hatreds." In Chicago, Rabbi Joseph Stolz denounced the "savages" who brayed for war. Several Irish and Italian clerics indicated it might be "sinful" for American Catholics to fight Spanish Catholics.[40]

Theodore Roosevelt, whose politics and saddle itch sometimes overrode his common sense, wrote to a fellow Harvard alum, "The *Maine* was sunk by an act of dirty treachery on the part of the Spaniards *I* believe." Roosevelt though, was not completely delusional, admitting, "[O]fficially it will go down as an accident." As usual, John D. Long took the right measure of the public pulse. "In this, as in everything else," he confided to his journal, "the opinion of the individual is determined by his original bias. If he is a conservative, he is sure it was an accident; if he is a jingo, he is equally sure that it was by design." His own judgment, based on the information thus far received, indicated "that it was an accident."[41]

Over three days, beginning on February 16, the *Washington Evening Star* conducted a poll of naval officers on duty in the capital. By a large majority the respondents attributed the explosion to an accident; most of the minority pointed to a mine; and a few thought a bomb had been smuggled into the ship. Lieutenant Frank Friday Fletcher at the Naval Torpedo Station, Newport, Rhode Island, wrote to his colleague Lieutenant Albert Gleaves, "Everybody [here] is gradually settling down to the belief that the disaster was due to the position of the magazine next to the coal bunkers in which there must have been spontaneous combustion." He was absolutely right, but would anyone of consequence listen?[42]

On February 17, Havana turned out for the burial of nineteen members of the *Maine*'s crew, all that had been recovered up to that time. Everyone who mattered was there: Captain General Blanco, General Parrado, Admiral Manterola, the bishop of Havana, the mayor and the Autonomy Council. The bodies, covered with flowers, lay in state in the Civil Government Building. The service, conducted with majestically somber ecclesiastical and military ceremonies, so moved Captain Sigsbee, he thought it "inconceivable that a greater demonstration could have been made."[43]

When John D. Long turned to the critical task of appointing a court of inquiry, upon whose verdict likely depended the ultimate question of peace or war, he discovered the navy maintained established procedures for handling exactly this sort of predicament. The fact that the explosion had occurred at Havana was completely incidental; had it been Norfolk, Brooklyn, or Pearl Harbor, the process would have been the same. The naval courts of inquiry were (and remain) fact-finding bodies charged to investigate material cases where the evidence is unclear, where crime or criminal acts are suspected, or where serious misdeed exists without certain guilt. From the court's findings, the convening authority, in 1898, be it the president as commander in chief of the army and navy, the secretary of the navy, or a squadron commander, would decide if further action was warranted. The court contained a maximum of three officers, with a fourth serving as judge advocate. If the conduct or character of an officer was under investigation, the three members were, if possible, to be of equal or superior rank to the accused.

Either President McKinley or Secretary Long could have convened the court. But to separate themselves politically from any repercussions over the verdict, both backed away. Instead, Long ordered Rear Admiral Montgomery Sicard, commander in chief of the North Atlantic Squadron, to act as the convening authority. On February 16, a day after the explosion, Sicard appointed four men from his flagship *New York:* her commanding officer, Captain French Ensor Chadwick; the executive officer, Lieutenant Commander William Potter; and watch and division officer Lieutenant Edward Capehart. Lieutenant (junior grade) Frank Marble was named judge advocate.

This composition was likely chosen because Sicard thought it should be done quickly. The flaw was that none of these men were senior to Captain Sigsbee, he being number thirty-nine in the captains list and Chadwick, at the bottom, number forty-five. Long overruled this initial membership, selecting as president of the court Captain William T. Sampson, number four in the list, currently skipper of the battleship *Iowa,* and a highly regarded officer and ordnance specialist. Chadwick and Potter remained on the court, but Lieutenant Commander Adolph Marix, the *Maine*'s original executive officer, was detached from the Brooklyn Navy Yard as judge advocate. As ultimately constituted, this court of inquiry held some of the best, most intelligent officers in the navy.

Admiral Sicard issued the precept on February 19, authorizing the court to meet in any ship of the North Atlantic Squadron, to explore "diligently" into all circumstances surrounding the destruction of the *Maine,* to determine whether she had been lost by negligence or action of any of her officers or crew, and to report if any further procedures were to be initiated against any individual. Captain Sigsbee, Lieutenant Commander Wainwright, and the ship's navigator and chief engineer each had the right to be present at all sessions. The following day, the court boarded the lighthouse tender *Mangrove* and departed Key West for Havana.

Spanish authorities were convinced the United States, and its navy, had far too much political capital at stake to conduct a fair examination, and for the briefest time they pinned their hopes on the appointment of a joint commission of inquiry. But given the hair-trigger consequences of the slightest Spanish complicity, the American public could not accept the arrangement. Writing to Secretary Long, Theodore Roosevelt argued that the administration's and the navy's critics "would undoubtedly seize upon a joint investigation as an excuse for denouncing us . . . asserting that we were afraid to find out the exact facts." He was quite right. Considering the inflamed opinion raging across the country, fanned by hysterical elements of the press, and, Roosevelt said, "the excited—almost turbulent—state of Congress," for Americans, only their own investigation would serve to answer the question.[44]

Yet even while the *Maine* burned, and hours before Captain General Blanco received instructions from Madrid "to gather every fact you can to prove the *Maine* catastrophe cannot be attributed to us," Admiral Manterola had formed his own court of inquiry headed by Captain Pedro del Peral y Caballero. To say the least, this was an extremely difficult task, because no clear conclusion could be reached without American cooperation regarding its shipboard routine, the contents of and access to the wreck, and a fair amount of technical data of the ship itself. It also raised some serious questions of international law. The battleship *Maine,* no matter the locus, was United States territory. But the wreck of the *Maine* presented a wholly different set of circumstances, and was stripped of legal prerogatives normally conceded in a foreign port. The detail generally held that with the departure of the crew, "which give life to the ship . . . also disappear the immunities they hold."[45]

Under this assumption, pressed by Captain General Blanco, Spain alone controlled the inquest. The United States took the position that a wreck per se did "not destroy the organization which gave life to the force." The immunities still pertained, and "only final abandonment could cause the ship to lose its character as a public [i.e., U.S. Navy] ship." The "mere absence for the moment" of the crew did not constitute abandonment. Indeed, on the morning after the explosion, at Captain Sigsbee's insistence, the United States flag had been hoisted to the mainmast. Spain, for the sake of amity, yielded the point. Grateful, the U.S. State Department promised to provide the Spanish naval court with English interpreters and all reasonable assistance to reach its verdict.[46]

On February 17, the Spanish tribunal, with its own experts, closely inspected the wreck. The officers deduced that the explosion had chanced in a forward magazine, between the fireroom bulkhead and the foremast, and "from the effects observed . . . the explosion was on the inside." But they could not be absolutely certain until divers conducted a full underwater investigation.[47]

Witnesses examined by the Spanish court sustained the theory of an internal explosion. Lieutenant Julio Perez, commanding officer of the *machina,* reported seeing a "brilliant illumination" ascending from the *Maine* at the precise time of "a terrible explosion." From the shape of the smoke, fire, and colored gases rising from the ship, he surmised its magazines had blown. He had been looking directly at the ship at the time and saw no eruption of water by the hull, which would have been a sure indication of a mine.[48]

As Captain Peral reported, had there been a mine detonation, "a certain quaking," in proportion to the amount of explosives used in the device and its nearness to the harbor bottom, would have been felt ashore. Every Spanish witness was asked if he experienced the quaking or noticed a water spout by the hull; none did. Also, there were no dead fish on the surface of the water, a common result of mine explosions.[49]

From March 2 to March 18, save for Sundays and saints' days, Spanish navy divers inspected the wreck. No rivers empty into the harbor basin. Consequently the bottom is soft mud and the waters are filthy, making any examination problematic and almost literally a hand-over-hand process. But what the Spanish divers found was significant. There were no ruptures in the battleship's double bottom, and, forward of the boilers, the hull plates were bent outward; "the entire vessel forward appears open," noted their report, "having undoubtedly burst toward the outside." Thus, it had been an *internal* explosion.[50]

Captain Peral, in his summary, completely dismissed the mine theory. First, there was "the utter impossibility" that a "submarine" mine of the magnitude to explode the *Maine* could have been manufactured without the complicity or knowledge of the Spanish naval authorities. Second, the detonation of a mine was produced either by contact with its target or by an electrical impulse from a remote-control box. The sea and wind in Havana Harbor on the night of February 15 were dead calm and "did not allow any motion of the vessel"; hence the "collision" theory "must be rejected." As for electric current, "no traces of any wire or station have been discovered." Also lacking were the customary phenomena of an underwater explosion: no gas bubble, no water column, no dead fish. What left the Spanish investigation open to question, however, was the divers' remarkable error in failing to identify the ship's keel as bent into the shape of an inverted V, the apex thrusting upward through the armored deck—something anyone looking for clues of an external explosion would account as obvious proof. Incredibly, the chief Spanish diver reported that the keel "did not appear to have suffered any damage."[51]

In the waning afternoon of February 16, the gunboat *Fern* arrived in Havana with relief supplies for the survivors of the *Maine*. What the crew saw obscenely sticking through the foul harbor water held no resemblance to the stately battleship of the day before. The twisted iron of a junkyard began amidships, where the funnels would have been. The fore part of the superstructure had blown up and out to starboard, folding back on itself, carrying with it the bridge, the pilothouse, a 6-inch gun, and the ten-inch-thick, nickel steel conning tower, which crushed everything beneath it. A broad surface lying uppermost was identified as the overhead of the berth deck. On its white paint, visible beneath the filth, were the impressions of two human bodies. Parts of others still drifted ashore, collected by crews from the Spanish warships. Forward, where the forecastle had been, three clumps of metal were identified as portions of the berth deck, armored deck, and the ship's bottom.[52]

On February 20, the United States Navy's court of inquiry convened aboard the *Mangrove* in sight of the wreck. The panel kept to a single incontrovertible fact—the explosion that destroyed the ship had occurred in one or more of the forward powder magazines. This presented four logical possibilities: internal accident, internal sabotage, external accident, or external deliberate act. The statements of Captain Sigsbee and his officers disposed to the court's satisfaction the probability of the first two explanations.

These men testified that temperatures of the magazines and bunkers were routinely checked according to standing regulations. The ship's fire alarms worked—in fact, they worked too well, having gone off at lower temperatures than their setting. The ship maintained proper procedures for disposing fireroom ashes and flammable wastes, and for stowing paint. Discipline had been excellent, and no one had any reason to believe a member of the ship's company had deliberately engaged in sabotage.

The wreck itself offered the best evidence. Yet the extremely difficult, indeed life-threatening, conditions of investigation showed that the U.S. Navy's divers were at times no better than their Spanish counterparts in describing the underwater picture. What was plain, though, was that the *Maine*, forward of amidships, was blasted open and outward like a sardine can, the forecastle completely separating itself from the rest of the vessel, capsizing to starboard. On the port side, a great portion of the ship's bottom had disappeared, as had the starboard turret and its pair of 10-inch guns. The most baffling, or conclusive, evidence, depending on one's predisposition to internal or external cause, was the condition of the wreckage near frame 18, the steel rib just forward of the foremast, right by the massively exploding magazines. The keel here had been driven upward, in the inverted V, to the level of the main deck, a thrust of about thirty-four feet. What had caused this seemingly impossible contortion?[53]

When the navy divers proved incapable of adequately describing the wreck scene on the harbor bottom, the court called Ensign Wilfred Powelson of the *Fern*, a certified naval architect. Could the explosion of the magazine alone have caused the keel to bend this way? Or, asked Captain Sampson, "suppose it was a mine," and if so, how did it get there? Powelson, armed with a set of the *Maine*'s drawings, refused to answer "such a difficult question" based on hypothesis.

The battleship's watch and division officers, when asked about "any hostile demonstrations afloat . . . of boats approaching the ship that had to be warned off," all responded, "None whatever." As to the telltale water column thrown up by a mine: "Did you see any water thrown up?" Lieutenant John Blandin, the officer of the deck at the time of the explosion, was asked. "Not a particle."[54]

Nearly forgotten in the maelstrom of the *Maine* explosion was the grudging Spanish reciprocation of sending the armored cruiser *Vizcaya* to New York. She had sailed from the Canaries and was at sea on February 15, the day of the explosion, ignorant of the disaster. Three days later, in dense fog, the cruiser appeared off Point Pleasant, New Jersey. Spanish consular officials were beaten to her by reporters, who after being welcomed aboard by Captain Antonio Eulate, informed him of what had happened. Originally she was to have berthed off lower Manhattan, but given the tense atmosphere, the cruiser was given a safer mooring down the bay at the naval anchorage by Tompkinsville, Staten Island. Eulate conducted himself with impeccable diplomacy. Declaring the *Vizcaya* in "deep mourning," with flags at half-mast, he was able to avoid the standard public appearances and keep the ship closed to visitors. The New York *World* was unimpressed, warning its readers that "while lying off the Battery, her shells will explode on the Harlem River and in the suburbs of Brooklyn." The Navy Department also had its qualms. Commodore Francis Bunce at the Brooklyn Navy Yard received orders to pay particular attention to the movements of inventor John P. Holland's recently launched submarine across the Hudson River, at Elizabeth, New Jersey. If she made any suspicious movements, Bunce needed to warn Captain Eulate of the menace; of the submarine, if necessary, he was to "seize her." In the end, nothing happened. Eulate, unescorted, drove in a carriage up lower Manhattan to the Spanish consulate and remarked that the "beauty of American women" was what most impressed him about New York. On February 24, the *Vizcaya* cast off and turned without ceremony to Havana.[55]

The destruction of the *Maine* did not plunge the nation immediately into war, yet it did create an atmosphere in which escape from war was virtually impossible unless one of the three parties—Spain, the United States, or the Cuban Junta—blinked. None did. The American public, already aroused by the Dupuy de Lôme scandal, was driven to new heights of hysteria. Interventionists were stimulated to renewed activity, and the Junta doubled its pressure on friendly legislators. Democrats, aping the Republican opposition of the Cleveland years, increased their attacks on the administration for doing, or not doing, whatever happened to be momentarily fashionable. The populist free-silverites were all for the conflict: war meant inflation of the currency, and wasn't that what free silver was all about? Republicans divided between interventionist, expansionist jingoes on one side and increasingly isolated antiwar conservative business interests on the other. In the melee, William McKinley lost control of the national agenda. Never a strong leader, always deferring to the supposed "will" of the people, he had burned his last chance with inaction over the Dupuy de Lôme letter. With the president unable to steer the ship of state, the nation lurched toward the path of war.

Public disgust with Spain's conduct in Cuba intensified. "Everything is under suspense," wrote John D. Long. "Public sentiment is very intense." Three mass meetings in Buffalo alone demanded a declaration of war. The Naval Veterans' Association of Brooklyn offered its services in any fight with Spain. In Lehigh, Pennsylvania, college students drilled under a banner stating, "To Hell with Spain." The tide of intervention swept across the national consciousness, and William McKinley was not the man to hold it back.[56]

On February 23, the president received a discouraging letter from Stewart Woodford in Madrid. The ambassador had just come from an extremely disappointing audience with the queen regent. She and her government, indeed all Spain, refused to concede that American support to the Cuban rebels was not at the heart and soul of the insurrection, instead believing "that the rebellion only lives because of our sympathy and assistance." Woodford doubted this fantasy could be altered, or that Spain was prepared to offer any further concessions of substance. Should the Sagasta ministry even try, the country faced an internal revolution incited by the army and its ultranationalist allies. Of the cabinet, Woodford believed that Minister of *Ultramar* Moret genuinely desired a solution short of armed conflict with the United States. As for Gullón and the hard-liners, "They prefer the chances of war, with the certain loss of Cuba, to the overthrow of the dynasty."[57]

. . .

John D. Long, the cabinet officer most in the news since the *Maine* tragedy, was also the brunt of antiadministration letter writers whipped up by the jingo press. "Who is to blame but you McKinley & Hanna & Reed," accused one correspondent from Chicago. It was Long and his friends—"the moneyed people of the U.S."—who held the nation back. Long and "demagogues" like him "caused" the explosion of the *Maine,* and then did nothing about it. "Why on earth don't you resign you *old fossil,*" another wanted to know. Long had digested enough of this bile. He wasn't sleeping well, his nerves were edgy, and he badly needed one of the little vacations that so invigorated his body and spirit. On Friday, February 25, he confided to his journal, "I was half inclined to go away for a little while. I have therefore taken the afternoon off."[58]

Long put some thought into this. The last time he had taken time away from the office, Roosevelt had maneuvered Commodore Dewey into the Asiatic command, causing a fair amount of political mischief and distractions the secretary could have done without. To make certain that Roosevelt stuck to the jobs on his desk blotter, Long penned a note setting out exactly what he expected, or more to the point, what he did not expect, of his impetuous assistant, who for this sunny Friday afternoon would be in the position of "acting secretary of the navy."

The politician-poet, the happy, mellow twinkler who once composed *Bites of a Cherry,* dipped a gold nib in the inkwell of his stand-up desk and, in a flowing hand on eagle-marked stationery, admonished Theodore Roosevelt: "Do not take any such step affecting the policy of the Administration without consulting the President or me. I am not away from town and my intention [is] to have you look after the routine of the office while I get a quiet day off. . . . I am anxious to have no unnecessary occasion for a sensation in the papers."[59]

The time away proved a tonic to the hypochondria-prone secretary. Long had lately taken to "mechanical massage," a contraption operated by a Washington osteopath, who strapped the secretary into an electric chair that soothingly jiggled his stomach and legs. It was most satisfactory for his nerves and digestion; Long came away refreshed. By his own account, he "walked the streets in an aimless way" until, contentedly weary, looking toward a night of sound sleep, he ambled back to his apartment at the Hotel Portland.[60]

No one could leave Theodore Roosevelt in a position of executive authority and believe for one minute in unruffled routine. In Long's absence and in rapid succession, Roosevelt dispatched a message to the House Naval Affairs Committee demanding immediate legislation authorizing the enlistment of "an unlimited number of seamen." Following that came instructions to the chief of the Bureau of Ordnance to ship thirty-two 6- and 5-inch guns from Washington to the Brooklyn Navy Yard for mounting on auxiliary cruisers. To Commodore John Howell, now commanding the European Squadron, went secret orders to keep his coal bunkers full and his small force continuing its observations of Spanish naval movements along the Iberian Peninsula. Most important were the "secret and confidential" instructions telegraphed to Commodore Dewey. Except for the ancient sidewheeler *Monocacy*, Dewey was to concentrate the Asiatic Squadron at Hong Kong and keep his coal bunkers full. Following that, "in the event of declaration of war [with] Spain, your duty will be to see that the Spanish squadron does not leave the Asiatic coast, and then offensive operations in the Philippine Islands." Not only did Roosevelt not confine himself to the "routine of the office"; he had issued orders of the highest political and strategic import, orders that would affect the course of empires. Revisionists to the contrary, Roosevelt's orders to Dewey were not part of an imperialist cabal to get a jump on the "large policy" of American expansion. A naval attack on the Philippines in a war with Spain had been contemplated at least since the previous summer in the Naval War College scenarios. Long was aware of it and had endorsed the operation, should it come. Roosevelt's action in triggering the movement, though certainly beyond the scope of his nominal duties, was a sensible act of military preparedness. Later, without apology or qualm, Roosevelt explained to Henry Cabot Lodge of this day, which he always considered constituted his "chief usefulness" to the Navy Department. "When I was Acting Secretary, I did not hesitate to take responsibilities . . . because I was willing to jeopardize my position in a way that a naval officer could not."[61]

Saturday morning John D. Long woke after "a splendid night." He looked forward to a busy day "both because I feel so much better, and because . . . I find that Roosevelt . . . has come very near causing more of an explosion than happened to the *Maine.*" That the secretary was more than a little angry is beside the point. "He has gone at things like a bull in a china shop," Long wrote, as people always would about Theodore Roosevelt. But very significantly, he was more piqued by Roosevelt's method, "which is most discourteous to me, because it suggests that there has been a lack of attention, which he is supplying," than he was by the substance of his actions. Long clearly conceded Roosevelt's "forceful habit is a good tonic" for a conservative man as "myself." That day, on resuming his office routine, Secretary Long elaborated on his assistant's prescription for all squadrons. The South Atlantic, European, Asiatic, and North Atlantic Squadrons were to "[k]eep full of coal, the best that can be had." The navy, if nothing else in the government, was preparing for war.[62]

In Madrid that Saturday, Premier Sagasta dissolved the Cortes, ostensibly to hold elections and increase his Liberal parliamentary base. The new body would not convene until April 25, a month away, coinciding with the Cuban rainy season. Military operations would halt, and Spain had another excuse for prolonging the pacification of the island. On Sunday, John D. Long joined the McKinleys and a few guests for dinner at the White House. Afterward, one of the ladies sang "psalm-tunes at the piano in a melancholy voice, and the rest of us grumbled a faint accompaniment."[63]

The following day, Monday, February 28, the *Maine* court of inquiry began sessions in the federal courthouse at Key West, taking testimony from the ship's surviving junior officers and enlisted men. After the officers testified, Captain Sampson administered the oath en masse to the seventy-odd sailors and marines. Lieutenant Commander Marix, the judge advocate, intoned the prescribed phrases covering the loss or grounding of a United States naval ship and stated that if those present could fault anyone on board the *Maine* during the night of its destruction, "let such officer or man step to the front." No one moved. Every man thus affirmed under oath no knowledge of crime or dereliction of duty. The question of shipboard accident, as far as the U.S. Navy was concerned, was closed.[64]

Long met with the president and Judge Rufus Day at the White House that evening. The topic was a message from Consul General Lee in Havana indicating "some probable explanation of the explosion." There were two points Lee was certain of: the magazine explosion in the *Maine* had been detonated by a crude external mine, and the Spanish government was innocent of any complicity. Clearly Lee had gotten this from an informed source, close to the court of inquiry, because this was precisely its line of thinking. Long, for one, was immensely relieved. "I believe war will be averted," he wrote optimistically.[65]

Naturally, the secretary looked for a peaceful outcome, but at the Navy Department, wishing rarely got in the way of reality. On March 1, as part of the general concentration of U.S. naval forces, movement orders east came to the battleship *Oregon,* at Bremerton, Washington. In the Pacific she was wasted power. Even without reinforcements already slated—the cruisers *Baltimore* and *Charleston*—Dewey commanded more than enough to beat the Spanish navy in the Philippines. Two days later, Long ordered the ancient wooden steam sloop *Mohican* to load ammunition at San Francisco, steam "at once" for Honolulu, and transfer the cargo to the *Baltimore.* At the Philadelphia, Brooklyn, and Boston navy yards came instructions to "enlist seamen, firemen, and petty officers," crews for the laid-up cruisers *Columbia* and *Minneapolis*—the fastest ships in the fleet.[66]

With naval preparations well under way, the McKinley administration tried tightening the diplomatic thumbscrew on Spain. Judge Day made sure Ambassador Woodford communicated the degree of anti-Spanish sentiment cresting across the United States since the publication of the "insulting and insincere" Dupuy de Lôme letter and the loss of the *Maine.* It created a situation "very grave, which will require the highest wisdom and greatest prudence on both sides to avoid a crisis." Sagasta and his ministers shrugged, responding with thin complaints against certain "objectionable newspapers," and suggesting the removal of Consul General Fitzhugh Lee from Havana. The Spanish government appeared suspended in a dream, seemingly incapable of divining the escalating climax rushing upon them.[67]

Perhaps the Spanish understood too well. But in the diplomatic arena, their main weapons were obfuscation and delay. They began working a scam on the guileless Stewart Woodford, a good cop/bad cop playlet with Minister of *Ultramar* Moret and Foreign Minister Gullón as the actors. Cabinet splits were magnified for Woodford's benefit, leading him to believe Moret spoke for a shadowy appeasement faction against the hard-line followers of Gullón. Woodford bought it, and believed Moret would go to any length to avoid war, "even if he has to sacrifice himself."[68]

Moret had recently confided to the Austro-Hungarian minister that in a worst case scenario—that of the Americans recognizing a republic of Cuba—the Sagasta government, faced with war or "great domestic dangers," would "throw down the gauntlet" and accept war with the United States. This confidence, too, came with more than one face. Moret voiced his "*ardent* hope" that friendly European powers would, at the last moment, diplomatically intervene, forcing the Americans to back down, compelling the rebels to accept some sort of negotiated settlement. Barring that, if war came, but before any real damage had been done, the powers might coerce the Americans to submit the Cuban mess to an international "court of arbitration." President Cleveland had demanded such from the British over the Venezuelan boundary dispute; why should this be any different? Haggling could go on for years, and surely the Cuban rebels would tire and accept autonomy. Spain now began moving on a parallel track: bluffing the United States into endless waiting, while at the same time marshaling diplomatic support in Europe.[69]

On Friday, March 5, an impatient John D. Long brooded over recent events. He and the entire administration had been vastly relieved on hearing of the court of inquiry's prevailing opinion that Spain stood untainted in the disaster. Long was anxious to receive the formal report. But the thorough Captain Sampson refused to be pushed. Not until the U.S. Navy's divers were finished, perhaps in two weeks, could the panel frame its final conclusions. "Busy and exacting," Long described these days. The Carson City (Nevada) *Appeal* reported truthfully, "Many people are for war on general principles, without a well-defined idea of why or wherefore." Long and Roosevelt conducted daily meetings with members of the congressional naval affairs committees. Letters passed back and forth between the Navy Department, foreign ship builders, and financially strapped governments offering warships for sale. On March 6, Long placed the Bureau of Ordnance on an emergency footing, approving a $4 million ammunition order, over half its peacetime fiscal-year budget.[70]

Largely against his will, President McKinley, whose benign leadership had all but evaporated, entered the fray. On March 6, he called "Uncle Joe" Cannon, the foulmouthed, steely hayseed from Illinois, chairman of the House Appropriations Committee, to the White House. Without any preliminaries, he came straight to the point. "I must have money to get ready for war. I am doing everything possible to prevent war, but it must come, and we are not prepared."[71]

Cannon himself opposed war with Spain. In a noisy House debate he castigated those "gentlemen who are loudly shouting for war . . . agonizing to shed their blood in selling supplies to the government." Nonetheless, he now believed war had become inevitable, and sensibly demanded a high degree of preparedness. Cannon had already reviewed Treasury accounts. An outright withdrawal of $50 million, he told the president, could be done without additional taxing or the issuance of bonds. Would the president draft a note requesting the funds? William McKinley refused, on the tissue-thin excuse that so long as the United States attempted a negotiated settlement with Spain, a presidential entreaty might be interpreted as a war message, and he would stand accused of "double-dealing," no different than the cynical Dupuy de Lôme.[72]

Ever the weaving politician, McKinley suggested instead that the Appropriations Committee introduce the measure on a motion of its own. Cannon nodded; yes, his committee could do that. But the president's political water came in a heavy bucket, and Cannon was not about to carry it by himself. If the president wanted a committee vote on its "own" motion, McKinley, at the very least, needed to draft the language. The president, Cannon later remembered, "walked over to the table and wrote on a telegraph blank a single sentence: 'For the national defense, fifty million dollars.' . . . [A]nd I put the slip of paper in my pocket."[73]

The so-called Cannon Emergency Bill, appropriating $50 million "for the national defense and for each and every purpose connected therewith," came to the House floor on Monday. After seventy-three speeches in its favor, it passed by 311 votes. On Tuesday, this time without oratory, the legislation cleared the Senate with 76 yeas, and 0 nays. "Joe," asked Speaker Reed, as he and Cannon walked out of the Capitol to the streetcar stop, "why did you do it?" Cannon explained his rationale of preparedness, and Reed nodded his massively bald head, admitting, "Perhaps you are right. Perhaps you are right."[74]

In one fell swoop, William McKinley had, for the moment, captured the national agenda. Acclaim for the measure was as near universal in the United States as anything could be. Even William Jennings Bryan publicly supported the bill, more than hinting that had the administration not gone ahead with it, the Democrats would have maximally exploited the issue in the November midterm elections: "Humanity demands that we shall act," said the past and presumptive presidential candidate. The New York *World,* no friend to the administration, thought it "a most prudent action [for a] nation that wants peace so much that it will fight for it if necessary." This would show Europe that the United States really possessed a "soul above mere money making." The *New York Times* considered the act "a pacific measure of great merit and potency." John D. Long thought of the wider potential of the bill, "the appreciation of what it would be to come in conflict with such a power as ours." Something like this, the appropriation of $50 million dollars, not as a credit or loan, but in hard cash, "will have a mollifying influence on Spanish public sentiment."[75]

In Madrid, the evening dailies announced the bill's unanimous passage in the Senate; the Spanish reaction went quite beyond Secretary Long's hopes of calm—in fact, it took their breath away. "It has not excited the Spaniards," Woodford cabled, "it has stunned them. To appropriate fifty millions out of money in the Treasury, without borrowing a cent, demonstrates wealth and power. Even Spain can see this. . . . The ministry and the press are simply stunned."[76]

The lion's share of the money, nearly $30 million, went to the navy, most of it to purchase warships and auxiliary vessels. The best of the lot were two Brazilian cruisers, the 6-inch-gunned *Amazonas* and the unfinished *Almirante Abreu,* at Newcastle, Scotland. The *Amazonas* had already been commissioned into the Brazilian navy, and lay with her complement on board ready to sail home. The U.S. naval attaché in London bought both of them on the spot. Long cabled Commodore Howell at Lisbon to move "at once" to Newcastle and hoist the United States flag over the ships.

The Navy Department swarmed with agents anxious to unload anything that floated and could mount a gun. "Sight was not lost,"

Long wrote after the war, "of the fact that Spain, too, was anxious to buy, and that it was more desirable that we should pay a high price for a ship than to permit it to pass into the Spanish service." The large and complicated administration of vetting and acquiring this off-the-shelf navy fell to Assistant Secretary Theodore Roosevelt. And, of course, in matters like this, there was no man better. Given the paucity of prime naval tonnage on the market, the navy improvised, buying or leasing one hundred merchant ships, from transatlantic liners to private yachts, fitting and arming them as auxiliary cruisers, gunboats, colliers, and supply vessels. In addition to these, the service obtained fifteen cutters from the Revenue Marine, four lighthouse tenders, and two U.S. Fish Commission vessels.[77]

Right after passage of the $50 million bill, Secretary Long organized the Naval War Board to advise on strategy, operations, and war plans. Its membership, for the moment, comprised Roosevelt as chairman, Arent Schuyler Crowninshield of the Bureau of Navigation, Caspar Goodrich of the War College, Chief Intelligence Officer Richardson Clover, and Captain Albert Barker.

The War Department received $19 million from the bill. Most of it went to the Corps of Engineers and the Ordnance Department for coast defense, a strategic shield that, if completed, assured the free mobility of the fleet, unconstrained by having to protect East and Gulf Coast harbors from Spanish naval bombardment.

But the army's five existing artillery regiments had nothing approximating the personnel required to garrison the coastal fortifications, much less man the field and siege batteries required for expeditionary service. For the past dozen years, secretaries of war along with the army's commanding generals and chiefs of artillery had badgered Congress to provide at least two more artillery regiments to the rolls. Previously, Democrats had been hostile to any increase in the regular army, and Republicans, on principle, refused to spend money on what they considered unnecessary. Now, swept by the tide of the $50 million bill, to say nothing of pressure applied by chambers of commerce in coastal cities, Congress acted. On a personal plea from Secretary of War Russell Alger, Speaker Reed brought the issue to a nearly unanimous vote on March 7. President McKinley signed it the next day, and the army started recruiting for the new 6th and 7th Artillery regiments. Thus reinforced, the regular army's artillery mustered about six thousand men, still barely adequate even as a cadre for the coastal defenses to be completed during the year.[78]

In the six weeks between the passage of the $50 million bill and the onset of hostilities, the War Department devoted relatively little attention to organizing a large army for the invasion of Cuba. It wasn't only because of Russell Alger's laxness, or his lame excuse that "no part of this sum was available for offensive purposes—even for offensive preparation." John D. Long held no such confining views of the navy's lion's share of the money, and when examined closely, neither, in many cases, did the War Department. Alger's statement to the contrary, the army accomplished significantly more than its own political head, or its critics, gave it credit for, but much less than it could have done.

On passage of the bill, preliminary steps were taken toward organizing and equipping an expeditionary force for foreign service, the first time since the Mexican War of 1847–48. At its own arsenals, the Ordnance Department increased and accelerated production of rifles, bayonets, slings, and cleaning gear, purchasing from private manufacturers over 12 million rounds of small-arms ammunition. Army contractors were put on notice to be ready to fill large orders for cartridge belts, knapsacks, and sundry field equipment on short notice. The quartermaster general adopted similar measures by speeding work at uniform depots, buying quantities of cloth and materials for tentage and clothing, and contracting for the manufacture of equipment. The army surgeon general got orders to prepare for large emergency purchases of medical supplies, and Congress was requested to appropriate for additional surgeons to the Army Medical Department. In early April, Secretary Alger and Quartermaster General Marshall Independence Ludington met with leading wagon manufacturers, warning them to expect large orders soon and to begin assembling army wagons, especially the big six-mule type, immediately. Alger also sent a quartermaster officer to St. Louis with orders to form twenty pack trains, each of seventy-five mules, telling the officer, "You had better buy good ones, for you'll probably go to Cuba with them!" In the same period, the Quartermaster's Department began sewing ten thousand experimental tropical uniforms, for the army had none. Finally, preliminary plans were prepared for chartering and converting merchant steamers into troop transports.[79]

On the operational and intelligence side, the Adjutant General's Office dispersed maps and intelligence reports on Cuba, Puerto Rico, and the Philippines, the likely theaters of war, to all commands. On March 11, Secretary Alger created the Department of the Gulf, placing mobilization for a Cuban invasion under its new commanding general and staff. Joint army-navy planners studied railroad lines and Gulf harbors to select a port of embarkation for the expeditionary forces. Late in the month all field and siege artillery batteries began moving to posts east of the Mississippi River. On April 1, General Miles directed all but three of the regular army's twenty-five infantry regiments to prepare for campaign service.[80]

Although the field army and the bureaus of the War Department were not caught as flat-footed as has often been thought, these preparations went nowhere near the readiness level obtained by the navy. One reason *was* Russell Alger's crippling definition, limiting offensive preparations from the use of the $50 million. But more importantly, hardly any person, military or civilian, who knew what he was talking about, saw the need for a vastly increased army. This war, to be fought chiefly for islands within the strategic geography of North America, was to be the navy's show, and intelligent people understood. It was strictly according to Mahan: The navy that controlled the sea dictated the outcome.

Neither General Miles, nor the adjutant general, nor the department and field commanders contemplated exponentially expanding numbers of citizen volunteers as had been necessary to fight the Civil War. The National Guard could garrison the coast defenses. The tiny regular army, counting the two new artillery regiments, numbered 27,316 officers and enlisted men. By simply increasing the number of regiments and staff functions, a well-found, well-trained expeditionary force of 75,000 to 100,000 men, under regular army command, would be enough to mop up Cuba and Puerto Rico after the navy destroyed the Spanish fleet. Miles, the senior field commanders, and War Department bureau staffs dictated their war preparations on the assumption of rapidly equipping and assembling this rather modest but wholly appropriate army. The *Army and Navy Journal,* an influential weekly reflecting a high order of professional opinion, summed it up: "With a regular Army of sufficient strength to form the fighting line, and with the organized militia for local service, we should have a force quite sufficient for our needs against Spain." But no one in the regular army took account of domestic and National Guard politics.[81]

After the immediate flurry of the $50 million bill, all attention shifted to the *Maine* court of inquiry. Once the examination of the survivors had been completed, the wreck itself remained the final witness for the origin of the explosion. The court returned to Havana for additional reports from divers and naval constructors. The court also examined Commander George Converse, skipper of the cruiser *Montgomery.* A man with thirty-seven years in the navy, Converse also had considerable experience in torpedoes and mining. He was convinced there had been an outboard explosion that triggered the main blast in the forward magazines. It was the only explanation for the upward shove of the bottom plating and the keel's twisting into the inverted V. In his opinion it was a crude underwater mine, probably filled with gunpowder, placed on the harbor floor. Judge Advocate Adolph Marix put a theoretical question: Might it have been possible for an internal explosion to tear out only the ship's sides and contort the wreck into exactly its present condition. It was a query that seemed phrased for the historical record, because the court understood that someone had to ask it in order to dispose of the shipboard-accident theory. Unintendedly, it also revealed that the court quite understood the hypothesis in which an internal explosion might account for each and every aspect of the wreck. The answer was certainly not scripted, but Commander Converse found it "difficult" to comprehend how the *Maine*'s damage could have been configured solely by an internal explosion. Marix then asked if the type of mine Converse had described—low technology, low order of explosive— might by itself have detonated the magazines in the manner indicated by the wreck? Here Converse drew back. No, he didn't think so.[82]

During the week of March 13, the Spanish navy threw a small scare into its American counterpart. Measures for a coming war with the United States, though nowhere approaching the preparations emanating from the $50 million bill, nonetheless took some steps forward. The U.S. embassy in Madrid cabled reports of a Spanish torpedo flotilla of three destroyers, three torpedo boats, and an auxiliary cruiser making ready to cross the Atlantic to Cuba, or perhaps Puerto Rico. A second division of similar makeup was reported in an early stage of preparation. "Locomotive" or "automobile" torpedoes, as they were then called, were absolutely the latest thing in naval strike weapons, and torpedo craft were the one area where Spain held a nominal superiority over the United States. The flotilla's movement indicated the beginnings of a Spanish naval concentration in the Caribbean and justly troubled members of the Naval War Board and senior fleet officers. Theodore Roosevelt lectured the president, arguing "that we ought to treat the sailing of those Spanish torpedo catchers exactly as a European power would the mobilizing of a hostile army on its frontiers." If the *Maine* court of inquiry could send an advance copy of its report to the board "at once," the navy would have a better idea of the immediate political situation and could advise countermeasures accordingly. Even the sane, sober Captain William Sampson urged Secretary Long to pass along a warning to Madrid that the U.S. Navy reckoned the intended voyage of the flotilla to the Caribbean as a hostile act and would sink the vessels if they appeared. "Self preservation demands such a course."[83]

The Spanish torpedo craft hadn't the stamina or the coal to steam across the Atlantic unaided. Buffeted by seas and plagued with engine breakdowns, they limped into port at the Cape Verde Islands. As a precursor to war, they proved a dud. Not so a little-heralded half-hour speech in the U.S. Senate, delivered during a pause in a sleepy debate over public health service hospitals.

The Senate, pleased to be relieved of the tedium, gratefully allowed Redfield Proctor, the "marble king of Vermont" and patron of Commodore Dewey, to expound on his recent visit to Cuba. But accustomed to flaming oratory on the subject, the members sat back with less than craning enthusiasm. The result, however, was totally electrifying. "I merely speak of the symptoms as I saw them," Proctor said in dry, passionless tones, with a self-deprecation that only enhanced his words. He had met with Consul General Lee, and with the U.S. consuls at Matanzas and Sagua la Grande; with municipal *alcaldes,* and the Cuban professional class; with Captain General Blanco at his Havana palace; and with the *Maine* court of inquiry aboard the *Mangrove.* He did not confer with the Junta in the United States, nor did he closet himself with Cuban rebels on the island. If anything, Proctor, a businessman of substantial private wealth, might be thought inclined toward an anti-intervention stance. "I went to Cuba," he said, "with a strong conviction that the picture had been overdrawn; that a few cases of starvation and suffering" had been sensationalized and "stimulated" by the press and its "highly cultivated imagination." The pictures of sick and starving *reconcentrados* he had seen in a religious tract "must be rare specimens, got up to make the worst possible showing."[84]

To the contrary, Proctor witnessed exactly the horrific scenes, "plenty as bad or worse," and many he considered too awful even to be photographed. The Spanish governed only "just what their army sits on," nowhere else. Everywhere outside Havana, he found only "desolation . . . distress . . . misery . . . starvation." The fortified towns garrisoned by the Spanish army he compared to "prison yards" of "foul earth, foul air, foul water, and foul food, or none." Hospitals were indescribable. Children, he went on monotonously, were horribly deformed with skeletal hunger, swollen eyed, "abdomen bloated." The Cuban people, "the entire native population," were locked to the death in a struggle for freedom "and deliverance from the worst misgovernment of which I ever had knowledge." It was an unmistakable call for American intervention, invoked by a member of the Republican conservative establishment, President McKinley's core constituency.[85]

"It is just as if Proctor had held up his hand and sworn to it," said a Senate colleague.[86]

The inhuman ghastliness, described utterly without emotion or affect, did more to inflame Americans than three years of Frederic Remington's atrocity art in the *New York Journal*. Intervention now assumed the noble repose of the Lincolnesque Proctor, summoning a crusade to eradicate evil. Though Proctor took no role in coercing the administration in its Cuba policy, his speech legitimized intervention for those groups hitherto opposed. Wall Street, until then objecting to war, fearful of undermining the recent economic recovery, now saw no financial disaster in a short conflict. Proctor's speech, wrote the *Wall Street Journal*, "made the blood boil." The big money men, the railroad, oil, iron, coal, and steel men, the bank men, the trust men, were "feeling militant." Religious institutions found the senator's apocalyptic address reason enough to about-face. Intervention *was* a noble, humanitarian service, and to strive for Cuban independence must be the will of God; "a day of the Lord, a judgment day, is at hand," said the Presbyterian *Interior*.[87]

It was assumed with convincing evidence that Proctor, a friend and frequent guest at the White House, partner of many "little talks" with the president, also spoke the president's mind. But actually, this was not the case. William McKinley was the next to last American to admit the inevitability of the crusade to separate Spain from Cuba. The last was Czar Reed, Speaker of the House; commenting on the marble king of Vermont's speech, he archly observed, "A war will make a large profit for gravestones."[88]

The *Maine* court of inquiry finished its Havana sessions aboard the *Mangrove* and reconvened in the more sumptuous quarters of Captain Sampson's battleship *Iowa* at Key West. Sampson saw no need to keep the administration ignorant of facts and findings thus far concluded, and while organizing the final report, he drafted an unsigned abstract. Secretary Long was informed that three of the *Maine*'s officers would arrive in Washington on the Saturday morning train bearing the preliminary document.

From Madrid, the president received no encouragement in a wire from Stewart Woodford, who depicted the Spanish capital as "despondent." Business stagnated, shares tumbled on the *bolsa,* and the exchange rate for the peseta in London and Paris rose sharply. "Bread grows dearer," wrote the ambassador. Woodford was blunt in his suggestion that the United States must make Spain understand it had reached the limits of patience over Cuba: "The Spanish mind is so ingrained with '*mañanaism*' that few Spaniards ever act until they have to act."[89]

Woodford also broached a subject that had occupied a good many American minds for a century: purchase. "The thought of sale is today in the air of Madrid." Spain, he calculated, was economically finished, "tired out and exhausted, threatened with practical famine," from endless money tossed down the Cuban sinkhole. Woodford thought that the Spanish people would thank the queen regent for her courage and wisdom should she "dare" to part with Cuba without going to war. He asked permission to pursue the matter if the opportunity presented itself.[90]

The next day Woodford reported a "long and heated" meeting of the Spanish cabinet. The army and navy ministers, threatening resignation, had urged an immediate step-up in war preparations, because, with every passing day since the $50 million bill, the military power of the United States increased, with a concomitant decline in Spanish prospects. Minister of *Ultramar* Moret, as usual, argued for the peaceful diplomatic solution. Premier Sagasta "positively" declared himself for peace in Cuba and with the United States, on any terms consistent with Spanish honor, which of course meant no agreement, but it sounded good. For the moment, the peace faction, such as it was, held the advantage, and threats of resignation were withdrawn. The time had come, said the minister of *ultramar* to the American minister, for some very frank intercourse, not between ministers of crown and republic, but between equal men, "for full and free understanding."[91]

At the American embassy, the two talked informally for over an hour. Moret wished to know if Woodford, as a personal favor, would ask President McKinley "to advise" the Cuban rebels to put down their arms and accept autonomy? No, Woodford said, he could not do that. Spain had coldly refused the president's good offices when they had been officially presented six months ago. American self-respect prohibited a second offering, except at the authoritative request of the Spanish government, and if such an appeal were made, Spain must expect the United States to maintain "a very free hand" in its labors.[92]

On the twentieth of March, Sunday, Judge Day advised Woodford of the *Maine* court of inquiry's preliminary findings. It judged the battleship had been destroyed by a mine, planted by persons or agencies unknown. Spain held no culpability for the act. But the fact that it happened in a Spanish harbor devolved upon her the responsibility for general maritime security, which had been breached. The full report would arrive any day and forthwith be submitted to Congress with no demur. The attitude in the United States, Day cautioned, was "very acute." If Spain took prompt action with a sincere apology and reparations, "such as the most civilized nations would offer," Day thought "everything" might still be settled peacefully. That expressed, Rufus Day turned hard-line. It had been said before, and again, but this was the last time. American forbearance could no longer continue. Unless Spain restored an "honorable peace," ending Cuba's slow death, and gave the wretched people "an opportunity to take care of themselves," the president, having "exhausted" all diplomatic avenues, would lay the entire matter before the Congress. Day pointed to April 15, a little more than three weeks away, as "none too early a date" for Spain to accomplish what she had not been able to do in three years.[93]

The president, however, wavered. The time for an ultimatum had not yet come. Pouncing on the court of inquiry's absolution of Spain in the actual explosion, McKinley, in a rather wily plan, considered sending the final, signed report to Congress without comment, simultaneously demanding a large indemnity from Spain. He would then request a huge congressional appropriation for Cuban relief. The antijingoists, the Democrats, and what remained of the peace factions could legitimately embrace this effort as a substitute for armed intervention. And if enough men swayed, the matter could be debated for a month, to the start of the Cuban rainy season, giving the president a few *more* months to snatch a diplomatic resolution. McKinley really didn't expect to carry this off, but a respectable show of strength in the Congress and press might just restore national direction to the White House.

It was a lost fight from the start. The wait for the *Maine* report took on the aspect of waiting for a jury verdict in a murder case. A Virginia mob burned twin effigies of William McKinley and Mark Hanna. The president's photograph was hissed in theaters and in some places torn from office walls. At the Washington press corps' annual white-tie Gridiron Dinner, Assistant Secretary of the Navy Theodore Roosevelt snarled through horse teeth at Mark Hanna, "We will have this war for the freedom of Cuba in spite of the timidity of the commercial interests." At theaters and popular music halls, audiences sang "The Star-Spangled Banner" after every performance. Patriotic orators speechified at the end of vaudeville bills. Crowds dusted off Civil War songs and sang "Rally Round the Flag."[94]

Walking in the evening with his attending physician, army Captain Leonard Wood, himself a close friend of TR, William McKinley asked with asperity, "Well, have you and Theodore declared war yet?"

"No, Mr. President," said Wood, "we have not, but I think you will, sir."

The ex-sergeant and major of Ohio volunteers shook his head. "I shall never get into a war, until I am sure that God and man approve.

I have been through one war; I have seen the dead piled up, and I do not want to see another."[95]

On Monday, March 21, the president and the judge advocate of the court of inquiry into the destruction of the United States battleship *Maine* appended their signatures to the document aboard the USS *Iowa*. Nearly three hundred pages in length, it was wrapped in sailcloth, heavily sealed, and given over to the care of Lieutenant Commander Marix, escorted by three *Maine* officers.

Their train pulled into Washington's Pennsylvania Station at 10:30 P.M. on March 24, where they found a sizable crowd waiting. The four tired, somewhat disheveled officers had been on "watch and watch"—four hours on duty, four hours off—since leaving Key West. A sharp-elbowed ensign pushed his way through with the message that Secretary Long would receive them in the morning, at regular hours. With the young officer in the van, propelling aside reporters, the party jostled to a hack stand and boarded closed hansom cabs to the Ebbitt House. Lieutenant John Hood, ex-senior watch and division officer of the *Maine*, clutched the parcel to his chest, one hand on the revolver under his coat.

In the morning, Marix took the report to the Navy Department, meeting first with the department's judge advocate general. Together they entered Long's office, where the document was placed in a leather mail pouch. Long and Marix then walked across Seventeenth Street to the White House, delivering it to President McKinley in the library. The cabinet arrived, and for the entire day the statesmen gravely considered the report, and its implications and repercussions.

The court's conclusions filled only a few pages. The *Maine* had been destroyed by two explosions: the first, the one sounding like a gunshot, lifted the forward end of the vessel, bending the keel into the inverted V, forcing up the bottom plating. In the court's opinion, these phenomena could only have been caused by "the explosion of a mine situated under the bottom of the ship," parallel to the foremast, "and somewhat on the port side." This explosion then detonated one or more of the forward magazines, whose eruption, the second blast, had literally blown the forward third of the ship out like a cherry bomb in a sardine can.

The court found no proof, or even circumstantial evidence, of a Spanish conspiracy, and no physical confirmation of a mine beyond manifestly thinking it so. Consciously or not, the court of inquiry, composed of senior officers of the United States Navy, men of unimpeachable probity aggregating 137 years of service, could not concede the possibility, as the Spanish report had correctly done, of an internal accident. That conclusion was "not acceptable" to either the service or the McKinley administration. Captain French Ensor Chadwick, with one other member of the court, who remains to this day unknown, initially believed the internal-accident theory. But after hearing testimony, Chadwick later said, they became "convinced otherwise against their prepossessions." In the end, after hundreds of pages of testimony, findings, and conclusions, the court had butted up against a wall, "unable to obtain evidence fixing the responsibility for the destruction of the *Maine* upon any person or persons."[96]

In a futile attempt to divorce the two issues—the *Maine* and Cuba—President McKinley decided to let the report sit in the White House over the weekend before sending it to Congress with a brief endorsement, omitting any reference to Cuba. This he planned in a separate message for Cuban relief, then another missive, outlining headway toward the hoped-for diplomatic solution. Politically, this was not fruitful. The president might be of a mind to split the two issues, the *Maine* from Cuba, but to the public they were conjoined, one and the same.

In Madrid, the day before the *Maine* report arrived in Washington, Foreign Minister Gullón, with Moret as his interpreter, took pains to assure Ambassador Woodford that Spain most certainly would do the right and honorable thing regarding the battleship, once it possessed all the facts. He also let Woodford know of the Sagasta government's pique at the new, overtly hostile American attitude. In diplomatese, Woodford sought to disabuse the foreign minister of such thoughts. America's perspective had not changed; it was simply weary with Spanish promises for Cuba that remained only that—promises. "Questions of humanity and civilization," Woodford lectured, "require that permanent and immediate peace be established and enforced."[97]

The next day, Moret, always eager and optimistic in his role of pacifier, called on Woodford for another of their man-to-man talks. He proposed that the question of an "early and honorable peace" be submitted to the autonomist Cuban parliament for solving. It was scheduled to convene in Havana in early May, and when Woodford inquired about Spanish military operations between now and then, likely to be full bore as they were the last until the onset of the rainy season, Moret proposed an immediate "armistice or truce," provided the United States could persuade the Cuban rebels to accept and abide by it. But what if the rebels refuse? Woodford asked. Moret had an answer to that. The United States and Spain together would compel "both parties"—insurgent and autonomist—to accept a settlement imposed by the two powers.[98]

On Friday, March 25, Gullón personally stated to Woodford his "very earnest" desire that the *Maine* report not be sent to Congress, but be resolved "as the subject of diplomatic adjustment" between Spain and the United States. He reiterated "that Spain would do in this matter whatever was just and right." To Woodford's surprise, Gullón, the ostensible hard-liner, repeated the proposal offered by Moret, to send the peace question to the Cuban autonomist parliament. Given this opening, Woodford asked if the Spanish government, provided the rebels agreed at their end, would grant an immediate armistice, which Moret had proposed the day before. Gullón hedged; he could not answer so grave a question without consulting Sagasta and the cabinet—though personally, he confided to Woodford, he feared such an armistice was "impossible." Spanish diplomacy had sunk to the level of a shell game.[99]

Spain's historic habit of procrastination did her no good this time. Had Sagasta's government granted the armistice immediately, as Moret initially proposed, with or without rebel cooperation, it would not have had to embarrass itself by doing exactly that two weeks later, and in a far weaker position diplomatically. The *Maine* report was not scheduled for delivery to Congress for another three days, and if President McKinley could have inserted into his message an official Spanish offer to suspend hostilities, a truly dramatic breakthrough for which McKinley could take credit, it just might have stretched the endless parleying through the summer rainy season to the following autumn. But all Woodford received were shrugs and promises of action when the autonomist parliament convened in early May.

Not good enough. In Washington, Republicans and Democrats were hot for intervention. Each viewed a potential war as a political unifier for its own parochial ends. The Democrats envisioned the conflict as a means of ending their frustrating domestic defeats at the ballot box. William Jennings Bryan, the nominal party leader, warned reporters that if the administration did nothing, the Democrats would maximally exploit the issue at the next election. For the Republicans, the jingoes were already all for it, and the waverers saw intervention as the only way to remove Cuba, as one senator said, from the "steamroller of public clamor." Moreover, should war come, wrote Henry Cabot Lodge, "we will not hear much of the currency question in the elections." Judge Rufus Day was accosted in his office by a senator, waving his cane, banging on the table, yelling at the assistant secretary of state, "By————! Don't your president know where the war-declaring power is lodged? Well tell him, by————! that if he doesn't do something Congress will exercise the power and declare war in spite of him! He'll get run over and the party with him!" Senator William E. Chandler of New Hampshire, one of the leading Republican war hawks, was on the mark, fearing if negotiations were prolonged, the Republican Party would suffer a very damaging split, permitting the temporarily united Democrats to overwhelm the GOP in the November congressional elections. Chandler, secretary of the navy during the Chester Arthur presidency, held an accurate measure of the coming conflict. A war with Spain, he told a colleague, would last between fifteen minutes and ninety days.[100]

On Sunday, one day before he sent the *Maine* report to Congress, William McKinley closeted himself with the dwindling Senate Republican peace faction: Mark Hanna, Eugene Hale, chairman of the Naval Affairs Committee, and three of the Republican "Big Four": Nelson Aldrich, John Spooner, and Orville H. Platt. On their advice, the president composed a broadly worded not-quite-ultimatum and wired it to Woodford in Madrid; it would be the last substantive proposal offered by the United States for a political solution in Cuba. It was literally Spain's final chance to disengage, without further bloodshed or credit drain, with her honor and the remainder of her still-considerable empire intact. The next day the *Maine* report would go to Congress, red meat in the cage. Said Senator Platt, "I think the President himself believes that the people of the United States will not tolerate much longer the war in Cuba and that, if he cannot end it by negotiations, the people will insist that he shall do so by force." If the

administration's diplomatic pains did not achieve "absolute independence" for Cuba, "nothing" could restrain Congress from "declaring
for intervention, which is the same thing as declaring war." Like
Chandler, Platt had got it exactly right.[101]

William McKinley, after mouthing the usual boilerplate of suffering, starvation, and horror, reviewed the Cuban morass over the past
three months, since the proclamation of autonomy, especially Spain's
total failure to pacify the island. "There is no hope of peace through
Spanish arms," the president said. Once again he offered himself as
mediator, but now with a caveat. He would only lend his prestige and
good offices if Spain immediately revoked *reconcentración* and offered "the Cubans full self-government." If Spain and the rebels together asked for his intercession with a peace treaty, "the President
might undertake such office of friendship."[102]

Woodford was instructed to present three general conditions for a
presidential intercession: an armistice until October 1, through the
rainy season, during which time President McKinley would attempt
to mediate a final peace; an immediate repeal of *reconcentración;*
and finally, penned as an aside for Woodford, to "Add, if possible,"
the half-masked ultimatum that if terms of peace were not settled by
October 1, the president would presume upon himself the role of
"final arbiter" between Spain and the Cuban rebels. "Prompt action" by Spain on these demands was most "desirable."[103]

This was a lot for Woodford to digest, and extremely ambiguous
besides. Did "full self-government" really mean that, or would Spain
preserve a vestige of sovereignty? Woodford drafted a wire seeking
clarification.

Rufus Day's response was likely the most important communication from Washington to Madrid during the weeks of the final crisis.
Autonomy, he reiterated, had brought no peace. The United States
must support complete Cuban liberation from Spain or remove itself
from the equation, which, given the state of clamorous public opinion,
was impossible. Given that dilemma, and William McKinley's reluctant permission, Day advanced America's aim regarding Cuba, demanding that Spain surrender the island, now. "Full self-government,"
he answered, "would mean Cuban independence."[104]

Though unaware of the details, the American press knew that a
note of great consequence had been delivered to Spain. Calling it an

"unmistakable ultimatum," Hearst's papers forecast a message from the president to Congress "next week" asking for the power to intervene in Cuba. In Madrid, Captain Tasker Bliss, the American military attaché, had spent the last three days working practically nonstop enciphering and deciphering the cable traffic between the embassy and the State Department. Taking the pulse of Americans and Spaniards in the city, he wrote to his wife, "Today it is generally said that chances are 99 for war and 1 for peace."[105]

Monday, March 28, the day the *Maine* report was delivered to Congress, had been awaited with extraordinary anticipation. The president had not spoken out on the *Maine* issue, and the public scarcely had an idea of where the administration stood. There were no press conferences as such, and the president's communication to the people was largely limited to formal messages to Congress and staged oratory before friendly crowds. The president's opinion was usually garnered from surrogates, especially his congressional leaders. There had been no intimation of William McKinley's closely guarded belief regarding the *Maine*. As one biographer said, "[T]he war spirit had flowered in a void of Executive guidance."[106]

The American public and press had "confounded" the issues of Cuba and of the *Maine,* no matter how dearly the president wished to keep them separate. The crisis, ascending since the passage of the $50 million bill and now peaking with the imminent publication of the *Maine* report, demanded that President William McKinley speak, as his biographer said, "in the accents of authority"—in other words, to be a president, not just look like one. If McKinley wished to divide Cuba from the *Maine,* a politically brilliant stroke if he could accomplish it, he must face the Congress and people squarely and "sternly disown the unworthy impulse of revenge," declare his resolution to act on behalf of suffering Cuba, and publicly articulate the demands he had just presented to Spain. This was McKinley's last chance to risk everything on a bold assertion of his authority and leadership, and he flubbed it.[107]

On Sunday, he dictated the presidential letter to accompany the *Maine* report. He expected Spain to do the right thing; its honor, and "the sense of justice of the Spanish nation," decreed no less. The message ended with the president's assurance that he would advise Congress on the pace of the negotiations then carrying forth in Madrid. "In the meantime deliberate consideration is invoked."[108]

The nation reacted with a collective gasp of incredulity. A "deeply ominous silence," wrote the *New York Herald*. Here was nothing of firm purpose, nothing around which the president's congressional supporters could rally, no leadership for a country rapidly girding for war. It was the same oatmeal they had heard since inauguration day. The president, said an observer, had fallen victim to "his great political defect of silence." As William McKinley vainly sought to sever the *Maine* from Cuba, so the nation disconnected his pallid words from the report itself.[109]

Readers devoured the technical jargon as proof positive that Spain was guilty of premeditated slaughter. The country, outraged by calamity, surged to a height of united patriotism only seen on the eve of crusading wars. As the *New York Times* said, "It would have been as easy to end the War of the Revolution at Bunker Hill or the Civil War at Bull Run as to turn back now." The president's measured tone and reserved phrases of "deliberate consideration" acted precisely opposite to his intention. Future vice president Charles Dawes observed "great indignation among the more radical members." That night, McKinley's secretary, George Cortelyou, wrote "[T]he feeling in Congress today is not so good as it was."[110]

Actually it was worse than that. The congressional reaction was so uniformly negative that McKinley was intimidated into holding off his request for Cuban relief appropriations, fearing it would furnish a vehicle for war resolutions. The Democrats were again united, this time over immediate recognition of the "Cuban Republic," a concept endorsed by the populists and silverite Republicans, presenting a solid block against the administration's peace endeavors. Fifty House Republicans, caucusing under the label *"reconcentrados,"* protested Speaker Reed's procedural interference with the will of the majority and defiantly asserted the exclusive function of Congress to declare war. A delegation of "war" Republicans descended on the White House demanding an instant Cuba message. McKinley tried to fob them off with Woodford's plea for just a little more time. "I don't believe a word of it," sneered a particularly noisome legislator. "Wall Street doesn't want a war and you are doing their bidding." Shocked by the venom, the president did what he did best, put his hand over his heart and declaim platitudes, which in the context of the verbal stab was too true. "My whole life," he replied, "is an answer to that statement."[111]

On Tuesday, March 29, Woodford presented the semi-ultimatum to the Spanish government and muffed his assignment. Woodford, an amateur at high-level diplomacy, had thus far conducted himself admirably, and probably none could have done better, until now. In order to spare Spanish sensibilities, he never explicitly mentioned the words "full self-government" as one of President McKinley's nonnegotiable terms, and certainly not the clarification of that phrase that he had specifically asked for, and that Day had quickly supplied: "Full self-government . . . would mean independence."[112]

On receiving the American proposals, Sagasta and his cabinet agreed at once that *reconcentración* should be terminated forthwith. As policy it had been an unmitigated disaster, and Captain General Blanco had more than once pleaded with the government to eliminate the fortified camps, at the very least. On the other hand, the cabinet resolved never to accept American mediation or arbitration on Cuba. The bargaining point came down to granting an armistice to the rebels, and on this, the Spanish cabinet divided. Moret and the doves favored it; Gullón and the hawks were opposed. The army, represented by the war minister, was outraged at the suggestion that Spain make the offer herself. The cabinet resolved that Spain could not grant an armistice at the injunction of the United States, but it might gracefully accede to offer a truce at the behest of the rebels or the European powers in concert. And then, of course, they needed to delay the announcement for a few days, a tactical disaster as it turned out. Woodford was told he had to wait until the thirty-first to receive the cabinet's decision.

Had Judge Rufus Day not been nearly bald, he might have torn his hair over this; not over Woodford's lack of candor—he didn't know about that—but at the Spanish dawdling. They were incapable of understanding the white-hot, war-ready temper in the United States. Calming himself, he cabled Woodford that so long as the envoy had already agreed to the thirty-first, he should not go back on his word. But this was the end; the administration would suffer no more—to use Woodford's term—*mañanaism*. It was of the "utmost importance" to get Spain's answer then. Nothing, repeat nothing, would be delayed beyond that date. Woodford must grasp the gravity and convey to the Spanish "that a resolution for intervention may pass both [houses of Congress] in spite of any effort which can be made."[113]

On March 31, Woodford met with Sagasta and Gullón, Moret serving as interpreter. Spain would submit the entire question of the *Maine* to an international court of arbitration. On *reconcentración*, per the government's instructions, Captain General Blanco had lifted the *bando* in the four western provinces. (Actually, the day before, Blanco had entirely abrogated *reconcentración* throughout Cuba, authorizing the "country people . . . to return with their families to their homes, and to dedicate themselves to all kind of agricultural labors.") Further, the Spanish government appropriated 3 million pesetas to assist in the recovery of the *reconcentrados* and expressed its willingness to accept whatever additional aid the United States wished to offer. These were the simple items. On the trickier question of an armistice, Spain agreed to accept "at once" any suspension of hostilities offered by the rebels, which, given that war between Spain and the United States loomed as inevitable, the insurgents were not inclined to do. On "full self-government," it remained the old story, which Sagasta now finessed to support of the Cuban autonomy parliament, "without any lessening or diminishment of the powers reserved to Spain"; in other words, nothing changed.[114]

A telegraph had recently been installed in the White House, and Woodford's cable started clicking over the wires at 10:30 P.M. The president and his dinner guests, Day, Mark Hanna, Russell Alger, and Interior Secretary Cornelius Bliss, waited until well after midnight for the full text. Woodford found it difficult to accept the failure of his mission: "a sorrow to me," he said, "for I have worked hard for peace." It had all turned, he thought, on a question of "punctilio." Spanish pride would not permit them to propose or offer an armistice—it would bring on a revolution. Yet Woodford had been told this so many times that he at last understood Spain's methods. Always they claimed they had reached the final point of compromise, and always they inched forward another bit. Weeks ago they had denied a problem even existed with *reconcentración* and hinted at war if even a trace of responsibility for the *Maine* touched them. Now they had retreated completely on the first point and offered to place the other before an international tribunal.

But what Woodford and probably every other American diplomat or statesman failed to comprehend was that the loss of Cuba, or any part of the overseas empire, hinged on far more than "punctilio." It was an enduring part of Spanish mythology that the empire had been bestowed by God as a reward for the *reconquista,* the liberation of the Iberian Peninsula in 1492 from Islam. On a more terrestrial plane, no thinking Spaniard believed the fragile constitution, in place only since 1875, could survive the shock of losing Cuba without a fight. "The army is still the controlling factor in Spanish politics," Woodford explained, "and the attitude of the army constitutes the real danger today."[115]

In the most serious diplomatic-military crisis since the Civil War, the American nation looked to the president with varying emotions ranging from hope to disgust. Once holding the limelight for a brief moment at the passage of the $50 million bill, William McKinley was again irrelevant to the national agenda. "Mr. President," pleaded Vice President Garret Hobart, "I can no longer hold back the Senate. They will act without you if you do not act at once." In the House, the word "peace" was treated as a dirty epithet. When a former New York governor asked Speaker Reed if he could not do more to halt the bellicosity of the members, the Czar told a reporter, "He might as well ask me to stand out in the middle of a Kansas waste and dissuade a cyclone."[116]

William McKinley became a prisoner of his natural political passivity. Paralyzed with indecision, he found sleep impossible, and desperately needing it, took to his wife's medicine cabinet for patent narcotics. His haggard face sagged, eyes darkly circled. He jumped at unexpected noise. At least two intimates reported him crying at times. John D. Long confided to his journal, "He has been robbed of sleep, overworked; and I fancy that I can see his mind does not work as clearly and directly and as self-reliantly as it otherwise would."[117]

In Rome, on Saturday, April 2, Spanish ambassador Merry del Val received a discreet approach from Cardinal Rampolla, Vatican secretary of state. Accounts from Washington reported conditions as "very grave," with President McKinley apparently "helpless" against the will of Congress for war. As Rampolla saw it, the difficulty lay "in who should ask for a suspension of hostilities." From his Washington correspondent, the cardinal had the impression McKinley was well disposed to accept the intercession of the Holy See. But before he undertook any mission, Pope Leo XIII needed Spain's assurance that such an armistice was "acceptable to the national honor."[118]

When Stewart Woodford was confidentially, and falsely, informed by Gullón that the Vatican had responded to "a suggestion of the President," he experienced a surge of renewed hope. Spain, Gullón whispered, would accept papal mediation if the United States first agreed to withdraw its menacing concentration of naval forces from Key West once the rebels were granted an armistice. Spain, the foreign minister said, was ready to accede because the pope's motives were "not political but humane." But before the cabinet accepted, Gullón needed an immediate answer regarding the American ships. Woodford cabled the information to the president: "If conditions at Washington still enable you to give me the necessary time," he was certain that before October, "I will get peace in Cuba."[119]

Woodford's cable brought a collective knitting of brows in the White House and State Department. Papal intercession; what was he talking about? This could not be allowed to proceed further. Given Protestant America's views of a pope-ridden Spain, this could easily bring the administration some acute and wholly unnecessary embarrassment. "The President," Day shot back, "has made no suggestions to Spain except through you." As for the armistice, what Spain offered "is simply an invitation to the insurgents to submit." If Spain was reconsidering its position, it must be so stated immediately *and* be accepted by the rebels, or else no deal. Regarding the navy, "the disposition of our fleet must be left to us." Though Woodford was doing a more than passable job in his unenviable position, Rufus Day showed increasing exasperation, demanding to know, "Would the peace you are so confident of securing mean the independence of Cuba?" Day, Woodford, everyone knew in their heart it would not. Events were unstoppable. "The President," Day ended, "cannot hold his message longer than Tuesday."[120]

William McKinley was not a blameless innocent in the papal misunderstanding. He had conducted several conversations with the influential Archbishop John Ireland of St. Paul, Minnesota. The prelate was now in Washington in an unofficial Vatican diplomatic capacity, and the president knew this. McKinley not only informed Ireland of the conditions Spain must meet in Cuba, but actually said he would be glad of any help the Vatican might offer. He could not, of course, say any of this publicly. Thus when Cardinal Rampolla uttered the phrase "at the suggestion of the President," there was more than a grain of truth to it.

On Monday, April 4, Archbishop Ireland paid a visit to the Spanish embassy for a meeting with the new minister, Luis Polo de Bernabé. Ireland, better than the Spanish diplomat, or for that matter the Spanish foreign ministry, grasped that unless Spain bit the bullet and exited Cuba with the best negotiated conditions, she would end up with nothing. He pleaded with Polo to urge his government to declare the armistice now. If the insurgents refused to reciprocate, so what? Let them for once assume the responsibility for perpetuating Cuban misery. The minister refused. Spain, he told the archbishop, had already given away all that was "compatible with national dignity."[121]

In the midst of the scurrying, hole-and-corner diplomacy, William McKinley composed his long-awaited Cuba message to be delivered to Congress. Vaguely, the president asked for only a simple congressional resolution, "to take measures to secure a full and final termination of hostilities between the Government of Spain and the people of Cuba," i.e., authority to intervene militarily to bring the desired peace. He would advise Congress not to recognize the existing rebel "government," proposing instead an eventually independent country that the United States would welcome at a future date into the family of nations.[122]

That evening, McKinley presented the draft document to a cabinet meeting, indicating he would pass it to Congress on Wednesday. "I suppose," mused John D. Long, "it is the best he can do." Earlier that day, Long had ordered Captain Sampson at Key West to take possession of the telegraph office, placing a "discreet and judicious" officer in charge, permitting no transmission to Cuba of any message relating to the actions of the president or Congress.[123]

On Tuesday evening McKinley sent for his most trusted advisers: Day, Long, Attorney General John W. Griggs, and Cornelius Bliss of Interior. A telegram had just come in from Woodford suggesting "a possible new phase" in the rush to arms. Spain had blinked, maybe. Citing the pope's interest in a peaceful solution and the coming of Passion Week, the queen regent, Woodford reported, had proclaimed an "immediate and unconditional suspension" of hostilities in Cuba. It would take effect as soon as the rebels accepted and would continue for six months. "I dare not reject this last chance for peace," Woodford wrote. McKinley, however, did. Though he "highly" appreciated the queen regent's desire for peace, he could no longer dally in his constitutional duties of transmitting to Congress the entire matter of dealing with Cuba that had been festering on the executive desk, his and Cleveland's, for over three years. If Spain were truly offering an armistice, well and good—he would communicate the fact in his congressional message to be delivered in the morning, and no more.[124]

On Wednesday morning, at an earlier hour than was usual for the conduct of high-level diplomacy, a little morality play unfolded in a small White House ceremony. The legates of the European powers—Great Britain, Germany, France, Russia, Austria-Hungary, and Italy—in cutaway Prince Albert coats and striped trousers presented themselves before the president. In and of itself this was a historic occasion, it being traditional for the American president and secretary of state never to receive representatives from a combination of European states acting in concert.

This time, however, William McKinley graciously heard them; they had come, after all, on a mission of peace. Yet everyone present knew the play was performed for the historical record, and nothing else. Lord Pauncefote, the British envoy and senior member of the cast, read aloud the note that had previously been vetted by Judge Rufus Day. It was "a pressing plea to the feelings of humanity and moderation of the President and of the American people" that further negotiations would lead to peace and a final settlement "for the re-establishment of order in Cuba." McKinley answered with a formal statement expressing identical hopes, but voiced America's exasperation with the "indefinite . . . insufferable" morass. The gentlemen were ushered out with polite bows and the honeyed thanks of the president and his senile secretary of state, John Sherman, summoned for one of his last public duties.[125]

In midmorning there was another delay. Word came from Fitzhugh Lee in Havana that if the address suggested "the possibility of war," American lives there were definitely in danger. He begged it be delayed until Monday, April 11. Long, who was at the White House, understood the dilemma, noting, "In this extremity it is always a matter of shying between Scylla and Charybdis. The country is so clamorous for action that the President cannot delay longer." Waiting for the message were Congress assembled in joint session and over ten thousand spectators, jamming the galleries, corridors, and streets around the Capitol.

It showed a degree of courage for the president to summon a congressional delegation to explain yet another delay, this time to evacuate Americans from Cuba. Although the legislators understood, the delegation assumed, as one of William McKinley's biographers said, "an attitude toward the Executive scarcely less menacing and peremptory than its defiance of Spain." Extremely angry, McKinley called for George Cortelyou and handed him the presidential Cuba address, ordering him to "put that in the safe until I call for it." His historic faith in the public's opinion, in the complete willingness of Americans to do the right thing, had been shattered. "The people," he sighed, "must not be unreasonable." In the evening, John D. Long wrote of "the intense excitement" in the House and Senate, "who in their turn, are violently pressed by their constituents for some positive action. Just what action, nobody seems to know."[126]

On Friday and Saturday, the eighth and ninth of April, the representatives of the European powers in Madrid pushed the Spanish hard, not only to steer a general course for Cuban pacification, but to accept the specific conditions demanded by the United States. Though a ministerial crisis threatened to bring down the government, the Sagasta cabinet authorized Captain General Blanco to grant an immediate armistice, with or without the rebels' agreement. Woodford jubilantly telegraphed President McKinley that peace was now truly at hand.

The president had first gotten the news from Archbishop Ireland, and for one small moment he believed that he had really pulled it off. But the crash of reality came very quickly, and it was the same story, soon revealed by Minister Polo de Bernabé. Spain had actually not granted anything, but had merely given Blanco the authority to implement a truce if conditions permitted. It was all a meaningless gesture, meant to placate Europe and garner diplomatic support, to buy time to bolster the army's defenses in Cuba against an external foe, and to augment the fleet with warships desperately repairing in French shipyards. The false concession availed Spain nothing.

Then on Sunday, April 10, Spain played a last card, too late. She now was forced to act in humiliation, where only weeks ago, she could have taken exactly the same steps from a position of relative strength. Captain General Blanco proclaimed an unconditional armistice in Cuba! Polo de Bernabé rushed to the State Department to inform Rufus Day, declaring "in each locality hostilities are declared to be suspended in the territory of the island of Cuba." But when Day asked whether Spain would surrender to the United States on the ultimate question regarding Cuban sovereignty, the Spanish diplomat had no choice but to utter a stiff "No."[127]

The president was privy to the armistice information as well, coming directly from Woodford in a personal letter that concluded, "I hope nothing will now be done to humiliate Spain." The Spanish government, Woodford continued hopefully, "is loyally going to go as fast as it can and as far as it can." McKinley summoned his senatorial allies, and together with the cabinet, the men agreed that Spain's last efforts had come too little and too late. The president would tag the information to the end of the Cuba message, but that was all. The lack of American diplomatic and political leadership had come full circle to impasse. It was not for lack of trying, but of imagination. They had allowed themselves to be jerked around for three years by masters of the diplomatic game. Cleveland, Olney, McKinley, Sherman, Day, and Woodford were neither stupid nor feckless men, but they entirely lacked global imagination. A more mature Theodore Roosevelt might have accomplished the desired end. But no one in his right mind would have trusted TR to conduct sensitive diplomacy in 1898.[128]

On Monday morning, April 11, the cabinet gathered informally "at the President's" to find McKinley putting the final touches to the Cuba message. Listening to the document read through, John D. Long hoped against his expectations to hear the utterance of a "satisfactory termination" of the Cuba problem "without armed intervention on our part." Rather, he heard only a surrender of initiative, a shift of "excitement and tension" from the White House to the Congress. Of the president's whole statement, Long had "a little feeling that its conclusion was somewhat indefinite and hardly a sequitur from the argument which precedes it."[129]

William McKinley's "war message," as befitted the man and the magnitude of the issue, was a long one, seven thousand words, read by a relay of clerks from the well of the House of Representatives. For once, according to Henry Cabot Lodge, the Congress listened "with intense interest and profound silence." To those who expected more, either of peace or of war, there was disappointment. Reviewed instead was the whole history of American-Spanish negotiations, culminating in Spain's unsatisfactory response to the ultimatum of "full self-government" for Cuba. With the spurning of this "last overture" for a pacific solution, President William McKinley abdicated the authority of his office; "the Executive," droned the clerk, "is brought to the end of his effort."[130]

Quoting from Ulysses S. Grant, Grover Cleveland, and his own 1897 annual message, McKinley asserted that "in the name of humanity, and in the name of civilization, in behalf of endangered American interests which give us the right and the duty to speak and to act, the war in Cuba must stop." A standing wave of applause swept through the House chamber. Then came the peroration. He asked Congress to "authorize and empower" him to take whatever measures necessary "to secure a full and final termination of hostilities" between Spain and the "people of Cuba," the authority to establish a stable Cuban government, and "to use the military and naval forces of the United States as may be necessary for these purposes."[131]

This was the original end of the address. As an afterthought, McKinley inserted two small paragraphs concerning the Spanish armistice, which he hoped would receive the same deliberate attention the Congress paid to all other points. If the "suspension of hostilities" offered by Spain achieved results, then good; if not, it only served as further "justification for our contemplated aims."[132]

Was it a war message or not? The ambiguity detected by John D. Long was evident in the implicit possibility of yet more negotiations. The nonrecognition of Cuban independence assured a hot congressional debate for many days, and might work in the president's favor, giving time for yet another last-minute Spanish concession. Also, significantly, President McKinley did not ask Congress to declare war. Far from it—he only asked only for the large discretionary powers to use the armed forces of the United States in his constitutional capacity as commander in chief.

Reaction to the message was predictably mixed. According to the *Washington Star*, Democrats generally thought it "a great disappointment to the American people." Republican Joseph Foraker of Ohio, a leading Senate war hawk, told the paper he "had no patience with the message, and you can say so." Hearst's sheets pronounced that the president had "profoundly disappointed the American people; instead of a call to arms," he had "sounded a summons to retreat."

Pulitzer's *World* severely condemned McKinley's failure to emphasize the *Maine* or to demand Cuban independence: "The real grounds for intervention are . . . because Spain murdered our sailors and insulted our flag." It characterized the president as personifying "quibbling, straddling, humbug and hypocrisy." Theodore Roosevelt was struck by the president's intentional omission of recognizing the Cuban insurgent government, and asked Senator Lodge to push for it. "Otherwise we shall have more delay and more shilly-shallying."[133]

Conversely, the consistently anti-interventionist New York *Evening Post* thought the president had "confounded his blood-thirsty followers." The proadministration *New York Tribune* did not agree with John D. Long that the speech was a non sequitur, instead discovering a message "logical and consistent." The *Journal of Commerce* was quite happy "Congressional belligerents" had not "bullied the President into proposing the recognition of the Cuban Republic," and "did not close the door to hope" for peace without war. Further, it actually claimed to understand "a perfectly clear and definite national policy of neutral intervention," as if it were somehow different from a war.[134]

In Madrid, Barcelona, and Valencia, incited by provocateurs as diverse as Weyler's partisans, Carlist pretenders to the throne, and antimonarchist republicans, sullen crowds took to the streets. The military press called loudly for war with America, as did even responsible Madrid dailies. The official attitude of Sagasta's government was resolute denunciation of McKinley's message and a promise of no retreat. The only sane voice, it seemed, belonged to aged, feeble Marshal Arsenio Martínez Campos, who offered to form a coalition government to maintain the peace *and* Cuba. Instead, Spain insisted on a course that resulted in war and nothing.

The initiative was now firmly with Congress. On April 13, House Democrats offered a resolution recognizing the "Cuban Republic," a move defeated by a forty-vote Republican majority. Under Reed's guidance, it then overwhelmingly passed a resolution endorsing McKinley's message, authorizing intervention in Cuba to end the war and install a stable, native government. To that end, the armed forces were placed at the president's disposal.

The Senate was even more belligerent. The Foreign Relations Committee reported a resolution demanding Spanish withdrawal from

Cuba and promising the island eventual independence. This was acceptable to the administration until "Fire Alarm Joe" Foraker inserted an amendment recognizing the Cuban republic "as the true and lawful government of that island." The amendment passed with bipartisan support and was inserted into the resolution. Proponents argued that it was the only way to prevent the president scheming to avoid war in order to shield the holders of $500 million in Spanish bonds. On April 16, the full Senate voted to accept the amendment and one other in its resolution.

Senator Henry Teller of Colorado, the most decent of men, a liberal Republican turned Democrat, antijingoist to the core, kept America honest. Lest its policy stray from the stated position of ultimate independence for Cuba, Teller thought it best to insert "That the United States hereby disclaims any disposition or intention to exercise sovereignty, jurisdiction, or control over said island" except in the course of bringing it peace, "and asserts its determination, when that is accomplished, to leave the government and control of the island to its people." No one had the courage to oppose this, and the final Senate resolution passed 67–21, with both the Foraker and Teller amendments intact.[135]

The House vote on what would become a joint resolution of Congress was scheduled for Monday, April 18, and administration spokesmen told reporters the president might exercise a veto if it came with Foraker's clause, but hinted that once fighting actually started between the United States and Spain, recognition of a Cuban republic might indeed be feasible.

The House of Representatives had to deal with its own version of the Foraker language, that of Democrat David Turpie of Indiana. The primary purpose of the radical Republicans and their Democratic collaborators was not merely to secure independence. Recognition of a Cuban republic was meant to bind William McKinley to a course in which there could be no negotiations. Spain, they knew, would refuse to sit at the same table where Cuba was given official recognition. Their purpose was nothing less than the expulsion of Spain from the Western Hemisphere.

On Monday morning the House voted 178–156 to adopt the administration's principles in the joint resolution. The Senate held out until the afternoon, when it bowed to the threat of a presidential veto, voting to strike the Foraker amendment and simply demand Spain's immediate withdrawal from Cuba. Proponents of recognition accepted the partial victory, William E. Chandler of New Hampshire saying, "[H]aving accomplished our object [intervention], we did not think it was wise to go further and delay proceedings and thus play into the hands of the peace men by continuing to insist upon specific recognition."[136]

The next day, April 19, the joint resolution passed the Senate by 7 votes, and the House by 311–6. For William McKinley it was a significant political achievement, reasserting presidential primacy in foreign affairs at a time when a raging Congress and inflamed public opinion dictated the opposite. The defeat of the Foraker and Turpie riders introduced a degree of reconciliation into the final draft of the joint resolution. Citing the "abhorrent conditions" existing in Cuba that constituted a "disgrace to civilization," and whose circumstances culminated in the destruction of the *Maine,* and stating that these conditions "can no longer be endured," the legislators resolved, first, that "the people of the island of Cuba are, and of right ought to be, free and independent." Second, the United States demanded that Spain "at once" renounce its authority and government of Cuba, and withdraw its armed forces from the island. Third, the President of the United States was "directed and empowered" to employ the nation's "entire land and naval forces" and to summon the "militia of the several states" to carry out the resolutions. Fourth and finally came the language of the Teller amendment abjuring any American motive to absorb or annex Cuba to itself.[137]

In Madrid, the Sagasta government considered even official notification of the joint resolution a supreme insult and did everything in its power to avoid receiving it in either Washington or Madrid. Polo de Bernabé got instructions to request his passports the instant President McKinley signed the document. Gullón telegraphed the Spanish embassies in Europe denouncing the decree, "which in denying Spanish sovereignty and threatening armed intervention in Cuba, is equivalent to a declaration of war."[138]

"An unusually busy morning," wrote John D. Long on Wednesday, April 20. A large number of senators and representatives had called at the Navy Department, among whom were a party of Pennsylvanians urging the secretary to adopt Pennsylvania anthracite coal instead of its usual West Virginia bituminous. "It is interesting," he noted, "how every section of the country . . . has an eye on the main chance."[139]

At 11:24 A.M. in the cabinet room of the White House, President McKinley put his name to the joint resolution. Simultaneously, an ultimatum, a real one this time, was prepared and telegraphed to Woodford in Madrid, and also delivered to Polo de Bernabé for transmittal to the Spanish government: "If, by the hour of noon on Saturday . . . the 23rd day of April, instant," Spain had not communicated "a full and satisfactory response" to the demand to quit Cuba as manifested in the joint resolution, the president would "proceed without further notice" to employ the army and navy of the United States "to such extent as may be necessary to carry the same into effect." When Polo de Bernabé read the note he informed Secretary of State Sherman that his continuation in Washington had become impossible. Once McKinley's signature appeared on the joint resolution it was war, and he asked for his passports. "I leave tonight for Canada," he wired the foreign ministry.[140]

In the late afternoon, accompanied by Rear Admiral Sicard and Captain Crowninshield, Long walked across Seventeenth Street to the White House. Secretary of War Russell Alger and General Nelson Miles, the army's commanding general, were already there. It put Long in mind of what must have been similar scenes in the first days of the Civil War, thirty-seven years ago, "when President Lincoln was surrounded by military advisors who were all at sixes and sevens. . . . At any event the burden is likely to fall upon the navy." Returning to the department, Long knew that Admiral Sicard, only just recovering from another bout of chronic malaria, was in no condition to undertake the premier wartime command. He transferred Sicard to the war board, and in his stead appointed Captain William Sampson of the battleship *Iowa* to the rank of acting rear admiral and command of the North Atlantic Squadron, a move that met with universal approval in the service. At the end of the day, Long telegraphed Sampson at Key West "to move at once to Blockade Cuba, which, of course, is the beginning of the war."[141]

In Madrid, the queen regent and government quickly reconciled themselves to war with the United States. Moret, though he did not dissent, thought it still possible for Blanco and the Cuban rebels to agree on at least some innocuous terms and for McKinley to advocate "extended autonomy," whatever that meant. The cabinet tally for war, however, was unanimous, and the queen regent ratified the vote, agreeing to summon the Cortes into special session and place Spain on a full war footing. At the meeting's adjournment, Moret cabled to Blanco in Havana, "Consider war as declared. Hostilities will begin immediately."[142]

Woodford received notice of the joint resolution in a wire from Sherman at 2:30 A.M. on the morning of April 21, and the text itself, in plain language, one hour later. At 7:30, he was notified by Gullón of his "painful duty" to transmit that Spain had severed diplomatic relations with the United States upon the president signing the joint resolution. Further, Spain refused to receive the resolution's follow-up ultimatum, "which would constitute a fresh offense." Woodford understood, limiting his intercourse to asking for his passports and making arrangements for himself and the embassy to leave Madrid on the afternoon express for Paris. Woodford telegraphed all American consular offices in Spain to inform them of the break in relations and turned the embassy, United States interests, and the safety of its citizens in Spain over to Great Britain. "I then removed the United States seal from the front of the legation offices," he reported.[143]

Woodford and the legation staff boarded the 4 P.M. Paris express. As the train passed northward out of Madrid, a mob threw stones. Tasker Bliss observed the minister, dejected by the ultimate failure of his commission, "in a very abbreviated undershirt, six-shooter cocked in hand, his mustache bristling, prepared to fight the whole Spanish army."[144]

On April 22, in Washington, William McKinley, pursuant to the authority granted him in the joint resolution to employ the armed forces, declared a blockade of the north coast of Cuba, on either side of Havana, from Bahía Honda to Cárdenas, a distance of 125 miles, and of the port of Cienfuegos on the south coast. The following day, in accord with congressional action empowering the president "to raise a volunteer army," McKinley issued a call for 125,000 men for two years' service, "unless sooner discharged," to fight the war.[145]

On April 25, a rainy Monday, McKinley met with the cabinet to discuss his congressional message requesting an actual declaration of war. Secretary of State John Sherman, senile, isolated from the decision making, and totally opposed to the conflict, submitted his resignation. John D. Long thought it "rather a sad termination of one of the most useful careers of American statesmen."[146]

Long had another resignation on his mind, and instead of melancholy, this one stoked his anger. Assistant Secretary of the Navy Theodore Roosevelt had determined to quit, "in order to go into the army and take part in the war." Long thought it juvenile foolishness. TR had been of enormous use to the secretary and the department, "a man of unbounded energy and force. He has lost his head to the unutterable folly of deserting his post where he is of the most service and running off to ride a horse, and brush mosquitoes from his neck on the Florida sands. And yet," Long quite knew, with an eye to destiny, "how absurd this will all sound, if by some turn of fortune he should accomplish some great thing and strike a very high mark!"[147]

The communication requesting a formal declaration of war that William McKinley sent to Congress on April 25 enumerated a short sequence of cause and response. Spain, rejecting "the reasonable demands of this Government as measures of hostility," had refused to receive the joint resolution, and instead severed diplomatic relations. These actions, McKinley said, demonstrated on their face "an existent state of war." Wasting not an hour, Congress moved to apply the legal boilerplate: "That war be, and the same is hereby declared to exist, and that war has existed since the 21st day of April AD, 1898, including said day, between the United States of America and the Kingdom of Spain."[148]

The same day, on the other side of the world, the U.S. Revenue cutter *McCulloch* sped out of Hong Kong for Mirs Bay, up the coast. Her captain held a telegram from Secretary Long to Commodore Dewey: "War has commenced between the United States and Spain. Proceed at once to Philippine Islands."[149]

CHAPTER 5

MANILA BAY

Here, in the shallow waters of the bays thus formed, could be
seen, drawn up in line, the fleet of Spain.
—*Commander Asa Walker, USS* Concord,
May 1, 1898

At 5:15 I made signal that our squadron open fire. The enemy
answered immediately.
—*Rear Admiral Patricio Montojo y Pasaron,*
May 1, 1898

On December 31, 1897, the steamer *Gaelic* of the Pacific Mail line
stood into the harbor of Nagasaki, Japan. Commodore George
Dewey was aboard, eager to take up his duties as commander of the
Asiatic Squadron. The next morning he boarded his flagship, the protected cruiser *Olympia,* handsomely outfitted in her peacetime white
and buff. The four 8-inch guns in turrets fore and aft, ten 5-inch quick
firers, and a top speed of over twenty-one knots attested to her ranking as the best of her type.

Rear Admiral McNair met Dewey at the gangway, and the two flag
officers spent the weekend transferring squadron records and discussing station business. On Monday morning, January 3, 1898, the formal change of command took place on the *Olympia*'s quarterdeck. At
two bells in the forenoon watch, 9 A.M., the crew mustered aft in their
dress blue uniforms, officers in their universal anachronism of naval
regalia: cocked hats, frock coats, and golden-knotted swords. Admiral

McNair, his flag lieutenant, flag secretary, and aide marched aft and faced the flag. Commodore Dewey and his personal staff appeared on deck a moment later. At the port rail, six side boys and the full marine guard snapped to attention at the order of the ship's skipper, Captain Charles V. Gridley. Marine drummers beat two ruffles, and the band crashed into the "Admiral's March."

McNair spoke briefly, turned to his successor, proudly informed him of the first-class state of the ships and men, and gave his last command to haul down the blue, two-starred rear admiral's flag. Commodore Dewey stepped up and stiffly saluted. He put on reading glasses, took his mandate from the secretary of the navy out of his breast pocket, and spoke the sentences to the assembled company. Dewey turned to Captain Gridley and pronounced his first order. The broad blue pennant with the single star rose to the peak. The saluting gun commenced firing, eleven guns for a commodore—the new commander in chief of the Asiatic Squadron.

The little squadron, not yet reinforced for the developing crisis with Spain, was scattered all over the station. The cruiser *Boston*, one of the original "ABCD" quartet of the new navy, watched events at Chemulpo (Inchon), Korea, monitoring the explosion of Russian and Japanese conflicts in the hermit kingdom. The gunboat *Petrel*, called the "baby battleship" on account of her heavy armament of four 6-inch guns, was due at Canton (Guangzhou) for the Chinese New Year celebrations, where potentially dangerous antiforeign demonstrations were expected. The ancient side-wheeler *Monocacy*, built during the Civil War and still armed with old muzzle-loaders, patrolled the lower Yangtze River at Shanghai.

"Things look decidedly squally out here," wrote Dewey to his son a day after taking command; "I should not be surprised to see a general war at any time." The powers, East and West, were carving up the prostrate body of defenseless imperial China. Great Britain, Germany, Russia, France, and Japan had scooped out large chunks for naval bases, railroads, mining concessions, and trading zones, eyeing one another with the deadly suspicion of thieves splitting the loot.[1]

For the United States, however, the threat of war in Asia had nothing to do with dismembering the Chinese colossus, but with delivering a quick jab to the Spanish empire in the Philippines. Dewey well understood he had been selected for that singular purpose, and it was never far from his thoughts. When still in Washington at the Board of Inspection and Survey, Dewey had been anxious over the ammunition stocks of his new command, which were below even peacetime requirements. The next allotment wouldn't arrive out on the station for six months. With Roosevelt's assistance, Dewey convinced Secretary Long and the Bureau of Ordnance to ship a first allotment, thirty-five tons, in the gunboat *Concord,* scheduled to join the force in February; the remainder would wait until the cruiser *Baltimore* came out in the spring as the relieving flagship.

On January 28, the nagging ammunition deficiency critically escalated on Dewey's receipt of the departmental order to retain enlisted men whose time of service was about to expire. It could only mean that relations with Spain had taken a dangerously new turn. The *Concord* arrived at Yokohama inside of two weeks, then turned for Chemulpo to spell the *Boston.* Dewey, his magazines more comfortably full, decided to head south for Hong Kong, a much better place to begin any operations against the Philippines.

He was at sea in the *Olympia* when the *Maine* blew up, and did not learn of it until anchoring in port on February 17. Although the telegram from Secretary Long stated the explosion had been "by accident," Dewey knew that in the poisoned climate of American-Spanish relations it did not matter. Before the sun set, he dispatched a wire to the U.S. consul general in Manila, Oscar Williams, requesting timely intelligence on Spanish warships in Manila Bay and on "what . . . changes there have been in the land defenses of that port in recent years."[2]

On February 26, the *Olympia* and *Petrel* anchored with their colors half-masted, in mourning for the dead of the *Maine.* That fateful day of Secretary Long's "afternoon off," Dewey received the concentration order from Acting Secretary Roosevelt: "Order the squadron except *Monocacy* to Hong Kong. Keep full of coal. In event of declaration of war, Spain, your duty will be to see that the Spanish Squadron does not leave the Asiatic Coast and then offensive operations in Philippine Islands. Keep *Olympia* until further orders." Dewey cabled to the ships at Chemulpo to expedite the ammunition transfer and join the flat at once. Dewey placed the ancient *Monocacy* into reduced commission at Shanghai, most of her officers and seamen making up personnel deficiencies in the squadron. Shortly, the fast, heavily gunned cruiser *Raleigh* came through Suez from the European Squadron as reinforcement.[3]

For the next six weeks Dewey kept the command fully occupied with overhauls, engineering repairs, and drills. He took pains to keep his captains abreast of the latest developments in diplomacy and the fact that war could be declared at any moment, and impressed on all the necessity of keeping their provision larders and coal bunkers full. Commander Asa Walker, skipper of the *Concord,* scanned the wires from the Navy Department, "indicating from day to day a closer approach to the border line between peace and war."[4]

Beginning in early March, Dewey initiated a regular correspondence with Oscar Williams, the resourceful U.S. consul general in Manila. At his post only a month, and lacking the military experience of Fitz Lee at Havana, Williams proved a most useful conduit of hard intelligence. Optimistically, he reported that "any two U.S. ships could enter the port, silence the forts and capture the city." The forts of Manila proper, he noted, were "too antiquated to merit consideration in modern war." Those works defending the harbor entrance were another matter and were fitted with several up-to-date guns taken from warships under repair. The Spanish squadron he reported as well provisioned, with full crews. Of extreme importance to Dewey was Williams's assurance, for the most part correct, that Manila's seaward approaches, "the bay and its channels," had not been mined, because the insulated arming wires hadn't yet arrived from Spain. To camouflage the reports from Spanish prying, the transactions were disguised as personal letters between Williams and Ensign Harry Caldwell, Dewey's flag secretary. "Two or more spies watch me constantly," the consul wrote in midmonth, "and my clerk is the son of a Spanish colonel." Williams was certain that duplicate keys to the consulate and its safe were "in the possession of persons who have no right to them."[5]

Politically, the Philippines, like Cuba, was in the throes of rebellion, though somewhat more contained by the authorities. Still, Spanish assertions of putting it down were equally groundless. "Pacification here," Williams noted, "is a foolish unfounded claim. The rebels are stronger than ever and as domestic clouds darken in Spain they have more confidence." An insurgent republic had been proclaimed, and armed rebels drilled on the main island of Luzon, as well as on the islands of Cebu and Panay. "All agree," Williams advised the State Department, "that a general uprising will come as soon as the present governor-general embarks for Spain." The consul thought that once the Spanish naval forces had been knocked out, the United States could "annex the islands before next Sunday."[6]

Since being discovered by Magellan almost four centuries before, the Philippine Islands had been governed by that peculiarly Spanish combination of brutality, beneficence, and ineptitude. Until 1821, the Philippines had been administered not from Spain, but from Mexico as an appendage of a colony, maintaining maritime and economic ties to Spain's possessions in Central and South America. Once these broke away from the mother country in the early nineteenth century, the Philippines languished at the farthest end of Spain's diminished world empire. It had suffered the most rampant exploitation of land and resources by the Catholic Church's monastic orders, and virtual slavery of the overwhelmingly rural population. The Philippines had not even Cuba's meager representation in the Cortes, and the population was considered little more than animals. Rebellion was put down by the harshest measures, the public firing squad in the town square and that particularly disgusting Spanish appliance, the garrote, being the common responses.

Oddly or not, it was not against Spain per se that the Filipinos periodically revolted, but against the Catholic Church and its mendicant orders. "*Viva España! Abajo los frailes!*" ("Long live Spain! Down with the friars!") was the common cry. By the nineteenth century, the monkish orders owned nearly half a million acres of the best land in the northern islands of the archipelago and a lot of commercial property in the heart of Manila. They rented fields to natives as sharecropped land, and the monks took actual control of the villages themselves, levying taxes and acting in all respects as the civil government. Locals were pressed into building roads, churches, and convents much as if they were slaves, which for all intents they were.

The catalyst of the latest revolt against Spanish rule was the prodigious Dr. José Rizal—poet, philosopher, physician, artist, and a man widely traveled throughout Europe. Of milder revolutionary tendencies than the Cuban José Martí, Rizal preached advancement through education and the economic development of the islands. In 1896, he was arrested, thrown into solitary confinement, and charged with treason. At his trial, evidence was fabricated and Rizal was sentenced to death by firing squad. The execution was a huge social event for the Spanish population of the city, who came out in all their finery for a breakfast party on the battlements. Crowds of native Filipinos also turned out, held at bay by Spanish artillery and bayonets. Driven in a tumbrel to the Luneta park fronting the ancient walls of Manila, Rizal was not allowed to face his executioners. By a supreme act of will, when the volley struck him in the back, he managed to twist his body and die facing the sun.

In the terror that followed the execution, two hundred rebel leaders were butchered, the result of an informant—the sister of a member of the *Katipunan* ("Patriots League")—who betrayed the revolution to a priest during her confession. Hundreds more were tortured by crushing of their bones or hanging by their thumbs—Spanish colonialism at its repulsive worst. The governor and captain general, Camilio Polavieja, stated that "for the traitors no punishment seems to me adequate and commensurate with the magnitude of the crime they committed against their king and country."[7]

By the end of 1896, the rebels in Cavite Province south of Manila numbered twenty thousand men, and perhaps ten thousand more on the rest of the main island of Luzon. Badly armed, if at all, having no uniforms and no training, they faced ten thousand Spanish regulars and native levies. Within weeks, most of Luzon was a battleground, with members of the Catholic religious orders being the particular objects of the rebels. When caught, they were literally cut to pieces, boiled in oil, roasted over fires, or at the very least harnessed to farm carts and made to do the work of beasts in the fields. In their hundreds, the monks fled to Manila. On the battlefield, Spanish arms proved as futile as in Cuba. Battles "won" rarely amounted to victory, for the rebels merely scattered. Polavieja asked for reinforcements and was refused; none could be spared from the war in Cuba. When European newspapers in the region began to document the horrors of Spanish repression, Polavieja was finished, poor health being the official reason.

He was replaced by the more amenable Captain General Fernando Primo de Rivera, under orders to end the rebellion by arms or guile, but end it in any case. He brought with him twenty-six thousand more troops from the homeland.

In December 1897, General Primo de Rivera engineered the truce of Biyak-na-Bató, a hamlet north of Manila, with the leadership of the rebel "provisional government," which was headed by a charismatic street fighter, twenty-nine-year-old "President" Emilio Aguinaldo. In return for eight hundred thousand Mexican dollars and a promise of Spanish amelioration of the most egregious of its colonial offenses, the Philippine rebel leaders agreed to surrender their weapons and exile themselves out of the islands. In what should not have been a surprise, the Spanish reneged on the reforms, Primo de Rivera and his colleagues pocketing half the money; the rebel chiefs set to squabbling over the rest.

When the U.S. Asiatic Squadron began assembling at Hong Kong, Aguinaldo and his compatriots, who had taken up residence there, at once understood the possibilities of enlisting the United States in the cause of Philippine independence. Aguinaldo approached the Americans through Commander Edward Wood of the *Petrel,* though who initiated the contact is murky, as is much of the intercourse between United States authorities and the insurgent exiles. As Aguinaldo wrote, the Americans wished the rebel leaders to return to the islands to mobilize their forces for military operations against Spain. When Aguinaldo asked what the United States planned once the Spanish were driven out, Wood, according to the rebel, replied that America as "a great and rich nation . . . neither needs nor desires colonies." Aguinaldo suggested this be put in writing, and Wood declined, having no authority to enter into high matters of state. Dewey flatly refuted Aguinaldo's version of these meetings, telling a Senate committee, "They seemed to be all very young, earnest boys. I did not attach much importance to what they said or to themselves."[8]

When war was declared, Aguinaldo, then in Singapore, was contacted by U.S. Consul General E. Spencer Pratt. Through an interpreter, he entreated the rebel to ally himself with the United States, whose victory was not in doubt. Again Aguinaldo asked, "What can we expect to gain from helping America?" This time the reply bore the stamp of legitimacy. "America," said the consul, "will give you much greater liberty and much more material benefits than the Spaniards ever promised you." When Aguinaldo, who equated the statement as assuring independece, requested this, too, in writing, Pratt declined, explaining he lacked the official authority to propose policy or speak on behalf of the government. He did, though, have a bit of diplomatic ammunition to bolster the claim of America's non-involvement in the Philippines' future. "You need not worry about America," he said. The Teller amendment attached to the congressional joint resolution for America's military intervention in Cuba disclaimed any intent of permanent possession once the Spanish were driven away and the country pacified. "As in Cuba, so in the Philippines," Pratt is alleged to have said. These conversations, differently remembered by the participants, would have great consequences for the subsequent history of the Philippine Islands.[9]

Aguinaldo, so he claimed, agreed to the consul's proposal to fight, but only if Dewey tendered the invitation. Pratt cabled the commodore in Hong Kong, stating that Aguinaldo and the "insurgent leaders" desired to join the Americans in the fight. Dewey replied, "All right; tell him to come on." So far as Dewey was concerned, that was the end of it. He had far more important matters to tend to, "and I attached so little importance to Aguinaldo that I did not wait for him. He did not arrive, and we sailed . . . without any of the Filipinos, although I told these young men they could go if they wanted to. They did not go."[10]

From the day of receiving Assistant Secretary Roosevelt's order of February 25 to "Keep full of coal," Dewey, as a sensible commander, faced the "grave question" of coal, provisions, "and other necessaries for a squadron [seven thousand] miles distant from any home base." The moment war was declared, various national declarations of neutrality would severely prohibit the squadron's ability to obtain critically needed fuel. He had already contracted for the best ship's coal on the local market. In the first week of April, Dewey requested, and Long so authorized, permission to purchase a civilian collier and five thousand tons of coal, direct from England if necessary, and to commission the vessel as an armed U.S. naval auxiliary. The British collier *Nanshan*, with three thousand tons of good Welsh coal, had just come into harbor, and Dewey bought the ship and her cargo on the spot. Three days later he did the same with the freighter *Zafiro* and a small sailing collier, whose seven hundred tons of coal he loaded into the larger vessels along with ninety days' provisions. Dewey thought better than to commission them into the navy. Even with one or two light guns they would be useless in a fight, and worse, as naval vessels, they were subject to the neutrality laws. Instead, he registered the ships as American merchantmen, keeping their English crews, augmented for signaling and discipline with one junior officer and four men each from the *Monocacy*. Also reinforcing the squadron at this time was the U.S. Revenue Marine's armed cutter *McCulloch*, en route to the U.S. West Coast—a most useful addition it turned out.[11]

With the necessary supplies in hand, Dewey needed a place where, in time of war, he could stockpile his stores and have a base for repairs. Hong Kong was out of the question, because Great Britain, as Dewey noted, "would immediately be held accountable by Spain" for any laxity in enforcing neutrality laws in favor of the United States. Other European enclaves posed the same problem, but not so China. "Chinese neutrality," said Commander Asa Walker of the gunboat *Concord*, "was considered a vanishing quantity." Thus Dewey ordered the *Monocacy*'s skipper secretly to arrange for the use of Mirs Bay (Tai Pang Han), thirty miles up the coast from Hong Kong's New Territories, a place "independent of international complications."[12]

In the last fortnight leading up to war Dewey made every endeavor to calculate the strength of the Spanish squadron, an effort Commander Walker described as "at best, but partially successful." The American forces were indisputably superior in all respects, but Consul Williams notwithstanding, there was no really accurate intelligence regarding the defenses of Manila Bay, or its strategic key, Subic Bay just to the north. If the bay was well fortified with coastal guns and minefields, the Spanish could balance their long odds afloat by a substantial margin. For a time, masters of incoming merchant ships to Hong Kong related that on exiting Manila Bay, they had been forced to take pilots, "who steered courses quite different" from the usual ship channels, "giving the impression that they were pursuing tracks to avoid mine fields." According to Commodore Dewey, if the morale of the Asiatic Squadron had not been of the "highest standard," the scuttlebutt going around Hong Kong and in the press claiming the Spanish defenses had transformed the city and bay into something "quite impregnable" might have had an ill effect. In the Hong Kong Club it was not possible to get bets on American success even at heavy odds. Dewey attributed a remark to a British officer whose mess entertained the squadron at dinner as, "A fine set of fellows, but un-happily we shall never see them again."[13]

On April 19, in accord with measures taken throughout the navy, the squadron covered up its peacetime white and buff with the dull green-gray "war color." The following day in Washington and Madrid, diplomatic relations between the United States and Madrid were severed. In the early hours of Friday, the twenty-second, came the ominous cable from Secretary Long informing Dewey that while war had not been formally declared, peace remained the thinnest of protocols: "The naval force on the North Atlantic Station are blockading Cuba." The receipt of this message raised some fears regarding the safety of the *Baltimore,* expected to arrive any day. "It would have been a telling stroke of strategy," wrote Lieutenant John Ellicott, one of that ship's watch officers, "for the Spanish squadron in the Philippines to intercept this single cruiser in overwhelming numbers and capture or sink her with her invaluable munitions of war." She was especially vulnerable on the final leg of the passage, between Formosa and Hong Kong, but Ellicott and Commodore Dewey had no need to worry. The Spanish had neither the capability nor the offensive mindset to embark on such an audacious coup.[14]

On the afternoon of April 22 the *Baltimore* was spotted off Kowloon, and by evening had anchored safely in the harbor. In addition to the badly needed ammunition in her magazines, the ship carried Commander Benjamin P. Lamberton, slated as the new skipper of the *Boston.* But that cruiser's present commanding officer, the ailing Captain Frank Wildes, simply refused to give her up on the very eve of battle. Dewey keenly understood, and instead of causing unnecessary dissension and ill feeling among his officers, he appointed the luxuriantly whiskered, "sunny, hopeful" Lamberton as squadron chief of staff in the flagship. Dewey had already arranged docking facilities for the *Baltimore;* still, he had only forty-eight hours for the crew and dockyard hands to scrape the ship's bottom, fill her coal bunkers, and repaint the vessel gray.[15]

As war hourly grew nearer, Consul Williams in Manila, after ignoring three State Department warnings to quit his post, finally departed on receiving a "peremptory" request from Commodore Dewey. His position had indeed become dangerous, the Spanish authorities even notifying him they could no longer guarantee his safety from the mob or an assassin. All of Spanish Manila was, after its fashion, girding for war. The latest rumors, publicly proclaimed from all churches, indicated that the United States government was begging for papal intercession to rescue it from defeat by Spanish arms. On April 23, turning over the consulate and American affairs to his British counterpart, Williams boarded a commercial steamer for Hong Kong.

That day the government of Great Britain issued its proclamation of neutrality. In Hong Kong, the governor-general ordered Commodore Dewey to depart Her Majesty's waters with all his ships by 4 P.M. Monday, April 25. At the bottom of the document, he penned, "God knows, my dear Commodore, it breaks my heart to send you this notification." Giving himself as much time for preparation as possible, Dewey, on Sunday, sent his two colliers, with the *Boston, Concord, Petrel,* and *McCulloch,* to Mirs Bay, a movement mockingly interpreted by the Manila press as "hiding their flag," wasting coal and hoarding ammunition. Dewey needed to wait until the last moment for the *Baltimore* to complete her docking, and also for one of the *Raleigh*'s engine circulating pumps, under repair ashore, and the expected arrival of Consul Williams.[16]

By 9 A.M. on the next day, without Williams or the machinery, the *Olympia, Baltimore,* and the limping *Raleigh* formed column and stood out of harbor with their bands playing "The Star-Spangled Banner." British sailors climbed the rigging of their ships, and convalescing soldiers in the hospital hulk cheered the Americans out. Left behind as a communications link were the commodore's flag secretary, Ensign Harry Caldwell, and the chartered tug *Fame.*

At deserted Mirs Bay, the squadron took on ammunition from the *Baltimore,* the ships' crews exercised at the guns, and the command was placed on a war footing with double watches, battle shutters clamped over the air ports, and all external lights extinguished at night. The ships also began stripping large amounts of woodwork—spars, chests, hatch covers, anything that could splinter in battle—and stored the stuff aboard the colliers. Yet according to Lieutenant Carlos Calkins, the *Olympia*'s navigator, so much joinery remained in the ships that the sensible precaution "appeared suggestive rather than final."[17]

Shortly after noon at Hong Kong, two hours after Dewey had sailed for Mirs Bay, there arrived the anticipated message from Secretary

Long: "War has commenced between the United States and Spain. Proceed at once to Philippine Islands. Commence operations at once, particularly against the Spanish fleet. You must capture or destroy. Use
utmost endeavors." Caldwell leaped aboard the *Fame* and chugged
into Mirs Bay at 7 P.M. that evening. He found the commodore in his
cabin, seated at a green-felt-covered table, studying a chart of the
Philippines. "Here is a cable from the Secretary, sir," he reported, laying the envelope down. Naturally, Dewey would have preferred to
leave, if not immediately, then at least at first light. But he was constrained to wait on Consul Williams, who might bring last-minute intelligence, and for the *Raleigh*'s circulating pump, without which her
speed was cut nearly in half.[18]

Waiting, Commodore Dewey, his captains, and staff readied themselves mentally for the task quickly coming to hand. As to the Philippine Islands themselves, there was just not that much useful
information readily available. Dewey called the place "terra incog-
nita." Investigating the Navy Department files prior to leaving Washington, he found the most recent documentation dating from 1876.
Even on the Asiatic Station most of the gleaned details were anecdotal,
according to Lieutenant Calkins, "blending scientific fragments with
travelers' tales," and "vague" consular reports dealing chiefly with
commerce. While at Hong Kong, Dewey dispatched his aides to buy
every available chart of the "Eastern Archipelago" and its surrounding
seas. Calculating the known qualities of Spanish resources likely to be
deployed against the squadron, Dewey realized that no strong defensive
combination of enemy sea and coastal forces existed, or was likely to be
in place in the near future. A fair amount of study went into the volume
titled *Estadio General de la Armada,* the Spanish naval directory, which
not only classified the ships in the Philippines with their nominal armament and characteristics, but with "elaborate candor" documented the
service, accomplishments, and decorations "in every detail" of the
Spanish naval officers the squadron was about to confront. Significantly, wrote Lieutenant Calkins, Dewey and the squadron officers entered into no "minute comparisons" of enemy vessels or executive
personnel. That the Spanish maintained a greater total of theoretically
serviceable combatant ships (eleven to the Asiatic Squadron's seven,
counting the *McCulloch*), mounting nearly as many modern rifled guns
of 5-inch caliber and above (about fifty to the Americans' fifty-five),

and that these ships were further backed by supposedly powerful shore batteries ringing Manila Bay did not really count for much in the equation. Nor did popular opinions that conceded overmuch to claims of Spanish prestige and moral superiority. The material and professional rot that permeated the Spanish armed forces and empire after four hundred years ran deeper than even the most pessimistic of projections. "Our confidence" in victory, Calkins said, "was founded on national and personal qualities and convictions."[19]

The war cable from Secretary Long with its order to destroy the Spanish fleet was clear enough; the question remained, Where was it likely to be? Naval opinion generally credited the Spanish naval forces in the Philippine operational area with a small radius of action, incapable, Calkins said, of "enterprises overseas." They had, however, a dozen harbors within a day's steaming of their main arsenal and navy yard at Cavite in Manila Bay. But given the natural tendency of Spanish arms against dispersion, plus the fact that war with the United States could do nothing but revive and strengthen the Philippine rebellion in the environs of the colonial capital, the problem of locating the main body of enemy naval forces was easily solved, "and relieved our chief anxiety." It had to be in Manila Bay. Or more exactly and logically, in the "natural sortie harbor" for its operational defense, Subic Bay, thirty-five miles to the northwest, on the seaward shoulder of the Bataan Peninsula. A Spanish naval force at Subic threatened the rear and communications of any hostile squadron attempting to drive a passage into Manila Bay, compelling a division of its assets between them, and inviting individual defeat.[20]

On April 26 a report came from the American consul in Singapore of recent Spanish mining activities in Boca Grande Channel, the main entrance into Manila Bay. This agreed with the accounts provided by Consul Williams just prior to his departure and by the merchant ship captains in Hong Kong. After some thought, Dewey and his commanding officers dismissed the threat as negligible. The great depth of the channel made the planting of electrically detonated "submarine" mines a task for real experts. Even if they were simple floating mines of the contact variety, they would quickly deteriorate in the tropical waters and become ineffective. Finally, the officers agreed that the many warnings to merchant mariners of compulsory pilotage and "spectacular zigzag courses" were, in effect, "crying wolf," and intended to frighten "a presumptuous enemy." Dewey considered it all "a specious bluff."[21]

The next day, April 27, the *Fame* came into Mirs Bay bearing Consul Oscar Williams and the *Raleigh*'s circulating pump. Dewey signaled for all captains to repair on board the flagship. According to the latest information, Williams reported that when he left, the greater part of the Spanish fleet had been concentrated in Manila Bay, in the general vicinity of the Cavite navy yard. Also, in addition to the coast artillery emplaced before the city proper, new guns had been mounted at Cavite, the tip of the Bataan Peninsula, and on the island of Corregidor in the mouth of Manila Bay. Furthermore, he had been informed that Boca Chica Channel, the bay's regular northern entrance, had been "extensively mined." Last, on the day before Williams's departure from Manila, the large steamer *Isla de Mindanao* had arrived from Spain, her holds full of coastal guns, ships' torpedoes, and, so it was reported, threescore mines and their appurtenances. Once this information had been digested, the various commanding officers returned to their ships, and the signal was hoisted to the yardarm of the *Olympia* to "prepare to get underway." At four bells in the afternoon watch, 2 P.M., the squadron, fires spread under all boilers, heaved in its anchors and steamed out of Mirs Bay on a smooth sea, under a "favoring sky," and set course for Manila Bay.[22]

Back on the fifteenth of March, around the time the short-lived sailing of the Spanish torpedo flotilla sent its scare through the U.S. Navy's Atlantic commands, Captain General Fernando Primo de Rivera summoned his principal officers to Manila headquarters for a conference on the defense of the Philippine archipelago. Strategically isolated from Europe, with no realistic hope of reinforcement, the approximately thirty thousand Spanish regular troops, the seventeen thousand questionable Filipino levies, and the naval squadron were on their own against anything the Americans could throw in their direction. In reality, the defenders could not do much more than concentrate their strength in the neighborhood of Manila, the bay, and its strategically associated environs.

The blueprint for the defense of the capital dated from 1885, updated in 1892. The centers of resistance were the masonry bastions of the old walled quarter of Manila itself, the fortifications surrounding the Cavite arsenal and navy yard along the eastern rim of the bay a dozen miles to the south, and Subic Bay to the northwest on the Bataan Peninsula. Additionally, a defensive position was prepared in central Luzon as a rallying point should Manila fall to an external invader. To protect the capital against internal rebel attack, a series of fifteen strong points, similar to the large blockhouses along the *trochas* in Cuba, were constructed around the city's landward approaches, north, east, and south. The defense of the west side of Manila and its seaward access was the principal responsibility of Rear Admiral Patricio Montojo y Pasaron and the inadequate naval forces under his command.[23]

Like many of his comrades in the senior reaches of the Spanish navy, Montojo, who had been in the navy since 1852, participating in actions against Peru, the Islamic Philippine Moros, and Cuban rebels during the Ten Years' War, was utterly defeatist in his attitudes and outlook for the coming struggle; it is difficult to see how he could not be. At the captain general's conference, Montojo stated categorically that his "poor squadron would not be able to withstand the onslaught of the American ships." When asked what steps could be taken to avert this catastrophe, the admiral, with circumlocutory logic, suggested fortifying Subic Bay "if only temporarily . . . so that our fleet may repair to it and there await the enemy, provided they come at all, keeping the fleet in readiness, in case Manila should be assaulted, to hasten there [to Manila] at night and attack the Americans unexpectedly" when so ordered by the captain general, adding "that the time is propitious for such a maneuver, counting on the hostile squadron being somewhat fatigued by that time." These were hardly the sentiments of a responsibly confident commander, or even a clear-thinking one.[24]

Montojo suggested closing one of Subic Bay's two channels by sinking blockships, and covering the other with properly sited coastal guns and a minefield. Thus protected, his ships might then "engage in battle with the Americans." With commendable energy a joint army-navy commission journeyed to Subic to determine the best positions for fixing four modern 5.9-inch breech-loading rifles originally intended for defense of the Cavite navy yard. Their replacements were expected to arrive in the steamer *Isla de Mindanao*. Montojo also dispatched six hundred tons of coal to Subic and ordered a condemned transport and two old merchantmen sunk in the eastern channel. When the commission reported that Isla Grande, the misnamed small island dividing the bay's entrance into its component channels, was most suitable for the guns, Montojo ordered the work to proceed.

For the next few weeks he received progress reports from the Subic station commander, Captain Julio Del Río, who claimed that when not disturbed by rebels, the work "never stopped a minute." This, however, was extremely misleading. The admiral also received collateral reports from his ordnance officers complaining that until the engineers completed pouring cement for the guns' foundations, the carriages could not be mounted. As to when that would be, the engineer in charge could not say, nor could he report on the status of the labor thus far completed. Montojo seems to have compartmentalized these disturbing accounts into different mental pigeonholes because he fully trusted that everything was going according to plan—a big mistake.[25]

Still, he was under some apprehension; writing on April 11 to the minister of marine, Admiral Sigismundo Bermejo, in Madrid, he complained, "I am without resources, or time." A delusionist of the first order, the minister replied that Montojo must substitute for his deficiencies by "zeal and activity." Less than a week later, Montojo asked, "How many days free from molestation have I for installing new batteries and obtaining men?" He received no answer, but within two days Bermejo ominously informed him, "Circumstances demand the closing of ports with mines," to which an exasperated Montojo responded, "Your excellency is aware that I have no mines." Not to worry, soothed the minister, seventy were on the way in the *Isla de Mindanao*. The man in Madrid sincerely regretted he could not do more for his brother flag officer, "for I am positive hostilities will break out on Sunday."[26]

At this critical juncture, the home government chose to replace General Primo de Rivera as governor and captain general with General Basilio Augustín. With only the briefest time available to organize the Philippines for war against the United States, there was little of actual substance that could be done. Civil servants and Spanish nationals were enlisted into the military services, and special courts were created to punish treason with death.

Manila, a city of three hundred thousand people, metropolitan hub of the Spanish empire in Asia, sprawled astride the Pasig River, on the east end of a large pear-shaped bay 120 miles in circumference. Portions of the old city walls, south of the river, dated from the late sixteenth century, but these were mostly rebuilt and elaborated following the capture and hostage ransom of the city by the British in 1762. In a dozen or so years prior to the Spanish-American War, they had been modernized to a certain degree. In all places the walls were of masonry, thirty to forty feet high, fifty feet thick, filled with packed earth over casemates. Fronting the walls a fifty-foot-wide moat drew its water from sluice gates to the Pasig River.

Atop the walls, and extending into the southern suburbs, were mounted 226 guns of every pattern, from up-to-date coast artillery to bronze pieces on wooden carriages that would not have been anachronistic in the Spanish Armada of 1588. Fully 164 of the guns were obsolete muzzle-loaders. The best of the coast artillery were four modern 9.4-inch breech-loading rifles, mounted behind massive, permanent earthworks twenty feet high and thirty feet thick, one each fronting the northern and southern bastions of the city walls, and two in battery along the Luneta park, the city's fashionable promenade south of the walls. These guns were augmented by nine 8.3-inch muzzle-loading howitzers from midcentury, which, given a bit of luck and a lot of skill, might have some effect against a modern hostile fleet. Of the sixty-odd remaining breech-loading pieces, most had been "modernized" in the past thirty years out of eighteenth-century muzzle-loading antiques.

At Sangley Point, the outer tip of the crab-clawed peninsula holding the Cavite arsenal and navy yard, Fort Sangley, a permanent, modern, semihexagonal work, contained two 5.9-inch-rifled breech-loaders, though because of high sills below the barrels they were prevented from aiming at targets inside two thousand yards. At the Cavite arsenal itself, the only piece of value was one 4.7-incher taken from the gunboat *Don Antonio de Ulloa,* then under repair.

The forward defenses were concentrated in the mouth of Manila Bay. The entrance, ten miles wide, obstructed by a number of rocks and islets, is divided into two main channels by the island of Corregidor: Boca Chica (Little Mouth) to its north and Boca Grande (Big Mouth) to the south. Tadpole-shaped Corregidor, head facing the sea, held three 8-inch muzzle-loading rifles as well as a signal station and quarantine hospital. Two mainland batteries on the southern tip of Bataan across Boca Chica held three 7-inch muzzle-loading rifles and two 6.3-inch breechloaders. A mile south of Corregidor's tail, in Boca Grande Channel, Caballo Island held three 5.9-inch guns taken from the cruiser *Velasco*. The Boca Grande Channel itself is divided between Caballo Island and the mainland by El Fraile (the Friar) rock, and mounted three 4.7-inch naval guns from the gunboat *General Lezo*. Finally, at Punta Restinga on the southern headland of the entrance were a trio of 6.3-inch muzzle-loaders. Thus, in all, from the mouth of the bay to the city walls, there were but a dozen guns of any practical utility for the defense of the city.[27]

On April 24, war already having been declared, Admiral Montojo resolved to take his squadron to Subic Bay and there challenge the Americans in battle. Telegraphing his intentions to Captain Del Río, Montojo proved incapable of directly ordering what he needed done to receive and support his ships in their preparations for combat. Instead, he trusted that Del Río, "with the slight and feeble resources upon which we can count, will do everything possible to guard the honor of the flag and the navy." Though requesting regular progress reports on the fortifying of this most critical forward position, Montojo could not bring himself to demand particulars. "Go on, sir," he penned in futile hope, "ordering and equipping as much as you think necessary for the common purposes which concern our interests." With Spain's senior naval commander issuing this sort of babble, the outcome of the contest could not be in doubt.[28]

Captain Julio Del Río was no idiot; in fact, Lieutenant Calkins considered him "a man of ability"; perhaps he was so, once. But it is clear that he was no longer up to his best endeavors. Years of butting his head against the unyielding wall of Spanish bureaucratic obstinacy had taken its toll. Del Río had chaired the original Spanish naval commission that investigated the strategic defense possibilities of Subic Bay in 1891. "If the voice of reason is heard," he wrote then, "we await the enemy at Subig. If certain material interests prevail, we await him off Manila." Given the latter scenario, Del Río prophesied, "The enemy admiral, if he finds Subig empty, will then stand for

Manila." When successive boards of investigation recommended Subic as superior in every respect to Manila, a start was made for a naval station at the village of Olongapo. A floating dry dock had even been ordered from Scotland, and was ready for shipment in early 1898. Yet the Spanish naval bureaucracy in the Philippines adamantly dug its anchor into Cavite, loath to depart the social and political nexus of metropolitan Manila for the comparative exile of Subic Bay. After eight years of struggle to transform Subic Bay into a naval station in anything but name, Del Río had given up. By the spring of 1898, he had honed his labors to the exquisite art of official communication, and he did nothing to prepare on the eve of battle, or to inform his chief, Admiral Montojo, of that fact.[29]

This was not all. Del Río divined the minutest analysis of the Spanish official mind and its workings in a crisis situation. Once the hostile force determined to enter Manila Bay, there was no means of preventing ingress, "unless it is opposed by another squadron of at least equal strength," not the collection of Spanish antiques and curiosities currently available. Finally, he asked, when the enemy had shouldered his way through Manila Bay's ill-sited coastal guns, and the minefields had harmlessly drifted away, "Where is our squadron? If it is at Cavite he attacks the arsenal, and our squadron, which is almost motionless, suffers helplessly until its annihilation is complete."[30]

At 11: A.M., April 25, Admiral Montojo stood on the bridge of his flagship, the cruiser *Reina Cristina,* took a breath, and called out the traditional departure command—"*Larguen en el nombre de Dios!*" ("Let us go in the name of God!")—that had sent Spanish fleets to sea since the time of Christopher Columbus. Rounding Sangley Point in straggling order, heading for the Boca Grande exit, there followed the flagship's smaller cousin *Don Juan de Austria,* the gunboats *Isla de Cuba* and *Isla de Luzon,* the dispatch vessel *Marqués del Duero,* and at 3,260 tons, Montojo's largest ship, the leaky, white-painted, composite wood-and-steel cruiser *Castilla,* station ship at Cavite, where she should have remained. Even Montojo recognized this, considering her nothing more than a floating battery, incompetent of maneuver. Still, he brought her along, hoping to put her guns to use defending Subic Bay against the Americans.[31]

The British naval historian Herbert Wilson called them a "miserably heterogeneous" collection, and so they were. Paper statistics aside, their gunnery quotient was less than half that of Dewey's squadron, and Montojo's fastest ships, at fourteen knots, were slower than every one of their foes save the *Petrel*. En route, the *Castilla* admitted so much water into her machinery spaces through her propeller-shaft bearing that the crew, laboring day and night, had to plug the gland with cement, "finally making the vessel water-tight," Montojo noted, but also making it "absolutely impossible to use her engines." She was put under tow of the transport *Manila*. With that immediate problem taken care of, Montojo gave thought to the defenses of Subic Bay, where the four valuable 5.9-inch guns originally intended for Sangley Point had been shipped. If they were not already mounted, said a Spanish naval officer, "they soon would be, but the admiral was to suffer a terrible disappointment and deception."[32]

Arriving at Subic on the twenty-sixth, Admiral Montojo got the stunning news, "which did not relieve my anxiety," from Captain Del Río that no, the guns had not been mounted, but he assured his admiral, "they would soon be finished"—in about six weeks! Nor, Del Río matter-of-factly explained, had much else been done, except for sinking the hulks in the east channel. Some gunpowder mines were planted, but soon enough the rebels had fished them up for their explosive contents. The iron shells lay impotent on the beach. In the store shed were some fifteen more, doing nothing.[33]

It was with "much disgust" that Admiral Montojo realized what was in effect a professional betrayal by his subordinates at Subic Bay, "so that the squadron would have . . . to bear the attack of the Americans with its own resources." With a fatalistic naïveté, hoping the Americans would dally before making their assault on the islands, Montojo stationed the *Castilla* as an immobile, floating battery to cover the west channel, "and give us time for more preparations." But on Thursday, the twenty-eighth, he received a cable, sent the day before, from the Spanish consul in Hong Kong: "Enemy's squadron sailed at 2 p.m. from the bay of Mirs, and according to reliable accounts they sailed for Subig to destroy our squadron and then will go to Manila."[34]

With the Yankee enemy wasting no time, indeed coming right for him, Montojo summoned a council of his ships' captains to determine their course of action. The admiral, defeatist beyond reason, did not wish to remain in Subic Bay, whose strategic geography still offered the best location of battle. His annulling reason was its twenty-two fathoms of water: "Our vessels could not only be destroyed, but they could not save their crews." The entire council agreed, except Captain Del Río, the officer whose inaction had created the intolerable situation. The commanders considered their present position "insupportable," and opted instead to return to Manila, "in order to accept there the battle under less unfavorable conditions." In midmorning, April 29, first giving orders to Del Río to burn the coal stocks, then sending ahead the *Don Juan de Austria* to collect and fill with sand enough barges to protect the *Castilla*'s waterline in the coming action, Admiral Montojo led his scraggly line out of Subic Bay.[35]

Once back at Manila that evening several options presented themselves in declining order of desirability. If Admiral Montojo's premier concern was the life and safety of his crews, and there is no reason to suppose otherwise, his best recourse to prevent slaughter was to land his guns, men, and everything else of use, to bolster the defenses of bay and city, and prepare his ships for demolition. The Spanish would have to move fast if they were going to adopt this method of accepting battle, because if the American squadron had left Mirs Bay on the twenty-seventh, as the consular cable reported, it might already be off the entrance to Manila Bay. But the Spanish national character, its overbearing reliance on points of honor, prevented both brisk work and the self-destructive nature of this option.

The next best alternative, and one which Montojo inclined toward, was to deploy the squadron in defensive positions under the protection of the heavy batteries, the 9.4-inch coast artillery, fronting the city of Manila. This would have put more heart into the Spanish defense ashore and afloat and provided opportunities for concentrated fire upon the enemy ships that did not obtain otherwise. But Admiral Montojo and Captain General Augustín, either independently or in concert, prohibited the squadron from adopting this stand before the capital because, as Montojo explained, "far from defending it, this would provoke the enemy to bombard the plaza." This insane decision proved fatal to any remaining shred for the prospect of Spanish success. In Mahanian doctrine, damage to Manila from ships' guns could not, from the Spanish national perspective, be compared to the certain loss of its naval squadron, and with it, the Philippines. Neither Augustín nor Montojo understood that Spain's very fate was at stake, not just a three-hundred-year-old colonial city. *This* was the real and great risk Augustín and Montojo assumed when they eliminated the combined ship-and-shore defense option. In the end, Admiral Montojo and his captains "unanimously" decided on the worst possible scenario, to take position in the Bay of Cañacao, between Sangley Point and Cavite, "in the least possible water," where the shore batteries could not depress to fire on targets at ranges less than two thousand yards.[36]

All the ships but the *Castilla,* who retained her white hull, had been painted dark gray, and their topmasts, yards, and rigging were taken down to decrease danger from splinters. In a shallow arc extending eastward a mile from Sangley Point, the ships anchored, springs to their cables, enabling them to shift their broadsides a few degrees in either direction, or to slip them "instantly." Nearest the point lay the immovable wooden *Castilla,* port broadside to the foe, her hull protected by sand-filled lighters. The remainder of the best fighting ships—the cruiser *Reina Cristina,* the gunboats *Isla de Cuba* and *Isla de Luzon,* and dispatch vessel *Marqués del Duero*—rode with their starboard broadsides presented. Within Cañacao Bay, sheltering behind Sangley Point, Montojo stationed the small cruiser *Don Juan de Austria* and her sister ship, the stationary, engineless *Don Antonio de Ulloa.* In Bacoor Bay, in the lee of Cavite, farthest from danger, were the out-of-commission *Velasco* and *General Lezo,* having neither guns nor boilers, and the armed transport *Manila.*[37]

At 7 P.M. in the evening of April 30, Admiral Montojo received a warning from the cable station at Subic Bay that two enemy ships had entered, found nothing, "and from there they sailed with course for Manila." As the hours slipped away, the mail steamer *Isla de Mindanao* nosed her way into Cavite. Montojo advised her master to head directly for Singapore, and thereby save his vessel. He had only until midnight, for certainly by then the Americans would be off the entrance channels. The skipper could not do it, there being no authorization from the home office to alter his scheduled passage. With a sigh, Montojo suggested—for that was all he could do—that the steamer anchor in the shallow waters of Bacoor Bay. When the stroke of midnight brought the change of watch to the huddled Spanish ships, those men on deck distinctly heard the dull boom of cannon fire in the direction of Corregidor. At 2 A.M., Admiral Montojo was handed a cable reporting the enemy's vessels returning the fire of the shore batteries in Boca Grande. After notifying the commandants of the Cavite arsenal and Sangley Point forts to prepare for battle, Montojo signaled his squadron. Fires were spread under the boilers, ammunition was brought up to the guns, "and everything in proper place, we waited for the enemy's arrival."[38]

On quitting Mirs Bay on April 27, Commodore Dewey deployed the Asiatic Squadron in two parallel columns, the warships, flagship *Olympia* in the van, to port, and Revenue cutter *McCulloch* leading the colliers to starboard. Fleet speed was maintained at a leisurely eight knots, both to provide underway training in formation steaming to the engineers, and to enable the slow *Petrel* and the auxiliaries to keep pace. When the last smudge of land dropped under the horizon, all hands not on watch were called to muster, and they listened to their officers read aloud a proclamation from Captain General Augustín.

It is a remarkable document, and objective people must wonder if the Spanish political and military commanders truly believed their own pronouncements. Because if not, then a lot of men died for a cynical pursuit of honor that could have been otherwise preserved without bloodshed. The "North American people," as Augustín proclaimed, "composed of all the social excrescences, have exhausted our patience and provoked war with their perfidious machinations, with their acts of treachery, and with their outrages against the law of nations and international conventions. . . . Your indomitable bravery will suffice to frustrate the attempt to carry them into realization." The fight, Augustín promised, would be "short and decisive. The God of Victories" would give Spain a triumph "brilliant and complete . . . humiliating and blasting the adventurers" in pay of a country "without cohesion or a history." As for the tools of the foe, the captain general harped on the fact that the lower decks of the U.S. Navy contained a good many immigrants: "A squadron manned by foreigners, possessing neither instruction nor discipline . . . with the ruffianly intention of robbing us," Spaniard and Filipino alike, of all means of life, liberty, and honor. And once the Yankees dropped anchor in Manila Bay, their only intent was "to kidnap those persons whom they consider useful to man their ships [and] to be exploited" on America's farms and in its factories. "Vain designs! Ridiculous boastings!"[39]

When the officers finished reading this extraordinary text to their respective crews, the men were informed of the mission: the Asiatic Squadron was bound for the Philippines, "to capture or destroy the Spanish fleet." From each ship, ringing cheers floated over the sea. Captain General Augustín could have done nothing better for the already high American morale.[40]

A direct course was set for Cape Bolinao, on Luzon's northwest coast, and no attempt was made at concealment. As if in peacetime, lights were shown at night, and the ships freely exchanged signals by lamp. The easy voyage across the East China Sea was spent, as Commander Asa Walker of the *Concord* remembered, "in more careful and complete clearing ship for action." The ripping out and tossing overboard of flammable woodwork continued nonstop. Overheads, wainscoting, bunks, furniture, all went over the side. "Turpentine, alcohol, shellac and varnish chests were committed to the vastly deep, wringing the hearts of the executive officers as only the loss of such necessary articles in a ship's housekeeping could do." Lieutenant Bradley Fiske, the *Petrel's* navigator, recalled his principal memory of the passage to the Philippines as being "the enormous quantity of woodwork flung overboard by the ships. It seemed as if the *Baltimore*, for instance, never could possibly have held the amount of woodwork she threw over." In Revenue cutter *McCulloch*, overeager mess attendants threw most of the mess tables into the sea, and thus obliged the crew to eat sitting on the deck until well after the battle. "The sea," said Lieutenant Ellicott of the *Baltimore*, "was strewn for fifty leagues with jettisoned woodwork unfit to carry into battle." In the flagship *Olympia*, however, one sailor noted that none of this was carried to extremes. "The commodore knew best what we were going up against, and we didn't tear out anything, just covered it with canvas and splinter nets." Metropolitan Club member George Dewey was not about to sacrifice needlessly.[41]

In addition to ridding the ships of flammables, Dewey ordered preparations he had learned from his hero, David Glasgow Farragut. Aboard all ships, anchor chains were garlanded in front of exposed gun positions and wrapped around ammunition hoists. Splinter nets were spread under and about the ships' multitude of wooden boats.

Medical officers "overhauled" their surgical instruments, and hundreds of yards of bandage gauze were disinfected.

On the third night at sea, in the first inky hours of Saturday, April 30, the squadron made a perfect landfall off Cape Bolinao, where, said Lieutenant Calkins of the *Olympia,* a "dark mass and a rank tropical odor revealed the great island." Daylight unveiled miles of mangrove swamp, backed by ridges of rock covered with scrub trees, with high peaks visible farther inland. Steaming almost due south in sight of the rough coastline, before the sun appeared over the mountains, Dewey signaled for the *Boston, Concord,* and a bit later the *Baltimore* "to proceed at full speed and explore Subig Bay." As Commander Asa Walker remembered, this is where the rumors picked up in Hong Kong had indicated the Spanish fleet would be deployed, and indeed, such had been Admiral Montojo's original intention.[42]

The *Boston* leading, the ships steered at full speed straight for the unblocked main channel, and though wary of mines, they kept as close inshore as possible. Walker described Subic Bay as "a most beautiful sheet of water, completely landlocked." No hostile ships visible from the mastheads, the *Concord* reconnoitered the arms and inlets, which Walker described as surrounded by massive hills, clothed from base to summit in "tropical verdure." Of the enemy, or in fact anyone, "[n]ot a sign of human life was visible, not even a canoe broke the calm waters of the bay." The *Concord* signaled "Nothing in sight," and the ships passed out of Subic and rejoined the squadron by the turn of the first dog watch, 4 P.M. Commodore Dewey, listening to the flagship's signalmen reading the *Boston*'s flag hoists, exclaimed to the watch standers on the bridge, "Now we have them!"[43]

As the sun's orange ball set westward over the vast reaches of ocean that is Pacific in name only, Dewey ordered the squadron to heave to and signaled for all captains to repair aboard the *Olympia.* The orders were simple, to the point, and could have been written by Farragut himself; these men needed no elaboration. "Very well, gentlemen," Dewey said to the assembly in the wardroom. "We shall enter Manila Bay tonight. You will follow the motions and signals of the flagship." The squadron, in column, would penetrate the entrance through Boca Grande Channel, each ship showing one hooded light at her stern, as Asa Walker remembered, "and engage the enemy's forces, should they be found."[44]

Dewey's nephew, Lieutenant William Winder of the *Baltimore,* raised the identical concern Farragut's officers had voiced prior to the Battle of Mobile Bay, the peril to the admiral himself as he led the squadron in dangerous waters. "We think the bay is mined," said the lieutenant, and he volunteered to command the deep-draft collier *Zafiro* to sweep ahead. "I could soon find out if the bay is mined," he stated, "and . . . clear a way for the squadron." Farragut, to his everlasting self-reproach, had given way. Dewey would not make that mistake. "Billy," he answered kindly, "I have waited sixty years for this opportunity. And much as I like you . . . mines or no mines, I am leading the squadron myself. Good luck my boy."[45]

In darkness, perfect silence prevailing, the squadron stood slowly down the coast, through bright moonlight, passing clouds, the occasional lightning flashes, a brief shower of warm rain—a tropical night out of literature. Asa Walker, on the bridge of the *Concord,* thought the ships resembled "dim ghosts . . . barely distinguishable to the ocean itself." At 9:45 P.M., the squadron went to general quarters. "The guns were all ready," said Lieutenant Bradley Fiske of the *Petrel,* "considerable ammunition was on deck, and the men lay or sat or stood by their guns. The night . . . rather dragged. There was nothing to do, for all preparations had been made." On the port hand, two or three miles away, he saw the vague outline of Bataan. Forward, the dim light over the stern of the *Raleigh* showed her position in the column; astern he could see nothing of the *Concord.* And there were almost no noises, "nothing to hear except the sound of the engines and the swish of water along the sides." At seven bells in the evening watch, 11:30 P.M., Lieutenant Calkins, the *Olympia's* navigator, brought the Asiatic Squadron to the mouth of Manila Bay, on course into Boca Grande Channel, heading for El Fraile rock.[46]

Everyone was tense, Dewey included. In the stifling heat, eyes searched the night for enemy signals, ears pitched for the sound of the first coast defense gun, for the horrible possibility of running full speed into a minefield. Dewey heard men talking in anxious whispers, and to break the tension, he turned to Captain Gridley and said in a voice loud enough for anyone around the bridge to hear, "A fine night for a smoke, eh, Gridley? It's a pity we can't light up." It loosened things up a fraction. At five minutes to midnight, when the jagged bulk of El Fraile bore starboard a half mile, Lieutenant Calkins shifted fleet course to the northeast, well and truly into Manila Bay. So near did the ships scrape by the rock, that one or two needed to sheer off a bit to give it a wide berth.[47]

At ten minutes past midnight, May 1, just as the *Petrel,* fourth ship in the column, swung on the new course, signals began flashing between Corregidor and Lasisi Point on Bataan, quickly followed by a soaring rocket shot from Corregidor into the sky. A second later, said Asa Walker, "the scream of a shell and the boom of the discharge of a cannon" opened the ball. The shell exploded in the water between the *Raleigh* and *Petrel,* "though *each* man in *each* ship was satisfied, in his own mind that it passed just between the masts of his own vessel." "Well, well," joked Commodore Dewey to Captain Gridley, "they did wake up at last." At that moment—after, not, as is often written, before the Spanish opened fire—the soot in the *McCulloch*'s smokestack caught fire, sending up a towering column of flame, "rendering her visible," Asa Walker said, "for miles as a beacon." There was little time to fret over that, as the rear ships in the column answered the battery on El Fraile. The *Raleigh* responded first with a shot from her after 5-inch gun, and even the *McCulloch* banged away with her 6-pounders. It was all over in a few minutes, and the squadron passed silently on, into the wide, placid waters of Manila Bay, unscathed, not a man injured. Dewey initially intended to anchor by the north shore until morning, but since the exchange of fire, he preferred to keep under way. Fleet speed was reduced to four knots so as to arrive off Manila, thirty miles dead ahead, by first light. Half the men were allowed to sleep at their guns and battle stations. "The decks were sprinkled with sand" for soaking up the blood, wrote an *Olympia* sailor, "and it would get into eyes, ears, and nose, scratch the skin and occasionally someone would stroll over your recumbent form, as leisurely as if on parade."[48]

At 3 A.M., May 1, the city lights of Manila became visible to watch standers on the various ships' bridges. The *McCulloch* and her two charges withdrew northward, out of range of the shore batteries. At eight bells, 4 A.M., the turn of the watch, all hands were roused, and coffee, beans, and hard bread were served to the crews. Commodore Dewey ate the same meal, less the beans. He had been drinking cold tea throughout the night, and the coffee did not mix well. According to his aide, newspaperman Joseph Stickney, a junior naval officer

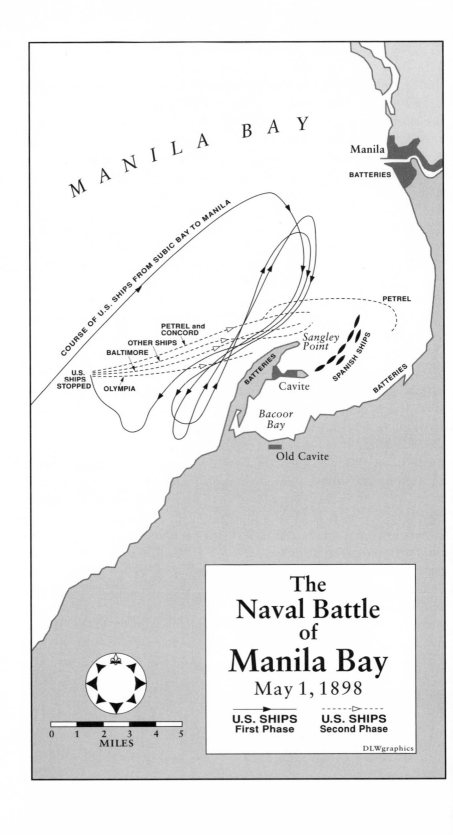

MANILA BAY

Manila

BATTERIES

COURSE OF U.S. SHIPS FROM SUBIC BAY TO MANILA

PETREL

PETREL and
CONCORD

OTHER SHIPS

BALTIMORE

*Sangley
Point*

SPANISH SHIPS

BATTERIES

U.S.
SHIPS
STOPPED

OLYMPIA

BATTERIES

Cavite

BATTERIES

*Bacoor
Bay*

Old Cavite

The
Naval Battle
of
Manila Bay
May 1, 1898

U.S. SHIPS
First Phase

U.S. SHIPS
Second Phase

DLWgraphics

0   1   2   3   4   5
MILES

during the Civil War and now signed on as a volunteer, "Commodore Dewey was as completely upset as if he had been a youngster just going out of port into a heavy sea on his first cruise. . . . [H]e threw up nearly everything."

"Slowly," Asa Walker remembered, "the night drew on to a close and the ruddy light in the east proclaimed the approach of day." Signals ascended the *Olympia*'s halyards, and were repeated in each ship as the hoists were spotted: "Prepare for general action," followed by "Form in single column" and then "Close up," which latter remained flying through the day. When the *Olympia* signaled to "execute" the first order by hauling it down, from every masthead and peak of the American ships "the folds of 'Old Glory,' " said Asa Walker, "were given to the morning breeze"—battle flags, large national ensigns, for the purposes of morale and to indicate friend from foe in the smoke and din of action. In the *Raleigh*, Lieutenant Hugh Rodman noticed the signalmen bending on additional flags that might find a place aloft, "and quite a number were run up," tied in small bundles with a "slippery hitch," but not immediately broken out.[49]

Standing steadily on, the squadron reached a point less than six miles from the city, now bathed in the flat sunshine of an early May dawn. Bradley Fiske made his way to the *Petrel*'s bridge and was greeted by a smiling Commander Wood, who said simply, "All right." The rumors had it that the Spanish fleet would base their defense off the Manila breakwater, under the guns of the main coastal batteries. But all Fiske could see ahead were "a great number of masts . . . very indistinct." The sound of one or two very distant big guns came over the water, and he watched smoke grow and dissipate along the waterfront. Commander Wood pointed to starboard, toward Sangley Point, about six miles off. "The Spanish fleet is over there," he said. Fiske strained his eyes through a glass and saw "a few indistinct shapes that looked like ships." There was absolutely no undue excitement. Looking about the ship, Fiske saw the crew calmly loading their four 6-inch guns; "a few were getting some coffee and crackers at the galley and the scene about the deck was as quiet and peaceful as I had ever seen it."[50]

From the *Olympia*, the Spanish line was observed in its slightly ragged, inwardly bent line, as Lieutenant Calkins noted, "in front of the white buildings of the arsenal." Dewey, wearing a light tweed "traveling" cap, a golf hat really, took his place on the open bridge, near to Lieutenant Calkins on the compass platform, as the lieutenant called out the ranges and navigated the squadron into battle. Captain Gridley reluctantly climbed inside the steel conning tower just below; it would not do for both the flag officer and the ship's captain to be killed by a single lucky shot to the bridge. Three miles from the Manila breakwater, Dewey ordered a ninety-degree turn to starboard. In lockstep precision every vessel turned in the wake of her next ahead, and at four-hundred-yard intervals the ships—*Olympia, Baltimore, Raleigh, Petrel, Concord,* and *Boston*—headed straight for the enemy. It might as well have been a naval parade passing in review in front of the city walls of Manila and the batteries along the Luneta. The shore batteries continued their fire. Lieutenant Rodman watched a heavy shell, probably from one of the 9.4-inch guns, strike exactly in the wake of the *Baltimore* just ahead. "If this shell had hit," he wrote, "it would have done a tremendous amount of damage. . . . Had the enemy allowed for the ship's speed in sighting their guns, the shot would have struck on the waterline and no doubt have seriously crippled her."[51]

The four leading vessels in the line stood disdainfully on, making no reply. The *Concord* and *Boston,* however, without slackening speed, lobbed a few shells into the batteries—according to Asa Walker, "to let the enemy know that we were not there solely to become targets." Once the batteries in Manila proper opened fire—and they continued to waste ammunition, hitting nothing over the next five hours—the city was deprived of any right of immunity against hostile bombardment. Thus, it was liable to destruction by the American ships, without itself contributing in any way to the defense of the Spanish naval forces. At the end of the day, the chief of the Spanish fortress artillery shot himself, as Lieutenant Calkins said, "to expiate his failure." The Asiatic Squadron, undaunted by fire, continued steadily southward, with the Spanish fleet, distant four miles, bearing broad on the flagship's starboard bow.[52]

At five o'clock, the Spanish guns on Sangley Point opened fire, their shots falling short and to starboard of the *Olympia.* The American ships remained silent. Minutes later, two mines exploded in the water, again short of the flagship. They did no damage, nor did they slow the American advance. "Evidently," Dewey said to his chief of staff, "the Spaniards are already rattled." At 5:15 the Spanish squadron began shooting, its fire becoming rapid and uncomfortably close as the American ships advanced, still at nearly right angles to the enemy. When the range came down to 5,500 yards, a little longer than he would have wished, but necessary in light of the unbelievable tension that wrapped itself around every ship and man, Dewey bent over the brass mouth of a speaking tube to the conning tower just below; it was 5:22 A.M. when he said, "You may fire when you are ready, Gridley." From the *Olympia*'s signal yards the flags whipped out: "Engage the enemy." Over the cruiser's starboard bow, a single 8-inch gun boomed, hurling its shell toward Sangley Point, where the Spanish ships were wreathed in billows of white gunsmoke. At a deliberate speed of about eight knots, the flagship steamed at the head of the column for another mile, at which point Dewey ordered hard right rudder. The squadron swung west, to starboard, unmasking its port-side batteries. In the *Raleigh,* Lieutenant Rodman now saw the little bundles of extra bunting break "from every masthead or other place aloft where a flag could be flown . . . as though it were a gala occasion and not the beginning of a historic battle." Bands in the *Olympia* and *Baltimore* began playing "The Star-Spangled Banner," and officers and men stood to attention as the music drifted back along the squadron column. As the last note disappeared through the splashes of the enemy's shells, Rodman remembered, "simultaneously there came a rousing cheer, and the guns opened on the enemy."[53]

Clustered in the bight of Cañacao Bay, Admiral Montojo's ships were as ready as Spanish ships could ever be for battle. Crews gave the regulation cheers for God and Spain, and the crimson-and-gold flags of Spain whipped from the mastheads. With a professional eye, Admiral Montojo noted the steadiness of his enemy, who had not deigned to reply to the Manila guns or the battery at Sangley Point, instead standing on, to engage their "principal object," his own squadron. At 5:15, Montojo signaled his ships to commence firing, to which "[t]he enemy answered immediately." Those ships that could, slipped their cables, and as the admiral reported, "started ahead with the engines, so as not to be involved with the enemy." This phrasing is difficult to understand. Montojo might have feared being rammed, a distant but not unthinkable threat, or was concerned to present a moving rather than a stationary target. If this is the case, his anchored formation at the beginning of the battle is incomprehensible.[54]

When the American battle line turned to starboard, its three leading cruisers concentrated their fire, as Montojo immediately saw and
felt, "almost entirely . . . [on] the *Cristina,* my flagship." From the
outset it received crippling punishment. An exploding shell in the
forecastle decimated the crews of four rapid-fire guns. It hit and splintered the foremast and wounded the helmsman on the bridge; his
place was taken by a lieutenant, who manned the wheel to the end of
the fight. A second shell blew up in the berth deck, setting fire to the
crew's seabags and effects.[55]

In a desperate venture to alter the course of a battle barely begun,
Montojo ordered the flagship to close with the *Olympia.* With smoke
and steam pouring out forward, amidships, and astern, the *Reina
Cristina* lurched ahead, out of the rapidly disintegrating Spanish line.
She was doomed. The range shortening by the second, the enemy
ships "covered us with a rain of rapid-fire projectiles." The steam
steering gear was destroyed, and the ship had to be worked by main
force on a manual wheel, as in the days of sail. Nine men fell to a single shell on the poop deck. The mizzenmast head was shot off, bringing down the national colors and the admiral's flag; both were
immediately replaced. A shell exploded in the wardroom sick bay,
"covering the hospital with blood, destroying the wounded who were
being treated there." The after magazine caught fire, driving off the
men at the manual steering gear. The smokestacks were riddled, and
the after stack toppled crazily forward. A large-caliber shell blew up
in the fireroom. The few undamaged broadside guns continued shooting until only 2 men remained unhurt, "as the guns' crews," Montojo
reported, "had been . . . called upon to substitute those charged with
steering, all of whom were out of action." Nearly half the crew of 352
men, including 7 officers, being killed or wounded, "I gave the order
to sink and abandon the ship before the magazines should explode."
Signaling for the *Isla de Cuba* and *Isla de Luzon* to rescue the living
from the *Reina Cristina,* Admiral Montojo quit his flagship and resumed command from the *Isla de Cuba.* The *Reina Cristina* turned
her head to shore and sank to the level of her main deck.[56]

For the rest of the Spanish fleet, the morning had not been much better. The *Castilla,* half her guns ashore as coast defenses, broke her
moorings, slewed around, and presented her toothless starboard side to
the enemy. She suffered severely, with 23 men dead and 80 wounded.

She was riddled with shells and repeatedly set afire; with flames bursting through the deck fore and aft, her commanding officer ordered her abandoned and scuttled. Her crew was taken off by boats sent out from Cavite and the *Don Juan de Austria*. The latter ship was herself on fire and heavily damaged. The *Isla de Luzon* had three guns knocked out; the stationary *Don Antonio de Ulloa* had but two guns left, and was struck by a shell that disabled something like half her 150-man crew, including the captain. The *Marqués del Duero* was left with one engine working and one main battery gun.[57]

The time was 7:30. The battle had been fought for over two hours, with the Americans steaming at will back and forth across the gutted Spanish line, when suddenly, on the fourth pass, the Asiatic Squadron hauled off to the northward, out of range. Admiral Montojo ordered his surviving ships to take shelter in Bacoor Bay, behind the town and arsenal of Cavite, "and there to resist to the last moment, and that they should be sunk before they surrendered."[58]

The American officers knew, Lieutenant Calkins said, "that our . . . cruisers could defeat all the vessels that Spain had in the Philippines," especially if they chose the suicidal huddling within easy range of open water, where the Asiatic Squadron could maneuver and fire at will. From the *Olympia*'s compass platform, Calkins watched the Spanish ships steam "about in an aimless fashion, often masking their comrades' fire, occasionally dodging back to the shelter of the arsenal, and now and then making isolated and ineffectual rushes . . . which had no rational significance except as demonstrations of the point of honor."[59]

Because the *Olympia* drew twenty-four feet, Lieutenant Calkins considered it safe to bring the squadron just inside the five-fathom line marked on his chart. As a result, the range dropped down from 4,000 yards to as little as 2,500 yards when closest to Sangley Point. In a small way, this favored the Spanish, because it presented targets for their much more numerous lighter guns. On the other hand, it increased the difficulty of the 5.9-inch coastal guns on Sangley Point, which could not depress their barrels for close-in fire.[60]

As the American battle line became "fairly engaged" in its first pass along the Spanish front, a small steam launch, with a big Spanish flag over her stern, darted out from behind Sangley Point and crossed the *Olympia*'s bow. "There could be but one interpretation" of her presence and movements, said Lieutenant Calkins; she was a Spanish torpedo boat intent on attacking, "and she had to be treated as such." Guns ranging from 5-inch rapid-fire to .50-caliber Gatlings, marines with rifles in the fighting tops, and even one or two main battery shells dismembered the "reckless" craft, yet she still floated, dead in the water, drifting ashore at Sangley Point. Every American participant in the battle thought she was a torpedo boat. She certainly appeared so. And some reports indicate there was a second boat. It turned out otherwise. "[N]o deadly microbe," said Calkins, but an English-owned market boat, bound for Manila, manned by local Filipinos.[61]

At the end of the westward leg, the *Olympia* turned hard astarboard, the squadron following, and countermarched over the same ground, pouring an uninterrupted fire into the Spanish ships, which were no longer in any kind of formation. In the *Raleigh,* third ship of the column, Lieutenant Rodman felt the men below in the powder division needed to know what was happening topside, "lest they become a little restless." Descending the ladders into the ship's bowels, Rodman heard the distinct sawing of a fiddle, accompanied by guitars, and found in the forward magazine and handling room "the men of the powder division strung across the deck, dressed in abbreviated gunny-sack *hula* skirts, burlesquing a dance and singing in chorus . . . *There'll be a Hot Time in the Old Town Tonight.*" On spying the officer, the sailors began a wild scramble to return to their stations. Rodman, however, was highly amused. "Men, we've got 'em on the run," he told them. "I don't know what that tune is you were playing"—it was the first time he had heard it—"but it's a corker; keep it up. I want the music to reach the upper deck." And through the rest of the battle, the strains of the popular song rolled up through the ammunition hoists "and cheered the men at the guns."[62]

After two hours of steady bombardment, there was no clear evidence of the destructive American fire on the remaining Spanish ships. The enemy, according to Lieutenant Calkins, "had seemed to flinch." There was a discernible slackening of their fire. But the pummeling meted out, though starting fires and explosions, had apparently caused no ship-killing damage. He observed the Spanish gunners "had neither gained not lost; they could drop shells close alongside or they could send them soaring aloft." Each American ship appeared within its own "charmed circle," and not a large one either, "since one seemed to count a hundred shells within a ship's length during the two hours of combat." Spanish shells "burst before our eyes," scattering deadly showers of steel splinters that cut rigging, ripped apart boats, and deeply scored any standing woodwork. A fire in the *Boston*'s hammock nettings, among the crew's clothing, was quickly extinguished, though much smoke caused onlookers to think her more than superficially injured. The *Baltimore* received the most damage. One 4.7-inch shell struck the hull on the starboard side, penetrated the armored deck, rattled about inside the ship, and exited through the after engine room hatch combing, where it struck a 6-inch gun, putting it out of action. The mad thing continued its flight, hitting a box of rapid-fire ammunition, exploding several charges that slightly wounded eight men.[63]

To the American officers, it was also evident the Spanish were wasting a lot of ammunition. "Our practice was evidently much better than that of the Spaniards," said Lieutenant Fiske of the *Petrel*, who called the fall of shot from the gunboat's masthead, "but it did not seem to me that it was at all good." Much of this Fiske attributed to difficulty in obtaining exact ranges, and the fact that individual gun captains felt compelled to fire as fast, rather than as accurately, as possible. Problems also accrued with the new "smokeless" powder, which only substituted red for white smoke. Newfangled instruments like the *Olympia*'s electric range finder quit after the first shot, and her turret telescopic sights needed constant cleaning from smoke and powder residue. Shooting became obstructed by great mounds of empty brass shell cases piled on the decks.[64]

At 7:35, when the squadron was well into its fourth pass, steaming west to east—when "victory was already ours, though we did not know it," reflected Commodore Dewey—he received a report from Captain Gridley, "startling as it was unexpected," that the *Olympia* had but fifteen rounds left for each of her ten 5-inch guns. This could be shot off in five minutes easy work. "It was a most anxious moment for me." He decided to haul out of range temporarily and redistribute the squadron's ammunition, if necessary. From the *Olympia*'s halyards flew the signal "Withdraw from action." As Mr. Stickney, the commodore's volunteer aide wrote, "the gloom on the bridge of the *Olympia* was thicker than a London fog in November."[65]

Yet even as the ships hauled out to the northward, it became evident the Spanish were suffering terribly; their shooting, with the useless exception of the Manila shore batteries, had entirely ceased, and fires were seen raging out of control on several of the ships. It also was quickly ascertained that reports of an ammunition shortage were erroneous. It should have been that fifteen rounds *per gun* had been fired, about 40 percent of the *Olympia*'s 5-inch stores. A check of the 8-inch magazines showed a promising week's fighting time of ammunition, and the 6-pounder rapid-fire guns were equally stocked. But it was also the start of a legend that still finds believers. In order to keep up the morale of the flagship's crew, Mr. Stickney, on being asked by a sailor why the squadron had retired from action, passed the story that the commodore had ordered the retirement to give the hands a meal. It immediately elicited the sailor's prayer to Commander Lamberton, the chief of staff, "For God's sake, Captain, don't let us stop now. To hell with breakfast!"[66]

Once the ammunition matter had been cleared up, and men looking around them saw all still fit and present (and began cheering themselves hoarse), it dawned on everyone, commodore, coal heaver, and Lieutenant Calkins alike, that "breakfast was not a thing under such circumstances to be despised." No one had eaten anything since the coffee and hardtack at four o'clock reveille, nearly four hours past, a meal, Calkins thought, that "seemed to belong to a different historic epoch." Though victory was certain, no one knew that yet, and the fighting might go on for the rest of the day with uncertain result. This opportunity might not present itself again, and Dewey took it, as Calkins said, "to give his squadron the increased fighting power which would come to his 1,700 men from full bellies." Up the *Olympia*'s halyards went the signal "Let the men go to breakfast."[67]

Hove to, engines stopped about five miles off Sangley Point, Dewey signaled for his captains to repair aboard the flagship. The Spanish had fired such a storm of shells that each skipper thought it was his own ship's incredible luck to have escaped anything but superficial damage; the others, however, could hardly have been so fortunate. But there was almost nothing to report. The *Boston*'s boats were all holed and splintered; the *Baltimore* had eight men slightly wounded and one medium-caliber penetration of the hull; all vessels had suffered some rigging cut away and topside dents; that was all. The squadron had come through unscathed and in complete fighting trim.

While the men rested, and the enemy shore batteries continued their desultory, ineffective roars, dropping the occasional shell within a hundred feet of the American ships, it could be seen from the various bridges that the Spanish line was melting away: the *Castilla* in flames, the *Reina Cristina* exploding as her magazines finally took light, and the smaller vessels scurrying for shelter behind Cavite in Bacoor Bay.

Commodore Dewey pondered his next move. To blockade the city and bay was the logical step, and he considered basing the squadron at Mariveles on the tip of Bataan. But when it became clear that only a shattered remnant of the enemy remained to oppose total occupation of the entire bay, Dewey resolved to reopen the battle. The *Baltimore,* being closest to Sangley Point, headed the line upon the signal "Attack the enemy's batteries." Going dead slow until she found the range at 2,200 yards, the *Baltimore* stopped engines and opened a deliberate, accurate, destructive fire on the shore guns and the *Don Antonio de Ulloa* anchored in Cañacao Bay.

The Americans, reported Admiral Montojo, formed a half circle of death and "opened . . . a horrible fire which we answered as far as we could with the few cannon which we still had mounted." There remained but one alternative for the Spanish admiral: to scuttle what little endured in futile combat, saving only the flag, his personal pennant, the contents of the paymaster's safe, the breech blocks of the ships' guns, and the signal books. That sad task done, Admiral Montojo, his leg bleeding from a splinter wound, retired with his staff to the convent of Santo Domingo de Cavite, where he telegraphed his preliminary report to the captain general at Manila. For the defenders of Cavite arsenal, it was no better. The enemy, in the words of its commandant, Commodore Enrique Sostoa y Ordoñez, was "directing against it a furious and destructive cannonade." The shore guns were either knocked out, or could not bring fire to bear in return, leaving the place without means of defense. Spanish sailors and marines, armed only with rifles, formed in ragged groups "in expectancy of a landing." The wounded men of the Spanish ships who lay suffering ashore "were forsaken; each instant the fierce fire of the enemy added to their number."[68]

Around 11:30 Dewey ordered the light-draft *Concord* and *Petrel* to round Sangley Point and pass inside Cañacao and Bacoor Bays on either side of Cavite and burn whatever remained of the Spanish fleet. The *Petrel* fired a few shots at the *Ulloa*, whose flag still flew, but she had been abandoned sinking. Further inside, the *Petrel* opened fire on ships whose masts and upperworks peeked above the red-tiled roofs at the navy yard. At 12:30 P.M., after two or three shots, said Commander Wood, "firing through the public buildings at ships behind the mole," the crimson-and-gold Spanish flag was hauled down and the white flag run up.[69]

Commodore Sostoa concentrated his men behind the south wall of Fort San Filipe, "the only shelter left the undefended arsenal." This, too became untenable the moment the *Petrel* turned the point, enfilading "the refuge with her guns, firing with impunity." Having nothing left with which to resist, deserted by the local army garrison, whom the commodore bitterly denounced ("which fired not a single shot during this terrible slaughter"), seeing his casualties uselessly mount under the *Petrel*'s relentless target practice, Sostoa ordered the white flag of capitulation hoisted over his command. Immediately the *Petrel* signaled this fact to Commodore Dewey and the squadron. All ships ceased firing. It was twenty minutes past one o'clock. From the flagship *Olympia* came the signal "Prepare to anchor," followed ten minutes later with "Anchor at discretion." Captain Nehemiah Dyer of the *Baltimore* preserved the moment in his report: "The victory was complete."[70]

Seven men under the *Petrel*'s executive officer, Lieutenant Edward Hughes, went ashore in their only undamaged boat. He found the "greatest confusion" in the yard. Surviving crews of the sunken Spanish ships still carried arms, and were "constantly falling in and moving about; yet there was no evidence of any desire to continue the fighting." They made no resistance to Hughes burning their vessels, a dangerous mission, because the Spanish had left gunpowder lying everywhere, with trains of the stuff leading into the magazines. Instead, Hughes noted, "they were rather inclined to assist with their advice and evinced a desire to surrender to the first officer they met." Hughes and his men opened the sea cocks and set torches to the *Don Juan de Austria, Isla de Cuba, Isla de Luzon, Marqués del Duero, Velasco,* and *General Lezo*. The unarmed coast survey vessel *Argus* was spared.[71]

When the *Petrel* nosed into Bacoor Bay to where her keel just scraped bottom, Lieutenant Bradley Fiske and half a dozen men went ashore on the stone quay. He saw for the taking some "nice-looking tugs and launches," very useful for salvage and inshore patrols. Advancing toward him along the waterfront were two dozen Spanish officers. Milling about farther off "was what looked to me like a small army of soldiers drawn up in regular formation under arms, and a crowd of sailors, who did not seem to be in any formation whatever." Fiske and the Spanish officers exchanged "punctilious" salutes and spoke to each other in French. Fiske described the beaten men as "somewhat excited," and having two worries: Would the American squadron reopen fire; and could the Spanish sailors return to their ships, "which they had abandoned in such haste that they had left behind their pocket money, and the pictures of their families, and all their clothes."[72]

Fiske told them the Americans would respect the white flag so long as the Spanish did likewise. This was very gratifying, and the Spanish raised a shouted *"Americanos siempre caballeros!"*

To assist the handful of the *Petrel's* bluejackets in carrying away the small craft, Fiske ordered the idle Spanish hands to help clear away. "This they did without any objection, and I soon had a number of our enemies pulling and hauling . . . like good sailors." By nightfall, the Asiatic Squadron steamed toward Manila, lighted on the short journey, Fiske wrote, by the "brilliant flames of the ships of our conquered foes."[73]

The Manila batteries that had kept up a persistent, though utterly ineffectual, firing during the entire day were now subdued into awed silence. Off the Luneta, Dewey anchored in his flagship and Consul Williams was sent aboard a British steamer with a letter for her master to deliver, via his own consul, to Captain General Augustín. The note included warnings, threats, and requests: Any torpedo boats hiding in the Pasig River must surrender; if the shore batteries reopened fire, Dewey would bombard the city; and lastly, Dewey promised to leave intact the Manila–Hong Kong telegraph cable if he was permitted to use it. Augustín, in reply, knew of no torpedo craft in the river, but if there were, his honor would not permit their surrender. He agreed on the shore batteries, saying they would not shoot unless the Americans did so first. But he would not compromise on the use of the cable. That being the case, the *Zafiro* fished it up in the bay and cut it, severing the Philippines from the rest of the world until August 22, ten days after the end of the war.[74]

The anguish of the Spanish population of Manila following the naval disaster was compounded by a gripping fear of bombardment by the victorious enemy. Since Dewey had been reported leaving Mirs Bay, more than four thousand Spaniards, including the family of the captain general, had fled north on the Philippines' only railroad, to the end of the line at Gagupan on Lingayen Gulf. Still, at the cooling dusk, as the American ships lay tranquilly off the Luneta, hundreds of people crowded down to the waterfront, onto the very ramparts mounting the useless coastal guns, to stare at the enemy's vessels and listen to the music of the *Olympia*'s band playing "La Paloma" and other Spanish songs. It was then the Spanish colonel in chief of the Manila coast artillery shot himself in the head, irredeemably dishonored by disgraceful failure.

Sometime after the turn of the midwatch, in the first hours of May 2, a steam launch put off from Manila, prompting the squadron to man its battle stations for torpedo attack and illuminate the craft with searchlights. The launch, however, came with a Spanish military official who boarded the *Olympia*. He requested of Commodore Dewey permission to order the guns on Corregidor not to fire on American ships passing in and out of the bay. This was granted. He was placed aboard the *Raleigh*, which, with the *Baltimore*, made the rounds of Manila Bay's entrance forts, demanding their surrender. Each capitulated and their garrisons were paroled. Landing parties from the cruisers went ashore, disabled the guns, removed the breech blocks, and destroyed the ammunition. They also swept for mines in the Boca Chica Channel between Corregidor and Bataan. Eventually they found some, eighty feet down, sitting on the bottom, useless.

With sunrise on May 2, a Spanish flag was seen flying over the Cavite arsenal and navy yard. Commander Lamberton and the *Petrel* went to investigate. On landing, he found the defenders—naval infantry, sailors, and soldiers—under arms as though nothing had happened the day before. In reply to Lamberton's astonishment and stiff questions, Commodore Sostoa y Ordoñez calmly answered that the colors had been lowered, and replaced by the white flag during the battle only as a token of temporary truce. Lamberton would have none of that, telling the Spanish officer that if the white flag was not rehoisted the *Petrel* would open fire and destroy all military targets in Cavite. Sostoa begged for time to consult Madrid, or if that were not possible, the authorities in Manila. Out of the question, said Lamberton. The only thing under consideration was unconditional surrender of all personnel, military facilities, and arms. He returned to the *Petrel*, giving Sostoa some time to think it over. Just before noon, the white flag reappeared over the arsenal, and the whole garrison evacuated and trudged up the coast to Manila. The navy yard, an asset beyond price, was immediately taken over by the squadron.[75]

Having of necessity cut the telegraph cable, Dewey could only communicate with the Navy Department from Hong Kong. For this he used the Revenue cutter *McCulloch*, which departed Manila on Thursday, May 5, reaching Hong Kong two days later. She carried two messages from the commodore to Secretary Long, the first being dated May 1: "The squadron arrived at Manila at daybreak this morning. Immediately engaged enemy and destroyed the following Spanish vessels . . ." Tolling that naval list, he informed the secretary of the uninjured state of the Asiatic Squadron, and the "few men slightly wounded." The message ended with a request for immediate replenishment of ammunition by fast steamer from San Francisco.[76]

The second message, dated Wednesday, May 4, indicated Dewey's precarious position, because victor or not, a naval squadron cannot hold ground. "I have taken possession of the naval station at Cavite, Philippine Islands," he began, "and destroyed its fortifications." So, too, the defenses at the entrance to Manila Bay, and the cable was cut. As far as the operational scene went, "I control bay completely and can take city at any time, but I have not sufficient men to hold." The squadron was doing splendidly, in "excellent health and spirits." Not so the Spanish; 250 of their military sick and wounded from the battle were being "cared for and protected" by the squadron's surgeons and hospital corpsmen in the Cavite naval hospital and U.S. Marines of the new Cavite garrison. "Much excitement at Manila," Dewey concluded. The place, on account of unwonted extravagance, was running scarce of food and provisions. And again, he reiterated his dire need of ammunition.[77]

In the United States, sparse accounts of the Asiatic Squadron had taken up a few column inches in the daily press; for most Americans in 1898, the Philippines might as well have been the moon. They knew, if they read the papers, that the squadron had been forced by international law out of Hong Kong and had departed the China coast to battle the Spaniards in Manila Bay. They also knew that Commodore Dewey was on his own. Every foreign port was closed to him, save for emergency coaling to his nearest home port. Of direct news there was none. There was as yet no transpacific cable, and all news from East Asia needed to come roundabout from Europe.

The first account of the Battle of Manila Bay to arrive in Washington was a Spanish report, indeed Captain General Augustín's telegram to Madrid sent at the time of Dewey's temporary withdrawal to count his ammunition and give the men breakfast. It was printed in the American papers on May 2, and made it clear that the Spanish had suffered badly. But the wording also indicated they had given as good as they got. "Our fleet," said Augustín, "engaged the enemy in brilliant combat. . . . They obliged the enemy, with heavy loss to maneuver repeatedly. At 9 o'clock the American squadron took refuge behind the foreign merchant shipping. . . . Our fleet . . . naturally suffered severe loss." The effect of this somewhat dire result was modified before much time passed by additional Spanish dispatches based on messages from Admiral Montojo. These were far saner accounts, but still claimed "that the American squadron received severe damage in the engagement." At least two of Dewey's ships were reported sunk.[78]

The first American account came just prior to the cutting of the cable, the Manila correspondent of the *New York Herald* reporting to the home office the annihilation of the Spanish fleet and the apparently uninjured state of the Americans. But there was nothing official; that would need wait until the *McCulloch* arrived at Hong Kong. Nearly a week passed with rumors that the Navy Department was withholding information to hide the severe losses to Dewey's ships. Secretary Long was obliged to issue a statement denying the rumors and promising a full disclosure the moment the official account arrived at the department.

At dawn on Saturday, May 7, the third assistant secretary of state, asleep on a cot in the State, War, and Navy Building, was handed a

message of four words: "Hong Kong McCulloch Wildman." Rounseville Wildman was the acting U.S. consul in Hong Kong, but it was
the ship's name that sent the bureaucrat running up the corridor to
the Bureau of Navigation. The Western Union cable handed to Secretary Long was typed in cipher, and anxious minutes lapsed before he
read the decoded text. Assistant Secretary Roosevelt, cleaning up the
last details of office before going into the army, leaned over the shoulder of the code clerk and brought Dewey's victory message to the mob
of reporters pushing against the door. Long's official statement to the
fifty newspapermen came as an anticlimax.

It is an understatement to say that wild celebrations erupted na-
tionwide on the publication of Dewey's reports and their elaboration
in the press. Manila Bay was hailed as the greatest naval victory in history, and Dewey as the equal of the transcendent Nelson. The commodore was immediately promoted to acting rear admiral, erasing the
slight at his appointment six months back. Congress voted ten thousand dollars for a Tiffany sword for the victor, and bronze medals for
the men of the Asiatic Squadron. A Dewey craze swept the country;
along with Theodore Roosevelt, he became one of the only two popularly remembered figures of the Spanish-American War, and his
order—"You may fire when you are ready, Gridley"—stands with
"Remember the *Maine!*" as one of the only repeated quotes of the war.

John D. Long was unstinting in his praise. "No man could have
done better or deserved more. Had the enterprise failed, it would
have been his ruin." And here was the nub. Not only would Dewey
have been disgraced and humiliated, but the United States would have
as well. Not everyone put his money on the Asiatic Squadron when it
departed Hong Kong; history held too many instances of guaranteed
victory turning to ashes in an afternoon. William McKinley and his
advisers, most of them veterans of the Civil War, remembered the cry
of "On to Richmond!" choking in the dust of the rout from Bull Run.
If the Americans had been repulsed, or even temporarily checked, at
Manila Bay, the European powers would certainly have rushed in
meddlesome concert to extricate Spain from its dilemma with the
United States. The victory was far-reaching in the extreme, not so
much because a colony had been snatched from Spain at literally no
cost, yet, but because the United States had planted itself as a player
of paramount consequence in East Asia, to be reckoned with by other

empire builders with an eye to the region—certainly, Germany, and most dangerously, Japan.[79]

But these enormous geopolitical consequences were lost in the near-term tumult of the operational victory. Any value placed by the European powers on the prowess or even worth of the Spanish navy was largely shattered. As Captain Chadwick said, Europe no longer spoke "of sitting in judgment upon the United States. . . . The victory at once gave a new aspect to the whole subject of the war."[80]

CHAPTER 6

WHEN JOHNNY WENT MARCHING OFF

Our condition was similar to that of Wellington in Spain, when he wrote, "[A small] army well equipped, disciplined, officered, and instructed is far more effective than a larger one without these essential conditions."
—*Major General Nelson A. Miles, USA, July 1898*

The energetic measures and sense of emergency manifested by the navy since the very beginning of the Cuban crisis found no equal measure in either the War Department bureaus or the U.S. Army in the field. Before the *Maine* explosion, it stood content with its primary duties of defending the coasts and patrolling the Rio Grande. What occupied most of the time of line and staff officers consisted of accelerating the deadly slow rate of promotion and abandoning dusty, company-sized posts on the vanished frontier.

On April 1, 1898, the authorized strength of the army stood at 28,747 officers and enlisted men, against a U.S. population of 73 million people, the smallest proportionally under arms at the beginning of any war, except the Revolution of 1776. Just over half of the army's regular personnel were allotted to its twenty-five infantry regiments, two of them, the 24th and 25th, being composed of black enlisted men and white officers. The cavalry counted ten regiments, the 9th and 10th being black units. The artillery, given the impetus of the $50 million bill, now stood at seven regiments, each an unwieldy amalgam of fortress, siege, and light batteries.[1]

Staff functions were exclusively confined to ten administrative and technical War Department bureaus, each headed by a brigadier general, advanced to his post by strict seniority. Primus inter pares in stature and influence came the Adjutant General's Department, the conduit of orders, commands, and assignments, and the custodian of archives and records. The Inspector General's Department inspected and reported on the army's proficiency, discipline, and leadership, together with judging the suitability of its arms, clothing, and equipment. The Judge Advocate General's Department, or Bureau of Military Justice as it was also termed, served as the reviewing authority for courts-martial and courts of inquiry, and was the source of legal advice for the Secretary of War. The Quartermaster's Department maintained responsibility for barracks and quarters, transportation of troops and equipment, and procurement and distribution of most supplies. The Subsistence Department held sway over purchase, content, and distribution of rations. The Medical Department was custodian of the army's health and hygiene. The Hospital Corps, composed solely of 706 enlisted men, served as stretcher bearers and also performed nursing functions. The Pay Department's officers traveled endlessly around the country distributing wages. Mapping and construction of field and permanent works was the province of the Corps of Engineers. The Ordnance Department tested, selected, bought, or manufactured in its own plants the army's weapons, and distributed all arms, ammunition, and related appurtenances. The most junior of the staff organizations was the Signal Corps, charged with maintaining communications via telegraph, semaphore, pigeons, and other devices, including tethered balloons.

The bureau system meant an extremely centralized organization, with all important decisions emanating from its offices. It created mountains of paperwork and long delays, and worst of all, it deprived individual troop commanders of the power and authority to act independently, stifled thinking beyond the mundane movements on a company parade ground, and inhibited all coordinated planning between combat arms. Though the combat arms—infantry, cavalry, and artillery—were a tough, efficient lot as individuals and small units, there was virtually no combined arms training, and no maneuvers or concentrations of troops beyond a handful of infantry companies or cavalry troops. There were no formations above the regiment, and no officer who had not served in the Civil War had any experience with, or had even seen, any unit as large as a brigade, to say nothing of a division or an army corps. Thus constituted, the army was at a severe disadvantage in organizing and mobilizing for war.

At the top of the pyramid stood Secretary of War Russell Alger, vain, egotistical, often lazy and evasive in difficult situations. He was not the utter incompetent often depicted and later scapegoated for the army's deficiencies in the war. But he lacked the administrative experience in managing a large organization and became overwhelmed under the sheer weight of responsibility for supervising the mushrooming expansion of the army in the crisis.

Since 1895, the professional head of the army, the senior major general, holding the honorific of commanding general, was Nelson A. Miles, an infantryman who signed up as a volunteer in the Civil War and collected vast experience during the decades-long Indian wars. As commanding general, Miles shared with Secretary Alger the authority to pass on all orders, and directly oversaw the training and deployment of the infantry, cavalry, and artillery. He also maintained more or less direct control over the offices of the adjutant general and inspector general. A man with commendable qualities of leadership, he had grown irritable with age and had difficulty working with his War Department colleagues and political superiors. Ambitious, hugely egotistic, a "brave peacock" according to Theodore Roosevelt, designer of his own uniforms, he was prone to confuse his own personal and political agenda with high principles of state and service. Miles and Alger detested each other to a degree that served the army and nation no good. What their official relationship was is conjectural, but in most cases Alger held the advantage because the bureau chiefs lined up behind the civilian secretary of war as the best means of preserving their fiefdoms and prerogatives against the demands of the commanding general. It was no way to run an army.[2]

Unlike the navy, the War Department did not get serious about the threat of war until the passage of the $50 million bill, and then only in a halfhearted way because of Russell Alger's strict interpretation of its "defense" rather than offensive-minded language. Yet, given the undoubted maritime nature of the coming war, the army's role was very much dependent on the actions of the navy. In the total absence of general staffs for either service, but recognizing the necessity for some sort of joint planning agency, in late March secretaries Alger and Long delegated their respective intelligence offices to coordinate navy and army war plans into a degree of compatibility. While it lacked the sophistication of Continental planning staffs, by the beginning of April, each service clearly understood its probable mission in the coming war with Spain.

On March 12, the influential *Army and Navy Journal* editorially stated, "With a regular army of sufficient strength to form the fighting line and with the organized militia for local service, we should have a force quite sufficient for our needs against Spain." In accord with this thinking, the War Department undertook a campaign for the type of "expansible" army long advocated by service reformers. The department found its congressional ally in Representative John Hull, Republican of Iowa, chairman of the House Committee on Military Affairs. Agreeing with the regulars, Hull considered the National Guard, as then constituted, a useless body for offensive combat, and strongly supported increasing the active army instead. Following the success of the artillery bill adding the 6th and 7th regiments to the line, Hull introduced legislation providing an organization of three battalions of four companies each to infantry regiments, rather than the ten-company alignment in place since before the Civil War.

Simultaneously, the Adjutant General's Office had prepared a similar measure, and the whole package, generically called the "Hull bill," was submitted to Congress on March 17. The act was intended to conform to long-standing army doctrine and was meant as a permanent service reform, not just a temporary crisis substitute for the existing structure. Essentially it combined reorganization of the infantry with an expandable enlisted force. At the time, each infantry regiment held ten companies, eight theoretically fully manned and two as officer cadres, where duties entailed training National Guard units or teaching military science in colleges. The Hull bill combined the eight companies into two battalions, and formed the two cadre companies into the nucleus of a third battalion, which, "in time of war" and by order of the president, would be mobilized to full strength, with two new companies created.[3]

The bill also authorized the president in wartime to enlarge the regular army into a striking force of 104,000 men by increasing the enlisted force of each infantry company, cavalry troop, and artillery battery. The additional officers required to staff this growth would come from promoting commissioned and noncommissioned officers, and from lists of civilians selected by the president. In calling for volunteers, recruiting areas for each regiment would be geographically designated, something long sought by army reformers and intended to make the regulars more popular by associating each regiment with a specific region, very much on the British and German models. The bill also soothed the sensitive issue of increasing the regular army in peacetime by keeping the third battalion unmanned, save in time of war. The actual increase of the peacetime establishment saw the addition of twenty-five majors, one for each infantry regiment. The promotion of twenty-five captains to the elevated rank to fill these vacancies would speed up promotion of the junior officers and place much needed younger men in command of companies. As written, the Hull bill was good law on its merits for the time, well suited to the army's requirements in the war with Spain.

Accompanying the bill was a letter from Secretary Alger to Congress explaining how the War Department, under the proposed legislation, could mobilize in a short time all the troops needed for a campaign in Cuba. In any emergency, the department could arrange the standing enlisted force to bring one or two battalions of each regiment up to full-strength war levels and equip these units for immediate service. The remaining battalions, now reduced to officer and NCO cadres, would travel to their assigned mobilization areas and fill up with recruits. After a few weeks of basic training under the eyes of professionals, they might be rendered fit for service and, trained and equipped, join the expeditionary force on active campaign. Alger, stressing the progressive theories of the late Colonel Emory Upton, more or less the Mahan of the army, noted that "the superiority of such a force made up of professional officers and noncommissioned officers skilled in their respective duties, over a hastily organized body, officered by men new to the service . . . would be incalculable."[4]

Both the Hull bill's sponsors and influential senior army officers made it abundantly clear that state volunteer and National Guard units would have no part in any attack on Cuba. Hull told reporters his bill was expressly designed to make the regular army the cadre for any future volunteer forces. A few days later Adjutant General Henry Corbin said, "An Army capable of expansion from a peace basis of

27,000 to a war footing of 104,000 would answer all ordinary demands." If National Guardsmen wished to partake in the campaign, he urged them to enlist in the expanding regular regiments. Similar sentiments were expressed by the army hierarchy, who maintained limiting the guard to coast defense duties only.[5]

With the full weight of the administration behind it, the Hull bill seemed to sail through the legislative process. Adjutant General Corbin served as the bill's manager, the leading newspapers pressed for its adoption, and House and Senate sponsors predicted early, favorable congressional action. The *Army and Navy Journal* anticipated "speedy and practically unanimous passage." The House took up the bill on March 23, adding amendments that required the immediate reduction of the regular army to its peacetime strength upon cessation of hostilities, and also a declaration of war by Congress prior to any presidential order for expansion. The key provisions, however, survived. By the end of the month, the United States military situation seemed quite in hand. The navy had concentrated, and the army was preparing to defend the coasts, was accumulating weaponry and gear, and was ready to enlarge itself on receiving the presidential order.[6]

The glitch and eventual death of the Hull bill arose over controversy about the National Guard and its wartime role. After the blowing up of the *Maine,* the guard had responded enthusiastically, and without waiting for War Department orders, units began recruiting up to their paper strength of just over 115,000 men. Supplies were accumulated, and war plans, after a fashion, were drawn up in expectation of a call to invade Cuba. In reality, the guard was sorely below strength, its equipment scarce and obsolete, its men with only the meagerest training. It would take just as long to get these units ready for campaign as it would completely new formations recruited from civilian life.

The state governors, as commanders of their respective National Guard regiments, would never surrender the tremendous opportunities for patronage served up by the opportunity to appoint officers to a popular war. Guardsmen and their powerful political allies in the Congress and state legislatures began agitating for a law to permit the president to use state troops in wartime for any sort of national service. Led by Ohio and Pennsylvania congressmen, the attack on the

Hull bill was launched. Their immediate objections to the legislation, so they said, were that units from inland states would probably not be called into service, so their members would be forced to join the regulars as individuals if they wished to see action.

Guardsmen, who considered themselves socially superior to regular army enlisted men, found this prospect degrading. Guard officers could not serve at all unless they surrendered their state commissions, an inconceivable action. Moreover, the Hull bill, by eliminating a need to call for volunteers, excluded the guard from what it considered its rightful place in the military arena. Guardsmen, who voted in solid blocks during state elections, placed extremely heavy pressure on their congressmen to defeat the Hull bill. These legislators, together with southern Democrats, who still resented the regular army and its role in Reconstruction, and populists, who feared an enlarged regular army as an agency of internal repression, formed a powerful league against the War Department and the regulars. With them as the enemy, the Hull bill never had a chance.

In addition to having purely military and peacekeeping functions, the National Guard formed a strong social entity fiercely opposed to any scheme whereby the identity of its formations was lost. Units elected and dismissed their own officers, and the thought of serving under regulars, over whom they held no influence, was pure anathema. In New York, a member of that city's elite 7th Regiment told a reporter, "One of the reasons that we would not go willingly into the Regular Army is that we would have to serve under West Pointers. For a self-respecting American of good family to serve as a private, corporal, or sergeant under a West Point lieutenant or captain is entirely out of the question. . . . To fight for my country as a volunteer in the regiment that I love would be a glorious pleasure, but to serve in the Regular Army and do chores for some West Pointer—well, I would rather be excused."[7]

On April 6, goaded by urgent appeals from Adjutant General Corbin, Congressman Hull brought the bill to the House floor. In two days of endlessly repetitive debate it was sanctimoniously demolished, denounced by Republican and Democrat alike. To self-indulgent applause from the galleries, speaker after superpatriotic speaker denounced the "immorality" of using only regulars in their bid to monopolize the glory of victory. In honeyed and graveled tones, the moral virtue and fighting spirit of the volunteers were extolled over the mercenary spirit of the regulars, who were born of the lower classes and fought only for pay. The volunteers, said a New York Democrat, "are no hirelings, no mercenaries; they fight for the defense of home and country, for principle and glory, for liberty and the rights of man. . . . They do not menace our liberties or the stability of our free institutions."[8]

The next day, the Hull bill died in the House. From the perspective of the War Department, it could not have come at a worse time; war was only a matter of weeks away. But even with its defeat, the army planned on an expeditionary force for Cuba of around one hundred thousand men. Realizing, however, the political fallout of relying solely on regulars, the department altered the composition of this force to include a large state volunteer contingent. A few days after the bill's demise, Hull received a conditional agreement from the guard and its adherents to a revised measure. The infantry reform would remain, but wartime expansion of the regular army enlisted force was to be limited to approximately sixty thousand men.

On April 9, two days after the Hull bill crashed in defeat, General Miles, assisted by the Adjutant General's Office, drew up plans for a Cuban expeditionary force consisting of most available regular units: twenty-two infantry regiments, five of the cavalry, and all of the light field artillery batteries—in all, about thirty thousand men. He recommended to Secretary Alger a mobilization in one large camp, where they could be "carefully and thoroughly inspected, fully equipped, drilled, disciplined, and instructed in brigades and divisions, and prepared for war service." In addition to the force of regulars, Miles foresaw forty thousand to fifty thousand volunteers or guards to reinforce the coast defenses, "or for construction of the large force that may be required in the future." The president might call on the states for the first volunteer contingents the moment Congress declared war, drawing as many volunteers as possible from existing guard units. Further calls would follow if necessary.[9]

In accord with Miles's thinking, Russell Alger on April 13 appointed a coordinating board for the mobilization of the regulars and forty thousand volunteers for field service, plus an additional twenty thousand volunteers for the coast defense. The board recommended concentrating the regulars either at a single camp or at the Gulf ports of Tampa, Mobile, and New Orleans. Just as soon as they could be mustered into federal service, the volunteers could join the regulars, with the force organized into larger units—the brigades, divisions, and corps of a field army. If the War Department desired a single gathering point, the board recommended Chickamauga Battlefield Park, Georgia, a reservation established during the Cleveland administration as a maneuver area for both regulars and the National Guard. The place could accommodate up to fifty thousand men and had both good water and rail connections to the Gulf ports.

On April 15, from eighty separate posts, from Vermont to Oregon to the Rio Grande, the regulars began to move. On departmental orders, they were to equip themselves "fully for war" and take with them all available wagons from their garrison stations. Within a week, fast-moving troop trains pulled into Chickamauga and the Gulf ports.

The selection of a few large camps rather than a multitude of small ones was due to several factors, not least of which was their proximity to the scene of the presumptive campaign, Cuba, and the acclimatization of the troops to a semitropical climate, which they would provide. As well, the War Department's supply and medical bureaus did not have the personnel or camp gear to deploy otherwise. But, as Russell Alger said, another reason was the desirability of placing the volunteers in the same camps with regulars, "in order that they might benefit from the example and instruction of seasoned troops." Alger also had some larger purposes in mind, reasons emanating from the rancor surrounding the Hull bill. "Home influences," he told an investigating committee after the war, "tended to retard military discipline." As circumstances and strategy evolved, Tampa became the preeminent place of the regular army, "on account," Alger said, "of the shipping facilities at that point and its comparative short distance from Cuba, rendering any movement of the troops possible on short notice." Tampa, however, with its minimal rail and port infrastructure, was never intended as a permanent base of training or embarkation, and it became the worst of all possible worlds.[10]

In mid-April, as the regulars deployed, the War Department negotiated an agreement with the National Guard on the method of raising volunteer units. Since many of the guard leaders were already in Washington to lobby against the Hull bill, they were available for a White House conference with the president, Secretary Alger, and generals Miles and Corbin. Together these men hammered out the legislation that governed the call-up of the volunteers. What emerged was a volunteer army to serve alongside the regulars. The president limited the first call to sixty thousand members of the National Guard, men eighteen to forty-five years old, apportioned by state population, with any full unit volunteering as such to be accepted by the army as a whole and kept under the command of its own officers. With the guard agreeing to accept federal service under these conditions, the War Department could still exercise considerable control, the volunteers having to adopt the same organization, regulations, and pay as the regulars. To the president went the power to appoint all general and staff officers of volunteers, but lesser officers remained the prerogative of the state governors.

The president received his authorization to call for volunteers on April 22 and for the increase of the regulars four days later. The War Department planners crafted a congressional bill providing for the organization of army corps, each to consist of three divisions, the divisions formed of three brigades containing three regiments. Time of volunteer service was slated at two years or the duration of the war. Acting under this authority, President McKinley issued the first call on April 23, though instead of the 60,000 men desired by the War Department, he asked for 125,000, beyond the total manpower of all National Guard units. This was a mistake; the nation hadn't the means to train and outfit such numbers. In all likelihood it was done so as not to repeat Lincoln's error of calling for insufficient men at the very outset of the war. The president might also have done it to impress Spain with the military potential of the United States, or merely to go all the way in the bargain with the National Guard. In any event, the helter-skelter mess the War Department found itself in during the next weeks and months can be traced largely to this superfluous call for unneeded men. By the act, the president also had the authority to enlist specific units from company to regimental size, "possessing special qualifications, from the nation at large." It was this that permitted the formation of three volunteer cavalry regiments, one of which, the 1st U.S. Volunteer Cavalry, nicknamed the "Rough Riders," became the most famous unit of the war. In total, the volunteer army, apportioned by population to the states, territories, and the District of Columbia, amounted to 119 regiments, plus

10 battalions, of infantry; 5 regiments, plus 17 troops, of cavalry; 16 batteries of field artillery; and 1 regiment, plus 7 independent batteries, of heavy artillery.

By the second law, that of April 26, the regular army was increased to 62,527 men, but as a wartime measure only. As General Miles saw it, the volunteer legislation "had a bad effect upon the enlistment of the Regular Army." Volunteers naturally preferred their own organizations, and it became difficult to recruit men "in the regular service, which it was most essential to have rapidly brought up to its authorized strength." A third piece of legislation, the act of May 11, permitted the enlistment of 10,000 "immunes"—men supposedly resistant to yellow fever—organized into 10 regiments, and 3,500 engineers formed into 1 brigade.[11]

The 125,000 men taken under the first call came primarily from members already enrolled in National Guard units. These men, however, needed to volunteer as individuals, since under the Constitution, the guard could only be ordered into federal service to repel invasion, to execute the law upon the order of the president, or to suppress insurrection. The Spanish-American War was none of these, and to circumvent the Constitutional prohibition, and still give the guard priority in enlistment, the law of April 22 provided that guard units would be mustered first, if the men volunteered as a unit and if the unit came at full capacity. Thus in the telegrams assigning state quotas for the volunteer army, governors were informed, "It is the wish of the President that the regiments of the National Guard or State militia shall be used . . . for the reason that they are armed, equipped and drilled." Governors were queried as to what additional gear they needed and when their troops would be ready for muster into federal service.[12]

The response to the call was immediate, though varied. Some governors refused to permit their militias to be mobilized and instead formed new units. In Minnesota, for example, which organized three regiments of infantry under the first call, a National Guard jealous of preserving the excellent Civil War reputation of its units refused to permit their being given the same numbers; there would be no 1st Minnesota Volunteer Infantry in this war; the Minnesota regiments began their numbering with the 12th Regiment.

Popular enthusiasms led to some bizarre ideas. Buffalo Bill Cody published an article titled "How I Could Drive Spaniards from Cuba with Thirty Thousand Indian Braves." Frank James, brother of out-law Jesse James, asked for command of a company of cowboys. The *New York Journal* proposed forming a regiment of noted athletes, with boxer "Gentleman" Jim Corbett and baseball great Cap Anson in the ranks: "Think of a regiment composed of magnificent men of this ilk? They would overawe any Spanish regiment by their mere appearance." A Colorado matron proposed a cavalry troop of women.[13]

Around nine thousand black men entered the volunteer army, most into four immune regiments. Only three states—Alabama, Ohio, and Massachusetts—formed black regiments in the first call, and only Company L, 6th Massachusetts Volunteer Infantry, saw combat. The McKinley administration, however, paid special attention to black manpower. Nearly two hundred thousand black men had served in the Union army during the Civil War. But most National Guard units did not accept black applicants, and those states that did gave preference to white units to fill their quotas. Black organizations quickly objected to their underrepresentation in the volunteer army. It was believed, as it had been during the Civil War (and would be in World Wars I and II) that honorable military service would win for blacks greater respect in society as a whole and would assist in their struggle for equality. In response to mass meetings and agitating petitions over the exclusion of blacks sent to the White House and Congress, President McKinley, in his second call for volunteers on May 11, accepted black units from Alabama, Illinois, Kansas, North Carolina, and Virginia; these were generally organized around existing state militia units, and some even had black officers who held state commissions, or former black regulars elevated to volunteer officers. The only black West Point graduate then serving in the regular army, First Lieutenant Charles Young, accepted a commission from Ohio as major and commanding officer of the 9th Battalion, Ohio Volunteers.

Naturally the War Department tried to assemble the best-trained and -equipped guard units for rapid movement into Cuba. In the first days of May it asked the state governors to outfit their units one at a time, rather than simultaneously, so as to get a few well-found formations ready for immediate action. As volunteers streamed into the camps, the adjutant general canvassed the nation seeking the readiest formations. On May 12, General Corbin reported to the secretary of war that thirty infantry regiments and four field artillery batteries, mostly guards from the Northeast and upper Midwest, had been mustered into federal service and at least partially equipped for active duty. Most of these were sent to Chickamauga Battlefield Park.

Most of the guard units were at their peacetime quota of around half that prescribed by law for the volunteer formations, and of these existing members, anywhere from a third to half refused to enlist or failed the army physical examination. Large states might have overcome this by combining units, as did small New England states, but for the most part, this was politically unthinkable. Instead they reached their authorized strength by enlisting raw recruits, many of whom were later found medically unfit for duty. What eventually resulted was a volunteer force consisting of a mass of undrilled civilians, commanded by National Guard officers, and stiffened with a thin cadre of old militiamen and one or two regulars per regiment. Hardly what the country needed at the time.

On April 27, the War Department began its recruitment and assembly of the army as created by the congressional acts, making a special effort to bring the regulars up to their authorized strength. Regimental commanders received orders to form their third battalions, and all branches were to fill up cadres and recruit to the limit of the wartime establishment. Regiments received permission to send recruiting parties where they wished, and the organization that was first in any given region had the exclusive right to draw on its manpower. The regulars, however, were severely hampered by the competing attractions of the swollen volunteer service and could not fill their ranks fast or adequately enough for the coming offensive. Hundreds of regular officers accepted appointments in the volunteers, usually with increased rank. When given the choice, most prospective enlistees preferred to enlist in the volunteer units, attracted by the easier discipline and the opportunity to serve with friends and neighbors. By the end of May, the regular army had managed to sign up only 8,500 men of the 36,000 needed to bring it to its wartime capacity. Not until late August, after an armistice with Spain had been signed, did it attain the desired goal.

The *Army and Navy Journal* described the "scramble for high commissions" in the volunteer army as "a sight for the gods." As in the unseemly rush during the Civil War, Secretary Alger's office was jammed with applicants demanding command of every formation from a brigade to an army corps. The president had only about fifty of these plums to distribute, and the seekers numbered about twenty times that. Adjutant General Corbin was inundated with a stack of letters "that reaches almost to the ceiling." "Everyone," said the *Journal,* "who has ever carried a musket . . . seems bent on getting a high command."[14]

While the regulars sought recruits and the volunteers mustered in their states, political pressures inherent in the system began influencing the composition of the army. When the Adjutant General's Office apportioned the state quotas to obtain a proper balance of line and supporting components, it ignored the organization of existing militia units. Thus some states found it impossible to send all the men of their quota, while others ordered to furnish cavalry and artillery simply did not have them. It resulted in another rush on the War Department by governors and legislators demanding changes in the state allotment, and for the most part this was accommodated to the detriment of the army. For in the dash to placate the guard and state politicians, certain militia units were excluded from the call so that others, more fashionable, might go instead. Formations the army really needed, such as attached signal and hospital companies of the various state regiments that did not exist in the regular establishment, often went missing.

Once the composition of each state contingent had been settled, they mustered at a central point for enrollment to federal duty. The state troops left their home districts to cheers of crowds, bands, cannon, and blowing steam whistles. Usually they spent a week at a state collecting camp, drilling and undergoing medical examinations. A mustering officer, sent by the War Department, swore each unit, company by company, into the national service. This went very quickly, and by the end of May, most of the 125,000 volunteers of the first call had been mustered in.

To its credit, the War Department lost no time in organizing and equipping the gathering host. On May 6, the department issued orders for the deployment of the volunteers. Under these directions, thirty-seven regiments of infantry, plus assorted cavalry and artillery units, assembled at newly named Camp Thomas at Chickamauga Battlefield Park, and twenty-four more infantry regiments with their cavalry and artillery contingents moved into Camp Alger in Falls

Church, Virginia. Smaller volunteer assemblages were sent to San Francisco for shipment to the Philippines, and to San Antonio, New Orleans, Tampa, and Mobile. A general reserve of forty-seven infantry regiments, seventeen cavalry troops, and twenty-four artillery batteries remained in their respective states under command of the army's geographical departments.

To meet supposedly increased manpower requirements, in good part prodded by the unforeseen circumstances in the Philippines, on May 25 President McKinley issued a second call for 75,000 men, which would increase the total of the volunteer army to 200,000. A number of these men were used to fill out the quotas of understrength outfits from the first call. However, only 40,000 had been mustered under this provision when orders came to cease recruiting in August, following the signing of the armistice.

The act of April 22 reorganized the army into a system of eight corps, each, so far as was practicable, of three divisions. On the twenty-third, the regulars at Chickamauga Battlefield Park were organized into a provisional corps under command of Major General John R. Brooke. Two weeks later, in General Order No. 36, the final framework was published providing for the establishment of seven army corps: First through Eighth, with the Sixth not activated. Of these, the First in Puerto Rico, the mostly regular Fifth in the campaign of Santiago de Cuba, and the Eighth at Manila would see active service against Spanish arms.[15]

Almost a quarter of a million men needed to be fed, equipped, clothed, and housed. Nearly everything was in short supply, and some items simply did not exist. The War Department had enough modern Krag-Jorgenson rifles and carbines to arm the expanded regulars and perhaps two thousand more for the volunteers. But the rest of the army had to make do with a decade-old Springfield single-shot rifle that fired a heavy .45-caliber black powder slug. Inspections of National Guard troops often revealed their arms in bad condition, rusty and incapable of lasting through a campaign. There were numerous instances of units arriving in camp without even these obsolete weapons, and there were occasions at Chickamauga Battlefield Park of sentries walking post with broomsticks.

The War Department was doomed to glaring blunders, and these were magnified by the speedup in the mustering of the volunteers. But neither the defective organization of the department nor the unexpected requirements for feeding and outfitting the coming masses can account for the failure to prepare the volunteers with the most basic outfits in their home camps. Quartermaster General Ludington and Secretary Alger compounded the problem with weak leadership at the top. Ludington repeatedly asked the number of militiamen for which he had to make arrangements, to which Alger first responded with the number of 30,000, then 80,000. Ludington's first hard information came with the president's call for 125,000 men. And from Alger there had been no response to the quartermaster general's timid suggestion that "possibly I ought to be doing something."[16]

It did not go well, especially in the beginning. The volunteers came in quickly, but for the most part they were appallingly outfitted, and reports of their battle readiness were overoptimistic to say the least. "[M]any of the States," said General Miles, "have made no provision for their . . . militia, and not one is fully equipped for field service." The administration had been duped by state propaganda that the large majority of the first 125,000 men had at least some rudimentary drill and the basic equipment of a soldier. New York regiments lacked mess kits and shelter tents. Several governors greedily withheld their equipment altogether, and their regiments entrained for camp in civilian clothing. By late May, regular commanders at Chickamauga and Camp Alger disgustedly reported not a single state regiment ready to take the field.[17]

Stockpiles of everything were virtually nonexistent at the outbreak of the war, and the Quartermaster's Department, with only fifty-seven officers assigned to it, was hopelessly overwhelmed. Of everything there was only enough for a three-month supply of the regulars as then constituted, 26,000 men, plus perhaps 10,000 more. Yet overnight, it was called upon to supply over a quarter of a million men. The volunteer units had no consistency about them on their arrival at camp. Some units had almost nothing; others came fairly well arrayed. The "worst from some states are better equipped than the best from others," said General Miles. Some companies came in mixed uniforms, while in others there was only civilian clothing. Writing to Secretary Alger from Tampa, Miles continued, "Several of the Volunteer regiments came here without uniforms; several came without arms, and some without blankets, tents, or camp equipage." A fair amount of the blame for that lay with staff officers of the volunteer regiments, who, with little or no experience in their duties, simply did not know how to requisition what was needed.[18]

To assure the rapid outfitting of formations designated for the initial attacks on Cuba and the expedition to the Philippines, the Quartermaster's and Ordnance departments gave these units first claim on all scarce supplies. When the six-mule wagons began arriving from the manufacturers, most were dispatched to Tampa, while other camps had to make do with only enough wagons to haul supplies from the railheads to the regiments. The chief of ordnance later established special expeditionary depots at Tampa and San Francisco, from which all units ordered to those ports could draw their necessary weapons, ammunition, and accoutrements. To keep these fully stocked, shipments to other camps were delayed. Beginning in late May, the commanders at Chickamauga Battlefield Park and Camp Alger adopted the same principle, filling up only those units to be called for expeditionary duty at the expense and shortage of all others. There was no other choice.

Few shortages produced more suffering for the troops or were more difficult to overcome than the lack of tropical uniforms for the invasion forces intended to fight in the Caribbean and the Philippines. Before 1898, the quartermaster general had issued no special uniform for hot-weather service, and men stationed in the warmer parts of the American South and Southwest had worn the standard blue woolen with only minor modifications. The nearest thing to a lightweight summer uniform was a brown canvas fatigue, first issued in 1883. Early in April, on Miles's recommendation, Quartermaster General Ludington adopted a variation of the fatigue for troops slated for campaigning in hot climates, and the army contracted for an experimental lot of ten thousand sets. A month later, Ludington encountered frustrating delays when he tried to order additional lots. Ludington wanted them not of canvas, but of the light khaki textile so successfully adopted by the British for use by their forces in India, but no American firm could weave or dye that fabric. A number of the troops did receive the brown fatigue uniform, but the only use made of it, said an infantry officer, "was to put the blanket-roll through the legs of the trousers, thereby adding to the weight of the roll, without perceptible benefit to the soldier." With the exception of the privately fitted out Rough Riders, the U.S. forces that fought the Spanish-American War made do with a reduced-weight, though still beastly uncomfortable, standard blue woolen shirt, trousers, and blouse, augmented by large issues of light cotton underwear.[19]

In all of their prewar planning and in a good amount of it done during the war, the armed services toiled without political guidance or objectives from the administration. President McKinley never revealed his ultimate plans for the future of Cuba, if indeed he maintained any. For the navy this lack of direction proved no great hindrance. Their mission was clear: to seek out and destroy the Spanish fleet, capture its merchantmen, and blockade and bombard the enemy's coast. For the army, however, the administration's political objectives would determine the course and scale of its war efforts. If the administration saw fit to merely provide arms and logistic aid to the Cuban rebels, enabling them to defeat Spain on their own and then establish an independent state, there would be no need for a large American expeditionary force. American war planners believed this direction would be best and most energetically achieved by severing Spain's sea communications with Cuba, using the navy.

But a large-scale land campaign by the United States against the Spanish army in Cuba was another matter entirely, requiring far greater preparations of every imaginable sort. Yet in the dearth of political ends from the administration, the United States Army was forced to base its contingencies on its own evaluation of the military situation in Cuba. Initially, it leaned toward sending a small force of regulars to support the rebels on their home ground, a scenario endorsed by the Cuban Junta, who feared too large an American military presence as a threat to ultimate independence, which indeed it proved to be. Thus the basis for the army's prewar strategy was to employ maximum American naval strength against Spain and the bare minimum of land forces. In reality, it did not turn out too differently.

There was also the matter of the bad timing of the war. It had come at the very beginning of the rainy season, or, as Russell Alger termed it, the "sickly" season. It was determined, he said, "that the wisest course would be to devote the summer to organizing, equipping, and drilling the volunteers" while making "harassing incursions" along the Cuban coast as opportunity presented. This view was endorsed by General Miles and most senior U.S. Army officers.[20]

There was a rather large hitch to this, however. Given the fact that the war was primarily to be the navy's show, and no thinking person doubted that, the fleet needed the freedom to roam the seas without worrying about the security of its bases or the vulnerability of the American East and Gulf coasts to Spanish raids. But of more than 2,000 heavy guns and mortars stipulated in prewar estimates for the defense of the coast, only 151 had been mounted by April 1, and these held less than twenty rounds per gun.

On April 4, a small, joint army-navy planning committee submitted its war plan to the service secretaries. Endorsing the blockade scenario of Cuba, it suggested that a modest army expedition seize a port through which supplies could be funneled to the rebels. They doubted the necessity for a big invasion, especially during the rainy season, an extremely dangerous undertaking. If, however, the administration decided on the latter course of action, they recommended a strike at the main Spanish strength at Havana with an assault force of fifty thousand men, all regulars, and a follow-up descent on Puerto Rico to deny Spain a vital Caribbean naval base.

The navy had its own ideas of how the army might be employed, based in part on the concentration of the Spanish fleet not in Havana, but at the Cape Verde Islands off the bulge of West Africa, where it could neither be blockaded nor brought to action by a preemptive American thrust at Cuba. Early in April, Captain William T. Sampson of the *Iowa*, soon to be named acting rear admiral in command of the North Atlantic Squadron, in conference with his fellow captains, forwarded a plan to capture Havana by naval action alone. Without great danger to his ships, Sampson believed, he could silence the city's coastal batteries and compel its surrender under the threat of bombardment. Whatever regular troops were available in the United States could then occupy the city. The enormous political and military fallout of so singular a victory early in the conflict could not be overestimated—if it could be done. But Secretary Long refused permission. He would not countenance exposing the squadron to damage by shore fire until the Spanish fleet itself was met and beaten. Sampson countered with a vigorous defense of his plan; the risks, he iterated, were small to the reward gained. He sympathized with Long's concern, but at the same time, "I regard it as very important to strike quickly and strike hard as soon as hostilities commence." Sampson's arguments apparently convinced the War Department, for on April 15, when Russell Alger ordered the regulars concentrated for action, he sent the infantry regiments directly to the Gulf, where they could more easily embark to support and follow up the naval attack.[21]

On April 18, General Miles presented Secretary Alger with a formal proposal opposing Sampson's coup de main at Havana and stressing the army's small-force concept. The general was not "sanguine" about the prospects for an immediate grand-scale incursion into Cuba; the United States had not the men for it in any case. Once the navy had secured control of the sea around the operational theater, Miles recommended the insertion of a moderate-sized force. Properly handled, they could do the enemy "the greatest injury with the least possible loss to ourselves. . . . [W]e can compel the surrender of the [Spanish] army on the island of Cuba with very little loss of life." Besides that, it "was utterly impossible" to organize a large invasion force, properly equipped, before the onset of the rainy season. During this initial small-scale operation, the rest of the army, regulars and soon-to-be-called volunteers, would mobilize and train in "healthful camps" in the United States until such time, the autumn, perhaps, when it was feasible for major operations in Cuba.[22]

At first impressed by Captain Sampson's plan, William McKinley now swung against it and shied away from an early invasion. On April 20, the day he signed the congressional joint resolution, the president called a cabinet meeting that was also attended by senior officers accompanying the service secretaries. General Miles argued against sending battleships against coastal forts while the enemy's fleet remained afloat and stressed the army's need to prepare before any major action was undertaken, telling the president that "there was not enough ammunition left in the United States to last an army of 70,000 men in one hour's serious battle." It was decided instead to initiate a close naval blockade through the summer while simultaneously sending arms and supplies to the rebels and possibly harassing the Spanish with small coastal raids by the army. Somewhat annoyed at the army's inability to do more than prepare, especially as the navy had been on a virtual war footing since the *Maine* explosion, Secretary Long confided to his diary, "I am inclined to think that if war actually comes, the country will demand that our soldiers make a landing and do something." Theodore Roosevelt felt the same, telling the navy's Captain Robley "Fighting Bob" Evans, "If only the Army were one-tenth as ready as the Navy, we would fix that whole business in six weeks before the sickly season was under way, but what will happen now I don't know."[23]

To supplement the blockade, the War Department set to preparing an expedition to Cuba. A "reconnaissance in force," Miles called it, for the dual purpose of showing the flag and bringing some aid to the rebels, "in order that they might continue to wage warfare against the Spanish troops." On April 29, Miles ordered Brigadier General William Rufus Shafter, the rough-hewn, corpulent commander of the Fifth Corps, to assemble at Tampa a force of six thousand regular infantry, cavalry, artillery, and assorted support units for overseas service. Sailing on chartered transports under navy escort, it was intended to land on the south coast of Cuba at Cape Tunas, about seventy miles east of Cienfuegos. Marching inland, this force theoretically could rendezvous with rebel troops under Máximo Gómez, and once joined, transfer weapons and supplies carried from the United States. Additionally, Shafter would collect invaluable on-site military intelligence and, if the opportunity arose, cooperate with Gómez in local raids against the Spanish. He was, however, to avoid major battles. After knocking around in Cuba for a few days, the regulars would reembark in their transports and return directly to the United States.[24]

The expedition never sailed, for on the very day Miles issued the orders, Admiral Pascual Cervera's squadron of four armored cruisers and three destroyers sailed from the Cape Verde Islands and disappeared into the Atlantic void. The Spanish fleet's destination and purpose being unknown, the U.S. Navy could not afford to deplete its forces to convoy Shafter's reconnaissance sortie to Cuba. The mission was canceled, but Shafter was ordered to continue his preparations nonetheless. By the end of the first week of May, he had assembled his six thousand men and seven steamers at Tampa Bay, ready to move when orders at last would come; he would wait some time.

Military operations in the Caribbean failed to keep pace with events. After the first heady news from Manila, plans for invasions of

Cuba and Puerto Rico, so impetuously laid, were now unavoidably delayed in a maze of complex frustrations. At a joint service and cabinet conference in the White House on May 2, it was decided to enlarge Shafter's command at Tampa to fifty thousand men. Its new mission was to seize and fortify the port of Mariel, where the western *trocha* met the sea, just west of Havana, as the commencement of a major operation to besiege the Cuban capital, the center of Spanish power in the Western Hemisphere. Russell Alger unwisely suggested the War Department could be ready for this action inside a month, the campaign to begin just as soon as the men and transport shipping were available, and without any regard to the onset of the rainy season.

With the support of the North Atlantic Squadron, General Shafter's regulars would operate as the vanguard for the operation, grabbing Mariel and fortifying it as a beachhead and base camp. Then, just as fast as they could be sent, the volunteer regiments would join the regulars, and when they reached their maximum of around fifty thousand men, the whole force would advance on Havana from the west and south. Cooperation with the Cuban rebels did not enter into this scenario. Recent liaisons with rebel leaders and minor gunrunning operations along the Cuban coast had finally brought the administration to realize that the rebels' military strength and their alleged desire to test the Spanish army in the field in real combat had been grossly exaggerated.

At a Friday, May 6, cabinet meeting, Navy Secretary Long, not quite honestly stating his service's readiness to provide escorts in spite of the Spanish fleet being at sea, pushed the army to move before it was ready. "I present[ed] a letter to the Secretary of War," he wrote later that day, "stating that the Navy is ready to convoy any force of forty or fifty thousand men to Cuba, and urging the War Department to take active steps." Russell Alger took offense, "very naturally. He intimates that the War Department will take care of itself without any interference from the Navy." Long was awaiting miracles if he expected the army to conform to the navy's timetable. Actually, the fundamental reason for the decision not to go forward immediately with the Mariel operation was the volunteer army. The forty or fifty thousand trained men Long had referred to simply did not exist, and both the secretary of the navy and President McKinley were seemingly blind to this fact.[25]

Yet opposing an attack on Havana was fraught with political danger. To shy from this course might open William McKinley to a new battle with the congressional jingoes. But there was no real option, not yet anyway. Puerto Rico was strongly suggested by General Miles, but advancing that far into the Caribbean left a long, exposed seaward flank, ripe for interdiction by the Spanish cruiser squadron. Thus Havana, for want of any other plum, had to be the target.

Nonetheless, Russell Alger could not dodge the preparedness issue any longer—there was no way he could produce an army of volunteers sufficient for the strike in the short time frame demanded by the administration. When he finally owned up to it, the president and others were surprised and more than a little put out. Physically, Alger was failing under the strain; he had difficulty keeping up with the cabinet meetings and appeared tired and unequal to the tasks at hand. Alger, the single cabinet member who had postured as a hawk on the whole war question, exposed himself to severe criticism, and Long raked him over the coals: "He has been the most active of all members of the Cabinet for war. For two months he has been saying that he would have his army ready in ten days—whereas, in fact, not a volunteer has left his state, and in my judgment there has been a striking lack of preparation and promptness."[26]

Not only Long, but the naval service as a whole could not help prodding the army to move along. The blockade had absorbed most of the navy's first line forces, and the available number of ships was insufficient to close the many small ports along Cuba's south coast; through them, a trickle of supplies continued to get through to succor the Spanish garrisons. Though food prices shot up and there was much belt-tightening among the hitherto well-fed Spanish population and armed forces, it did nothing to break their resistance. "Spaniards starve well," wrote Theodore Roosevelt to ex–navy secretary Benjamin Tracy. If the blockade dragged on through the summer, the fleet would be prone to hurricane damage. Blockade duty was hard on the ships, constantly bringing mechanical breakdowns. Naval officers increasingly demanded the army do something to relieve them of the odorous task of steaming back and forth across a harbor mouth, or sitting at anchor, eating coal in the dank humidity of coastal Cuba. At the very least, the army might grab an opportune port where the fleet might shelter, coal, and repair on-site; Guantánamo Bay was suggested.[27]

The lack of army preparedness became a regular feature of the *Army and Navy Journal*. "To invade Cuba," it noted in late May, "requires an army, and whoever may be held responsible for the result, the fact remains that we have no army. We have some excellent raw material for one, that is all." Comparisons in the training camps offered striking opportunities to gauge differences between the regulars and volunteers. "No aggressive campaign should be attempted with anything less than a Regular Army," the *Journal* correspondent noted. "The Volunteers, even when they are a picked lot of men, as in the 71st New York, are plainly not in condition for hard work in the open field."[28]

Fresh assessments downgrading the danger from tropical diseases also reinforced the navy's demand for a more aggressive operational attitude on the army's part. In May, army Surgeon General George Sternberg and his staff decided they had overestimated the hazards of campaigning in the rainy season. As a result of reports from Americans living in prewar Cuba, it was incorrectly deduced that high death rates in earlier Cuban campaigns by British troops and the current mortality rate of the Spanish army resulted more from poor sanitation than from any elemental deadliness of the climate. Sternberg and others argued that if American soldiers ate proper food, camped on high ground, and kept themselves clean, they could march and fight in Cuba in relatively healthy circumstances. This conclusion was based on the widely held theory that malaria and yellow fever were filth-bred diseases.

There were also international considerations that dictated an early invasion of Cuba. As the weeks of May slipped by, it became increasingly unlikely that Spain would risk a fleet action in the Caribbean. Instead, if they were smart, the main units of the Spanish navy would remain in home waters, counting on the unreadiness of the U.S. Army to force a period of inactivity. During this phase, European powers friendly to Spain might intervene on her behalf. If this was Spain's strategy, it could only be frustrated by quick, decisive action in Cuba. Thus, in the week following May 9, the War Department pushed forward preparations for the Mariel-Havana expedition, ordering all regular units at Chickamauga Battlefield Park to move south to Tampa, reinforcing General Shafter's command to about twelve thousand regular troops.

Though Russell Alger's inability to manage his mammoth task was becoming apparent to all, the president still counted on the secretary to get the volunteers ready within a month's time. Alger himself knew this was an impossibility, telling a reporter, "It is one thing to be a National Guardsman with all the convenience of a few days in camp once a year, and another to buckle down to the duties and hardships of real soldiering." Still, President McKinley decided on a major Cuban offensive even before most of the troops required for its operations had been mustered into federal service, and optimistic reports from Shafter at Tampa confirmed the administration's faith in an early attack.[29]

When the War Department canceled the reconnaissance in force on April 30, it also ordered Shafter to continue preparing his command for an assault on Cuba, with suggestions that he consult with the navy at Key West to determine what operations might be feasible in the near future. Shafter dispatched one of his divisional commanders, Brigadier General Henry Lawton, to confer. The navy let it be known that small expeditions to the north coast of Cuba might be conducted at any time, and further, the big reconnaissance was also possible, but not both at the same time—they hadn't enough ships to convoy simultaneous operations. On Lawton's return to Tampa on May 7, Shafter informed the War Department that the uncertainty of the Spanish fleet's whereabouts dictated prudence, and he did not consider it wise for his command to sail in a single body. He did, however, let the department know his whole force of regulars would be completely fitted out for expeditionary duty by May 12, and any time thereafter he was prepared to land and "take possession of, and hold permanently, some point on the north coast of Cuba to be used as a base of operations."[30]

In response to this information, Alger and Miles dictated orders to embark Shafter's troops, along with reinforcements to be sent from Chickamauga and other camps, and to "seize, fortify and hold Mariel" or another "most important" point on Cuba's north coast. Shafter would command the vanguard of fifteen thousand regulars for Mariel, and Miles, the main body of fifty thousand–plus volunteers for the assault on Havana itself. But on the thirteenth all orders were suspended to await naval developments. The Spanish cruiser squadron had been spotted west of Martinique. The War Department actually greeted the arrival of the Spanish with relief, as it provided them with an excuse to postpone a campaign they were not ready to launch.[31]

By the time the War Department had issued its concentration order on May 6, framed to execute the military strategy formulated at the April 20 cabinet meeting, the character of the war, and particularly the army's mission, had undergone a radical change. This, in the main, was the result of Dewey's victory at Manila Bay and the dramatic revelations it brought of the weakness and inactivity of the Spanish navy. Dewey's message that he could take the city of Manila at any time if he had the men to do it opened a new and wholly unexpected front in the war. On May 3, at Alger's request, General Miles presented a plan for sending five thousand men to Manila. The proposed force, intended only to secure the city, contained two battalions of the 14th Infantry, the regimental band, two troops of the 4th Cavalry, three volunteer infantry regiments, and two heavy batteries of volunteer artillery. By May 13, when Dewey formally requested the dispatch of a Manila garrison, the troops were already mustering in San Francisco.

By the second half of the month, the administration had greatly increased both the size and the importance of the Manila expedition, and Alger informed the staff bureaus to make provisions for at least a doubling of the force. On May 12, Major General Wesley Merritt, the second ranking officer of the U.S. Army, was appointed its head. Merritt, a handsome Civil War veteran, was at the time chief of the Department of the East at Governor's Island, New York. The Philippine appointment surprised many who expected someone of his stature and experience to be sent to the supposedly more important Caribbean theater of operations. Four days later, the War Department designated the new command the Department of the Pacific, with jurisdiction over the entire Philippine archipelago. On May 29, Merritt's force was increased to twenty thousand men, and in June it was designated the Eighth Army Corps.

The political reasons behind the expansion of the Philippine expeditionary force, from merely taking and holding Manila to occupying the whole island group, are obscure. Since Dewey's victory, businessmen and politicians interested in expanding American influence in

East Asia had demanded annexing the Philippines as a military and commercial outpost. But even while he ordered the expeditions, President McKinley gave little sign of whether he agreed with these views. A common, and probably true, anecdote has the president looking closely at the globe in the Cabinet Room to find the Philippines. If so, it is not likely that a sound set of principles, expansionist or not, was formed by the administration. General Merritt was as confused as anyone over the president's direction. "I do not yet know," he asked, "whether it is your desire to subdue and hold all of the Spanish territory in the islands, or merely to seize and hold the capital."[32]

Generals Merritt and Miles also disagreed as to the objectives of the Philippines expedition. This came to a head in mid-May over the number of regulars to be included in the enlarged force; Merritt demanded twice as many as Miles wished to assign. These seasoned, trained men, Merritt insisted, were completely necessary for the task of "conquering a territory 7,000 miles from our base, defended by a regularly trained and acclimated army of from 10,000 to 25,000 men, and inhabited by people, the majority of whom will regard us with the intense hatred born of race and religion."[33]

In defense of his own estimates, Miles accused Merritt of exaggerating the size of the Spanish forces opposed to him. As to the mission, military and political, Miles was under the impression the Philippines expedition was to be limited in scope: "The force ordered at this time is not expected to carry on a war to conquer extensive territory." Rather, he lectured Merritt, it was to establish "a strong garrison to command the harbor of Manila, and to relieve the . . . fleet under Admiral Dewey with the least possible delay." The number of men allotted was already three times what Dewey recommended for taking and holding Manila.[34]

President McKinley's formal instructions to General Merritt, couched in a letter to Russell Alger, implied the opposite: an extensive campaign. He mentioned "acquisition and control of the bay," but also regarded the expeditionary force as "an army of occupation to the Philippines for the twofold purpose of completing the reduction of Spanish power in that quarter and of giving order and security to the islands while in the possession of the United States." But as with most everything, McKinley left unclear any long-range design. Though he did direct the establishment of an American military government, he like as not hadn't settled on any permanent policy, and frankly, there was no reason to at this early stage. The president had simply taken the logical military step, the exploitation of a successful attack with fresh reinforcements. The failure to define the political objectives, however, did lead to large complications for the commanders who came on the scene later.[35]

Henry Cabot Lodge, an expansionist who flew his colors proudly, had no doubt of the president's eventual path, not from any clear utterances, but on an interpretation of remarks similar to those in Merritt's orders. "Unless I am utterly and profoundly mistaken," he wrote to Theodore Roosevelt, "the administration is now fully committed to the large policy that we both desire." The administration might not have known its own mind yet, but Lodge had discerned its future exactly.[36]

Though army operations in the Caribbean had been suspended until the naval situation shook itself out, the administration still remained committed to a major push against Havana, this in spite of Miles's disapproval of launching an operation during the rainy season. Instead, he favored flank attacks against weaker Spanish positions in eastern Cuba and Puerto Rico, which he claimed would destroy Spanish power in the Caribbean at a much smaller cost to the United States. "The cry," he wrote after the war, "was 'On to Havana!' as it had been . . . 'On to Richmond!' " in the Civil War. "This became so intense that even the conservative administration was over persuaded."[37]

The president, Miles thought, "had evidently been misinformed" of the acute dangers of going straight at Havana. There were 125,000 Spanish troops in the vicinity with 100 field guns, besides the 125 heavy pieces of ordnance in the surrounding fortifications. Spanish soldiers had about a thousand rounds of ammunition per man, while U.S. forces hadn't enough ammunition to fight one battle.[38]

Yet until the last days of May, and in spite of Miles's objections, the administration remained committed to the Havana operation. The offensive would begin as soon as the navy disposed of the Spanish squadron, enough troops were trained and equipped, and sufficient steamers were chartered to bring them to a point off Mariel. President

McKinley received advice from some quarters urging an attack without waiting for the volunteers, the argument being that as soon as Cervera's squadron was defeated, a force of 12,000 regulars could seize and hold a base from which the army could aid the rebels and from which the main force, once it had been assembled, could sally and deploy for the Havana attack. It seems likely that both Alger and McKinley were inclining toward this view.

By mid-May, up to five regiments a day were arriving at Tampa, and the place, never intended as anything but a sand crusted winter resort town, became exceedingly overcrowded. General Shafter was forced to open satellite camps at Lakeland and Jacksonville. At the same time, Miles urged Congress to appropriate $350,000 for entrenching tools, road-building machinery, and railway equipment for the army of invasion. The quartermaster general increased orders for tropical uniforms, hammocks, and rubber sheets. But the army's preparations for Havana were scarcely under way when the Spanish navy threw a wrench into the works, causing a major shift of strategic movement.

Having been spotted on the eleventh of May in the neighborhood of Martinique, Admiral Cervera's elusive squadron slipped away and was not sighted again for three days, this time at Curaçao, where they took on some desperately needed coal. But the U.S. Navy's scouts were few in number and poorly deployed, and once again Cervera disappeared. On May 19, eluding a strong American naval force on the south coast of Cuba, the Spanish squadron entered the harbor of Santiago de Cuba, and was thus reported to Key West by an American agent in the Havana telegraph office.

So long as this naval force remained intact, it kept Spanish resistance alive in the Caribbean, the cockpit of the war. It was erroneously supposed to be operating at its full power and steaming capacity, and in the political and command councils in Washington and Tampa, it was felt that if given favorable circumstances, Cervera might yet again slip away and do considerable damage. But with the army's assistance at Santiago, it was believed that the navy could eliminate this threat. Troops landing east or west of the town could storm the entrance batteries, enabling the American fleet to clear the minefields, steam into the harbor, and annihilate the enemy squadron. A movement against

Santiago de Cuba would bring diplomatic as well as military benefits. This was clearly a mission the regulars could do alone, or nearly so, and with the massive volunteer army nowhere near ready for active service for the Havana operation, the Santiago scenario presented an assured opportunity to establish a solid foothold in Cuba's second largest city—one, moreover, that maintained no railroad link to the main Spanish forces in the Havana region. Cuban rebels infested the hinterland around it, and the city garrison, if attacked by U.S. forces, would fight with no hope of significant reinforcement. Thus, Santiago presented an easy plum for the Fifth Army Corps now assembling in its thousands at Tampa.

On May 26, to adjust national strategy to the new naval situation brought on by the Spanish squadron at Santiago, President McKinley convened a council of war with Long, Alger, Miles, and the Naval War Board in attendance. It was decided to cancel the Havana operation for the time being and instead to attack Santiago de Cuba and Puerto Rico. For Miles, always opposed to the direct Mariel/Havana venture, it was a personal victory. As usual, Secretary Long was critical of the War Department's shortcomings. At the last cabinet meeting, Alger had promised seventy-five thousand men ready for Cuba; "now [Alger] says they are not prepared and won't be for two or three weeks. Alger . . . does not seem to have things in hand," Long continued in his diary entry for the day. "He is apt to promise a great deal more than he can execute, simply because he is not thoroughly informed as to his own resources and preparations."[39]

In a series of memos, the first of which he drafted the day of the conference, General Miles outlined the new campaign. The available force of regulars could attack Santiago now and, by use of their siege guns, aid the navy in the destruction of the bottled-up Spanish squadron. Once it had done its main task, and reinforced from the United States if necessary, it would attack Puerto Rico with naval support. Miles expected Puerto Rico would fall without much fighting. Once that venture was concluded, the army and navy should return to Cuba and capture the deepwater ports on the island's northeast coast. Through these, the United States could supply large quantities of matériel to the rebels, whose main forces operated in the region. But Miles now overreached himself, concocting a truly bizarre plan. Along with these supplies, he suggested landing a contingent of from ten thousand to fifteen thousand regular cavalry and artillery. This highly mobile force, assisted by freshly supplied Cubans, could then drive west, across the fever-free central plateau, and overrun the Spanish garrisons in its path.

Miles's allied army, once it finished its victorious march, might then bring Havana under siege. At the end of the rainy season, if Havana did not surrender at the threat of bombardment, the volunteers, now fully equipped and with three months' training, could land near the city and complete the destruction of Spanish power in Cuba.

Wisely, at Alger's vehement urging, the president rejected the loonier aspects of Miles's plan, throwing out completely the westward march of the combined U.S.-Cuban forces. The logistic nightmare attending such an operation boggled the mind. The government hadn't the shipping to transport the fifteen thousand horses needed for the venture, and even if it did, U.S. army animals could not live off the land; they needed high-grade forage, oats and hay, up to ninety tons a day, which would have had to be carried through one or two small ports and over Cuba's execrable roads. Alger also pointed out that many of the towns slated for capture along the line of march were strongly fortified, and without infantry the column would surely bog down in futile frontal attacks of cavalry against walls. It was all too stupid for words. Why, Alger wanted to know, should the army march 350 miles overland to Havana, if that was the objective, when they could steam 90 miles in a day from Key West? Sensibly, the administration adopted only the saner portions of the scheme, opting to attack Santiago at once with the regulars of the Fifth Corps at Tampa, then strike Puerto Rico immediately after Santiago fell.

The size of the armies (with their gear) sent to attack Santiago, Puerto Rico, and Manila depended absolutely on the number and capacity of the ships carrying them. This was the responsibility of the quartermaster general, who in army regulations was accountable for all forms of transportation, including oceangoing vessels. Long before the campaigns were mapped out, General Ludington began his search for suitable ships. In fact, a month before the declarations of war he had his New York depot commander surveying shipping lines operating between East Coast ports and the Caribbean. Once the administration committed to a descent on Cuba, quartermasters on the East and Gulf coasts, aided by navy officers, began inspecting vessels for charter. Ships were hired at fixed rates per day proportional to their tonnage. They were officered and crewed by their civilian companies, and their contracts obligated them for food for the army officers but not the enlisted men, nor for coal and water; the government took care of those needs.

When the ships were turned over to the army, they were hastily refitted by contractors who knocked together flimsy tiers of wooden bunks in the cargo holds. The army had almost no experience in this sort of work. The navy had conducted an extensive study of merchant shipping for military purposes in 1890, but it was ignored. As a result, the too few transport vessels were inadequately ventilated, crowded, and to a great degree unhygienic. "These ships had to go at once," said the quartermaster at New York. "I would have anywhere from three to five days to take a ship and fit her up to go to sea. . . . It was a rush order." Many ships left New York for Tampa with workers still aboard. Foreign flag ships were prohibited for military charter under international law, and patriotic American shipowners strenuously lobbied Congress to prevent their temporary transfer to U.S. registry. Further reducing the range of vessels was the type engaged in the Caribbean trade, from which most came. The fast, roomy Atlantic liners, which would have been perfect for the task, drew too much water to enter Cuban or Puerto Rican harbors. Thus the quartermaster general had to rely on what the trade provided; small, slow merchantmen, largely unsuited for carrying large numbers of men and animals.[40]

In preparing the transport fleet, Ludington was hampered by the administration's changing Cuba strategy and his natural reluctance as a supply officer to buy anything that might not be needed. Attempting to conform to the plans of the War Department, he initially chartered only enough steamers for Shafter's original six-thousand-man reconnaissance force. The sudden decision in early May to attack Havana with seventy thousand men necessitated a hurried expansion. The quartermaster general now began chartering every available merchantman to transport at least twenty-five thousand men, the projected first wave of the invasion. By the end of May, thirty steamers were on hand at Tampa.

The expedition to Manila presented problems of a different sort. The small number of American flag vessels operating in the Pacific made chartering especially difficult. Most of these ships were also away from their home ports on long voyages to Asia or South America, and their owners could deliver them to the army only one by one as they returned from distant ports. Still, most were large passenger liners, built and fitted out for long voyages to hot climates, and were thus far better suited for the transport role than the Caribbean coasters. By June 30, fourteen steamers, with a capacity of fourteen thousand men, were available for the Eighth Corps. Even so, for a seven-thousand-mile voyage, extra ventilators had to be constructed, and the installation of electric lights, extra bathing and toilet facilities, and galleys large enough to prepare two hot meals a day was required. Each ship carried fresh meat, either frozen in special refrigerators or on the hoof, and each vessel was fully staffed and equipped with a sick bay, surgeons, and Hospital Corpsmen.

Carefully selected ports of embarkation were necessary for the various expeditions. San Francisco did perfectly well for the Manila operation, with enough trackage, docks, and warehouses to fully service an endeavor of any size. But nothing so good was available for Cuba and Puerto Rico. For Caribbean operations, the War Department required a port easily defended against naval raids, yet sufficiently near the target for logistic purposes. Florida had few large cities or extensive railroad trackage, while the Gulf ports of New Orleans and Mobile were too far away, and on the wrong side of Cuba for the projected Havana operation. Thus, as a historian has said, "almost by administrative gravitation," the army selected Tampa on Florida's west coast as the port of embarkation for Cuban operations.[41]

A city of twenty-six thousand people, Tampa, despite its grievous shortcomings, possessed a number of the elements required by the army for a Caribbean-facing base. Besides lying closer to Havana than any other usable American port, it sat at the head of a deep bay, safe from enemy raids. Large steamers were able to navigate its twenty-one-foot-deep main shipping channel, and up to thirteen vessels could theoretically load at the main wharf. There were, however, ten miles of sandy, roadless country crossed by a single railroad track that separated the regiments and their mountain of stores encamped in the piney woods around Tampa city from the docks at Tampa's port. This bottleneck created infinite difficulties, which the army was unable to surmount, in the embarking of the Fifth Corps for Cuba. "The port had not been at all prepared to handle the amount of property or the numbers of men and animals that were concentrated there," said Captain John Pershing of the 10th Cavalry.[42]

Throughout May and June, Tampa, town and port, presented an intolerable spectacle of congestion and confusion, which overloaded the port's fragile operating capacity. "Mounted officers and orderlies ploughed their rushing way through great heaps and dunes of ever-shifting sand," remembered an infantry officer, "leaving behind them stifling clouds of scintillating particles, which filtered through every conceivable crevice and made the effort to breathe a suffocating nightmare." Neither the War Department nor General Shafter placed a single man in charge of the port, nor gave anyone ultimate responsibility to coordinate the work between the staff departments and the line regiments. After the decision had been made to attack Havana, the department, without regard for Port Tampa's limited facilities, poured an unending flow of men and equipment into its crowded spaces. Jammed railroad cars backed up to Columbia, South Carolina, five hundred miles north. Delayed arrival of bills of lading forced supply officers to open hundreds of cars and thousands of crates merely to determine what lay inside. By the middle of May, over a thousand cars crammed the Tampa yards, yet they were being emptied at only three a day. General Miles, who arrived at Tampa on June 1, described "over 300 cars loaded with war material along the roads about Tampa, but the invoices . . . have not been received, so that the officers are obliged to . . . hunt from car to car to ascertain whether they contain clothing, grain, balloon material, horse equipments, ammunition, siege guns, commissary stores, etc." He reported fifteen cars of uniforms sidetracked miles from the city for weeks, while the volunteer regiments in Tampa were "suffering for clothing."[43] Also the siege train was scattered through "hundreds" of cars on side tracks.

The chaos reached even more absurd lengths when the two rival railroads that served the city engaged in a bitter feud as they attempted to monopolize the profitable army traffic. It climaxed when the Plant line, which controlled the single track to the port, refused to allow its competitor's cars to pass along it. Plant workers only ceased this intolerable interference when the army threatened to seize the railroad and run it themselves.

When the Rough Riders arrived at Tampa after a hot, dusty four-day ride from San Antonio, Lieutenant Colonel Theodore Roosevelt, the regiment's second-in-command, remembered, "[W]e disembarked in a perfect welter of confusion . . . everything connected with both military and railroad matters was in an almost inextricable tangle." No liaison officers met the Rough Riders' trains, nor were there any instructions as to where they were to camp, and there were no rations for twenty-four hours. The officers had to buy the regimental food locally, out of their own pockets, and "to seize wagons in order to get our baggage taken to the camping ground which we at last found had been allotted to us."[44]

During all this, the army waited, training and organizing after a fashion, hoping, praying by the minute that the navy would find the Spanish squadron so they could leave this chafing, sweating place for Cuba. The Fifth Corps generals and staffs—except for old General "Fighting Joe" Wheeler, West Pointer, ex-Confederate cavalry officer, and lately a U.S. congressman, of the Cavalry Division, whose head-quarters tent rose from a dusty field, marked by a cavalry guidon—established themselves in the garishly Moorish brick monstrosity of the Tampa Bay Hotel, constructed by the same Morton F. Plant who owned the railroad. "Only God knows why Plant built an hotel here," said one general, "but thank God he did." Along its wide terraces ranks of rocking chairs comforted senior officers whose chief duty seemed to be sipping gallons of iced tea, marking time waiting for the navy to do something, while they renewed old friendships. "This was the rocking-chair period of the war," said correspondent Richard Harding Davis. When they were not nodding off on the porch, their life at the hotel centered around the lobby bulletin board. Officers, correspondents, and foreign military attachés stood eight deep, as Davis noted, "peering over each other's shoulders as each new telegram followed fast and was pasted up below the last." "After reading these dispatches for some weeks," Shafter's aide, Lieutenant John Miley commented, "one was in a frame of mind to expect anything."[45]

A few miles back in the sandy pine woods, beyond the silver-painted minarets of the hotel, slept up to twenty thousand men of the Fifth Corps. Of the enthusiastically amateurs soldiers, Davis noted the opposing gripes of the 71st New York and the 2nd Massachusetts, two of the best volunteer units in the whole muster. The great complaint of the 71st was the abundance of beans in the diet. "Beans for breakfast, beans for lunch, beans for dinner," said a New Yorker, "what t'hell." The Massachusetts men thought otherwise. "And as for beans," bitched one, "they don't give you enough to fill a tablespoon."[46]

Davis found the regulars a different set, men who regarded camp life and soldiering as a "business, and as nothing more." And that was the vast gulf dividing the two forces. Davis thought the regulars as fine a body of troops as any in Europe. "[T]he discipline was so good that it obtruded itself; and the manner in which each man handled his horse or musket, and especially himself, made you proud that they were American soldiers, and desperately sorry that there were so few of them."[47]

After May 19, when the Spanish squadron was tentatively identified in the harbor of Santiago de Cuba, things began moving at a faster, though no more coherent, clip. On Thursday, May 26, Shafter received from General Miles preliminary instructions: "Be prepared to load on transports 25,000 men." The movement of this expedition depended on further intelligence of the Spanish squadron. As Lieutenant Miley noted, this telegram, though unspecific as to any operational details, indicated the period of waiting and suspense had come to an end. "This was the first intimation General Shafter had that the troops at Tampa would be sent against Spanish forces" to confront them directly, not merely as a reconnaissance force. As yet there was no hint of the objective, but there were some guesses it might be Puerto Rico.[48]

For the Fifth Corps, the Quartermaster's Department had assembled a force of thirty-one transports, two water boats, and a collier. After prodding by the chief of engineers, three small steam lighters were obtained, as well as a deep-sea tug and a pair of decked barges for use as landing craft. On receipt of Miles's warning telegram, Shafter, to his chagrin, realized this seagoing aggregate hadn't the capacity to carry twenty-five thousand men, their animals and gear; at the very most, it could take seventeen thousand, and that only if very stripped down. Only the regulars, the Rough Riders, and two volunteer infantry regiments, the 71st New York and 2nd Massachusetts, could go. The cavalry, save one troop, would leave their horses. The

siege guns must also stay, as must tons of regimental baggage and hospital stores. Confusion and congestion reigned supreme.

Starting on May 29, the day the Spanish squadron was positively
identified in Santiago, the preliminary orders were fleshed out with
logistic and operational details. "Go with your force to capture garrison at Santiago and assist in capturing the harbor and fleet," ordered
General Miles. As to the units to be embarked, Miles now broadly indicated "an effective force" of regulars and volunteers, supported by
siege guns, howitzers, mortars, and "two or four field batteries." As
for cavalry, Shafter could now take as many dismounted troopers as
he desired. Draft animals were to be limited to the least amount required to haul the guns, "as it is expected that you will go but a short
distance inland." The troops he ordered to have five hundred rounds
of rifle ammunition per man, with two months' worth, if possible, in
reserve, and if Shafter could manage it, "you can load supplies to six
months if practicable."[49]

At 2:30 A.M. on Tuesday, May 31, the adjutant general, "by order"
of General Miles, telegraphed to Shafter his definitive operational instructions: to load his command on their transports and, under naval
escort, proceed "to the vicinity of Santiago de Cuba," where, under
naval "protection," he would land east or west of that place "and
move up to the high ground and bluffs overlooking the harbor . . . as
shall best enable you to capture or destroy the garrison there"; to provide protection to naval minesweeping forces, "or with the aid of the
navy capture or destroy the Spanish fleet." Shafter was urged to accomplish these tasks with the least possible delay. He was also given
permission to request assistance from the rebels, "especially as scouts
and guides," but was warned against putting "too much confidence"
in anyone outside of his own command. Once the Santiago mission
had been completed, Shafter was to reembark his men and head to the
port of Banes, around Cape Maisi on Cuba's northeast coast, and
await instructions. "When will you sail?" ended the order.[50]

The resort atmosphere of Tampa town vanished in the tumult of
loading the ships. Shafter's quartermaster put three shifts of laborers
to work hauling stuff out of the railroad cars, moving it to the pier,
and then aboard the transports. The streets and ways along the railroad between the camps and the waterfront were transformed into a
barbarian-like movement of wagon people, with cursing muleteers,

teamsters, and quartermasters, "all dusted with hay, dirt and anger." Interference from Washington served to compound the inevitable snafus. Navy Secretary Long, fearing the Spanish squadron might escape before the army's arrival, pressured the administration to order Shafter to sail immediately, with whatever troops he had embarked. General Shafter, attempting to comply, tried to rush too many men through the rail bottleneck to Tampa's port too quickly. The embarkation turned into a huge, ponderous stampede. Regiments appropriated one another's trains and rolled onto the dock in the wrong order for boarding. Largely on their own, without any assistance from the totally overwhelmed Fifth Corps staff, the regiments sorted themselves out and boarded their ships in the greatest confusion, their baggage piled into the holds in willy-nilly heaps.

Captain Pershing and others of his 10th Cavalry Regiment were appalled; no competent commander would have permitted this sort of chaos. The troopers broke camp and managed to get a first-class excursion train, fitted with lavatories and ice-water spigots. But they had no rations. When Pershing as regimental quartermaster tried to make local arrangements, he was told it was bad for business to feed black soldiers. The 6th Infantry had food enough, but their train had last hauled cattle, and the men in the stock cars stood ankle deep in manure under a semitropical sun while they were shunted about in the baking midday heat.[51]

The 10th Cavalry was assigned to the transport *Leona,* along with the headquarters of the 2nd Cavalry Brigade and most of the 1st Cavalry. Pershing found the vessel in "reasonably good shape." The hold had been thoroughly disinfected and bunks or hammocks erected or slung wherever cargo permitted. "Better arrangements might have been made with more time," he said, "but everyone was so eager to go and so fearful of being left behind . . . that almost any conditions would have been accepted without grumbling."[52]

The 71st New York boarded the *Vigilancia.* The regiment's Private Charles Post described the berthing arrangements: The bunks had been built so hastily "that the earnest contractor in his effort to speed the war along, do his bit, and, make, perhaps, a little margin of tidy profit, had put two boards twelve inches wide into the bottom of each bunk. Thus he saved one board for himself out of the three he was paid for." With each four-tiered bunk thirty-six inches wide, the occupant had the choice of lying over twelve inches of open space in the middle, or dividing it half and half on either side.[53]

According to Lieutenant Colonel Roosevelt, the Rough Riders were informed the expedition was to start out "for destination unknown" immediately; they were to go with it, but the horses, save the personal mounts of senior officers, must be left behind. On June 7, the regiment received word the force was to sail at daybreak, "and that if we were not aboard our transport by that time we could not go. We had no intention of being left, and prepared at once for the scramble which was evidently about to take place." As one knowledgeable about such things, Roosevelt figured that each regiment of a known size would be assigned to a transport of a given tonnage and capacity. The Fifth Corps quartermasters must have arranged that each regiment and its transport "should meet in due order on the dock, [so it] ought not to have been difficult." But no planning of this sort was done, "and we were allowed to shove and hustle for ourselves as best we could." Ordered to be at a certain track with all their gear at midnight to board their train for Port Tampa, the regiment duly arrived, but the train did not. While the men slept on the ground, Roosevelt and the regimental commander, Colonel Leonard Wood, army doctor, lately President McKinley's physician, now promoted up in the volunteer organization, wandered about searching for information, "which no one could give." They bumped into several brigadier generals, and once even came upon General Miles, "but nobody knew anything."[54]

Some regiments managed to board their trains, and some did not, but as Roosevelt noted, "as none of the trains started this made little difference." At 3:00 A.M., the Rough Riders were ordered to march to an entirely different siding, "and away we went." But there was no train here either. At the first hint of dawn, a string of empty coal cars rattled by, "and these we seized," using "various arguments," to back down the nine miles to Port Tampa, where they chugged in, filthy with coal dust.[55]

The transports, anchored in midstream, slowly came alongside the pier for loading. The trains, however, were unloading wherever they happened to stop, with no attention whatever being paid to the vessel on which the soldiers were to go. Wood and Roosevelt could find no one who knew their ship, or where it was. Colonel Charles Humphrey,

Shafter's quartermaster, who should have known and should have been supervising the entire operation, was not to be found, and the quay, Roosevelt said, "was crammed with some ten thousand men, most of whom were working at cross purposes." After an hour, they found their ship, the *Yucatán,* anchored in midstream. Wood jumped into a stray launch and boarded her. At the same time, Roosevelt learned she had also been allotted to the 2nd Infantry and the 71st New York. Roosevelt ran full tilt to the coal train, left a strong guard with the baggage, and double-timed the regiment to the pier and up the gangways, "just in time to board her against the Second Regulars and the Seventy-first, who had arrived a little too late."[56]

By midday, June 8, most of the troops were crammed into the berths and decks of the inadequate vessels. But they were not to sail for another week and sweltered away in Tampa Bay while the navy investigated a rumor that Spanish raiders had escaped from Santiago. At last, on the evening of June 13 came the welcome order to start. A bare seven weeks since the outbreak of the war, seventeen thousand men of the U.S. Fifth Army Corps were on their way to Cuba. One by one, the thirty-odd steamers, escorted by a naval covering force, weighed anchor and slowly steamed out of the bay: as Roosevelt remembered, "the bands playing, the flags flying, the rigging black with the clustered soldiers, cheering and shouting to those left behind on the quay and to their fellows on the other ships."[57]

CHAPTER 7

VIVA ESPAÑA!

The object of military operations is final success and not
proofs of valor.

—*Captain Victor M. Concas y Palau,
commanding officer,* Infanta María Teresa

Spain had no chance of winning the war, though with some anticipation and bold, intelligent military leadership she could have protracted the conflict and caused the United States a fair degree of embarrassment and perhaps even a tactical check or two before the inevitable weight of American arms brought the war to its conclusion. The Madrid government, debt burdened, with scarcely any ready cash and with dried-up credit, was placed at a severe handicap when compared to the United States, with its overflowing coffers and its burgeoning manufactories, against which Spain could not hope to compete. She was also at an extreme disadvantage geographically, an ocean removed from the cockpit of war in the Caribbean, and without any real means of succoring her large army in Cuba.

Spain's armed forces, considering the deepening crisis with the United States, especially following the *Maine* explosion, remained entirely unready. Captain Victor M. Concas y Palau of the armored cruiser *Infanta María Teresa* wrote that "not the least preparation was made, either on land or on the sea . . . while the whole world was under the impression that we were frantically getting ready for a struggle to the bitter end."[1]

Compared to the tiny U.S. Army in April 1898, the Spanish official count of her men under arms at home and abroad numbered
something more than 400,000 men. There were in Cuba some
196,000 veteran soldiers, about 4,500 more in Puerto Rico, and
51,000 in the Philippines. Having been engaged for the past three
years, the Cuban garrison had been acclimated to the region, and
should have been expected to give a good account of itself on the
battlefield. The Spanish soldiers on the island were experienced campaigners, well supplied with small arms, smokeless powder, and field
artillery.

Most of the Spanish forces in Cuba were widely distributed
through the western and central provinces, principally in and around
Havana, Matanzas, Cárdenas, Cienfuegos, and the railroads connecting these cities. The remainder, around 36,000 men, were scattered in
small garrisons in Oriente Province. Concerned wholly with battling
the insurgent bands, the Spanish military leadership made no plans to
conduct a land campaign against an external foe, and with the exception of the extensive coastal fortifications at Havana, the Spanish
army faced inward, against the rebels.

Apparently concentrated at strategic points, the army was actually
frittered away in penny packets, many of which maintained no land
communications with one another, linked only by coastal shipping.
Town defenses were built to repel attacks by lightly armed rebels, and
were not designed to withstand a regular infantry assault backed by
heavy artillery and engineers. The proper land strategy for Spain in
early 1898 was to pull back and consolidate at a few central positions,
ready to react aggressively against the invader. But for practical and political reasons, Spain could not do this. Concentrating forces in this
manner would have been a tacit surrender of the countryside to the
rebels. Even if Spain opted for this course, there were no supplies available in the large cities beyond that for their regular garrisons, a problem
made even worse by the devastation of the countryside. The army, save
in the Havana region, depended on overseas shipments of food into the
island, and a naval blockade of Cuba could well starve it into surrender
in a matter of months. Spain was also precluded from logical massing
of troops by the lack of a good road network and a dearth of draft animals and wagons. Thus they had little choice but to hunker down in
their blockhouses until overwhelmed by superior American force.

The Fifth Army Corps landing unopposed at the wooden pier, Daiquirí, Cuba, June 22, 1898. The abandoned Spanish block-house can be seen in the center. (Harper)

Hotchkiss battery and the black Cavalry in action against the sh at Las Guásimas, Cuba, 24, 1898. (Harper)

A pack mule collapses into a muddy ditch along the *camino real* between Si-boney and the American lines besieging Santiago de Cuba. (Appleton)

The 71st New York Infantry fording
one of the streams during the advance
on the San Juan heights, July 1, 1898.
(Appleton)

The fortified stone church, El Viso, a
Spanish blockhouse at El Caney.
(Appleton)

The 7th Infantry during the bloody assault on El
Caney, July 1, 1898. The stone church, El Viso,
is seen at the top of the hill, center. (Harper)

Brigadier General Hamilton Haw
hatless, center, personally leadir
brigade against the Spanish right
at San Juan Hill. (Harper)

The Morro castle at the entrance to Santiago de Cuba. The scuttled Spanish cruiser *Reina Mercedes* lies in the foreground, not quite blocking the channel. (Appleton)

The Spanish armored cruiser *Almirante Oquendo*, with a torpedo boat alongside. She, the *Infanta María Teresa*, and the *Vizcaya* formed a handsome class, but all were destroyed at the Battle of Santiago. (Harper)

Admiral Don Pascual Cervera y e, the brave, despairing com- er of the Spanish cruiser squad- ʰat suffered utter defeat at the of Santiago. (Harper)

ɔanish armored cruiser *Vizcaya* dur- r visit to New York, following the explosion, February 1898. (Harper)

The Spanish armored cruiser *Cris[tóbal]
Colón*, in her unsuccessful attempt [to es]cape during the Battle of Santiago, J[une]
1898. Her main guns had never be[en in]stalled. (*Century Magazine*)

What remained of the *Vizcaya*
following the Battle of Santiago. (Appleton)

The scarred hulk [of]
Almirante Oquendo, [east]
of Santiago, July 3, [1898.]
(Appleton)

Major General Nelson A. Miles, Commanding General of the U.S. Army. Egotistical, ambitious, and an Indian fighter par excellence, Miles pushed for a peripheral approach toward Spanish power in the Caribbean, and was the chief proponent and commander of the Puerto Rico expedition. After the war he caused a major scandal with his unsubstantiated charges of "embalmed beef" issued to the troops. (Haskell, London, 1899)

Major General Wesley Merritt, the second-ranking officer in the U.S. Army. He commanded the Eighth Army Corps in the Manila campaign. (Haskell)

A well-turned-out regiment of Spanish infantry marches through Mayagüez, Puerto Rico, to engage U.S. forces. (Harper)

Towed by navy steam launches, U.S. field artillery disembarking in native craft at Manila Bay. (F. T. Neely, New York, 1899)

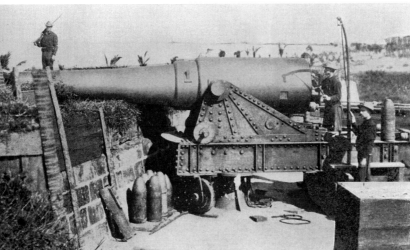

One of the four m Krupp 9.4-inch c guns defending M U.S. troops stand following the city' render, August 13, (Neely)

U.S. troops in Manila by an eighteenth-century muzzle-loading smoothbore cannon, "modernized" by the Spanish into a breech-loader. (Neely)

Spanish bicycle troops of the Manila garrison—for their time, highly mobile infantry. (Neely)

o insurgent troops d for inspection. As , American military n of these soldiers igher than for the rebels. (Neely)

Emilio Aguinaldo, leader of the Filipino insurgents. He always insisted American officials had promised Philippine independence in return for their help against the Spanish. (Collier)

Camp scene, south of Manila, midsummer 1898. The 14th Infantry lining up for chow. The soldier in front is grinding coffee. (Minnesota Historical Society)

Fort San Antonio de Abad following its bombardment and capture by the Americans during the battle for Manila, August 13, 1898. (Neely)

Spanish prisoners of war foll the American capture of M August 13, 1898. (Neely)

A hospital tent at Camp Wikoff, Montauk, Long Island, August–September 1898. (Appleton)

Only around Havana was there a system of roads, infrastructure, defenses, and supplies that permitted a converging of forces equal to the area under defense. In 1895 when Captain General Martínez Campos arrived on the island, he found the city virtually defenseless against a seaward attack, having but half a dozen short-barreled 11-inch guns, twenty years old, and some old iron howitzers, described by a Spanish artillery officer as "perfectly useless for a combat against foreign squadrons."[2]

Anticipating trouble with the United States, Martínez Campos persuaded the Spanish government to invest heavily in the coastal defenses of Havana. By the time war bloomed, thirty-two guns, including four 12-inch Krupp rifles, were pointed seaward, though so poorly positioned that the U.S. Navy could have dropped its anchors within sight of the boulevards and opened a bombardment against which the Spanish gunners could but feebly reply. In the shipping channel entrance were placed three lines of various types of electrically detonated and contact mines, as well as a pair of Whitehead torpedo tubes, supported by a powerful battery of searchlights and heavy steel cable that was stretched across the entrance at night.

The city's landward defenses, facing rebels or an advancing army rather than warships, held twenty-four thousand garrison troops with 104 pieces of field artillery, in addition to an infantry division with its own thirty guns. In all, Havana and its suburbs held about sixty thousand fighting men, excluding the small naval force of one disabled cruiser and a few score small gunboats and steam launches. Martínez Campos had also appointed a military commission to study strengthening and modernizing the stone bastions that for generations had guarded the entrances of Matanzas, Cienfuegos, and Santiago de Cuba. Plans were submitted, but there was no money, and practically all the work in preparing up-to-date defenses was spent on Havana.

The war for Cuba—and the Philippines and Puerto Rico as well—would depend, in chief, not on the strength and number of soldiers in the field, but on who controlled the sea, and here Spain had not the slightest chance of success. Falling into a fatal mode of military fantasy, in 1895 Spain adopted a new rating system for its navy that was wholly unrealistic and went far to dupe the nation and even foreign naval observers, who should have known better, into classifying the Spanish navy into a much higher material category of strength and readiness than it deserved. Simply, they uprated all cruisers of nine thousand tons and above into "first-class battleships"; armored and belted cruisers at a stroke became "second-class battleships"; and so on down the list, every vessel being upgraded beyond its nominal capability. Thus in 1898, the Spanish navy possessed one true battleship, the slow, short-legged *Pelayo* (called *El Solitario* in the service), and she was undergoing modernization in France; but the register lumped with her the dubious and incomplete armored cruiser *Emperador Carlos V,* giving Spain two first-class battleships, plus nine second-class battleships (which were no such thing, two of them being broadside ironclads of midcentury vintage), seven first-class cruisers, and thirteen second-class cruisers. All this was done without any regard to the age of the ships, their condition, or ability to steam and fight at anywhere near their stated capacities.

It proved a terrible delusion. What the Spanish navy possessed on paper and what was actually ready for even limited service in late April 1898 were two entirely different matters. She had no battleships ready for sea, and only four armored cruisers, and one of those, the Italian-built *Cristóbal Colón,* lacked her main armament of four 10-inch guns; wooden dummies sat in their place. There were no large protected cruisers of the *Olympia* type, and only twelve small cruisers and gunboats. Of Spain's vaunted torpedo forces, numbering thirty torpedo gunboats, destroyers, and torpedo boats in the official list, those actually ready for service were counted at eleven, and even these would shrink markedly when put to the test at sea.

In training, discipline, education, seamanship, and engineering, the Spanish navy was woefully behind its American enemy. Most of the large ships maintained a complement of Scottish engineers, who left the Spanish service on war being declared, with the result that steaming endurance and engineering efficiency dropped alarmingly. With only a small amount of exaggeration did a Madrid newspaper claim, "The Americans for a year have been preparing for war. . . . We have had but one target practice and that over a year ago. This was limited to expending the least possible amount of ammunition. Half our vessels have not cleaned their bottoms for a year. . . . The Americans are constantly making voyages in all seas with their vessels, so that they have a trained *personnel* for the machinery. We have the greatest scarcity of engineers, and hardly any stokers at all."[3]

In short, the Spanish navy was a disorganized collection of antiquated junk, unfinished vessels of dubious worth, and scarcely serviceable ships in commission. Its senior officers maintained no vigor of the initiative, but only a fatalistic outlook that envisioned no future but defeat. To aggravate these systemic weaknesses, only the vaguest operational plans were prepared in advance of hostilities. Everything was done haphazardly, in response to a popular clamor to do something, anything. There was no cooperation between the Spanish army and navy, and when war erupted, bases at home and in the colonies were without stores, provisions, ammunition, or coal. What ships were in commission were scattered on both sides of the Atlantic.

In October 1897, fifty-nine-year-old Vice Admiral Pascual Cervera y Topete, a much beloved man of high honor and courage, though utterly pessimistic and defeatist in his outlook, took command of Spanish naval forces at Cádiz. In the navy since age nine, he had seen much service during Spain's endemic civil wars, was under fire in Indochina, and fought against Chile and Peru in the Guano War of midcentury. He saw extended service in the Philippines and against Cuban rebels during the Ten Years' War. Cervera was the first captain of the battleship *Pelayo*, and served a period as minister of marine. Since 1896 he had held the rank of vice admiral, the senior Spanish naval officer afloat. His force consisted of the armored cruisers *Infanta María Teresa*, toothless *Cristóbal Colón*, and the modern British-built destroyers *Plutón*, *Furor*, and *Terror*. When reinforced by the armored cruisers *Almirante Oquendo* and *Vizcaya*, these would eventually become Spain's expeditionary fleet for operations in the Caribbean against the United States. Gazing over his inadequate command, Cervera held no illusions. Spain, he presciently wrote to his cousin in January 1898, two weeks before the *Maine* blew up, had become trapped "in one of those critical periods which seem to be the beginning of the end."[4]

Prior to his appointment, Cervera was visited by a reporter at Cádiz. "You appear to be indicated . . . for the command of the squadron in case war is declared," the man stated. "In that case," Cervera responded, "I shall accept; knowing however, that I am going to a Trafalgar." When the reporter asked how that catastrophe could be avoided, Cervera responded that unless he was permitted to expend, prior to hostilities, fifty thousand tons of coal in maneuvers and ten thousand projectiles in target practice, "we shall go to a Trafalgar."[5]

On February 12, Cervera indicated to the minister of marine, Rear Admiral Sigismundo Bermejo, his preoccupation with the hideous prospect of war with the United States and requested intelligence relating to American naval movements, as well as charts, plans, and "routes of what may become the scene of operations." What, he wanted to know, "will be the objective of the operations of this squadron?" Would it be called upon to defend the Iberian Peninsula and Balearic Islands, the Canaries, or Cuba? Or would his mission be to harass the coasts of the United States, "which would seem possible only if we had some powerful ally." He needed to know the government's plans of campaign, if indeed they had any. Finally, in case of war, where was the squadron to receive its supplies? Because here, at Cádiz, Spain's premier naval base, "strange to say . . . we have not even found 4-inch rope, nor boiler tubes nor other things equally simple." He required this information immediately, since, as the U.S. Navy was at least three times stronger than Spain's, "[t]he best thing would be to avoid the war at any price; but on the other hand, it is necessary to put an end to the present situation, because this nervous strain cannot be borne much longer."[6]

In response to Cervera's plea, Bermejo submitted to the admiral a general plan of operations so outlandish as to defy logic. While the navy retained a force of unfinished cruisers, obsolete ironclads, and some modern torpedo vessels in the vicinity of Cádiz, Cervera would sail to Cuba with the main units of the Spanish fighting fleet, taking no account of their material readiness: the battleship *Pelayo* still refitting in France, the unfinished *Emperador Carlos V*, the *Cristóbal Colón* without her 10-inch guns, and the three sister armored cruisers *Infanta María Teresa*, *Almirante Oquendo*, and *Vizcaya* with her foul and barnacled bottom. Accompanying this fleet were three modern destroyers and three torpedo boats. If all vessels had been in condition for active service, with topped-off coal bunkers, full armament, ammunition, clean boilers and bottoms, complete and well-trained crews, plus a train of colliers and a well-found base in the operational theater, the U.S. Navy would have had quite a job on its hands. But such was not the case.

Once in Cuba, this fleet, in conjunction with the "larger" vessels of the Havana naval station, was to take up positions to cover the channels between the Gulf of Mexico and the Atlantic, "and try to destroy

Key West." If this succeeded, Bermejo went on to say, "the blockade could be extended to the Atlantic coast" of the United States, cutting its communications with Europe. All this grandiose nonsense was of course predicated, the minister cautioned, on the outcome of naval battles, "in which it will be decided who is to hold empire of the sea."[7]

To Minister Bermejo's wildly optimistic ideas, Cervera responded patiently on February 16, the day after the destruction of the *Maine*. "It seems to me," he cautioned, "there is a mistake in the calculation of the forces we may count upon in the sad event of a war with the United States." He knew the *Pelayo* and *Carlos V* would not be ready in time, and the midcentury ironclads *Numancia* and *Lepanto* were obsolete beyond measure. The *Colón,* the minister had to be constantly reminded, had not her main battery, "and if war comes she will be caught without her heavy guns." As for the ships of the Havana station, "they have no military value whatever." In pointing out these obvious flaws to the ministerial plan, Cervera took pains to say that he was not goaded by a spirit of faultfinding, "but only by a desire to avoid illusions that may cost us very dear." With the Spanish navy at so much of a material disadvantage, it seemed to him "a dream, almost a feverish fancy, to think that with this force . . . we can establish the blockade of any part of the United States."[8]

Putting his finger on some very unpleasant conclusions, Cervera stated that a campaign against the United States, for the present time, must either be wholly defensive in nature, or else come to disaster. If Spain were to take the offensive, he could only envision some raids on the American coast with his fastest vessels. As for a naval battle, "It is frightful to think of the results . . . even if it should be a successful one for us, for how and where would we repair our damages?" Of course, he would do whatever was ordered, but the minister and government must "analyze the situation such as it is, without cherishing illusions which may bring about terrible disappointments."[9]

Bermejo replied a week later, admitting that perhaps he was "somewhat" optimistic in his outlook, but if Spain could avoid hostilities with the United States until the end of April, the disparity in naval strength might well balance itself out, if only slightly. Yet, he admitted, holding off that long could be very difficult in light of domestic politics. "We have to reckon," the minister said, "with the excitable nature of our nation and the evil of a press which it is impossible to

control." Indeed Spain was being whipped into excitement by a press
that fed the people a diet of claptrap on the superiority of the Spanish
navy over that of the United States. A former Spanish navy minister
went so far as to claim that "as soon as fire is opened the crews of the
American ships will commence to desert. . . . Ship against ship, therefore, a failure is not to be feared."[10]

Spanish public and official opinion held that they had nothing to
lose by fighting, even though Cuba was already lost. Spain, they reasoned, even if defeated in war, could do incalculable damage to American seaborne commerce, seriously injuring if not destroying the U.S.
Navy in the process, and could teach the Yankees a salutary lesson.
This would be infinitely better than rolling over and giving up the
ghost of Cuba without a struggle; honor demanded it. That being the
predicament, Bermejo assured Cervera he would see about obtaining
sufficient funds to get his ships into some sort of fighting trim before
the conflict opened.

Cervera was not impressed, and in late February he submitted a series of letters filled with the hard facts of the disparities between his
command and the U.S. Navy in the Atlantic. Arguing that the prime
purpose of naval operations is to obtain command of the sea (pure
Mahanian doctrine), a situation obtained only by defeating the enemy
in battle or blockading him in port, he asked Bermejo, "Can we do
this with the United States?" He provided his own answer for the
minister: "It is evident to me that we can not." Even if God granted
Spain a victory at the outset, the resulting battle damage would force
his ships out of action for the remainder of the war, while America
could easily repair her damage, aided by "powerful industries and
enormous resources." Thus, *when,* not *if,* the Americans gained command of the sea in the Caribbean cockpit, they might easily establish
bases in Cuba, and from there directly conduct operations against the
Spanish forces on the island. Without command of the sea, Spain
would find it extremely difficult, if not impossible, to reinforce her
army in the Antilles.[11]

Finally, on February 26, Cervera sent a courageous and impas-
sioned missive admonishing Bermejo that they, as professional naval
officers, owed the country their honest beliefs, not fantasies cooked
up in ministerial chambers. Cervera found himself unable to keep
silent about the truth, and did not wish to be an "accomplice in ad-

ventures which will surely cause the total ruin of Spain." And for what? he demanded to know. To defend Cuba, "an island which was ours, but belongs to us no more." Because even if they managed to retain it legally as a result of the war, it was in reality lost already, and with it an incalculable amount of Spanish treasure and the shiploads of irreplaceable young men who had died "in the defense of what is now no more than a romantic idea."[12]

Despite his entirely candid statements, Cervera could not budge the government in its determination to send heavy naval forces to the Caribbean. Bermejo disputed Cervera's calculation of the inferiority of the Spanish fleet compared to the Americans', arguing that the United States would find it difficult, if not impossible, to station its entire first-line naval forces in the Caribbean because of commitments in the Pacific and its need, political as well as military, to protect its coastal cities against attack. Therefore, Spain could close the gap in naval strength. And Bermejo chided Cervera for not factoring into his pessimistic calculations "the effect of homogeneous [ships' crews], well trained and disciplined, as against the United States crews of mercenaries."[13]

In vain Cervera argued on March 7 that U.S. naval forces in the Pacific and Asia were not intended to take part in Caribbean operations—true with one significant exception, the battleship *Oregon*, though he had no way of knowing that at the time. Thus it was a hollow trick to subtract them from an equation in which they were no factor. After another mournful litany of ships not ready, of shortages in ammunition, of guns in disrepair, Cervera disputed Bermejo's estimate of Spanish public opinion. He was inclined to believe the "immense majority of the Spaniards wish for peace above all things," but this majority had kept silent and permitted a militant minority to dictate a suicidal nationalistic policy.[14]

The Spanish government began its naval deployments on March 13, predicated on the dual mission of protecting the Spanish coast from bombardment and defending Cuba against invasion. The first units were the three destroyers and three torpedo boats of the torpedo flotilla, commanded by Captain Fernando Villaamil; sailing from Cádiz to the Canaries, they were to go on to St. Vincent in the Portuguese Cape Verde Islands off the bulge of West Africa. This was the movement that had so exercised Theodore Roosevelt and the

American naval command, who considered it an overtly hostile act worthy of retaliation.

On April 1, the concentration to the Cape Verdes continued. From Havana, the armored cruisers *Vizcaya* and *Oquendo* were ordered to the islands. Something would have to be done about the former ship, Cervera complained, as she had not had her bottom cleaned in eight months and trailed a full lawn of sea grass and barnacles along her hull, cutting her speed to something like fourteen knots. The Spanish navy, pined Cervera to Bermejo, was planning "like Don Quixote, to fight windmills and come back with broken heads." If he was compelled to steam to the Caribbean, the Americans would force a battle Spain could not hope to win. His plea to remain in the eastern Atlantic fell on deaf ears, especially as the government had just received a telegram from Captain General Blanco in Cuba warning, "Detention of flotilla at Cape Verdes leaves our coasts unprotected." This warning had far greater influence with the ministry than any of Cervera's complaints and observations, and for all intents it guaranteed the sending of Cervera's squadron to its doom in the Caribbean.[15]

Bermejo issued Cervera his initial sailing orders on April 7, directing the Cádiz cruisers to the Cape Verdes. Bravely the admiral stated his ships were ready for any duty, but what that entailed he as yet hadn't a clue. "No doubt," he replied to his orders, "Government has formed its plan; I must know it without fail if I am to cooperate with it intelligently." As for Cuba, he inserted almost as a non sequitur, he no longer would even mention its fate, "because I have anticipated it long ago."[16]

Admiral Cervera steamed into St. Vincent harbor on Thursday, April 14, with the flagship *Infanta María Teresa* and the defanged *Cristóbal Colón*. Coaling began immediately. On the Monday following, April 18, Cervera received his orders regarding the probable destination of the squadron, and it was not Cuba, but San Juan, Puerto Rico, a much closer destination, and one that had the advantage of forcing a division of enemy forces away from the Cuban blockade. Here, Bermejo promised, Cervera would find "every kind of supplies, including ammunition." Cervera raised objections; to him, any objective across the Atlantic pointed to useless defeat. He was grateful the squadron was not being sent to Cuba, but he had no illusions about Puerto Rico either, and he saw no need for its naval reinforcement. If that island remained loyal to Spain, he advised, "it will not be such an easy task for the Yankees; and if it is not loyal, it will inevitably follow the fate of Cuba." So what was the use?[17]

Not a day passed that the gloom-ridden Cervera did not seek to edify the minister regarding the true state of the squadron. The torpedo boats' machinery was in terrible condition, with the *Ariete*'s boilers practically unserviceable, "so that this vessel, instead of being an element of power, is the nightmare of the fleet." As for the modern destroyers *Plutón, Furor,* and *Terror,* their bows could not face heavy seas, crumpled like foil, and required stiffening material placed within their hulls. On the nineteenth, Cervera received his final reinforcements when the *Vizcaya* and *Almirante Oquendo* arrived from the Caribbean, the first in no way up to undertaking a campaign without a thorough docking, scraping, and painting. But this was not done.

Admiral Cervera convened a meeting of his second-in-command, Commodore José Paredes, the chief of staff, and ships' captains aboard the *Colón* on April 20, putting to them the question: "Under the present circumstances of the mother country, is it expedient that this fleet should go out at once to America," or should it remain to protect the Iberian coast, the Canaries, "and provide from here for any contingency?" The gallant response, Cervera noted, was the first and natural desire of the captains "to go resolutely in quest of the enemy and surrender their lives on the altar of the mother country." But to embark on that approach was to abandon Spain to her fate.[18]

That said for the sake of history and conscience, the discussion became general regarding the probable consequences of a campaign in the West Indies. The great disparities between the opposing naval forces were put on the table, as were the very scanty resources available in Cuba and Puerto Rico, no matter the hollow promises of the naval ministry. Considering the grave implications of a defeat, thus permitting the enemy to approach the Spanish homeland "with impunity," the officers unanimously agreed to inform the government that a concentration of force in the Canaries was substantially preferable to a death-or-glory voyage into the Caribbean. It would also give them time to dock and scrape the *Vizcaya* as well as complete the myriad other tasks typically not done. "Any division of our limited forces at this time and any separation from European waters would involve a strategic mistake," they advised, and they were right. By sending the squadron to the West Indies, what remained in home waters could not defend the coasts against determined enemy attack.[19]

Captain Concas of the flagship *Infanta María Teresa* would write after the war: "The object of military operations is final success and not proofs of valor." It was, however, useless to discuss this point because it could never be understood by the Spanish people. He fully comprehended that once Admiral Cervera's squadron was destroyed, and it would be if sent to the Caribbean, the war could not continue, though this, too, could not then be fathomed by the Spanish public or its politicians. Dividing Spain's skimpy naval resources, sending half across the ocean to certain destruction or, at best, nullification by blockade in port, was so enormous a strategic mistake that if it had been brought about by enemy action, "it alone would have been sufficient to make a name for the hostile admiral who accomplished this by virtue of his maneuvers." And here Spain was doing precisely that, handing the enemy its fleet on a plate to be devoured virtually at will.[20]

The day after the conference of captains, Admiral Cervera reported to the minister the squadron's readiness to return to the Canaries; he was totally rebuffed. "You will go out with all the forces to protect Puerto Rico," he was told in no uncertain terms. The phrase "Am going north" was to be his coded message to the government that the squadron had sailed for the West Indies. Nothing if not persistent, Cervera refused to go quietly into that good night. "The more I think about it the more I am convinced that to continue voyage to Puerto Rico will be disastrous." His ships' captains, he told Bermejo, were of exactly the same opinion, "some more emphatically."[21]

Captain Fernando Villaamil of the torpedo flotilla invoked his privilege as a member of the Cortes to make a direct appeal to Premier Sagasta. He considered the loss of the squadron an unmitigated disaster for Spain, elaborating, "Whilst we as seamen are ready to die with honour in the fulfillment of duty, I think it an undoubted fact that the sacrifice of this naval force will be as certain as it will be fruitless and useless." In response he received an inane telegram from Colonial Minister Moret: "God bless you."[22]

What was probably the final nail in the coffin came on April 22, the day after the Spanish declaration of war, from Captain General Blanco in Havana. He reported public spirit among the Spaniards in Cuba as very high, with "great enthusiasm among all classes." But if the people became convinced the squadron was not coming to their rescue, "disappointment will be great, and an unpleasant reaction is possible."[23]

At long last, on April 23, in response to Cervera's unrelieved pessimism, Minister Bermejo summoned a conference in Madrid of Spain's naval hierarchy: one admiral, four vice admirals, eight rear admirals, and five captains. The meeting was hastily called, and the participants were not informed of its object and had no time to prepare their judgment. Bermejo explained that the government planned to send Cervera's squadron of four armored cruisers plus the torpedo flotilla to Puerto Rico, the island being in great danger of attack and poorly defended. All other ships would be kept in Spain to be deployed as the developing situation dictated. Cervera, the conferees were told, was wholly in opposition. They were also advised of Blanco's telegram that Spanish morale in Cuba was of "the very best spirit for resistance," but that this was due in great part to expectation of the arrival of the squadron.[24]

Four of the participants opposed sending the squadron, but the majority voted for its immediate departure, either as constituted, or reinforced with the yet unfinished *Emperador Carlos V,* carrying her workmen aboard if necessary. The only sop given to Admiral Cervera was permission to employ the widest latitude in choosing his route to the scene of operations and in executing the plan on his arrival in the Caribbean. Cervera's letters to the ministry were apparently not shown at this meeting, and for this lapse Minister Bermejo deserves severe censure. It was unwise to keep in command an officer who spent a fair amount of time protesting the government's desires, right though these arguments were. One of the admirals who voted to send the squadron to the West Indies should have been chosen in Cervera's stead, even at that late date. Though the sudden relief of Cervera would have led to some disorganization in the squadron, the fact that he was unutterably opposed to his mission and without confidence in the government should have dictated his removal. But Madrid was blind to this reality. "Opinion," telegraphed Minister Bermejo at the conclusion of the conference, "is that the four battleships [sic] and three destroyers should start immediately for West Indies."[25]

It was the worst decision Spain could have made. She had several far better options that, from a military vantage point, might very well have yielded something other than bitter fruit. It would have taken a government far less in thrall to popular clamor—and a stern realization that despite the army's powerful influence in domestic politics, the colonies were irrevocably lost. For Spain's weak government, more concerned with maintaining its monarchical system than with an intelligent manner of waging war, it was too much to ask. The first, and simplest, option was to keep its fleet in home waters as a "fleet in being," which by mere existence exercises an influence over its foe beyond nominal capabilities. (Russia had done this in the midcentury Crimean War, and so had Germany in the more recent Franco-Prussian War. However, in these cases, neither regime had overseas colonies in which were trapped large bodies of troops, nor were their governments prone to listen to popular shouts of "Something must be done!")

It was obvious to all that America was going to have to organize and drill thousands of new volunteers for ground combat. Equally, she would have to transport them across the open sea to Cuba and Puerto Rico at great risk, unless she could obtain and hold complete command of the Caribbean Sea prior to these movements of invasion. Although this outcome was inevitable, given the disparity of naval forces in favor of the United States and the offensive nature of its senior naval officers, Spain could have thrown in several embarrassing wrenches before the inevitable weight of the enemy's force and aggressive character made itself felt. As a first, basic policy step, it should have been decided that, until she could put all her armored vessels into operational condition, it was the better part of valor to act strategically on the defensive.

This was the general plan proposed by Admiral Cervera and Captain Concas, and it offered Spain the best outcome she could get, with the least possibility of debacle. It entailed concentrating Spanish naval forces in the Canary Islands, building up the base with supplies and war matériel, and sending Spain's warships there as they became ready for active campaigning. This would have provided a secure and permanent foundation of operations. Not only did a Spanish force in the Canaries—a classic fleet in being—pose a constant menace, even if only perceived as such, to America's Atlantic coastline; it also prevented powerful American naval units from leaving the vicinity of Hampton Roads to participate in the blockade of Cuba. As a potential threat, it would also have forced the American military command to question whether their expeditionary force might sail to Cuba or Puerto Rico unmolested.

A more proactive option was to raid or threaten to raid the U.S. Atlantic coast somewhere north of Boston, something over which the American authorities, military and civilian, felt a good deal of anxiety. How practical this course was is admittedly questionable. The only Spanish ships even barely capable of the operation in late April were the *María Teresa, Oquendo,* and *Cristóbal Colón,* and two of these were not properly outfitted with ammunition, while the third still lacked her main guns. If the Spanish waited, however, until the end of May, the *Vizcaya* could have been docked and scraped, the *Carlos V* gotten ready for service, the *Colón* received her battery of 10-inch guns, and fresh ammunition for all the ships obtained. With full bunkers and a deckload of coal, this force could have steamed at an economical speed three thousand miles from the Cape Verdes to Boston or Portland, Maine, lobbed a few shells, and escaped from there to Halifax. Once there, under the international laws of neutrality, they could have demanded to buy enough coal to get them back to Spain. The popular panic generated on the coast would have been unimaginable. On the downside, the snail's pace of Spanish coaling, taking a week instead of a day or a bit more, would have given the U.S. Navy's Flying Squadron time to steam at full speed from its Norfolk base to blockade the Spanish ships in a neutral port.

Whether or not this scenario had played out to its end, the sheer presence of an ostensibly powerful Spanish force off the American coast would have led to a popular demand for the recall of at least part of Admiral Sampson's squadron from the Cuban blockade. Also, if the Spanish government had spread reports that the battleship *Pelayo* and whatever else could have been cobbled together in late May were also moving ostentatiously westward, then secretly retired them home, the seacoast panic would have been palpably increased.

Yet a third opportunity was to seek out and destroy the battleship *Oregon,* then making her famous voyage around Cape Horn, up the east coast of South America, to the operational seat of the war in the Caribbean. At the very beginning of hostilities, three of the Spanish armored cruisers and three destroyers might have been used to bring her to battle somewhere north of the bulge of Brazil. Though with the facts now known, the probability of a Spanish victory is doubtful, it was possible that these six ships, with their theoretically powerful torpedo capability, could have inflicted severe enough damage on the *Oregon* to put her out of action for months, providing great exultation in Spain and a terrible blow to the prestige of the United States and its newly vaunted navy. Further, even a partial victory over the *Oregon* could have given political cover to the Spanish government and naval hierarchy to pursue the prudent program of the fleet in being in the Canaries, repairing the ships returned home after the action, and providing time to ready the *Colón, Vizcaya, Pelayo,* and *Carlos V* for active service.

Lastly, if the dispatch of Admiral Cervera's squadron was the only course palatable to the Spanish government and naval ministry, then it was absolutely essential to send better than a few ill-equipped ships, with defective and missing guns and ammunition, and no means of replenishing provisions or coal. It was imperative for the government to delay at least another month until the *Carlos V* was ready for sea, the *Vizcaya* was docked, the gunnery faults were made right, and three more destroyers were added to the flotilla already at the Cape Verdes. While these preparations were taken in hand, Spain might have prepared for coaling contingencies in the West Indies, placing colliers along the Venezuelan coast and at Cienfuegos and Santiago de Cuba. Steaming with full bunkers from the Canaries, then coaling off Venezuela, Cervera could have made directly for Cienfuegos, brushing aside or destroying the small American blockading force currently there. This would have been a much harder nut for the Americans to crack than the eventual terminus of the Spanish squadron at Santiago de Cuba. Cienfuegos maintained direct rail communications with Havana, enabling army reinforcements to be shuttled back and forth almost at will, and a blockade would have been a far more protracted endeavor, as would the eventual land campaign.

But Spain did none of this, and thus was doomed to fight a war without being able to inflict a single check on the enemy. On April 23, after receiving word of the decision of the Madrid meeting, Admiral Cervera telegraphed Minister Bermejo, "Though I persist in my opinion, which is also the opinion of the captains of the ships, I shall do all I can to hasten our departure, disclaiming all responsibility for the consequences." These final complaints to Madrid were as useless as they were pathetic. New problems arose. The after main battery turning gear of the *Almirante Oquendo* "does not obey," Cervera informed the minister; "we continue to work incessantly." On the twenty-fourth, Cervera was informed that colliers were ordered to meet him in San Juan, Puerto Rico, and that he could accept or decline battle as he wished. This was hardly an option, not with the *Vizcaya*'s bottom resembling a kitchen garden. She was now, Cervera said, "nothing but a buoy and I cannot abandon her."[26]

For five days the squadron coaled with inferior stuff at St. Vincent. Captain Concas ruminated that there "was no way out of the dilemma." The idea of returning to Spain contrary to orders "was fermenting in the minds of all," especially Captain Díaz Moreu of the *Colón,* as "the only salvation of the country." The ships' captains, though they supported this in theory, knew if they carried out this sensible precaution, the "ignorance prevailing in Spain" was so great that not only would these brave men be punished, "but also ridiculed, and no one would understand that it was a heroic resolution and a sublime sacrifice." There was no choice but obedience, which for Spain meant the inevitable loss of her fleet and thus her empire.[27]

On April 28, Cervera received a telegram from Minister Bermejo informing him that Havana and the north coast of Cuba were under blockade, but San Juan was "so far free." As for the domestic scene in Spain, "quiet and harmony" reigned. The nation sent its enthusiastic greetings, and the ministry was expending great activity in fitting out the rest of the fleet.[28]

Admiral Cervera responded the next day with a terse coded wire, the prearranged signal: "Am going north." At 10 A.M., he heaved in his anchors, pointed his bows west, and disappeared into the Atlantic void.[29]

At 10 A.M., April 29, said Captain Concas of the flagship *Infanta María Teresa,* "we lost the Portuguese Islands from view to the eastward." Four armored cruisers, one without her main battery, and three destroyers, whose flimsy hulls and poor engines were no match for the Atlantic seas, plowed west. No auxiliaries sailed with the squadron, no light scouting cruisers, "and worst of all," according to Concas, "no colliers." Three had been ordered to rendezvous with the squadron in the West Indies; two would be captured, and the third missed the encounter point. The order of the squadron's sailing was in double column, with the *María Teresa* leading to starboard and the *Cristóbal Colón,* flying the broad pennant of the second-in-command,

Commodore José Paredes, to port. To obviate the need for coaling at sea, and to keep their delicate machinery in basic order, the destroyers were towed. But this had not been taken into account when the torpedo flotilla had originally departed Cádiz for the Cape Verdes, and the destroyers were not properly equipped for towing. "They require special bridles for that purpose," said Concas, "which were to be found neither at the arsenal nor on the market." Towing, a difficult operation in the best of situations, became a small nightmare. The craft yawed continuously, lines parted, and "much valuable time was lost." It was, however, infinitely better than coaling at sea from the cruisers, which, owing to the long swells caused by the fresh breezes, was a difficult and dangerous operation. The *Vizcaya*, with its foul bottom, was the only ship that did not tow; as it was, her coal consumption, even at the fleet speed of only seven knots, was so much greater than the other ships "that we were all alarmed about it."[30]

On May 10, two days east of the Caribbean's Windward Islands, the tows were cast off. The cruisers formed line astern of the flagship with the destroyers forward in line abreast, a good formation to meet an enemy. Fires under all boilers were lit and fleet speed was increased to eleven knots. But this proved impossible to sustain on account, said Concas, of "injuries" to the destroyers' engines. Admiral Cervera now detached the *Furor* and *Terror* under their commander, Captain Villaamil, to Martinique with instructions to obtain coal from the colliers supposed to rendezvous there and to learn most especially the latest war news. Villaamil also carried a message to be wired to Minister Bermejo announcing the squadron's safe arrival with "spirit excellent" in the West Indies. Cervera also requested an increase of credit, for the squadron's pay was due and he did not wish to exhaust the specie that constituted his funds aboard. The destroyers had been ordered to dash in at twenty knots, but after a few hours the boilers of the *Terror* became fouled and she wallowed helplessly in the open sea. Villaamil left her, knowing the squadron would come upon the craft soon enough, and he headed west in the *Furor*.[31]

The exact landfall of the squadron, Martinique, was not known to anyone outside of its executive command because Cervera, "fearing some indiscretion," had not even notified the government of his plan to touch land there—though he had hinted at it when he telegraphed Bermejo from the Cape Verdes that "at principal ports . . . where these ships are likely to touch, we should have confidential agents to give me authentic information." Cervera hoped to learn not only the enemy's previous movements, but also their mode of campaign, and even possibly their current maneuvers and ship distribution. It was natural for him to suppose that Spanish consuls were on the alert to provide this intelligence. But when Villaamil arrived at Martinique's Fort de France, he found the Spanish consul "was in the country."[32]

According to Captain Concas, Villaamil was received "ungraciously" by the island's French governor, and would not have gotten any news were it not for the captain of the Spanish hospital ship *Alicante*, who passed on the reports printed in the daily press; this was all Villaamil could obtain, and there was no coal either. The expected collier was not there, and the governor denied the Spanish permission to buy any in the port. Aside from these bad tidings, Villaamil was jolted to learn the American auxiliary cruiser *Harvard* lay across the island at St. Pierre and had doubtless learned of his presence. At midnight, May 11, Villaamil weighed anchor and, assisted by the *Alicante*'s boats and searchlights, sped to sea to alert the admiral.

The prearranged hour of meeting the returning Villaamil had passed, and great anxiety blanketed the squadron. "Silence," said Concas, "was imposed upon the ships, which were advancing with all lights extinguished" except for a screened lamp at the stern. The crews were at their battle stations. Shortly before 2 A.M., May 12, they spotted the signal of the *Furor*'s searchlight bouncing off the clouds. An hour later Villaamil was aboard the flagship, and Cervera learned of the disaster at Manila Bay, the presence of an American cruiser at Martinique, the rough dispositions of the Cuban blockade, and that major elements of the enemy's fleet were cruising off, if not already bombarding, San Juan. So much for the government's initial plans for the squadron to put in to Puerto Rico; and worse yet, Villaamil continued, there was no coal in Martinique. In view of this gloomy report, Admiral Cervera had no doubt that his arrival in the West Indies had been telegraphed by the Yankee cruiser, "that we were right on the scene of the war," Concas recalled angrily, "and that the enemy had gained control of it, without any opposition whatever."[33]

Cervera continued westward, entering the Caribbean between St. Lucia and Martinique, where he intended to leave the *Terror* with orders to repair her boilers, then try to catch up with the squadron, or to make for the nearest Spanish port. A few miles west of Martinique, Cervera halted and called a conference of captains, at the same time coaling his destroyers from the cruisers in the relatively calm seas. It was decided to head southwest, off the coast of Venezuela to the Dutch island of Curaçao. Why Curaçao, which lay in the opposite direction from San Juan and Havana, and from where the squadron could only make it to the south coast of Cuba? Captain Concas explained that for some time it had been reported that the United States had been negotiating the purchase of the island of St. Thomas in the Danish Virgin Islands, just east of Puerto Rico, and they had reason to suspect the Americans had a coaling station already in place. Even if just one American merchant ship were there, the enemy fleet, "which we had been told [correctly] was at San Juan, would be notified . . . and the U.S. squadron was certain to cut off our passage." If they then continued on to Puerto Rico or Havana from their southern position in the Caribbean, an encounter with the North Atlantic Squadron would likely have taken place at sea, with the Spanish at least four hundred miles from a friendly port.[34]

In the case of a battle, said Captain Concas, with enemy forces being overwhelmingly superior, "our ships, if even slightly injured, were hopelessly lost" and would be hunted down in a remorseless chase. Thus, San Juan "we had to discard altogether," because the Americans could take it whenever they pleased; and so, too, Havana, "which we had to suppose to be well guarded [blockaded]." Cienfuegos was an option, and not a bad one either, being in rail communications with Havana and on a direct route from Curaçao. But Concas called Cienfuegos a "veritable rat trap, very easy to blockade . . . [and] with no fortifications to amount to anything."[35]

The only remaining solution was Santiago de Cuba, "the second capital of the island," Concas went on, which the squadron command reasonably supposed "well supplied with provisions and [coast] artillery in view of the defensibly favorable conditions of the harbor entrance." Better yet, to Concas's thinking, this end of the Cuban coast offered opportunities for sorties on stormy days and an open sea for operations once they had coaled, resupplied, and repaired after the voyage. Thus Curaçao became their way station. Besides, back at the Cape Verdes, Cervera had been promised a collier there, and as they were less than five hundred miles away from Santiago, this detour to the southwest added only two hundred miles to their ultimate destination. "It was decided to proceed to Curaçao."[36]

The destroyers deployed on the flagship's beam, fires were spread under all boilers, and the ships made ready for any emergency. The squadron reached the island of Curaçao on the morning of May 14, and was immediately halted at the harbor entrance by the Dutch colonial authorities. After what Concas called "lengthy and unpleasant negotiations," the governor admitted only two ships, under the stipulation that they might remain no more than forty-eight hours, severely limiting the coal they might take on board. The *Infanta María Teresa* and *Vizcaya* entered port. Though Concas says the crews worked "frantically," they were able to get only four hundred tons of coal aboard, and "also such provisions as we could obtain" in the time allowed. In the harbor, for the men aboard the two ships, the night was filled with high anxieties, "when we interpreted every noise as an attack upon our comrades." And there was no way for them to leave for the open sea either, because at dark the harbor entrance was sealed shut by the lowering of a drawbridge.[37]

In the meantime, Concas and the squadron officers understood the "sad fact" that their anxiously looked for collier was not coming, nor was there any new war news. At daylight on May 16, the two cruisers exited port, formed line with the squadron, and at an economical speed due to the low bunkers of the *Almirante Oquendo* and *Cristóbal Colón,* shaped course for Santiago de Cuba, "which the admiral indicated by signals to be our destination." Cervera timed their arrival for daybreak three days hence.[38]

First light on May 19 saw the squadron off Santiago without having encountered a hostile ship. The destroyers reconnoitered the coast for a space and the cruisers entered the harbor, casting anchor at 8 A.M. The *Oquendo* had less than 100 tons of coal left. Awaiting Cervera were a couple of telegrams from Minister of Marine Bermejo. The first replied to the admiral's message from Martinique. The squadron's credit had been increased by £15,000 so the sailors could be paid on time. There was "[n]othing new in the Peninsula," and the enemy had bombarded San Juan. Unbelievably, he also told the admiral that the hospital ship *Alicante* at Martinique had a load of coal for the squadron on board. This when the captain of that ship, who proved extremely helpful within his limited means, made absolutely no mention of it to Villaamil.

There was also more coal on the way to Santiago in the chartered British collier *Restormel,* which should be there directly.[39]

There was another telegram from Bermejo, almost an afterthought, dated May 12, but Admiral Cervera claimed never to have seen it until his return to Spain after the war. The Spanish government, unhinged in its martial ardor after the defeat at Manila Bay, now had second thoughts about sending the squadron to the West Indies. Cervera's orders from the navy minister were "amplified," giving him the option of returning to Spain if he considered that operations in the Americas were a fruitless mission. Even if Cervera had read these new instructions, Captain Concas thought it was too late. The squadron hadn't the coal to return to Spain. "It is madness in time of war," he wrote, "to send a squadron out to sea [without colliers], as it would be madness to send an army corps into a campaign without provisions and cartridges except as the soldiers might carry in the knapsacks."[40]

Whether Admiral Cervera saw this cable or not, Captain General Blanco in Havana and his confrere, General Manuel Macías, governor general of Puerto Rico, did, and they were not happy about it. Blanco was shown the telegram after asking the Havana naval commander, Admiral Manterola, of the latest news of the squadron. "If this should happen [the recall of the ships]," he wrote the new colonial minister, Vicente Romero Girón, the situation in Cuba would become "wholly untenable, and I could not prevent bloody revolution in this capital [by Spanish *peninsulares*] and whole island." Everyone was already very put out by the squadron's delay in arriving. If the squadron were defeated, he and the *peninsulares* could live with that, "it would increase here determination to vanquish or die; but if it flees, panic and revolution are certain."[41]

Within the cabinet in Madrid, the shock of the defeat at Manila Bay had brought on a ministerial crisis. Moret in the colonial office, Foreign Minister Gullón, and Admiral Bermejo in the navy ministry found themselves under attack—Bermejo being blamed for the disaster in the Philippines and the unpromising scenario unfolding in the Caribbean. Premier Sagasta appealed for continued national dedication and reorganized his government. In the foreign ministry, the Duke of Almodóvar replaced Pío Gullón; Vicente Girón took the colonial portfolio; and Rear Admiral Ramón Auñón, a real fire breather, knocked Bermejo from the navy ministry.

CHAPTER 8

HUNTING CERVERA

We've got them now, Graham, and they'll never go home.
—*Commodore Winfield Scott Schley, May 29, 1898*

Within a few days of Admiral Cervera's disappearance into the oceanic emptiness, and even amidst the celebrations of Dewey's victory at Manila Bay, a sudden nervousness jittered along the U.S. eastern seaboard. A telegraph operator in Newfoundland thought he heard gunfire at sea and the report flashed down the Atlantic coast. Merchant skippers started reporting strange ships off Fire Island, and the whole North Atlantic suddenly filled with dubious sightings of Spanish cruiser squadrons. The idea spread that Admiral Cervera's ships would suddenly appear off New York or Boston threatening bombardment. New battleships being built in the Norfolk area were thought to be in danger from Spanish torpedo boats, and valuable scouting cruisers were detailed to Hampton Roads as harbor defense vessels. "The calls made upon the [War] Department for immediate rescue from the advancing Spanish fleet," said Secretary Alger, "were pathetic in their urgency. . . . They wanted guns everywhere, mines in all rivers and harbors on the map."[1]

Assistant Navy Secretary Roosevelt, before he resigned his office, pacified congressmen who wanted ships sent "to protect Portland, Maine, Jekyl Island, Narragansett Pier, and other points of like importance," by sending them a Civil War monitor, manned by New Jersey Naval Militia. It satisfied Portland "entirely!" Though as TR noted, "It would have been useless against any war vessel more modern than one of Hamilcar's galleys." Members of Congress who had actively opposed building the new navy now came loudly demanding protection. And it was not only elected officials who came; a stream of chambers of commerce presidents and boards of trade members piled "every species of pressure to bear" on the administration, persuading it to a large degree to "adopt a most fatal course—that is to distribute the navy."[2]

It might have been a joke to send the rusting monitor to Portland, but it was no laughing matter to weaken the North Atlantic Squadron by siphoning off some of its best ships to sit eating coal at Hampton Roads, under the misnomer of the "Flying Squadron." The naval war would be won or lost in the Caribbean, not off Martha's Vineyard or Norfolk. Even if Cervera managed to lob a shell into Boston or Portland it was of no great military import. He could not sustain the operation without a ready supply of coal, and he did not have that.

The Flying Squadron, at first composed of the navy's fastest cruisers, was intended to dash out from its centrally located base at Hampton Roads and intercept the enemy attacking a coastal city. Yet owing to the detachment of its swiftest vessels, the cruisers *Columbia* and *Minneapolis,* early in the conflict, and their replacement by the battleships *Massachusetts* and *Texas,* the Flying Squadron was hobbled to half its original speed. And while its gunpower increased mightily with the addition of the battleships, their detachment from the main North Atlantic Squadron in the Cuban blockade denied Admiral Sampson some necessary brawn required for heavy slugging with the Spanish navy. For six frustrating weeks, from the beginning of the war until mid-May, the Flying Squadron sat at Hampton Roads, looked upon, as Theodore Roosevelt said, "with hysterical anxiety by the Northeast and its representatives in Congress as a protection against a Spanish attack."[3]

Commodore Winfield Scott Schley commanded the Flying Squadron, and he seemed a good choice. A dashing, imperial-goateed officer with a fine Civil War record, Schley had seen more recent action in Korea, had rescued a starving Arctic expedition, and was captain of the *Baltimore* during the Chilean crisis of 1891, though he did not really show to his best there. His most recent duty had been as chairman of the Lighthouse Board, and in that capacity on March 20, 1898, he called upon Secretary Long to offer the navy his tugs and tenders. Summoned back by telephone later in the day, Schley thought the call was to arrange the transfer of vessels. Instead Long offered him command of the Flying Squadron, to be formed immediately. When asked when he could assumed command, Schley answered, "Tomorrow." The dashing Schley, an officer far more widely recognized than the obscure clubman George Dewey or the dour, professorial William T. Sampson, was likely pushed on Secretary Long by Theodore Roosevelt as a counterweight to the conservative influence in the Bureau of Navigation, and frankly, as a dashing sop well calculated to allay the unreasonable public fears of a Spanish raid on the East Coast. If anyone could intercept Cervera, it would be Commodore Winfield Scott Schley.[4]

Until Admiral Cervera's position was disclosed on the western side of the Atlantic, each passing week saw public tension increase, making Schley a virtual prisoner at Hampton Roads. Schley used the time to drill his ships and men. After the *Maine* report reached Washington in late March, the squadron had been on notice for one hour's steaming, and remained in this state for thirty-seven days. Subcaliber firing practice, ammunition-handling drills, and endless coaling occupied the crews.

On April 13, Schley fired a signal gun from his flagship, the armored cruiser *Brooklyn,* recalling all hands from shore, and the Flying Squadron put to sea. According to the chaplain of the *Texas,* "The windows at the hotels went up, and the ladies were seen looking out at us, and in a little while they were all down at the beach." The women crowded into small boats to bid their husbands a tearful good-bye. But one reporter noticed the composure of Mrs. Schley and rightly surmised the squadron was not leaving for the theater of war. The commodore merely intended steaming a short distance to the drill grounds, fifteen miles away off the Virginia capes, to test his big guns in a lively sea. A day and a half later, the squadron was back in Hampton Roads.[5]

Even before the opening days of the conflict, tall, lean, stooped Rear Admiral William T. Sampson, the ordnance and gunnery expert, lately chairman of the *Maine* board of inquiry, whom the correspondent Richard Harding Davis described as looking more like a "calm

and scholarly professor of mathematics" than an admiral commanding a fleet of warships, strove to prepare his forward base at Key West
and to drive into shape a heterogeneous blockading fleet that at any
moment might encounter a hypothetically powerful enemy of great
speed and surmised torpedo prowess. Spain had good bases at Havana and San Juan to service her squadron in the West Indies, if they
were well provisioned, and Sampson had no reason to doubt it. Given
that, he formulated a basic plan to blockade Havana, forcing the
Spanish squadron to anchor in San Juan, where, in a surprise attack,
he would sink it at its moorings.[6]

But he would take the Havana strategy a step further than simple
blockade: he would knock out the forts at the harbor entrance,
threatening the city with bombardment and forcing it to surrender. At
the end of March he outlined his method to Secretary Long. "My
present plan contemplates an attack [upon Havana] the very moment
the dogs of war are let loose." But, he added, his force, as presently
constituted, might not be up to it: the battleship *Indiana* was off re-
tubing her boilers, and the flagship, the armored cruiser *New York*—
though one of the best of her type anywhere—was only a cruiser,
"hardly suitable for such work," Sampson said, "though she would
have to do her share if it were to be now." To ensure success, he
begged the return of the *Massachusetts* from Schley's Flying Squadron, where it sat immobile at Hampton Roads. "I am convinced,"
Sampson told the secretary, "that the country has nothing to fear
from an attack along our northern coast." Long knew that too, but he
bowed to the popular furor and refused to detach the battleship from
her shackles.[7]

Long, advised by the Naval War Board, was not all that impressed
with his fleet commander's ideas regarding attacks on coastal batteries. The rule of thumb since before the Civil War had been one gun
ashore equaled four afloat, and the Spanish certainly had that equation at Havana, and 12-inch guns at that, which if well served could
cripple the North Atlantic Squadron before the war was a week old.
The only way Long would countenance this sort of action was if "the
more formidable Spanish vessels should take refuge within those harbors." Should that prove to be the case, "rigid blockade" and the use
of torpedo boats could accomplish the desired result just as well without risking the battleships. There was another reason as well: the immediate lack of available American troops to occupy any captured

stronghold of size. Lastly, Long did not want a war-damaged fleet jamming up his navy yards and dry docks before the capture or destruction of "Spain's most formidable vessels." Sampson had to be satisfied with this mind-set, and conservative though it was, it was thoroughly correct.[8]

On April 21, the *New York* anchored outside the reef at Key West, and Rear Admiral Sampson convened a meeting of his captains to await the war-message cable from the Navy Department. When nothing happened, the captains made ready to return to their ships, but Sampson bid them to stay. "So," remembered Captain Robley "Fighting Bob" Evans of the battleship *Iowa*, "over our fresh cigars we sat and listened to the quiet words of our clearheaded commander, while the wind howled and the ship pitched and rolled in the choppy sea." Just before midnight a torpedo boat raced out from the town with a coded cipher: "War declared; proceed to blockade the coast of Cuba," from Cárdenas east of Havana to Bahía Honda on the west, a distance of 145 nautical miles. "Do not bombard," the instructions ended.[9]

On receipt of the orders, Sampson signaled all ships inside the reef to come out immediately. Lights were placed on the navigation buoys, and by them and ships' searchlights, all vessels ready for duty exited the harbor and lay hove-to by the flagship. At 4:58 A.M., she hoisted the signal "Form order of cruising." Before daylight, Evans recalled, "every vessel of the fleet was under way, formed in double column, and headed for the coast of Cuba." It was really a remarkable achievement, for in less than four hours from the receipt of the order, the navy showed its state of readiness by actually starting for the enemy's coast. "Fortunately for the country," Evans said, "we were in much better shape than the people thought we were." The edge of Cuba came into sight in late afternoon, and the first Spanish merchant ships were seized on the high seas. Havana, from the ships' decks and bridges, appeared in a blaze of lights. A few signal guns were fired from the shore, and then Morro castle went black. The war at sea had begun.

John D. Long anticipated the blockade would produce three key results: First, it would cut off food and supplies to the Spanish army in Cuba. There would be no concomitant injury to American forces. Second, it would destroy Spanish seaborne commerce, the sole artery that connected Spain to its New World possessions. Third, it would oblige Spain to send relief to her colonies, with the consequent strain of conducting a war over three thousand miles from home bases. These were lofty and appropriate goals, but Admiral Sampson's meager force, depleted by the formation of the so far useless Flying Squadron, plainly limited the scope of operations to that portion of Cuba's northern coast within easy steaming range of Key West. There was no question, at the time, of stationing anything but small scouts off the southern ports of Cienfuegos or Santiago de Cuba, not unless the Flying Squadron were untied from the feckless duty of coast defense, and domestic politics would not yet permit that.

The main blockade around Havana formed a semicircle at distances of six to ten miles from the harbor mouth. From the first day to the last, the city was zealously barricaded, and only three small ships in the first few days ever broke through into the port. The Cuban capital, however, never really felt the pinch of starvation, though food prices rose and the poor suffered accordingly. Havana and its immediate environs could easily have withstood a year's blockade before being compelled by an empty larder to surrender, for as Theodore Roosevelt had said, "Spaniards starve well." The most important result of the blockade was that it prevented Admiral Cervera's squadron from even attempting to enter Havana or operating anywhere along Cuba's north coast. That alone made it effective.

If Admiral Sampson was hampered by a lack of warships for a complete blockade, he was inundated by a flock of press boats that hovered around the fleet in its every movement. Before the declaration of war, he had beseeched Secretary Long: "It is considered best . . . to forbid all press associations being in squadron." Long, who had a keen eye to public relations, turned this down. At Key West, the leading papers and wire services all operated at least one fast boat. The Associated Press correspondent aboard the flagship *New York* had four at his command. Because Admiral Sampson was woefully short of suitable dispatch vessels of his own, he was often forced to employ the press craft to carry messages to cable stations during active operations. He was also strained to use his torpedo boats for this postman duty, something for which they were not at all designed. It was recognized by everyone, said Captain French Chadwick of the *New York*, "that if they were to be kept ready for the work for which they were built, they should be carefully nursed

rather than knocked about in the tossing sea of the Florida Channel."
Yet information in war is paramount, and "any sacrifice must be
made to this end." A bit later, when a number of armed yachts were
commissioned, the admiral was better served, but he never truly over-
came the burden of not having sufficient dispatch boats to communicate with distant ships of the squadron or the Navy Department
through the various Caribbean island cable stations.[10]

On April 27, Sampson took the *New York,* the monitor *Puritan,*
and the cruiser *Cincinnati* off the Havana blockade and steamed down
the coast to Matanzas to give his crews the smell of gunpowder under
near-battle conditions. The Spanish were reported to be constructing
some earthworks on a point by the city, and the admiral wished to demolish them. After a speed run to the east (relatively speaking, since
the *Puritan's* top speed of twelve knots kept a check on the rest), the
three ships steamed slowly toward the harbor entrance. With a long
glass, spotters on the bridges and fighting tops could see Spanish soldiers two miles away standing on a long earthen mound. The correspondent Richard Harding Davis was aboard the flagship and later
remembered that at the sounding of the general quarters bugle,
"Everyone seemed to have been caught just at the wrong end of the
ship and on the wrong deck, at the exact point farthest from his division. They all ran about for about a minute in every direction, and
then there was absolute silence, just as though someone had waved a
wand over each of them and had fixed him in his place."[11]

From the forebridge, Captain Chadwick ran down the ladder to
the portside 8-inch gun, shouting to the young ensign in charge. The
waist gun was chosen for the opening shot because of the intense rivalry existing between the fore and after turrets—Chadwick did not
wish to favor either at the expense of the other's morale. "Aim for
4,000 yards, at that bank of earth on the point," the captain yelled,
then ran back up the ladder to the bridge. At first Davis tried keeping
track of the shots, "but soon it was like counting falling bricks. The
guns seemed to be ripping out the steel sides of the ship. . . . The thick
deck of the superstructure jumped with the concussions and vibrated
like a suspension bridge when an express train thunders over it. . . .
The noise was physical, like a blow from a baseball bat."[12]

The low-riding *Puritan,* her decks lashed with two feet of water
in the swells, appeared to have waves running in and out of her gun

turret ports, which was not unlikely given the configuration of the monitor type. To Davis, though, the flames and smoke from her guns came right out of her waterline, "so that it looked to us as though she were sinking and firing as she sank." The *Cincinnati* fired her broadsides "as rapidly as a man can shoot a self-cocking revolver." For nearly an hour the bombardment continued, the range coming down to three thousand yards. The reply of the Spanish field guns had no effect. Admiral Sampson claimed to have destroyed the earthworks, but the Spanish only admitted to the death of a mule. In early afternoon, the ships sailed away to the west, back to the Havana blockade, the men having smelled powder and taken fire in return.[13]

A more serious encounter took place on May 8 and 11 at Cárdenas, some miles east of Matanzas. Three small Spanish gunboats were reported sheltering in the harbor and Lieutenant John Bernadou took the torpedo boat *Winslow* to flush them out. Outside the harbor, the gunboats *Wilmington* and *Machias* waited. The *Winslow* fired sixty rounds from her 1-pounder guns at point-blank range, but the Spanish vessels refused to chase her, remaining safely inside. Three days later, the Americans returned, this time bringing the armed Revenue cutter *Hudson*. The torpedo boat and cutter entered the bay, finding one of the Spanish gunboats lying by a wharf among some merchant shipping. The *Winslow*, being of the lighter draft, steamed virtually alongside; nearing the dock, however, it passed a number of red buoys, and Bernadou realized too late they were range markers for a Spanish masked battery. The Spanish gun vessel fired one shot, the signal for the battery to open fire. The *Winslow* was quickly disabled by guns firing smokeless powder, impossible to spot. Her steering gear destroyed, rudder jammed, she had to maneuver by her engines alone. Lieutenant Bernadou himself was badly wounded in the groin. The forward boiler was pierced and a shot struck one of the torpedoes on deck, though it did not explode. The port engine stopped, and the *Winslow* wallowed helplessly. The *Hudson* came to her rescue and threw a towline, which parted, then tried another, which succeeded in hauling her out of danger, but not before a Spanish shell exploded among a group of the *Winslow*'s men who were passing ammunition. A young ensign was killed, two seamen were mortally wounded, and four others less so, making eight casualties in a crew of twenty-five men.

A second skirmish took place on May 11, off Cienfuegos on the south coast. Five underwater telegraph cables touched there, running eastward to Santiago and ultimately connecting Havana with Madrid. The cruisers *Marblehead* and *Nashville,* with the Revenue cutter *Windom,* came to cut them. Two steam launches and two sailing launches were put over the side, each armed with a 1-pounder gun and a detachment of marines to keep the Spanish down. While the *Marblehead* opened fire on the cable house, the *Nashville* and *Windom* beat the bushes and woods, which were infested with Spanish infantry. The cables, "heavy armored" things six inches in diameter, could be clearly seen on the bottom. The first was grappled when only ninety feet from shore; several feet were cut away, and an effort was made to drag it into deep water, cutting off as much of the end as possible and puncturing the insulation with sharp awls. Through furious enemy rifle fire that peppered one of the boats, the second cable was hooked within sixty feet of the beach. By the time the third cable was grappled, men in the boats were falling fast—one was dead, three were fatally wounded, five less seriously so. Though grappled, the third cable was ordered dropped. It was far too dangerous to continue. The steam launches took the other two in tow and, keeping up a fire on the beach, withdrew to the ships in deep water. It was a heroic and necessary operation, but Havana remained in telegraphic contact with Spain through the war.[14]

On April 29, with news of Cervera's departure from the Cape Verdes, the Navy Department issued orders to its fast, big scouts, the auxiliary cruisers *Harvard, Yale,* and *St. Louis,* all formerly transatlantic liners, chartered into the navy. The *Yale* was assigned to the waters around Puerto Rico, while the other two were given a patrol line immediately west of the chain encompassing the Windward and Leeward Islands, a six-hundred-mile-long stretch of ocean extending roughly from St. Thomas in the Virgin Islands to Trinidad off the Venezuelan coast. The *Harvard* had specific instructions to enter Martinique if no information on the Spanish fleet had come in by May 10. These orders were, according to Captain Chadwick, "most judicious" in their character and were an almost perfect forecast of Spanish intentions and movements. But they erred in their estimate of when the Spanish would enter the Caribbean, allowing a much higher turn of speed for their ships and, thus, an earlier date of arrival in the war zone. The miscalculation enabled Cervera to elude his hunters for over two weeks.[15]

On the day of the scouting orders, Admiral Sampson also received news of Cervera's sailing. He thought the Spanish admiral would make either for San Juan or for a port in eastern Cuba, and he decided to cut him off in the Windward Passage between eastern Cuba and Haiti or, failing that, to catch the Spanish at anchor at San Juan, coaling, unready to receive an attack. He intended to take along the bulk of the Havana blockade force: armored cruiser *New York*, battleships *Iowa* and *Indiana*, monitors *Amphitrite* and *Terror*, cruisers *Detroit* and *Montgomery*, and the torpedo boat *Porter*, plus a collier and a tug. The ships were prepared for battle with chain cables wrapped around ammunition hoists and sandbags piled at vulnerable points. Night was already falling when the squadron rendezvoused eighty-five miles east of Havana. The tublike monitors were an immediate problem: because of their small coal bunkers and very inefficient engines, the monitors had to be towed by the *New York* and *Iowa*. But Sampson could not dispense with them; there were no other armored ships at hand, and there would be nothing else until the department found the courage to shake the Flying Squadron loose from its apron strings at Hampton Roads, or the battleship *Oregon* finished her circumnavigation of the Western Hemisphere and reached the Caribbean war zone. The night was one of extreme difficulties. Towlines snapped and leaky boilers in the *Indiana* and *Detroit* promised the squadron would not reach San Juan by May 8 as Sampson wished.

On the morning of May 7, north of Cap Haïtien, Haiti, past the halfway mark to San Juan, the admiral sent the *Montgomery* and *Porter* into port to glean from the cable station any news of the Spanish that might have come from the Navy Department. At first there was nothing, but then the *Porter* came out with several telegrams giving erroneous reports of Spanish vessels coaling and loading ammunition in the Virgin Islands. There was also an annoying reminder from Secretary Long to Admiral Sampson: Do "not risk so crippling your vessels against fortifications as to prevent from soon afterward successfully fighting Spanish fleet."[16]

In the early hours of May 8, a captains' conference aboard the flagship ended with a decision to continue on to San Juan since nothing definite had been received regarding Cervera's movements. Sampson felt the risk justified extending his line of communications to the near breaking point from Key West, if by so doing he could prevent the Spanish admiral from coaling and repairing unfettered in a fortified harbor. To Sampson, just to wait was out of the question. Had he either remained off Havana or continued steaming about the Windward Passage while Cervera coaled at San Juan, and had the Spanish then appeared off the American East Coast, one could imagine the public outcry. The decision to continue on to San Juan was a difficult one, Captain Chadwick said, but Admiral Sampson had accurately forecast the Spanish intentions. "He judged the activity and energy of the Spanish commander by his own," he said. The only flaw was that the Spanish could not stick to the timetable afforded them by their foes. Sampson, even with his dragging monitors, was too quick off the mark.[17]

Naturally and unavoidably a flotilla of press boats hung along with the squadron. Sampson fully recognized the insatiable demand of the American public for information and did not impede these craft beyond military necessity. The present movement east demanded secrecy to the fullest, and in the main the press understood this. (There was an exception, a report from Cap Haïtien that "eight warships passed this harbor this morning going east," which was published in New York, along with a chart showing the squadron's exact position. When this became known to the admiral, the correspondent was banished from the squadron.) But Sampson needed to employ the press boats as dispatch vessels, for lack of anything better. While still off Cap Haïtien, he sent the Associated Press's *Dauntless* into port to deliver his messages, and she returned with startling news: the battleship *Pelayo* and the cruiser *Carlos V* might possibly join Cervera in the Caribbean in about two weeks, and the Spanish had been spotted at Martinique. (This latter was premature.) The blockade of Cuba and the safety of Key West itself might be in real danger if the Spanish managed to slip by to the west while Sampson was still operating so far east. "Therefore," cautioned Secretary Long, "you should be quick in your operations at Puerto Rico."[18]

At noon, May 9, Sampson's squadron stood northwest to give the impression of returning to Havana, and when well out of sight of land, he turned east again. After two hours the *Amphitrite*'s engines seized up and she was delayed until the evening. The *Indiana,* with leaky boilers, could not make over seven knots, and the situation got worse when the crown sheets of one of her boilers collapsed. At that point, the towline between the *Iowa* and the *Amphitrite* snapped, the bitter end knifing like a whip into the *Iowa*'s stern cabin, lacerating the arm of Captain Evans, miraculously not killing him, and forcing the squadron to stop until another line could be made fast. The torpedo boat *Porter* now needed a tow to conserve her coal, and the *Terror* passed her a line, presenting the curious sight of the flagship *New York* towing two ships in tandem. These delays were infuriating in light of Long's dictum of not tarrying around Puerto Rico and Sampson's belief that Cervera would have arrived in San Juan on May 8, the day before.

Worse was yet to come. Before dawn on the tenth, the towline between the *Iowa* and *Amphitrite* parted again, requiring the squadron to slow to five knots until another could be made fast. In early afternoon the *Terror*'s steering gear broke down, and again the squadron barely moved through the water for two hours during repair.

In the admiral's cabin, William Goode, the AP reporter, was recording how Sampson deplored the necessity of having to take the confounding monitors, designed solely for harbor defense, on deep-sea operations for which they were thoroughly unsuited when "suddenly, there was a report like the firing of a 4-inch gun just over our head. The flagship shook as if she had been jerked out of water." Before the deck steadied, there was a second loud report. Goode jumped, thinking the enemy had been sighted. But Admiral Sampson ruefully shook his head. "I am afraid she is gone," he said. "Who's gone?" the reporter asked. "The *Terror,*" the admiral replied, picking up his cap and going on deck. As it happened, the monitor's steering gear had gone out of whack again. She sheered to starboard, carrying both hawsers, just missing the flagship's stern. After stopping nearly two hours, new lines were passed, the squadron lying motionless all the while.[19]

They were still three hundred miles from San Juan and it was a disheartening piece of business that reflected no credit on anyone except the unhappy crews of the monitors, who labored, Captain Chadwick said, "in these monstrosities of ill design and construction."[20]

To fight a battle was easy work compared with the ceaseless heat, the toil of carrying broken towlines, and the everlasting sweep of green seas across their low decks, "which made life aboard the monitors a living hell to officers and men." The timetable for reaching San Juan was now shot to hell, and Sampson determined to engage the harbor batteries whether the enemy squadron was in port or not, a clear snubbing of Secretary Long's orders. Goode asked, "If you don't find the Spanish fleet at San Juan will you take the city?" The admiral hesitated a second: "Well, if they want to give us the city, I suppose we can't refuse it." Chadwick thought there was a bit more to it than this. The admiral, he believed, felt San Juan should not be left behind to the possible occupation of the Spanish squadron. Taking the city knocked out one of Spain's two true naval bases in the Caribbean. If he were successful in capturing the city, Sampson intended leaving the monitors in possession and transporting the surrendered Spanish garrison away in the auxiliary cruiser *Yale.*[21]

In the early evening of May 11, as the squadron neared San Juan, the admiral shifted his flag to the battleship *Iowa* because of its ability to take the heaviest knocks—and because of Sampson's natural desire to be in position to command the situation under any circumstances. The plan of battle, supposing the Spanish ships to be in port, was sent around to every ship. The heavy ships would advance in this order: *Iowa, Indiana, New York, Amphitrite, Terror.* The cruiser *Detroit* was to take a point one thousand yards ahead of the flagship. The tug *Wompatuck* would take a position five hundred yards off the flagship's bow, tug and cruiser constantly taking depth soundings with the lead and signaling immediately if the ten-fathom line were crossed, indicating shoaling water. In the rear the cruiser *Montgomery* would deal with any outside fire from the enemy and keep an eye out for torpedo boats. Admiral Sampson's torpedo boat, the *Porter,* had orders to torpedo any enemy vessel (especially the armored cruisers) that attempted to exit the harbor.

The admiral stipulated two objects for the attack: first, the Spanish ships, if they were there, and second, the guns of the ancient Morro castle looming over the harbor. As usual, woodwork, according to Captain Chadwick, "had been ruthlessly torn out" and thrown overboard, until the sea was covered with the wreckage for hundreds of miles. So much of it later washed up on the island coasts that Captain

General Blanco reported an American ship had been wrecked somewhere in the area.

Eight days after the ships' departure, at 2:30 A.M., May 12, the lights of San Juan were seen in the far distance. There was plenty of time before daybreak and the men were roused and given breakfast. The city of San Juan at the time held 30,000 people and was built at the end of a long sand-spit island running east-west, in the lee of which lay the harbor. At the extreme western tip rising on top of 100-foot vertical bluffs loomed the Morro castle, one of the most imposing seventeenth-century fortifications built by the Spanish to protect their American empire. According to then current information, the defenses consisted of a formidable seventeen 5.9-inch breech-loading rifles and ten 9.4-inch breech-loading howitzers—heavy, ship-battering metal if well manned—along with the usual collection of 100-year-old Spanish antiques of no value. The island garrison consisted of 4,500 troops plus several thousand local volunteers, though the San Juan defenders themselves numbered only 600 men.[22]

The squadron steamed forward into the dawn at a bare four knots. The city appeared out of the shadows as an ocher-walled, red-roofed checker of houses sprawling over an east-west ridge. At the eastern end the ridge fell away into a sandy beach, soon lost in a swamp. Along its front, trade winds blew massive waves against rising cliffs that rose into the ancient fortifications; "and there," wrote a reporter in the squadron from *Scribner's* magazine, "stood the ancient Morro Castle, at once a fortress and a hopeless prison for political prisoners." The Spanish defenders showed no sign that they had spotted the fleet, and no flag flew from the battlements.[23]

Ahead of all chugged the little tug *Wompatuck*, towing a boat with a red flag nailed to an improvised mast, which was to be anchored at the ten-fathom line, giving the squadron a fixed turning point to serve when smoke had obscured the landmarks ashore.

At five o'clock the bugles and klaxons sounded general quarters for the squadron. "The call was heard," wrote the *Scribner's* man, "and away they ran." A few minutes later "we saw the ensigns begin to rise to the trucks of the masts and staffs all over the fleet—holiday ensigns, work-a-day ensigns, ensigns for use in foul weather; new ensigns and ensigns that were old and patched." Even Admiral Sampson's blue flag was replaced by the national colors on the *Iowa*'s masthead, and was rehoisted on a smokestack guy wire.[24]

The moments ticked by until, in the dim dawn light, a few merchant masts could be seen in the harbor; it was clear, immediately, that the Spanish squadron was not in residence. But Admiral Sampson was not about to turn around and go home. At a quarter past five, the *Iowa* took a deep plunging roll, and the sharp crack of a 6-pounder gun from her forebridge signaled the squadron to commence firing. Surprise was apparently complete, and a full eight minutes elapsed before the Spanish replied. The ships steamed in a counterclockwise oval, a formation soon disrupted by the slowness of the monitors in making their turns. To prevent the expenditure of useless small-caliber ammunition against the Spanish castle walls, the admiral signaled, "Use only large guns." The *Scribner's* reporter, experiencing the operation in the *Indiana*, noted that "with every discharge of a great gun, the ship beneath it shivered under the recoil." Spectators on the press boats two miles away felt the tremble "as one feels an earthquake shock."[25]

The squadron formed up for its second and third passes. This time, not only were projectiles hitting the base of the castle walls, though doing little enough damage, they were passing through and over it into the town. The Ballaja barracks caught a shot, indicated by a cloud of red brick dust followed by a black ball of fire smoke. Within minutes there were seven fires burning in San Juan. In all the Spanish suffered 13 killed ashore, for a total of 113 casualties, most of them civilians. (After the war Captain Chadwick was informed by a Spanish officer that had the American squadron remained half an hour longer, the terror of the inhabitants and the consequent pressure on the governor would have compelled him to surrender.)

From the opening gun until the Spanish fired the last round of the morning, marksmanship on both sides was nothing to be proud of. The aim of the American big guns was particularly poor, for many of the shots aimed at the Morro splashed in the water at the foot of the bluffs. The primitive range finders gave only horizontal distances and made no allowance for the height of the target above the water. The 5-inch guns on the cruisers, however, were, as the *Scribner's* man reported, "handled more like sporting weapons, and so sent home their shots." These repeatedly drove the Spanish gunners from their pieces. But if American practice won no medals, the reporter went on, "an adjective for the marksmanship of the Spaniards is lacking." With only one or two exceptions no Spanish gunner took any other aim "than an attempt at a line shot." Seemingly no adjustments were ever made. In every case where a shot struck near a ship, the next shot from the same gun invariably hit at least twice as far away.[26]

Two American ships were hit. A 5.9-inch shell caught the *Iowa* on her port side abreast the aft 8-inch turret, wounding three men, passing through the sailing launch, and holing numerous deck fittings. Shell fragments did considerable damage to the joinery work of the forebridge, and splinters narrowly missed Admiral Sampson and Captain Evans. The *New York* was struck on the portside superstructure deck, killing one man at the waist 8-inch gun, wounding four others, and wrecking a boat and searchlight. The only other fatality was a man aboard the monitor *Amphitrite* who succumbed to the heat.

It was all over before nine o'clock. In the ships the fatigue of all hands, up since 3 A.M. and not having eaten since the turn of the morning watch an hour later, made rest and food necessary; a veritable one-sided target practice in the tropics was still a body-mauling exertion. Captain Chadwick watched numbers of both officers and men throw themselves down and, "sunk with fatigue," fall asleep immediately.[27]

Admiral Sampson, though he sincerely felt he could force the surrender of the town, understood that his main objective was the Spanish squadron, which was, in all probability, not too far away. He could not wait around while arrangements were made for the arrival of an American garrison, and unless the town and fortifications were occupied immediately, it had no weight in comparison with meeting the Spanish fleet. It was also clear that news of the American operation in Puerto Rican waters would cause Admiral Cervera to head elsewhere, and Havana always loomed in American minds as his primary goal, especially as the bulk of American naval power was now one thousand miles to the east, and the Flying Squadron at Hampton Roads was of no immediate help.

There was also the practical matter of the monitors and their extreme want of mobility—he could not just leave them here without army support. Thus Admiral Sampson decided to withdraw to Havana. In late afternoon, he returned to the *New York*, ordering the *Montgomery* to St. Thomas, sixty miles away, to get the latest news. The squadron, after stopping to bury its two dead, stood out to sea, course westward. Although the bombardment of San Juan did not accomplish very much in material terms, the presence of such a powerful American force off Puerto Rico did spook Admiral Cervera, causing him to eliminate the island as his primary objective in the West Indies. His options for any port along the northern rim of the Caribbean—Havana to San Juan—had disappeared in the smoke of naval gunfire.

But where was he? The Spanish squadron had sailed from the Cape Verdes nearly two weeks ago, and not a true word since. That was soon to change. On May 11, a day before the San Juan bombardment, Captain Charles Cotton brought the big auxiliary cruiser *Harvard* into St. Pierre, Martinique, fully expecting to depart in the morning for St. Thomas, 350 miles north on the return leg of his patrol line. While he was ashore with the American consul that evening, an urgent telegram came from the island capital at Fort de France stating that a Spanish destroyer (Villaamil with the *Furor*) had sailed into port about three hours before. Later that night, Cotton, preparing his report to the Navy Department, was visited by a French naval officer with official word of the Spaniard's arrival, and also that she intended to depart later that night. Under the strictures of international law, the *Harvard* needed to wait twenty-four hours before she could leave port in the enemy's wake. Being thus detained, and prevented from his scouting duties, Cotton sent a marine officer with the consul to Fort de France by rowing boat to get what information they could of the Spanish forces now obviously in the area.

They returned the following morning by steamer, and Cotton informed the department that "they saw and counted, hull down in the offing five [*sic*] large steamers" plus, in the harbor, the hospital ship *Alicante*. This information arrived in Washington that evening, May 12, and was elaborated on the morning of the thirteenth in the *New York Herald,* as "eight warships and seven torpedo boats."[28]

Captain Cotton, however, once he was permitted to sail, did not; unfortunately considering himself under blockade by a vastly superior Spanish force, he opted to remain in port, "that we may be such a bait . . . until the approach of one of our fleets." But the Spanish had slipped away.[29]

In the meantime, Admiral Sampson, steaming slowly westward from San Juan, received vague reports from a press boat at St. Thomas that the enemy fleet had returned to Spain—reports likely stemming from the instructions in the ministerial telegram Cervera never received. To Sampson, it was not out of the question, and if true, there was but one thing to do: return to San Juan and take it. He sent the torpedo boat *Porter* into Puerto Plata on the Dominican coast with a question to the department, "Is it true the Spanish ships are at Cádiz?" It was not until midafternoon on the fifteenth that *Porter* returned with cables from Secretary Long. The Spanish, he informed the admiral, were now off Curaçao, and American scouting cruisers were approaching the Windward Passage to cut Cervera off from the south coast of Cuba. But just as importantly, the Flying Squadron was now en route to Key West, and Sampson was ordered to join it there with all possible speed.[30]

On May 16, Cervera stood 135 miles north of Curaçao, about one-quarter of the distance to Santiago de Cuba, heading north at seven knots. For Sampson, just north of the Windward Passage, it was impossible to believe that the enemy's ships, all rated at not less than twenty knots, had been brought to such a pathetic condition. By noon on May 16, he was looking straight down the Windward Passage, 160 miles from Santiago de Cuba, the Spanish still 500 miles off. There is little doubt that once Sampson received word of the enemy at Curaçao, his own probable course was the south coast of Cuba. To his scouts— *St. Paul, St. Louis, Harvard,* and *Yale*—he signaled of the Spanish squadron, "Destination unknown, probably Santiago de Cuba," and he positioned the vessels accordingly. But though he would have preferred to station himself off Santiago immediately, he was obliged by the department's orders to return to Key West.[31]

Arriving there on May 18, Sampson found the welcome sight of the Flying Squadron busily coaling. Commodore Schley boarded the *New York,* and it was decided to send him and the Flying Squadron to the south coast of Cuba, to Cienfuegos, where it was presumed the Spanish were ultimately headed, since its rail communications to Havana made it a far better spot to hole up than isolated Santiago. Meanwhile, he and the North Atlantic Squadron would remain off Havana. So it was that at 8 A.M., on May 19, about the same hour Admiral Cervera anchored his vessels in Santiago de Cuba, Commodore Schley in the armored cruiser *Brooklyn*, with the battleships *Massachusetts* and *Texas* and the armed yacht *Scorpion*, set sail for Cienfuegos.

Several hours after Schley sailed, an unconfirmed telegram arrived at the Navy Department from the manager of the cable station at Key West. Before the war the man had arranged to receive intelligence from the Havana telegraph office by means of a private code, and the department was notified, "Five Spanish ships have entered the harbor of Santiago." The information was taken to the Naval War Board, but was not considered reliable by Admiral Sicard, who could not imagine Cervera putting into a port that lacked rail communications with Havana. In the first hours of the twentieth, however, the Navy Department sent word to Admiral Sampson that "the report of the Spanish fleet being at Santiago de Cuba might very well be correct." They strongly advised that instructions be sent to Commodore Schley to head there "with his whole command," leaving one small vessel at Cienfuegos. According to Captain Chadwick, this information was too ambiguous and caused much "perplexity" in Admiral Sampson's mind. The source of the intelligence was unmentioned, and the admiral did not feel justified in stripping the Havana and Cienfuegos blockades on what might be just a rumor.[32]

The following day, Sampson decided to reinforce the Flying Squadron with the navy's most powerful vessel, the battleship *Iowa*, along with the cruiser *Marblehead*, gunboat *Castine*, and some lesser craft, including the collier *Merrimac*. Sending Schley two copies of the recent telegram from the department regarding the Spanish at Santiago, one via the *Iowa*, the other in the fast torpedo boat *Du Pont*, Sampson nonetheless made no changes in the disposition of the Flying Squadron in its blockade of Cienfuegos. Sampson and Secretary Long, until they were convinced otherwise, supposed the Spanish vessels to be carrying a significant amount of war material to Cuba; if that were so, Santiago could not be the destination. They must either put into Cienfuegos and load it on rail cars, or make for Havana directly. If it later developed the Spanish *were* at Santiago, it would not be difficult to assemble the fleet there, "and completely blockade it."[33]

A few hours later came confirmation that Admiral Cervera and the Spanish squadron were indeed at Santiago de Cuba. While ashore at the fleet headquarters in Key West, Sampson's assistant chief of staff,

Lieutenant Sidney Staunton, met with a Captain Allen of the army Signal Corps, who was in charge of the Key West cable censorship office. As Staunton told it, "He called me aside and told me he had very, very important information that he believed to be correct." Staunton must keep it a secret from everyone, except Admiral Sampson and the immediate staff, since the man who passed the information would likely lose his life if it were disclosed. On the night of May 19 to 20 had come further intelligence from the agent in Havana that the Spanish squadron had positively entered Santiago de Cuba. Staunton returned to the *New York* and reported to Admiral Sampson.[34]

Somewhat ambiguous orders to Commodore Schley were immediately cut and sent out in the *Marblehead*, directing him to steam for Santiago, "if you are satisfied they are not at Cienfuegos." He was directed to proceed "with all despatch, but cautiously," and if he found the enemy at Santiago, to "blockade him in port." Perhaps realizing these orders might be misconstrued, giving Schley unnecessary options, Sampson sent another set in the armed yacht *Hawk:* "It is thought the Spanish squadron . . . still at Santiago, as they must have some repairs to make and coal to take." The scouts *St. Paul* and *Minneapolis* were on their way as well, he was informed. The skipper of the *Hawk* was firmly instructed to impress upon Commodore Schley, "as from the admiral," the need of getting off to Santiago as quickly as possible because the place could only be a way station for the Spanish—no competent commander given the mission of reinforcing Cuba would make for that port as a permanent refuge.[35]

Commodore Schley and the Flying Squadron had covered the 520 miles from Key West to Cienfuegos in sixty-four hours, arriving off the entrance to the bay just after sunup on May 22, averaging a little less than nine knots an hour. Shortly after, the torpedo boat *Du Pont* joined the force, followed by the *Iowa* later that morning, both bearing the probable news of the Spanish fleet at Santiago. On shore, the Spanish were visible busily mining the harbor entrance, and there was a great deal of smoke. Schley did not conduct a close reconnaissance of the harbor, but notified Admiral Sampson of a few disagreeable facts. First, he said, "anchorage not visible from entrance"; in fact, it was. Second, he said he expected great difficulty in coaling because a storm was bringing constant swells; "other problems easy compared to this one, so far from base." And finally, "I would state that I am by no means satisfied that the Spanish squadron is not in Cienfuegos." Under these circumstances, Schley thought it "extremely unwise to chase up a probability at Santiago de Cuba reported . . . no doubt as a ruse." He intended to remain off Cienfuegos, he said, availing himself of every opportunity to coal. These disturbing messages indicated to the admiral that his orders carried in the *Hawk* and *Marblehead* had failed to reach the Flying Squadron by the early hours of May 23, or if they had, then Schley had discounted them. Schley's actions off Cienfuegos marked the beginning of a series of highly controversial acts by the commodore that would lead to a court of inquiry into his conduct after the war.[36]

On the morning of the twenty-fourth, the *Marblehead* came up, carrying Admiral Sampson's orders to quit Cienfuegos. As her skipper, Captain Bowman McCalla, later said, he boarded the *Brooklyn* and informed Commodore Schley "that the Spanish force . . . had been reported authoritatively in Santiago" since May 19, last Thursday, and was still there on the day he sailed from Key West, Saturday afternoon. Schley wouldn't buy it. The Spanish, he thought, must be at Cienfuegos. Though he had still not reconnoitered the harbor entrance to find out, he did have a Jamaica newspaper obtained from a civilian steamer which indicated the Spanish had sailed from Santiago to Cienfuegos, anchoring there just before the Flying Squadron's arrival on the scene.[37]

McCalla informed Schley that he had brought arms, ammunition, and dynamite for the insurgents in the area, and if he could deliver his cargo, "I would at once find out whether the Spanish fleet was in Cienfuegos." The commodore agreed. The *Marblehead* and armed yacht *Eagle* headed to a point thirteen miles west of the harbor entrance and located a force of rebels on the beach. They soon verified the Spanish were not in Cienfuegos. The *Eagle* returned to the Flying Squadron to alert the commodore.

In the early evening Schley handed the commanding officer of the torpedo boat *Du Pont* a packet of messages to the Navy Department for transmission at Key West, with Admiral Sampson, his immediate senior officer, listed only as an informational addressee. Coaling off Cienfuegos, Schley maintained, was "very uncertain." His collier *Merrimac,* not having underway replenishment gear, was unsuited for the job, and it was very difficult to coal at sea with the running northeast swells banging the armored sides of the warships against the beat-up collier, especially the *Texas* with her large, protruding gun sponsons. The *Merrimac*, a relatively new ship, built in Scotland in 1894 and acquired by the navy in December 1897, was a lemon. The Associated Press correspondent aboard the *Brooklyn* recorded of her, "[I]t was a cause of favorable comment any day . . . if, at least, every five hours, she did not report some trouble with her boilers, engines, or steering gear." Schley was in great need of two more colliers equipped with hoisting engines and buckets for "fast work." He was now sure the Spanish were not here, and he intended to communicate this to Admiral Sampson by cable from St. Nicolas Môle, Haiti, across the Windward Passage from eastern Cuba, where he might also coal his ships in smooth water. He ended his dispatch with, "On account of short coal supply in ships, cannot blockade them if in Santiago." But he signaled the squadron to form column, course south by east. Just as the sun dipped, the flags soared up the *Brooklyn*'s halyards: "We are bound to Santiago."[38]

Admiral Sampson choked when he read this. The battleships and the *Brooklyn* had all left Key West with full bunkers, or nearly so. The *Texas*, the *Marblehead*, and the yachts might run short and could be detached with the *Merrimac* to St. Nicolas Môle, but the rest should have no trouble, and coal enough to blockade Santiago for a considerable period.

The Flying Squadron covered the 315 miles to Santiago averaging a bit more than six knots an hour on account of water coming into the *Eagle*, which had to be bailed with buckets, no pumps being aboard. At 5 P.M. on May 26 they reached the longitude of the harbor entrance, at a point 22 miles to the south. Three American scouts, the *Minneapolis*, *St. Paul*, and *Harvard*, patrolled off the port, but on sighting the Flying Squadron's smoke, they quit their station and steamed to investigate, leaving Santiago free of an inquisitive eye for many hours. The *St. Paul*'s captain, Charles Sigsbee, late of the *Maine*, came aboard the *Brooklyn* to report. "Have you got them, Sigsbee?" asked Commodore Schley, referring to the elusive enemy. "No," Sigsbee answered, "they are not here. I have been here a week, and they are not here." An oddly uninformative answer, given that early the day before, the *St. Paul* had overhauled and captured right at the harbor entrance the British collier *Restormel* bringing coal to Admiral Cervera's squadron. Sigsbee and Schley should have surmised that where there was a collier, there must be the Spanish fleet. (According to international law, Sigsbee had to send this modern ship to Key West for adjudication by a prize court rather than keeping her for use by the blockading forces on the south coast of Cuba.)[39]

In the early evening, the *Merrimac* signaled another engine break-down; the valve stem of her intermediate cylinder had broken off, and it would take hours to repair. The armed liner *Yale* took her in tow. Schley's coaling problems mounted. The triple-screwed scouting cruiser *Minneapolis* reported her machinery in bad shape and her coal bottoming out. To the query of whether she had enough to make Key West, she answered, "Just enough." To Schley it seemed to magnify the coal problem out of all proportion. But keeping the *Minneapolis* or sending her back to Key West didn't matter to the sum strength of the Flying Squadron. Nor did he seem cognizant of the actual coal left in the bunkers of his battleships and the flagship *Brooklyn*. Apparently, on account of the difficulty of coaling at sea from the broken-down *Merrimac*, Schley now opted to quit the blockade, leaving only the *St. Paul* off the entrance to the bay. Just before 9 P.M., he signaled the squadron, "Destination Key West via south of Cuba and Yucatan Channel." They would start as soon as the *Merrimac* completed her repairs. According to a respected British historian, when this signal first became visible to the Flying Squadron, it was taken for a joke, the flags spelling out "via s" seeming to mean "via Santiago." Only when the letters "o-u-t-h" were read was it understood the blockade was to be abandoned. "All hands on the *Iowa*," said Captain Robley Evans, "were greatly surprised at this unexpected retreat, and I for one was absolutely in the dark as to its meaning."[40]

At the time Schley signaled his intention to return to Key West, the principal ships of the Flying Squadron still maintained a respectable coal endurance. The *Brooklyn* held a minimum of ten days' coal, the *Massachusetts* and *Iowa* eight days', and the *Texas,* five. And this did not take into account the 4,300 tons in the *Merrimac*. Indeed, if the Flying Squadron had enough fuel to return to Key West, it certainly had enough to remain at Santiago until further supplies arrived or the sea calmed. At worst, the ships could have gone in shifts to coal at sea in the lee of St. Nicolas Môle. Commodore Schley, a brave and re-sourceful veteran officer, seemed to have lost his faculties for no known reasons.

Fortunately, though it did not appear so at the time, the hemp towing hawser between the *Yale* and the *Merrimac* parted four times, and only after a full day of backing and filling in sight of Santiago was a steel cable made fast. This delay made it possible for the *Harvard* to catch the squadron before it left altogether. It was carrying a message from Secretary Long, who was in great perplexity over the actions of the commander of the Flying Squadron. Schley had been chosen specifically because of his dash and impetuous manner. Now he seemed to be funking it in the face of the enemy. It was inconceivable that either Dewey or Sampson would throw up excuses of this sort: in essence, "Can't coal, going home." What Schley needed was a good kick in the pants. "The most absolutely urgent thing now is to know positively whether the Spanish division is in Santiago," Long lectured, because if it was, as all intelligence indicated, then an immediate movement by the army and navy had to be made on the city. As for Schley's coaling situation, he "must surmount" the difficulty by "ingenuity and perseverance." The department was relying on him. If the Spanish were inside Santiago, they must "not leave without a decisive action."[41]

Schley sent his response to the secretary via the *Harvard* through Kingston, Jamaica, and it was not the sort of "Damn the torpedoes, full speed ahead!" thing that won wars. According to Schley, he simply could not remain on station with the *Merrimac*'s broken-down engine. "Have been absolutely unable to coal" on account of very rough seas and "boisterous weather." He "regretted" his inability to carry out the department's orders, "earnestly as we have all striven to that end," and he signed off with, "I am forced to return to Key West . . . for coal. Can ascertain nothing certain concerning enemy." Hardly the stuff of a great commander.[42]

In Santiago, Admiral Cervera was fully alive to the difficulties of his situation. The bottoms of the *Vizcaya* and now the *Almirante Oquendo* as well were foul, and he required more than 600 tons of fresh water for his ships' boilers—a very perplexing matter since the handful of Santiago water barges carried but 6 tons apiece and could make but two trips to the squadron a day. But most of all, he desperately needed coal and provisions. Cervera, writing to the new minister of marine, Rear Admiral Ramón Auñón, informed him that "if it [the squadron] does not receive any [coal], it must succumb; if we are blockaded before we finish taking coal, which is scarce, we shall succumb with the city." And what coal there was, was extremely hard to put aboard. Even with army help, the squadron could not heave more than a total of 150 tons a day, and this when each ship burned 5 tons per day just for routine operations such as cooking, lighting, operating winches and steam launches. Even coaling baskets were lacking, and the men had to carry the stuff aboard in sacks.[43]

On May 21, one day before the Flying Squadron reached its point off Cienfuegos, Admiral Manterola in Havana queried Admiral Cervera on the condition of the squadron and other critical matters. He needed to know if Spain intended to send more warships and munitions and supply convoys, "so that if we can count on nothing more than we have," proper contingency plans might be formed. The local naval forces, which Cervera had been told in the Cape Verdes he might count on for support—advice he wisely ignored—were out of the scheme. The two cruisers, *Alfonso XII* at Havana and *Reina Mercedes* at Santiago, Manterola stated, were "wholly useless," and there was but one gunboat ready for sea duty. As for supplies, he had two months' worth for his own forces, such as they were. Mistakenly, he had counted on Cervera and "numerous convoys of provisions and stores of every kind" to replenish Cuba with military necessities. Painfully, Cervera replied that the six ships of his squadron were all that Spain intended to send in the matter of men-of-war. As for replenishment convoys, he didn't believe such a thing had "been thought of at all, since I have always been told that I should find everything here."[44]

On Monday, May 23, a number of telegrams arrived for Cervera from Captain General Blanco, indicating that strong U.S. naval forces had concentrated before Cienfuegos, and that since midmorning of this day "almost the entire horizon" as seen from the Havana fortifications was free of hostile ships, save four gunboats to windward. This could only mean the north coast blockaders were on their way south; though actually they weren't, not for a few days yet. The disappearance of the bulk of Admiral Sampson's force was due strictly to the happenstance of coaling at Key West or chasing strange sail, which temporarily took them off station. But these cables, coupled with the fact that since Saturday at least one American scout had been spotted off the Santiago harbor entrance, prompted Cervera to call a council of war on Tuesday. His senior officers were briefed on Admiral Manterola's news regarding the dismal lack of assets and Blanco's intelligence on the whereabouts, actual and supposed, of the enemy's squadrons. Inasmuch as each of these forces individually was superior to the Spanish, Cervera wanted opinions on what should be done under the circumstances. Cervera seems to have wanted some assurance as to the correctness of his own decision, for according to the text of the meeting, the admiral had decided without the council to depart Santiago for San Juan; messages had already been sent there requesting a collier and asking that the transatlantic steamer *Alfonso XIII*, laden with war stores of every sort, be held.[45]

Had they wished to proceed, it would have been as good a time as any. Schley was preoccupied at Cienfuegos, and the American scouts off Santiago, still ignorant of the Spanish presence, never numbered more than four fast but weakly armed vessels, of which only one, the *Minneapolis*, was a true warship. (With one 8-inch and two 6-inch guns, she could not have prevented any escape.)

But the council demurred, unanimously considering it an impossible task with their own speed cut to fifteen knots on account of the *Vizcaya*, and concerned that they had only been able to take on one-third of their coal. The conferees also raised the matter of a reconnaissance and its consequences. This might be required, a cruiser or destroyer having to exit and return with information of the enemy in the immediate vicinity, and strangely, such coming and going would be bad for morale. Why this was necessary, with the Morro castle signal station having a sea view to the horizon for twenty miles, is unclear. In the end, taking all into account, it was considered too dangerous to risk for the "few advantages" that might accrue from reaching San Juan. They would remain at Santiago, refitting from the thin stores in the port, and take advantage of the first good opportunity to escape the place, "at present blockaded by superior [*sic*] forces." The ships' fires were banked.[46]

The following day, Cervera, in a letter to General Arsenio Linares Pombo, commander of the eastern district of Oriente Province, was already rueing his decision to remain. "It is much to be regretted," noted the admiral, that in spite of the council's negative conviction, he had not stuck to his guns and sailed when all boilers were alight and precious coal awasting. He cabled the minister of marine with a wholly pessimistic report. "We are blockaded," he informed the government. But this was not quite true. The enemy's scouts had yet to discover him, and Schley's Flying Squadron was still a day's steaming away. But as Cervera analyzed the situation, there was nothing for the squadron to do but to take up defensive positions to protect the harbor from naval assault by the enemy. If another opportunity to escape presented itself, he would try it, but "it will only be a matter of changing this harbor for another where we would also be blockaded."[47]

On Thursday afternoon, May 26, right about the time Commodore Schley arrived under the horizon, Admiral Cervera held another council of war. Now it unanimously voted to sail for San Juan, and orders were passed to spread fires in all ships and be ready to sortie at 5 P.M. But three hours before this, the semaphore on the Morro reported the presence of three American scouts, and doubt once more entered the admiral's mind. The officers were again convened, and this time the problem that concerned them was the sea swells, the same condition that had allegedly prevented the Flying Squadron from coaling at sea. It might adversely effect the *Colón,* who with her deep draft could well touch bottom. The pilot who brought the squadron into port was sent for, and he agreed it was too dangerous to attempt given the state of the sea and wind. Cervera put the question to his officers: "Is it expedient to risk the *Colón* being injured, or should the sortie not be effected, awaiting more favorable circumstances?"[48]

This time the vote was not unanimous. Most favored staying. But Captain Concas of the *Infanta María Teresa* and Captain Joaquín Bustamante, the chief of staff, were all for going out. Pilots, they argued, were notoriously squeamish about the slightest risk and always left large room for error. Bustamante argued that the enemy was not yet in strength off the harbor, with just the lightly armed scouts in evidence; but tomorrow "they [heavy ships] are almost sure to be." To tarry and accept battle against superior odds "seems to me almost inhuman." If they were to wait for a better situation, there would be nothing left but to capitulate with the surrender of the city when food ran out in a month. "This last solution," he told the assembly, "is to my mind even more inadmissible than . . . the former." Even at the risk of losing the *Colón,* he argued, they could extricate three cruisers and the destroyers. If the *Colón* touched bottom and could not make it out, it would be better for her to remain disabled at the harbor entrance as a floating battery "than for us to await what I fear is in store for us."[49]

Admiral Cervera, in his own words, "reserved his opinion." And his dithering proved fatal, for after May 28, no further opportunity other than suicide for the Spanish squadron presented itself. It is highly ironic that at the precise hour Cervera had given for the sortie—5 P.M.—the American scouts left to chase Schley's smoke over the horizon. Had the Spanish put to sea, Cervera could only have regarded the empty waters as providential, leaving the path clear to San Juan without hindrance or even detection. Not for another two days did the Flying Squadron truly establish the blockade of Santiago, by which time even the laggard Spanish could have put into San Juan. Thus, the chances of Cervera's escape, though to what end, save perhaps a return to Spain, were fair enough on the evening of May 26.

During the afternoon of May 27, a press boat joined the Flying Squadron with news that Admiral Sampson had already left the Havana blockade for Santiago de Cuba. Though Schley continued on his westward course for several hours (what would after the war be termed, infamously, his "retrograde movement" away from Santiago and toward Key West), this news, wrong though it was, finally turned him around. In another stroke of luck, the *Brooklyn*'s engineer force had been sent aboard the *Merrimac,* fixing the valve stem; though still under tow, she could now steam on her own power at seven knots. At 7 P.M. Schley signaled the *Texas,* "If collier is cast off do you think you could coal tonight?" Her captain, the redoubtable Jack Philip, answered, "We can try." The same signal was made to the *Marblehead:* "Yes," came the reply. Ten minutes later the *Brooklyn* signaled the squadron, "Stop." As an augur of good fortune, the weather moderated, easing the task of coaling at sea. The ships labored through the night, and before noon the next day, they were done. By the early evening of May 28, the Flying Squadron, topped off with coal, began the blockade of Santiago de Cuba.[50]

Schley's dilatoriness, his "retrograde movement," before settling down in front of Santiago stunned Admiral Sampson when he heard of it. "Had the Commodore left his station," he wrote to Secretary

Long several weeks later, "he probably would have been court-martialed, so plain was his duty." The conduct had been "reprehensible." In fact, so contentious were Schley's evolutions, that a respected naval historian, Edgar Stanton Maclay, in a 1901 book intended as a text for the Naval Academy, termed them "timidity amounting to absolute cowardice." The statement was frankly libelous, but it served as yet another rationale for convening the postwar court of inquiry into Schley's performance.[51]

While the Flying Squadron coaled, Admiral Sampson determined to go to Santiago himself. He handed orders to the skipper of the cruiser *New Orleans,* a new and very welcome addition to the fleet, one of the ships bought from Brazil while fitting out in Scotland, and equipped with modern smokeless powder and rapid-fire 6-inch guns. The orders were for Commodore Schley, directing him "to remain on the blockade of Santiago at all hazards." He must take the utmost precautions the Spanish did not break out. Taking the collier *Sterling,* the *New Orleans* left for Santiago, while Admiral Sampson steamed first to Key West to get a thorough update on the situation and events from the latest cables.[52]

John D. Long, stymied by Schley's behavior and fearing the Flying Squadron might not hang around, cabled Schley that he must remain off Santiago unless it was "unsafe" for his ships to do so. He also suggested taking Guantánamo Bay and using it as a coaling station. If, however, Schley needed to do the unthinkable—quit his station at Santiago—he had the department's authorization to sink the *Merrimac* as a blockship in the harbor entrance, something Sampson's staff had also pondered. But at all events, "You must not leave the vicinity of Santiago de Cuba," save for the safety of his ships, "or unless Spanish division is not there."[53]

At 2 A.M. May 28, Admiral Sampson anchored outside the reef at Key West. At the time, the Flying Squadron was engaged in its night coaling from the *Merrimac;* Schley had now resolved to remain on station and not return to Key West, though Sampson knew nothing of this. On the morning of the twenty-eighth, Sampson was told by Long that if the Spanish were indeed at Santiago—and where else could they be at this point in the game?—the navy intended "to make descent immediately upon that port" with ten thousand American troops to be convoyed by Sampson's ships. How long, the secretary wanted to know, would it take the admiral to get to Santiago? As Captain Chadwick remembered it, Admiral Sampson hesitated not a second before replying, three days. "I can blockade indefinitely," he added. As soon as he received the go-ahead, he would sail with the *New York* and the just arrived battleship *Oregon*. When orders to do so did not arrive, Admiral Sampson sent a cable in which he stressed that Schley's failure to blockade Santiago "must be remedied at once, if possible. There can be no doubt of the presence of Spanish Squadron at Santiago."[54]

The admiral and the secretary of the navy could breathe with some relief when, in the midafternoon of May 29, they received a cable from the *Yale*. The *Merrimac*'s engines had been repaired and coal was now a less critical problem for the Flying Squadron. Schley would hold his position off Santiago until the fuel of his large ships reached their lowest safe limit; they would then fill up at St. Nicolas Môle, not Key West. The relief in the *New York* and the Navy Department was palpable. "Congratulate you on success," telegraphed the admiral to the commodore. "Maintain close blockade at all hazards, especially at night." Early that evening Secretary Long sent his permission for Admiral Sampson to quit the Havana blockade and steam for Santiago. It was, he noted, "very desirable." As for Guantánamo Bay, as a sheltered coaling and repair station forty miles east of Santiago, which would relieve the fleet from having to cross the Windward Passage to St. Nicolas Môle or returning to Key West, "[t]he seizure immediately is recommended."[55]

That day, Long also sent a "Get off your duff" telegram to Commodore Schley, now dutifully blockading Santiago though still without any concrete information regarding the maddeningly evasive Spanish squadron. If its presence were not "ascertained immediately," said Long, by whatever means, the whole hide-and-seek affair "would be discreditable to the navy." The point was hammered home that all naval and military movements in the Caribbean theater of war depended on this information, and Washington needed it immediately.[56]

But the secretary, had he wished, could have gone off on holiday that afternoon and been assured of a positive outcome, because at dawn, the *Marblehead* had signaled from close inshore: "Just caught view of Spanish warship in harbor entrance." Soon after, the *St. Paul*—after chasing strange lights that turned out to be snooping press boats—informed the flagship, "In the entrance, apparently coming out, two men-of-war resembling armored cruisers with flags at each mast-head." Up to every fighting top in the Flying Squadron men scampered with long glasses. There was no doubt of one of the black-hulled ships, the *Cristóbal Colón,* easily recognizable by her single mast amidships between her twin funnels. Indeed, she had been anchored there for four days without being spotted; the other was the *Almirante Oquendo.* Commodore Schley turned to the Associated Press man standing beside him on the forebridge and spoke the truth: "We've got them now, Graham, and they'll never go home."[57]

Schley called his captains to the *Brooklyn* and explained that if the Spanish came out, he planned to concentrate all his fire on the enemy van. A testy moment passed when Captain "Fighting Bob" Evans of the *Iowa* asked if the commodore intended the squadron to fight motionless, simply firing at the enemy as they exited the harbor, or to steam directly at them. "What do you think I'd do?" an annoyed Schley answered. "We'll get just as close to that entrance as we possibly can, the instant we see them making a move to come out, and I don't think they'll get very far." But the Spanish made no moves, and the Flying Squadron spent that day and the next steaming back and forth across the mouth of the harbor.[58]

On Tuesday, May 31, in midmorning, Schley finally decided to attack the *Colón* at her anchorage and in the process get the Spanish to reveal the position of their coast defense guns. These did not amount to much. On the high and jungled eastern bluff of the entrance, whose precipice rose two hundred feet from the sea, was the stone and masonry Morro castle. Its armament did not compare with what Havana had, or even Manila or San Juan: just five 6.2-inch muzzle-loading rifles converted from 150-year-old bronze smoothbores. On the lower western side of the harbor mouth, naval ratings manned the Socapa battery of two fairly modern 6.2-inch naval rifles taken from the dismantled cruiser and Santiago station ship *Reina Mercedes,* as well as two more at Estrella, just inside the Morro. Army artillerists stood behind three 8-inch muzzle-loading howitzers. Lower down the hill near the water were small, rapid-firing pieces, intended for defense of the double line of mines protecting the entrance.

The commodore shifted his flag to the *Massachusetts,* and following the noon meal, the squadron heavy ships stood on a northeasterly heading to a range of seven thousand yards. The action took about half an hour, the Flying Squadron scoring a near miss on the useless *Reina Mercedes,* another near the *Colón,* which according to her log, exploded by the stern, "making dents in the side and cracking some bowls in the round-house." The Spanish sent one shell through the upper works of the *Massachusetts,* which splashed on the far side.[59]

"Well, the dagoes are getting a little better," said one American sailor.

"Oh," replied his mate, "give them a year and they will learn to shoot."[60]

These comments aside, the officers of the *Colón* considered their day a success. The Americans, they noted in the log, retired "in disorder," two of them needing "convoying" by the *Brooklyn.* In truth, hardly any damage was done by either side.[61]

Late on the night of Sunday, May 29, Admiral Sampson steamed from Key West to Santiago 550 miles away, taking with him his flagship, the *New York,* battleship *Oregon,* torpedo boat *Porter,* and the yacht *Mayflower.* He took the eastern route, through the Bahama Channel and Windward Passage, meeting the *Yale* and *St. Paul* homeward bound for coal and with copies of messages sent at St. Nicolas Môle, the most important of which was "Enemy in port." Pounding along at thirteen knots, the admiral signaled to the *Oregon,* "Can you keep up thirteen knots?" to which the battleship answered, "Yes, fourteen if you wish."[62]

At 6:30 in the morning, June 1, Admiral Sampson and his reinforcements hove up to Santiago, finding the Flying Squadron steaming in an east-west line in the face of the harbor mouth. From that moment, said Evans of the *Iowa,* the "beginning of the end was in sight."[63]

CHAPTER 9

EMPIRE BUILDERS

Life between decks became almost intolerable.
—*Captain Charles Clark, USS* Oregon

The Navy—in my opinion—wants to stop grubbing in machine shops and get up somewhere where it can take a bird's
eye view of military truths, and see them in their relations and
proportions.
—*Captain Alfred Thayer Mahan, member,*
U.S. Navy War Board, August 31, 1898

She was built at San Francisco's Union Iron Works, the first U.S. battleship built on the West Coast and the third of the trio of "sea-going
coast-line" battleships authorized by Congress in 1890. They were
ships that left behind forever America's naval tradition of commerce
raiding and coastal defense; now a blue-water fleet and global responsibilities would be the order of the day. Named the *Oregon* at
her launching in October 1893, she was commissioned into the navy
on July 15, 1896, to become arguably the most famous ship to come
out of the Spanish-American War. The *Oregon's* feat of steaming
around the Western Hemisphere assured, as nothing else could—not
Mahan's writings of an America looking outward, or Henry Cabot
Lodge's and Theodore Roosevelt's advocacy of the "large policy" in
diplomacy—the eventual United States' building of the Central American isthmian canal, which provided the ability to transfer the battle

fleet from ocean to ocean and guaranteed American hegemony over two continents.

The destruction of the *Maine* made it only a matter of time before the *Oregon* was ordered east from the Pacific. She lay at Bremerton, Washington, on March 7, having just had bilge keels bolted to her bottom, when the order came from Secretary Long: "The situation is getting worse"; head for San Francisco and load with ammunition. She got there in five days, and orders awaited her to sail for the next port, Callao, Peru. "The crew is to be constantly drilled," the secretary ordered. On the seventeenth, the *Oregon*'s skipper, Captain B. J. McCormick, in the words of the official report, found himself "condemned by medical survey," and he was replaced in command by the able Captain Charles Clark, a veteran of thirty-eight years' service. The *Maine* court of inquiry report was expected any time, and "the crew of the *Oregon* hoped for war."[1] Excitement on board was intense, according to Lieutenant William H. Allen, one of the ship's watch and division officers.

Averaging nearly eleven knots, the ship made Callao on April 5. But the entry into equatorial waters took its toll. As Clark related, "[L]ife between decks became almost intolerable, for to the tropical heat was added that generated by the ship's boilers, kept at a full head of steam." Lectured by the chief engineer never to permit salt water into the boilers, something Clark nonetheless did on occasion to allow more drinking water to his men from the distilling apparatus on board, he said, "I felt it was asking almost too much of the endurance of the crew." To use only salt-free distilled water in the boilers "meant not only reducing [the crew's] drinking supply, but that the quantity served out would be so warm as to be quite unpalatable." Still, the consequent deprivation of drinking water, Clark said, "was borne without a murmur." The tiny amount of ice made on board was given to the firemen and coal passers, who worked in a living hell of fire and intolerable heat.[2]

As Lieutenant Allen remembered, it became impossible for the men to sleep on the berth deck, so they moved their hammocks to the main deck and turret crowns, a situation that continued even to the latitude of the Strait of Magellan. In the compartments directly above the engines and boilers, temperatures reached 115 degrees, and in the ammunition passages, 140 degrees. Yet only one man of the engineering force succumbed to the heat during the entire voyage.

From the time of leaving San Francisco, clearing the ship for action and gunnery drills were the order of the day. The ship crossed the equator on March 31 with all the attendant gross ceremonies of misfortune for the uninitiated pollywogs by the salty shellbacks of King Neptune's court. "All land lubbers were treated to a shave and a bath," said Lieutenant Allen, "and were given certificates showing that they were now free to pass Neptune's kingdom, and bespeak for them good treatment." The ship's band kept already high spirits elevated. There was dancing nearly every evening, and officers met nightly in the wardroom to play whist, "pajamas being the customary uniform."[3]

From Callao, Clark informed the department that if he coaled at Punta Arenas, at the southern tip of Chile in the Strait of Magellan, he could make it all the way to Montevideo, maybe even Rio de Janeiro. Because of the hard navigation in the strait and reported movements of a Spanish torpedo gunboat—the *Temerario,* a 562-ton vessel of a reputed nineteen knots speed—near Montevideo, he asked that the gunboat *Marietta,* already at Callao, accompany him for the voyage. Permission was granted by the secretary, who added, "Keep secret your destination." As for the Spanish vessel, the crew hoped they might encounter and sink her. Clark agreed with this opinion, especially if she were met in the Strait of Magellan, for she could be there for no other purpose than to attack his ship and, according to Lieutenant Allen, "[H]e would sink her, war or no war."[4]

Though outwardly the Peruvians seemed friendly to the Americans, it was reported that a plot was afoot among the Spanish residents of Callao and Lima to sink or blow up the ship. In consequence, Clark doubled the number of marine sentries, who now manned their posts armed. The *Oregon*'s steam launch patrolled around the ship day and night, and no boats were permitted to approach without proper consent. The coal bunkers were packed to their 1,640-ton limit, and the decks piled with another 200 tons in sacks.

Pounding south into the gray wintry seas of the Tropic of Capricorn, the ship, Clark said, "dipped her bows deep in foaming surges." Entering the Strait of Magellan, the ship was hit by violent winds. Thick, scudding clouds hid the rockbound shores close by, and with night coming on it seemed to Clark unwise to keep going. Yet, he remembered that, "with the ship driven before the gale as she was," it was impossible to get correct bearings on their position, and making a safe anchorage became largely a matter of chance. He decided to anchor anyway as the lesser of evils. The first of two anchors was let go, and it ran furiously through 125 fathoms of chain before it could be checked. But she held fast through the night in the raging maelstrom.[5]

During the forenoon of the next day the ship was chased through the strait by heavy, blowing snows, with sheer cliffs on either side, at points scarcely a mile wide, and bottomless depths below, but "there could be no pause or hesitation in this exciting race," Clark recalled. The weather cleared and the sun shone brilliant rainbows on the masses of ice around them as the battleship swept past the old wrecks of two steamers "that had left their bones to mark the perils of the passage." At night, they anchored in Punta Arenas. Clark had last been there thirty-two years before, in the escort for the monitor *Monadnock*, the first American armored vessel to round the continent on her way to the Pacific. Now he was commanding officer of the second such vessel to perform that duty, albeit in the opposite direction.[6]

The coal, for which the government had paid the exorbitant sum of twenty-two dollars a ton, came in a hulk under a load of reeking raw wool, and it was unbelievably hard and dirty work, on top of the usual drudgery of coaling, to get the stuff aboard. The *Marietta* joined up, and both ships departed Punta Arenas on April 21, the day Spain declared war. On the way out of the strait and up the coast, Captain Clark exercised both ships by throwing empty casks over the side for target practice. Nearing Rio de Janeiro, he left the slower *Marietta* behind and arrived at the great port on April 30, getting the first news of the war and rumors of a battle at Manila. Telegrams from the Navy Department indicated the *Temerario* was in the neighborhood, possibly heading his way. "This was disturbing information," Clark wrote. "If the torpedo boat should arrive and had an ordinarily enterprising commander, I felt he would not hesitate to violate a neutral port," if by so doing he could cripple or sink one of the enemy's principal vessels. Indeed, the United States had done exactly that in the Brazilian port of Bahia during the Civil War, when the American sloop of war *Wachusett* opened fire, boarded, and captured the Confederate raider *Florida* right under the noses of the Brazilian authorities. With coal lighters alongside, the *Oregon* steamed up the bay of Rio to a point two miles above the regular warship anchorage. By leaving the anchorage to the Spaniard, Clark assumed that any move it made in the *Oregon*'s direction would be inherently hostile, giving "me the right to turn our guns upon her."[7]

The Brazilians showed a friendly face, no doubt enhanced by the fact that the United States had just bought their auxiliary cruiser *Nictheroy* (a ship that proved, at first, a bad bargain, having defective engines), and she'd been placed under Clark's command. On May 1, while the *Oregon* underwent some machinery repairs, Clark received a cable from Secretary Long telling him of Admiral Cervera's disappearance into the Atlantic and stating, "Four Spanish cruisers heavy and fast, three torpedo boats" had sailed from the Cape Verdes westward, "Destination unknown." But their objective might well be to corner the *Oregon* as she made her way northward from Rio. Long left it to Clark's discretion how to avoid the enemy and reach safety at Key West or some other haven. "The general trend of these telegrams," Clark thought, "made it plain that the Department felt our position was critical." Long also did not wish to take the responsibility of forcing Clark to face seemingly unequal odds in a fight; whether to stand and fight or run, he "left the decision to me."[8]

Clark appreciated the consideration but would have much preferred to be backed by definitive orders. Thinking over the situation with "utmost care," he concluded that if the Spanish squadron was headed for the West Indies, then the *Oregon*'s presence in those waters was imperative. If, on the other hand, Admiral Cervera was making for the bulge of Brazil with the idea of intercepting the battleship, he could undoubtedly, by making his designed speed of twenty knots, reach that point before the *Oregon*. But Clark did not think the Spanish would take this option, especially as there was a good chance of missing the battleship altogether, an extremely likely happenstance in the days before aircraft and radar. But "if they did come upon us, we would give them a good fight." Clark decided to head north from Rio, come what might.[9]

Calling his officers, he informed them that if the ship fell in with the Spanish squadron, he intended to make a running fight of it, hoping to string out the enemy in a high-speed stern chase. In such a battle, his after 13-, 8-, and 6-inch guns had the range and weight of metal over the Spanish; in fact, even in a fight broadside to broadside, the *Oregon* outgunned the entire Spanish force. On May 4, the *Oregon, Marietta,* and *Nictheroy* sailed from Rio, leaving the just arrived *Temerario* snugly safe in a harbor backwater, where she uselessly remained for the rest of the war. Finding his two consorts a drag, Clark left them to their own devices and pushed on alone. He called the crew aft and read to them the Navy Department's cables regarding the possible movements of the Spanish. If the combat took place, Clark assured his men that "we would at least lower Spain's fighting efficiency upon the seas, and that her fleet would not be worth much after the encounter." The crew cheered "as though the fleet had already been sighted and a victory assured."[10]

From Bahia on May 8, Clark assured the Navy Department of his optimism to "beat off and even cripple" the Spanish squadron. Long responded with orders to clear Brazil altogether and head to the West Indies for coal at once. There was no news of the Spanish; no one knew where they were. On the tenth, the *Oregon* quit Bahia, rounded the bulge of Brazil at Cape St. Roque, and laid a course for home waters.[11]

Eight days later she steamed into Carlisle Roads at Bridgetown, Barbados, and anchored. Adhering to strict neutrality under international law, the governor allotted the ship twenty-four hours, reckoned from daylight the next morning. Clark also received the uncheering if inaccurate news that Admiral Sampson had attacked San Juan and been driven off. There came too the "pleasing intelligence that the Spanish fleet," increased in the rumor mill to eighteen vessels, "was waiting for us outside." Surmising this was all rubbish, Clark spread the word around town the ship would remain in port until 2 A.M. the following morning. But before 10 P.M., he cast off his coal lighters, and with lights showing, followed a conspicuous course westward, into the Caribbean; he then doused his lights and headed north for the Florida coast.[12]

Having gleaned the latest news of the position of U.S. naval forces, Clark opted to make for Florida's Jupiter Inlet, telegraphing the department of his arrival. From there he could either join Sampson on the north coast of Cuba, or Schley on the south. On the night of the twenty-fourth, the rays of Jupiter Inlet Light House streamed out to the ship like the fingers of a hand welcoming her home. Clark sent a boat ashore to wire the department, and Secretary Long replied that if the ship was in good shape, it should make for Key West; if not, for Hampton Roads. On Friday, May 27, the *Oregon* anchored outside the reef at Key West, having steamed 13,792 miles in sixty-six days, averaging over eleven knots an hour, a singularly outstanding achievement. Coaling commenced immediately.

The replenishment was carried on through the next day. Then the ship got under way to join the force off Havana, presenting to the blockading ships—dressed in their Sunday inspection whites—a filthy, coal-begrimed appearance. "But her reception was none the less hearty," remembered Lieutenant Allen, "and amounted to an ovation." Each ship in turn cheered the newcomer, and bands crashed out in music-hall tunes, the most popular, again, being "There'll Be a Hot Time in the Old Town Tonight." The *Oregon*'s stay off Havana was brief. The next morning, she departed with Admiral Sampson, the *New York,* and the armed yacht *Mayflower* for Santiago de Cuba.[13]

In the autumn of 1897, fifteen-year-old Lyle Evans Mahan, son of retired navy Captain Alfred Thayer Mahan, suffered an untimely heart attack. After the New Year his father decided to take the family to Europe to aid the boy's recuperation. When the *Maine* blew up and the navy turned into a hive of activity, Assistant Secretary Roosevelt, who kept up a continuous correspondence with Mahan, lobbied Secretary Long to recall the officer to active duty, so as to have him immediately available for consultations should war erupt. Long wasn't sure; Mahan was too difficult a character to have hovering close by. He refused TR's urgings. But from a distance Mahan, through Roosevelt, did try to steer the department to adopt the course of concentrating the entire fleet at Key West, able simultaneously to blockade Cuba and to fall back on the East Coast should the Spanish move aggressively in that direction, something Mahan did not consider probable given the Spanish mind-set. "I entirely agree with you with all my heart about local coast defense," wrote TR. "I shall urge and have urged the President to pay absolutely no heed to outcries for protection from Spanish raids." But this sane advice was futile.[14]

Mahan and his family arrived in Rome a few days before the declaration of war. On April 25, the day after the American Congress made it official from their side, a U.S. embassy messenger handed Mahan a telegram from the Navy Department: "Proceed to United States immediately" and report to the secretary. For security reasons,

Mahan shaved his beard and temporarily adopted the name "A. T. Maitland" for the return journey. Walking into the department's offices at the State, War, and Navy Building across the street from the White House, Mahan was greeted by Secretary Long, who informed him of his desire that he serve on the Naval War Board. Its composition was at that moment in flux. The original chairman, Assistant Secretary Roosevelt, had resigned to enter the army, and two other members, including the navy's chief intelligence officer, were slated for duty with the fleet. This left rear admirals Sicard, late the North Atlantic Squadron commander, and Crowninshield of the Bureau of Navigation as the only members—now to be joined by Mahan. The resignations of the original members had clouded the board's mission and responsibilities. Roosevelt had given it political clout and legitimacy; the chief intelligence officer had provided a vital insight into the thinking of the enemy. But with their resignations, there were, even with Mahan now on board, just three elderly officers without a clear mandate of obligation.

The board, said the *Army and Navy Journal,* "seems to be whatever the members make of it." According to the unkind editorial, its main objects were "uttering warning cries" and prodding the administration into "this or that" course of action. "Every little while," the *Journal* continued, "we hear of one or more of them going to the White House and urgently impressing upon the President something which they think he ought to do, which he seems to listen to amiably, and then does not do. Then at other times they turn up before the Secretary and fiercely prod him, the result of which is that he gets his hat and escapes as quickly as possible." The *Journal* feared the board might actually undertake to supervise the fleets directly, a sort of aboriginal office of the chief of naval operations, an entity still seventeen years in the future. The *Journal,* and it was not alone even among naval thinkers, held the opinion that only the commander on the spot had the necessary wisdom and stature to direct his forces. Should the board take such presumption, the normally sane *Journal* commented, "its abolition should promptly follow."[15]

Truth to say, Mahan's first disgruntled reaction to the board was that it ought to be disbanded. The Navy Department had so little regard for its functions that it provided no proper meeting room. To his aged mentor, Admiral Luce, Mahan wrote, "When I arrived we were under the eaves of the Department Building in a room with one window, which theretofore had been used as a lumber room for books no longer needed for the library." As the board was intended to "furnish the Department with brains for the trivial and secondary purpose of carrying on the operations of the war, the high eligibility of this pasture for broken down books 'turned out to grass' was immediately clear."[16]

On Mahan's second day of his new service, he at once discerned that Sicard, who became chairman on TR's departure, was not up to the job. A "clear headed man for Bureau work," Mahan commented, "but very second or third rate for what we had to do." Before any public differences arose with his colleagues, and there were bound to be a number given Sicard's and Crowninshield's inherent conservatism, Mahan respectfully suggested to Secretary Long that he abolish the board and constitute in its place a "council of war . . . with corporate responsibility." Auguring the position and status of the future chief of naval operations, Mahan proposed the appointment of a single officer, "assisted by experts in various lines," each responsible for the authoritative opinions now theoretically supplied by the War Board. He understood that under the law, as now constituted, the secretary of the navy, a political appointee, was the man with that "single officer" accountability. But with so many "varied and onerous" duties upon his shoulders, an overwhelming amount of technical information needed to come from precisely those officers intimately familiar with the subjects, subjects that only "military seamen can possess. . . . Professional opinion," Mahan stated in his brief, should come to the secretary, not as the result of a majority vote, but with the far weightier sanction of "a single competent man." Mahan forwarded the recommendation to the secretary via Admiral Sicard, who sent it on without comment. Whether Mahan felt he should be the "single competent man" is impossible to say.[17]

John D. Long, no revolutionary, turned Mahan's proposal aside and opted to continue the War Board without change. It was not a formal body, he told critics; it had no rules or regulations. Its members were officers in whose judgment the secretary "has confidence, and they act merely as advisers." The principal function of the board was to collect information about the enemy and furnish it to the squadron commanders afloat. "The Secretary of the Navy," he told the *Army and Navy Journal,* "is not bound by its advice."[18]

Actually, by the time Mahan joined the board on May 9, there was little to be done in the realm of strategic planning. A brief morning's work at Manila had eliminated Spanish power in the Pacific, and Mahan's notion of concentrating the fleet off San Juan to await Cervera had come to nothing. The principal Atlantic dispositions were already formed prior to Mahan's arrival, and the only real movement of large import occurred with the discovery of Admiral Cervera's force off Martinique. On May 12, in response to that sighting, the board recommended, and Secretary Long approved, the logical realignment of naval forces, moving the Flying Squadron from senseless coast defense to the active theater of operations in the Caribbean.

This is not to say the War Board served no legitimate function, for it was of large help to the secretary. Each day reports from all naval sources poured into its office/meeting room, and from these the members deliberated and made their decisions, casting their ideas into proper orders for Long's signature. Yet it could never get out from under mindless criticism. The board, Mahan wrote to a friend, was "the most unpopular and ridiculed body of men in the country." If Dewey could do the job without any interference from Washington, said the naysayers, so could Sampson and Schley. Both of these commanders, it was said by Senator Pasco of Florida, were being unduly checked in their freedom of action by meddling chair warmers in Washington. "It was a good thing that Dewey cut the cables," he said. "Both Sampson and Schley ought to take a hint in this respect."[19]

Even the generally sane and progressive *Army and Navy Journal* took up the hectoring. Sampson and Schley, it said, must be given "full liberty of action" without any interference from the War Board or other "paper strategists." If the board's officers were more competent than the flag officers afloat, then put them in command "and place the responsibility on them." Did anyone, the *Journal* argued, believe that Dewey could have accomplished his deed "if he had been at the end of a wire running into the Navy Department?"[20]

On the other hand, the New York *Sun,* a big fan of Mahan's, pitched into Secretary Long for presuming to employ his own insight against that of the board's professionals. If he could reject their advice, then what good was it? If the board was merely advisory, then what was the need for the Navy Department's own Office of Naval

Intelligence? "The simplest way out of the difficulty," the paper said, was to abolish the board altogether and appoint Mahan chief of naval intelligence. The sniping on both sides, however, quickly subsided after the first week of July, when the Spanish squadron was utterly destroyed at Santiago.[21]

In late August, as the war drew to a close, Secretary Long penned a letter of honest appreciation to Rear Admiral Sicard, and through him to Crowninshield and Mahan. He virtually gave the War Board full credit for the real direction of the naval war. The secretary noted the "intelligence, the wise judgment, the comprehensive forethought and the unfailing competency" to meet every contingency. Long thought that the board had made no errors in the larger scheme of things, and through it, he had been able to exercise proper control of the Navy Department "over all movements in the field."[22]

Mahan, while agreeing at the close of the war that the secretary "had the sound sense to see that he was being well served by a number of capable men . . . and to allow them scope," was nonetheless piqued that Long should have written so flatteringly of Admiral Sicard, the board's nominal head, when he, Mahan, had been its real brains. "I feel now," Mahan wrote Admiral Luce, "very much like the teacher who after laborious explanations, receives from one of his boys one of those answers we see in the funny columns of a newspaper."[23]

CHAPTER 10

BLOCKADE

Fire all torpedoes!
—*Assistant Naval Constructor
Richmond P. Hobson, USN, June 3, 1898*

On Thursday, June 2, the day following his arrival off Santiago, Rear Admiral Sampson reorganized and positioned the fleet for the formal blockade of the port. The ships of the old Flying Squadron, now designated Second Squadron, remained under Commodore Schley, while the admiral exercised direct command over the First Squadron, the old North Atlantic Squadron ships previously under him, and general command overall. Tactically, Sampson shaped his blockade forces in a semicircle around the harbor mouth, to a distance of six miles by day and somewhat closer at night. The smallest ships took their posts at the ends of the half circle a bare two miles from the cliffs fronting the harbor channel. Toward the apex came the more powerful cruisers, armored cruisers, and battleships. At the median of the semicircle lay the battleship *Iowa*. Schley and the Second Squadron held the western quadrant; Sampson and the First Squadron formed the eastern. "If the enemy tries to escape," the admiral noted in his order, "the ships must close and engage as soon as possible, and endeavor to sink his vessels or force them to run ashore in the channel."[1]

In the last days the admiral spent on the Havana blockade and during the voyage to Santiago, the idea had percolated through the flagship

340

of stopping up the Spanish in port by use of a blockship, specifically the collier *Merrimac*. The practical methodology of the task Sampson assigned to a young member of his staff, twenty-eight-year-old Assistant Naval Constructor Richmond P. Hobson. Hobson devised an ingenious plan to use "torpedoes," as he called them—actually reduced charges of 8-inch shells, ten of them, each holding seventy-eight pounds of gunpowder in a copper tank to be affixed to the collier's port side twelve feet below the waterline. Anchors were to be dropped fore and aft, holding the ship in position athwart the narrowest part of the channel, the sea cocks would be opened, and at that moment, the torpedoes would be fired by means of a magneto generator, blowing in her side. If it went as planned, the *Merrimac*, with two thousand tons of coal still inside, would go down like a rock in little more than a minute, corking the Spanish like a bug in a bottle.

Originally, Hobson intended to disguise the ship as one of Spain's chartered colliers that had missed the fleet rendezvous at Martinique and Curaçao and was now being hotly chased by the American blockaders. In a convincing play to be performed by night, the fleet's searchlights would dance around the ship, illuminating a Spanish flag; guns would fire wide; pitch would be tossed into the fire box to produce billows of camouflaging smoke; and hooting whistles would blow distress calls; all meant to convince the Spanish to hold their fire until it was too late. But this charade was canceled. A close examination of the harbor chart convinced Hobson of the extreme difficulties of night navigation. Some light was needed, and the operation, he concluded, would best be run at dawn.

For a crew, Hobson estimated that beside himself, six men (later increased to seven) would suffice for the job, "with the simplest form of duty for each member to perform": one man at the wheel, two at the anchors to cut the lashings with axes, two to tend boilers and engine, two to aid with firing the torpedoes. Signaling the men for their various tasks, which had to be done with near split-second timing, could be done by pulling on cords tied to their wrists. The men, of course, must all be volunteers, and were, it was hoped, to escape over the side into an old catamaran dropped overboard at the last moment. If they were lucky, they'd be picked up in the teeth of the Spanish guns by the *New York*'s steam launch, dangerously stationed right in the harbor mouth.[2]

Three of the men came from the *Merrimac*'s own crew, the rest out of a call to the fleet that produced a tremendous response. The signal had gone from the flagship seeking volunteers "for a desperate and perhaps fatal expedition." From the *Iowa* came the reply, "Every man on this ship wants to go"; the *Texas* responded with, "We can give you 250 volunteers"; from the *Brooklyn,* "Two-thirds of the . . . crew are fighting for first place." Hobson was besieged with junior officers begging for a chance at death or glory.[3]

While the crew was assembled, the *Merrimac,* already lashed to the *Massachusetts,* which was coaling from her, was stripped of everything not nailed down, except the leavings of the wardroom lunch. All through the night of June 1 to 2, the work of stripping the ship and arming her with her last deadly cargo went forward. Seven hundred tons of water were admitted into the double bottom as additional ballast. A hitch developed when Hobson discovered the fleet hadn't a single electric magneto generator, which would have enabled the torpedoes to be fired from the bridge. Instead, they now had to be hooked up to batteries, a much less certain process, and detonated from the ship's rail, far more dangerous. Hobson, to assure a fail-safe alternative should the batteries or anything else misfire, asked Admiral Sampson for two warheads from the *New York*'s arsenal of locomotive torpedoes, the self-propelled type fired from tubes, to be placed in the *Merrimac*'s hold. The admiral shook his head: "I cannot let you have them, two hundred pounds of guncotton on the inside would blow everything to the devil."[4]

At 4:00 A.M., June 2, with the crew clad only in flannel underwear, the engine-room hands in loincloths, and Hobson alone in uniform, the *Merrimac* began her run to the entrance—and was anticlimactically pulled up short by the torpedo boat *Porter.* Admiral Sampson had sent it to abort the mission, fearing it was too near daylight for safety. "One could see a cloud of gloom and disappointment pass over the men," Hobson recalled. "No one spoke a word." He ordered them to lie down and sleep, while he took the wheel and headed for the *New York.* Here a temporary relief crew boarded, giving Hobson's men the chance for a breakfast of scalding coffee and hardtack, "a superb combination," he said. "It is inconceivable how revivifying it was."[5]

Aboard the flagship, Hobson, Sampson, and Captain Chadwick argued over the best time for the mission. Over and over the two senior officers tried to convince Hobson to make the attempt at night, but he refused; light was necessary to navigate, and the escape of the crew must come second to the success of the operation. It was finally agreed to make the try in the last stages of the moon, and if this proved too dim, Hobson obtained permission to continue with the rising sun, without fear of recall. Again he asked for locomotive torpedo warheads, and again Admiral Sampson refused, explaining that everything and everyone would go to the "devil." During the afternoon, the eight men, keyed to an extremely high pitch, found it impossible to sleep or to get anything inside themselves but coffee. The flagship's executive officer sent down a basket of provisions and a large bucket of the strong black coffee that was the only thing the men could keep down. Hobson himself took a shower to relieve the tension. Officers pressed upon him oranges, bottles of cordial, pistols; it was a mission of suicide, of that no one had a doubt.

At the turn of the second dog watch, 6:00 P.M., Hobson and his seven men left the New York for the Merrimac, Admiral Sampson at the gangway being the last to say farewell. The collier lay just outside the night blockade line, about four miles from the harbor entrance. Again Hobson ordered his men to catch some impossible sleep while he scanned the horizon: the Brooklyn was almost white in the moon, and the Texas, her dark side toward him, looked dark, squat, and mean. Every detail he had gone over with his men, all petty officers of long service: when to open the sea cocks, when to let go the anchors, when to detonate the torpedoes, when to jump over the side.

Half an hour after midnight, the men took more coffee, and this time Hobson forced them to eat a sandwich from the basket provided by the flagship; men always do better in battle with a full stomach. Hobson ordered the engine ahead, and the men stripped to their life jackets, underwear, and loincloths, strapping on firearms. The ship steamed to the harbor entrance, responding to wheel and throttle "as if animated." As it left the blockading vessels behind, the outline of the Morro and other objects ashore became clearer. Because the ship was outlined in brilliant moonlight, all hope of surprise was long gone if the Spanish were awake and alert to the danger steaming down upon them. Hobson ordered full speed to the engine and for the helmsman to steer for a white patch to the left of the Morro, inside the channel, the Estrella battery.[6]

The Morro loomed to starboard in the moonlight, and on the port hand, the Socapa battery came into view. The ship was now five hundred yards from the entrance, and still neither a hail nor a shot broke a stillness mitigated only by the thrumming wheeze of the collier's engine. "The silence," Hobson noted, "was ominous." Unless they struck one of the mines in the entrance, there was no way now that the Spanish could prevent their progress. No matter what happened, the flood tide would carry them in, and even with a mortal wound, the ship held enough excess buoyancy to reach the narrowest part of the channel. Hobson ordered the engine stopped; he would glide the rest of the way. They moved one more ship's length, 322 feet nearer their goal, and then, at last, came a shout and the flash of gunfire to port.[7]

Another shot passed astern. Hobson stared through his night glasses and dimly saw a small picket boat firing away in the shadows. They'd pass a ship's length apart, if that. One rapid-fire gun on the *Merrimac*, Hobson knew, "could have disposed of the miserable object in ten seconds." But they had been stripped away with the rest of the fittings and appendages. Unmolested, the Spanish picket continued to fire. Now from starboard, the Estrella battery, just upchannel from the Morro, opened her guns. "Very well," said Hobson on receiving the report from Deignan, the man at the wheel, "pay no attention to it." A shot struck the bridge. The *Merrimac* nosed ahead another two lengths. She was now well into the channel, the looming Morro cutting off the sky to starboard. The swells of the flood tide took her within thirty feet of the Morro rocks before she recovered by swift work of the wheel and continued on. But at the last possible moment a shot from the Estrella battery smashed into her stern, destroying the rudder head and carrying away the steering chains. All control was lost.[8]

Hobson yanked one of his cords three times, Murphy in the bow swung his ax, severing the anchor hawser, and down it went. The ship moved with the tide at six knots, the anchor dragged through the muck, and on the *Merrimac* lurched. As previously ordered, Murphy moved aft and fired his torpedo without further instructions. From the muffled explosion Hobson could tell the ship's collision bulkhead had collapsed. If only he could let go the stern anchor in time, the ship might still ground in her proper position at the narrowest part of the channel. Torpedoes two and three should have been fired, but there was no sound of them. Hobson yelled down from the bridge, "Fire all torpedoes!" The noise of the Spanish guns made it impossible to be heard. Again and again he shouted down to fire. Charette, the sailor in charge of that operation, climbed to the bridge. The cell batteries had been shattered, all except for number five—then in a flash, that went off. And that was it for the torpedoes, two out of ten. The ship would not go down like a rock, unless the stern anchor could hold her. Hobson decided to handle that personally. He ran aft, and his heart sank. The shells that had crushed the stern, carrying away the steering gear, had also taken the anchor chains. If only Admiral Sampson had allowed him to carry the torpedo warheads packed with guncotton, he could have blown the whole ship up right there. But on she drifted, enveloped in smoke, the Spanish guns shooting furiously. "For noise," Hobson said, "it was Niagara magnified." The firing was intense and rapid, but so inaccurate in the night that friendly fire from the Socapa guns killed and wounded a score of Spaniards in the Morro. These casualties made the Spanish think a real warship was forcing entry, perhaps even the *New York;* the possibility of it being an unarmed collier was inconceivable, for nothing but a warship could put up such a fight![9]

Heavy bumps under the ship and towering columns of filthy black water showed where the Spanish had detonated their mines, eight of them, protecting the channel, leaving only four, something the American naval commanders would have paid dearly to learn. Ahead to port and starboard, the cruiser *Reina Mercedes* and destroyer *Plutón* fired their locomotive torpedoes. None hit, but later it was found that one of them still contained its dummy drill warhead. In such haste had the Spanish been to fire, they had neglected to replace it with a live one. The *Merrimac* drifted on, out of the critical part of the channel, hardly blocking it at all, and slowly settled to the bottom, only her mast tops and funnel cap showing.

As she slowly went down, Hobson ordered his men to abandon ship. Only one man had taken a wound in the firing, though all the rest, including Hobson, were sorely banged up in leaving the wreck. After clinging to the catamaran until the sun came up, they were rescued personally by Admiral Cervera in his barge and taken first to the *Reina Mercedes,* where they were treated as heroes, fed and clothed, and had their wounds taken care of. The Spanish refused to believe they had not fought a regular warship or that the sailors were regular bluejackets of the U.S. Navy. Men such as these must be "desperadoes" at best, or even mercenaries specially recruited for the job. In the afternoon, Hobson and his crew were rowed ashore and marched up the steep path to medieval prison cells in the Morro.

On the day of the *Merrimac's* foray, Captain General Ramón Blanco received the most remarkable communication from War Minister Miguel Correa. The serious situation in the Philippines, with Dewey blockading the bay and American troops doubtless on their way to take the city of Manila, compelled the archipelago's military and naval reinforcement by Spain. Therefore, the minister went on with Alice in Wonderland logic, "the only thing we can do is to send all the ships of Cervera's squadron that can get out of Santiago." But before the government could give the insane order, it needed to know Blanco's opinion as to what effect this withdrawal would have in Cuba. Correa assured Blanco that the movement to the Philippines would only be "temporary." As soon as the object was attained—presumably, the destruction of Dewey's squadron and the lifting of the blockade—Cervera could return to Cuba, "without loss of time and strongly reinforced" (from where and by what the minister did not say). There was no discussion of how Cervera, without a sure supply of coal and with foul-bottomed ships that barely made it into Santiago, was to break out of a heavily blockaded port, steam halfway around the world, and engage even an ostensibly inferior enemy squadron that was fully aware and deployed.[10]

Blanco responded with a straight face. He would be failing in his duty if he concealed the fact that Cervera's departure "would be of fatal effect on public opinion," and he doubted whether he could control the situation if such were the case. The *voluntarios* were already "much exercised" over the inadequacy of the naval forces sent from the home country and were only "kept up" in their fervent morale by hopes of a second squadron of reinforcements. He feared a *voluntario* mutiny if they learned that instead of more naval forces to Cuba, the opposite, a withdrawal, was in the works: "the repression would necessarily be bloody." Worse, he could not count on the army to suppress the revolt if it happened. "Loss of island certain," he concluded, "in view of horrible conflagration it would kindle here."[11]

• • •

At 7 A.M., June 7, the American fleet stood in toward the harbor entrance of Santiago to deliver the first of many more or less ineffectual
bombardments of the city and its fortifications. Admiral Sampson
pretty much knew they would bear little fruit—the Spanish works
were situated too high. In the day's meager result, the *Reina Mercedes*
was damaged; her executive officer, one soldier, and five sailors were
killed, and eleven were wounded. The *Vizcaya* and *Furor* were both
hit, but neither sustained serious injury. In marked frustration, Admiral Sampson wired the Navy Department, "If 10,000 men were here,
city and [enemy] fleet would be ours within forty-eight hours. Every
consideration demands army movement."[12]

Awaiting that, the admiral turned to a goal more within his immediate reach: taking Guantánamo Bay. Forty miles east of Santiago, in
American hands it would prove a godsend to the fleet as a forward repair and coaling station, relieving ships of the necessity of coaling at
sea or making the laborious back-and-forth passage to Key West. The
bay itself was defended by one small Spanish gunboat, the *Sandoval,*
and a small stone work, Fort Toro, midway up the bay, mounting a
handful of ancient bronze smoothbores. In Guantánamo city, the center of the coffee and sugar industry in eastern Cuba, eighteen miles in
from the bay and linked to it by rail, sat a Spanish garrison of six
thousand men, commanded by General Felix Pareja. They were completely cut off from the forces in Santiago by surrounding rebels, and
so dire was their predicament that they were down to half rations,
and even these could last but a month.

Just before the Americans cut the Guantánamo cables, Pareja received orders to hold the place to the last bullet. Spanish commanders
expected the main enemy force to land here, just as the British had
done in 1741, and then march overland to Santiago. As Pareja never
got any further instructions, he was entirely ignorant of what was
happening, and his forces remained isolated and useless in the grand
scheme of the Santiago campaign. (Even if Pareja had marched his
men to Santiago and reinforced the garrison, not enough food existed
to feed them there either.)

On June 7, the *Marblehead* and the auxiliary cruiser *Yankee* sailed
into lower Guantánamo Bay, drove the *Sandoval* into its upper end,

and destroyed Fort Toro. With that, the scout *St. Louis* arrived to cut the cables. In a communication that never reached them, Pareja informed his chiefs in Santiago that the Americans now utilized the bay "as if for a harbor of rest, they having anchored as if in one of their own ports." Ships, though, cannot hold ground, and troops were needed to secure the harbor for its uninterrupted use. It was time to send in the marines.[13]

As early as April 16, Secretary Long had ordered an expeditionary battalion of marines scraped up from the East Coast naval stations and placed under the command of Civil War veteran Colonel Robert Huntington, commandant of the marine barracks at the Brooklyn Navy Yard. Marine quartermasters planning well ahead purchased a three-month supply of engineering stores (axes, wheelbarrows, shovels, wire cutters, and small wagons), rushing the stuff to Brooklyn, where the battalion had assembled, a total of 24 officers, 633 men, and four 3-inch landing guns. On June 10, in oppressive heat, the battalion unloaded on the east side of Guantánamo Bay from the cruiser-transport *Panther.*

Taking position on a small hill known as Camp McCalla (for the commander of the *Marblehead,* who was in overall charge of the operation), the marines, in the midst of settling in, were hit by a force of 300 Spanish infantry. Two men in an outpost plus the battalion's naval surgeon were killed before rifle and machine-gun fire from the battalion, supported by naval gunfire, drove the enemy off. Huntington and several of the older officers in their heavy blue woolens were in a state of near collapse from the heat and humidity.

At Commander McCalla's suggestion, Huntington moved his men from the exposed crown of the hill, where they were subject to Spanish potshots, to the forward slope closer to the beach. On June 14, acing on the suggestion of a rebel officer, a force of 160 marines and 50 Cubans marched six miles inland through atrocious country and attacked the Spanish holding Cuzco Well, the only drinking water on the east side of Guantánamo Bay. Caught between marine and Cuban fire, the enemy were driven off with at least 60 dead and wounded; the well and heliograph station were destroyed. From that point, the eastern side of the bay remained wholly free of Spanish troops, and the fleet had its forward base for the remainder of the campaign.

Though it was only a skirmish in the large strategy of things, the little action at Guantánamo held enormous significance for the future of the Marine Corps. With the rise and growth of the new navy, the continued existence of the corps had been thrown into doubt. There was no longer a legitimate need for the small detachments of marines that served on battleships and cruisers to keep discipline, and they were much resented by the crews as taking up space better filled by sailors. But the skirmish at Guantánamo Bay opened new vistas of actions to seize forward bases for the fleet, a mission that remained with the Marine Corps through World War II.

One day after the fleet bombardment of Santiago's fortifications, Admiral Sampson issued an order stipulating that searchlights be directed on the harbor entrance all night, every night. It was one of the most important decisions of the war, as it removed from Admiral Cervera's mind any thought of making a night escape and it also removed American fears of a night torpedo attack, though it does not seem that the Spanish ever maintained any serious thought of this.

As it happened, on the very day of the searchlight order, Admiral Cervera held yet another of his captains' conferences. Chafing at inaction, Captain Joaquín Bustamante, the chief of staff, took into account the lack of provisions in Santiago and the overwhelming strength of the enemy fleet. He suggested the squadron take advantage of the present darkness of the moon "and resolutely effect the sortie." The destroyers would go out first and head at their best speed into the gap between the *Texas* and the *Massachusetts,* the top of the western half of the blockading circle. Next would come the *Colón,* "heading straight for the *Brooklyn*" a bit further west. Then the remainder of the cruisers would dash out, on opposite headings to the southeast. This division of forces, Bustamante reasoned, should "create confusion in the hostile fleet," enabling the Spanish to save at least half their ships. In his opinion, this suicidal dash was "vastly preferable" to that "other solution," rotting at their moorings and surrendering with the city as it starved on. If only part of the squadron survived the foray, he argued that Havana should be the rendezvous; if all made it, then San Juan. Why he chose Havana at all, being farther away, difficult to reach, and closer to American bases, is not clear.[14]

Captain Victor Concas suggested that if the *New York* or the *Brooklyn*, the two fastest enemy ships, "should at any time disappear," a squadron sortie should be attempted immediately. Or it should be tried in the darkness of the new moon, with the "whole squadron united," all ships following the same course—not, as Bustamante had it, in virtually opposite directions. The rest of the commanders objected. Citing the "impunity" of the enemy in approaching the harbor entrance, and the partial blocking of the channel by the *Merrimac*, they were opposed to going out at all. Militarily, they felt the most important service of the squadron was to aid in the defense of the harbor and city.[15]

On June 9, the skipper of the dispatch vessel *Dolphin* reporting in from St. Nicolas Môle with messages from the Navy Department handed Admiral Sampson a bizarre telegram dated at Key West the day before. According to it, the yacht *Eagle* in the Nicholas Passage on Cuba's northwest coast had spotted a strange armored cruiser and two destroyers, and for a time had actually been chased by one of the latter. In reality, the larger ship was the British cruiser *Talbot*, which bore a superficial resemblance to the Spanish ships of the *Infanta María Teresa* class; the smaller "destroyers" were actually U.S. vessels en route to the blockade. This mistaken identity, and others, would hold up the sailing of the Fifth Corps at Tampa for nearly a week until the situation sorted itself out. The day after, another incident, this time in the Windward Passage, had the *Yankee* spotting up to eight hostile vessels, including a battleship. These devolved into the *Scorpion* and the *Panther* bringing the marines to Guantánamo, and two supply ships. The War and Navy departments, in panic, requested Admiral Sampson to "scour" the appropriate waters with armored ships taken from the Santiago blockade. Was he sure all the Spanish vessels were still tightly holed up? The admiral had no confidence in the sighting reports, knowing the "ghost" fleets for what they were, his own vessels, and considered the consequent delay in sending the army expedition "most unfortunate."[16]

Instead of detaching ships to hunt will-o'-the-wisps, the admiral sent Lieutenant Victor Blue on a reconnaissance foray inland. With the aid of Cuban rebel scouts, he landed at Aserraderos, a few miles

west of the harbor, climbed the hills, and came within nearly complete
visual range of the Spanish ships. "Decided relief," noted John D.
Long on receiving the admiral's account of Blue's mission. The army
could now sail. "The navy has had all the fun so far," wrote General
Miles to his sister, "and I only hope that peace will not be declared
without giving the army a chance at both Cuba and Porto Rico as
well as the Philippines."[17]

The navy was to have one more bit of "fun." After repeated requests, the dynamite cruiser *Vesuvius* joined the blockading forces off
Santiago. A graceful, yachtlike vessel, the ship mounted three 15-inch
pneumatic dynamite-throwing tubes that stuck out of her foredeck at
a fixed angle. Each could lob a two-hundred-pound package of dynamite about three miles. On the first day of her action, she loosed one
salvo only, but it was enough for Admiral Cervera to withdraw his
destroyers to safer positions behind the Socapa battery. Lieutenant
José Müller of the Spanish navy inspected the damage and reported
the dynamite had cleared a swath twenty meters in circumference on
the Socapa heights. "It looked as though a road had been opened
across the mountain."[18]

The fleet had done its job bottling Cervera in port. Now it was up
to the army to flush him out. On June 14, the expedition forces sailed
without incident.

CHAPTER 11

THE SANTIAGO CAMPAIGN

They say the first man who landed inquired the way to Santiago. I don't know whether he did or not, but the first organized command which reached the shore took the road to Santiago, and didn't stop until they got there.

—*Major General William R. Shafter,*
United States Army

We cannot hope for help either from within or without; we cannot hope for provisions [or] ammunition, and without these the soldier[s] cannot be fed and cannot fight—a sad and desperate situation for men who ask for nothing else and whom fate seems to pursue.

—*Lieutenant José Müller y Tejeiro, Spanish navy*

During the week of the ghost squadron chimera, the sun beat mercilessly down over the transports in Tampa Bay. Those ships carrying horses and mules were brought dockside, and the animals were unloaded and walked to stockyards two miles away; they, at least, were spared the suffocating holds. "We were much disappointed," said Sergeant Horace Wayman Bivins of the 10th Cavalry, "as we were expected to leave for Cuba. . . . The question was asked by thousands: 'What is the trouble?' " General Shafter allowed the men of the expedition daytime liberty ashore, where most of the enlisted ranks partook of the questionable pleasures in the shanties and tents of "Last Chance Street," magically erected like a Western boom-town right alongside the pier. Doors leading to certain establish-ments above dubious "restaurants" never stopped swinging. It was evident, said an observer, watching men button their trousers, that "no one was allowed to dawdle." Aboard the transports, one diver-sion was swimming over the side in the warm waters of the bay, where, a reporter noted, "The women here are frequently con-fronted by embarrassing situations, but they turn their faces the other way and leave the bathers undisturbed. This is not Narra-gansett . . . and bathing suits are neither accessible nor desired." There was also a fair amount of prohibited gambling, and im-promptu concerts by the various regimental bands. But mostly, the men stood around yarning, or slept in any corner they could find on deck, anywhere but those jammed, three- and four-bunk-high black holes below. Over the bulwark of the *Yucatán,* someone had hung a sign, "STANDING ROOM ONLY," to which another wag added, "AND DAMN LITTLE OF THAT."[1]

The heat also added to the stench of several quarters of chemically treated beef (a private experiment by a packing company, at no ex-pense to the government) that were stowed under canvas on the *Yu-catan's* foredeck. The stench of what quickly became known as "embalmed" beef was overpowering, indeed nauseating. Lieutenant Colonel Roosevelt of the Rough Riders reported the matter, and the mess was soon tossed into the bay.

Some naval escort vessels came up on the eleventh, giving credence to the rumor of roaming Spanish warships, but indicating as well that events were about to progress. Finally, on Monday, June 14, the an-chor chains were again heaved short, steam was raised, and the order given for the third and last time to get under way. This time the scene was "neither picturesque nor moving," reported correspondent Richard Harding Davis. In contrast to the aborted movement of June 6 and again two days later, there were no bands, no crowds on the pier. "The men who were going to die for their country did not swarm in the rigging and cheer the last sight of land." They had already done that twice. From the deck of the headquarters ship *Segurança,* Davis watched three "colored women and a pathetic group of perspiring stevedores and three soldiers [who] represented the popular interest" in the departure of the convoy. But once moving through the water,

leaving the entrance to the bay, those aboard the *Yucatán* broke into
the most popular song of the day:

There'll be a hot time in the old town tonight,
where you knowed ev'rybody and dey all knowed you,
and you've got a rabbit's foot to keep away de hoodoo.[2]

The convoy that formed into three ragged lines under the annoyed
nudging of the naval escorts was no mean formation; in fact, it would
be the largest military force ever to depart the United States until
World War I. Twenty-nine transports and six auxiliary vessels carried
819 officers and 16,058 enlisted men, in twenty-three regiments of
regulars and three of volunteers, plus 959 horses and 1,336 mules. The
artillery counted sixteen 3.2-inch field guns, four 7-inch siege howitzers, four 5-inch siege rifles, eight 3.6-inch mortars, two Hotchkiss
1-pounder mountain guns, four Gatlings, and an experimental dynamite gun. There were, in addition, a small balloon detachment for
battlefield observation, 112 six-mule wagons, and eighty-one escort
wagons, but only seventeen ambulances. Supercargo included 30 civilian clerks, 272 teamsters and mule packers, 107 stevedores, 89 reporters, and 11 military attachés.

In the evening of the following day, off the Dry Tortugas, east of
Key West, the convoy straggled along over the bluest cobalt sea to rendezvous with the naval escort commanded by Captain Henry Clay
Taylor in the battleship *Indiana*. Taylor's gunboats had an awful time
keeping the convoy closed up, and the transports, at their impossibly
close intervals of four hundred yards between bow and stern and eight
hundred yards side to side in three columns, couldn't do it. Merchant-
ship masters were used to the complete opposite, keeping as safe and
far as possible from anything afloat, and this sort of close-order drill
was nightmarish to them, reeking of danger and collision. Inevitably,
after two nights at sea, the convoy lost most of its cohesion, as well as
a steam barge and a tug. It was also very strung out, perhaps fifteen
miles front to rear.

Entering the narrowest part of the Old Bahama Channel on Cuba's
north coast, General Shafter asked Captain Taylor to stop to allow
stragglers to re-form, but Taylor refused: not here, where any re-
sourceful Spanish torpedo-boat skipper could dash out and do his

worst, especially at night. But lest all formation be lost, Taylor agreed to slow the convoy to six knots, the warships constantly signaling "Close up" to little avail. A hail through the megaphone brought either no answer or universal shouting, good-naturedly yelled by the crew and embarked troops, for whom this was truly a great adventure. Theodore Roosevelt wrote to his sister Corinne, "If the Spanish had any enterprise they would somewhere or other have cut into this straggling convoy . . . but they haven't any and so we are safe."[3]

To Richard Harding Davis, the convoy presented no aspect of the warlike, no battling "through the waves on its errand of vengeance and conquest." It had the sea completely to itself, undisturbed by either Spanish torpedo boats or coastal guns, which it often passed in full view, though out of range. The escorting warships reminded him of "swift, keen-eyed, intelligent collies," darting in and out of the wallowing columns, rounding up a herd of stupid sheep, treating them "with the most punctilious courtesy and concealed contempt." A lot of the problem of straggling could have been alleviated by having a junior naval officer on board each of the transports to help the civilian captains read signals and keep their ships in correct position in the formation. Alfred Thayer Mahan said it best when he observed, "The committing of transport service to the army is radically vicious in theory. . . . The navy ought to have total control of such commands and movements."[4]

As in ages past, water was a large problem for both men and animals. A water schooner was towed behind the *Yucatán*, but she so slowed the vessel that both were always in the straggling rear. On the *Segurança*, Richard Harding Davis found the water so bad he could not even shave with it. "It smelled like a frog-pond or a stable yard, and it tasted as it smelt." Officers who could afford to drank bottled water or tea. The enlisted men, however, were condemned to the slop, or had to pay a ship's steward five cents for a glass of the civilian crew's distilled water. The regular drinking water was stowed forward, in rows of great casks lashed to the forecastle, and held a sluggish mixture of charcoal, "for health's sake," said Private Charles Post of the 71st New York aboard the *Vigilancia*. To him, it looked like muddy glycerin and tasted like the ship's bilge. Not only did it look and taste awful, it stank, having been put into casks six weeks before. The crew told the soldiers, perhaps truly, perhaps not, that the casks formerly held everything from pickled fish to kerosene. If the troops could not filch some water from the crew's supply, or buy a glass from an officer's steward, they tried to make the stuff palatable by mixing in lemon drops.[5]

Food was not much better, for officers or enlisted men. Davis, a privileged and internationally renowned correspondent, messed with the officers of the *Segurança* and found the fare provided by the shipping company "villainous; the enlisted men . . . were much better served by the Government with good beans, corned beef, and coffee." Private Wells of the Rough Riders lacked even that. "Our travel rations," he wrote in his diary, "we find are not sufficient because the meat is very bad indeed. . . . If we had been given canned corned beef, we would have been all right, but instead . . . we have been issued horrible stuff called 'canned fresh beef.' There is no salt in it. At the best it is stringy and tasteless; at the worst, it is nauseating."[6]

Private Post of the 71st New York ate corned beef and was quite satisfied. "Cooking on the *Vigilancia* was simple," he recalled. The "required" number of cans of meat were dumped into a wash boiler, some hardtack was broken into it, and a steam hose from the engine room was aimed into the tub and turned on. "It was not bad; the steam seemed to soften the hardtack, and perhaps it was the boiler scale from the fire room below that gave a tang to the corned beef." Coffee was made the same way. The estimated number of bags was poured into the wash boiler, and steam was turned into it until the water boiled. "The process," Post said, "involved a vast bellowing and gurgling of the steampipe and the water butts, as they battled to produce coffee." The problem was when the men had their corned beef, they could not have coffee, for the company had only one washtub.[7]

In between cramped drills and inspections, the men loafed and sang a lot, each company seeming to have a natural song leader. Sometimes it was an old melody, like "Banks of the Wabash" or "Sweet Marie." But more often, it was the mode of the times, such as "I Don't Like No Cheap Man," or the ever popular "Hot Time," which led all others. Not to know popular songs of the day, whether one could carry a tune or not, said Private Post, "was the mark of an illiterate."[8]

On the nineteenth, the convoy, badly strung out, turned south into the Windward Passage. Men noticed the shadows on deck shifting, and Cape Maisi came into sight off the starboard sides. "A long blue ridge came over the horizon," wrote Private Post, with mountains coming right down to the shoreline. Palm-thatched settlements dotted the narrow beaches. Davis, who as dean of the correspondents had seen most of the world, could still rhapsodize about indigo seas and mountains with the green of corroded copper. Colonel Leonard Wood of the Rough Riders, like his executive officer, Theodore Roosevelt, understood the wider implications of the vista, writing to his wife of the "great maritime picture" as the ships steamed by the cape, "the commencement of a new era in our relations with the world."[9]

At sunrise the next morning, June 20, Taylor sent the torpedo boat *Ericsson* to communicate with the fleet off Santiago. In a few hours the Morro came visible from the transports, as did the gray warships of the blockading fleet. Sailing along the coast the convoy passed the hamlets of Daiquirí and Siboney, and above these habitations, on all the hills overlooking the water, sat the Spanish blockhouses. Then came the harbor entrance of Santiago. "We could see the pinkish ocher of the ancient forts that guarded it," said Private Post. "They looked like the toy forts made for children." Watching from the beach, a Cuban rebel officer said, "No scene could be grander or more thrilling than that moving spectacle after three long years of struggle in the jungle." Fifteen miles offshore, the convoy stopped to await its slow coaches and to contemplate General Shafter's decision of where to land the expedition. To help with this and to discuss coming operations, Captain French Chadwick, Admiral Sampson's chief of staff, came out to the *Segurança* to confer.[10]

The most important feature of this shipboard meeting was a lack of communications between the army and navy on the objective, though neither service realized it at the time. Chadwick pressed home Admiral Sampson's view that the army had come to assist the navy in taking the harbor forts, thus enabling the fleet to clear the minefields and steam into the harbor to destroy the Spanish squadron within. Chadwick, Sampson, indeed, the entire naval hierarchy always believed General Shafter had sanctioned these goals. "General Shafter gave the most cordial assent," wrote Secretary Long after the war, "and stated that he had no intention of attacking the city proper, that here [the harbor entrance] was the key to the situation." To the navy's way of thinking, a landing somewhere east of Santiago, then a march over the coastal road, would bring the army in behind the Morro and its attendant works. The navy could directly support such an advance, keeping within several hundred yards of the army's seaward flank. It sounded simpler than it was. The coast road was hardly more than a goat path in places, where troops would be forced to march in single file, inviting enfilading fire down their column from any determined defender. There was, however, an ore railroad that ran parallel to the road for ten or so miles between Siboney and Aguadores, a little less than three miles east of the Morro. But at Aguadores, the small San Juan River emptied into the sea through a steep gorge, which was crossed by a long iron railroad bridge, and no one could assume the Spanish would leave it intact (though, in fact, they did).[11]

But unbeknownst to the navy, General Shafter had decided on another plan. He had chosen Daiquirí as his landing spot. An iron-ore shipping hamlet with only the most rudimentary docking facilities, Daiquirí lay about eighteen miles east of the Santiago harbor entrance. Once it was taken, Shafter's forces would strike inland against Santiago itself. To march for any distance along the coastal road, he later claimed, "never for one minute met with my approval." After the war, Captain Chadwick concluded that Shafter's decision was the result of incorrect information from the War Department and Cuban rebel sources that indicated the harbor mouth and its fortifications were heavily defended by the bulk of the Spanish forces. Such a situation, if correct—which it was not—would have left the city itself without adequate protection. Actually there were about four hundred men, mostly artillerists, in the Morro castle and its attendant batteries on the east face of the harbor mouth.[12]

Writing with hindsight, Captain Chadwick felt that with better planning, the army and navy together could have accomplished both goals—taking the harbor forts and the city. The squadron's one thousand marines, aided by Cuban rebels (whose cooperation, the Americans soon learned, was never a sure thing) and naval gunfire, could land west of the harbor at Cabañas and assault the Socapa battery, which held at most four hundred men. In a combined movement, General Shafter would advance an infantry brigade along the coast road from Daiquirí, making use of the railroad for part of the way, attack the Morro from the rear, and still have nearly fifteen thousand troops for the main attack on Santiago. But careful interservice

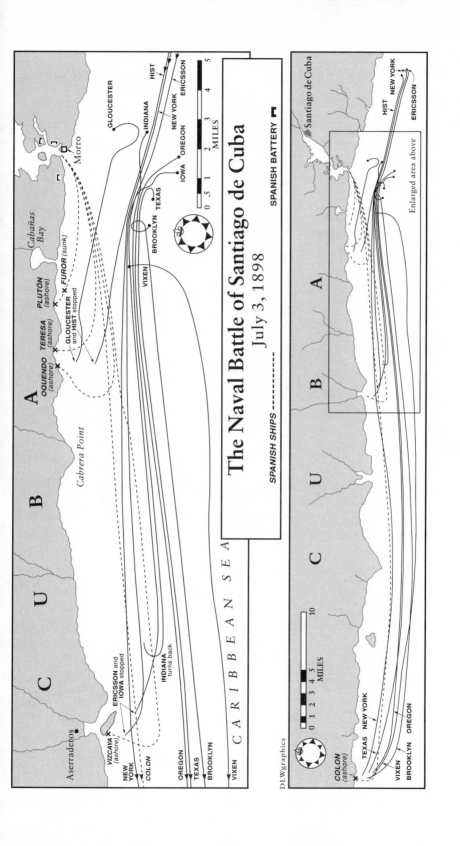

The Naval Battle of Santiago de Cuba
July 3, 1898

SPANISH SHIPS ------------

SPANISH BATTERY ◼

MILES
0 .5 1 2 3 4 5

Enlarged area (main map) labels:

C U B A

Cabañas Bay

Cabrera Point

Morro

Aserraderos

VIZCAYA (ashore) ✗

OQUENDO (ashore) ✗

TERESA (ashore) ✗

PLUTÓN (ashore) ✗

FUROR (sunk) ✗

GLOUCESTER ✗ and HIST stopped

ERICSSON and IOWA stopped

INDIANA turns back

NEW YORK

COLON

OREGON

TEXAS

BROOKLYN

VIXEN

GLOUCESTER

INDIANA

IOWA

OREGON

NEW YORK

ERICSSON

HIST

CARIBBEAN SEA

Lower (overview) map labels:

C U B A

Santiago de Cuba

Enlarged area above

HIST

NEW YORK

ERICSSON

COLON (ashore) ✗

TEXAS

NEW YORK

VIXEN

BROOKLYN

OREGON

MILES
0 1 2 3 4 5   10

DLWgraphics

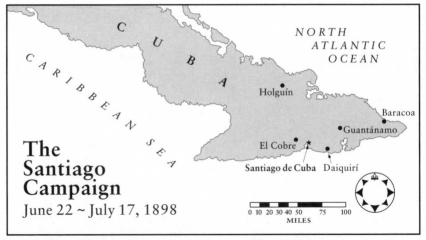

The Santiago Campaign
June 22 ~ July 17, 1898

NORTH ATLANTIC OCEAN

CARIBBEAN SEA

C U B A

Holguín

Baracoa

Guantánamo

El Cobre

Santiago de Cuba   Daiquirí

0 10 20 30 40 50   75   100
MILES

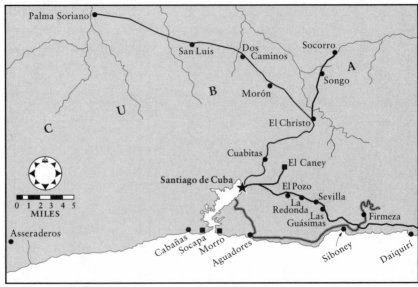

Palma Soriano

San Luis

Dos Caminos

Socorro

A

Songo

B

Morón

U

C

El Christo

Cuabitas

El Caney

Santiago de Cuba

El Pozo

Sevilla

La Redonda

Las Guásimas

Firmeza

Asseraderos

Cabañas   Socapa   Morro

Aguadores

Siboney

Daiquirí

0 1 2 3 4 5
MILES

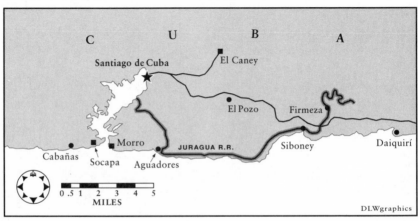

C   U   B   A

Santiago de Cuba

El Caney

Morro

El Pozo

Firmeza

Cabañas

Socapa

Aguadores

JURAGUA R.R.

Siboney

Daiquirí

0 .5 1   2   3   4   5
MILES

DLWgraphics

operational collaboration lay well in the future, in the coming century, and even in World War II there were major kinks.

General Shafter's decision to land at Daiquirí and move inland to his objective, the city of Santiago, derived primarily from his conviction that the task had to be accomplished quickly; if it were not, the army would be decimated by yellow fever. He had studied the British expedition to Santiago in 1741; they had landed at Guantánamo and in their march to Santiago, lost two thousand men. "With this example before him," Secretary of War Russell Alger wrote, "he realized that the sole chance of success would lie in the very impetuosity of his attack" on Santiago itself. Once the city fell, everything else around it would collapse.[13]

With army and navy confident in their independent thinking and secure in the assumption that the other party held to the same view, the *Segurança* headed westward along the coast, eighteen miles to Aserraderos, for a meeting ashore with Admiral Sampson and General Calixto García, commander of the revolutionary forces in eastern Cuba. It would have been more convenient to confer aboard the *New York*, but García had been aboard the flagship the day previously and had been so seasick that he had to be confined to a bed. Thus the conference was held at the headquarters camp of General Jesús Rabí, in the hills above Aserraderos. Included in General Shafter's party were the British and German military attachés and several correspondents, including Frederic Remington and Richard Harding Davis. There was no military escort other than the Cubans who met them on the beach and hauled the longboat over the surf, cheering, carrying the officers ashore on their shoulders, pressing upon them coconuts, limes, and mangoes. Rebels in every state of rags formed in ranks to present arms. The camp was some distance up in the hills and mules were provided. For the poor beast that bore the three hundred pounds of General Shafter, "one had to have compassion," wrote a Cuban officer, "it giving profound groans of anguish during its ascension, because of the cargo with which it had been punished that summer morning."[14]

The assembly was held under a palm-leaf roof, the leaves hanging down to form the walls of the structure. Shafter sweltered in his blue uniform; Sampson looked a little more comfortable in white duck. García—tall, imposing, with high boots, white hair, mustaches, and a deep bullet wound between his eyes as a result of a botched suicide attempt years before while a Spanish prisoner—confirmed that Daiquirí was probably the best place to land, and he promised a thousand insurrectos, General Demetrio Castillo's men, to harass the enemy at and near the landing site. It was also arranged to make a feint at Cabañas, west of the harbor, with Brigadier General Jacob Kent's 1st Division and its transports simulating the movements of a landing. Simultaneously, the navy would transport, under blind Spanish eyes, Castillo's rebels and eventually most of García's command, nearly three thousand men, from Cabañas east to the Daiquirí area. García offered to place his forces under General Shafter's orders. But this Shafter wisely refused, for with command came responsibility for Cuban movements, uncertain at best. However, he assured the rebel leader he would be very glad to accept his "voluntary" services, in return for which Shafter donated nine thousand rations and several thousand rounds of ammunition to the rebels. The meeting proved the high point of American-Cuban relations on the battlefront during the entire campaign.

Back aboard the *Segurança,* General Shafter composed his landing order. Brigadier General Henry Lawton's 2nd Division, supported by the Gatling gun detachment, would land first, followed by Brigadier General John C. Bates's independent brigade in support. Joe Wheeler's dismounted Cavalry Division would come next, then Kent's division brought over from its exercise off Cabañas, and last, the mounted squadron of the 2nd Cavalry. If strong enemy resistance was encountered, the light artillery, the 3.2-inch field guns, were to be landed alongside the troops in the steam lighter *Laura;* if not, the guns would come ashore later. Each man was to carry his full field gear and three days' rations, with the coffee already ground, a full canteen, and one hundred rounds of ammunition. In conclusion, the general wished "to impress officers and men with the crushing effect that a well-directed fire will have on the Spanish troops." To foster confusion among the Spanish as to where the landing was actually to take place, the navy undertook to bombard the coast on both sides of Santiago, from Cabañas on the west, east to Daiquirí. The movement ashore was scheduled for the morning of June 22. Shafter wished personally to hand each senior officer his landing orders, but early on the twenty-first the rains began, accompanied by rough seas until noon, and the transports scattered to such an extent that Captain Taylor was obliged to herd them together for the brigade and division commanders to repair aboard the *Segurança*. What was planned as a morning meeting did not begin until noon, and several of the officers did not reach the headquarters ship until nightfall.[15]

Even if major operational questions remained unanswered, tactical cooperation by the fleet, with its limited means, in putting the army ashore was a factor of the highest order. The Fifth Corps had been originally organized and outfitted to land at the port of Mariel, near Havana, a place with facilities to handle a flotilla of small boats, having a dock, breakwaters, and other necessaries of anchorage for the transports, artillery, and the expedition's animals. Nothing prepared the troops, horses, and mules to swim for the shore, or to land in ships' boats, over open, perhaps fire-swept beaches three miles from the sides of their vessels. Indeed, prior to its sailing from Tampa, Secretary Long begged "leave to enquire" how the army intended to get itself ashore. In a burst of uncharacteristic pettiness, he opined, "[I]t is obvious that the crews of the armored ships . . . as will be called upon to remove Spanish mines and meet the Spanish fleet in action cannot be spared for other purposes and ought not to be fatigued in the work incident to landing of the troops."[16]

Admiral Sampson, however, could not just stand by; without the active help of the fleet, the army could sit roasting in its transports for days or weeks more, a logistic impossibility given the lack of water for the animals. On Sampson's orders, the fleet provided three armed tugs, and its battleships lowered a dozen steam launches, each with a 1-pounder rapid-firing gun, and forty pulling boats to assist the landing. Captain Caspar Goodrich in the armed liner *St. Louis* had charge of the operation. Together with the army's steam lighter *Laura*, these various craft had a capacity of around 1,500 men, nearly a third from the *St. Louis*'s boats alone.

The navy's boats, each with its coxswain and crew of two to four men, gathered under the lofty sides of the *St. Louis* at 4:30 A.M. A dozen pulling boats lined up behind each steam launch, making fast to each other fore and aft. The "string" then received orders to make for its designated transport. The boats were to be loaded carefully, and the soldiers first aboard were directed to sit on the bottom. Those on the thwarts needed to be prepared to use their rifles on the enemy if they appeared on the beach during the run in. Once loaded, the strings of boats took position astern of one of the three tugs for the dash ashore. When the "blue peter" flag was hauled down from the tug *Wompatuck*, where Goodrich exercised tactical command of the operation, the strings of boats would steam ahead, sweeping the beaches with their 1-pounder guns. A small wooden pier was the objective for the first boats of the first wave.[17]

That night, aboard the *Yucatán*, the officers of the Rough Riders lifted their glasses in a macabre toast: "To the officers—may they get killed, wounded, or promoted." Excited men aboard the transports watched numerous fires along the shore and ridges from Siboney to Daiquirí. Were they signals by the Spanish alerting the coastal forces to repel an invasion? No one had a clue as to their reception on the morrow.[18]

"I shall commence landing this morning," General Shafter wrote to Admiral Sampson. "It is my intention to proceed from Daiquirí to Santiago as rapidly as I can. . . . The animals are in absolute need of some rest, and for that reason I may not get very far to-day." This message, though not completely obvious, should have dispelled the navy's notion that General Shafter intended to take the coast road to the gates of the Morro and there assist in destroying the coastal fortifications. It was clear, almost, that he was heading inland to attack the city itself.[19]

Daiquirí was a mean little hamlet on a small bay, actually barely an indentation in the coastline, sixteen miles east of the Santiago harbor mouth, and about the same distance overland to the city, to which it was linked by a single, virtually impassable trail. The place had been developed by American mining companies to service the iron pits of the interior, what the Spanish called the "mineral region." It had no harbor or even a breakwater. But there was a dangerous iron dock for dumping ore into waiting ships. It was too high for landing troops from small boats, though feasible for the transports. All but one of the ships' captains refused to approach it. Next to the dock was a small, slimy wooden pier, in disrepair, that extended about forty feet into the sea. The immediate area inland had a good supply of drinking water coming down in iron pipes from streams in the hills. There was some open ground behind the village, suitable for re-forming the troops after they got ashore and for establishing a supply dump and animal corrals. As generally is the case along this part of the Cuban coast, the heights, dominated by Mount Losiltires, with its block-house, commenced at the water's edge, and it was a fine place for a spirited, bloody defense, should the Spanish so choose.

Five miles west along the coast was Siboney, where General Shafter might make use of the railroad, which, heading westward, terminated at the harbor of Santiago between the city and the Morro. A squalid, salt swamp habitation, Siboney held the railroad shops, a company infirmary, and a number of buildings that might be called a village. Other than a small headland that broke the wind and surf, it had no landing facilities whatever.

At 4:30 A.M., Captain Goodrich piloted the *St. Louis* to within a mile and a half of the iron pier. At 14,910 tons, she was easily twice the size of most of the convoy steamers, and Goodrich explained that he took this exposed position "in order to demonstrate to the trans-port captains that the approaches were perfectly safe."[20]

Amphibious warfare, the ship-to-shore movement of troops in a hostile environment, is the most difficult of all military operations. There were major difficulties attendant on this landing; for one, it had not been done, even in training, since the Civil War, and no one really had a clue. But it was carried out with far less disorder than might have been the case—for instance, if the Spanish had defended the beaches. The convoy, naturally, was spread all over the sea, many of the ships five miles and more from the beach. The *Knickerbocker,* car-rying most of the 2nd Massachusetts Infantry of Lawton's 2nd Divi-sion, was lost altogether and did not appear until the afternoon. Goodrich considered the overly cautious conduct of the merchant captains the most significant obstacle encountered during the landing, and one that would have been "largely avoidable" by the simple ex-pedient of placing a naval officer aboard each vessel to assume re-sponsibility for movement. It also took quite a time for the army steam lighter *Laura,* with a capacity of over three hundred men, to make her appearance in the transport debarkation area, "disarrang-ing" Goodrich's operations even more.[21]

The boat strings proceeded to their transports. Accommodation ladders were lowered, and men burdened with horse-collar packs, rifles, haversacks, and cartridge belts gingerly stepped into the heaving small craft. It was like jumping into an elevator that kept moving up and down between floors. By nine o'clock, most of the 8th Infantry, the leading unit of the invasion, were in their boats—enough, Goodrich considered, to warrant heading for the beach. "Soon the sea was dotted with rows of white boats filled with men bound about with white blanket rolls and with muskets at all angles," wrote Richard Harding Davis, "and as they rose and fell on the water . . . the scene was strangely suggestive of a boat race, and one almost waited for the starting gun."[22]

The cruiser *New Orleans,* leading the bombardment ships off Daiquirí, opened fire on the beaches, "heavy enough," Goodrich noted, "to drive out the whole Spanish Army in Cuba had it been there." The *Wompatuck* and tug *Suwannee* added their light rapid-fire pieces, sweeping the jungle to either side of the pier and dock. There was no return fire. After about thirty minutes, a group of horsemen waving a Cuban flag appeared on the beach—Castillo's men. From the *Segurança,* General Shafter hoisted the signal to cease firing, and almost immediately after, the first steam launch and its string of boats reached the wooden pier, men scrambling up the slippery piles for the forty-foot run to dry land.[23]

Once the first boatloads hit the pier, or grounded off the beach, the debarkation continued as fast as the distance of the transports from the shore and the speed of the boats permitted. The crews had got the knack of quick loading, and a navy beachmaster directed traffic ashore. When the *Laura* got into operation, three companies at a time could leap onto the pier and double-time off to re-form inland. By early afternoon, albeit in somewhat of a jumble, a good part of Lawton's 2nd Division: the 8th, 17th, and 22nd Infantry regiments, plus part of the 2nd Massachusetts—had landed without a single casualty.

Ironically, in the house of the late Spanish commander, an unfinished letter to General Arsenio Linares, commanding the Fourth Army Corps and eastern Oriente Province, was found. The writer assured his chief that he was "abundantly able to resist any attack at Daiquirí, either by land or sea." Indeed, with his three hundred men, he could have done it and turned the beaches into a bloodbath for the Americans. But the Spanish garrison evacuated the town before dawn, and not a shot was fired in its defense. Daiquirí, and the following day, Siboney as well, were handed as bloodless gifts to the norteamericanos.[24]

The correspondents aboard the Segurança itched to get ashore, but General Shafter's landing order confined all persons to remain afloat who were "not immediately on duty" with the units listed in the debarkation until the beach was declared secure. Richard Harding Davis took issue with Shafter directly, saying that the order assigning only fighting men to the boats "will keep back reporters." True, Shafter replied, but this prudence did not manifest any "unfriendliness" to correspondents, only a desire "to be prepared as far as possible to return the fire of the Spaniards," should they put up a fight for the beaches. Davis, according to a senior staff officer, misread Shafter's "intense anxiety" about enemy action for hostility toward the press, and persisted in arguing. "Finally," recalled the officer, "Mr. Davis said he was not an ordinary reporter, but a 'descriptive writer.' " At this, Shafter's patience, never his long suit, gave way. The spaniel eyes narrowed. "I don't care a damn what you are," he said through gritted teeth, "I'll treat you all alike." Davis never after gave General Shafter a drop of good ink. Watching the playlet from nearby, another pressman remarked, "[T]here are many necessary evils in this world. Among others are newspapermen. From the moment of issuing that order, pencils began to be sharpened," and Shafter's reputation suffered forever for it.[25]

Landing the expedition's horses and mules posed an enormous problem, one that would not have occurred had the expedition gone to its original destination, the port of Mariel. But when the Spanish squadron had put in at Santiago, that changed everything. Only a few animals were landed the first day, mostly senior officers' horses, but they paid a price, and half a dozen drowned, including Theodore Roosevelt's Rain-in-the-Face. The horses were led to an open cargo port, and as they looked down into the sea, a blacksnake whip stung them from behind and over they went. Buglers on the beach sounded "Stables," "Boots and Saddles," "Fours Right," "Charge"—anything the beasts found familiar to give them direction. Many became dazed and hysterical; boats would race toward a panicked animal to enable a trooper to throw a rope about its neck and lead it to the beach. After a few horses were lost, strict orders were given that three or four were to be tethered together and towed ashore by boat. It was much slower, but there were no further losses after the first day. The animals, after a few hours of rest in the corral behind Daiquirí, soon recovered and, as Shafter's aide, Lieutenant John Miley, said, "all seemed ready for their work."[26]

According to General Shafter's debarkation order, the Rough Riders were scheduled to land much later in the day with the Cavalry Division. But it soon became apparent to Lieutenant Colonel Roosevelt that much of the exercise had become "go as you please." As luck had it, the armed yacht *Vixen*, commanded by TR's former aide in the Navy Department, passed close by the *Yucatán*, and the skipper offered to pilot the transport within a few hundred yards of the beach. Thus the Rough Riders landed well in advance of the rest of the division, and some of the infantry as well. But there was a price: the *Yucatán* steamed off, taking most of the regimental baggage with her before any attempt was made at unloading. Roosevelt found himself with only a yellow mackintosh, a toothbrush, and several pairs of glasses sewn into the linings of his tunic and hat.[27]

General Joseph Wheeler, second-in-command of the expedition, had come ashore with his Cavalry Division. Noticing the Spanish flag still flying over the blockhouse on Mount Losiltires, he sent several Rough Riders scampering up the hill to hoist the American colors. The sight of the flag engendered wild jubilation in the troops assembling on the beach and those still in their transports. A correspondent wrote, "A quarter of an hour of whistle shrieks, cheers, yells, drum flares, bugle calls and patriotic songs were sent up." When the cacophony ceased, there came the strains of "The Star-Spangled Banner" from the band of the 20th Infantry. Soldiers on the beach and still afloat stood quiet until the bandsmen finished the song, and then, continued the reporter, "three full-lunged hurrahs crashed against the hill, and the salute to the flag was complete." By day's end, six thousand men were ashore, with only two fatalities, a pair of 10th Cavalry troopers drowned at the pier by the weight of their equipment. The army, reported Captain Goodrich, was now "abundantly capable of holding its own."[28]

Instead of encountering defending Spaniards, the men on the beach found hundreds of Cuban rebels, portions of Castillo's division, whom Roosevelt described as "a crew of as utter tatterdemalions as human eyes ever looked on, armed with every kind of rifle in all stages of dilapidation." Roosevelt saw in a moment they would be no use once the fight became serious, but hoped they might be of some help in scouting.[29]

On an operational and personal level, the Cubans proved a big disappointment to the expedition. The propaganda of the Junta in the United States had prepared the Americans to expect a ragged bunch of eager fighters in the Valley Forge mold, primed to come to grips with the enemy and needing only the assistance and supplies of the United States to overthrow the Spanish yoke.

Much of the animosity that arose shortly after the initial contact with the Cubans on the beach was cultural. Well over half the rebels, especially in Oriente Province, were black, and in the Jim Crow era of the United States, the American soldiers, representatives of a racist society, took their prejudices ashore with them. General Shafter looked upon the insurgents as "grazing" on American largesse. That should not have surprised anyone. After three years of the most bitter privation, they had found in the U.S. Army their new quartermaster, and nothing was safe from their pilferage or begging. Picking up on that theme, the commanding officer of the soon to arrive 34th Michigan Infantry "failed to find any Cubans who are not what you would call human vultures." "The Cubans in my opinion are not worth fighting for," said a 9th Cavalry major, "but of course everybody knows that." Major Arthur Wagner, the army's chief intelligence officer, found the rebel soldiers better disciplined and equipped than he'd expected, but "it was not until later . . . that I discovered that, whatever their merits as bushwhackers might be, they were practically useless in battle." On the racist level, Lieutenant John Parker of the Gatling Gun Detachment found the typical Cuban insurrecto, "cannot be trusted like the Indian, will not work like a negro, and will not fight like a Spaniard." These views were fairly universal within the Fifth Corps. Overall, the Cuban rebel forces performed somewhat better than the U.S. Army gave them credit for, but nowhere to the degree initially expected of them.[30]

At 4:00 P.M. on the afternoon of the landing, General Shafter ordered Lawton to advance west seven miles along the coastal path to Siboney, which the Spanish had precipitately abandoned at the time of the naval bombardment. Once there he was to encamp, entrench, and stay alert for any Spanish counterattack that might come down the road, the *camino real,* from Santiago to the northwest. Seven miles on a map was vastly different from the reality of the Cuban track. The exposed hard coral ran up and down steep little hills, and the tropical sun was intense enough to stun a local, to say nothing of unacclimated troops in government-issue blue flannel. Even when the road meandered off into shaded coconut groves, the trapped humidity and clouds of insects were torture. Soon blanket rolls, coats, and cans of food littered the path—and were immediately appropriated by the "grazing" and delighted Cuban rebels. Too tired and late to complete the march, Lawton camped on the trail for the night, the men sheltering from the rain in their two-man "dog tents." As was to be expected from troops in their first night in enemy territory, fire discipline left much to be desired, and there was much shooting by sentries at jungle noises. But the men had other enemies to contend with than the Spanish—fearsome land crabs. "The fight lasted all night long," said a 17th Infantry private, "and [they] almost drove us from our position, outnumbered as we were dozens to one in the darkness and ceaseless rain. . . . To be awakened from a doze of exhaustion . . . with land crabs clinging to one's ears and hands and creeping all over the body is not soothing to the nerves."[31]

General Lawton got his men up before dawn, and by sunrise his leading units had marched into Siboney, to be met by a few "scattering" long-range shots from the hastily retreating Spanish. Siboney provided a good defensive position at the base of the *camino real,* which led directly to Santiago. It was also a fairly good place to land troops over a gently shelving beach, protected by its small headland, and General Shafter ordered the remaining transports to complete their unloading here rather than at Daiquirí.

Lawton, Medal of Honor winner in the Civil War, reported that the Spanish withdrawal was so hastily done that if he had had a squadron of mounted cavalry at the front, he might have bagged the whole lot, which he estimated at 600 to 1,200 men. Some mounted Cubans did pursue the enemy rear guard and succeeded in capturing several carts of supplies. Later in the day most of Castillo's command renewed their skirmish on the Spanish rear, but were driven off.

. . .

While the American Fifth Corps was rapidly consolidating its position, hindered only by nature, what of the Spanish? What preparations had they made to defend Santiago de Cuba, the second city of the Pearl of the Antilles, now also the sheltering haven of Admiral Cervera's cruiser squadron? For it was upon this fetid city of 30,000 souls that the fate of the Spanish empire now depended. There were about 36,000 troops in Oriente Province, of which 28,300 came directly under Major General Arsenio Linares, commander of the Fourth Army Corps. But this figure is quite misleading, for it was impossible to concentrate anywhere near this number to face the enemy at and around Santiago.

The Spanish forces were widely dispersed over twelve thousand square miles in garrisons large and small, many of them isolated from the central command, and each other, as much by the nature of the terrain as by the rebels. Many could reach Santiago only by sea, an impossibility once the blockade had been established. Overland traffic was extremely problematic, most of the few roads that existed being not much more than what Americans would call trails. Even those that were called *caminos reales* were only equaled, said Captain Chadwick, "by that of the roughest mountain roads in the southern part of our own Appalachian Mountains."[32]

As far back as early April, weeks before the declarations of war, Captain General Blanco, with keen intuition, though on what basis is impossible to fathom, had informed General Linares that the Americans intended to land an army at some point in eastern Cuba for the purpose of launching an attack on Santiago. He recommended the construction of coastal and inland batteries at both Santiago and Guantánamo to repel assaults by sea and to check any bands of Cubans that might operate in conjunction with the American forces. It was arranged for Linares to journey to Havana for conferences with the military leadership, but owing to the rapidity of diplomatic events in late April, this was not done.

After some correspondence between the two generals regarding transfer of the garrisons from Oriente's northeast coastal areas and Guantánamo to Santiago, it was decided to reinforce Guantánamo with three companies of the Cordoba Regiment from the northern region and to take from Guantánamo six companies, about 1,200 men, from the Talavera Regiment, to bolster the defenses of Santiago. Prior to the blockade of Santiago, no further efforts were made to reinforce its garrison, except to move a few companies of troops from the inland towns surrounding the city to positions around the harbor.

In early June, however, once Admiral Cervera had been firmly sealed in port by the blockade and it was evident that an American attack was coming, it was announced that two or three battalions would be ordered down from Holguín, a major provincial town seventy miles to the north. Announced but not done. At the same time, Linares considered moving a battalion of infantry, some mountain artillery, and engineers over from Guantánamo. This order was never effected either. Thus on the day the Americans landed, the Santiago garrison and its immediate environs counted but 12,096 men, augmented by 1,000 sailors landed from Cervera's ships and under the command of the chief of staff, Captain Joaquín Bustamante. The only reinforcements for Santiago, 3,600 troops, started out from Manzanillo on a ninety-mile trek the day of the Daiquirí landing, but appeared too late to influence affairs on the battlefield.[33]

Linares's operational plan of defense comprised two lines. The first, the beach line, started five miles west of the harbor mouth at Punta Cabrera and ran east along the coast twenty-two miles to Daiquirí, the far extremity of the position. The second extended inland to defend against the rebels and protect the railroads, water supply, and what remained of the cultivated zones to the north and northeast, from where the city obtained its produce—though there wasn't much of that, now nothing but some mangoes. Yet, because of the waterworks, Linares was compelled to hold this northern line in some strength against the rebels, rather than concentrating farther south and east, against the Americans coming up along the road from Siboney.

These "lines of observation," as they were called, were far too extensive for solid coverage and effective defense, and Linares frittered away sizable forces in a needlessly strong position in the rolling country on the west side of the harbor. Intuition and military astuteness should have told him the Americans would not attack from this direction, it having no direct access to Santiago on the opposite side of the bay. When the bulk of García's insurgent forces were secretly evacuated by the fleet from this area to Daiquirí, small detachments were left behind to harass the Spanish, and were completely successful in fooling Linares as to their strength, so much so, that 980 men of the Asia Regiment sat by uselessly, playing no part in the crucial battles that erupted east of the city. Besides these positions guarding the landward approaches, Linares needed to garrison the harbor forts on both sides of the entrance with upwards of a thousand men.

Toward the end of April, Spanish engineers assisted by the infantry began fortifying the eastern landward approaches in front of Santiago. These fieldworks on the San Juan heights, about four thousand yards in total length, consisted of two or three lines of trenches and breastworks protected in front by extensive barbed-wire entanglements and occupying the crests of the hills and ridges immediately surrounding the city. The trenches were deep and well excavated; in many cases the dirt had been carted away, so there was no sign of them visible to an observer even at a distance of five hundred yards. These lines were reinforced with the ubiquitous Spanish blockhouse at key points and were kept in mutual communication by heliograph.

Until the arrival of the American expedition, it was only their fleet that had been the antagonist, and powerful though it was, it threatened only the harbor entrance, and even there it was kept back by the minefield. But now a hostile army had appeared off Santiago, an army with field artillery and naval gunfire from a fleet that completely controlled the sea, enabling that army to be supplied and equipped without hindrance. Further, that invading army had the support of the Cuban rebels, who more or less controlled the countryside. Santiago was doomed, and Lieutenant Müller of the Spanish navy knew it. "We cannot hope for help either from within or without; we cannot hope for provisions [or] ammunition, and without these, the soldier[s] cannot be fed and cannot fight—a sad and desperate situation for men who ask for nothing else and whom fate seems to pursue."[34]

Following the American landing at Daiquirí and the advance to Siboney, Linares ordered the coastal garrisons east of Santiago moved inland and the mining region abandoned. The rear guard of this precipitate withdrawal, led by Brigadier General Antero Rubín, was ordered to concentrate on the *camino real* up from Siboney, along the ridge at Las Guásimas, having gathered all the small detachments in the blockhouses along the way, until the Spanish had slightly more than two thousand men in the position. In the decision to abandon the coast east of Santiago—indeed the whole mining district, excellent defensive territory where a good fight could have been made—General Linares somewhat lamely explained to his troops, "I did not wish to sacrifice your lives in vain in unequal battle, with musket fire, against the pompous superiority of the enemy, who was fighting under cover of his armored ships."[35]

While Linares had taken certain questionable defensive measures in preparation to receive the American advance, virtually nothing was done to provision the city of Santiago to withstand the rigors of war and siege. Nearly a month had passed between the declaration of war and the arrival of the first American warship off the port, but no food came in after April 25. This was inexcusable. There were several Spanish merchant vessels in the port, and Jamaica lay only 110 miles away. For at least three weeks following the declaration, these ships could have made the journey with near impunity, coming back laden with provisions. The Spanish authorities made only one attempt to send supplies into the city, a small schooner with a cargo of butter, potatoes, cornmeal, and onions, which was quickly peddled at wildly inflated prices. The German steamer *Palaria*, not wishing to run the Havana blockade, dropped off 1,700 sacks of rice at Santiago, and that was the end of provisions until the city capitulated. By the time the American expeditionary force arrived at Daiquirí, Santiago was down to 180,000 rations of flour, 197,000 of rice, 149,000 of chickpeas, 79,000 of kidney beans, 96,000 of wine, and 150 cattle on the hoof. The army alone required 360,000 rations a month. This was apart from Cervera's two thousand sailors, who had come short-rationed to begin with, and a civilian population of thirty thousand people. This left the army, navy, and civilians on very short rations. The starvation that quickly ensued turned the city into a typhus pesthole. Lieutenant Müller saw dogs and other animals just drop dead in the street, "and the worst thing was that their carcasses were not removed. I also saw . . . a dog throw himself upon a smaller one and devour him."[36]

The army eventually saw its rations reduced to rice "bread" and rice boiled in water, which, Müller said, "the soldiers could not stand." After May 29, with the port permanently blockaded, it was clear that both the army and the population were cut off from any succor for as long as the war lasted, and must inevitably capitulate or starve. In his defense, given this situation it is difficult to see how General Linares could have concentrated more men from outlying towns than he already had in the city and its immediate environs; he simply had nothing to feed them with.[37]

In the Alameda, the city's central park, military bands played on Sunday evenings to keep up the spirits of the populace. The Plaza de Armas, where the troops formed for parades on Thursdays and Sundays, always drew large crowds. "People fond of giving sensational news, especially those who took pleasure in inventing it," Müller observed, "had a wide field and plenty of material to satisfy their desire." Children played at war, pelting each other with stones, "divided into parties in command of a Cervera of ten summers or a Sampson of twelve Aprils." The various corps of volunteers swelled with citizens flushed with martial ardor. "The city," said Müller, "was full of sabres, machetes, stars, and galloons. . . . Even the clerks of the guardhouse and employees of the Civil Guard armed themselves with carbines and machetes." Müller believed that not even in Berlin, the world's most military city, were there more uniforms about in the streets.[38]

A collection fad developed in the city—the buying, selling, and trading of unexploded ordnance from the American naval bombardments. People, Müller said, sought them as souvenirs "of an event which does not happen often in a lifetime." Some collected only small-caliber ordnance, 6-pounder shells and the like; others sought only those of 8 inches and above; still others "wanted to make a collection of all sizes." As the bombardments continued through June, "people began hearing them all the time; the falling of a chair, the closing of a door or window, the noise of carriage wheels in the distance, the crying of a child—everything was taken for gunshots."[39]

According to General Shafter's orders—actually written to Lawton, but also addressed for the sake of unforeseen contingencies to the "senior officer at the front," which happened to be Wheeler, the expedition's deputy commander—the Cavalry Division was supposed to follow Lawton's infantry to Siboney. While Lawton advanced up the *camino real* in the direction of Santiago, Wheeler was to remain in the town and supervise the rest of the landing. But Wheeler interpreted the order creatively; he was, after all, the "senior officer at the front." Aside from that, said a friend, Wheeler never stayed in one place long enough "for the Almighty to put a finger on him." In his own words, the ex-Confederate cavalry general held an intense desire to be the first to meet "the Yankees—dammit, I mean the Spaniards."[40]

Wheeler, accompanied by his aides and some Cubans of Castillo's division, rode ahead of everyone, indeed even Lawton's advance guard, along the trail from Daiquirí to Siboney. Arriving at the village just as the Spanish withdrew up the *camino real,* he discovered the enemy moving into position along the ridge at Las Guásimas. With Castillo's assistance, he conducted a reconnaissance of the area and determined to attack the enemy as early as possible the following morning, the twenty-fourth. Castillo promised eight hundred men to assist in the fight. From Daiquirí, Wheeler ordered forward to Siboney Brigadier General Samuel Young's 2nd Cavalry Brigade, consisting of the 1st and 10th regulars and the Rough Riders.

In midafternoon, the Rough Riders, bringing up the rear of the brigade, began their march. Lieutenant Colonel Roosevelt, in command of the 1st Squadron, found it a hard one. The regiment was not in the best of shape for the trek. Many of the men being cowboys and ranchers—over two hundred of them—most had never done much walking. "The heat was intense," TR remembered, "and their burdens very heavy." Yet there was very little straggling. Colonel Wood kept up a fast pace, for he was determined to get ahead of the other regiments "so as to be sure of our place in the body that struck the enemy next morning." Junior officers tramped alongside their men, encouraging them by example. Private Ogden Wells of D Troop noted in his diary the furnacelike sun, and that the "packs were like lead. At last we could stand it no longer and we began to throw away our blankets; after the blankets went cans of meat, then our coats and underclothes, until some only had their guns and ammunition left, for these were essentials." It was nightfall by the time the regiment slogged into squalid Siboney, Wood positioning it at the very front of the brigade command. Too exhausted to sort the men into proper formation for a night bivouac with an enemy less than three miles away, Roosevelt said, "we simply drew the men up in column of troops, and let each man lie down where he was."[41]

It was the onset of the rainy season and black thunder clouds gathered, but the men had time to boil coffee and fry some bacon and hardtack for dinner. "The officers, of course," wrote TR, "fared just as the men did." Hardly had the regiment finished eating when the rains came. Officers and men sheltered themselves as best they could for the two hours the tropical deluge lasted; "then the fires were relighted and we closed around them, the men taking off their wet things to dry them, as far as possible, by the blaze."[42]

Brigadier General Antero Rubín, after concentrating his forces and brushing off several bothersome ambushes by Castillo, arrived at the Las Guásimas position early on the twenty-third to find Linares waiting for him. Las Guásimas, with the deserted hamlet of Sevilla just behind it, had once been a fairly busy community, but was now a godforsaken overgrown ridgeline after three years of revolution. The place was identified only as the junction of the *camino real* that crossed the ridge on the way to Santiago and a jungle footpath that paralleled the road a mile to the westward. As a defensive location, it could not have offered the Spanish better. The ridge, with a jutting salient in the center, covered both the road and the path at right angles against any attacker approaching Santiago directly inland from Siboney. The lay of the land permitted enfilading fire from hidden positions, which were reinforced by stone breastworks flanked by small blockhouses.

Linares and Rubín stationed their forces in three lines. The first, just forward of the road-footpath junction, its left on the road and its right extending across the path into the jungle, incorporated three companies of the Puerto Rico Provisional Battalion and one of *voluntarios* in a strong natural site along the ridge itself. The second line, three companies of the San Fernando Regiment, one of railroad troops, 80 *guerrilleros,* and two rapid-fire field guns, deployed on the flat ground behind the first position in front of the ruined houses of Sevilla. The third line, a mile and a half farther back and sited at the hamlet of Redonda on the *camino real,* was formed of five companies of the Talavera Regiment, one *voluntario* company, and perhaps 30 mounted *guerrilleros.* In all, the Spanish defenders at Las Guásimas amounted to 2,078 men.[43]

Linares remained at Las Guásimas for only a short time before retiring to establish his field headquarters at El Pozo ("the well") on the *camino real,* roughly midway between Las Guásimas and Santiago. The Spanish forces had scarcely taken their positions in the morning when Castillo, who had constantly harried Rubín during his retrograde movement to Las Guásimas, attempted to envelop the first line on the ridge, but he was easily beaten back. A second Cuban attempt was made in the afternoon, but with artillery support from their rapid-fire guns, the Spanish achieved the same result, throwing Castillo back down the road toward Siboney.

In the meantime, Linares grew apprehensive lest the Americans push westward from Siboney along the coastal railroad to Aguadores and, with naval gunfire support, force a crossing of the San Juan River. From there they could march inland, up the railroad to Las Cruces on the bay, which formed virtually the southern suburbs of Santiago, between the city and the harbor forts. This fear so took hold of Linares's thoughts that he illogically decided to abandon the strong position at Las Guásimas and further withdraw his forces into the entrenched barbed-wire lines immediately in front of Santiago that centered on the ridge on either side of a rise known as San Juan Hill.

On the evening of June 23, Linares ordered Rubín to withdraw from Las Guásimas the next day. He had sent to Santiago for a mule train and carts, which, he informed Rubín, would be at Sevilla sometime that evening. Immediately on their arrival, Rubín must have his sick, wounded, and supplies ready to move to Santiago with the pack train escort. Rubín's movement orders dictated that the withdrawal commence after breakfast the following morning. He was to march with his whole command to Santiago, reporting to new positions in and around San Juan Hill. Anticipating an enemy attack at the same moment as he began his retreat—a very dangerous situation—Rubín brought up two companies of the Talavera Regiment from his third line as reinforcements along the ridge at Las Guásimas and began preparations to evacuate his sick and wounded.[44]

On his arrival at Siboney on the evening of the twenty-third, General Young sought out Wheeler and from him learned of the rearguard engagement between Castillo and the retiring Spaniards earlier in the day. Castillo, who was present at several of these informal councils of war, thought the Spanish would likely fall back on Santiago during the night. But he had also received word from his advance scouts that the enemy, rather than continuing their withdrawal, were, in fact, reinforcing their rear guard at Las Guásimas. Young deemed it essential that he obtain positive intelligence of the position and movements of the enemy to his front and asked Wheeler for permission to conduct a reconnaissance up the *camino real* and its parallel path as far along as Sevilla early the next morning. Castillo promised to assist the operation by providing 800 men.

It was Young's plan to advance along the *camino real* with one squadron each of the 1st and the 10th cavalry, having for support a battery of four Hotchkiss quick-firing mountain guns, a total, less the gunners, of 464 men. For the advance up the parallel trail a mile westward, Young detailed the two squadrons of Wood's Rough Riders, about 500 men, with two mule-packed Colt machine guns. Wood was to keep a sharp lookout, to open fire on the enemy when encountered, and, once engaged, to connect his right flank in the gap between the trail and Young's left on the road, while at the same time extending his own left into the jungle in an attempt to turn the enemy's right flank.

When Lawton got wind of Wheeler's projected movement, he attempted to contact General Shafter and have it annulled. This was partly out of pique at having been outfoxed by the diminutive "Fighting Joe" in who would meet the enemy first. Shafter, however, was still aboard the *Segurança,* and sea conditions made it impossible to communicate by small boat in the time remaining. Still, it had clearly been General Shafter's intention that Lawton, not Wheeler, have temporary command ashore; the "senior officer present" order was merely a contingency should Lawton become incapacitated or made temporarily absent, and was not meant to replace his authority with Wheeler's.

In an order written from the *Segurança* on June 23, but not seen by divisional commanders until sometime following the skirmish at Las Guásimas, General Shafter made it plain to his immediate subordinates that he considered it "impossible" to advance any distance on Santiago until adequate supplies had been accumulated on the beach dumps. Until then, the commanders were to establish strong positions near a good water supply, "and make yourselves secure from surprise or attack." As for the position of the units, the somewhat hazy order dictated that Lawton, supported by Brigadier John Bates's independent brigade, "will be in front" (westward along the railroad toward Aguadores or north, facing Las Guásimas, it did not say). Kent's 1st Division, then landing at Siboney, would take position in and "near" the village, while Wheeler's dismounted cavalry remained "near" Daiquirí. Horsed or not, the Cavalry Division, more lightly equipped than the infantry and schooled in scouting and reconnaissance, should have been given the advance position in front of Siboney, with orders to gain contact with the enemy. The ancient horse soldier Wheeler understood this and, upon his old, skinny shoulders, assumed the responsibility of realigning the corps, at least as far as the Cavalry Division was concerned.[45]

Young's brigade was shaken out of its blankets at 3:00 A.M., many of the men having to put on wet clothes from the night before, bolting down a breakfast of coffee, bacon, and hardtack. The tough Indian-fighting regulars of the 1st and 10th took it all in stride, but it took nearly three hours for the Rough Riders to get ready as they had almost no field training to prepare them for this sort of operation. At 5:45 Young, astride a mule, led the column of regulars out of Siboney up the *camino real*. The road had been there at least fifty years, and perhaps originally deserved the name, being adequate for wagons of any size all the way to Santiago nine miles to the northwest. But now, like everything else in Cuba, it had fallen into disrepair and was passable to nothing more than horses, cattle, and two-wheeled carts. The marshy valley up which the road meandered to the Cobre hills was spotted with stagnant pools and lined with sparse clumps of coconut palms. The air was hot and close, clouded with mosquitoes, and branded by the foul, rank stink of decaying vegetation.

Wood started the Rough Riders up the path fifteen minutes after Young's regulars moved out. They exited Siboney, swinging along in column of fours, but before the huts were out of sight, the regiment stretched out into single file. Wood and two correspondents, Edward Marshall of the *New York Journal* and Richard Harding Davis of *Scribner's*, were mounted. Roosevelt at the head of his squadron, just behind Wood's command group, walked, leading his horse Texas. At the top of the first rise, they came upon an outpost of the 22nd Infantry, Lawton's point unit on the trail, who reported the Spanish definitely at Las Guásimas, because they had heard them felling trees all night and strengthening their positions. The going became tougher as the path led through thick underbrush, covered by swarms of flies, gnats, beetles, and land crabs: "a footway walled in barbed wire," said a historian of the regiment.[46]

At 7:30, Young halted his column in an open glade. While the men rested, a small scouting party went forward and discovered the enemy entrenched behind their stone breastworks. They were a little to the left of front, some in rifle pits, some stretched out in the heavy jungle, some off in the remains of what was once a large ranch. Blockhouses flanked the whole position. Young brought up his Hotchkiss guns, placing them nine hundred yards from the ridge, and deployed his men in open order of skirmishers, the 1st Cavalry to the front, the 10th in support. But to allow Wood, who had a much more difficult march, time to come parallel, Young delayed the attack a few minutes, sending a Cuban guide across the ravine that separated the regulars from the Rough Riders, "in order that the development on both flanks should begin simultaneously." Of Castillo's promised eight hundred Cubans, there was not a sign. The Cuban general had decided to sleep in that morning and could not be disturbed. During this brief intermission, Wheeler rode up to Young's side, surveyed the ground, and made no changes in the dispositions. Young took the time to examine the enemy through his glasses and, as Wheeler noted, "prepared to develop his strength."[47]

Wheeler, surveying the Spanish lines, had seen occasional straw hats along the ridge and was in some doubt as to whether they were indeed the enemy, or Cubans. He suggested opening fire with the Hotchkiss guns. At 8:00 A.M., Young gave the order, and Wheeler got his answer. "The fire," he said, was very different from what I had seen before. Thirty-three years ago we fought at short range. Here we commenced at 700 or 800 yards." The Spanish replied with volleys, so frequent and hot on the Hotchkiss guns that Young was forced to order them under cover for a time. "The fire of the enemy," Young said, "was almost entirely by volleys, executed with the precision of parade." The ground he had to cover to reach the ridge was a mass of jungle growth, with barbed-wire fences that remained unseen until tripped over. "It was impossible for troops to keep touch along the front, and they could only judge the position of the enemy from the

sound and direction of his fire." The first line of the 1st Cavalry returned fire on the yet unseen foe. Young rode on his mule along the
front, exhorting, "Don't shoot until you see something to shoot at."[48]

The men obeyed, and fire discipline was excellent. But as the 1st
Cavalry wriggled forward, the 10th did likewise, and both became entangled in the same firing line, until confusion was nearly complete. But
the regulars did not hesitate. Suffering some casualties, the two regiments, which eventually counted eight dead and eighteen wounded, advanced forward toward the Spanish positions in the terrible heat of the
jungle battlefield. Finally, close under the enemy's guns, they opened a
heavy fire and charged to the crest of the ridge. "Our lines advanced
very rapidly to the top of the hill," remembered the first sergeant of the
10th Cavalry's E Troop. "All this time the Spaniards kept up a heavy
and terrific fire on our lines." But once the ridge was carried, the Spanish breaking pell-mell for the rear, Young's men, though utterly exhausted, occupied the ground. Had a force of mounted cavalry been at
hand, he reported, "the fruits of our victory would have been more apparent."[49]

A good part of that victory was due to the action of the Rough
Riders, fighting unseen across the jungle ravine to Young's left. Wood
set a punishing pace, fearing his arrival at the junction of the trail
and the road would be too late for him to effect a flanking attack. Before the regiment had gone two miles, the strain on the men was evident, and blanket rolls, knapsacks, and the occasional man fell from
the column. "At the time," said Roosevelt, "I was rather inclined to
grumble to myself about Wood setting so fast a pace, but when the
fight began I realized that it had been absolutely necessary, as otherwise we would have arrived late and the regulars would have had
very hard work indeed."[50]

About twenty minutes after starting out, Wood stationed Captain
Allyn Capron Jr.'s L Troop as the regimental advance guard. A no-
nonsense, scientific, professional soldier, Capron was the son of
Captain Allyn Capron Sr., who commanded an artillery battery in Lawton's division. Capron appointed Sergeant Hamilton Fish, the biggest
man in the regiment, along with four men, to serve as the point. Following L Troop came Wood and his staff, then the rest of the command
in single file. So narrow and dense was the trail that it was impossible
to place flankers on either side of the march, for they could not possi-

bly keep pace with the column. At the very head, one or perhaps two Cuban guides scouted warily.[51]

The march continued for over an hour, with short rest stops when Capron came hurrying back along the trail. Wood halted the column at a slight rise and rode forward, passing the word back along the column to keep silence in the ranks. He then went ahead with Capron and disappeared into the jungle. Ten minutes later the two men reappeared on the trail, both very anxious to start the regiment moving. The Cuban guides had come across a dead Spanish *guerrillero* on the trail. According to Castillo's intelligence, the enemy had to be close by, probably less than five hundred yards away. Wood called his squadron commanders and staff, pointing to where a good eye could just make out the Spanish earthworks in the bush. Orders were passed down the line to load the Krag carbines, which none in the regiment had ever fired before. Wood ordered Roosevelt to deploy with three troops of his 1st Squadron to the right of the trail and advance. Wood deployed the 2nd Squadron to the left, where the ground was somewhat more open. One troop was held in general reserve in the center, "and the command," Wood noted in his report, was "ordered to advance carefully."[52]

The regiment had barely begun its movement when General Young opened the battle to the right with his Hotchkiss guns; then a crash to the immediate front of the Rough Riders announced the fight was on and evidently very hot. The Spanish opened a terrible volley on the advance-guard L Troop, killing Captain Capron and Sergeant Fish in the first shots. The Cuban guides at the head of the column disappeared, as did the Cuban muleteers with the Colt machine guns at the rear of the column, leaving the animals to wander about on the fringes of the battle. Roosevelt, seeing L Troop hotly engaged—indeed nearly ambushed—"hurried my men abreast of them," across a barbed-wire fence into the ravine that separated the Rough Riders from the regulars.[53]

"Perhaps a dozen of Roosevelt's men had passed into the thicket before he did," wrote Edward Marshall of the *New York Journal* in a prophetic article. "Then he stepped across the wire himself. . . . It was as if that barbed-wire strand had formed a dividing line in his life, and that when he stepped across it he left behind him in the . . . path all those unadmirable and conspicuous traits which have so often caused him to be justly criticized in civic life, and found on the other side of it, in that Cuban thicket, the coolness, the calm judgment, the towering heroism, which made him, perhaps, the most admired and best beloved of all Americans in Cuba." Marshall would write these words from a wheelchair; he was shot in the spine and rendered a paraplegic at Las Guásimas.[54]

Roosevelt moved right into the bush, but due to the Spanish use of smokeless powder, he could not tell where their fire came from—all he knew was they were not as close as had first been thought and were much higher in elevation than his own men. Seconds later, the jungle parted and TR found himself in a clearing looking out at the *camino real*, with Young's column under heavy fire below and to the right. The Spanish, though, still remained invisible. Their Mauser bullets flew over the heads of the Rough Riders with a disconcerting buzz, and men instinctively hunched their shoulders, ducking their heads as they moved slowly forward. Wood, in this action, received the nickname "Old Icebox" for his utter contempt of personal danger. One trooper remembered that at no time during the action at Las Guásimas "did I see Teddy Roosevelt or Wood in a prone position. Both of these officers stood up at all times to observe the deployment of troops and the enemy through binoculars."[55]

Calling up his last troop, Wood gave the order to advance very slowly. Coming up to a small blockhouse, they drove the Spanish out of a strong position in the rocks. By now they were able to distinguish the enemy three hundred yards to their front. The Spanish volleys doubled in their intensity, and here the Rough Riders took most of their eight killed and thirty-one wounded for the day. Up to Roosevelt's side came a panting Richard Harding Davis, armed with a carbine, and he pointed up the ravine onto the ridge. "There they are, Colonel, look over there, I can see their hats near that glade." Roosevelt examined the position through his binoculars and gave the order, "Rapid fire!" The Spanish, now under the twin fires of the regulars and the Rough Riders, quit their first line, hightailed it farther up the ridge, and ran to another spot. TR said, "[N]ow we could make out a large number of them."[56]

Though Roosevelt did not fully realize it, he had performed extremely well. By engaging and driving back the enemy's center, he had exposed their forces holding the top of the ridge to a cross fire from the rest of the Rough Riders on the left and frontal fire from the regulars on the right. The way was now open for a general advance of the whole line.

After they had driven the enemy from their initial position, the firing died down in front of Roosevelt's men, though not along the rest of the front. In a few minutes Roosevelt spied a body of troops crossing the ravine from where the Rough Riders had just driven the enemy. They were quickly made out as Young's men extending the line into the center. Not wishing to get fired on by friendly forces, Roosevelt ordered a sergeant to climb a tree and wave the troop guidon; immediately, one of the regulars did the same, and thus contact was established on the inner flanks. Roosevelt, however, unable to pursue the foe because of the impenetrable viny growth directly to his front, left two troops to hold the center and took G Troop back to the left by the trail where fighting was still in progress. He was very uncertain where the main body of the enemy was holed up and of what he should do, "but I knew it could not be wrong to go forward." He badly needed to find Wood and get new orders, for he "was in a mood to cordially welcome guidance."[57]

He hadn't seen Wood since the beginning of the fight, when some of the men had begun cursing at the Spanish fire and Wood had growled, "Don't swear—shoot!" When Roosevelt led G Troop back to the path he found the bulk of the regiment spread out in a thin skirmish line, advancing over comparatively open ground, each man taking advantage of what cover he could find, while Wood, "Old Icebox," strolled about the field, leading his horse. Major Alexander Brodie of the 2nd Squadron, who had commanded the left at the beginning of the action, had been badly wounded, and Roosevelt, on Wood's command, now took charge of the regiment's left flank, with orders to continue the advance; "so over I went."[58]

Roosevelt now commanded the left, Wood the center, and Wheeler the right flank on the *camino real*. On the bugle order "Charge!" nine hundred dismounted cavalrymen broke cover and swarmed up the ravine. Well spread out, Roosevelt, with troops D, E, and F, advanced through the high grass of an open forest. "A perfect hail of bullets was sweeping over us as we advanced." Taking fire from the deserted ranch to their right, TR grabbed a carbine from a wounded man and tried some shots himself. The sun blistered down and the men were exhausted. The bush became thicker, and Roosevelt lost contact with Wood in the center. He ordered a halt and began firing into the ranch. Then came cheering from the right, which he supposed was Wood's charge, "so I sprang up and ordered the men to rush the buildings ahead of us." A moment of heavy firing from the enemy, all of which went high, and then silence. Panting and out of breath, TR's men found nothing but a pile, actually heaps, of empty Mauser cartridges and two dead Spaniards, shot through the head.[59]

"Like ants shaken from a biscuit," said one of Roosevelt's biographers, the Spaniards had leaped from their rocky defenses and bolted for Santiago. Wheeler, the wizened old Confederate, stood up in his stirrups. "We've got the damn Yankees on the run!" he wheezed in a thin yell. For a very brief time the Spanish attempted to form another line by the village of Sevilla, but this too broke. "Large masses of them were seen to retreat rapidly," Wood noted in his report, "and we were able to distinguish parties carrying litters of wounded men."

Wood ordered his men in the center to cease fire, advance, and take the ground. What remained of any Spanish resistance between Sevilla and the hamlet of La Redonda, another mile and a half further along the road, collapsed. The Rough Riders halted, and physical contact was established with Young's left. The skirmish had been won. But as Wood said, "[O]ur troops were too much exhausted and overcome with heat and hard work" to continue the pursuit to the very outskirts of Santiago, which they might have done had fresh reserves been immediately available. "I think," Wood continued, "we could have captured a large portion of their forces, as they seemed completely disheartened and dispirited." Spanish losses amounted to ten dead and twenty-four wounded.[60]

On the left of the Rough Rider line, the extreme left of the American position, the firing had died out, but Roosevelt, who commanded here, was still entirely ignorant of what had occurred in the center and the right. He did not know whether this was just a lull in the fight, whether he might be attacked by the Spanish volleys again, or if the enemy had indeed run for it. A straggler came up with the disconcerting news that Wood had been killed, which meant the regimental command now devolved upon Roosevelt's shoulders. Assuming the worst, TR hastily set about taking charge. He ordered pickets out to the front and the left, sent men to fill canteens, and dispersed the forces immediately in his purview in a long line in the defile of a sunken trail that provided some cover should the Spanish reopen fire. The broken-down ranch buildings he hastily converted into a battlefield aid station, placing inside a dozen wounded and those suffering from heat exhaustion. He then started moving toward the center, where he found Wood very much alive, and also reinforcements—the 9th Cavalry and units from Lawton's division coming up at the run along the trail and road. Brigadier Adna Chaffee, puffing at the head of his brigade, was "rather glum," TR noticed, "at not having been in the fight."[61]

According to one account, Lawton was so furious at being usurped as commander of the van that he accused Wheeler of deliberately circumventing his authority. "I was given command of the advance," he reportedly said, "and I want you to know that I propose to keep it, by God, even if I have to put a guard to keep other troops in the rear." Wheeler shrugged his bony shoulders; truthfully, he had never seen Shafter's position order keeping the Cavalry Division at Daiquirí. But like the good soldier he was, he had discerned an opportunity and had taken it. In any event, the seizure of Las Guásimas and the villages beyond it provided far better and more extensive camping grounds for the corps, with a good supply of water, than the cramped, swampy area around Siboney. Almost immediately, Bates's independent brigade moved up, then Brigadier Hamilton Hawkins's 1st Brigade of Kent's 1st Division. Two days later came the remainder of Kent's forces, along with the mounted squadron of the 2nd Cavalry and two batteries of light artillery.[62]

On General Antero Rubín's failure to repel the American attack, General Linares took personal command at El Pozo, covering the rout of his troops with artillery until Rubín's entire force passed into the Santiago lines. The fact that General Linares had no intention of making a determined stand at Las Guásimas, after giving up the landing beaches without the slightest opposition, better than anything thus far indicated the extremely poor quality of Spanish generalship. Had Wheeler not been so quick on the march, there would have been no skirmish. But equally, had Linares determined to hold the position, bringing on the battlefield the two thousand–plus men he had in the immediate vicinity, it might have taken all of Wheeler's and Lawton's divisions to dislodge them.

Having failed to contest the landings from the heights overlooking
the beaches, Linares should have resolved to make his second stand at
Las Guásimas and fight a battle for Santiago. Tactically, the Las Guásimas position was a very strong one, with its range of hills and ridges
almost at right angles to the road and trail. Had the position been occupied in force and a determined stand made, the bulk of the Fifth
Corps, while waiting for the necessary supplies to unload over open
beaches preparatory to the formal attack, would have been compelled
to occupy a very cramped position around Siboney with much difficulty in supplying the whole command with adequate water.

The Las Guásimas site was also of great strategic importance. Had
Linares massed his forces there, behind stone breastworks, flanked by
blockhouses—all of which were already in place—General Shafter
could not possibly have advanced on Santiago, either by the coastal
road to Aguadores, which would leave the enemy on his right flank,
or frontally through Las Guásimas, until he had driven the enemy
from that position by a frontal attack on a very limited expanse. So
long as the Las Guásimas position was held by the Spanish, the Americans were powerless to intercept any reinforcements that might come
from Guantánamo or Holguín should the Spanish bestir themselves
to move from that direction. Moreover, holding Las Guásimas kept
safe the water supply of Santiago at the reservoir at Cubitas north of
the city.

Once Las Guásimas was given up, it was clear marching for the
Americans all the way to El Pozo, halfway to the city, where there was
good, well-watered ground to camp the corps. There was neither difficulty nor risk for Linares in concentrating at least double the forces
originally at Las Guásimas. Had he understood there was hardly a
Cuban rebel west of Santiago, and virtually none in the cultivated region, he could have moved the entire Asia Regiment into the Las
Guásimas area, and still have left more than sufficient garrisons in the
harbor forts and at Aguadores to prevent any enemy movement in
that direction, which would have been extremely difficult in any case
while he held the line at Las Guásimas.

As it was, Linares did none of these things, and the action at Las
Guásimas provided a sharp morale boost to the American forces. No
one in the American command maintained the slightest notion that
they had caught the Spanish in the middle of a retreat. What they saw,

and experienced, was a nearly three-hour fierce struggle against a sturdy enemy who seemed very anxious to hold his ground, and indeed could have, if his senior officers been worthy of their rank. At the beginning of a campaign, nothing inspires a soldier more than a victory; nothing is more depressing than a defeat. The American expeditionary force had been given a present of the beaches and, at minimal cost, the road to Santiago.

CHAPTER 12

SAN JUAN HILL

The heights must be taken at all hazards. A retreat now would
mean a disastrous defeat.
—*Lieutenant John D. Miley, aide-de-camp
to General Shafter, July 1, 1898*

For six days after Las Guásimas, the army rested in bivouac while
General Shafter looked after his supplies, which quickly became as
large a problem as the enemy before him. The Fifth Corps had been
organized and equipped for a campaign in the open country around
Havana, with relatively good roads and use of the sheltered harbor of
Mariel for landing men, equipment, and stores. None of this was
available at Santiago. Daiquirí and Siboney in comparison were mere
clusters of huts in an indentation of shoreline that offered some difficult access to the interior, nothing more; they were by no means even
sheltered anchorages. Every bullet and biscuit had to come in over
open beaches, often through high surf.

Movement through the hinterland was all but impossible for large
bodies of troops unless they kept to the bad roads and trails. There
was but a single direct road from Siboney to Santiago, the execrable
camino real, over which the entire army and its baggage had to pass.
At best it was nearly impassable for the heavy six-mule army wagons.
The daily rains that began about a week after the army landed
blocked the road with flooding streams and transformed whole sections, where wagons sank to their axles.

Neither on land nor at sea did General Shafter have the transportation or equipment to overcome these obstacles. In response to his repeated pleas, the War Department began chartering additional tugs, sending them to the war zone with barges in tow. Most of the barges were wrecked in the surf, and during the greater part of the campaign, the Fifth Corps was reduced to one steam lighter, the indispensable *Laura,* to land rations, ammunition, wagons, and other heavy equipment. Of the two hundred wagons brought along, perhaps half remained in the ships' holds because the Cuban roads could not handle them, and there were not enough landing craft to bring them ashore anyway.

After Las Guásimas, many of the troops had been off the transports for three days and the rations they carried had been nearly consumed. As the wagons were still being unloaded and set up on the beaches, details from individual units, with a mule or two, were ordered into Siboney to carry out as many rations as possible. By June 25, however, mule pack trains were completely fitted out and began carrying food to the troops up the *camino real* from Siboney and Daiquirí. The orders cut over General Shafter's signature parceled twenty-five six-mule wagons and one mule pack train of seventy-five animals per division, five wagons to Bates's independent brigade, and fifteen wagons and one pack train as the Fifth Corps ammunition detachment. One wagon was allotted to each cavalry troop, one to each of the four light artillery batteries. The remaining wagons and one pack train remained the province of corps headquarters.

Much delay was experienced with the big wagons, because they had been broken down at Tampa for loading aboard ship, and now had to be assembled on the beaches. So long as the troops were close to Siboney, it was thought the pack trains alone could carry enough rations, and during June 24 and 25, efforts were made to get more men ashore rather than wagons and supplies. But relying primarily on the mules was soon found to be insufficient, especially as Brigadier General H. M. Duffield's Michigan brigade of four thousand reinforcements was expected daily. Urgent orders were issued to Colonel Humphrey, the corps quartermaster, to unload sixty wagons without regard to anything else needed and erect them at Daiquirí. Loaded with rations and forage, they were sent in equal measure to the divisions.

The original plan of assigning wagons to individual divisions proved unsatisfactory. All the wagon teaming, as well as the mule packing, had to be done on the single road leading inland from Siboney, and with transportation divided into independent wagon and mule trains, directed by as many different individuals, confusion and delay were the inevitable result. When Duffield's brigade landed on June 27, it brought with it two additional pack trains, and a complete reassignment of transportation was made. Two pack trains were given to each division, one to Bates's independent brigade, and all the rest of the transportation—wagons and mules alike—was placed under the command of a single officer, Captain Edward Plummer of the 10th Infantry. All wagons were assigned to corps headquarters, where communications existed in every direction, and subdepots were established for forage, rations, and ammunition. Plummer received his instructions directly from General Shafter, and transportation and supplies were dispatched to where they were needed most.

If this plan for supplying the entire command had worked, the troops would have had ample stores of every kind. But the *camino real* soon became blocked by wagons stalled in the mud or breaking down, delaying the entire operation into the night, and sometimes even the next day. There were barely enough wagons and mule trains for the corps under favorable conditions. Streams near the front beyond Las Guásimas rose after the daily rains and could not be forded until the next day, forcing the loaded wagon trains to spend the night hitched on the road. Teamsters and muleteers soon began contracting malaria and dysentery, and these conditions were serious enough to further impair the supply system. Sick teamsters were generally replaced by soldiers who could handle a six-mule team, but it was not so easy to replace a mule packer, who required training, not to say a certain patient disposition. It forced General Shafter to limit severely the amount and type of supplies sent up to the troops, now basically restricted to ammunition, medical stores, hardtack, canned meat, and coffee. Everything else, including the heavy artillery, was left either on the beach or aboard ship.

As the men became adversely affected by the climate, so too did the horses and mules. "Day by day," said Shafter's aide, Lieutenant Miley, "these animals sickened and became unserviceable, but often kept going until they dropped in their tracks." They also quickly wore out their shoes. Within a week of landing, Shafter telegraphed the War Department for six thousand pounds of mule shoes and four hundred pounds of nails.[1]

It was soon apparent that only the most basic elements of the ration—hardtack, tinned meat, coffee, and sugar—could be provided to the troops with any certainty. Whenever possible the rest of the ration—bacon, potatoes, onions, and canned tomatoes—was brought forward, but doing so sorely interfered with the ability to supply the four basic items. There were instances when individual regiments, usually the volunteers, found themselves without any rations for a day or more, although this was the result of their commanders or quartermasters not making proper arrangements to draw sufficient for three days at a time.

Theodore Roosevelt wrote of the deprivation: "We were not quite given the proper amount of food, and what we did get, like most of the clothing issued us, was fitter for the Klondike than for Cuba. We got enough salt pork and hardtack for the men, but not the full ration of coffee and sugar, and nothing else." Requisitioning a wandering mule on his own, TR organized a few unofficial expeditions to Siboney to expropriate some stores and brought back beans and canned tomatoes. Recalling the episodes, he wrote, "A silly regulation forbade my purchasing canned vegetables, etc., except for the officers; and I had no little difficulty in getting round this regulation, and purchasing (with my own money, of course) what I needed for the men."[2]

Captain Chadwick in his history of the war also pointed to the necessity of something more than biscuit and canned meat, the three "primal necessaries for the well-being and contentment" of the troops being onions, potatoes, and tobacco; "on these with bacon the soldier and sailor can live and be happy." Of the lot, he ranked tobacco first. Men, he said, "should never be called upon to undergo the nervous strain of a campaign without a full supply of this most essential element of their content and well being." The want of almost anything else would have occasioned less grumbling in the ranks. Correspondent Richard Harding Davis agreed. "The men before Santiago, who were forced to go without their stimulant for four days, suffered just as greatly as a dipsomaniac who is cut off from alcohol. Regulars paid two dollars for a plug which usually cost them eight cents. Those who could not get tobacco at all smoked dried grass, roots, and dry manure."[3]

There was some attempt to improve the *camino real*. For the first few days after the landing, Bates's brigade furnished work details clearing out boulders and filling in some of the more atrocious holes. This job was soon turned over to the engineer battalion, which up until June 27 had been engaged in building piers at Aserraderos and Siboney. Additional men were provided by the volunteer regiments. Brush was cleared from both sides of the road, the swampy portions were corded with palm logs, drainage was improved, and some new trails were cut as sidings for damaged wagons. A few small bridges and culverts were constructed with what material came to hand. Had the engineers been able to bridge the larger streams, they would have greatly improved the capacity of the road. But this and all other work was hampered by lack of any transportation for the engineer battalion. They had brought none with them and received none on their arrival. Not being able to transport it, they left their bridging gear aboard the steamer *Alamo*.

Thus the Fifth Corps would exist in a sort of self-imposed privation: fighting its subsequent battles and siege on scanty and monotonous rations, sleeping in dog tents, if they were lucky, and cooking in their individual mess gear and the odd pot because the company cookstoves were not brought up to the front. If they fell sick or wounded, they received the merest attention from one ill-equipped, understaffed field hospital. In battle they would assault fortified positions supported only by Gatling guns and obsolete, nearly useless light field pieces. Most everything needed to remedy this situation lay a few hundred yards offshore, in the holds of the steamers, for lack of anything to bring the matériel ashore, or once there, to carry it to the front. Significant amounts of gear and stores stayed on board until after the war, the ships returning home with these items. In one instance, a shipload of tropical uniforms, enough to outfit the entire corps, arrived at Siboney on July 10 and lay untouched for two weeks while the troops sweltered in their woolen trousers and flannel shirts.

The health of the command, however, remained excellent for a time. The regimental camps were set up by streams that supplied abundant good water, and the food supply, if monotonous, was at least steady after the first few chaotic days. The successful action at Las Guásimas raised troop morale, and the whole command was keen for another battle, little realizing the desperate fight that lay ahead.

On June 26, Shafter, who still commanded afloat from the *Segu-rança,* sent a note to Sampson outlining in general terms his plan of op-erations. "I mean to advance on the road from Sevilla Wednesday [June 30], without fail toward Santiago." He intended to put a "large force" into the village of El Caney, northeast of the city on the Santiago-Guantánamo road, and another contingent farther west near Cubitas in the cultivated region athwart the city's water pipeline, "making my attack from the northeast and east." He hoped Sampson would use a naval bombardment to prevent enemy reinforcements from coming up on his left along the Aguadores railway bridge, but urged him not to de-stroy the bridge, as the army might eventually need it.[4]

Beginning on the twenty-fifth, the corps began moving forward be-yond Sevilla. Every unit carried three days' rations that, combined with the rest of their gear, made for excessively heavy packs and caused many a man to throw away articles that were later badly needed. As Lieutenant Miley said, "As far as possible it was seen that nothing was carried which was not absolutely necessary, so if any-thing was left on the way the loss was keenly felt later." As there was not enough room for all the troops to camp comfortably, Wheeler rec-ommended the command march even further toward Santiago, into the region of El Pozo, about three miles short of the city. Shafter as-sented to this, though he directed the impetuous cavalry general to ex-ercise "great care" not to bring on another engagement. The artillery and mounted squadron of the 2nd Cavalry were placed well to the front, according to Miley "in the most convenient places." Lawton's 2nd Division was furthest ahead, near El Pozo, with the Cavalry Di-vision close behind. Kent's 1st Division remained further back at Sevilla. Miley described the new bivouacs as comfortable; the water in the streams was "clear and pure, ample for all purposes and a lux-uriant growth of grass was everywhere, which helped out the forage supply very considerably."[5]

Serious reconnaissance of the area immediately in front of the Spanish defenses began on June 26, a work undertaken mainly by the corps' chief engineer, Colonel George Derby. In addition, Wheeler and Lawton with their staffs were constantly at the same task. Gen-eral Shafter especially wanted information on the roads and trails from El Pozo to El Caney because, Miley said, "he thought it likely that he would send a division by that road to assault the town."[6]

Also on the twenty-sixth, the chief signal officer, Major Frank Greene, established a telephone system. The line ran from Daiquirí through Siboney to the extreme front at El Pozo, connecting the supply dumps with the troops. Whenever the command moved forward, the line followed, enabling General Shafter to communicate at all times with his division commanders. The coastal cable from Santiago to Guantánamo was also discovered at this time, and was fished up and carried to Siboney. The Guantánamo end was spliced on ocean cable to St. Nicolas Môle, and by this means Shafter had direct access to the War Department in Washington.

Taking immediate advantage of the system, the general notified Secretary Alger, "There is no necessity for haste, as we are growing stronger and they weaker each day. The health of the command as reported to me by the surgeon is remarkable." To Wheeler, he reiterated, "Under no circumstances, unless you are attacked, must any fight be precipitated. . . . A waiting policy is one that we can afford, at least for a few days to carry out strictly."[7]

On June 28, Shafter's policy of waiting for further reinforcements—the remainder of Duffield's Michigan brigade—was placed in jeopardy when he was informed that 8,000 Spanish regulars, with an abundance of beef cattle and other supplies, were advancing at a rate of twelve miles a day toward Santiago from Manzanillo in the west. This was Colonel Federico Escario's column of 3,660 men, mostly infantry, with 250 cavalry, two field guns, and a pack train of sixty mules, the only reinforcement the Spanish would receive at Santiago, and they would not arrive until too late to alter the situation. Shafter was now unwilling to wait. Although the equipment of the Fifth Corps was far from complete and scarcely more than three days' rations had been accumulated at the front, he believed the time had come to attack.

In the meantime, Lawton and his 3rd Brigade commander, Brigadier General Adna Chaffee, had reconnoitered the area around the village of El Caney, four miles north of El Pozo, determining it was "an important position which was necessary to be occupied" because it straddled the wagon road between Santiago and Guantánamo, from where the Spanish could logically be expected to draw reinforcements. Lawton thought he could take the place with his division in two hours. On June 28, at Shafter's temporary headquarters at Siboney, Lawton and Chaffee presented the idea to the commanding general, who approved, but ordered them not to attack until corps headquarters had come permanently ashore, scheduled for the next day, and the general attack plan for Santiago had been drawn.[8]

As Chaffee later testified before a Senate commission, "I did considerable reconnoitering." A large force of 1,200 Cuban rebels had reported to him for outpost duty. They were men who knew every trail in the country and "they were of great service to me"—a statement at odds with the accounts of many American participants of the campaign. For two days, using a portion of the Cubans and four companies of infantry, Chaffee worked on the road that branched off the *camino real* and connected El Pozo to El Caney, making it at least passable for artillery. "We had to get out of the brush and use picks and shovels and everything of that kind," he recalled. "The road was simply a mule track, and a difficult mule track at that."[9]

On June 29, General Shafter came ashore to establish his headquarters near El Pozo. Early the following morning, along with his adjutant general, Lieutenant Colonel Edward McClernand, Colonel Derby the chief engineer, Lieutenant Miley, and other staff, Shafter rode forward to El Pozo to observe the Spanish positions in front of Santiago. He had an excellent view of the enemy's lines, the trenches, and the blockhouse, along the crest of the San Juan heights, and also the ranch buildings on what became known as Kettle Hill to the right and slightly to the front of the main position. The party rode forward until they came upon some Cuban pickets who informed them of the Spanish outposts about two hundred yards farther on.

This single reconnaissance, upon which General Shafter based his attack plan, received severe criticism from Major Arthur Wagner of the Military Information Bureau, the army's intelligence arm. He argued that Shafter's viewing the region west of El Pozo resembled nothing so much as Moses' observation of the Promised Land from Mount Pisgah, and that it provided nothing of worth. A half dozen small patrols, he maintained, "directed to push forward until the enemy was touched upon or his position absolutely discovered, would have resulted in gaining information that would have saved an infinitude of trouble."[10]

Shortly after Shafter's return to headquarters, the divisional commanders were summoned. Wheeler, ill with malaria, was represented by his 1st Brigade commander, Brigadier General Samuel Sumner, who assumed temporary command of the Cavalry Division. The attack on the Spanish lines would go forward the next day. Shafter thought it might even result in the capture of the city. Believing in Lawton's contention that he could take El Caney in two hours, his 2nd Division would open the attack at daybreak, supported by Captain Allyn Capron Sr.'s battery of four 3.2-inch guns, and if necessary, Bates's independent brigade. Thus, nearly half of the Fifth Corps would be engaged upon what was little more than an outwork, an important one to be sure, but one that could have been dealt with by masking it with a reinforced brigade, rather than an entire division plus supports. In any event, once Lawton had secured the position, his whole force was to come by the El Caney–Santiago road and form on the right of Sumner's Cavalry Division for the general attack on the city.

Kent's 1st Division and the Cavalry Division were ordered to advance as far as El Pozo, where gun pits had been dug for Captain George Grimes's light battery of four guns. Moving in the morning by the El Pozo–Santiago road just as soon as Lawton was well engaged, Sumner's dismounted cavalry needed to ford the Aguadores and San Juan Rivers, turn to the right, and deploy in line before Kettle Hill, his left resting on the Santiago road. Kent, following Sumner down the same road, was to advance bearing left, fording three streams, the Aguadores twice, before coming to the San Juan in front of San Juan Hill, with his right flank connecting with Sumner's left on the road. Both were then to await the arrival of Lawton before advancing to the attack up the heights.

There were several major flaws in the plan: not enough artillery, a poor division of force, and the fact that two divisions had to advance down a single Cuban jungle road and debouch from it into open country completely enfiladed by the enemy entrenched in the San Juan heights to their immediate front. Richard Harding Davis, no fan of General Shafter's, claimed Chaffee knew that it would be impossible for the army to break out of the road leaving the jungle and enter the open country before the heights without great loss. Chaffee had suggested that trails be cut off the road leading into the open, so that the whole force of the two divisions could be marched out upon the hills simultaneously. "Of course, the enemy knows where [that road]

leaves the wood," he said; "they have their guns trained on the open-
ings. If our men leave the cover and reach the plain from [that road]
alone they will be piled so high that they will block the road."[11]

For the remainder of the corps, Duffield, in command at Siboney,
was ordered to send the 33rd Michigan at dawn along the railroad
to the iron bridge at Aguadores, and there make a "vigorous attack"
on the five hundred or so Spanish supposed to be in place, providing
the double task of fooling the Spanish commanders into thinking the
main attack was being made along the coast and preventing the
enemy forces at Aguadores from being shifted inland to support their
main lines along the San Juan heights. Shafter's only mounted contingent, the squadron of the 2nd Cavalry, was to await orders near El
Pozo. The remaining two batteries of light artillery were uselessly stationed near headquarters, likewise to await orders. General García
with his rebel force was requested to move along the El Caney–Santiago road, passing west of the town, and to take up a position north of
Santiago so as to prevent the entrance of Escario's reinforcements,
something he did not succeed in doing.

The lay of the land did not favor the attacking forces. The one
known road, the *camino real,* leading directly from El Pozo to Santiago, followed the Aguadores stream, and frequently the stream bed
itself, and had to be forded several times. A mile west of El Pozo, the
Aguadores joined the Guaymas creek, and a bit further on, it entered
the steep-banked, waist-deep San Juan River, which continued down
to the coast at Aguadores. The whole vicinity of the stream area was
covered with dense brush. After crossing the rivers near the San
Juan–Aguadores fork, there was cleared ground within range of the
Spanish guns on the heights, and the road became slightly sunken at
this point. But here it was bordered on the left, through which Kent's
division was to deploy, by a six-stranded barbed-wire fence, made
fast to the trunks of growing trees and thick overgrown hedges. On
the right of the road lay Kettle Hill; on the left, San Juan Hill, upon
whose 125-foot summit sat the Spanish blockhouse. Between the two
hills ran a small valley with a large pond at its bottom.

After the war, Brigadier Chaffee, a grizzled, hardened old Indian
fighter inured to privation in the field, described the area in harsh
terms. "The army was forced to operate in a sea of brush that was
thicker, more dense, more difficult to penetrate than any place I had

ever seen in my life. This brush is high and so thick as to exclude the circulation of air. There is no road, properly speaking in Cuba, mere trails, called roads, that would not permit of a column marching any distance except by [single] file. The men marching along these trails were, as it were, melting. . . . [A]fter the rain set in, the tramping of the men simply made it muck."[12]

At 3:00 P.M. on Thursday, June 30, the general order was passed to all units to break camp and march to their jump-off points for the attack the next day. Why the order had been given so late in the day, and virtually at once to all units, is impossible to comprehend; it made for a needless, confounding mess. "It was as though fifteen regiments were encamped along the sidewalks of Fifth Avenue," wrote Richard Harding Davis, "and were all ordered at the same moment to move into it and march down town. If Fifth Avenue were ten feet wide, one can imagine the confusion."[13]

By the headquarters tents near El Pozo stood a crowd of foreign military attachés, each in his particular uniform, a small knot of Cuban rebel generals, white-coated officers from the flagship *New York*, and a small army of journalists and photographers. A double file of soldiers trod slowly along the sides of the muddy road, while up and down dashed mounted aides, splashing the men with dirty water, shouting important orders from their respective generals: "You will come at once, sir"; "You will not attempt to enter the trail yet, sir"; "General Sumner's compliments, and why are you not in your place, sir?" As the concentration lurched ahead, the Signal Corps' hydrogen-filled observation balloon began its ascent; Davis noted that "its great glistening bulk hung just above the tree tops, and the men . . . picking their way along the trail, gazed at it open-mouthed."[14]

And the Spanish? The withdrawal that began on June 22 with the American invasion and continued on the twenty-fourth with the engagement at Las Guásimas finally ended three days later, when the Americans spotted a long yellow pit opening on the hillside of San Juan, and watched straw sombreros bobbing up and down. For three days the pits grew in length and number, in plain sight from the hill at El Pozo. It was a wonder that General Shafter did not order his artillery, meager as it was, to interfere with this work. "The encounter is at hand," announced General Linares in a general order to his troops, "and it will take place under equal conditions. Your military virtues and your valor are the best guarantee of success. . . . The nation and army look to us." He called on the men—regulars, *voluntarios, guerrilleros,* and city volunteers alike—to stand firm at any cost. There would be no vacillation, no thought of retreat, "but only of saving the honor of our arms. . . . *Viva España!*"[15]

After the retirement from the mineral district and Las Guásimas, Linares made only a few changes in the general disposition of his forces; he still attempted to hold every point around the city, be it actually threatened or not. Unaware of the transfer of the bulk of rebel forces from the west of the city to the east, he kept a significant number of troops, the entire Asia Regiment, and a company of *voluntarios,* the whole amounting to 1,233 men, sitting useless west of the Socapa. Linares fielded over 10,000 men for the immediate defense of Santiago and its precincts, most of which should have been concentrated on the San Juan heights and El Caney, the points clearly to be assaulted by the Americans, but this was not done. In the forward trenches on the crests of San Juan and Kettle hills were a total of 521 men, regulars from the Talavera Regiment, *voluntarios,* and two Krupp field guns that formed the whole of Linares's effective artillery. Three companies of the Talavera Regiment, numbering 411 men, together with an ancient, "modernized" bronze cannon and a 4.7-inch naval gun, created the second, main line around Fort Canosa, at the junction of the roads from El Pozo and El Caney leading into Santiago. A third line of 140 mounted *guerrilleros* formed on a hillock near the fort. Behind these defenses, within the city, and surrounding it in a semicircle from northwest to southwest were 4,352 soldiers, sailors, city volunteers, and municipal firemen. Of these, perhaps 800 to 1,000 were sick in the military hospital. At the time of the battle, Captain Bustamante, with a company of 125 sailors, came from the northwest corner of the semicircle to take position in the second line of defense behind San Juan Hill.

At El Caney were 520 men of Brigadier General Joaquín Vara de Rey's San Luis Brigade, consisting of three companies of the Constitución Regiment, 40 men of the Cuba Regiment, 50 *voluntarios,* and a company of dismounted *guerrilleros.* The village of low, palm-thatched houses rose on a moderate hill. Six wooden blockhouses protected the approaches to the west and north, connected by short trenches with wire entanglements to their front. The key to the village and its defenses sat on a hillock about five hundred yards to its southeast—an old stone church, El Viso, heavily loopholed for rifle fire, fronted by a deep trench. It was a naturally strong position, and so recognized by the Spanish, who according to the British military observer, Captain Arthur A. Lee, "had arranged its defenses with the greatest care and no mean skill."[16]

Around 3:00 P.M., June 30, Lawton's division tramped up the El Pozo–El Caney road to their night bivouacs, halting behind a ridge about a mile southeast of El Caney. The men set up hasty camp in their tracks, preserving strict silence and lighting no fires. As Captain Lee remembered, "Our chief fear . . . was that the Spaniards at El Caney would learn of our advance and evacuate the place before we could surround and capture them." In the light of the next morning's events, this anxiety proved a fancy, for the enemy had no notion whatever of retreating "and was apparently quite as anxious for a fight as we were." Shortly after daylight, July 1, the division threaded its way through narrow, slippery paths and over a succession of razor-backed ridges, and closed in on the town.[17]

The deployment for the attack went easily enough. Chaffee's brigade—the 7th, 12th, and 17th Infantry regiments—took up position six hundred to eight hundred yards from El Viso on the east side of the village. Brigadier William Ludlow's brigade of the 8th and 22nd regulars, plus the 2nd Massachusetts, marched to the southwest side to seize the El Caney–Santiago road, cutting off the escape of the garrison. Two of the regiments of Colonel Evan Miles's brigade, the 4th and 24th Infantry, were held in reserve angling toward the southeast. The remaining unit, the 1st Infantry, and a mounted troop of the 2nd Cavalry deployed in support of Capron's battery a little over a mile to the south of the village.

At 6:00 A.M., Lawton's men could see the red-and-gold Spanish flag flapping lazily on its staff above El Viso, and a number of enemy soldiers, in their light blue uniforms and white straw sombreros, lounging outside the fort's gate. They seemed remarkably indifferent

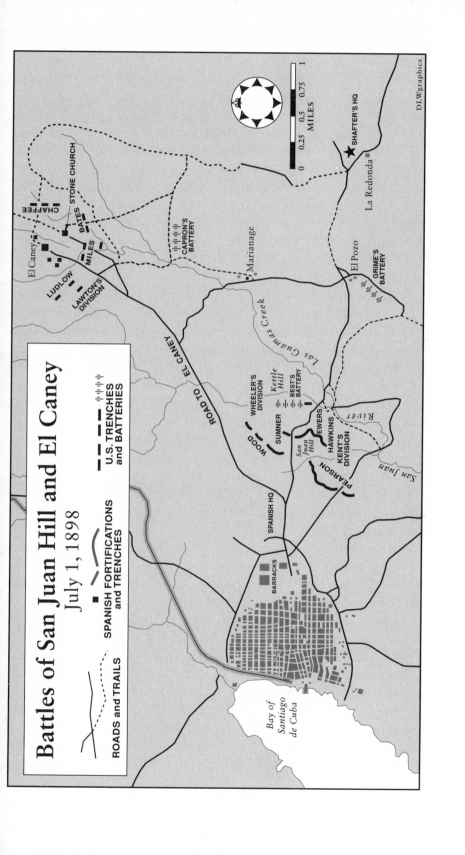

Battles of San Juan Hill and El Caney
July 1, 1898

ROADS and TRAILS

■ **SPANISH FORTIFICATIONS and TRENCHES**

▬ **U.S. TRENCHES and BATTERIES**

DLWgraphics

MILES

0   0.25   0.5   0.75   1

CHAFFEE

STONE CHURCH

BATES

El Caney

MILES

LUDLOW

LAWTON'S DIVISION

CAPRON'S BATTERY

Marianage

El Pozo

GRIME'S BATTERY

La Redonda

SHAFTER'S HQ

Las Guanaos Creek

WHEELER'S DIVISION

Kettle Hill

BEST'S BATTERY

SUMMER

WOOD

EWERS

HAWKINS

San Juan Hill

KENT'S DIVISION

PEARSON

San Juan River

SPANISH HQ

ROAD TO EL CANEY

BARRACKS

Bay of Santiago de Cuba

to the Americans coming right up to their approaches, though they watched with apparent interest the deployment of Captain Capron's battery, which showed black against the small green clearing where the guns were unlimbered. Half an hour later, the silence was broken by a white puff of smoke from one of Capron's guns, and before the sound reached the ears of the infantry lines, as Captain Lee recalled, "the Spaniards outside the fort had vanished with the rapidity of prairie dogs." Simultaneously, a row of white sombreros "sprouted from the ground like mushrooms," marking the position of the glacis in front of the fort, and the deep rifle pits and trenches around the village.[18]

This first shot was thought to have been fired at a column of Spanish cavalry advancing in a lane near the town. (Actually it was a bunch of Cuban refugees from Santiago, but fortunately the shot overreached.) In fact, Capron's artillery was much too distant from its main target, El Viso, to have any real effect. The Spanish had no artillery for counterbattery fire, and it would have been safe to bring the guns closer. The shots scattered; there were no forward observers to correct the fire. There was no doctrine for it anyway, since all U.S. artillery operated under the direct-fire principle—see the target and shoot—and for most of the battle, the guns did little damage. A correspondent wrote that the Spanish in their trenches "minded the shells bursting over and around them as little as though they had been bursting snowballs." As Chaffee later said, "There was not sufficient artillery there to demoralize the garrison."[19]

For the next fifteen minutes, though Capron's guns kept up a leisurely fire on El Viso, this so little disturbed the white hats in the trenches that it was suggested they were dummies. "Our belief in the fighting qualities of the Spaniards died hard," remembered Captain Lee.[20]

Chaffee, on gaining the reverse slope of a little grassy ridge that overlooked the village from the north and east, deployed his brigade: the 12th Infantry on the left, 7th on the right, and the 17th in reserve behind the 7th. The Spanish had no outposts at El Caney, and this position was occupied without resistance. From the crest, the men could see into the town; no sign of life prevailed, save a few wisps of smoke from the thatched shacks. To their left was the cone-shaped hill of El Viso, smooth and steep, "and on its extreme tip," said Captain Lee, "the little mediaeval fort perched itself like a hat."[21]

All three of Lawton's brigades now advanced. Ludlow, on the far left, whose horse was shot from under him, pushed within a hundred yards of the town, drawing heavy fire from two blockhouses to his front. On the right, Chaffee moved the 12th Infantry beyond the blockhouse in his path, giving and taking heavy volleys from the Spanish trenches as the enemy slowly pulled back from their forward lines to the main position at El Viso. For three hours, the fight was continuous. The Spanish powder was smokeless, and even with the best field glasses it was impossible to detect the position of Spanish sharpshooters firing from the loopholed church, the trees, huts, and blockhouses. On the other hand, the smoke from Capron's battery hung over the ground like haze. In the face of murderous volleys from the Spanish trenches, the American skirmish lines edged closer—all but the 2nd Massachusetts, whose old-style single-shot black-powder Springfield rifles made them special targets for the enemy, and they were pulled out of the front and kept in reserve for the rest of the day.

About ten o'clock, when it was evident to Lawton, and everyone else, that El Caney was not going to fall in the promised two hours, there came a slight lull in the battle. Bates's brigade had come up to reinforce the attack, taking position on the southeast, between Miles and Chaffee, and bringing the American strength to 6,653 men. Lawton, having made his position secure in the face of Spanish opposition infinitely greater than expected, passed the word to cease firing and for his men to take food and water. Two men from the 12th Infantry crept forward with wire cutters and passed along the whole brigade front, taking cover behind some bushes and folds in the ground to cut the barbed wire before the enemy's trenches.

At eleven o'clock the battle resumed in all fury. From the grassy ridge, Chaffee ordered the 17th Infantry to advance up a slightly sunken road bordered with hedges on either side. No sooner did they break the cover of the ridge crest and deploy to the right through a gap in the hedges than they were struck by killing volleys from the trenches. The regimental commander was hit three times, and his quartermaster killed at his side. The 17th withdrew into a hollow and extended further to the right. The 7th Infantry was even less fortunate. It advanced until its firing line stretched along the entire crest of the grassy ridge, less than three hundred yards from the enemy trenches. It was exposed to a terrible cross fire from the village and from the blockhouses. For hours the men lay without flinching, the sun scorching their backs, suffering heavy losses from an enemy who was practically invisible and to whom they could not reply effectively. More than one hundred of Chaffee's men lay dead or wounded in the sunken road, with little shelter, barely fifty yards behind the firing line.

Captain Lee dashed over to where the 7th was fighting. On nearing the sunken road and seeing it full of men lying down, he asked an officer if they constituted the regimental reserves. "No, Sir," said the man, "by God they are casualties." Lee counted more than one hundred dead and wounded laid out in as many yards of the road, "and so close were they that one could only pass by stepping over them." Seeing his strange uniform, several asked pathetically if he was a doctor. "I could but shake my head and they would instantly relapse into their strained intent attitudes." The heat in the sunken lane was terrible, well over ninety degrees. There was neither shade nor breath of wind, and the wounded lay sweltering in the sun, "till the head reeled with the rank smell of sweat and saturated flannel." Lee considered one of the worst features of the battle to be the lack of enough medical personnel of all types, from frontline aid men to stretcher bearers to regimental surgeons. For hours the badly wounded lay unattended in the sun, often bleeding to death. The regimental dressing stations were located three quarters of a mile to the rear, and they tended only to those who could make it back, the slightly and walking wounded.[22]

It was a most anxious hour. The battle was at a stalemate. In front of the San Juan heights, Kent's and Sumner's divisions crouched in their lines of departure, suffering needless casualties, waiting for Lawton at El Caney to finish what was supposed to be the preliminary to the general engagement. And there was no end in sight. A black soldier of Miles's 25th Infantry wrote, "[T]he Americans were gaining no ground, and the flashes of the Spanish Mausers told us that the forces engaged were unequally matched, the difference of position favoring the Spanish." One correspondent watched a line of some "fifty or sixty light-blue clad [Spaniards] . . . standing in a trench," in the middle of which a young officer stood with drawn sword, unprotected to the belt, "and sometimes, as he stood up, exposed to the feet." The Spanish soldiers in the trench rose at the word of the officer's command, delivering volley after volley, "full in our faces; standing as they did so," visible to return fire, "grimly facing death, drawing their dead up and out of the trench as they fell to make standing room for living men."²³

At this critical point, around one o'clock, Lawton received a desperate message from General Shafter ordering him to break off the engagement at El Caney and bring his division to Sumner's right flank to support the main attack on the San Juan heights, for which Shafter had not a single rifleman in reserve. "I would not bother with the little block-houses," read the order. "They can't harm us. Bates' Brigade and your division and García should move on the city . . . from the right of the line. . . . Line [in front of San Juan] is now hotly engaged." Later Shafter admitted, "I was fearful I had made a terrible mistake in engaging my whole army at 6 miles interval, and I sent word to Lawton to come to [Sumner's] right and help there."²⁴

But the final assault on El Caney was about to go forward, and Lawton would not, and indeed could not, disengage. To do so at this juncture would crush morale. He disregarded the order and pressed on.

By this time, Capron's battery had gotten the range of the El Viso fort, shot away its flagstaff amid vociferous American cheers, and begun knocking great holes into the walls. But the Spanish garrison still fought furiously. From the trenches below the church, on which the artillery had no effect, the Spanish poured repeated volleys at everything appearing on their front. Chaffee's brigade suffered badly; stretches of cleared land along his front exposed him to a raking fire from El Viso and a blockhouse to the northwest, but by quick rushes, the 12th and 17th Infantry dashed across the killing ground. At 2:30, the 12th Regiment reached the foot of the hill in the defile just below the Spanish rifle pits.

Miles's brigade was brought up on the south side, the 4th Infantry on the left, the 25th Infantry on the right. They advanced 200 yards through a grass field hidden from the enemy at El Viso by a double row of trees until they came to a barbed-wire fence. Men with clippers made the breaches and the regiments tore through, into an open pineapple patch. They were well in range and view and the Spanish poured a murderous volley into the regiment. "Ye gods! It is raining lead," recalled an officer of the black 25th. "The line recoils like a mighty serpent, and then, in confusion, advances again! Men are dropping everywhere! . . . The bullets are cutting the pineapples under our very feet. . . . How helpless we feel! Our men are being shot down

... and we, their officers, can do nothing for them." Officers in the pineapple patch held a quick consultation and decided there was but one thing to do—advance! The firing line was no more than 150 yards from the south side of El Viso. Orders were given for only sharp-shooters to fire, and twoscore men poured lead into every rifle pit, door, window, and firing slit in and around the church. The Spanish were now clearly shaken and rapidly becoming demoralized by con-stant battle against ten times their number. Bareheaded, some without rifles, they ran from the trenches into the church. "Our men," said the officer of the 25th, "are shooting them down like dogs."[25]

Chaffee gave the order for the 12th Infantry to charge the fort. Pushing rapidly up the ravine that skirted the east side of the vil-lage, they swung into line and dashed up the hill. In a moment they swarmed over wire fences and across the trenches, wrote Captain Lee, "like a hive of angry bees." Amidst the cheering of the rest of the line, they drove the enemy "helter-skelter" over the crest. Actually, the first man into El Viso was the Hearst correspondent James Creelman, who showed great courage, summoning the Spanish inside to surrender, and was shot through the shoulder in his successful attempt to re-cover the Spanish flag lying on the ground outside.[26]

In front of the 25th Infantry, which was making a simultaneous charge, a Spanish soldier appeared in the gateway of El Viso showing a white flag, but he was shot down before the firing could be stopped. A second Spaniard took up the flag and he too fell. When the hill and El Viso were finally taken at around three o'clock, the troops, Cap-tain Lee noticed, "ran around like schoolboys, cheering and waving their hats; the officers were shaking hands and congratulating each other." Then it dawned on everyone that while El Viso had fallen, the garrison in the town and the blockhouses had stayed put, keeping up fire on the El Viso hill. There was no cover, and the mixed-up regi-ments lined up around the church and began pumping fire into the blockhouses. The 25th Infantry rushed forward, changed direction left, and charged the nearest fortlet. "Men are still dropping by the wayside," wrote the regimental officer, "but on, on, up, up they go, those dusky boys in blue!" The Spanish were now falling over them-selves to get out, streaming out of the northwestern end of the town.[27]

The Spaniards' last stand at El Caney was at a blockhouse at the western entrance to the town along the Santiago road. Here a small band of soldiers held the road for hours and died like heroes. "Their officers," said correspondent James Archibald, "appeared to court death, for they exposed themselves uselessly while urging their men to fight." General Vara de Rey rode his horse up and down the line, and in the last minutes, while trying to rally his men in a church plaza, he was hit in both legs. Helped onto a stretcher, he was instantly killed by a bullet in the head. Two of his sons also died in the fight. The mounted squadron that sat unused at Capron's guns would have been invaluable to pursue and cut down the retreating enemy, but as it was, the Spanish suffered badly enough from the crossfire of Ludlow's brigade, and only 103 of the original 514-man garrison survived to make it back to Santiago. Dead were 248; the rest were prisoners of the Americans.[28]

Captain Lee, taking stock, saw a gruesome sight. The trench surrounding El Viso was floored with dead Spaniards, horribly contorted, with staring, sightless eyes. Others littered the slope, terribly mutilated by shellfire during the latter part of the fight. Those killed in the trenches had all taken shots through the forehead, "and their brains oozed out like white paint from a color tube."

At 3:45 P.M., the firing died away, and the Americans were at last in possession of El Caney. It had cost them 81 dead and 360 wounded.[29]

At 3:00 A.M., July 1, one hour before reveille, General Shafter summoned his adjutant general, Lieutenant Colonel McClernand, to his tent. The obese commanding general was nearly prostrate, incapacitated with gout and the exertions of the reconnaissance the day before. He ordered McClernand to take his place at the front, establish a battle headquarters at El Pozo, and, assisted by Lieutenant Miley, direct the action from there, keeping in touch with the general through field telephone and staff gallopers.

By seven o'clock, McClernand was at El Pozo, impatiently expecting Lawton to clear things up at El Caney; two hours, Lawton had promised. Kent and Sumner, their divisions stacked up along the *camino real,* their forward units being potted by Spanish fire, stood at his side. "Well," Sumner asked with some exasperation, "when are we going to begin this thing?" Soon enough, McClernand thought. It didn't take much convincing that El Caney was not going to be the easy prize Lawton had predicted. He feared if the fight went on much longer there, the Spanish might reinforce the village, blunting the attack before the main assault on the San Juan heights commenced. At eight o'clock, he ordered Kent and Sumner to advance down the road and take position in front of the heights. Sumner's dismounted cavalry was to move at once, cross the Aguadores stream, execute column right, and deploy in front of Kettle Hill, with their left resting on the *camino real*. "What am I to do then?" Sumner asked. "You are to await further orders," came the answer. Kent would follow, and after fording the Aguadores and San Juan rivers, align his men directly in front of San Juan Hill, with his right on the road, and his left extending beyond the extremity of the heights.[30]

Captain George Grimes's battery of four 3.2-inch guns, which had taken position on a hill to the left of El Pozo, opened fire at a range of about 2,500 yards. Like the American artillery at El Caney, it was not effective; indeed, it was counterproductive. The billows of white smoke from the black powder immediately disclosed the position to the Spanish on the heights, and Grimes received a heavy return fire from the pair of smokeless Krupp field pieces that constituted the whole of the effective Spanish artillery. After forty-five minutes, Grimes ceased firing.

Following the first fording of the Aguadores, which had to be crossed within a half mile of leaving El Pozo, the troops of every unit became a congested mass into which the Spanish, though the Americans were still invisible to them in the jungle, kept up a desultory yet effective fire. The initial deployment was described by a British correspondent: "first came the Cubans"; once a little down the road, they branched off to the right "and disappeared for the day. Then the [dismounted] cavalry; then the balloon led by a rope . . . Two men held it down by a cross bar, and two men walked in front of it holding stays . . . like [that] of a Foresters banner . . . then the infantry."[31]

Because Leonard Wood had been posted to command the 2nd Cavalry Brigade on Brigadier Young's coming down with malaria, Theodore Roosevelt now led the Rough Riders. In the coming battle, he remembered his men as "greatly overjoyed, for the inaction was trying." TR recalled his orders being of the "vaguest kind," simply to march down the road, assemble to the right, and attach his right flank to Lawton's left, an impossibility at the time. On the march down the road, there was a stoppage in front every few minutes, and Roosevelt ordered his men to sit beside the track and loosen their horse-collar packs. The heat was unwaveringly fierce as they passed through the still, close jungle that formed a wall on either hand. Occasionally they came upon an open space where some regiment was stalled, apparently out of its proper place in the advance. These troops would then file into the road, breaking the cavalry's line of march. As a result, the Rough Riders merely followed the trail of the regiment ahead, usually infantry, thrust into the interval. Leonard Wood described this movement forward from El Pozo as "a dense mass wholly unprotected and without any definite plan of action." In the dreadful heat, Roosevelt hurried his men across the Aguadores ford, marched half a mile to the right, through a hot fire from the heights, and halted at a sunken lane in front of Kettle Hill. The 1st Cavalry Brigade to his left was already in a stand-up fight. TR sent back to Colonel Wood for orders.[32]

Kent's 1st Division following the cavalry had a bad time of it. There were frequent halts for the men to drop their blanket rolls and natural delays in fording the streams, and all the while Spanish were shooting at them from the heights. "These delays under such a hot fire grew exceedingly irksome," Kent said, and he pushed the head of his division as fast as possible toward the San Juan River in column of twos, paralleled in the narrow way by the cavalry. This quickened the forward movement of the division and largely aided his getting positioned for the attack on the heights. Yet, owing to the badly congested condition of the road, the progress of the bulk of the division was painfully slow. Kent sent a galloper to the rear to hurry on the rest of the troops.[33]

When about half of the Cavalry Division had crossed the Aguadores ford and Kent's division was jammed in the road, taking heavy fire from the heights, the Signal Corps observation balloon, with Lieutenant Colonel Derby, the chief engineer, and Lieutenant Colonel Maxfield of the Signal Corps in the basket, approached the Aguadores ford amidst the crowd of troops struggling to cross. By message drop, Derby reported to General Shafter that the head of Kent's division had halted on the road, within four hundred yards of the San Juan River, and was taking heavy fire.

The balloon flight was a good idea that went mostly bad. Sent up in the middle of the advancing troops, it was the one thing the Spanish could easily see, and everything under it became their general target. "A Spaniard," said Richard Harding Davis, "might question if he could hit a man, or a number of men, hidden in the bushes, but he had no doubt at all as to his ability to hit a mammoth glistening ball only six hundred yards distant, and so all the trenches fired at it at once." The 1st and 10th Cavalry regiments, packed together just behind the balloon, received the full force of the rifle volleys, and the Krupp shrapnel had been timed to explode just over their heads. These men were in a position where they could neither take cover nor reply to the fire, and their soldierly qualities were greatly strained.[34]

Colonel Derby had determined to push the balloon right up to the skirmish line, ascending to one thousand feet, reporting on the movements of the army to General Shafter as the regiments advanced on the heights. But when the balloon reached the Aguadores ford the guy ropes became entangled in the trees, affording the Spanish a stationary target. It was "drilled with as many holes as a pepper box," wrote a reporter; "it began to grow flabby, to curl up, to lose its shape. Then it came down limply, having rendered enough disservice for the day." Perhaps not as bad as the correspondent thought. Just before the balloon fell, Derby discovered a hitherto unknown trail branching left off the *camino real,* crossing the San Juan River just below its junction with the Aguadores. The discovery led to a movement that not only relieved the congestion of troops on the main road, but enabled Kent's march to speed up appreciably.[35]

The leading regiment of Brigadier General Hamilton Hawkins's 1st Brigade, the 71st New York, was immediately ordered to take the trail, which would have delivered them into their proper place on the left of the brigade. But, Kent said, "the enemy's fire, steadily increasing in intensity, now came from all directions, not only from the front and the dense tropical thicket on our flanks . . . but from shrapnel." When thrown into this narrow way, with shot and shell from an unseen enemy falling all around and among them, the regiment's foremost battalion broke and recoiled in confusion on the formations behind it. It was a sore misfortune to place these volunteers in so exposed a position, but they were the first to the trailhead, and there was no choice. It would have been a serious trial for seasoned regular troops under highly trained officers. Russell· Alger aptly noted, "[I]t is not to be wondered that for the moment it demoralized these inexperienced soldiers whose officers were little better qualified than they for such an emergency." At this perilous moment, officers of Kent's staff formed a cordon behind the reeling battalion and urged it forward. They were not successful, and Kent personally ordered them to lie down in the thickets on either side of the trail, clearing the way for the 2nd and 3rd battalions coming up in better order.[36]

At his headquarters tent General Shafter fell prey to increasing anxieties. The heat, gout, and likely the onset of malaria didn't help matters. The firing at El Caney continued without letup, and that from the San Juan heights increased in volume and killing effect. It was clear to him and everyone else in the Fifth Corps that the Spanish, despite all expectations, were fighting one hell of a battle. According to the overoptimistic plan, the thing should have been concluded hours ago, and yet there was no indication of the slightest progress. Given the topography of the battlefield, there were no brilliant tactical moves to spring on the enemy. He had committed his only reserve, Bates's brigade, to El Caney, and that had not resolved the matter. Kent and Sumner were still lurching down the road, spilling into open fields under heavy fire and trying to find some cover from where they could return bullet for bullet. Ammunition was running low at the front, and care of the many wounded had gotten beyond all control. It was now that Shafter sent the "little block-houses" message to Lawton to disengage at El Caney. But Lawton could not do it, and the fight in front of the San Juan heights devolved on the leadership of individual brigade, regimental, and company commanders.

Trying to deal with the situation of the 71st New York, Kent ordered his 2nd and 3rd brigades under colonels E. W. Pearson and Charles Wikoff to hurry their men up front. It was twenty minutes past noon when Wikoff's brigade—the 9th, 13th, and 24th Infantry regiments—shouldered aside the frightened men of the 71st and entered the branching trail, stepping over prostrate forms, forcing their way to the front. As they advanced along the narrow path under a hail of Mauser fire, the sight of the mounting dead and wounded was enough to make the bravest recoil. But with the indomitable, bespectacled Wikoff at their head, they did not waver.

Reaching the banks of the San Juan, the men leaped into the waist-high water, waded the stream, and clambered up the opposite bank in sight of the enemy and with a clear view of the blockhouse and entrenchments on San Juan Hill scarcely more than five hundred yards ahead. Wikoff flung his brigade into position along a sunken way on the far bank. While personally directing the deployment of the 13th Infantry (the lead regiment), totally oblivious of the enemy fire, exposing himself without the slightest cover, Wikoff was shot through the body. He died fifteen minutes later. Lieutenant Colonel Worth of the 13th, forthwith took command of the brigade, and under a terrific fusillade continued the placement before he, too, fell severely wounded. Lieutenant Colonel Emerson Liscum of the 24th Infantry assumed charge and was soon knocked to the ground badly injured. Finally, Lieutenant Colonel Ezra Ewers of the 9th Infantry "won" command of the brigade.

Pearson's 2nd Brigade came running up on the 3rd's heels. His 2nd and 10th Infantry regiments deflected to support Ewers's brigade, forming the extreme left of Kent's line facing the heights. The remaining regiment of the brigade, the 21st Infantry, continued down the *camino real* to uphold Hawkins's 1st Brigade on the right.

While Ewers's brigade formed line on the left, Hawkins's 6th and 16th Infantry regiments moved along the main road to take their positions on the divisional right wing. After crossing the Aguadores and San Juan fords, they deflected left into a small triangular meadow bounded by the sunken road on the far bank and the converging streams behind that formed the San Juan River. Between Hawkins's and the Spanish positions on the heights, the front was obstructed by a fringe of trees and the six-strand barbed-wire fence made fast to their trunks. Hawkins had hoped that when he exited from the thicket of the road and crossed the river, he would be in position to enfilade the Spanish trenches. Instead, he found himself parallel and in full view of San Juan Hill. Russell Alger says that the only Cuban who actually took part in the battle accompanied the 6th Infantry, and with his machete he hacked a portion of the wire in the face of "savage fire" from the Spanish trenches. When he had made several breaches, the regiment advanced out of the sunken track into the grassy field and opened fire on the heights. This was answered by the whole Spanish right wing. In ten minutes, with no shelter, nearly one-quarter of the 6th Infantry Regiment, 127 men, lay dead or wounded. As the rest of the division had not yet gotten into line, for the 6th Infantry to attempt to hold this position would have resulted in its annihilation. Hawkins ordered them back to the sunken path. Without panic, the regiment fell back, carrying their dead and wounded.[37]

Meanwhile, Sumner and the Cavalry Division lay hunkered down, awaiting orders in what became known as the "Bloody Angle" in front of Kettle Hill, on the right of the line. Sumner reported the fire from the Spanish Krupp field guns as "passing over the command in column of twos." Richard Harding Davis said, "There was not a single yard of ground for a mile to the rear which was not inside the zone of fire." The men were ordered to lie down and not return fire, for they could not see from where it came. Behind the lines, hospital corpsmen drew the wounded back to the streams, where they stretched out in long rows, their feet touching the water's edge and their bodies supported by the muddy bank.[38]

By two o'clock, there were still no orders, nor any indication that Lawton would anytime soon finish at El Caney to connect with the cavalry's right flank, which yawned open and unsupported. Colonel Roosevelt's Rough Riders, lying in a sunken lane under the bank of the San Juan River, were suffering badly from the potshotting and the intolerable heat, and many of the men already showing signs of exhaustion.

The 2nd Cavalry Brigade formed the extreme right of the whole two-division front. The Rough Riders held the brigade right flank, the 1st Cavalry fought to their left, and the black 10th was just behind. In front of them was poised the 1st Brigade: the 3rd Cavalry Regiment on the left, 6th in the center, the black 9th Cavalry on the right. But the lines in the jungle were already overlapping in places, for the troopers simply could not remain still and kept edging forward. Roosevelt sent messenger after messenger to find Sumner or Wood, seeking permission to advance; he was just about to make up his mind that in the absence of orders the best thing to do would be to "march to the sound of the guns" when an officer came riding up with the "welcome" command "to move forward and support the 1st Brigade in the assault on Kettle Hill in front."[39]

It had already become unmistakable to Sumner and his officers that the division would have to advance on Kettle Hill or retreat under fire. Wheeler, aroused from his sickbed by the sound of the guns and feverishly wandering over the battlefield, sent a message to Colonel McClernand at El Pozo that "General Sumner wished to know if General Shafter's orders contemplated attacking entrenchments." Lieutenant Miley at Sumner's side sent his own message back to McClernand; "The heights must be taken at all hazards. A retreat now would be a disastrous defeat." McClernand replied that General Shafter's orders were for Kent and Sumner to "fight all their men if they could," adding, "From present firing I think Lawton is at it hard. Don't let him fight it out alone." Then, on his own initiative, Lieutenant Miley, in Shafter's name, ordered Sumner to advance the Cavalry Division up Kettle Hill. The tide of battle was about to turn.[40]

Sumner ordered his 1st Brigade to attack Kettle Hill with the 2nd Brigade in support. The red-roofed ranch houses at the summit indicated the objective, and the advance began at once. The troopers crawled along the ground, taking what cover they could find from brush and folds in the earth, and pushed forward in the face of galling fire. Roosevelt remembered, "The Mauser bullets drove in sheets through the trees and the tall jungle grass making a peculiar whirring or rustling sound." As the 1st Brigade moved forward, the 2nd came up to the skirmish line and became mixed with it. The men, standing upright, quickened their pace and rushed across the grassy field to their front, picking through a thick undergrowth and a wire fence at the foot of the slope, waded across the San Juan River, and charged.[41]

The instant Roosevelt received the order, he sprang on his horse, Texas, and began what he called his "crowded hour." He formed his regiment in line of troops, extended in open skirmish order, the right flank resting on a wire fence that bordered a sunken lane leading up the hill. TR had meant to go into battle on foot, as at Las Guásimas, but the ardent heat made it impossible for him to run up and down the line to superintend matters unless he was in the saddle. Moreover, when mounted he was able to see the men better, and they him. The skirmish line, which initially hesitated, moved forward under his exhortations, then quickened its pace, resulting in the rearmost lines of the regiment bunching together. TR rode through them, the better to lead from the front.

The six regiments of the Cavalry Division advanced intermingled—there was no real formation—and kept up a heavy fire on the Spanish positions around the ranch houses. Up Kettle Hill Sergeant George Berry of the 10th Cavalry bore not only the flag of his own regiment, but that of the 3rd Cavalry, whose color sergeant had been shot; he kept shouting, "Dress on the colors, boys, dress on the colors," as he followed his captain, who was running in advance of his troopers, waving his hat. The black 10th lost a greater proportion of officers than any other regiment in the fight, eleven killed and wounded out of twenty-two.[42]

With the 9th Cavalry to their front and the 1st to their left, the Rough Riders advanced up the hill. To their extended left, the 3rd, 6th, and 10th Cavalry regiments moved up between San Juan and Kettle hills. By the time Roosevelt reached the head of his regiment, they had angled somewhat to the left, becoming mingled with the 9th and some of the 1st, both of which were lying down shooting at the summit, their officers walking back and forth along the line. TR spoke to one of the captains here, saying that in his judgment, the hills could not be taken by fire alone, "and that we must rush them."[43]

The captain responded that his orders were to keep his men down where they were, and he could not charge without orders. Where was his colonel? Roosevelt asked, and when told he did not know, TR stated, "Then I am the ranking officer here and I give the order to charge." He did not under any circumstances wish to keep the men lying in the open taking fire that they could not effectively return. The captain hesitated to obey, the order not coming from his own commanding officer. "Then let my men through, sir," TR said, and he rode through the lines of the regulars, followed by the grinning Rough Riders. This embarrassment proved too much, and the 9th and 1st jumped to their feet. "The whole line, tired of waiting," Roosevelt remembered, "and eager to go forward . . . slipped the leash at almost the same moment." Everyone was "in the spirit of the thing," terrifically excited, adrenaline at the peak; the entire Cavalry Division, first haltingly, then faster, then at a rush, was on the move up. Roosevelt galloped ahead a few yards until he was sure the men were well started. Then he slowed, and completely exposed to the enemy fire, the only man mounted in the charge up Kettle Hill, advanced to the summit. From his higher vantage point he could already see the enemy running out of the ranch buildings, making for the rear.[44]

Forty yards from the crest he ran into a wire fence, jumped off Texas, and turned him loose. The horse had been nicked by several shots, one of which grazed TR's elbow. Almost immediately the hill was swarmed over by the cheering, yelling Rough Riders, the 9th Cavalry, and one squadron of the 1st. Most of the Spaniards had gone. One was captured in the buildings, another was shot trying to hide, and several others were cut down as they fled to the rear. But no sooner was the cavalry in possession of the hill than the enemy from the San Juan heights to their left and front opened a very heavy fire with rifle volleys and the two Krupp field guns, whose shells burst right overhead. Several of the men took shelter behind the huge sugar-boiling kettles from which the hill took its name. But from Kettle Hill's vantage point, the cavalry had an excellent view of the infantry advance up San Juan Hill and its blockhouse, and the obvious thing to do was wheel left and assist the infantry assault.

By forceful orders, Roosevelt assembled the milling men of four regiments, got them into some sort of line, and commenced volley firing against the enemy to their left front in the San Juan blockhouse and its surrounding trenches, where only the Spaniards' heads were visible. The cavalry was much shot up in the firefight; Colonel Hamilton of the 9th Regiment was killed, and Colonel Carroll, commanding the 1st Brigade, was wounded. Then, suddenly, above the crackling of their carbines, the cavalrymen heard a peculiar drumming sound, which they at first mistook for Spanish machine guns. Roosevelt listened intently and made out the noise as coming from the flat ground to the left. He jumped in the air, slapped his thigh, and with loud exultation shouted to everyone, "It's the Gatlings, men, our Gatlings!"[45]

By 1:00 P.M., the moment the cavalry swept over Kettle Hill and the infantry lay poised to begin its murderous advance up San Juan Hill, the Gatling Gun Detachment of three guns, under Lieutenant John Parker, had shouldered its way along the *camino real*, taking position in a clump of trees near the San Juan ford, about six hundred yards from the crest of the hill. The 71st New York greeted the guns' arrival by an eruption of cheering, which Parker disdainfully described as "an outburst of ignorant enthusiasm." The fire of the Gatlings lasted only eight and a half minutes, but it was enough to break the will of the enemy on the hill and in the blockhouse.[46]

Roosevelt could see the infantry of Kent's division slowly making its hellish way up San Juan Hill, and some of the Spanish were already abandoning the trenches. With the Gatling fire hosing the enemy, he ordered his men to cease firing and prepare to charge the Spanish positions on the San Juan heights to their left front. Thinking that the whole command would follow, TR leaped a wire fence and started off on the double. After he had covered a hundred yards, he turned around and found only five men had accompanied him. Bullets were ripping the grass all around—one of the men dropped dead, and another was badly wounded. There was no use in going forward with only three carbines behind him, and TR retreated under fire. Running back across the wire fence, he was "filled with anger against the troopers, and especially my own regiment for not having accompanied those men." With a look of injury and surprise, the Rough Riders called out, "We didn't hear you, we didn't see you go Colonel; lead on now, we'll sure follow you." Roosevelt wanted to take with him every man on the hill, and he ran down to where Sumner had his temporary headquarters. The general instantly agreed, promising to make sure no one hung back.[47]

The dismounted troopers of the various regiments rushed across the valley that separated Kettle from San Juan Hill. But long before the cavalry reached the crest, the Spanish had run off, save a few who surrendered or were shot down. "When we reached the trenches," Roosevelt said, "we found them filled with dead bodies in the light blue and white uniform of the Spanish Regular army. There were very few wounded. Most of the fallen had little holes in their heads from which their brains were oozing." As at El Caney, they had died with their faces to the enemy. Two Spaniards leaped from the trenches and fired in Roosevelt's direction, not ten yards away. As they turned to run, TR fired twice, missed the first, and killed the second.[48]

Kent's infantry massed in a confused state on the south side of the road facing the main Spanish positions on the heights. The 6th and 16th regiments had exited the thicket and deployed in a skirmish line, while six hundred yards to their front, the enemy continued to pour volleys across the intervening meadow. Immediately in front of the infantry was the six-stranded barbed-wire fence, which the men tried hacking away at with their bayonets. Brigadier Hawkins, whom a reporter described as a "tall and soldierly figure with white goatee and mustache, brilliant in the sunshine," exposed himself without fear. But his men were getting hit in their slow attempt to cross the wire. Farther to the left, Ewers's brigade was already breaking into the meadow; to the right, the cavalry was stumbling over from Kettle Hill.[49]

This was the moment of the Gatling guns. Hawkins ordered his bugles to sound the "Advance," and at the head of his brigade, he waved his hat and called out, "Come on! Come on!" The infantry, in the face of terrific, death-dealing volleys from the crest of the hill, and with the drumming of the "coffee grinder" Gatlings and the renewed fire from Grimes's battery at El Pozo at their backs, began to charge up San Juan Hill. First a handful, then a multitude of skirmishers poured out into the grass-covered valley, cheering, moving forward. As Hawkins wrote in his report, "The very audacity of the assault seemed to demoralize the enemy."[50]

The long, ragged line, with men concentrating in bullet-catching bunches in one place and leaving large gaps in others, lurched forward. The first few men gained the initial slope of the ridge, and with it, some comparative safety, as the enemy could not depress their fire from the summit. They had dug their trenches at the very top, rather than along the military crest, slightly lower down, where their volleys would have been far more effective. Still, the summit spit and flashed with flame. "The men held their guns to their breast and stepped heavily as they climbed," wrote Richard Harding Davis. Behind the first "line," or mass really, the various companies of the regiments spread out like a fan in single files ever moving forward and upward, through the tall, smooth grass, "with difficulty as though they were wading through water." At nearly every point in the advance, a man would suddenly sink or pitch forward, struck by a Mauser bullet, and disappear in the high grass.[51]

Captain Leven Allen, commanding C Company, 16th Infantry, of Hawkins's brigade, provided an excellent account. After coming through the jungle trail, mixing up with units of the 6th Infantry and 71st New York, the company found itself in the sunken road parallel to the grassy field, fronted by the six-stranded barbed-wire fence, which led to the heights. Ahead, about two hundred feet up the steep hill, they could easily see the blockhouse that formed the center of the Spanish position on the crest. Getting no orders, Allen directed his men to open fire on the enemy at long range, seven hundred yards. Other units crowded in, and Allen had great difficulty keeping his men together. They could not just stay there. Allen ordered his men to tear down the fence, something he heard other captains of his regiment shouting at the same time. It was nailed to the living trees of an overgrown hedge, and the men had nothing but their bayonets for the job, hardly the best tool. Yet the wire was partially beaten down in several places. Allen placed his foot on the fence, and called to his men, "Come on!" The company followed in driblets, as it was still very difficult to pass through the wire. Eventually, there were several companies in the open field, five captains at their heads, moving forward. "We were in plain view of the enemy," he reported, "and our men were falling fast."[52]

The advance continued steadily, without pause, until the companies were about two-thirds of the way up. At this critical juncture, shells from Grimes's battery, which had reopened fire from El Pozo, began bursting dangerously near. Allen was not disposed to halt, feeling the firing would stop in time for the final assault on the crest line. Some shells began falling between the advance and the Spanish trenches, but he urged his men forward, and they responded "most nobly." He could see some of the enemy abandoning their positions, and was at the point to press home the victory and take the crest when a great cry came from the foot of the hill: "Come back! Come back!" Bugles sounded the "Recall" and "Assembly." The men naturally hesitated, stopped, then began drifting back down the slope. The Spanish rousted by the Gatling guns and on the run, there had been nothing to prevent the final charge "save the loud mouths of those in the rear who became suddenly fearful for our safety."[53]

This sudden withdrawal lost precious time for the Americans, time that might have permitted General Linares to reinforce the heights with additional forces. Instead, he ordered a withdrawal, sending forward a company of mounted *guerrilleros* to cover the retreating movement of the riflemen in the trenches. To take the place of the *guerrilleros* in the second line, Linares ordered up a hundred convalescents from the military hospital. They were given arms and sent to Fort Canosa at the junction of the *camino real*–El Caney roads.

Captain Allen, hurling curses at the "wretches" below, ordered his company to lie down and collect their strength and breath. Just then he noticed another captain, with some men still higher up on the slope, waving his hat. Allen took this as a call for support and called out to his men, "Look at Captain McFarland and E Company! Who of C Company will go with me to the top of that hill in spite of hell and the battery?" The men near him sprang to their feet and plunged up the hill once more, only to find McFarland wounded, and his company coming slowly down. There were too few men to advance further, and Allen to his disgust fell back once more.[54]

But they were to go up yet a third time. Grimes's battery had finally ceased firing, though the Spanish riflemen in the trenches and blockhouse had not. Again the dark blue infantry line went forward, up the slope. When near the crest, broken fragments of the various regiments came together in a sudden burst of speed, and in a great, cheering rush stormed the crest of San Juan Hill. The Spanish appeared for a moment, outlined against the sky, poised for instant flight, and fired a last volley before being overwhelmed. Coming up in support on the right, to rush the blockhouse together with the infantry, were the 9th Cavalry and the Rough Riders, TR at their head. The "line" became a complete shambles of infantry and cavalry together, who fell on their faces along the crest and opened fire on the retreating enemy. Into the soft earth of the trenches were driven the yellow silk flags of the cavalry and the U.S. colors of the infantry. The men then collapsed as Davis watched, "and looked back at the road they had climbed and swung their hats in the air."[55]

Amid the unbelievable confusion "we found ourselves overlooking Santiago," Roosevelt said. While the troops were re-forming, one of Sumner's aides rode up with orders to halt the Cavalry Division in place, advance no further, and hold the heights at all hazards against the expected Spanish counterattack. Roosevelt had with him the elements of six cavalry regiments, which formed the right wing of the army, and being the senior officer on that part of the hills, he remained in command of the sector for the rest of the afternoon and night.[56]

The Spanish first-line trenches had been captured by two o'clock, and though the Americans held the ridgeline, it was still a tenuous position. There were no ready reserves to throw in should the Spanish counterattack, and ammunition was in desperately short supply—it was feared that Kent's division would run out by the end of the day. Ammunition, reported Lieutenant Miley from the front, needed to be "pushed forward with energy." Also the artillery and Gatling guns "must be pushed forward at once and strongly entrenched by night." Food was now a dire necessity as well, the men having eaten nothing since dawn. And Miley strongly urged Colonel McClernand to pull Bates's brigade out of El Caney and bring it to the heights "at once. We need fresh men and . . . ammunition to enable us to hold the hill. Urge everything forward."[57]

All during the afternoon and into the night the Spanish kept up a random fire of musketry and artillery on the position along the crest of the heights, at times reaching great intensity and causing some losses among the American troops. The fight between the two lines, facing each other at distances of from three hundred to eight hundred yards, continued at intervals until quite dark. In the course of this firefight, the Spanish made what Roosevelt called the only offensive movement he observed during the whole campaign. Some companies of infantry, a company of sailors under Captain Joaquín Bustamante, and a troop of mounted *guerrilleros* moved forward, seemingly in an attempt to retake a part of the line. But they advanced only a few yards before spirited rifle fire drove them back, Bustamante taking a fatal wound. "It could not be called a charge," Roosevelt said, "and not only was it not pushed home, but it was stopped almost as soon as it began, our men running forward to the crest of the hill with shouts of delight at seeing their enemies at last come into the open." Bustamante, in spite of the heat, had entered the battle in his service "blue-cloth" uniform, which easily distinguished him from everyone else in the attack. When Lieutenant Müller found him being carried back on a litter, "he was covered with blood, pale and disfigured, his eyes closed, and without his saber and revolver." Before being hit, his horse had been killed under him, and his cap shot away. At the military hospital, "in spite of his insignias of a [naval captain], nobody paid much attention to him . . . for over 300 wounded had been received, and they were still coming." In all that day, at El Caney and San Juan, the Spanish lost 593 men killed and wounded, including General Linares, who lost an arm. He turned over field command to the military governor of Santiago, General José Toral.[58]

Wheeler had left his sickbed and, carried in a litter to the battlefield, resumed command of the cavalry. In messages sent to the rear, he informed General Shafter that owing to the number of casualties, well over a thousand, and the natural drifting away of men to the rear, the right flank was dangerously weak should the Spanish opt to renew their attack that night. He estimated there were not more than three thousand effective men on the heights at the end of the day. Since Lawton had not yet come down from El Caney to take position on the right flank, the 13th Infantry from Kent's division took ground between the Rough Riders and the 9th Cavalry on the thin right of the line. Fortunately, there were some reinforcements. Green and untested, they were nonetheless warm bodies that could be thrown into the line as a last resort. The 34th Michigan and 9th Massachusetts, just landed at Siboney, were rushed up the *camino real* to the front, the former taking position behind Kent's division, and the latter extending his flank to the extreme left.

Wheeler, racked with malaria, took command on the heights as senior officer and ordered the entire line to entrench on the most advanced position. Wagons were sent to collect tools cast aside during the deployment. Throughout the night the digging was kept up by the tired, hungry men. The only thing to arrive promptly was ammunition, which was direly needed as the Spanish fire was incessant. Most everything else—the shelter tents, dry clothes, and the rations carried by each man—had been heaped in company and regimental piles stretching back for two miles on the road. Guards were detailed to keep watch over the gear. But during the battle, these men had been pressed to aid the wounded. As a result, everything became the property of the first comer, usually the Cubans, straggling in wake of the advance. Every effort was made to get food to the heights, and some actually arrived in the evening. But for many, their long fast would not end until the next day.

Morale began to slip. As Wheeler informed General Shafter, "A number of officers have appealed to me to have the line withdrawn and take up a strong position farther back, and I expect they will appeal to you." Wheeler would have none of it. "I have positively discountenanced this, as it would cost us much prestige." With the lines so thin, the many wounded, and universal exhaustion, he hoped the stragglers who had gone to the rear could be gotten up to the ridge that night. "We ought to hold tomorrow," he wrote, "but I fear it will be a severe day."[59]

At 1:30 A.M., July 2, Bates's brigade countermarched from El Caney and took position on the far south of the line, further extending Kent's left flank. The brigade had started out from Siboney on the evening of June 30, marched to Shafter's headquarters that night, and gone from there to El Caney. They had been in the thick of that fight for over two hours, and following the town's surrender had hurried back by the El Caney–El Pozo trail to the heights at San Juan, arriving a little after midnight. With the exception of six hours, during the night of June 30 to July 1, Bates had been continuously marching and fighting for nearly thirty hours.

The battles of El Caney and San Juan took much of the fight out of the Fifth Corps. Lieutenant Müller, who observed the battle, noted, "On the first of July the Americans fought without protection and with truly admirable courage, but they did not fight again as they did that day." The biographer of William McKinley, Margaret Leech, wrote of General Shafter's state, "One day's fighting had used up all his aggressiveness. He had broken his egg and spoiled his omelet; and sick in mind and body, he shrank from exposing his army to further combat."[60]

"Our casualties will be above 400," Shafter telegraphed to the War Department on the evening after the battle. Actually they were far greater. By the close of July 3, they had climbed to 225 dead and 1,384 wounded. The entire loss amounting to almost exactly 10 percent of the total force of 15,065 men engaged in combat. The loss in officers had been particularly heavy, 22 dead, 94 wounded. Of Admiral Sampson, Shafter asked, and received, the assistance of the fleet surgeons for the base hospital at Siboney, which held 385 wounded men by the end of the day.[61]

The care of the wounded left much to be desired, approaching a scandalous state. Clara Barton, who had come down in the Red Cross–chartered steamer *State of Texas,* went with her assistants into the field. The supplies aboard this ship became an invaluable addition. Ample army hospital supplies (except for ambulances) had accompanied the expedition, but the confusion and lack of organization in loading and unloading made locating and getting the stuff ashore an ordeal. The transports continued to wander off the beaches, and one, carrying the corps' reserve medical stores, hovered about the Morro for five days. The ship carrying the 1st Division hospital disappeared for a week, and no mention is made of hospitals for the 2nd or Cavalry divisions until after the cessation of hostilities. Large quantities of medical supplies remained aboard ships under orders to return to the United States without landing.

Seventeen ambulances had been loaded at Tampa, though only three seem to have gotten ashore in time for the battle. Fifty more, and their mules, had been left behind for want of space in the steamers. It was thought that the standard army wagon could do double duty of hauling supplies and the wounded and sick. The only field hospital near the front was that of Kent's 1st Division, moved to within 1,200 yards of the heights. As Captain Chadwick said, "It seemed an ideal camp, except for the daily rains and the polluted water supply."[62]

Outside of instruments, operating tables, and medicines, the resources of the 1st Division hospital were extremely limited. There was tent shelter for about a hundred wounded men, but no cots, hammocks, mattresses, or pillows. The limited supply of blankets was soon exhausted, and there was no clothing except for some three dozen shirts. "In the form of hospital food," wrote Red Cross volunteer George Kennan, "there was nothing except a few jars of beef extract, malted milk, etc."; and this was carried into the field by the divisional surgeon in his personal baggage, held in reserve for the truly desperate cases. The rest made due on bacon, hardtack, and beans.[63]

"All that a litter squad could do with a man when they lifted him from the operating table," Kennan continued, "was to carry him away and lay him down, half-naked as he was, on the water-soaked ground under the stars. Weak and shaken from agony under the surgeon's knife and probe, there he had to lie in the high wet grass, with no one to look after him, no blanket over him, no pillow under his head." Once a man had been treated in the field hospital, assuming he survived, he was taken to Siboney as fast as could be managed and there housed in the mining company premises until shipped out to the hospital steamer, *Olivette*. General Shafter soon ordered the conversion of two additional vessels into hospital ships.[64]

Duffield's feint attack on the Spanish position at Aguadores was anticlimactic at best. The troops, the 33rd Michigan, arrived by train along the coastal railroad near midmorning, protected on their seaward flank by the guns of the *New York*, *Suwanee*, and the armed yacht *Gloucester.* About 275 Spaniards held some trenches on the hill to the west of the railroad bridge over the San Juan River gorge, and these men disappeared once the ships opened fire. A corner of the local blockhouse was knocked off and the flagstaff shot away. Random firing was kept up by both sides through the early afternoon, when the Spanish brought up a small gun and fired several shells down the gorge. After the piece was rendered silent by the *New York,* Duffield's men boarded their train and returned to Siboney, making no further effort to either attack or hold the position.

As Wheeler had predicted, July 2 was a day of intense trial. Flooding rains in the night made conditions for the survivors on the crest and for the wounded truly hellish. The twelve miles of road between the front and Siboney were transformed into a mud slough, and resupply, except by mule pack train, was nearly impossible. On more than one occasion, heavily laden mules were swept away and drowned while attempting to ford the swollen streams. At around noon, Lawton, after a long, hard, roundabout march, brought his division into line on the San Juan heights, to the right of the cavalry. Thus, the whole army—its effectives anyway—was now positioned for the assault on the city.

During the entire day, though they made no attempt to retake the hills, the Spanish kept up a severe, continuous drumbeat of rifle fire, killing and wounding another 150 Americans on the heights. For their part, the U.S. troops were too near collapse from exhaustion to do much else than duck and take cover. The men had been without sleep for two days, and for the greater part of that time, under fire. Many had not been fed, their clothing was soaked through, and they scrambled about in the trenches on their hands and knees, "weakened by the fierce tropical sun."[65]

General Shafter, too, showed the ill effects of the battle. His health badly deteriorating, his three-hundred-pound bulk enervated by the heat, he knew his army had shot its bolt, and so had he. "Terrible fight yesterday," he wrote to Admiral Sampson. His line was entrenched about three-quarters of a mile from the city, but hadn't the strength for the final push. He begged the admiral to "make effort immediately to force [harbor] entrance to avoid future losses among my men, which are already very heavy. You can now operate with less loss of life than I can."[66]

Admiral Sampson's reply came in two parts. The first, written by his flag lieutenant, Sidney Staunton, reiterated the impossibility of forcing the harbor entrance until the mines were cleared, "a work of some time after forts are taken possession by your troops." Later in the day, the admiral replied personally. It was his hope that the army might still attack the shore batteries from the rear, leaving the fleet "at liberty" to drag the entrance for mines. But if the condition of the army was as dire as Shafter made out, "If it is your earnest desire that we should force the entrance, I will at once prepare to undertake it." He thought, however, and let the general know, that if the fleet failed in the attempt, everyone's situation, navy's and army's, would only be much worse for the botched effort.[67]

At 6:00 P.M., on July 2, General Shafter felt it essential to call together his senior officers to decide on a course of action. There was pressure on the general to abandon the heights, but it is impossible to say from whom. Such an option was militarily insane: to retreat after the objective had been attained at such cost would have been devastating to morale, to say nothing of having to do it all again with a substantially inferior force in the attack and the enemy greatly sustained by their successful defense. Reports of Spanish reinforcements came into headquarters hourly. Escario's column of three thousand–plus was a day's march from the city. In fact, that was all, though hobgoblins of thousands of arriving Spaniards badly spooked the general's mind.

Meeting with Shafter at El Pozo were Wheeler, Kent, Lawton, and Bates. Shafter opened the council with a statement that eight thousand Spanish reinforcements (the overblown estimate of Escario's column) were but a day's march from Santiago to the west. He reported large forces of troops at San Luis, less than fifteen miles north, as well as ten thousand at Holguín and seven thousand more at Guantánamo.

Though Shafter did not know it, this was all academic. The Spanish could not accomplish it. Beyond Escario's column, they hadn't the transportation for the movement of their forces, the Cuban roads being just as abominable in the rainy season for them as for the Americans. Save for Escario, nobody budged. Yet Shafter could not know that, either. "If they come down," he told his subordinates, "we shall have to get back, and I want an expression of opinion against anything that might come. If those forces take us in flank [the American right], which would not be difficult in our present exposed position, I will be held responsible."[68]

Bates, the junior, answered first. At the endmost left of the line, he did not think he could hold his present position without reinforcements. Then came Lawton's turn; "Hang on," he advised the commanding general, followed by Kent and Wheeler with the same sentiments. The conference lasted two hours, and at its close, Shafter opted for a compromise of sorts. The army would keep its present positions for the next twenty-four hours, and if conditions had not improved, he would again call on his officers for their views.[69]

The following day, Sunday, July 3, Shafter dispatched a gloomy telegram to the War Department. He reported Santiago invested by the Fifth Corps to the north and east, but with very thin lines; there was no real thought of an assault on the city anytime soon. Worse, "I am seriously considering withdrawing about five miles, and taking up a new position on the high ground between the San Juan River and Siboney."[70]

But soon afterward, in all likelihood supported by the opinions of his senior subordinates, Shafter got hold of his nerves and thought no more of retreat. Instead, in a move of high pluck, he sent a surrender demand to General Toral under a flag of truce: "Sir: I shall be obliged, unless you surrender, to shell Santiago de Cuba." Toral was warned to inform all foreigners, women, and children to leave the city by ten o'clock the next morning. Naturally, Toral rejected this first demand: "It is my duty to say to you that this city will not surrender."[71]

In Washington, Russell Alger considered July 3 "the darkest day of the war." Shafter's first messages of the battle, arriving at the War Department late on the night of the first, indicated "action is now going on," followed by a report of carrying the enemy's outer defenses, and "casualties will be above 400." Shortly after midnight, July 2, came another dispatch with Shafter announcing, "I fear I have underestimated today's casualties," and asking for a large and "thoroughly equipped" hospital ship "at once." Nothing further was received at the department that day. "But the air," Alger said, "was filled with foreboding rumors." Though there was no positive information, the press printed accounts of Shafter's illness, and Wheeler's as well, reporting incorrectly that yellow fever had appeared among the troops. For the administration, the need for news was too much to bear. Just after midnight, July 3, Alger telegraphed, "We are waiting with intense anxiety tidings of yesterday."[72]

When Sunday, July 3, dawned in Washington with no bulletins from the front, anxiety over the fate of the army gripped the country. All day, the War Department was thronged, Alger said, "by people prominent in political and private life," all apprehensively seeking the latest word. The papers and the Associated Press wire were full of half-truths and bare accounts, which the secretary and president, awake until almost sunrise, found deeply troubling, especially since they had heard nothing official from Shafter since his first telegrams on the night of the action. At eleven o'clock in the morning, Alger sent another message, instructing Shafter to "interrupt" all communications sent out by the correspondents and to make an official report to the War Department at the end of each day. Less than an hour later came the general's melancholy thoughts of withdrawing, which did nothing to assuage the pessimism permeating the capital.[73]

Worse yet, due to a telegraph operator's mistake, the message—which should have begun, "We have the town well invested on the north and east"—read instead, "Well invested on the north and east," implying that the enemy had succeeded in turning the army's right flank and was threatening its rear. This, taken in conjunction with the withdrawal language that followed, had a chilling effect on the administration. If Shafter was compelled to abandon his position, it would mean a catastrophic loss of American prestige abroad, to say nothing of encouraging the Spanish government to greater resistance. Nothing yet was known in Washington of Shafter's surrender demand to the Spanish, which would have alleviated some of the apprehension. In any event, the conditions at the front were regarded as too delicate to warrant any interference by the War Department in the exercise of Shafter's authority. "Of course," Alger telegraphed, "you can judge the situation better than we can at this end of the line." But if he could hold his lines on the heights, "the effect upon the country would be much better than falling back." These were only suggestions, Alger noted, and he left the decisions to the commanding general, ending, "We shall send you reinforcements at once." He would increase the Fifth Corps by another ten thousand men, and anything else the general wanted. It bucked up Shafter's spirits enormously. Later in the day, to the inexpressible relief of the administration, the correct version of the cable, "We have the town well invested," arrived at the War Department. On July 4 came the best news yet from the army: "I shall hold my present position."[74]

At 7:00 P.M., the War Department telegraphs clicked out yet another dispatch from the front. One of Shafter's cavalry officers had come in from the far right of the line, where he commanded an excellent view of the upper harbor. He reported that at 10:00 that morning, the Spanish squadron, in plain sight, had steamed down the bay, and shortly afterward came the sound of heavy naval gunfire. Soon, from Siboney, Shafter got news from Duffield that naval signals indicated the Spanish squadron "had escaped" and Admiral Sampson "was in pursuit." There was more. Yesterday the French consul had passed the information that in conversation with Admiral Cervera, the Spaniard had stated that "it was better to die fighting than blow up his ships in harbor."[75]

CHAPTER 13

FOURTH OF JULY
PRESENT

Papa, the enemy's ships are coming out!
—*Naval Cadet Herbert Evans, USN, July 3, 1898*

We have lost everything, the majority of us reaching the shore
absolutely naked.
—*Vice Admiral Pascual Cervera y Topete,*
commanding the Spanish cruiser squadron

Up the halyards of the flagship *New York* soared the signal flags,
"Disregard motions of commander in chief." The admiral, dressed in
summer whites, with leggings, stood on the quarterdeck, hardly rel-
ishing the coming hot ride up the brown hills from Siboney to meet
with General Shafter at his headquarters near El Pozo. Like the corpulent general, the pencil-thin admiral was not in very good health.
He was well-nigh worn out from the constant tension of the blockade. William Goode, the Associated Press reporter aboard the *New
York,* wrote of the "physical and mental strain [that] . . . had confined him once or twice to his bed, much against his will." The admiral was now also deaf in one ear, the result of the gun blasts during the
bombardment of Aguadores two days before.[1]

"Terrible fight yesterday," the gouty, despondent General Shafter
had written to the admiral the morning after the battle, pleading for
the navy to make an "effort immediately" to force the harbor entrance.
To this entreaty, which had festered since the day the army landed,

Sampson's staff responded with the navy's standard answer. It was impossible for the fleet to force the harbor mouth until the minefield was swept.[2]

But General Shafter remained puzzled; indeed, he was at a "loss to see why the navy cannot work as well as the army" in performing the task. Sampson replied directly. All right, he responded with exasperation, "If it is your earnest desire that we should force the entrance, I will at once prepare to undertake it." He was eager to cooperate in a combined operation, using the fleet's marines on the Socapa side, while the army tackled the Morro end of things. Captain Chadwick, the chief of staff, had gone ashore on Saturday, July 2, the day previous, to arrange a conference between the commanders to coordinate this combined action. Shafter's health did not permit him to come out to the flagship, nor did it permit of his taking the rough ride down from El Pozo to Siboney; hence the admiral had donned his leggings to meet the general at corps headquarters. The conference was scheduled for the morning of July 3.[3]

Admiral Sampson wasn't the only senior naval officer to be badgered with instructions and not very helpful advice by his army counterparts; Admiral Cervera found himself metaphorically in the same boat and with consequences far more dire. On June 20, the day the American invasion force hove into sight off Daiquirí, Captain General Blanco dashed off a communication to his chief, the minister of war in Madrid. The presence of Cervera's squadron at Santiago had changed the strategic locus of the war from a probable American attack on Havana and its environs to a campaign at the other end of the island. Blanco "regretted" the "independence" of Admiral Cervera, which prevented the captain general from "aiding" naval operations. If only he and Admiral Manterola in Havana had been consulted beforehand, and General Linares too, for that matter, "perhaps between us we might in the beginning have found a better solution than those now awaiting the squadron"—namely, either an unequal battle in the harbor, or a breakout for Cienfuegos, Haiti, or Jamaica, perhaps, "where it would again be closed in."[4]

It would, Blanco went on, be "preferable" for the squadron to make for Cienfuegos, or even Havana; or best of all, reinforced with the

Pelayo and *Carlos V,* have the whole aggregate return to Spain; "anything rather than [to] remain closed in Santiago with the prospect of having to surrender from starvation." The situation had now become "extremely serious," and he had no doubt the government in these "critical" circumstances would order what was best for the good of Spain "and the honor of our arms." To that end, Blanco respectfully suggested to the minister the uniting of the military and naval commands in Cuba "under one head," his own, asking that he be invested with the authority over all land and naval forces on the island.[5]

Blanco's request for authority over Cervera, and thus naval operations, was approved by Madrid, which also granted permission for the squadron to make a sortie from Santiago, though to where was left open. As a contingency measure, certain supplies were sent overland from Havana to Cienfuegos, and according to the fire-breathing minister of marine, Admiral Auñón, auxiliary cruisers would "be sent to hostile [American] coast" to act as a diversion for Cervera's exit from Santiago. This operation never went beyond the words of the minister's telegram.[6]

When Cervera received word of the change in command and the government's permission, in principle, for the squadron to attempt its escape, the admiral must have torn at his hair. Madrid had absolutely no concept of his plight; did they think the *yanqui* blockaders were paper ships? He cabled Auñón at the naval ministry: "As it is absolutely impossible for squadron to escape under these circumstances, [I] intend to resist as long as possible, and destroy ships in the last extreme. Although others [namely Auñón and his predecessor, Bermejo] are responsible for this untenable situation into which we are forced in spite of my opposition, it is very painful to be an actor therein."[7]

On June 24, Cervera assembled his senior officers, less Captain Bustamante, who was ashore in command of the naval landing force in front of Santiago. He read to them the cable approving the sortie and asked for views. In ascending seniority, the men categorically stated that any exit was "absolutely impossible." He then read the telegram of reply, and they agreed with their admiral that the government had indeed placed them in a very "painful situation." But no one really had any idea of what to do, besides resisting in the harbor if and when the American fleet forced the entrance. If the Americans did not so engage them, then they would blow themselves up rather than starve into surrender. What else was there?[8]

Now that the squadron was officially under the command of Captain General Blanco, Admiral Cervera felt it only right to let the man know what he had acquired. It was pretty much the same litany he had sung prior to leaving the Cape Verdes; nothing had changed, except for the worse. Of the 3,000 rounds of 5.5-inch ammunition, only 620 were considered reliable. The rest, his gunnery officers pronounced "worthless." Two 5.5-inchers in the *Vizcaya* and one in the *Almirante Oquendo* were defective, and the majority of fuses of all types and calibers were unserviceable. The *Cristóbal Colón*, of course, still lacked her main battery of four 10-inch guns and could not obtain them unless she returned to a European dockyard. The *Vizcaya's* bottom remained excessively foul, "and [she] has lost her speed." There was little coal left, and provisions enough to endure only until the end of July. Lest Blanco have any fantasies about a naval battle, Cervera stated bluntly, "Blockading fleet is four times superior; hence our sortie would be positively certain destruction."[9]

Notwithstanding the extreme pessimism of the admiral, Blanco needed something more regarding the naval plans: "rot at our moorings, then blow ourselves up" surely could not be all. On the day he received Cervera's assessment of force, Blanco contacted General Linares in hopes of ascertaining the admiral's true plans. "It is my opinion," Blanco telegraphed, "that [Cervera] should go out from Santiago as early as possible whenever he may deem best." According to his most reliable information, Santiago was blockaded by only seven warships. There were nine at Havana, yet two small merchantmen had had no trouble in running that blockade in the middle of the night. Blanco made no differentiation between the gunboats and small cruisers blockading off Havana and the battleships and armored cruisers at Santiago. Nor did he take into account that two small cargo vessels running out of Havana did not exactly represent Spain's naval power in the West Indies, ships that would have to exit a twisting harbor mouth with the enemy's searchlights full in their face. Cervera *had* to engage the enemy: "If we should lose the squadron without fighting," Blanco told Linares, "the moral effect would be terrible, both in Spain and abroad."[10]

When Linares put the questions to Cervera, the admiral answered bluntly. He had considered the squadron lost ever since it left the

Cape Verdes, "for to think of anything else seems madness to me." To Blanco's contention that because two freighters had run the Havana blockade, Cervera could break out at Santiago, the admiral responded, "There is no possibility of stratagem or disguise, and the absolutely certain result [of a sortie] will be the ruin of each and all of the ships and the death of the greater part of their crews." If he thought he had the "remotest chance of success" he would have made the attempt already (though in late May, when there were only weak scouts off the port, he did not avail himself of the opportunity); but even then, it would only have amounted to a change of trap. If the squadron could fight its way to Havana, it would be a different story entirely, but there was no chance of that; the enemy would run them down. "Today," he continued the lament to Linares, "I consider the squadron lost as much as ever, and the dilemma is whether to lose it by destroying it, if Santiago is not able to resist . . . or to lose it by sacrificing to vanity the majority of its crews." For himself, he was a man without ambitions, "without mad passions," and would undertake whatever had to be done, but "most emphatically," he told the general, "I shall *never* be the one to decree the horrible and useless hecatomb" that was the only possible result of a squadron sortie into the teeth of the American blockade. That was for Blanco to decide; the captain general wanted overall command, and now he had it. It was up to him "whether I am to go out to suicide, dragging along with me those 2,000 sons of Spain." With that he considered he had stated his aims.[11]

Cervera wrote to Blanco directly the same day. It was not true the blockade of Santiago was reduced to seven vessels. The principal enemy ships represented three times the gunnery strength of his own four cruisers. Again, he would never order the squadron out, but if Blanco so directed, "I shall carry it out."[12]

In response to these statements and sentiments, Blanco telegraphed Cervera on June 26 in a vain attempt to soothe the admiral's fears. "It seems to be," he began, "you somewhat exaggerate [the] difficulties of [a] sortie." The whole matter, as he envisioned it, was not a question of fighting, per se, but of escaping "from that prison in which the squadron is unfortunately shut." He believed it possible to take advantage of a dark night and dirty weather to break out and flee to wherever Cervera thought best. The fact that the admiral felt certain of Santiago's fall was an additional reason for flight, since it was infinitely preferable "for the honor of arms" to fall in battle.[13]

Blanco, however, then reversed himself on the entire matter: even if Santiago fell and there was no sortie, the destruction of the ships need not occur. They could surrender to the Americans as they had to the British in August 1762, when a dozen Spanish ships of the line capitulated at Havana to superior forces during the Seven Years' War. But, twisting his reasoning yet again, Blanco told Cervera that if his ships were captured at Santiago, the effect "in the whole world" would be disastrous, and the war would be considered over in favor of the enemy—which was exactly right. The "eyes of every nation," he said, were fixed on the squadron, and the honor of Spain rested on its rusty hulls. "[T]o my mind," concluded the captain general, "there can be no doubt as to the solution of the dilemma," especially as he had great confidence in its success. He would leave the route and destination of the sortie to Cervera, and the decision to leave any slow ships behind as well.[14]

Cervera was having none of this. If Blanco wanted a sortie, he would have to issue a direct order, not just something the admiral could construe as a strong suggestion. "I beg you will confirm the order of the sortie, because it is not explicit." It caused Blanco to take a small step back, and perhaps rethink it all. "Tell me candidly," he wrote the same day, "your opinion of [the] squadron, whether you believe it can go out and what solution seems best to you." Cervera did not reply directly, possibly in disgust, for what more could he say? He told Blanco of a communication just received from General Linares, that it was impossible to reembark the naval landing force from the trenches, upwards of a thousand men, until Escario's column arrived from Manzanillo. So at this point it was all problematic. Even if Cervera wanted to escape, he could not do so with half his crews ashore, men Linares refused to return.[15]

The following day, Blanco solidified his instructions. If it was at all possible, he would send additional reinforcements to the city, perhaps even raising the siege and achieving the "salvation [of the] squadron." If not, it would be necessary for the squadron to leave harbor in spite of all the difficulties Cervera had enumerated, and "which I appreciate." The plan, as he unfolded it to Cervera, would have the squadron sit in the harbor "and . . . provided it has provisions left," wait for a favorable opportunity to exit in whatever direction Cervera deemed best. But should the situation in Santiago become "aggravated," and its fall imminent, the squadron must sortie immediately, "as best it can," trusting its fate to the "valor and ability" of Admiral Cervera and his captains.[16]

There were practical difficulties of which Blanco was not aware. The scanty supply of coal at Santiago made it extremely difficult to keep in constant readiness for instant movement. For the big cruisers, it took twelve hours to work up a full head of steam from cold boilers. Even if the fires were banked at nominal levels in all boilers, just to be ready for the opportunity to make the dash, each ship would burn fifteen tons of coal each day. The instructions from Blanco, however, were now clear in Cervera's mind, and he assured the captain general that if a favorable opportunity presented, he would sortie, or if the city looked about to fall, to steam out of harbor at "the last hour, even though loss of squadron be certain."[17]

On Thursday, June 30, Cervera dispatched a request to General Linares citing Blanco's authorization for the sortie should the situation in Santiago become "aggravated." In Cervera's opinion, such a condition existed and he needed his thousand men now. Linares refused. He had no way of knowing how far the Americans would press their attack; thus "the moment when to notify" Cervera of the "aggravated" situation was impossible to calculate. Still, he would attempt to keep the admiral posted on the course of the battle, though if it turned out badly, "the moment would not be propitious" for reembarking the sailors. For Cervera, it was infuriating. The army, in the person of the captain general, had given specific orders for naval operations, yet General Linares, by refusing to return the landing force, made those operations impossible.[18]

On July 1, the day of the land battle, Cervera telegraphed Blanco before receiving news of the American victory, citing Linares's obstinacy in refusing to return the crews. These men were absolutely critical to the operations of the squadron; denied them, Cervera needed a modification of the sortie instructions. "As these ships cannot go out without the forces . . . the case might arise that I could not carry out your orders."[19]

At 7:00 P.M., with the Americans occupying both El Caney and the San Juan heights, Cervera convened a conference of his captains. In the place of the mortally wounded Joaquín Bustamante, Captain Victor Concas of the flagship *María Teresa* assumed the added capacity of chief of staff. Cervera, following a summary of the day's disastrous events, asked his officers their opinion as to whether the situation had indeed arrived in which the captain general had ordered the squadron to sortie; in other words, had their predicament become "aggravated"? The men were unanimous in their conclusion—yes it had, but it was also "absolutely impossible" to sortie without reembarking the landing force. General José Toral, who, on the wounding of Linares, had taken command of the garrison, maintained his predecessor's decision: the sailors could not be allowed to return to their ships—in the army's opinion, it would entail the immediate loss of the city. Given this, the captains concluded that in order to cooperate in the defense of the city, the only measure they could possibly accomplish was to block the harbor entrance and prevent an ingress by the enemy fleet. This impasse prompted Cervera's second telegram to Blanco that day. Noting again that the army refused to permit the withdrawal of the sailors from the inner line of trenches, he said: "Without them the sortie cannot be attempted." What did the captain general now advise?[20]

Very late in the day, Blanco replied with two cables fifteen minutes apart, each headed "Very urgent." In the first, he said Cervera was to reembark his crews, "take advantage of first opportunity, and go out with the ships of your squadron" to wherever Cervera thought best. He was authorized to leave behind any vessel whose lack of speed or other adverse circumstance prohibited optimum operations. For the admiral's information, he added that there were only three blockaders at Cienfuegos and nine at Havana, "none of them of great power." The second telegram indicated Blanco's great anxiety and his certainty that the fall of Santiago was only a matter of time. Cervera was urged to "hasten" the sortie before the enemy could take possession of the harbor entrance. Before daybreak the next morning, Saturday, July 2, Cervera received still further orders from the captain general: "In view of exhausted and serious condition of Santiago . . . your excellency will reembark troops of squadron as fast as possible, and go out immediately."[21]

Toral received messages about the same time. Blanco exhorted him to concentrate his forces and prolong the defense of the city, at all costs preventing the enemy from taking possession of the harbor mouth. If Toral could not hold out until the arrival of Escario's column from Manzanillo (which would enter Santiago the next day), he must gather together all troops and loyal citizens and fall back on Holguín or Manzanillo, "destroying what cannot be taken along and burning everything left behind, so that not the least trophy of victory will fall into the enemy's hands."[22]

At sunup that Saturday, July 2, Admiral Cervera called his captains to the flagship for their last council of war. Blanco had ordered the sortie, and the time for discussion was over; they had nothing else to do but to obey. It was agreed the sally should be made with all possible haste lest news of the movement reach the enemy. The hour was set for 4:00 P.M. that day, if the crews could be gotten aboard in time; if not, then the next morning.

Captain Concas believed there was no way to mask the movement within the harbor entirely—there'd be too much smoke for that—and he was sure the enemy would be aware of the foray within a few hours of the initial preparations. "We would thus lose the only hope which remained to us, that of engaging [the American fleet] before their engines were entirely ready."[23]

Cervera then issued his instructions for the coming battle. They were based on observation of the enemy's maneuvers during the blockade. The ships were generally aligned in a "great arc," and the space on the west side, between the *Texas* and the shoreline, was always occupied by the *Brooklyn,* the fastest of the enemy ships, and an armed yacht. Supposing, therefore, the *Brooklyn* was at her usual station when the Spanish came out, the *María Teresa* was to head straight for her, endeavoring to ram. While the American squadron grappled with the flagship, the remaining vessels, led by the *Vizcaya,* would pass to the westward along the coast and attempt their escape. Though to where was still an open question—Cienfuegos, perhaps, or possibly even Havana. The two destroyers, *Plutón* and *Furor,* were to place themselves under the protection of the cruisers and, as soon as they could, try to steam away from the action in the wake of the big ships, except, as Concas said, "in case a good opportunity should present itself."[24]

Admiral Cervera's words were greeted with enthusiasm by the senior officers. They clasped each other's hands, Concas remembered, "fervently, as [sailors] who knew how to meet death and destruction, from which no power could save us." The men uttered "harsh and well-merited" denunciations of the "statesmen" in Madrid who had placed them in this unenviable predicament, politicians who acted as if they owed nothing to God or their country; "and we swore that if anyone of us should survive he would defend the memory of those who perished in the encounter." Orders were passed to all ships to light their fires and be prepared to exit that evening, as soon as the landing force was aboard. Concas went ashore to give General Toral the sortie orders from the captain general.[25]

Beginning in late afternoon, the landing force returned to their respective ships, all except the *Vizcaya*'s, which were at the far western end of the defensive perimeter at El Cobre. It was very late and they were exhausted by the time they arrived at the fleet landing, prompting Cervera to postpone the escape to Sunday morning in order to allow everyone a night's rest. In great secrecy, Captain Concas and his engineering officers made all preparations for scuttling the flagship *María Teresa* should the ship be in danger of capture, "feeling sure it would be carried out." These arrangements could not be made public for fear of jeopardizing the morale of the crew.[26]

July 3 dawned foggy. In the stokeholds, fires were spread under all boilers, and in the ships' messes, the men were given extra rations. At 7:00 A.M., Concas took the small gunboat *Alvarado* to the harbor mouth to reconnoiter the enemy, whose ships could not be seen from the anchorage. The Americans were in their usual positions, though perhaps a little closer inshore. One of the battleships was missing (the *Massachusetts*, gone to Guantánamo for coal), and that was to the good.

Immediately on Concas's return and his report to the admiral, anchors were heaved in, and the signal for the action, "*Viva España*," flew up the halyards from the flagship. The hoist was answered with enthusiasm by all the crews as well as by the troops ashore. Battle flags, large gold-and-crimson national ensigns, were hoisted in the ships, and the *Infanta María Teresa* led the squadron out of the anchorage toward the harbor entrance. For the last time, the command rendered honors to its admiral, according to Concas, "saluting him with hurrahs that manifested the spirit of the crews, worthy of a better fate." With a rapidity that threw caution aside, the *María Teresa* advanced until abreast of the Estrella battery just inside the entrance from the Morro. Then came the loud crack of a rapid-fire gun from one of the enemy battleships. Not even out of the bay, the squadron had been discovered, and the Americans were converging with obvious great haste upon the head of the Spanish column.[27]

The Spanish had just completed making the turn at Diamond Bank, "amidst deathlike silence," Concas remembered, and all hands from the admiral to the lowest seaman were awed by the "magnificent spectacle" of the ships issuing from the narrow entrance; to port loomed the gray bastions of the Morro, and to starboard, the heights of the Socapa. On the bridge, outside the *María Teresa*'s armored conning tower (which Concas refused to enter, "in order, if I should fall, to set an example to my defenseless crew"), Concas requested permission from the admiral to open fire; it was given and the order passed. "The bugle," he said, heralded the commencement of the battle, "an order . . . followed by an approbation from all those poor sailors and marines who were anxious to fight; for they did not know that those warlike echoes were the signal which hurled their country at the feet of the victor." Concas now waxed with sentiments that would have brought a grunt of approval from Mahan, so exactly did they repeat the tenets of *The Influence of Sea Power upon History*. "The sound of my bugles," mused Concas, "was the last echo of those which history tells us were sounded at the capture of Granada. It was the signal that the history of four centuries of grandeur was at an end and that Spain was becoming a nation of the fourth class." Concas turned to Admiral Cervera. "Poor Spain!" he said to his "noble and beloved" commander. Cervera answered with only a pained glance and a shrug at his chief of staff. The gesture expressed that he had done everything possible to avoid what was about to descend on the squadron, and that his conscience was clear.[28]

Cervera and the chief pilot of the port, Miguel López, stood together. Immediately past Diamond Bank, López nodded to the admiral. "Admiral," he said, "the helm may be shifted now." Without shouting and without excitement, calm as usual, Cervera gave the order, "To starboard," and a moment later, "Fire!" Cervera turned to the pilot. "Good-by," he said, "go, and be sure you let them pay you, because you have earned it well."[29]

The second gun of the flagship's portside battery was the first to open fire. Then, Concas said, "we poured out a frantic fire with our whole battery," except for the forward 11-incher, which he reserved for the instant before ramming. In accordance with orders, he headed the *María Teresa* straight for the *Brooklyn*. The American armored cruiser wore to starboard, presented her stern, and let fly her after turret guns. The *Brooklyn's* sudden and unexpected maneuver brought the *Texas* and *Iowa* between the *María Teresa* and her intended target; to remain on course risked being rammed by the American battleships. After a hurried consultation between Concas and Cervera, it was decided to go about and race westward along the coast. For ten minutes, the *María Teresa* was entirely alone, her consorts still negotiating the shoals of Diamond Bank. The dead already lay torn about on her upper battery deck. Fire from the *Brooklyn, Texas,* and *Iowa* pummeled down. A pair of 12-inch shells from the *Iowa* slammed into her afterdeck, bursting the steam pipe of the main engine pump. Huge clouds of vapor poured out from her stern.[30]

The evening of July 2 and predawn of July 3 had passed quietly in the American blockading ships. In the *Iowa,* which was directly in front of the harbor entrance and could see well up the reach, the officer of the watch discerned six columns of smoke rising above the land. After a careful look, Captain Bob Evans dismissed it as nothing more than the Spanish ships freshening their fires, as they had done on several occasions. But as he later admitted, the *Iowa's* signalmen took the observation somewhat more seriously, and bent on the halyards signal No. 250, "Enemy's ships escaping," ready for instant hoisting.[31]

The sun peeked over the eastern horizon, heralding a fine Sunday, with a bit of early fog, as the American ships wallowed in their usual positions along the rim of the semicircle of blockade. On the western, Socapa, side, the armed yacht *Vixen* was closest to the shore. Then came the *Brooklyn, Texas,* and *Iowa.* The *Oregon* rode at the apex of the eastern quadrant; to starboard of her were the *New York, Indiana,* and armed yacht *Gloucester,* closest to the Morro, completing the arc. When Evans swept the sea with his sailor's eye, he thought the "rusty, lead-colored squadron looked very business like as it rolled gently in the long southern swell."[32]

The American ships were in varying states of engineering readiness, with only the *Texas* having steam in all fireboxes and the boilers on-line to the engines. The *Iowa*, on searchlight duty during the night, had allowed her fires to die down, and had instant steam for ten knots only. The *Oregon*, on the other hand, had fires under all her boilers, though not all were on-line. The *Brooklyn*, as was usual except in high speed or battle, had uncoupled her forward set of four engines. Three boilers had steam ready but the fires not fully spread. The flagship *New York*, whose forward engines were similarly uncoupled, had plenty of steam in three boilers, enough for twelve knots.[33]

It was Sunday, and in the ships the ritual of captain's inspection and the monthly reading of the Articles of War were progressing as if in peacetime. The blockade was infinitely boring. Skipper Jack Philip of the *Texas* later recalled that "a trip to Guantánamo for coal was a welcome relief, and a bombardment of the Santiago fortifications a joyous dissipation." Philip was halfway up the ladder from his cabin to the main deck when the electric gongs sounded the general alarm. Scrambling up, he saw the men running to their battle stations, "some of the officers who had been off duty buckling on their sword belts as they ran. I heard someone cry, 'They're coming out!' " He looked toward the Morro and saw three wreaths of smoke blackening the hazy blue sky over the harbor mouth. Her twin screws beating up a white wake, the *Texas* was already driving forward. From her halyards, as indeed now from every other ship's, whipped signal No. 250, "Enemy ships escaping." Just as Philip reached the bridge, the *Infanta María Teresa* poked her black snout around the point and fired. Almost immediately, one of the *Texas*'s forward 6-inch guns barked out. The Spanish breakout "was so long expected," Philip said, "that when it actually came, it was unexpected. I for one, did not dream . . . he would come out in broad daylight." The Spanish ships, he noticed, with their large battle flags, black hulls, and buff upperworks, "came out as gaily as brides to the altar."[34]

In the captain's cabin of the *Iowa*, Bob Evans had just finished breakfast with his naval cadet son, Herbert, visiting from the *Massachusetts*. He was sitting back and puffed on a cigar. The boatswain's mate of the watch had just struck three bells. One minute later, the general alarm shattered the quiet and rang throughout the ship. Young Cadet Evans jumped up and looked out the cabin port. "Papa," he yelled, "the enemy's ships are coming out!" Both started as fast as they could for the bridge. Before Evans reached the spar deck he heard one of the *Iowa*'s 6-pounder guns crack out. He snapped his head aloft and saw the signal flying, No. 250, "Enemy ships escaping."[35]

While the battle hatches rattled into place and the ship's dog, cat, and goat were safely stowed, the *Iowa*'s crew stopped for a second in their mad dash to general quarters to give a cheer to the *María Teresa*, Evans said, standing "boldly out." The *Iowa* had commenced fire at five thousand yards, closing the Spanish flagship on a rapidly converging course. Evans intended to ram either her or the second ship to come out, the *Vizcaya*, but he hadn't worked up enough speed for this and altered course westward to steer parallel to the enemy.

When the range dropped by half, the *Iowa*'s turret and starboard broadside guns crashed out. Evans kept his eyes on the *María Teresa* and observed "her broadsides follow[ing] each other with startling rapidity." Several Spanish heavy shells passed very close over the *Iowa*'s forward turret and conning tower. Their shooting, Evans said, "came with mechanical rapidity, and in striking contrast to the deliberate fire of the American ships. A torrent of projectiles was sailing over us, harmlessly exploding in the water beyond."[36]

In the flagship *New York*, already several miles east of the harbor entrance, Captain French Chadwick had been preparing to go ashore with the admiral when, at 9:35, he heard the distant sound of gunfire. The rumble was immediately followed, Chadwick remembered, by "a scurry on deck," and the call to battle stations. By the time he reached the bridge, the chief quartermaster had called out, "There comes another ship!" "Yes, they're coming out," said Admiral Sampson, and he gave the order to turn the ship and hoist the signal: "Close in toward harbor and attack vessels." The ship's gunners, who had stripped off their Sunday clothes, shouted down the ventilators to the black gang belowdecks, "For God's sake get those engines going! Make us move! Burn any old damn thing! Get us there! Get us there!"[37]

In the battleship *Oregon*, Lieutenant Edward Eberle, the fore turret commander, sat around the wardroom breakfast table with a group of "disheartened" officers. The officer of the deck had just sent down a message, gotten from a press boat, that the army had taken heavy losses in their battle for the San Juan heights, and the outlook was discouraging. At 9:25, the chief quartermaster sighted the masthead of a ship coming from behind Smith Cay. Immediately the general alarm rang out, signal No. 250 was hoisted, a 6-pounder gun banged out, and the ship's siren screamed. "For thirty-four long days and nights," Eberle said, "we had constantly watched that 'hole in the wall,' praying that Spain's fleet would come out and give battle; and having abandoned hope, here they were at last!" The *Oregon*'s men jumped about the decks, waving their caps, cheering, "There they come! There they come!" Under forced draft, the *Oregon* charged ahead, getting fast up to her full speed of fourteen knots to meet the enemy. The *María Teresa* was just abreast of the Morro when the *Oregon* opened fire with one of her 8-inch guns, to which the *María Teresa* responded, Eberle said, "with a shower of shell"; their fire "became furious."[38]

Sunday morning found the battleship *Indiana* holding the eastern end of the blockade line. She had spent the past two days coaling at Guantánamo, followed by searchlight duty from midnight to dawn, and her men were exhausted. The weather was quiet, the sea smooth, and the ship prepared for general muster, to be followed by church service. She lay with her head to the northwest, roughly facing the harbor mouth, the Morro distant about two miles off the starboard bow. At 9:30 came the boatswain's call to muster and the ship's company assembled in their cleanest uniforms. Captain Henry Clay Taylor, former president of the Naval War College, stood easily on his quarterdeck awaiting the executive officer's report that all was ready in the ship for the captain's eyes. The scene was so peaceful that it would have occurred exactly that way if the *Indiana* had been anchored in Hampton Roads. But that was very deceptive, for as Taylor remarked, "Under Admiral Sampson's wise and vigilant direction . . . we had grown day by day more eager and alert, until our . . . condition had come to that of complete and continuous readiness by day and night."[39]

In the perfect quiet of ship and sea, the crack of a gun and the fluttering of flags deciphered as signal No. 250 broke the reverie. "A second to realize the fateful meaning of the signal," said Taylor, "another to give the orders: 'Sound the general alarm!' 'Clear ship for action!' " Other orders were rapped out by department and division officers: "Turn on the current of the electric [ammunition] hoists!" "Steam and pressure on the turrets!" "Hoist the battle flags!" "Lay aloft range finders to the tops!" "Engines ahead full speed!" Ranges on the turret and starboard guns were set at four thousand yards. The time it took to break from muster to the point where all these frantic orders were carried out seemed to Taylor not two minutes. The impatience of all hands, however, made it seem much longer. The powder division had to pass down two narrow hatches to reach the magazines, their lieutenant harrying them through with exhortations of "They will all get away; two of them are outside the Morro already!" At this point, the men of the powder division simply "fell below," throwing themselves down the ladders in their eagerness to reach their posts, until, Taylor said, "the deck was swarming with bruised and bleeding men, staggering to their feet, and limping to their stations."[40]

Less time was needed for the men who manned the guns, and as they crowded into the 8- and 13-inch turrets, "their clothes seemed to fall from them, and by the time they had reached their stations, they were, for the most part naked to the waist." The Spanish squadron as it emerged from the harbor seemed for a moment to be heading eastward, toward the *Indiana*, and the "question of ramming," said Taylor, "and receiving a ramming blow demanded for a moment a strained and eager attention." Taylor gave orders for the forward 13-inch guns to check fire until he could determine whether or not the enemy was intent on ramming. If that were the case, these guns could crush a Spanish cruiser before the moment of contact.[41]

"Taking advantage of the exceptionally fine day," remembered Captain Francis Cook of the *Brooklyn,* he had given orders to the executive officer for the men to go to quarters at 9:30 A.M., then march them aft for general muster and inspection. "White mustering clothes" were prescribed for the men, and "all white" for the officers. The first call for quarters had just sounded. In his cabin, Cook laid on his bunk his last laundered white coat and was about to don it for the occasion, "when I heard the ringing voice of the executive officer . . . calling, 'Clear ship for action.' " As Cook had given no such orders, "I knew at once from the tone that it meant business." He ran forward to the forecastle and was told by the navigator that all systems were ready and connected for the captain in the conning tower. Cook rang down for full speed on the after engines, for steam on all boilers, and for the helmsman to steer for the head of the enemy column.[42]

Commodore Schley, after a turn on the *Brooklyn*'s deck, sat beneath an awning on the fantail. There came a yell from the navigator, Lieutenant Albon Hodgson, over a megaphone: "After bridge, there! Report to the Commodore and the Captain that the enemy's ships are coming out." The commodore ran forward, taking his place on a small wooden platform built outside the conning tower. The *Brooklyn* was heading toward the Socapa and the *María Teresa* when Hodgson called out from the flying bridge, "Commodore, they are coming right at us." "Well," said Commodore Schley, "go right for them." Five minutes after the first sighting, the *Brooklyn* opened a raking fire on the *María Teresa* with her portside battery at 1,500 yards.[43]

At this point Commodore Schley executed a highly controversial maneuver that might have turned the day into a catastrophe for the American fleet. As did the other ships, the *Brooklyn* steamed in the direction of the Socapa, concentrating on the harbor entrance to crush the head of the enemy column as it emerged. To starboard of the *Brooklyn,* the *Texas* and *Iowa* were coming up with a tremendous rush. The *María Teresa* seemed to be coming right at the *Brooklyn* when Commodore Schley ordered Captain Cook in the conning tower, "Put your helm hard-a-port." But Lieutenant Hodgson, the navigator, was immediately and rightly confused. "You mean starboard," he said. "No, I don't," snapped Schley, "we're near enough to them [the enemy] already." Hodgson was really perplexed now. "But we'll cut down the *Texas,*" he yelled from the flying bridge. "Let the *Texas* look out for herself," Schley responded.[44]

By this exceedingly dangerous movement, the *Brooklyn* increased her distance from the Spanish column and brought her starboard broadside to the bow of the *Texas.* Schley maintained after the war that the movement was intended to avoid the "blanketing fire" of the American battleships. As the *Brooklyn* sheered off to starboard to begin her 360-degree loop, she passed so close to the Spanish ships that Commodore Schley later said he watched men of the *Vizcaya* running out from one of her turrets into the superstructure. Without binoculars, he could "distinctly see the daylight between their legs as they ran."[45]

In a very few minutes, hard in the *María Teresa*'s wake, came the *Vizcaya, Cristóbal Colón, Almirante Oquendo,* and the two destroyers, *Furor* and *Plutón.* "Handsome vessels they certainly were," observed Jack Philip, "and with flags enough flying for a celebration parade." An officer standing with him commented, "They certainly mean us to think they have started out, at least to do business, but perhaps they have some white ones [flags] ready for an emergency." The array of Spanish flags and the brief comment on them caused the navigator,

Lieutenant Lewis Heilner, to look aloft, where he saw no battle flags flying from the *Texas,* only her national ensign from the stern. "Where are our battle flags?" he cried. Watching one of the *Texas*'s 6-inch shells throw a column of water over the *María Teresa*'s deck, Philip replied, "I guess they won't have any misconception about our being in battle." Heilner was not appeased. "What's a battle without battle flags?" he protested. The flags were in their locker, and the key was in the possession of the chief signalman, at his station in the foretop. "Then smash the locker," said Heilner. Philip nodded his agreement, "and at last we got our battle flags up. I don't know that the *Texas* fought any better after that, but the lieutenant was certainly happier."[46]

The action had fast become a general melee. Every one of the Spanish ships fired as she came broadside to the Americans, and steamed desperately westward; "the whistle of shells passing over our heads," said Jack Philip, "became unpleasantly frequent." While the *Texas* swung to port, west, parallel to the Spanish column, she saw the *Brooklyn,* a mile ahead, plowing up the water at a great rate, heading right for the harbor entrance, directly at the enemy ships. Smoke from the *Texas*'s guns hung so heavily about the vessel that, for a few minutes, Philip and his men could see nothing. "We might as well have had a blanket tied over our heads."[47]

A sudden whiff of breeze and a momentary lull in the gunfire lifted the pall, "and there, bearing towards us and across our bows, turning on her port helm, with big waves curling over her bows and great clouds of black smoke pouring from her funnels, was the *Brooklyn.* She looked as big as a dozen *Great Easterns,* and seemed so near that it took our breath away." Philip ordered both his engines back down hard, "and in a twinkling the old [*Texas*] was racing against herself. The imminent collision had been averted, and as the *Brooklyn* "glided past, all of us on the bridge gave a sigh of relief." Had the *Brooklyn,* with her particularly brutal ram bow, struck the *Texas,* the battleship would have gone down like a rock. Had it gone the other way, *Texas* ramming *Brooklyn,* it would have been equally disastrous. The *Texas* had a "soft" bow, not a ram, "and she would have doubled up like a hoop."[48]

From the decks of the *New York,* still a good deal to the eastward but closing rapidly, the vast clouds of gunsmoke had hidden every ship from sight. "Suddenly," said Captain Chadwick, "the *Brooklyn* emerged from this great white bank, standing apparently directly south, the sun shining brightly against her four hundred feet of lofty side." Shouts of lamentation went up from the *New York*'s crew; "The *Brooklyn*'s hurt." More than once Admiral Sampson said with deep concern, "What can be the matter?" Then a murmur of relief, followed by a great cheer, went up from the ship as the *Brooklyn* turned again westward, in the wake of the fleeing enemy.[49]

Straightened out on a westerly course parallel to the Spanish column, the *Brooklyn* steamed within point-blank range of the first three cruisers—the *María Teresa*, *Vizcaya*, and *Colón*. "We must stay with this crowd," Schley said as enemy shells fell around the ship, raising jets of water ahead, astern, over, and short; the roar they made was that of "express trains." For a short while, the enemy showing no overt signs of injury, the thought passed through Commodore Schley's mind "that after all of our precautions and waiting these fellows would get away."[50]

But only a minute or two after she had rounded Socapa Point, the *Infanta María Teresa* was already a shambles, on fire astern, with dead lying about her upper battery deck. An 8-inch shell from the *Brooklyn* exploded in Admiral Cervera's cabin, roofed and paneled in heavily varnished wood. It blazed up furiously. The same hit cut the fire mains aft, sending a torrent of water raining down on the boilers, causing, Captain Concas said, "alarm instead of extinguishing the fire raging above." Another 8-inch shell from the *Brooklyn* struck and exploded on the shield of one of the *Teresa*'s 5.5-inch guns, sending steel splinters aft along the upper deck with the most devastating effect. Two guns were put out of action and most of their crews as well. Then two heavy shells struck just underneath the after barbette and exploded in the torpedo flat, tearing out a huge hole in the starboard side. The ammunition hoists to the quick-firing guns broke down. Defective cartridges that were thrown on deck exploded. Electric primers missed fire. Firing pins blew out and pierced the gunners like spears. "And thus it came about," said Captain Concas, "that though the *Teresa* aimed a hot fire at the *Brooklyn*, the big American cruiser still drew ahead, uninjured."[51]

Standing unprotected on the bridge, Concas watched men fall all about him. "It was like hell on the bridge," said an officer. "Shells were bursting all around us." At this moment, while Concas was exhorting his men, "who were fighting furiously amidst the frightful chaos," and trying to ascertain what was happening aft—because from the forebridge it was impossible to see—he fell, badly wounded, along with two officers of the squadron staff, the three being the only ones left standing outside the conning tower. Fire broke out in the fore-castle, the upper works were riddled with shell fragments, and the crew became demoralized. The executive officer could not be found, and Admiral Cervera took over command of his flagship.[52]

The fire spread rapidly to the amidships portion of the vessel, and inasmuch as the fire mains were broken, the flames were impossible to stop. It moved "with great rapidity and voracity," Cervera said af-terward. He dispatched one of his aides and a party of men to flood the after magazine, but they found it impossible to penetrate through the passages owing to the dense clouds of smoke and steam escaping through the engine-room hatch. Concas said they all "perished, suf-focated by the steam." Cervera realized the ship was doomed, in real danger of blowing up. He called to him the second and third officers, and such of the lieutenants as were within hearing. It was agreed be-tween them that, to keep the ship from falling as a prize to the enemy and to save the crew, they would beach the ship. None thought the battle should continue.[53]

From the American ships, the *María Teresa* was seen to be lagging astern, smoke rolling out of her ports and deck hatches. Columns of smoke rose straight into the air as she lost speed and curved into the beach. "We have got one," said Schley through the conning tower slits to Captain Cook within. "Keep the boys below informed of all the movements. They can't see and want to know these things." Every few minutes, messages were sent down the voice tubes and the cheers of the men in the bowels of the ship reverberated up the ventilator shafts. When the *María Teresa* turned into the beach, "the cheering of the crew," Cook remembered, "could be heard amid the roaring of the guns." "Fire steady, boys," Schley shouted to the men at the quick-firers nearby, "and give it to them."[54]

At 10:35, an hour after she steamed boldly out of harbor, Cervera steered the *Infanta María Teresa* for a small cove near Punta Cabrera, about six miles from Socapa Point, and ran her aground. "We hardly had time to leave the burning ship," said the defeated admiral. The *María Teresa* presented an "awe-inspiring aspect," explosions following each other in rapid succession. Cervera believed it impossible to save anything from the burning carcass. "We have lost everything," he later wrote in his report, "the majority of us reaching the shore absolutely naked."[55]

The *Almirante Oquendo* was next. She was the last of the cruisers out of the harbor and the target of every American ship, now fully ready for battle. The turn at Diamond Bank under the solid fire of the enemy, said Captain Concas, who watched her from the *María Teresa*'s bridge, was done as if it were "an everyday occurrence." She was struck almost immediately by an 8-inch shell, which pierced the thin armor of the forward barbette hood. The gun turning gear jammed, and all but one man within was killed.[56]

Running the gauntlet between the *Brooklyn, Iowa, Indiana,* and *Oregon,* the *Oquendo* was struck repeatedly. In the after barbette the ventilation became so bad the men could not endure it. Two main fires broke out, one in the after torpedo flat, where an American projectile exploded a torpedo, completely wrecking that portion of the ship above the armored deck and severing the fire mains. The *Oquendo* staggered under the hail, and for a brief moment seemed actually to stop before lurching on. Lieutenant Adolfo Calandria, the senior surviving officer of the ship, came out on deck and "saw flames issuing forth from the officers' hatchway in the poop." Realizing the impossibility of controlling the fires aft owing to the proportions they had assumed, he went forward to report to the captain, and found him already making preparations to beach the ship.[57]

When the third round was about to be fired from the fore 11-incher, an 8-inch shell entered the barbette, tearing away the armor of the gunport, killing or wounding most of the men inside. At the fourth shot from the number six 5.5-inch gun on the port side, the breech burst, killing and wounding its full crew. By this time there were so many casualties in the portside battery, including their officers, that only enough hands remained to serve two guns, which continued to fire until the ammunition hoists broke. Firing from these guns continued, the rounds dragged up to their crews by a wounded lieutenant and two equally injured men.

The *Texas* was the recipient of that shooting. On her bridge, Jack Philip stood with a knot of ship's boys, whom he used as messengers in the battle, finding them more reliable than speaking tubes or the telephone. "I remember hearing one of these boys," Philip remembered, "a youngster, surely not over sixteen, in the very hottest of the battle remark to another: 'Fourth of July celebration, eh? A little early, but a good one.' " With enemy shells screaming about their ears, Philip decided to abandon the flying bridge for the navigating bridge, which surrounded the conning tower, and in whose lee the boys could shelter. It was fortunate they did, for a minute later, a shell from the *Oquendo* struck the pilothouse, exploding inside, wrecking the paneling and framing, blowing away the after bulkhead. A second round from the *Oquendo* exploded over the forward superstructure. The concussion lifted the bridge contingent off their collective feet. Philip recalled pitching up in the air, "with my coat tails flying out behind me." Not long after, a 5.5-inch shell struck forward of the ash hoist, smashing through the outer plating of the ship. The hit caused considerable excitement in the fireroom. Fragments of the shell dropped in. Hammocks and clothing caught fire and also fell below, causing such a gush of smoke in the fireroom that some of the men thought the ship was a goner. But there was no panic.[58]

Aboard the *Oquendo*, Captain Joaquín Lazaga ordered the magazines flooded on account of the fires, but the chief machinist was only able to reach the forward ammunition spaces. Fire had spread to the after deck, the result of burning wood from the officers' mess falling through the hatch of the ammunition hoist. It would have caused the explosion of the 5.5-inch magazine had not two seamen stopped up the hatches with wooden gratings and wet bedding.

The guns of four American ships, the *Oregon, Texas, Iowa,* and *Indiana,* at ranges of 5,500 down to 2,000 yards, pummeled the life out of the *Oquendo*. In the *Iowa,* recalled Bob Evans, "every gun on the starboard side roared and barked at the unfortunate Spanish ship. For a few minutes, she seemed to stop her engines, and as the smoke from our exploding shells and her own broadsides lifted, we all thought she would strike her colors, so deplorable was her condition."[59]

The *Oregon* closed in rapidly and, at less than a thousand yards, according to Lieutenant Eberle, "poured into her the hottest and most destructive fire of that eventful day . . . and as we drew her abeam, our guns raked her unmercifully."[60]

Lazaga, fearing the explosion of the after magazines, ordered his torpedoes fired, and with tongues of flame and smoke pouring from astern, he steered for the beach, two miles west of the *María Teresa*. Lazaga ordered Lieutenant Calandria to lower the flag, "but owing," the lieutenant said, "to the listlessness with which the order was given and partly to the natural vacillation of those who were to fulfill it, the distressing order was not carried out." It didn't need to be. The fire, which had assumed "gigantic proportions," caught the halyard, and the flag dropped into the flames. Both masts fell across the deck.[61]

With a quarter of the crew, about 120 men, dead or wounded, the remainder took to the undamaged boats and abandoned ship. Lazaga and a few men clustered on the forecastle, the captain refusing to leave. Then he fell to the deck, hands clutching his chest, and died of a heart attack.

"We have settled another," called out Captain Clark of the *Oregon* to Lieutenant Eberle; "look out for the rest!" This was answered by a mighty cheer, repeated through the ammunition passages and, as Eberle recounted, "down among the heroes of the boiler and engine rooms." It was the same in the *Brooklyn*. "Our crew," said Captain Cook, "in transports of joy born of such triumph, were cheering, and forcing their best efforts at the battery."[62]

At 9:30, just as in the big ships, the officers and crew of the armed yacht *Gloucester*, at the tip of the eastern rim of the blockade half circle, stood at quarters in their best clothes, drawn up for inspection. Lieutenant Commander Richard Wainwright, lately executive officer of the *Maine*, now skipper of the yacht, had gone below to the berth deck, "and was taking great pleasure in the tidy appearance of the ship . . . when I heard a shuffling of feet overhead, and a voice called down the hatch, 'They're coming out!' " Before he even had a chance to think, Wainwright had run to the bridge, where the executive officer had already rung down for full speed and forced draft on the boilers. The men were at their guns, and as Wainwright always had plenty of ammunition on deck, "we were ready for the fight at once."[63]

The yacht, formerly the *Corsair*, owned by J. P. Morgan, quickly worked up to her seventeen-knot speed, her greatest asset. With the heavy vessels engaged, Wainwright wondered where the enemy destroyers were. He was tempted to shoot under the stern of the last cruiser, the *Oquendo*, and try to damage her steering gear or propeller, but there was no time for this, for finally, in the wake of the Spanish cruiser, the *Furor* and *Plutón* made their dash. From the mast of the *Indiana* whipped the signal "Enemy gunboats coming out," which Wainwright misread as the order "Gunboats close in," which he instantly did. The *Indiana* fired her secondary guns "furiously" at the destroyers as they exited, at times coming so close to the *Gloucester* that an 8-inch shell grazed her bow. The secondary and light batteries of the *Iowa, Oregon,* and *Texas* added to the maelstrom at the harbor mouth.

As Lieutenant Commander Diego Carlier of the *Furor* remembered it, Captain Villaamil, who was on board commanding the destroyers, gave orders to head west at full speed, and guns were opened on the enemy. "But from the very first we received an enormous amount of fire from the majority of hostile ships and were struck by shells of every caliber." Within minutes her main steam pipe and a boiler burst, the starboard engine was put out of action, and she began going down by the stern. A large fire began in the engine room, and several more broke out around the little ship. The steering servomotor was wrecked and the ship's boatswain cut in two, with portions of his body becoming entangled in the steering gear. The decks were covered with the horribly mangled bodies of the dead and wounded. Men began jumping over the side, only to be sliced through by the thrashing propellers.[64]

As the *Gloucester* neared the destroyers, Wainwright glanced around his ship. "I can well remember my astonishment at not seeing any wounded or any sign of blood when I looked about the decks." Shells from the shore batteries in the Morro and Socapa had also been directed at the yacht. The automatic Maxim 1-pounders in the destroyers were the most serious danger to the *Gloucester.* Their fire could be traced by the splashes of the projectiles coming closer and closer. When they began to fall about twenty yards short, and the water stirred as if in a hailstorm, the fire ceased. Had they secured the range, and it was just the smallest elevation, the slaughter in the *Gloucester* would have been great.[65]

The executive officer called Wainwright's attention to the west, where the *María Teresa* and *Oquendo* were heading inshore. Wainwright thought they were attempting to escape by running inside the gauntlet of American ships and doubling back to the harbor. If that happened, the *Gloucester* would be exposed to enemy fire at close range and would doubtless be demolished. The only thing to do, Wainwright thought, was to close at high speed with the Spanish destroyers so they would be sunk along with him. A few minutes later, after Wainwright discerned the true intent of the enemy cruisers, he saw the *Plutón* slowing down and in serious trouble. A large shell from the *Indiana* struck the *Plutón* amidships, exploding her forward boilers, and killing every man but two in the fire and engine rooms. "The scalding water," said one of them, "stabbed the men like sword blades." From the *Iowa*, Evans watched as a "great column of steam fringed with coal and coal dust arose from her, fifty to one hundred feet in the air, and we knew [she] was done for." On fire, nearly cut in two, unmanageable, but still going ahead, the *Plutón* ran onto the rocks about four miles west of the Socapa, then sank to the level of her main deck.[66]

The *Furor* now turned on the *Gloucester*, her main antagonist. It appeared a critical situation. The Spaniard might succeed in torpedoing the yacht or escaping back up the harbor. The Spanish destroyer, however, continued in a large circle, and it was evident she was disabled and her wheel was jammed. The *New York* came thrashing up and pumped three 4-inch shells into the stricken craft. From the *Gloucester* flew the signal "Enemy's vessels destroyed"; the flagship gave three cheers and continued her chase after the cruisers.[67]

Captain Villaamil, having neither rudder nor engine power, on fire amidships and aft, half his crew dead—indeed, only eleven out of seventy-five were unhurt—ordered his flag and boats lowered. Hostile fire ceased, and two boats from the *Gloucester* came alongside. According to one of the yacht's officers, "a scene of horror and wreck confronted us. The ship was riddled by three and six pound shells. . . . She was on fire below from stem to stern, and on her spar deck were the dead and horribly mangled of some twenty of the officers and crew." Perhaps a dozen men were saved by the *Gloucester*'s boats before the wreck blew up and sank, taking Villaamil down with her.[68]

Wainwright then headed to the point west of the Socapa where he had last seen the *María Teresa*. He found her and the *Oquendo* aground near the beach, with white flags flying from all parts of the burning ships. Spaniards crowded in the bows and many were in the water. The *Gloucester* rescued an officer floating by on a small raft, kneeling with his hands raised to heaven; he proved to be the fleet surgeon. The *Gloucester* steamed between the wrecks, lowered her boats, and began the difficult rescue. A line was stretched from the *María*

Teresa's bow and secured to the beach. The *Gloucester*'s boats then ferried along this line, taking 8 or 10 men each trip—480 from the *María Teresa* alone, including Admiral Cervera. From the beach, where the prisoners were guarded by bands of Cuban rebels, a number of Spanish sailors were taken out to the *Gloucester*, Cervera being among them. According to the executive officer, "When Admiral Cervera came on board the *Gloucester* after his surrender ashore . . . he was dressed in a flat white sailor cap, a wet sack coat, an undershirt, and a torn pair of trousers which might have been discarded by a tramp." He was barefoot. There was no bugle to sound the proper flourishes for a vice admiral, and as all the yacht's boatswains were out of the ship rescuing prisoners of war, Wainwright could not even pipe the side for his erstwhile enemy. He held out his hand and congratulated the crestfallen admiral on his heroic fight. The *Gloucester*'s officers received Admiral Cervera and his staff with great courtesy, according to the admiral, "vying with each other in supplying our wants, which were manifold, for we arrived absolutely naked and half starved." The unwounded prisoners were herded into the bow, under an awning. Inasmuch as they equaled the number of the *Gloucester*'s own crew, many of whom were away in the boats, a "dead line" was stretched across the deck, and two sailors stood with loaded rifles at each end with orders to shoot anyone who crossed it. A Colt machine gun was aimed just over their heads.[69]

The *Vizcaya* had been ready for sea in the evening of July 2, the battle flags—one of them a beautiful silk banner presented by the Vizcaya historical association—being hoisted by the ship's officers, who were then addressed by Captain Antonio Eulate, who reminded them "of the obligations imposed . . . by the Ordinances, and the heroic deeds of our ancestors in our honorable career." After a prayer, "we received kneeling" the benediction of the chaplain. Following in the wake of the flagship, the *María Teresa,* the *Vizcaya* went to full speed on passing the Socapa and opened fire, as Eulate said, "very heavy at first, but gradually decreasing."[70]

Like the others, she was set afire early in the battle, the blaze beginning with a shell that exploded in Eulate's wood-paneled cabin. "I do not believe that a man in our ship did a cowardly act," said a Spanish officer, "but many of us were perfectly distracted. The flashes of exploding shells, the shriek and roar of the missiles passing over us, and the rattle of the lighter shot on the steel decks made a frightful din. It was impossible to think of or hear anything else." Officers screamed their orders for a while, but soon they could not make themselves heard, "and there were few to obey." In the fighting tops there were none but dead and wounded; the mainmast fell over, jamming the after barbette. The scenes belowdecks were appalling. The wounded were not sent below the armored deck, but treated in the sick bay, which caught fire. There were so many injured that the surgeons abandoned all efforts to deal with the mass of human suffering and fled to the upper decks. Fifty or sixty men were killed or wounded by a single hit on the forecastle.[71]

"The fire was terrific," remembered another Spanish officer; "shells were continually striking us at all points, and it seemed as if each shell started a new fire wherever it struck. Our men were driven from their guns by the rain of fire," and several were likely shot by their officers for leaving their posts in battle. Water came pouring into the engineering compartments, striking the revolving cranks, blinding the men with flying, scalding water and hot oil. The pumps became choked with debris and could no longer empty the bilges. The chief engineer was killed by escaping steam from ruptured pipes and the majority of his men either drowned or were horribly burned.[72]

To add to the ship's bad luck, she found herself alone, the *Colón* outracing her in a desperate attempt at her own escape. One of the *Vizcaya*'s 5.5-inch guns had to load seven shells before a serviceable round could fill the breech; another gun needed eight to find a good one. Every gun in the lower portside battery was put out of action, the majority dismounted and their crews all dead or wounded. In the upper battery, the 5.5-inchers, there were so many casualties that when only one gun stood able to fire, there were not enough men to crew it. "It therefore," said Captain Eulate, "became necessary to decrease the crew assigned to extinguish the fires that were constantly breaking out everywhere," to serve the piece. Eulate, knowing his ship was lost, lowered the silk flag and burned it, lest it become an enemy trophy, replacing it on the mainmast with another that was lost when the structure collapsed into the flames, devastating the after end of the ship.[73]

The *Vizcaya* still blazed away "viciously," according to Jack Philip, and at this time, the Americans took their only fatal casualty in the battle. On the roof of the *Brooklyn*'s fore turret, Chief Yeoman

George Ellis stood with a stadimeter taking the ranges of the enemy, when a shot from the *Vizcaya* took off his head. Commodore Schley, standing a few feet above, was spattered with bits of brain. Two seamen were about to heave the body over the side when Schley ordered them to cover it with a blanket.

By 11:50 A.M., the *Vizcaya* could no longer fire a gun on her port side, and according to Captain Eulate, "I wanted to try whether we could ram the *Brooklyn,*" her nearest antagonist. For a moment, the *Vizcaya* sheered off to port, the *Brooklyn* doing the same to avoid the collision. Eulate, wounded in the head and shoulder, staggered to the sick bay to have his wounds dressed. Faint from loss of blood, he turned command of the ship over to the executive officer, "with clear instructions not to surrender the ship, but rather beach or burn her." Her bow torpedo exploded in its tube, and a 13-inch shell from the *Oregon* raked the ship from stern to stem.[74]

The *Oregon,* according to Captain Cook of the *Brooklyn,* "was coming up in glorious and gallant style, outstripping all others. It was an inspiring sight to see this battleship, with a large white wave before her, and her smokestacks belching forth continued puffs from her forced draft." Her speed steadily increased to fourteen knots until the range to the *Vizcaya* dropped to three thousand yards. The *Vizcaya's* pathetic attempt at ramming placed her broadside to both the *Brooklyn* and the *Oregon.* Two 13-inch shells from the latter, one in the bow and one amidships, staggered the *Vizcaya* to starboard, sending up columns of steam and smoke.[75]

In the mortally wounded ship, Captain Eulate resumed command and convened the surviving officers, asking if any among them thought they could do more "in the defense of our country and honor." The unanimous reply was "No." Just after eleven o'clock, she turned inshore, heading toward a sandbar off Aserraderos, about fifteen miles west of the Morro.[76]

As the *Texas* drew up, the *Vizcaya's* stern flag came down, but one still flew from the foremast, and as the ship presented no white flag, some of the *Texas's* officers thought she might not have surrendered. Flames shot from her deck all along its length, and as she touched the sandbar, two tremendous explosions literally shook the ship to pieces. The men in the *Texas* began cheering. "Don't cheer, boys," admonished Jack Philip, "the poor devils are dying."[77]

As soon as the cruiser touched bottom, the only serviceable boat was lowered and brought the wounded ashore. Eulate remembered the sight of his ship in her death throes as "awe-inspiring." Ammunition exploded, flames rose above the funnel tops, and the side armor glowed red hot.

When Bob Evans realized he could not keep up the chase after the *Colón*, the only remaining Spanish ship, he cut his speed "in the cause of humanity," to save the crew of the *Vizcaya*. Many of her crew stood in water up to their armpits, the target of Cuban rebels ashore. "The sharks," Evans saw through his glasses, "made ravenous by the blood of the wounded, were attacking them from the outside." Many of the wounded were still on deck, crowding on the forecastle and poop and likely to be burned to death.[78]

Boats from the *Iowa*, torpedo boat *Ericsson*, and armed yacht *Hist* brought off 25 officers and 250 men, 5 of whom died in the boats. According to a *Hist* officer, many of the wounded were "horribly mangled," many with arms and legs torn off. "The salt water bath," he said, "had in many cases saved life by stopping the bleeding. When it was reported to Evans that the captain of the *Vizcaya* was coming alongside in one of the boats, he paraded the marine guard and made preparations to receive Eulate with all honors due his rank. "As the boat lay along the gangway," Evans said, "she presented a spectacle that could be seen only in war, and rarely then, I imagine." There was a foot of water in the boat's bottom, and in this rolled two men, terribly torn to pieces by shell fragments, the water red with their blood. In the stern sheets sat Captain Eulate, supported by an American naval cadet, and about his feet lay six wounded Spanish sailors.[79]

Seeing Eulate badly wounded, Evans hoisted a canvas chair into the boat to bring Eulate on deck. The marines presented arms and the officer of the deck saluted. Eulate slowly straightened himself up, "with an effort unbuckled his sword belt, kissed the hilt of his sword and with a graceful bow presented it to me." Evans refused it to the cheers of the battleship's crew, but he accepted Eulate's surrender, along with his officers and crew, as prisoners of Admiral Sampson.

Evans was taking Eulate to his cabin to have his wounds dressed, and when they reached the head of the companionway, Eulate turned, raised his right hand toward the wreck, and exclaimed, "*Adiós Viz-*

caya!" Just as he said this, the forward magazine blew, sending up a column of smoke visible for fifteen miles. In the cabin, Evans offered a cigar, "a Key West, but the best I had," and Eulate graciously accepted it. He then reached into the coat pocket of his sopping uniform and brought out, as Evans recalled, "a beautiful but very wet Havana cigar. He bowed, and handed it to me with the remark, 'Captain, I left fifteen thousand aboard the *Vizcaya*.' "[80]

For the flagship *New York,* the most direct line toward the fleeing enemy carried her close under the guns of the Morro and Socapa, and she was bracketed by shell splashes as she swept by. Turning to the admiral, Captain Chadwick asked, "Shall we answer them?" "No," replied Sampson emphatically, without taking his binoculars from the action, "let us get on—on after the fleet! Not one must get away." Yet after firing her passel of 4-inch shots at the *Furor,* all but the *Colón* had been bested. Several Spanish sailors called from the water alongside, "Amerigo! Amerigo! Auxilio! Auxilio!" ("Help! Help!") The flagship's course was altered slightly to avoid running them down, and to the cries for rescue, life rings were tossed over the side, and a seaman threw them the chaplain's wooden pulpit, still on deck awaiting the church service. Near 11:30, doing nearly seventeen knots on her after set of engines, the *New York* passed the *Indiana,* signaling her to return to the harbor mouth and resume the blockade.[81]

"We were rapidly increasing our speed," Chadwick reported; she was nearly up with the *Brooklyn, Oregon,* and *Texas.* And as it was evident that the *Colón* was going to provide a lengthy chase, the crew were dismissed from their battle stations for the midday meal.[82]

The *Colón* had passed her comrades and all the ships of the pursuing American fleet, giving the *Iowa,* Evans said, "two ugly blows" with 6-inch shells on her starboard bow. One exploded on the berth deck with tremendous force, "literally destroying everything in the dispensary, and setting fire to the linoleum which was cemented to the steel deck." The second hit went through the bow five feet above the waterline. Fragments struck the chain locker, cutting through a sheet chain wrapped around the forward 6-pounder ammunition hoist. The explosion of the shell caused a small fire that was quickly extinguished. The flying bridge was hit once with a minor-caliber round, as was the stern right on the waterline. There were three hits on the smokestacks, two on the after starboard 8-inch turret, and one on the after main battery turret, none of which did more than slightly dent the armor.[83]

While the *Texas* steamed past the *Almirante Oquendo,* Jack Philip watched as the *Colón,* "wiliest" of all the Spanish ships, outraced the *Vizcaya,* leaving her to her burning fate. "The *Colón* forged well ahead," Philip noted, "and was running like a greyhound for safety." Yet she kept so far inside, hugging the shore, that she was forced to follow the bights and sinuosities of the coast. It became a "test of engines, and not of guns, and we hoped to capture the ship uninjured." For nearly two hours, the chase, "grim and silent," continued over the smooth and foamless sea. The *Colón* was in a trap of her own making. The *Brooklyn* drew ahead, making for Cape Cruz to cut her off westward, the *Oregon* kept on her quarter, preventing a run to the open sea, while the *Texas,* astern, her black gang "working like beavers," scotched a doubling back.[84]

Commodore Schley was beginning to despair that the last of the enemy would escape when the *Oregon* came up on the *Brooklyn*'s starboard quarter, and to the armored cruiser's 8-inch guns, whose shells were falling just astern of the *Colón,* were added the battleship's 13-inchers and quick-firers. "I never saw such a fire and never realized what rapid gun fire really meant before," Schley later said, "because both ships were at that time a sheet of flame."[85]

At something like six thousand yards, "the firing was very fast," Captain Cook recalled, "the whistling of the shells incessant, and our escape with so little injury was miraculous, and can only be attributed to bad marksmanship on the part of the enemy." The *Brooklyn* was struck by twenty whole shot, and oftener by fragments and machine-gun fire. Her stacks were hit seven times, the flag at the mainmast knocked away. Minor-caliber hits struck all about the ship, especially her superstructure and upperworks. A 6-inch shell from the *Colón* pierced the hull at the berth deck amidships, throwing splinters in all directions, but failed to injure the men in the compartment. Another 6-inch shell and a 6-pounder struck the waterline armor belt but failed to penetrate. Aft, a 5.5-inch round hit the ventilator cowl, fragmented, and creased the roof of the after turret.[86]

The *Colón* was still outside effective gunnery range of her antagonists. The vessel's speed averaged nearly fourteen knots and at times reached seventeen. But the poor physique of her stokers and engineers prevented this pace from being kept. Eventually speed dropped to twelve knots, while the *Brooklyn, Oregon,* and *Texas* fast came up astern. Another reason for this slackening of speed, according to a British historian, was the drunken condition of the engineer force. They were given brandy prior to the fight, and at first performed well, but the reaction when it set in could not be controlled. A mutiny of sorts erupted below the armored deck, and the engine-room personnel, having enough of the fight, opened the steam escape valves. When the ship surrendered, several bodies were found in the stokeholds with revolver bullets in them, shot by their officers for attempting to leave their stations during battle.[87]

When the *Brooklyn* outpaced her comrades, the *Colón* switched broadside fire into her, but against the *Oregon* on her quarter, she was unable to bring to bear any but one gun on account of her lack of a main battery. When the *Colón*'s speed began dropping, the chief engineer reported the good coal was all but consumed, and he could provide revolutions for fourteen knots only for another three miles. This was disastrous, and according to Captain Díaz Moreu, "Everything was done to stimulate the enthusiasm and interest of the firemen." The situation could not have been more critical.[88]

At around 12:50, Commodore Schley ordered a wigwag signal made to the *Oregon:* "Try one of your railroad trains." The battleship, about half a mile to landward of the *Brooklyn* and right in the *Colón*'s wake, opened fire with her fore turret. After six rounds, which could only be answered by one gun in the *Colón*'s 6-inch battery, the 13-inch shells began passing over the target. For all intents, the battle was over. It was merely a matter of shortening the range for the "railroad trains" to begin plunging into the *Colón*'s deck. Though there was only one dead resulting from enemy action and twenty-five wounded, all the fight was taken out of her. Shortly after two bells in the afternoon watch, 1:00 P.M., the *Colón* fired a gun to leeward, struck her colors, and ran aground in the estuary of the Rio Tarquino, about fifty miles west of the Morro. When her hull touched bottom, Captain Díaz Moreu called his officers and explained to them that had they kept on their course for even a few minutes longer the ship "should have been in the greatest danger of falling into the hands of the enemy and becoming a trophy of victory, which was to be avoided at all costs."[89]

Captain Cook of the *Brooklyn* was sent by Commodore Schley to take the surrender of the prize. Shifting into a clean uniform, and "with a 'lick and promise' at hands and face, which were covered with perspiration and sulphur," he climbed into his gig. As he came alongside the *Colón,* some of her crew called out, "Bravo Americanos!" Cook found most of the Spanish officers on deck. Díaz Moreu, who spoke English, "received me pleasantly," Cook reported, "though naturally much depressed." "I surrender," the Spanish captain said. "You are too much for us." Commodore Paredes, the second-in-command of the Spanish squadron, stood by, overcome by grief, sobbing bitterly. As Cook left the ship, the Spanish officers drew themselves erect on the quarterdeck and saluted.[90]

The *New York* had finally come up, the admiral signaling each ship in turn, "Report your casualties." He was answered by Commodore Schley with "We have gained a great victory," and the report of one death, Ellis. Admiral Sampson could hardly believe it—only one fatality in the entire fleet.[91]

A boat from the *New York,* with Captain Chadwick aboard, was sent to the *Colón* to take possession of the wreck and arrange for the distribution of prisoners into the American fleet, less the ship's engineering force, which remained on board. Chadwick, who had brought with him one of the flagship's engineering officers and her carpenter, reported the ship taking water aft, and that but a small portion of her bow was actually aground. A repair party from the *New York* hastened to the prize. The work of closing her watertight doors was to no avail. As Chadwick reported, a large number of the sea valves "had been treacherously opened and the valves so broken as to make it impossible to close them." The ship slowly settled by the stern. In the evening she floated off the beach. Later, a line was made fast from the *New York*'s bow to the *Colón*'s. The *New York* now assumed the extremely delicate task of nudging the ship back up the beach to keep her from sinking. With rope fenders on her bows, she put her ram against the *Colón*'s starboard quarter and began forcing the ship in. Suddenly, however, the *Colón* lurched over and collapsed on her port side in shallow water, her starboard gun barrels pointing at the night sky.[92]

There was a bit of comic drama in the afternoon. The armed steamer *Resolute* had come west from Guantánamo bearing a cargo of mines to counter-mine the Santiago Harbor entrance. When off Daiquirí, she had spotted a large warship, painted a dingy white, with two prominent funnels and two military masts, standing to westward. At first sight she appeared to be a large Spanish cruiser, perhaps even the battleship *Pelayo,* to which she bore a striking resemblance. The *Resolute* steamed west at her best speed, her siren screaming, warning the transports at Siboney of the alleged intruder. The *Harvard* picked up the hue and cry. Near one o'clock, they came upon the *Iowa* and *Indiana,* and both battleships prepared for action. The yacht *Vixen* sped up to the *New York* with the startling message "I have seen the enemy." As Captain Chadwick remembered, this "for a moment shook the admiral's disbelief." The *Brooklyn* and *Texas* were signaled, "Prepare to chase."[93]

Captain Henry Taylor of the *Indiana* had dismissed his men from their battle stations on resuming the blockade. But when word of the strange ship came, the men were sent scurrying back. "We had already been three hours at the guns," he said, "preceded by several days of excessive fatigue [from coaling]; but the tremendous cheer with which our crew responded to this call for more fighting was . . . most convincing proof of the instinctive love of battle which has ever distinguished the American seaman." The *Indiana* was just at the point of opening fire at the stranger when, at a range of three miles, her signals were read: "I am Austrian." It was the armored cruiser *Kaiserin María Theresa.* "It was just in time."[94]

From the *Gloucester,* Admiral Cervera and the officers of the two sunken destroyers were taken to the *Iowa.* Evans paraded his full marine guard of 80 men. The ship's officers mustered on the starboard quarterdeck while the prisoners from the *Vizcaya* stood on the port side. The *Iowa's* crew swarmed in their powder-blackened whites over the turrets and superstructure. As Admiral Cervera stepped on deck, the marines presented arms, officers uncovered their heads, boatswain's pipes wailed, and the bugles sounded the proper honors for a vice admiral. "[A]nd as the distinguished officer, who had lost more in one hour than any other man has lost in modern times," said Evans, "stepped onto the quarterdeck, the crew of the *Iowa* broke into cheers." Cervera bowed his head in thanks for a full minute.[95]

Cervera, his officers, and his men were transferred to the *Harvard* and *St. Louis* for passage north to Annapolis for the officers, and Seavey's Island, Portsmouth, New Hampshire, for the enlisted men, where they were interned as prisoners of war. "There was no doubt in my mind as to the outcome," the Spanish admiral wrote to Captain General Blanco from captivity, "although I did not think that our destruction would be so sudden."[96] Concas placed the Spanish losses in the battle at 323 killed and 151 severely wounded; of the 2,227 officers and men present, this amounted to 22 percent of the ships' crews. Perhaps 120 sailors escaped ashore to Santiago.

"The fleet under my command," telegraphed Admiral Sampson from Siboney via Guantánamo to Washington, "offers the nation as a Fourth of July present the whole of Cervera's fleet."[97] It now hardly mattered that the Spanish still held out in Santiago, or in Havana for that matter. The battle had wrested for the U.S. Navy total control of the sea, and thus, according to Mahanian doctrine, had won the war in an afternoon.

CHAPTER 14

CAPITULATION

Santiago is no Gerona.
> —*Major General Arsenio Linares Pombo,*
> *July 12, 1898*

We may have to fight for it yet.
> —*Major General William R. Shafter, July 14, 1898*

Immediately after the battle for the heights on July 1, the San Juan positions taken by the assaulting American forces were, according to correspondent Richard Harding Davis, "painfully suggestive of Humpty-Dumpty"—the corps could never be put back together again. Along the top of the ridge of hills, little groups of soldiers, usually not more than a dozen to a clump, sprawled on their backs or sat with their elbows on their knees, panting for breath. By some miracle bestowed by the god of war, they had made it to the top and found themselves in sole possession of the Spanish trenches and blockhouses. "Well, hell, here we are!" was the general American sentiment during those waning hours of the day. But they hadn't the strength to move another step. Three hundred yards below, in the intervening defile that separated Santiago from the heights of San Juan, several thousand Spanish Mausers still sputtered "furiously," Davis said, "shrieking with rage."[1]

With the annihilation of Admiral Cervera's squadron, tension in the trenches relaxed perceptibly, and the constant spitting musketry from the Spanish lines slowed, then ceased nearly altogether. As the

467

commanding generals, Shafter and Toral, each sought for his own ends a cessation of hostilities, "we entered," Davis wrote, "into a more cheerful state of existence under the white flag of truce."[2]

Shafter, unable to manage the casualties he had already suffered and loath to incur additional wounded in a frontal attack on Santiago, conjured reason after reason to keep that dreaded day from coming. Actually, the city and its defenders no longer had any military value, not once the Spanish squadron had been destroyed. "Everybody," said Lieutenant Müller of the Spanish navy, "knew that calamity was not far off and was inevitable, for no provisions could be expected, either by land or sea." The arrival of General Escario's column from Manzanillo merely swelled the number of mouths that had nothing to eat, except boiled rice and rice "bread." The war, if it was for Cuba's freedom, thus was already won, militarily anyway; all Spain needed to do was surrender. Indeed, lest it suffer the further consequences of an attack on Puerto Rico, the surrender of Manila, even an ascent on the Canaries and a bombardment of Spain's coastal cities by the U.S. Navy, the Sagasta Liberal ministry was already extending tentative peace feelers. For his part, General José Toral, who had taken over command from the wounded Linares, was only too glad to accommodate the Americans, spinning out flags of truce to spare civilians the danger of bombardment, to exchange prisoners, endlessly to negotiate.[3]

As General Shafter informed Admiral Sampson of the situation on July 3, hostilities would likely be mutually suspended for three or four days, allowing for the return of wounded Spanish prisoners and for the exit of foreigners from the city. "Now," Shafter optimistically stated, "if you will force your way into the harbor the town will surrender without any further sacrifice of life." The fact of the minefields in the harbor mouth completely eluded him, as it would continue to do. The navy's reply came from Commodore John Watson, lately arrived from the Havana blockade and Sampson's second-in-command. No, he said, the fleet would not throw itself on the mines. As Sampson related to Secretary Long, Shafter's plea "shows a complete misapprehension of the circumstances which had to be met." In a report the next day to the War Department, Shafter called the navy's cooperation "not very encouraging."[4]

To the American soldiers in the trenches along the ridgeline, perplexed at the constant coming of white flags signaling neither peace nor war, the "virgin flags" of truce soon became the object of scorn. They reminded one regular of "two kids in a street fight, stopping after every punch to ask the other fellow if he's had enough. Why," he asked Davis, "don't we keep at it until somebody gets hurted?" Or as a Rough Rider cowboy cavalryman put it, "Now that we got those Mexicans corralled, why don't we brand them?" The flags of truce passed between the lines so frequently that the men compared them to the various editions of a daily newspaper: "Has that ten o'clock edition gone in yet?" or "Is this the baseball edition coming out now, or is it an extry?"[5]

The first flag of truce left the American lines on July 3, carrying General Shafter's initial surrender demand. As a result of that and subsequent cease-fires, with the exception of two short naval bombardments of Santiago, fighting along the front died away. Given time—and some sort of face-saving gesture on the part of the United States—Spain, General Shafter believed, would surrender. The problem now before him was to thoroughly invest the city, cutting off all hope of supplies or reinforcements from inland.

By July 3, dog tents, brought up to the front out of the piles left along the trails during the advance to battle, afforded the Americans at least a modicum of shelter from rain and scorching sun. Food, however, was monotonous, totally unsuited to a tropical climate, and hardly more than the basic ration of the hated canned meat, bacon if they were lucky, hardtack, sugar, and coffee. Living off the land was impossible. "The devastated country," Davis wrote, "afforded them as few comforts as a stretch of ocean." For three years, the hills and valleys between Siboney and the front had been swept equally by rebel and Spanish columns. There was not a cow for milk, nor a stray chicken to be had; not a patch of corn, nor kitchen garden of potatoes or peas. Wild mangoes grew, which if eaten raw made the men sick. Limes and running water were all that the land offered in support. In the trenches, a match was so precious a commodity that if a man had tobacco and lit his pipe with one instead of using the cooking fire, "you felt as though you had seen him strike a child." Writing paper was so scarce that orders and requisitions were made out in the margins of newspapers and on scraps torn from notebooks and on the insides of old envelopes. Everything came up short. One of Wheeler's stars of rank was cut from a tin cup, and the acorns of Roosevelt's hat cord had been hammered from a lead spoon.[6]

The dire lack of transport shipping added immeasurably to the supply problem. Up until July 3, the War Department had managed to charter only nine additional ships beyond those that had sailed with the original expedition from Tampa. Most of the vessels that carried the Fifth Corps from Tampa never made a second voyage, simply because they could not be unloaded fast enough once they got to Cuba. The navy helped somewhat by hauling a brigade for the Puerto Rico campaign in the big armed liners *Harvard* and *Yale,* the cruiser *Columbia,* and the captured Spanish steamer *Rita.* The lack of shipping for the army finally prompted Secretary Alger to purchase fourteen vessels, almost all of foreign registry, for $16 million. Most of these did not enter service until near the end of the war.

The dearth of tugs and steam lighters off Santiago made it impossible to unload the ships with any facility or speed. Shipmasters, gnawed by an inordinate fear of grounding, remained wary of approaching the beaches at Siboney and Daiquirí. To Adjutant General Henry Corbin, Shafter plaintively wired, "Transports go off miles from shore and there is no way of reaching them or of compelling them to come in. It is a constant struggle to keep them in hand." In response, though it had no real effect, Corbin passed President McKinley's directions "that you order transports to stand in by the shore and enforce demand." Short of a shot across their bows, there was no way. It was really only due to the steam lighter *Laura* that the corps maintained even the barest necessities and commissary stores.[7]

News of these difficulties made its way home via correspondents' reports, stirring up public outcries. Corbin telegraphed that Davis, in particular, had criticized both operations and logistics: "He says that some of the men in the trenches have been without food for forty-eight hours and without tobacco." The president, Corbin continued, viewed such dispatches as "unjust," but nevertheless, "the country will of course be distressed by the account he [Davis] gives." Shafter responded with the generally valid excuse that many of the troops had left their haversacks containing rations along the road during the advance to battle and it took some time to recover and distribute them. Some food was brought up to the front lines as early as the night of July 1. Still, Shafter confessed to difficulty: True, the troops were without tobacco for several days, "as it is only by the greatest exertion that coffee, sugar, meat, and bread could be gotten out. . . .

They had full rations except for twenty-four hours, when there was no coffee."[8]

Despite the numerous streams between Siboney and the front, there was a complete lack of facilities for washing clothes. One officer complained, "I do not at all mind other men's clothes being offensive to me, but when I cannot go to sleep on account of my own, it grows serious." The personal baggage of the officers had been left behind in the transports, and as the mule pack trains were desperately needed to bring up rations, the men never put on fresh underwear until able to buy some in Santiago after the Spanish surrender. "A tooth brush," Davis observed, "was the only article of toilet to which all seemed to cling, and each of the men carried one stuck in his hat band, until they appeared to be part of the uniform."[9]

When it rained, the water ran down the hills in wide streams, overflowing the trenches and washing over the men. During one week, officers and men camped near El Pozo stowed their clothing under dog tents and stood about naked until the sun came out again. When General Miles arrived at the front on July 12, he was as much amused as startled to see the regiment of District of Columbia Volunteers standing naked, saluting him as he passed their lines.

At least the road and trails leading to the streams were now, according to Lieutenant Miley of Shafter's staff, "free from dropping bullets." Men were taken out of the trenches to bathe in shifts "and this refreshed and inspirited the whole command," at least for a time. There was very little sickness yet, but the seeds of disease were there; in a few weeks it would prostrate the army, rendering it incapable of operations. Shafter dreaded increased casualty lists; indeed, he was unable to care for those wounded in the actions for El Caney and the San Juan heights. Arrangements for their care were left to the small and wholly inadequate medical corps. Shafter, by giving priority to unloading quartermaster and commissary stores, unfortunately deprived the regimental and division surgeons of most of their medical supplies. The single field hospital, the 1st Division's, consisted of a few tents with a few blankets, and no cots, mattresses, hospital clothing, or special food. The base hospital established at Siboney afforded little more than shelter from the elements, and even this was not sufficient for the eight hundred men who crowded its sheds just days after the battle.[10]

Shafter's own health was not of the best. Heat and gout and the general's great bulk had all taken their toll. "I am still very much exhausted," he wrote to Corbin on July 4, "eating a little ... for the first time in four days." But the news of the disaster to the Spanish naval squadron was like a tonic to the general; it had, he reported, "inspired everybody," and there was cheering from one end of the line to the other.[11]

The War Department, concerned for the general's health, gently inquired whether he would consider relinquishing command to Wheeler, or if that elderly officer was incapacitated, which he nearly was, to the next senior general officer, Kent. "Your continued illness brings sorrow and anxiety," wrote Corbin on Alger's behalf. As for attacking the city, the department understood the shaky condition of the Fifth Corps so soon after the battle. Shafter was not expected to undertake an offensive until he considered himself ready.

Criticism of Shafter had begun to worry the administration. To Alger's chagrin, the press reacted badly to the Cuban campaign. News stories alluded to Shafter's illness and the handicap of his "flesh." Some editorials broadly hinted at gross military blunder. The attitude at the front was not much different than in the press. "General Shafter is a fool and I believe he should be shot," jotted a soldier of the 16th Infantry. It was the same from senior officers, at least those who felt no constraints at speaking their opinions. "Not since the campaign of Crassus against the Parthians has there been so criminally incompetent a General as Shafter," wrote Theodore Roosevelt to Henry Cabot Lodge, "and not since the expedition against Walcherin has there been a grosser mismanagement as this."[12]

At nine in the morning of July 4, Robert Mason, the British vice-consul in Santiago, plus the Portuguese consul and the secretary to the civil governor of Oriente Province, met with Colonel Joseph Dorst of the 1st Infantry and Lieutenant Miley under a large ceiba tree, soon to be called the *árbol de la paz,* about six hundred yards in front of the American lines. The officials wished to know if the noncombatants of the city could come out unmolested to El Caney and be provided with food. Should the humanitarian request be granted by the American commanding general, they further asked that bombardment of the city, scheduled and announced for the next day in Shafter's surrender ultimatum, be delayed one day.

Mason explained the "dreadful conditions now existing among the inhabitants of Santiago." For the past two years no crops of consequence had been harvested, and the scenes around the consulates were "very distressing," especially since it was thought the American fleet was about to force its way into the harbor to bombard the city. Mason claimed there were about thirty thousand civilians in town, of whom more than half were women and children. He asked whether General Shafter would permit the old, infirm, and sick to be placed aboard the Spanish merchant ships in the harbor and have them moored to a point so as not to be placed under fire; whether trains filled with refugees could be run out of Santiago through the American lines north and south of the city; and finally, if some "guarantee of disposition of American troops" could be made for the safety of the civilians who fled the city for territory occupied by Cuban rebel forces. When Mason had finished, the secretary to the civil governor insisted on the broadest interpretation of the term "noncombatant" when indicating those who would be permitted by the Americans to leave the city. There were many inhabitants of Spanish birth and sympathy, he said, engaged in civil pursuits, who would be glad to leave if given permission.[13]

It was explained to the consuls that El Caney was hardly suitable, being badly shelled, with many Spanish wounded lying about, and also some of the dead still unburied. However, any civilians leaving Santiago, up to three thousand or four thousand, it being impossible to care for any more, would be permitted sanctuary there. The U.S. Army would provide the "rougher components of the ration," tinned meat, bread, sugar, coffee—exactly what the American troops ate. As for delaying the bombardment, General Shafter would have to consult his government, but the consuls and the Spanish civil officer should know that the alternative was hardly inviting, "being a very close investment and starving the garrison out." Should that be the case, the people who could find food in the city had better remain there, only coming out when provisions failed. If the civilians came out all at once, little could be done for them. General Toral would be informed of the American decision directly, and another meeting was scheduled for the next morning.[14]

At a White House conference on July 4, with the full military and naval hierarchies present, it was decided to send General Miles to

Cuba, if for nothing else than to buck up Shafter's flagging spirits. Miles was incredibly eager to be off. He had made small progress on his coveted expedition to Puerto Rico, which the administration had deferred until the end of the Santiago campaign. To bring that closure, he had a sound plan, quite in accord with the navy's, to land a force of troops and the fleet's marines on the western, Socapa, side of the harbor, and in conjunction with a push by Shafter on the east, force a surrender of the city. He would take with him the 3,500 men of Brigadier General George Garretson's brigade in the *Columbia, Harvard,* and *Yale.* With, as the *New York Tribune* put it, "elated demeanor," Miles rushed from the White House to make his preparations. His departure for the front was hailed with universal satisfaction, for it was taken for granted, though not stated in his orders, that he would assume command of the army in the field besieging Santiago.[15]

General Shafter carried on a busy correspondence with José Toral between July 3 and 5. He proposed to return the handful of wounded Spanish officers captured at El Caney if they would give their parole not to serve against the United States until properly exchanged. This idea had occurred to the general when he saw the certitude of the Spanish prisoners that they would be shot by the Americans after capture. Shafter contemplated the POWs returning to Santiago, telling of their good treatment, and creating a positive reaction in the Spanish forces against further, futile defense. Additionally, Shafter proposed a complete exchange of Spanish prisoners for those captured from the sunken *Merrimac,* the only American POWs held by the Spanish. Shafter also availed himself of the opportunity to renew his proposal for the city's surrender. "I would suggest," he concluded, "that, to save needless effusion of blood and the distress of many people you may reconsider your determination of yesterday [not to capitulate]. Your men have certainly shown the gallantry which was expected of them."[16]

Regarding the consular requests, Shafter had received permission from the War Department to act as he saw fit. He informed Toral that he would grant a day's grace before opening fire in order to spare the "poor women and children who will suffer very greatly by their hasty and forced departure from the city." As for the consular suggestions of placing the old and sick on the merchant ships, and the running of refugee trains, he also agreed to those. Toral, for his part, was grateful for the information regarding the wounded prisoners. He had no objection to receiving them, but he was not authorized to make any exchange; Captain General Blanco reserved that authority—but the request had been passed on to Havana. Regarding capitulation, "The same reasons that I explained to you yesterday, I have to give you today—that this place will not be surrendered."[17]

The return of the Spanish wounded took place on the afternoon of July 5, during a time of truce. Twenty-eight wounded men, four of them officers, were placed in ambulances and driven under military escort to a point near the city's defenses. The convoy was met by a force of Spanish troops who presented arms to the American escort. A large group gathered around the ambulances and removed the men. "The affair," said Lieutenant Miley, "made an excellent impression upon the Spaniards."[18]

On the night of July 4 to 5, the Spanish conducted a desperate attempt at blocking the harbor. The exit and destruction of Cervera's squadron had left the city virtually bereft of naval defenses. Though the contact mines were still in place, six electric mines had been taken up from the minefield to permit safe passage to Cervera's ships and had yet to be replaced; in fact, it was impossible to do so under the guns of the American fleet. The Santiago naval command, with Toral's assent, decided to sink the old cruiser *Reina Mercedes* in the channel narrows.

On the evening of the fourth, she was stripped and, under the command of Ensign Nardiz, a skeleton crew of deckhands, engineers, and two pilots made ready to sink her near the Morro. At midnight, Santiago was startled by heavy firing at the harbor entrance. The *Texas* had spotted the *Mercedes* and opened fire. The Spanish cruiser was struck by several 12- and 13-inch shells from the American battleships— excellent night shooting. The *Mercedes* listed over and, with her port rail under water, sank, but like the *Merrimac* before her, she was not in a position to block the channel. "The sacrifice was useless," said Lieutenant José Müller, "and the harbor was not obstructed."[19]

Lieutenant Miley had arranged to meet with the consuls on the morning of July 5, but before he could ride out to the ceiba tree, "the entire population had poured out of the city." The consuls said that, the day before, the people had expected the fleet hourly to force the harbor entrance, and the populace was prepared to flee at the first indication of its approach. The road to El Caney, Miley observed, "was filled with women and children and old men."[20]

Lieutenant Müller described the scene: "At daybreak . . . a compact crowd, composed for the greater part of old men, women, and children, though strong, robust men—some of them volunteers, now in civilian's clothes—started from the city toward El Caney . . . on foot, there being no carriages, nor wagons, nor vehicles of any kind, not even horses. . . . All these people were crossing the ditches and trenches by which the . . . road was cut and obstructed, all anxious to escape from the dangers of a bombardment." Many of the refugees were wealthy citizens of the city, "women not accustomed to such fatigues and hardships, which fear and terror alone enabled them to bear."[21]

Frederick Ramsden, the British consul, described the terrible scene on the road: "people flocking out, sick carried in chairs or as they could, children getting lost by the way." Convinced that their absence from the city would not be more than three days, the majority of civilians had nothing but the clothes on their backs and no provisions except what they could carry on their persons. Müller was told by many people that the houses in El Caney held at times eighty people, and in some up to two hundred. "As in the cemetery, each person," he noted, "had no more space than he or she occupied; and thus they were housed together, men and women, children and old people, white persons and black." The provisions for three days were soon exhausted, "money was looked upon with disdain and . . . gold was of no value." Trading there was, "but it was exchanging rice for coffee, hardtack for beans, or sugar for codfish."[22]

The bodies of those killed during the battle for the village on July 1 were only partly buried. Animal and even human carcasses were thrown into Las Guamas Creek, in which the refugees washed, bathed, and drank. The houses had no sanitary provisions of any kind, and doors were kept closed to prevent new invasions by lately arriving refugees. The atmosphere was terrible. Children, sick from lack of food, or from taking food they could not digest, cried day and night. Quiet or rest became impossible.

A town of two hundred houses had been invaded by about fifteen thousand people who counted on staying three days and remained for eleven. Müller claimed that week and a half at El Caney caused more deaths in the civilian population than three years of war. Deaths, which had numbered five a day, now jumped to not fewer than fifty. For lack of transport, the army was unable to provide anything but the barest subsistence, and the Red Cross ship *State of Texas* could add little more than that. That vessel's "many delicacies," as French Chadwick wrote, things such as oatmeal, malted milk, and beef broth, were reserved for the sick and wounded of the army. Near the end of their ordeal, Consul Ramsden drew up a petition, signed by a number of women, to General Shafter. In essence, they demanded that something be done to alleviate their situation, or arrangements made with the Spanish to allow them to return to the city, "where we would rather die from the shells or be buried under the ruins of our homes than perish slowly from hunger and disease, and the privations we are suffering." But suffer they did until, with the capitulation of the city, they were finally able to return.[23]

Notwithstanding the navy's most recent refusal to pass its armored ships over the minefield at the harbor entrance while the forts were still capable of interfering with the minesweeping craft, General Shafter sent off a cable to the War Department in the early hours of July 5. In nearly the same language he used two days before to the navy, he unburdened himself to Adjutant General Corbin: "I regard it as necessary that the navy force an entrance into the harbor . . . not later than the 6th instant and assist in the capture of the place. If they do, I believe the place will surrender without further sacrifice of life." If the army had to take the city on its own, then Shafter required at least 1,500 reinforcements "speedily." He was now, he informed Corbin, "in position to do my part."[24]

The reply from the War Department came before noon. In the absence of any general staff, to say nothing of the lack of existence of something as sophisticated as the Joint Chiefs of Staff, the fount of all solutions—if they could be called that—lay with the commander in chief, the president. Down the chain of command, through the secretary of war, Corbin was instructed to inform Shafter "to confer" with Admiral Sampson "at once for cooperation in taking Santiago." After this exchange of conflicting views, "you will agree upon the time and manner of the attack."[25]

Shafter knew nothing would come of trying to convince the navy to buck the minefield. There could be no agreement on this; the navy would not risk its ships. In the afternoon, he dispatched another telegram to the War Department, this time demanding that the "Navy should go into Santiago at any cost." If they did, he had no doubt the city would surrender at once. If the navy continued to demur, he cautioned, "the country should be prepared for heavy losses among our troops" in any attack. But Shafter was in no mood for battle. He informed Corbin that after speaking with the consuls, he would refrain from bombarding the city until more troops arrived. As for the refugees, "If it was simply a going out of the women . . . to places where they could be cared for, it would not matter much, but now it means their going out to starve to death or be furnished with food by us, and the latter is impossible now."[26]

Shafter's latest wires were shown to the president, who, after deliberating with Russell Alger and his professional military advisers, rightly concluded from the several telegrams that General Shafter recoiled from assaulting the Spanish positions, considering himself not strong enough with the forces immediately at hand. "This being the case," Corbin cabled back, "it is the better part of wisdom to await reinforcements. . . . [Y]ou must be judge of the time and manner of assault." Again, the president as commander in chief directed Shafter and Sampson to confer "and determine a course of cooperation best calculated to secure desirable results with least sacrifice."[27]

Then, in a note "strictly confidential to you," Corbin passed on a suggestion from Russell Alger. If the navy refused to undertake breaking into the harbor, Shafter might take one of his transports, cover the pilothouse with baled hay, attach an anchor to a towline, and grapple for the mine cables. Officer volunteers from the army were to be called upon for this duty, "to run into the harbor, thus making a way for the navy." The one certainty, said Corbin, was that "the navy must get into the harbor and must save the lives of our brave men that will be sacrificed if we assault the enemy in his entrenchments without aid."[28]

As a result of these communications, late in the afternoon of July 5, Shafter signaled to Admiral Sampson that he was "directed" by the president "to confer with you fully" on a joint attack on Santiago. Again, because of his gout and general unwellness, General Shafter was unable to ride down from his El Pozo headquarters to the coast at Siboney. "Can you not come here to see me?" he asked the admiral. For his part, Admiral Sampson also received a communication from Navy Secretary Long. In like manner, the admiral was instructed to confer with the army command "in order at once for cooperation in taking Santiago."[29]

To Captain French Chadwick, Sampson's chief of staff, the difficulty in the overall logic of General Shafter and his chiefs in the War Department of sending the navy to force an entrance into Santiago was the army's failure to appreciate more recent, larger strategic conditions of the war. They pardonably saw only Santiago before them, ignoring or dismissing the threat of a new Spanish naval squadron, commanded by Rear Admiral Manuel Cámara, sailing east in the Mediterranean. Consisting of the battleship *Pelayo,* the armored cruiser *Carlos V,* auxiliary cruisers, destroyers, and two troop-packed transports—nearly every remaining modern Spanish naval vessel—it was ostensibly bound for the Philippines. This fresh development, seconded by the arrival of an annoying, interfering German naval force in Manila Bay, needed attention. Orders had already been dispatched to Admiral Sampson to form "Eastern" and "Covering" squadrons with his armored cruisers and most of his battleships to reinforce Admiral Dewey in the Philippines and to harass the Spanish coast. Taking the matter further, Chadwick said, "War is sacrifice—both of men and material. Of men there were plenty; of the all-important material—ships—there was but little; no number of men within reason could in the circumstances weigh against a battleship." Inasmuch as the outcome of the war depended largely on the superiority of the U.S. Navy to that of the Spanish, Secretary Long naturally agreed with his commanders. On July 6, he wired Admiral Sampson instructions not to risk the loss of any armored vessels by mines "unless for the most urgent reasons."[30]

Because Sampson was ill and confined to his berth, it was felt unwise to inflict upon him the rough seven-mile ride from Siboney to El Pozo in the burning midsummer sun, or worse, a tropical downpour; Captain Chadwick would represent the admiral instead. In his preconference briefing, Chadwick was directed to place the navy's plan for taking Santiago before General Shafter: The marine battalion at Guantánamo, plus the various ships' marine detachments, in all about 1,200 men, should be landed at Cabañas Bay, about two and a half miles west of the harbor entrance. Supported by the fleet and the Cubans still in the area, they would assault and capture the Socapa battery. At the same time, an attacking force of the army could move on the Morro and the eastern batteries. As soon as the two positions were carried and the ground was safely in American possession, the navy would clear the minefield and steam into the harbor.

Chadwick arrived at El Pozo in midmorning. General Shafter, "ill and evidently suffering," lay on a cot in the glade where the head-quarters had been established; a single orderly was the only person near. Following an extended review of the conditions current along the front, which included the temporary truce for the exchange of prisoners due to end that day, Chadwick suggested laying stress upon the Spanish adherence to *pundonor*—saving face. Prior to any attack, Chadwick recommended, a combined Shafter-Sampson letter should be sent to General Toral, in which the totality of the American naval victory over the Spanish would be placed before him. With it should come a reminder of the consequent ability to destroy Santiago by naval gunfire. To prolong the sufferings of the Spanish troops and the populace by a defense, which in any case could end only in surrender, was useless. Chadwick suggested the letter embody a proposal to refer the question of surrender to Madrid, relieving Toral of a grave military and political responsibility.

Should the Spanish not surrender, the fleet would subject Santiago to a prolonged naval bombardment by its heavy guns. If this was not sufficient to bring the Spanish to terms, then the naval plan of a si-multaneous marine-army attack on the west and east harbor fortifi-cations would go forth, together with an effort to force the minefield with some of the smaller ships of the fleet. The bombardment was fixed for July 9, in three days.

At around the time the meeting adjourned, General Shafter was in-formed that Captain General Blanco had approved the exchange of prisoners. The names of three captured Spanish army lieutenants were sent to Toral, in exchange for Lieutenant Hobson of the *Merri-mac*; Toral would choose one. The enlisted men of the *Merrimac* would be exchanged for a like number of Spanish soldiers taken at El Caney or San Juan Hill. Lieutenant Miley represented General Shafter and a Major Irles appeared for General Toral. The reply from Toral with the name of the officer to exchange for Hobson had not arrived in time for the parley, and Miley took all three, prepared to give them up for Hobson if necessary. They, along with the seven enlisted men, were blindfolded while passing through the American lines. On arriving at the Ceiba tree, Major Irles indicated that First Lieutenant Arias had been chosen. Miley pointed the major's attention to Arias's slight arm wound and asked if this did not change his decision; it did not. A cartel of exchange was signed, and the negotiators waited for the arrival of Lieutenant Hobson and his crew.

The trail down which Hobson and his men came was a broad one, between high banks with great trees meeting overhead. For hours before they came in sight, American officers and men not on duty in the trenches waited along the sides, "broiling in the sun," as Davis said, "and crowding together as closely as men on the bleaching boards of a baseball field." Hobson, astride a skinny horse, came slowly along the road, wearing his blue navy uniform, against which his white prison pallor stood out. For a moment, he sat motionless. One of the regimental bands struck up "The Star-Spangled Banner." "No one cheered," said Davis, "or shouted or gave an order, but everyone rose to his feet slowly, took off his hat slowly, and stood so, looking up at Hobson in absolute silence."[31]

Then a red-headed soldier leaped down into the trail, shouting "Three cheers for Hobson," and the mob rushed him in wild welcome. The accolade was matched in fervor all along the route to Siboney.[32]

Following the exchange, Miley informed the Spanish that hostilities were to resume in an hour. But before that time was up, General Shafter made a third demand for surrender. Shafter's "suggestion" of surrender, Miley related, was made in a "purely humanitarian spirit," as he had no wish to "slaughter" any more men, American or Spanish. But unless this were arranged by noon, July 9, the fleet, which "is now perfectly free to act," would open a bombardment of the city. The three-day grace period, Toral was informed, was given to permit him to consult with his home government. Toral graciously accepted the provision.[33]

The next day, Shafter cabled the adjutant general in Washington. He hoped his reinforcements might soon arrive. "Not one in sight yet except for the two hundred recruits for the Second Infantry, who came a week ago." Also, where were the tugs, lighters, and steam launches that had been promised him ten days past? As for an immediate attack on Santiago by his own troops, "I do not consider my force sufficient to warrant an assault on the city, though I believe it would be successful, but at a fearful loss." So heavy did Shafter reckon his casualties in that endeavor that he considered it "criminal to hope for the end to be gained, which is merely the capture of a few thousand men and when we see that we are getting them by siege."[34]

During the lull in army operations before and after the battle for the San Juan heights, preparations went steadily forward in the fleet for an expedition to the Mediterranean and the Spanish Atlantic coast. This had first been broached by the Navy Department as early as June 18, when Admiral Sampson was ordered to detail an "Eastern Squadron"—the *Iowa, Oregon,* and *Brooklyn,* plus a strong division of auxiliary cruisers—for service in Spanish waters should Cámara's squadron pass Suez; "hold them for speedy orders," noted Secretary Long. The composition of the force changed from time to time, but the directives and departmental consternation over a Spanish squadron containing a battleship, against which Dewey would be well-nigh defenseless, remained palpable for several weeks.[35]

On June 26, the Navy Department cabled Commodore Watson, who would command the Eastern Squadron, to sail "as soon as Sampson gives the order," this time with the *Iowa, Oregon,* the cruiser *Newark,* and auxiliaries, for St. Michael, in the Azores, and thence to Tangier, Morocco. On June 28, Sampson, who had warned the department of the danger of reducing the blockade, was authorized to detain the *Iowa* and *Oregon* until the other armored vessels in the fleet had been fully coaled, so as to be able to hold his position off Santiago with sufficient force should Cervera opt to escape. "But you will hurry this," Secretary Long emphasized, "as the department desires to get these vessels to the East via Spain."[36]

By July 8, however, much of the dilemma regarding Cámara, and all of the questions concerning Cervera, had been resolved. Cámara had indeed reached Suez, was refused permission by the British to coal, then paid out £68,000 passage money to steam into the Red Sea, only to turn about, back into the Mediterranean. Yet the Navy Department still urged haste in assembling the Eastern Squadron, ordering the ships detailed to rendezvous at St. Nicolas Môle, Haiti. This directive was supplemented by a report from the American consul in Lisbon that the Spanish cruisers—the relic *Vitoria*, the newer *Lepanto*, and the auxiliary *Alfonso XII*—had been ordered to steam in the Strait of Gibraltar to counter the Eastern Squadron. By this time, Watson had hoisted his broad pennant in the *Oregon* at Guantánamo. On July 9, Sampson informed the secretary the Eastern Squadron would be ready to depart in two days.

In anticipation of Toral's likely refusal to surrender the city, Admiral Sampson offered the army ten 3-inch rapid-fire guns, together with crews. They were accepted at once. Then on the morning of July 10, General Shafter delayed the landing of the pieces at Siboney, telling the admiral that General Toral had just proposed abandoning Santiago and all its fortifications, if permitted to march under safe conduct with his entire command, its arms, and baggage to Holguín.

This startling development came as a result of the Shafter-Chadwick letter. As Toral explained, putting the best face on a bad situation, he proposed these terms solely in order to avoid further damage to the city, "useless shedding of blood, and other horrors of war." The loss of Cervera's squadron, he said, "in no way influences the defense of the city." In fact, quite the opposite, as it had been reinforced by Escario from Manzanillo. Toral now had at his disposal "sufficient men" to resist any attack. True enough, if deployed and led properly. He was also "well provided" with ammunition and water "in abundance," collected in cisterns, filled with the daily rains, "and rations for a reasonably long time." That was also correct, if only rice was on the menu. As for the threatened American bombardment, that "will only be felt by the house owners—foreigners, many of them—and many other natives whom the American army came to protect." Lastly, Toral played on Shafter's real fears of disease racking his army, signs of which had already begun. "The Spanish soldier is fully acclimated," Toral said; "your troops are not." Any American losses in an attack on Santiago would only be compounded "by the rigors of a bad climate and the sickness of the present season."[37]

Shafter immediately sent the gist of this message to the War Department, urging acceptance of the Spanish proposal. He did it without consulting anyone, though after transmission, he ran it by his division commanders, who to a man agreed with his views. Shafter's rationale pointed first to an immediate opening of the harbor, which in an instant would provide the Fifth Corps with all the stores still loaded in the transports, easing the logistic nightmare immeasurably; second, it permitted the return of the thousands of refugees suffering at El Caney; third, it saved great destruction of property, which a naval bombardment would entail; fourth, it at once relieved the command of a siege while it was still in good health for operations elsewhere, namely, Puerto Rico. As it was, there were three cases of yellow fever (actually probably malaria) in one of the Michigan regiments. "And if it gets started," Shafter warned, "no one knows where it will stop."[38]

As the general viewed it, the only downside of accepting Toral's proposition was losing some prisoners "we do not want and the arms they carry." Many, he believed, would desert to the American lines in any case. But Shafter did not think the administration would buy it. His reasoning, which might be operationally sound, was politically questionable; why let the Spanish off the hook? Shafter himself was of divided mind, telling Secretary Alger that the delay in operations due to submitting the Spanish request to Washington provided time to get reinforcements up from Siboney, as the first transports bearing them had just arrived. The Spanish "[i]n my opinion . . . will have to surrender unconditionally very soon after I open fire upon them."[39]

The reply from Washington was quick. According to Adjutant General Corbin, the administration had received Shafter's recommendation with "great surprise." After all, he had already told them he expected the enemy to surrender unconditionally now that their supplies and water had been interdicted. Following "careful consideration" by the president and secretary of war, Shafter was ordered to "accept nothing but an unconditional surrender"; furthermore, he should double his precautions to prevent a Spanish breakout toward Holguín. Responsibility for destruction to the city and the distress to the civilians, Corbin said, "rests entirely with the Spanish commander." Shafter now received somewhat more than a gentle kick. Corbin related Secretary Alger's orders, "that when you are strong enough to destroy the enemy and take Santiago that you do it." If he hadn't enough force for the operation, more reinforcements would be dispatched "at the earliest moment practicable." In the meantime,

Corbin ended, "nothing is lost by holding the position you now have and which you regard as impregnable."[40]

As soon as the reply came from Washington, Toral was informed of the U.S. government's rejection of his offer. Shafter, pro forma, again demanded unconditional surrender, requiring a reply by 3:00 P.M. the next day, the tenth; and if the answer was no, active operations would resume an hour later. Toral promptly refused to capitulate, and the latest truce ended.

Reinforcements had begun arriving on July 9: the 1st Illinois and 1st District of Columbia Infantry, and the 4th and 5th U.S. Artillery regiments. The supply of artillery was now ample; the question was how to get it the seven miles from Siboney to the trenches. It was never solved. Though eight 3.5-inch mortars with a very limited supply of ammunition were already in position in the center of the line, only two heavy siege pieces ever made it to the front before the final negotiations for surrender began.

The lines, however, were strengthened and shifted to the right, bracing Lawton's wing, extending it to completely encircle the city, preventing any attempt by Toral at escape or of reinforcements from entering. The 1st Infantry, previously held in support of the artillery position at El Pozo, moved into new positions on the right, as did the whole 1st Brigade of Kent's division. On the near right, in the gap between the cavalry and Lawton's divisions just north of the Santiago–El Caney road, General Shafter placed his new Illinois and Washington, D.C., arrivals. On the far northwest, García's Cubans guarded the hill passes. At some points, the opposing lines were not more than half a mile apart. "My plans for tomorrow," wrote Shafter to the adjutant general on the tenth, "are to keep up a bombardment of the trenches and city and to complete the investment on the northwest. . . . Should the opposition be light at any point [I] will push line nearer the city, but will not assault."[41]

Inside the city, the garrison was poorly clothed, still more poorly fed, and eight months arrears in pay, not that there was anything to buy. The remaining civilians, far from helping the soldiers, bolted their doors and windows, even, said Lieutenant Müller, "at the drug stores. The merchants, far from furnishing provisions to the army, or even to the hospitals, which stood so much in need of them, hid them carefully and official searches had to be made."[42]

Without any prospect of receiving help by sea, which was now completely controlled by the Americans, Santiago was surrounded by an army that continued to grow and receive supplies. As Müller saw it, the siege was exceptional for the fact that any reinforcements would have the opposite effect of their intended purpose—further straining the already nearly empty food supplies. There were some Spanish officers who suggested forcing a passage through the enemy's lines to Holguín. But this was fantasy. As Müller accurately noted, "One cannot break through lines and walk over armies equipped with modern muskets and guns." The Spanish command and rank and file knew they would be forced to surrender, "and that is only a question of days."[43]

On July 10, the navy opened a short bombardment of the city with 8-inch shells from the *Brooklyn* and *Indiana*. The Spanish responded in late afternoon with a vigorous rifle and artillery fire, which was returned by all the American field guns on the trench line, with, as Miley said, "much effect." The American infantry pretty much stayed hunkered down, and the firing was mostly done by the artillery. Shafter, in his report to the War Department, stated that if the next day's bombardment was not satisfactory, he would ask the navy to make an attempt at forcing the harbor. "I will not sacrifice any lives."[44]

Shortly after eight o'clock in the morning of the eleventh, the *Brooklyn, Indiana,* and *New York* opened a slow five-hour bombardment of Santiago. From the army lines, the shells could easily be seen falling into the city and fires starting. At the time, General Shafter claimed the firing to be "very accurate," but he later amended this to say, possibly out of spite, that the ships firing "had absolutely no effect on the town." Shafter's turnaround is disputed by the report of a board appointed by Admiral Sampson, who investigated the results following the surrender. Fifty-seven houses were hit, most of which were severely damaged and a good number destroyed. Even shells that did not explode "went through four walls, completely wrecking interior." Typical was the house at Calle de Bartholomé 29: "This house was a complete wreck, not even a portion of the walls were standing." In the Calle de Marina, along the waterfront, for a stretch of six hundred yards, the officers counted nineteen holes made by 8-inch shells. The board considered the full amount of damage "startling," with a great deal of property destroyed. At 12:45 P.M., firing ceased on signal from the army at the Siboney station: "I am going to put up a flag of truce."[45]

This latest came as a result of a cable from Adjutant General Corbin. In Washington, the fact that Shafter and his senior officers favored the Spanish offer to surrender the city was felt to be an ominous development; surely he would not let the Spanish just walk away. To make "unconditional" surrender more palatable to the Spanish, the president sanctioned a suggestion by Russell Alger that if they opted to capitulate the garrison as well as the city and its fortifications, the prisoners of war would be shipped home to Spain at American expense. Shafter was informed of this during the naval bombardment, and this was the proposal that now went forward with the flag of truce.[46]

General Miles, after an uneventful voyage on his way to seize Puerto Rico, had arrived off Siboney with the *Yale, Columbia,* and *La Grande Duchesse* during the naval bombardment. On coming in sight of the flagship, he signaled to Admiral Sampson his desire to land west of the harbor and move east to take the Socapa and its supporting positions from the rear—Sampson's dearest plan. The admiral immediately boarded the *Yale* for a conference with the commanding general. "I explained to him," said Miles, "the purpose of my presence and told him I desired the cooperation of the navy in the plan." Admiral Sampson offered every assistance of the fleet to cover the disembarkation of the newly arrived troops and to enfilade the Spanish positions with the ships' guns. Miles then landed with his staff at Siboney.[47]

The following morning, July 12, General Miles rode up the *camino real* to Shafter's headquarters at El Pozo. On arrival, Miles said, Shafter "sent by my direction" a communication to General Toral, informing him of the commanding general's coming with reinforcements and that the American generals desired to meet with him at any time agreeable at the regular place, the ceiba tree. Toral's replies, both to Shafter's demand of July 11 and to the latest missive, informed the American commanders that he had telegraphed the POW transport proposal to Captain General Blanco, and would be happy to meet with the Americans at noon the next day.[48]

"Rained very hard last night," cabled General Shafter to the War Department that morning, "and so far today." If the roads became too bad to transport rations to the front, and they were barely adequate for that task, "we will simply have to take the town by assault, without regard to what it costs." As yet, he complained, there was no attempt by the navy to force the harbor entrance: "They should be required to make a determined effort at once." How this was to be accomplished under the truce then in place—making such an action a violation of the rules of war—the general did not state, and in fact he had already signaled Admiral Sampson that the cease-fire would remain in effect through the thirteenth at least.[49]

Conditions along the front on both sides were awful. The onset of malaria, in most cases mistaken for yellow fever, in the Fifth Corps had now mounted to over a hundred cases, and the medical officers were undecided to what extent it might cripple the command. "This was the most serious feature of the situation," Miles wrote after the war, "and impressed me with the importance of prompt action." There had to be a surrender or an attack on the city; neither could wait any longer.[50]

At first, General Shafter and his senior officers tried to keep the fact of the fever outbreak secret from the troops, but this was impossible, not with a hundred men down with it. The army, said Lieutenant Miley, now knew "it would have to fight a foe more dangerous than the Spaniards." Medical science was still of the opinion yellow fever was spread by poor hygiene and other factors not related to the actual cause, the female *Aedes aegypti* mosquito. To contain the illness, General Shafter ordered the commanding officer at Siboney to burn all buildings designated as contaminated by the base hospital surgeon.

The rains were unusually heavy; as predicted, the roads were impassable to wagons, but as well, the streams were so swollen at times as to be unfordable by the pack trains. On the eleventh and twelfth, supplies were entirely cut off to the refugees at El Caney, and they were urged to quit the place for the mining district between Siboney and Daiquirí, where they could be supplied by rail. There were thousands of civilians at El Caney, however, who could not make the ten-mile trek, and most stayed put and suffered.

On the Spanish side, the situation in front of Santiago produced a full-scale policy rift between the government at Madrid and the army in Cuba. At the conclusion of the land and naval battles of July 1 and July 3, Premier Sagasta, desperate to end the conflict with at least a portion of the empire intact, opened an exchange of messages with

Captain General Blanco concerning future actions. At Havana, Blanco convened a conference of his commanders to arrive at a recommendation for the government. The military leaders in Cuba decided that, regardless of the outcome at Santiago, resistance should continue. Blanco cabled War Minister Correa that he could hold out in the island for many months yet, and that the army wished, as a matter of honor, to fight on.

To these unwelcome views, Sagasta responded that Spain had no option but to capitulate and get the best terms possible, the view of all but the most intransigently nationalist Spanish politicians. Domestic unrest, always lurking, might well erupt if the war continued with further disasters, which would also harden the Americans into presenting options the Spanish considered unacceptable. How, Sagasta wanted to know, would the army in Cuba react to the government's opening peace negotiations? War Minister Correa also pleaded with Blanco to give assurances that the army in Cuba would abide by the decision of the government. In the end, Blanco finally caved; on July 14, he gave notice that although the army wished to continue the fight, it would obey orders. But before this notice, and perhaps helping to cause it, came word from General Linares.

On July 12, Linares, temporarily overcoming the pain of the wound he received on San Juan Hill, deemed it his duty to write the captain general, and through him, War Minister Correa and the government in Madrid, of the true situation at Santiago, and "of these long-suffering troops." The enemy positions were now very close to the precincts of the city, and by the nature of the ground were looking down into the Spanish lines. The Spanish forces were "exhausted; large numbers sick; not sent to hospitals because [it] is necessary to retain them in [the] trenches; horses and mules without food and shelter." In heavy storms the rain poured incessantly into the trenches for twenty-four continuous hours. The men were without permanent shelter, rice was the only food, and they lived in one cotton uniform without the opportunity to wash it. There were many casualties, with high rates among junior officers and battalion commanders, which deprived the forces of necessary leadership in critical moments.[51]

In these conditions, Linares went on, it was impossible to break through the enemy's lines, and any attempt would cost a third of the garrison. If they were to break out, assisted by a relief column from

Holguín, it would be necessary for the latter to break the lines from the outside, something Linares did not think possible. Thus, "the situation fatally imposes itself; surrender is inevitable; and we can only prolong the agony." Any sacrifice was now useless—to what end were the troops fighting? The enemy could bombard the city at will, exhausting the defenders, without exposing his own men. The American fleet had the range of the city, "and bombards . . . by sections with mathematical precision."[52]

"Santiago is no Gerona," he continued, "a walled city, part of the mother country, defended inch by inch by its own children without distinction—old men, women, and children, who encouraged and assisted the combatants and exposed their lives." In contrast to that heroic seven-month stand against the French in 1809, "Here is solitude; a total emigration of the population," Cuban as well as Spanish, including the public officials. Only the clergy remained, "and they wish to leave the city today headed by their archbishop."[53]

The defenders of Santiago, said Linares, were not at the beginning of a campaign, full of enthusiasm and energy; they had been fighting for three years, and not only Cuban rebels, but climate, privation, and fatigue; "and now that the most critical time has arrived, their courage and physical strength are exhausted," and there was no means of regaining them. "The ideal is lacking," for the troops were defending the property of those who abandoned it in their very presence, "and who have allied themselves with the American forces."[54]

"The honor of arms" had its limit, and Linares appealed to the judgment of the government and the Spanish nation "whether these long-suffering troops have not saved that honor many times." If it was necessary to "consummate the sacrifice" of the city for reasons unfathomed, or if someone was needed to bear the responsibility for either surrender or destruction of the garrison, Linares was prepared to offer himself "loyally on the altars of my country for the one purpose or the other." His own modest reputation, he ended, was of little value when it came to a question of national interests.[55]

It was clear by now that submission was imminent, and the main point in the minds of the Spanish military commanders in Santiago was the salvage of at least some face. This would soon be made evident in communications from Toral to Shafter, but it is especially evident in the letter of Linares, which laid before the Spanish government, as Chadwick noted, "in all its nakedness the seriousness of the situation."[56]

Though surrender loomed, active American preparations went forward should negotiations fail. The disembarkation of the artillery continued, and arrangements were made to land the waiting reinforcements at Cabañas, about a mile west of the Socapa. There were a number of American officers and several members high in the McKinley administration who thought Toral was merely procrastinating to gain time, and Shafter was constantly urged to break off haggling and attack the city. But he recoiled from this, knowing the enemy must surrender if given enough time. Lieutenant Miley, observing the Spanish positions, had no doubt as to the difficulty of storming them. The inner trenches just outside the city were fronted by double lines of barbed wire, each line of six strands, and so erected that assaulting troops would be halted under a deadly fire. If the Spanish fought as desperately as they had done for San Juan Hill and El Caney, now on a much smaller front, concentrating their fire, the probable result was "something fearful to contemplate."[57]

Late in the evening of July 12, Toral communicated to Shafter, insisting on his earlier proposition to evacuate the city, "for the honor of the Spanish arms." In this, he trusted that his adversary's chivalry and sentiment as a soldier would make him appreciate "exactly" the situation, "and therefore must a solution be found that leaves the honor of my troops intact." Otherwise, General Shafter needed to understand that the Spanish would defend their positions and the city, as far as their strength permitted.[58]

At 2:00 A.M. on the thirteenth, Shafter relayed this message to the War Department, asking if any modification of the unconditional surrender dictum might be permitted him. He was "perfectly satisfied" the city could be taken, but if the Spanish fought, "it will be at fearful cost of life." To remain in front of the city, in essence doing nothing, until he felt unquestionably strong enough to attack, posed a threat from disease as great as that of Spanish bullets. The suffering of the refugees at El Caney was "intense." He was able to supply only enough food to keep them from starving, "and if rains continue I do not know how long I can do that."[59]

The reply from the War Department, from Secretary Alger himself, came, as Chadwick marveled, with "startling promptness," only fourteen minutes elapsing between transmission of the wire out of Guantánamo and the return from Washington. There would be "no modification" of the unconditional surrender demand. In regard to the navy's supposed hesitancy in forcing the harbor entrance, the secretary of the navy would be consulted "at once concerning the ordering of Sampson to assist you."[60]

That morning, Alger, in response to Shafter's telegram depicting the navy's supposed lack of ardor in forcing the harbor entrance, sent a memorandum to Secretary Long requesting that he order the fleet to force its way "at once" to aid the army in capturing the city. The reasons which made the navy's cooperation so necessary, Alger stated, were the heavy rains, the difficulty of supplying food to the frontline units, water-filled trenches, the danger of yellow fever, and the elaborate character of the Spanish defenses, which to take "by assault would require a terrible sacrifice of life." But as Shafter had done in his cable regarding the navy forcing the harbor, Alger also disregarded the fact that a battlefield truce was in place, making it impossible for the navy to accede to the demand, even had it been inclined to do so. To underscore this, Shafter, at around eight in the morning, signaled Admiral Sampson that he and Miles were to engage in a parley with General Toral within a matter of hours; the admiral, Shafter noted, should "have no firing until due notice."[61]

Learning thus of the impending negotiation, Admiral Sampson—who, as commander of the naval forces, held equal standing with General Shafter in any agreement made with the Spanish—shot off his own signal to the general stating that he expected to be represented in any conference arranging terms of surrender for the city. "Questions are involved of importance to both branches of the service," he noted.[62]

Notwithstanding Sampson's demand, sometime around noon, generals Miles, Shafter, and Wheeler, accompanied by a pair of staff officers, met with Toral, who came with two staff officers of his own, and Mr. Robert Mason, the British vice-consul, who acted as interpreter. Following the introductions and some conversation between Toral and Shafter, Miles got to the point. By rights, as commanding general of the American forces in the field, Shafter should have conducted the negotiations, and some have seen this as a sign of "a somewhat divided command." In any case, as the ranking officer,

Miles laid plain the American position. It was the determination of the government "that this position of the Spanish forces must either be destroyed or captured." Miles had arrived in Cuba with sufficient reinforcements to accomplish the object, and "any number of troops could be brought here as fast as steamers could ply, if it took 50,000 men." The American government, Miles continued, offered liberal terms, namely to return the Spanish garrison to Spain, and pointed out that this was the only way in which his forces could return, being on an island three thousand miles away from home.[63]

Toral responded that under Spanish law, he was not permitted to surrender so long as he had ammunition and food, that he was compelled to maintain the honor of Spanish arms. "My reply," Miles reported, "was that he had already accomplished that," and that Toral must surrender now, or take the consequences. Miles gave him until daylight the next morning to make up his mind. Toral pleaded for more time, saying it was impossible otherwise to communicate with his superiors and obtain their authorization. However, if the Americans wished, he still agreed to evacuate under safe conduct to Holguín, giving up the city, its defenses, indeed, all of eastern Oriente Province to the Americans. Miles agreed to extend the time for Toral's reply from dawn until noon.[64]

General Miles sent off a cable to Russell Alger: "The Spanish general today asked that some conclusion be reached that shall save his honor." Outlining Toral's proposal to evacuate the city and its defenses, he urged it on the secretary as "a great concession," which would obviate attacking prepared defenses fitted "with every device for protecting his [Toral's] men and inflicting heavy loss on assaulting lines." The refugee problem was out of control, and there were a hundred cases of malaria (still misdiagnosed as yellow fever, but serious enough) in the corps; under these particulars, he concurred with General Shafter, requesting that "discretion" be granted to the commanders in the field as to the terms of capitulation, especially in view of other immediate operations, namely Puerto Rico, in which the army and navy needed to participate.[65]

Shafter's own report to the War Department was a bit more emphatic regarding the Spanish surrender, echoing the administration's hard-line view, which he had no choice but to adopt. "Told him [Toral]," said Shafter, "that his surrender only will be considered," that he was without hope of escape and had "no right" to continue fighting. It was Shafter's opinion that his own truculence had made a strong impression on the Spaniard. If Toral refused by noon tomorrow, "I will open on him . . . with every gun I have," including naval gunfire.[66]

In Washington, Miles's cable counseling acceptance of the Spanish evacuation of the city alarmed President McKinley enough for him to call a special cabinet meeting with the professional military and naval advisers in attendance. As McKinley perceived it, both his options were unpalatable. Balanced against the risk of prolonging the ordeal of the Fifth Corps in siege and attack was the absence of certain victory by acceding to the Spanish offer of evacuation. The press was already refusing to accept anything less than actual battlefield success or abject surrender. Spain must not be permitted to dawdle, dragging her ancient feet for lenient terms; humanitarian and political grounds, as well as military, made any further delay at Santiago intolerable. However, there now leaked into the cabinet a distrust of General Shafter's firmness in bringing the siege to a close, and Russell Alger was much influenced by this new development.[67]

Navy Secretary John D. Long thought the War Department had reached a very awkward moment. "We had a long sit-down of two or three hours," he said of the cabinet meeting. "We are all pained at the delays at Santiago. . . . The commanding officers have been ordered over and over again to bring the matter to a head, but they delay— perhaps for good reason, although we are inclined to think the Spanish commander is tricking them along with truces and of terms of surrender."[68]

There was also a blowup, or as Long described it, "a pretty scrimmage" between the navy and army in the persons of Captain Alfred Thayer Mahan of the War Board and Secretary Russell Alger. Focused almost solely on Santiago, Alger had become intensely displeased at certain priorities given to the Pacific theater and to the greater strategic aspects of the war, especially the formation of the Eastern Squadron, which he saw as a large subtraction from the naval support the army could expect in the Caribbean. He worked himself into a fine lather at how the army at Santiago was being ignored and victimized by the navy in general and Admiral Sampson in particular. Long brushed this away as empty carping, noting in his diary, "We have furnished him transport to carry his men, on account of his own neglect in making provision for transportation. We have landed them; have helped him in every way we can; and have destroyed the Spanish fleet. Now he is constantly grumbling because we don't run the risk of blowing up our ships over the mines . . . and capturing the city, which he ought to capture himself." Captain Mahan lost patience, sailed into the secretary of war with real vehemence, and, as Long related, "told him he didn't know anything about the use or purpose of the Navy, and that he didn't propose to sit by and hear the Navy attacked. It rather pleased the President, who, I think, was glad of the rebuke."[69]

As a result of the cabinet meeting, Russell Alger communicated directly to General Miles, this in spite of previous arrangements to the contrary stipulated in Miles's orders that General Shafter would remain sole commander on the Santiago front. It was an insulting, indeed potentially dangerous division of command, another error that would not have occurred had there been anything like a functioning general staff. Alger granted Miles the alternative of offering the Spanish officers and men their parole, rather than making them outright prisoners of war, after which they would be shipped back to Spain with American assistance. He was to consult with Admiral Sampson and pursue a course of action jointly agreed upon; the "[m]atter should be settled promptly." Thus, as Miles wrote after the war, Russell Alger "left the matter to my discretion—to accept surrender, order an assault, or withhold same."[70]

Simultaneously, Secretary Long cabled Admiral Sampson with the results of the cabinet meeting. Informed that General Shafter "urges" and the secretary of war "urgently requests" that the navy "force harbor," Sampson was told to consult with General Shafter, "to do all that is reasonably possible to insure the surrender of the enemy." As to how the navy was to accomplish its end of the mission, it was left to the admiral to plot his own course, "except that the United States armored vessels must not be risked."[71]

Sometime before noon, July 14, Shafter received a communication from Toral with the latest word from Blanco. The captain general, "believing the business of such importance as the capitulation of that place [Santiago] should be known and decided upon by the government of his majesty," had requested an immediate answer from Madrid. Toral begged the U.S. commanders to hold their fire until the response came. In the meantime, Toral and Shafter might agree upon general terms of capitulation based on the repatriation of the Spanish garrison.[72]

At noon, Miles, Shafter, and a few staff officers met with General Toral and his small entourage. The Spaniard was prepared to surrender his command. It was an action approved by Captain General Blanco, who had authorized him to appoint commissioners to agree on clauses of capitulation, which he was prepared to do. But though he had received permission from Blanco, Toral still needed to secure the approval of the government in Madrid. Shafter would have none of this and demanded Toral surrender unconditionally immediately and without any further temporizing. The discussion continued, carried on by means of interpreters—Robert Mason for the Spanish, and Cuban volunteer staff officers for the Americans. Somehow, though erroneously, it was conveyed to Shafter and Miles that Toral had unqualifiedly surrendered without waiting for any approval beyond that of Blanco. The respective parties returned to their lines, each under its own misapprehensions of what had been understood. The next parley was scheduled for 2:30 P.M. Just before 1:00, Miles cabled Alger at the War Department, "General Toral formally surrendered the troops of his army corps and division of Santiago on the terms and understanding that his troops would be returned to Spain."[73]

At 1:15, General Miles signaled Admiral Sampson to send an officer to represent the navy during the coming negotiations. But before this could be done, a second signal came from Miles: "The enemy has surrendered." Thus Admiral Sampson, too, was under the misapprehension of a premature capitulation.[74]

The commissioners appointed by General Shafter to conduct further negotiations—Wheeler, Lawton, and Lieutenant Miley—believing that a surrender had already been made without qualification, drafted a rough accord of agreement for submission that seemed to embody the issues settled during the noon meeting. At the 2:30 conclave, the document was discussed point by point, and some slight modifications were made at the request of the Spanish: the word "capitulation" being inserted for "surrender" in all places of the instrument, the retention by the Spanish of the archives of the Military

Division of Santiago, and permission for the *voluntarios* and *guerrilleros,* fighting under the Spanish flag, to return to their homes in Cuba, rather than be shipped off to Spain. The only sticking point seemed to be retention of small arms, which the Spanish insisted on, as they would technically be under parole, rather than prisoners of war. This the Americans refused, but they promised to petition their government to allow the Spanish to take their small arms back with them to Spain. The administration rejected this, but a later wording in the articles permitted the Spanish to march out of Santiago bearing their arms to points of collection selected by the American commanders.

The surrender document covered all Spanish forces constituting "the division of Santiago de Cuba," i.e., east of a line running from Aserraderos on the south coast to Sague de Tanamo on the north; all these troops were under the command of General José Toral and included the Santiago garrison, their weapons and munitions of war, plus twelve thousand more soldiers stationed at Guantánamo, San Luis, Sague de Tanamo, and Baracoa. These garrisons had been, oddly enough, suggested in the cartel by Toral, and were not contemplated by the Americans in the original negotiations. "I was simply thunderstruck," said General Shafter, "that, of their own free will, they should give me 12,000 men that were absolutely beyond my reach."

The instrument of surrender contained ten clauses:

1. All hostilities between the opposing armies in the division of Santiago de Cuba "absolutely and unequivocally cease";
2. The capitulation include all the forces and war material in the noted territory;
3. The United States agree to transport all troops who so wished to Spain;
4. Officers be permitted to retain their side arms, and all ranks their personal baggage;
5. The Spanish remove, or assist the U.S. Navy in lifting, all mines and obstructions to navigation in the harbor;
6. General Toral deliver up without delay a complete inventory of all arms, munitions, and a roster of troops;
7. The Spanish be permitted to remove the military archives and records of the district;

8. All *voluntarios* and *guerrilleros* be permitted to remain in Cuba on condition of surrendering their arms and giving their parole;
9. The Spanish forces march out of Santiago "with the honors of war," depositing their arms at points agreed upon to await their disposition by the U.S. government, it being understood that the American commissioners would recommend their return to Spain;
10. The terms become operational on signing.

A codicil stipulated the immediate entry into the harbor of the Red Cross ship *State of Texas,* cooperation by both sides in the return of the refugees from El Caney, and the reopening of the water pipeline at Cubitas to the city.[75]

The agreement embracing all points was drawn in order to make it a final document. When at the 2:30 P.M. meeting under the *árbol de la paz,* the Americans asked if the Spanish commissioners were ready to sign, they hesitated, saying they had first to return to the city with a copy of the instrument to consult with General Toral. The meeting was adjourned until 6:00. When they reconvened, the Americans fully expected that nothing remained to be discussed and the agreement would be signed. For that reason, the Americans requested that the Spanish troops immediately evacuate their fortifications and trenches and begin the work of removing the mines from the harbor entrance.

But the Spanish commissioners stated they needed to adjourn until the following day, this time to consult with General Linares on certain points. To the Americans this was, as Lieutenant Miley said, a "remarkable request," as the Spanish had just come from speaking with General Toral. Moreover, the Americans knew that Linares, because of his wounds, was no longer in command. The American commissioners had come with full powers of negotiation and they presumed the Spanish had done likewise; now it did not seem so. "Hitch in negotiations," read Shafter's signal to Admiral Sampson; "we may have to fight for it yet."[76]

Something was amiss. The commissioners on both sides appeared to be working at cross-purposes. The Americans—Wheeler, Lawton, and Miley—were determined to press the negotiations to an end that night. It began to seem that the Spanish were stalling for time, or that there had been a misunderstanding on Shafter's part at his earlier meeting with Toral.

The situation was quite serious, for if an amicable conclusion could not be reached, the only alternative was to sever negotiations and re-open the battle. To help clear matters, General Toral came to the parley near midnight and explained his position, just as he had described it to General Shafter earlier in the day. Though he and Blanco were willing to surrender, he refused to proceed without Madrid's approval. Two or three days, he said, must elapse before an answer would come. He was as anxious as the Americans for a speedy resolution, but without the approval of Madrid, he would not surrender.

It was now obvious to the Americans that General Toral had been misunderstood; he had not really surrendered after all. Either that, or he had news of imminent reinforcements and was playing a false game. The meeting was adjourned until 9:30. During this delay, Toral met with the British consul, Frederick Ramsden. Toral admitted that he was now prepared to surrender without Madrid's approval, even if it meant a court-martial for premature capitulation. This was a very important point, for without the government's sanction of his actions, his troops might not be able to return to Spain.[77]

Nearing the appointed time, there was no doubt in the minds of the American commissioners that Toral was sincere in his declarations. It was necessary, however, to get to the bottom of the situation, for if there were grounds to suspect the Spanish were playing for time, the negotiations must be broken off quickly and offensive operations renewed. The Spanish draft was taken up for consideration as soon as it arrived.

The main object for the Americans was to get signatures on a document of capitulation in which the Spanish formally acknowledged their surrender, or unequivocal words to that effect. Now that the document had been purged of as many subjects of contention as possible, there could be no further delay. The ten main clauses were adopted and there was nothing to do but prepare English and Spanish copies for signatures. Given the primitive facilities, this was a long and tedious operation, and the final drafts were run off on a "typewriting machine" placed on a camp stool. By 3 P.M. all were ready. The Spanish commissioners signed the Spanish copy, followed by the American commissioners, and the same was done, in reverse order, on the English version. Each side also received unsigned copies in both languages for their respective commanders. All that was lacking was final word from Toral that capitulation, indeed, had occurred.

Yet there was still the nagging question of the Spanish small arms; as agreed, the Americans made a separate recommendation to their government. "Recognizing the chivalry, courage, and gallantry of General[s] Linares and Toral, and of the soldiers of Spain," the American commissioners unanimously joined "in soliciting the proper authority to accord to these brave and chivalrous soldiers the privilege of returning to their country bearing the arms they have so bravely defended."[78]

There was great anxiety in Washington. They did not understand the delays, and Alger awaited with "deep interest" the details of the surrender. Shortly after noon, he cabled Shafter, "Have you received the absolute surrender of the enemy? We are awaiting the conditions with impatience." Later in the afternoon, both he and Adjutant General Corbin suggested, "[I]s it not possible that Toral is gaining time to get reinforcements that may be on the way to assist him?" And finally, "It is not possible that you are entertaining the proposition of permitting the Spanish to carry away their arms. Such a suggestion should be rejected instantly."[79]

Shafter's reply to this reflected the pique frontline soldiers express toward politicians who attempt to direct a war from the halls of government. He certainly did not "entertain" permitting the Spanish to retain their arms. "They are to surrender them absolutely," as soon as the articles of capitulation were signed. What the Spanish desired, indeed begged, was that the commissioners and General Shafter intercede with the U.S. government to allow the arms to be shipped back to Spain with the garrison. Shafter regarded this as a "small matter." Such an intercession in no way bound the administration to this course of action, but he knew a refusal might mean the difference "between clearing 20,000 Spanish soldiers out of Cuba or leaving them to be captured later, and probably with much loss to ourselves."[80]

The politicians, though, were "impatient with parley," as Corbin put it in his evening cable to Shafter on July 15. Again he harped on the "arrangement" regarding the Spanish arms, pointing out that any such conclusion "had as well be abandoned once for all, as it will not be approved." Toral could not be permitted to dally any longer. "The way to surrender is to surrender," and this should be fully impressed on the Spanish commander. Corbin was careful to inform Shafter that he had sent this communication "as your friend and comrade," and not by authority of the president or secretary of war, "but you can be guided by it with entire safety."[81]

Both Shafter and Miles, the latter aboard his transport itching to get to Puerto Rico, could not have been more relieved when at ten o'clock in the morning of July 16, Spanish heralds rode through the lines under a flag of truce bearing the crucial letter from General Toral. He had finally received authorization from Madrid to capitulate, and asked General Shafter to designate the time and place where the commissioners were to meet "to edit the articles of capitulation on the basis of what has been agreed upon to this date." He also needed to know the stand of the U.S. government on the arms question; not that it would stand in the way of the proceedings, but it was a matter of honor that could not be ignored.[82]

Shafter acknowledged the letter immediately and asked that the Spanish withdraw their lines from the railway to Aguadores and along the American left flank. He also asked that Toral direct the removal of all harbor obstructions, or assist the navy in doing so, "as it is of the utmost importance that I at once get vessels loaded with food into the harbor." Shafter suggested the commissioners meet at midday at the usual place, but the time it took to pass this message through the lines made that impossible; the meeting would occur at 4:00 P.M. instead. In the meantime, work began on removing the harbor hazards.

At 10:15 A.M., Shafter cabled the War Department, "Spanish surrendered. Particulars later." To Admiral Sampson he signaled the same, asking that the admiral send someone to represent the navy in the proceedings.[83]

At 4:00 P.M., July 16, the final instrument of surrender was signed; there were no changes from the previous draft. When Toral announced to the commissioners his determination to destroy the gunboat *Alvarado,* the only naval vessel in the harbor, as Spanish regulations demanded, Captain Chadwick, who was present representing the navy, remonstrated hotly. It was a dishonorable act, he said, and "against the usage of nations"; Toral yielded the point. Chadwick also informed General Shafter that as Admiral Sampson's representative, he should sign the articles of capitulation, and indeed demanded to do so. This General Shafter refused, giving the astonishing rationale that no claim had been made by the army for the victory over Cervera in the battle of July 3. After the war, Chadwick wrote that this was "probably the only instance known of so prominent a departure from usage in combined operations, and in marked contrast to the procedure soon to be taken at Manila."[84]

The surrender of Santiago occurred on Sunday, July 17. At 9:00 A.M., the Spanish flag was hoisted over the Punta Blanca fort, saluted with twenty-one guns, and then lowered. Half an hour later, near Fort Canosa in the inner lines of the Spanish defenses, generals Toral and Shafter—the latter with a large staff and entourage of senior officers, including members of the fleet, and a troop of the mounted squadron of the 2nd Cavalry—reviewed a march-past of a company of Spanish infantry. The Americans presented arms and the band of the 6th Cavalry beat a march on its drums. Lieutenant José Müller of the Spanish navy described the morning as "beautiful, and the clearness of the sky formed a singular contrast with the gloom that enwrapped the spirit of our troops." When the march-past ended, the Americans remained in position while the Spanish left their trenches and moved to the city to deposit their arms at the artillery park. The Socapa and Estrella garrisons were taken by steamer to the Las Cruces pier and from there marched to the deposit point for their arms.

As the operation in the artillery park lasted for hours, Müller found it curious the see the "avidity" with which the Americans looked for anything the Spanish had left behind: insignia, buttons, and decorations, especially of the Constitución Regiment, which had fought so gallantly at El Caney. "It was noticed with what satisfaction they kept whatever articles they could gather. Some of them put on the crosses, covered with dirt and blood, that had adorned the breasts of the Spanish. . . . They showed the high conception which Americans forces had of the valor of our army." After the Spanish stacked their weapons, Lieutenant Miley saw the prisoners cooking horses that had been brought out of the city with them. American rations, however, were soon issued from the stores at hand. Once the supply ships entered the harbor the next day, it was easy to get rations to everyone, and until they were shipped home, the Spaniards ate as the U.S. Army ate.[85]

Wheeler described the surrender ceremony with the American generals drawn up in line from right to left according to rank and their staffs in the same manner, forming several successive lines. Shafter rode forward alone up to General Toral and presented him with the sword and spurs of General Joaquín Vara de Rey, who had been killed defending El Caney. "The Spanish troops presented arms, and the Spanish flag which for 382 years had floated over the city was pulled down and furled forever." The American officers and the cavalry troop then presented arms, after which the Spanish company wheeled left and marched back to the city. The American generals and staff officers rode into town in column of twos, Shafter and Wheeler in front, the other generals and officers following in order of rank, with the mounted cavalry troop bringing up the rear.[86]

One correspondent described the short journey into the city, over ground that they would have had to fight for had Shafter ordered an assault: "Between the lines, and especially as we neared the city, the conditions were terrible. All along the road were carcasses of horses, most of which still had the saddle, bridle, and in many cases saddlebags full of effects, on the dead animals." Shallow graves along the road had been scratched open by vultures and "the odor was horrible in the extreme." The first barricades were "cleverly conceived" barbed-wire entanglements that did not close the road, but compelled traffic to zigzag back and forth, so that any attempt at entrance would have been under a hail of fire, making it nearly impossible. Then came defenses of sand-filled barrels covering the inner trenches. Side streets were barricaded with paving stones and loopholed for rifle fire, as were the thick-walled houses, which made fine fortifications. "It would, indeed," said Wheeler, "have been a hard task for American troops, were they never so brave and courageous, to have taken a city by storm which was protected by such defenses as these."[87]

At the governor's palace, on which was painted "VIVA ALFONSO XIII," the Americans were met by a host of civic officials, including the governor, the archbishop, and the foreign consuls. The American party rode out to the plaza of the city, where thousands of Spaniards and Cubans had congregated to witness the ceremony. As the clock in the cathedral struck the hour of noon, the United States flag was hauled up the staff by three junior officers on the roof of the governor's palace. At that moment, Capron's battery fired a twenty-one-gun salute, the 6th Cavalry band struck up "Hail Columbia," and the 9th Infantry, drawn up in ranks in the plaza, presented arms.

A single incident marred the ceremony. For reasons only known only to himself, General Shafter had barred the press from entering the city to cover the formal change of authority. Most of the correspondents stayed away, but not Sylvester Scovel of the *New York Journal.* Somehow, Scovel managed to climb to the roof of the governor's palace. Very much to his indignation, he was ordered down by Lieutenant Miley. Scovel then loudly appealed directly to General Shafter, which was a big mistake, as the general's enmity toward the press was hardly a secret. According to one officer, "Some words followed, and I saw Scovel strike or attempt to strike General Shafter in the face." Shafter ordered Scovel placed under arrest, and he was hustled off to spend a pretty awful night in the ancient *calabozo,* among the rats and vermin.[88]

Up in the six-mile half circle of American trenches surrounding the city, the men lined the parapets and could see directly into the city as the flag went up. As Private Charles Post of the 71st New York wrote, "Miles of men in tattered and ragged blue; sick and well, waving and cheering and shaking hands. The war was over. Now we could go home. And what a dinner we would order!"[89]

Clearing the mines from the harbor mouth began early on Sunday, July 17. Originally, eighteen mines had been planted in the entrance channel: nine contact and nine electric, the latter equipped with remote firing positions ashore. Five of the electric mines had been blown attempting to sink the *Merrimac,* and seven of the contact mines had been taken up to allow Cervera's squadron safe exit from the harbor. To remove the remainder, Admiral Sampson sent the tug *Suwannee,* which had the heavy lifting gear to raise the mines, each of which weighed about a ton. The Spanish naval authorities gave every assistance. The electric mines were destroyed by sending a current through them and exploding them in position. Two failed to detonate. Their cables were then broken, sinking them to the bottom, and the keyboards were removed from the firing station ashore. The contact mines were simply lifted out. By July 19, the entrance was pronounced safe for any vessel. According to the officer in charge of the operation, "What would have happened to a ship attempting to run the mine field is problematical, but the chances were that she would have been sunk, for not withstanding the number of bad mines encountered, enough good ones were left to destroy her."[90]

The surrender of the large garrison at Guantánamo was accepted by General Kent. Lieutenant Miley received the assignment of taking the surrender and bringing in the six small Spanish garrisons in the immediate neighborhood of Santiago, the furthest of which, Palma Soriano, lay about forty miles from the city. Accompanied by Captain Rannes of General Toral's staff, two troops of mounted cavalry, an American and Spanish mule train with ten days' supplies, and a local guide, Miley set out on July 18 from El Caney to accomplish his mission. In his map case he bore a letter from General Toral to the local commandants notifying them of the details of capitulation, with directions to recognize Miley's authority as coming from General Shafter.

Miley began his ascent of the mountains that rose behind Santiago, a region that was almost entirely wilderness, so overgrown that any roads or trails had completely disappeared, and they traveled in single file. Once over the mountains, they came to a vast tableland 1,000 to 1,200 feet high. Before the devastation brought by the rebellion of 1895, this plateau had been divided into well-tilled plantations growing sugar, tobacco, coffee, and bananas. Now, save for the odd ruined dwelling, the farms had disappeared. The whole country was covered with rank grass, often as high as the back of a horse, and a scrubby growth of guava.

El Cristo was the first garrison of the march. Miley recorded both the Spanish garrison and the native population being overjoyed to see them: the garrison at the news of going home to Spain, and the locals with having something substantial to eat. Miley found the Cubans consisted almost wholly of women, children, and old men, all the able-bodied being off with the rebels.

At Dos Caminos, the commandant related that his immediate superior at San Luis had ordered him to resist capture to the utmost of his strength. Rannes, showing the man the letter from General Toral, convinced him to obey the orders of his ultimate senior officer. This he did, but not before warning Miley and Rannes that the commandant at San Luis had declared he would not surrender while he had a man left to fight.

From Dos Caminos, the column soon reached San Luis, halting three thousand yards from the trenches outside the town. Rannes rode forward alone, watching Spanish soldiers taking up their positions along the firing steps, and he spurred his horse forward, shouting orders not to fire. The Spanish second-in-command came out in front of the position, and Miley rode forward to meet him. Refusing to believe in the genuineness of Toral's letter, the officer declared the whole thing a ruse and denounced Rannes as a traitor. Miley informed the officer he would enter the town late that afternoon to receive the commandant's decision. Before that time, however, the commandant rode out with some of his staff, informing Miley he could not agree to surrender until he sent two or three officers into Santiago to learn for themselves the true state of affairs.

Miley considered it useless to argue the matter and agreed, one major concern being the condition of his column's horses and mules, which could badly use the respite offered. He detailed two troopers as escort, and the Spanish officers departed for Santiago. In late afternoon the following day, they returned with the news of the general capitulation. The commandant thereupon offered up his sword. Miley left one of his two troops of cavalry to collect the arms and to guarantee the safety of the prisoners of war from the rebels.

The following morning he pushed on with the remainder of his force over the trackless scrub to Palma Soriano. Heliograph communication between the towns indicated that if the Americans came, they would be fired upon. Miley paid no attention to this. In the afternoon the column halted two miles from his objective and was met by a Spanish staff officer, to whom Miley presented the letter from General Toral.

The commandant came out personally to greet the column, and in spite of the threats of the previous day, they were cordially received, actually better than in any other place. Miley engaged all the ox carts he could find and loaded them with the sick and wounded in the hospital, most of whom were from General Escario's column, having been felled in their brushes with the rebels during the march to reinforce Santiago. About two hundred *voluntarios* and *guerrilleros* were at Palma Soriano, and they gave their parole and arms.

Miley returned to Santiago on July 29 and two weeks later left by the captured merchantman *San Juan* to take the surrender of Baracoa and Sagua de Tanamo on the north coast of the province. This time he was accompanied by Major Irles of Toral's staff and a volunteer Cuban aide of General Chaffee's, who acted as interpreter. There were in addition three Spanish officers and a doctor in charge of the Red Cross stores. Thirty tons of rations were carried for the Spanish troops on the north coast, with twenty tons more for the forlorn garrison at Guantánamo. Outside Baracoa, the *San Juan* dropped anchor and Major Irles went ashore. He sent back word to Miley that the commandant was ready to surrender, but troops at the harbor guns were ready to fire at the first suspicious movement. Though nearly a month had elapsed since the capitulation of Santiago, nothing was known of that here. A surrender was arranged, but the Spanish refused to give up their arms until a garrison of U.S. troops occupied the town. There was no problem at all at Sagua de Tanamo. Everyone was delighted at the prospect of returning to Spain. On the wall of the commandant's quarters, Miley read a bulletin posted for the edification of the garrison. "It invited attention to two telegrams," he recalled, "one from the Spanish admiral at Manila, in which he described a wonderful victory he had won in the battle with the American navy, and the other from [Premier] Sagasta, sending the thanks of Spain to the admiral for his glorious victory."[91]

Transportation of all POWs to Spain was handled through British negotiators, who, on the day after the surrender of Santiago, opened talks on behalf of the United States with the Spanish government, and through it, the Spanish Transatlantica Company, whose ships carried home the Spanish soldiers. Passage costs, rations, and medical supplies were all provided by the United States. For the time of loading and sea passage, the ships were regarded as neutral and given safe conduct across the Atlantic. The first Spanish transport reached Santiago on August 8, leaving two days later with 1,038 officers and men. From August 10 through August 18, ten ships carried a total of 22,864 people, which also included families of officers, priests, and hospital nuns.

The type of administration for the conquered territory was laid out in a memo by President McKinley and sent to General Shafter for his "information and guidance." By direction, he was to proclaim the kindly intentions of the United States toward all peaceful and law-abiding citizens. They were to be protected in their persons, property, private rights, and relations. The transfer of authority to the United States was meant to bring a minimum of "derangement." The municipal laws were to remain for the present in force. Existing officials and courts, on accepting American supremacy, would continue to function under military supervision. The "native constabulary," so far as it proved practicable, would be preserved in their offices. "Our occupation should be as free from severity as possible," said the president.[92]

McKinley considered one of the most important matters falling under the jurisdiction of the military commander to be the treatment of communal property and the collection of revenues. To this end, it was "conceded" that all public funds and securities belonging either to the Spanish crown or to the Cuban "autonomous" government were ceded to the military occupying power "in its own right," and that all arms, supplies, and other "movable property" of the enemy governments might be seized. Shafter, and his representatives and successors, could use real property of the state, administering it for its own use, but were not to destroy it, save in case of military necessity. All means of land and water transportation and communications belonging to the enemy regime could be appropriated and their revenues used to defray the cost of the occupation. All churches and religious buildings, also those devoted to the arts and sciences, and all schoolhouses, "so far as possible," fell under the protection of the military commander. Further, all destruction or "intentional defacement" of such places, including historical monuments, archives, and works of science or art was prohibited, "save when required by military necessity." Private property would be respected and might be confiscated only for cause. The levying of "contributions" on the citizenry, though held as a right of conquest to compensate the cost of the occupation, should be accomplished in such a way "that it may not savor of confiscation." All ports now in possession of American forces were opened to the commerce of neutral nations, with customs duties to be collected by the military authority. Thus by these actions, the taxes and fees payable by the citizenry of Santiago and eastern Oriente Province to their former governments were now collected by the occupation forces.[93]

The city of Santiago sat in its own veritable fouling. Troops on the heights and sailors in the fleet watched hundreds of vultures circling over the city. The stench wafting out with the land breeze gagged the sailors on deck. The place "stewed in its misery and filth," a city of death, and it would take a sure hand to turn it around. General Shafter chose the best man possible as military governor, Brigadier General Leonard Wood, late of the Rough Riders and the 2nd Cavalry Brigade, a leader of the "large policy" of national expansion, and soon to prove a colonial administrator of the first rank. "The Commanding General directs you to take charge of the City of Santiago," read the scribbled order.[94]

On July 18, Wood rode at the head of his staff down the narrow streets into the city. At every turn, Wood remembered, emaciated, "ghastly-looking" people dragged aimlessly in search of a patch of shade. All about, "poisoning the air with foul exhalations," lay the rotting carcasses of dead animals piled among heaps of decomposing garbage, dung, and filth. Neighing with disgust, shying from the reek of corruption, the American cavalry horses trotted across open sewers clogged with foul water and human excrement. By the hundreds, the dead lay unburied.[95]

Refugees from El Caney streamed in from the countryside. The president's memorandum notwithstanding, there were no public funds, and the municipal courts and police had ceased to function. The city's medieval dungeons were packed alike with common felons, thieves, political prisoners, and the forgotten who had long served out their sentences. Visiting the main Spanish military hospital, Wood, a physician himself, found the reek in the wards "unsupportable." Heaps of infected clothing and blankets blocked the halls. In the courtyard, the well was polluted with human and animal skeletons, shoes, rags, and slime a foot thick. Wood's tasks were clear: feed the hungry, bury the dead, nurse the sick, and clean up the city.[96]

On any given day eighteen thousand to twenty thousand army rations were distributed to civilians, with canned meat, sugar, hardtack, and rice forming the basic diet. "All classes and all ages were represented" in the food lines, Wood wrote, "and the issue force worked from early in the morning until after dark, issuing and issuing, with no time to weigh things or bother about the exact amounts authorized or required. . . . Outside. . . . the soldiers, with their rifles used only as bars, strove to push the crowd back, to keep order and to protect the weak. . . . [T]hese were strange and very unusual sights for an American, and very unpleasant ones."[97]

Cleaning the city and disposing of the corpses—the death rate was over two hundred a day—were tandem projects, and for the task Wood found a remarkable individual. "Major" George Barbour held his rank by courtesy and to match it wore a uniform sewn by a fashionable military tailor. He just seemed to show up, full of stories about Buffalo Bill and Indian fighting. He also claimed a superintendency of New York City's street cleaners; for Wood, the references were good enough. Barbour was given a thousand civilians for the job. Every cart, wagon, driver, and laborer was pressed into service. All workers were given fair wages—part money, part rations. Those who refused to work soon learned, as Wood put it simply, "that there were things far more unpleasant than cheerful obedience."[98]

There were too many corpses for burial, and the bodies were hauled in carts to the outskirts of the city. On gratings built of railroad tracks, the dead were piled eighty high and layered with dry grass. Gallons of kerosene were poured over the pyres and the frightful heaps were torched to ashes. "It was the only thing to be done," Wood later wrote, "for the dead threatened the living and a plague was at hand."[99]

Day after day the black, nauseating columns of smoke palled in a monstrous cloud over the city. On a day when rains quenched the fires, kerosene ran short. When Barbour tried to buy more, he found the price had risen to a Spanish gold dollar a gallon. Wood called the merchants to his office in the governor's palace. "We have come to Cuba," he lectured, "at your call to relieve your distress. You are repaying our efforts by trying to make money out of us. . . . I call such conduct murder." The cost of kerosene fell to its normal level.[100]

The cobbled streets themselves ran bright with kerosene fires. But the civilian population treated Wood's measures with cynical indifference. "I do not understand you Americans," he was frequently told. "You are proud of your liberty and right to do as you please, yet here you walk into my house and tell me that I must clean my yard and sidewalk and how I must do it. Why, the Spaniards never would dare do such a thing." But Wood and Barbour were not given to debate. On more than one occasion, Barbour smashed down doors and publicly horsewhipped respectable citizens for making sewers out of the streets. By these means the death rate fell within a month from two hundred a day to thirty-seven.[101]

While Wood saw to conditions in Santiago, the health and vitality of the Fifth Corps plunged markedly. Theodore Roosevelt described conditions in the Rough Riders, a regiment probably in better health than most: "Very few of the men retained their strength and energy. . . . [T]here were less than fifty percent who were fit for any kind of work. All the clothes were in rags; even the officers had neither socks nor underwear. The lithe college athletes had lost their spring; the tall, gaunt hunters and cow-punchers lounged listlessly in their dog-tents, which were steaming morasses during the torrential rains, and then ovens when the sun blazed down."[102]

Shafter urged the War Department to hasten the shipment to Spain of the POWs in order that his own command, whose condition Lieutenant Miley accounted as "deplorable," might be returned to the United States. In the period just after the surrender, about half the troops had been attacked by malaria and dysentery, with several cases of the dreaded yellow fever and typhoid correctly diagnosed.[103]

The first step taken to check the spread of yellow fever was removal of the regiments to new camping grounds. Siboney, a sump if there ever was one, and where much of the yellow fever occurred, was first quarantined, then abandoned and burned. The Cavalry Division moved several miles into the interior. Roosevelt described it: "Through some blunder our march from the intrenchments to the camp on the foot-hills . . . was made during the heat of the day; and though it was only five miles or thereabouts, very nearly half the men of the cavalry division dropped out."[104]

It was directed from Shafter's headquarters that the camps be moved every few days, an awful drain on the men, who had constantly to heave about in the height of a Cuban summer. The decision, taken with the best medical opinion of the time, was meant as a health measure, to keep the troops from cases of yellow fever as they arose. By this, it was expected that in a short time the disease would be stamped out, and the command could then be sent, without danger of infection, wherever the War Department wished. To alleviate the suffering of the men on the lines and in the new camps, large Sibley tents were unloaded from the transports as soon as they entered the harbor. But the effect produced by the work of setting them up on new ground

increased alarmingly the number of men on the sick lists. Malaria convalescents were again taken with the fever, and the other maladies—
yellow fever, dysentery, and typhoid—increased. It quickly became
apparent that to keep moving the troops every few days simply weakened them and made them susceptible to illness.

On July 25 President McKinley was apprised of the "appalling situation" of the army around Santiago. In private letters, Lieutenant
Colonel Charles Dick and Colonel C. V. Hard, both of the 8th Ohio
Infantry, in which the president's two nephews served, urged the administration to get the troops out of Cuba before September, the
worst of the yellow fever season; not a moment's delay should be
countenanced.[105]

On August 1, the War Department acted, stirred by Shafter's reports of thousands of men on the sick lists—3,370 with various diseases on July 27, jumping to 4,290 by August 2. Some regiments, like
the 17th and 25th infantries, had 200 cases of malaria each, making them useless for active operations. Plans and reality smacked
head-on. There were not enough ships to evacuate the Fifth Corps in
a timely way, and their projected rest camp on Montauk Point, Long
Island, Camp Wikoff, was not ready to receive them.

To parse the dilemma, Army Surgeon General George Sternberg
was called in for consultations. Maintaining that yellow fever was
"impossible" above a certain altitude, Sternberg said the army could,
with precautions and if moved into the hills, stay in Cuba for a bit
longer. Shafter was again ordered to move the corps, this time into the
mountains at San Luis at the northwestern end of the railroad. "Then
we will move them north," said the adjutant general, "[to the United
States], as rapidly as possible. What do you advise? It is going to be a
long job at best to get so many troops away."[106]

At this point, moving to San Luis was a physical impossibility. The
troops were too sick to march, and the work of repairing the railroad
and its bridges was nowhere near complete. Even if this were done,
the rolling stock was insufficient to transport the whole command,
perhaps a thousand men a day, and would take until the end of August. At San Luis the camps would have been even less habitable than
those around Santiago, and with none of the facilities for the mountain of supplies necessary for the army's wants. Lieutenant Miley,
who was familiar with the area, noted the lack of water, and the fact

that the amount of rainfall was at least twice what the troops were experiencing around Santiago.

"In my opinion there is but one course to take," Shafter responded to the War Department, "and that is to immediately transport the Fifth Corps . . . to the United States. If it is not done, I believe the death rate will be appalling."[107] They should at once be put on board the transports and the movement begun as soon as the next day, August 4. If the War Department adopted a plan of waiting until the fever and rainy season were past before bringing the army home, "I believe there will be very few to move."[108]

The general convened a conference of the Fifth Corps' division and brigade commanders, accompanied by their medical officers, at the governor's palace in Santiago. All agreed that the entire command must be removed to the United States. A direct recommendation to the War Department by the chain of command was discussed. Shafter read aloud the letters from Secretary Alger and Surgeon General Sternberg regarding the movement of the army into the interior. It was met by stony silence. Roosevelt saw the dilemma. "They were almost all regulars and had been brought up to the life long habits of obedience without protest." Acting Brigadier General Theodore Roosevelt of the 2nd Cavalry Brigade took the initiative.[109]

So, during a break in the meeting and at the urging of his fellow officers, Roosevelt said, "I wrote a letter to General Shafter, reading over the rough draft to the various generals and adopting their corrections." But before these could be delineated, it was determined to send a circular letter, a "round-robin," on behalf of "all of us" to General Shafter. This letter, along with one signed by the chief medical officers of the corps, was sent along with Shafter's own letter to the adjutant general. It was signed by every divisional and brigade commander. Though he signed it, Lawton thought it a rather dictatorial demand aimed at the War Department, and he wanted it understood that Shafter had approved of it before it was sent on. He was also of a mind, perhaps unkindly, that "much of the fatal illness is due to homesickness and other depressing influences."[110]

The generals' and surgeons' reports, though written with General Shafter's approval, had been leaked to the press before Shafter laid eyes on them. The president, reading all this for the first time in the evening papers, was, according to Russell Alger, "very much excited and indignant." Overtures for peace had come from Spain and it was vitally important to conceal the military weakness of the U.S. occupation in its corner of Cuba. Now that had been blown into the open, with the barely camouflaged insubordination of senior officers as well.[111]

General Shafter received a sharp slap to his already shaky reputation when the Associated Press published the letters. Though Shafter said the leak was done without his knowledge, and "it was a foolish and improper thing to do," Secretary Alger replied that "it would be impossible to exaggerate the mischievous and wicked effects of the publications." The leak, Alger insisted, did nothing to hasten the return of the army, but only "brought terror and anguish to half the communities and neighborhoods in the land." Nevertheless, the public outcry did just what the generals wanted—it spurred the War Department to bring the army home. Havana was the only important military position left to Spain in Cuba, and this could await events, which as anyone could see were forecasting peace. Puerto Rico was to be dealt with by General Miles, who had new and healthy forces already at hand or on the way.[112]

On August 4, an order came from the War Department proposing to send five "immune" regiments for duty in Santiago, and movement was to begin at once on getting the Fifth Corps to Camp Wikoff on Montauk Point. Transports bearing the sick and wounded began returning to the United States in the first days of August. Several of the vessels were specially fitted for this purpose, but hardly enough, and even those that were so altered left much to be desired. Water on board was scanty, as it had been on the outward voyage, and the food, the basic army ration, was nearly impossible for the sick men to digest. When the *Yucatán,* carrying 150 men, docked at Tampa, the quartermaster at the port reported the men being almost without clothing and nearly starving. The *Seneca,* docking in New York, carried nearly 100 invalids, including 40 badly wounded men from the San Juan battle. They were packed into airless holds without attendants.

Naturally the complaints, which turned into a postwar scandal, fell on General Shafter. "We did the best we could under the circumstances," he wrote to the adjutant general; "I will not quietly submit to having the onus laid on me."[113]

Though Shafter could be blamed for some of the suffering and neglect of the wounded and sick in the field, the vaster guilt had to sit squarely on the War Department, which was completely unable, given its primitive staff apparatus and lack of adequate preparation, to outfit a major campaign overseas.

The first troops had embarked for home on August 7. General Shafter left with the last on the twenty-fifth. The Santiago military campaign had come to an end.

CHAPTER 15

PUERTO RICO

Porther Ricky . . . Gin'ral Miles' gran picnic an' moonlight excursion.

—*Mr. Dooley*

Lying east of Hispañola in the Greater Antilles, Puerto Rico was Spain's second largest possession in North America, a roughly rectangular island running about 108 miles from east to west and 40 north to south. The 1899 census showed a population of something less than 1 million people. Ponce, located on the south coast, was the largest city, with 37,535 citizens. However, the most important place, the military and political center of the island and residence of the governor and captain general, was San Juan, with just over 23,400 people, on the north coast.

Anti-Spanish agitation did not erupt in Puerto Rico, though certain political factions were pushing for various changes in the relationship with the mother country. The most influential leader of this group was Luis Muñoz Rivera, who favored Puerto Rican autonomy within the Spanish empire; only a few radical dissidents called for outright independence. A substantial number of Puerto Ricans, the so-called *incondicionalistas,* favored the status quo. In the fall of 1896, Muñoz Rivera visited Spain and sought autonomy; negotiating with the Liberal Party of Premier Sagasta, he successfully struck a bargain. In November 1897, as a side aspect of Spain's attempt at reforming its Cuba policy, Puerto Rico was granted home rule, and an autonomy government soon materialized.

An irrevocable charter authorized a Spanish-appointed governor general with limited powers to preside as the representative of Spain over the island's government. However, an elected insular parliament exercised the real political authority, and from this body, a cabinet would be chosen for executive direction. The governor general could not issue an order that did not have the signature of a local elected official, and even a measure of external autonomy fell to the proposed insular government. Given Spain's intractability over Cuba, it is surprising that the Puerto Rican autonomous government was granted the authority to make treaties with foreign governments and the island was subject only to those Spanish treaties that the insular parliament chose to accept. Autonomy proved far more palatable in Puerto Rico than in Cuba because it represented concessions quite far beyond local expectations.

On February 9, 1898, General Manuel Macías y Casado was appointed governor and captain general, and on March 27, the island elected its thirty-two-member parliament; it was dominated by *Muñocistas*. When war was declared between the United States and Spain, Macías immediately declared martial law and called for stiff resistance against the Americans: "Providence will not permit," he proclaimed, "that in these countries which were discovered by the Spanish nation the echo of our language should ever cease to be heard, nor that our flag should disappear from before the eye. . . . *Viva Puerto Rico,* always Spanish, *Viva España!*"[1]

The subject of Puerto Rico hardly arose in American political and expansionist circles during the diplomatic activity that led up to the war. The island was mentioned in Madrid by U.S. Ambassador Stewart Woodford in connection with a commercial agreement intended to regulate economic relations between the United States and Cuba, and that was about all. Prior to the war, all attention centered on Cuba, and the United States did not develop plans to annex Puerto Rico before the war, or indeed for some time thereafter.

The War and Navy departments gave consideration to operations against Puerto Rico as a natural adjunct to the Cuban theater. On April 4, when the joint army-navy board presented its plan of campaign, it based its assumptions on the fact that the navy would carry the principal load in the war, and favored an attack on Puerto Rico to deprive the Spanish of a useful forward base in the Caribbean.

Retired Major General John Schofield, former Commanding General of the Army and now McKinley's unofficial military adviser, favored initial attacks on Puerto Rico and the Philippines rather than going directly for Cuba, perceiving that success in these peripheral spheres might negate the need to assault Spain's principal and strongest colony, locus of her military strength in the Western Hemisphere.

An American thrust at Puerto Rico also figured in the strategic thoughts of Captain Alfred Thayer Mahan. Puerto Rico, he wrote, "would be invaluable as an intermediate naval station and as a base of supplies and reinforcements for both [Spain's] fleet and army; . . . if left in her undisturbed possession, it would enable her practically to enjoy the same advantage of nearness to the great scene of operations that the United States [has] in virtue of our geographical situation." He advocated an attack and reduction of the island as the "first objective" of the war. The effect of this would be to throw Spain back on the Iberian Peninsula for the logistic support of operations in Cuba, "thus entailing upon her an extremely long line of communications, exposed everywhere throughout its course."[2]

Had Spain been a more powerful opponent or acted with greater vigor at the outset in defense of her Antillean possessions, or had Admiral Cervera entered San Juan, as his original orders stated, instead of Santiago de Cuba, Puerto Rico would certainly have been a primary target for American forces, which would have threatened Spanish communications and thus, said Mahan, "retarded, if not actually prevented, [Spanish] relief of Cuba." But such was not the case. As Navy Secretary John D. Long noted, once Cervera was located in Santiago, "the Navy Department determined to concentrate our sea strength in the Atlantic upon Cuba particularly, and Porto Rico incidentally." Given that the United States had no outlying colonies and no lines of communication to defend, and with Key West only ninety miles from Havana, the Naval War Board rightly concluded, and Long agreed, that early conquest of Puerto Rico "promised no results commensurate with the sacrifice such action would entail."[3]

The most important advocate of a campaign in Puerto Rico was General Nelson Miles, who maintained a view very similar to Schofield's, believing that the war would develop largely as a naval duel. "It was a question," he said, "of whether our fleet would destroy the Spanish fleet or whether they would destroy ours." Given that, Miles wished to delay land operations, especially in Cuba, until the United States had unquestioned command of the sea. He was particularly concerned about the risk of tropical disease, a factor most dangerous in Cuba during the rainy season. Miles considered it of overriding importance to "operate against the Spanish forces by doing them the greatest amount of injury with the least to ourselves, harassing them during the sickly season . . . and taking such places [e.g., Puerto Rico] as we could during the rainy season . . . without endangering the lives of our own troops from disease." But the question of Cervera's whereabouts, and Dewey's precarious position in the Philippines, soon dominated the administration's councils, and Puerto Rican proposals were shelved for the moment.[4]

Late in May, however, with Cervera bottled up in Santiago, interest in an attack on Puerto Rico was renewed. The island's strategic significance now became apparent given that the campaign was being fought in eastern Cuba, rather than against Havana in the west. General Miles reacted quickly to this new situation. When he detailed his highly questionable cavalry campaign along the north coast of Cuba, he coupled it with an attack on Puerto Rico, both operations being preliminary to a major assault on Havana at the end of the rainy season.

Instead of adopting Miles's plan, the administration opted to concentrate its land and sea forces at Santiago de Cuba so as to destroy Cervera's squadron, the principal strategic Spanish asset in the Caribbean. It was a course of action that placed immediate pressure on Spain and promised a result that could easily lead to early negotiations for peace on terms highly favorable to the United States. Only with the primary naval thrust made at Santiago, and a victory expected, could President McKinley and his military and naval advisers consider the idea of mounting a second operation in the Antilles, an attack on Puerto Rico. With the blockade of Santiago, Havana became largely irrelevant.[5] By early June, General Shafter, who had yet to sail from Tampa, was informed that after completing his operations against Santiago, he was to reembark his command into their transports and be ready for further service—an attack on Puerto Rico.

General Miles, in Tampa to help sort out the preembarkation mess of the Fifth Corps, additionally busied himself with his pet plan for an invasion of Puerto Rico. On June 2, he cabled Secretary Alger that an attack there should immediately follow the Santiago campaign, providing the army and navy were in condition to continue operations. Miles, putting in his bid for command, recommended, "If it meets the approval of the government, as soon as this expedition [to Santiago] sails another can be immediately organized to reinforce the first and make sure of the capture of number two [Puerto Rico]." He requested that steamers be immediately gotten ready to transport fifteen thousand troops.[6]

Before receiving a response, Miles began concentrating forces in Tampa for an expedition against "No. 2." When the answer came, it emanated directly from the White House. Possibly, for a short time, thinking of conducting two operations, President McKinley wanted to know the earliest possible moment Miles could have an expeditionary force ready for Puerto Rico, "large enough to take and hold the island, without the force under General Shafter."[7]

Miles believed that thirty thousand volunteers could be assembled just as soon as transports became available. He then suggested leaving "No. 1" (Santiago) "safely guarded," and with the bulk of the Fifth Corps and naval assistance, taking "No. 2 first before it can be reinforced." His idea was to land this force at a suitable site in Puerto Rico and secure the island, then install sufficient men to hold it while freeing the rest for the assault on Santiago, which "can then easily be accomplished." This division of forces was out of all proportion to the results to be gained. Cervera was the prime objective, and until he was dealt with, absolute command of the sea was still in question, no matter how lopsided the forces. Alger telegraphed on June 6, "The president says no. . . . No. 1 must be taken first."[8]

McKinley's decision to launch the offensive against Puerto Rico at the conclusion of the Santiago operation had an immediate political effect. Concurrent with his approval of both strikes, the president secretly informed his ambassador in London, John Hay, that in lieu of demanding a cash indemnity from Spain at war's end, he would require instead the cession of Puerto Rico to the United States. McKinley rarely put his thoughts to paper, and whether he was influenced by large policy advocates, such as Senator Lodge, who wrote his friend Theodore Roosevelt, "Puerto Rico is not forgotten and we mean to have it," or by other considerations, is not known.[9]

On July 8, with Cervera destroyed and the fall of Santiago imminent, General Miles sailed from Charleston with 3,500 men in the cruiser *Columbia* and the armed liner *Yale,* the first contingent of the Puerto Rican expeditionary force. The talk of a general peace was already in the air, and the actual occupation of Puerto Rico was of prime importance if the United States were to insist upon Spain's yielding her Antillean dominions entirely. First, however, Miles stopped at Santiago, both to coordinate his naval assistance for Puerto Rico and to offer his troops in the final subjugation of eastern Cuba.

The impending appearance of an American invasion convoy off the shores of Puerto Rico prompted Captain General Macías to summon the insular parliament into session on July 17. Luis Muñoz Rivera led the government in adopting a wholly loyalist stance. "We are Spaniards," he declared, "and wrapped in the Spanish flag we will die." This reflected a political victory for the governor, who hoped the grant of autonomy would cement the loyalty of the island to Spain. But he had pitiably small forces with which to meet the American attack. About eight thousand Spanish regulars garrisoned the island. These were divided into five thousand infantry, seven hundred gunners, and the rest of other branches. There were also seven thousand to nine thousand local militiamen, poorly trained and unreliable. The island was divided into seven military districts, with the regulars scattered about in the major towns. Except for a few guns at San Juan, no artillery was available. Ponce and Mayagüez, the first and third cities of the island, had no defenses whatever. The Spanish navy had three gunboats, one auxiliary cruiser, and the destroyer *Terror,* which Cervera had originally left behind at Martinique.

In San Juan, Macías received plenty of advance warning as he made what preparations he could to resist the invasion. By the time Miles started for Puerto Rico, the Spanish had been accurately informed of his strength and intentions. On July 25, Macías got word from the colonial ministry in Madrid that the Americans intended to land at either Cape Fajardo on the northeast tip of the island, Arecibo on the northwest coast, or Ponce in the south, all of which, from one aspect or another, were logical choices. At the same time, Macías had orders from the war ministry to resist the invasion, as a firm defense might strengthen Spain's bargaining position at the end of the war, something already in sight.

Macías was faced with two options for defense. He could concentrate all his forces around San Juan to defend the center of government, or he might base his stand on strong points in the interior. The first solution was the more logical, as he had only a very limited number of reliable troops and could expect some local opposition to his forces in the interior. The second would likely slow the approach of the Americans to San Juan, a political consideration of some consequence. But faced with these two choices, Macías rejected both. He kept the bulk of his forces in the north, where he expected the American invasion to take place, but also placed two battalions at Ponce and Mayagüez, and another detachment in the interior, astride the good military road running down the island from San Juan to Ponce. Other small units he scattered about to give the appearance that no ground would be surrendered without a stand.

In the meantime, on July 15, the Navy Department dispatched orders to Admiral Sampson concerning the formation and sailing of the Eastern Squadron, orders that conflicted with the naval convoy General Miles deemed essential for covering his transports to Puerto Rico. Though Admiral Cámara and his force had reversed course from the Red Sea back to Spain, the Navy Department still intended sending the proposed Eastern Squadron to reinforce Dewey at Manila. Because the department still believed that Cámara's ships, when combined with those armored vessels remaining in Spanish ports, were, theoretically, superior to the Eastern Squadron, it ordered Admiral Sampson to organize a Covering Squadron, the entire force to be under his command until separating after coaling in the Azores. The Eastern Squadron was to continue to Suez and points east, and the Covering Squadron was to hold the Spanish coast under observation or do battle with the remaining Spanish vessels as the situation evolved. Inasmuch as the two squadrons contained virtually every fighting ship in Cuban waters, with the exception of the *Texas,* the cruisers *Cincinnati* and *Columbia,* and some gunboats and auxiliaries, there was hardly anything left to convoy Miles's transports to Puerto Rico and cover the landings.

On July 16, Miles signaled Admiral Sampson of his orders to equip an expedition of twenty-five thousand men immediately for Puerto Rico "in conjunction with the navy," saying he would be glad of an opportunity to consult regarding the enterprise, including the best point of disembarkation "and mode of accomplishing this object, in order that the army and navy may act in full concert." The two men met the same day aboard the New York, and Cape Fajardo, on the northeast coast, was selected as the projected landing site. A road extended westward to San Juan along the coast, permitting the army to advance overland under the guns of the fleet. Sampson duly informed the Navy Department that Miles had requested ships capable of "rendering very decided naval support." How this was to be accomplished while organizing the Eastern and Covering squadrons the admiral was at a loss to fathom. He suggested adding the New Orleans, currently blockading San Juan, to Miles's convoy, also the Cincinnati, and if necessary the three monitors Amphitrite, Puritan, and Terror. These, along with the Columbia and Yale, could deal with anything the Spanish might have ashore in the matter of artillery, even the largest of coastal guns, which did not exist in Puerto Rico.[10]

On July 17, Miles informed the admiral that he was ready to move on Cape Fajardo; all transports, whether in Cuban waters or departing from the United States, were to rendezvous there. He was anxious to sail and only awaited word from the War Department, which was expected momentarily. Miles's superiors, however, gave no approval for immediate action; they, along with the Naval War Board, seemed to feel the more urgent necessity was to occupy Nipe Bay on the north coast of Cuba's Oriente Province for use as an intermediate base. After the war, it was felt there was no way to account for that decision. Guantánamo was forty miles closer to the objective, Puerto Rico, and was healthy, commodious, and already in American possession. Nipe was still in Spanish hands, it was believed the place was mined, and there were some guns mounted in the harbor. To take and occupy Nipe might require weeks, needlessly delaying the Puerto Rico expedition, causing "much embarrassment and difficulty," as Miles said. He informed Admiral Sampson of this, and also that he had cabled the War Department several times that he preferred to go directly to Cape Fajardo, hoping the admiral shared this view.[11]

On the evening of July 17, the War Department threw another wrench into Miles's plan for an immediate assault on Puerto Rico with the three thousand troops of Garretson's brigade he had afloat with him off Santiago. In Russell Alger words, Miles's invasion with so few men "does not seem best, in view of the fact that you could not be reinforced for a week or ten days." About twelve thousand men in Charleston and Tampa were prepared to join Miles at any point he and Admiral Sampson designated. But until the issue of Nipe Bay was settled and reinforcements arrived in the theater, he was to stay where he was.[12]

Taking Nipe proved easier than Miles had anticipated. On July 18, in furtherance of the War and Navy departments' schemes, the gunboats *Topeka* and *Annapolis,* the armed yacht *Wasp,* and tug *Leyden* were ordered to Nipe Bay to take possession, lift any mines, and destroy the small Spanish gunboat *Jorge Juan* known to be in the vicinity. On July 21, they arrived off the port, finding the *Jorge Juan* anchored near the entrance. After a short period of fire, she began sinking and was abandoned by her crew. The *Topeka's* skipper was told by the mayor of the town that eight hundred Spanish troops were in the vicinity and the harbor had been sown with thirty mines, both electric and contact. But the next morning all Spanish forces had escaped to Holguín. In another stroke of luck, a dozen mines popped to the surface at the center of the harbor entrance and were destroyed by gunfire. The bay was soon secured, but no use of it was made for the Puerto Rico campaign, and virtually as soon as the action, such as it was, ended, the ships were ordered to rendezvous at Cape Fajardo preliminary to the landing.

Miles was not yet in receipt of the War Department's cable ordering him to wait for reinforcements before descending on Puerto Rico when, shortly after noon on July 18, he cabled them: the importance of the enterprise, he said, justified that a senior naval officer—with whatever vessels might be spared—be seconded at once to act under his orders. With more than a hint at the friction between Admiral Sampson and General Shafter, Miles cautioned, "The experience of the last five weeks should not be repeated." The president and War Department responded quickly, reversing their previous caution and giving Miles permission to land the troops aboard the *Columbia* and *Yale* at any point in Puerto Rico of his choosing. Miles was allotted the fullest discretion, but his determination of time and place of the landing must be made with the knowledge that reinforcements could not reach the area of operations for another five to seven days. Admiral Sampson's directives from the Navy Department mirrored those to General Miles, ordering him to provide the army with such assistance as necessary for the landing of troops and maintaining them once on the beach.[13]

In sending Admiral Sampson a copy of his movement order, Miles added that he was ready to move to Cape Fajardo without delay and requested a very strong naval force to accompany the transports, cover the invasion, and protect the flanks of the landing force during the critical period of occupying the beachhead. Also, he requested that the navy render all possible assistance in the overland movement along the coast from Cape Fajardo to the investment and capture of the harbor and city of San Juan and other seaports on the island. If Sampson thought it advisable, Miles would be glad to have the fleet's marines accompany his troops. Miles also considered it advisable "that a strong demonstration be made near the harbor of San Juan before the landing of troops off Point Fajardo."[14]

On July 20, Miles and Sampson again met aboard the *New York,* which lay at anchor at Guantánamo. The admiral, with his much greater knowledge of the abilities of ships' batteries, essentially differed with Miles as to what constituted "a strong force of naval vessels." Once more, he proposed that the *New Orleans, Cincinnati,* and the monitors, in addition to the *Columbia* and *Yale,* were more than sufficient to cover the landing at Cape Fajardo. There were simply no Spanish warships that could do the expedition any harm. The only one of importance, the destroyer *Terror,* was still undergoing repairs at San Juan. While Sampson was unable to understand the need for greater force, he was quite ready to send everything he could spare, and he agreed to include the vessels involved in the reduction of Nipe, plus the armed yacht *Gloucester.* Even without the monitors, such a force was enough to cover any landing at an undefended beach in Puerto Rico.

But Miles seemed not to credit this, viewing the situation only with reference to his own expedition and refusing to take into account the demands of the Cuban blockade, the Eastern Squadron, and necessary repairs to ships. Following the meeting, he telegraphed an extraordinary message to Secretary Russell Alger in which he complained of the navy's lack of cooperation in providing the warships he deemed vital for the safety of the expedition. Without them, the small Spanish gunboats known to be stationed in Puerto Rico could come out of harbor and attack the transports. "There are battleships enough here to enable us to land within cannon shot of the city of San Juan," he wrote. He requested that orders be sent to the navy to screen the landing of at least ten thousand troops without delay, as that number was expected in Puerto Rican waters within a week. Miles sent a virtual copy of this letter to Admiral Sampson, telling him that the ships allotted, especially the *Yale* and *Columbia,* could not silence a light battery of field artillery on the beach without jeopardizing the lives of the troops on board. That might have been true for the *Yale,* a converted liner armed only with 6- and 3-pounder guns, but the *Columbia* was a protected cruiser mounting one 8-inch, two 6-inch, and eight 4-inch guns, power enough to deal with any but permanent coast defenses. Discounting the presence of the *New Orleans* and the *Cincinnati,* which together carried seven 6-inch and ten 5-inch guns in their main batteries, Miles still did not consider the naval contingent sufficient. He requested "an additional and ample force" be immediately ordered to the invasion site.[15]

In Washington, Russell Alger brought Miles's telegram to the president, who, in Chadwick's words, "naturally yielding to whomever had his ear," took the side of General Miles. To Navy Secretary Long, the president sent Miles's message and accompanied it with his own ill-informed addendum: "It is evident to me . . . that Admiral Sampson is not proposing to furnish such assistance as I have heretofore directed." A brigade had already sailed from Charleston to Cape Fajardo, expected to get there inside of a week. If the navy continued with its "delays," those transports would reach that point without any protection, "which must not be permitted. . . . It seems to me," the president went on, blithely ignorant of the facts, that "a cruiser or battleship, or both should be detailed for this duty." Long, he said, was to issue the necessary orders "at once."[16]

The following day, as a result of the presidential dressing-down, Long wired a completely unwarranted rebuke to Sampson at Guantánamo: "The president directs that you send ships of war enough to enable Miles to land at Puerto Rico, and to remain there as long as needed to render assistance." The admiral was ordered to provide "at once the *Indiana,* the *Newark* or something of each class as good. . . . On the face of things you seem dilatory in this matter."[17]

Admiral Sampson shot back to the secretary of the navy as good as he got. He informed Long of his previous orders "to prepare all armored ships and certain cruisers" for service east; he had been led to believe the Navy Department regarded this as of "prime importance." He had also been ordered to send "a specified force" to Nipe to remove mines and hold the place as a rendezvous. "This was done," though he was informed only the day before that the army had decided to bypass Nipe, going directly to Puerto Rico. He had placed at General Miles's disposal two powerful cruisers (the *New Orleans* and *Cincinnati*) plus the Nipe force, the *Gloucester*, and three monitors. He had already told Miles that his orders from the Navy Department regarding the Eastern Squadron did not permit of anything further, which in any case was superfluous to the mission. But now that the secretary of the navy insisted, he would add the battleship *Massachusetts* and the auxiliary cruiser *Dixie* to the expedition. The admiral trusted this would satisfy the army's demands.

Long soon apologized. Sampson's dispatch was of "much value," delineating all that the navy had done for General Miles's expedition. The information provided was just what the department needed to set it, the president, and "you" right.[18]

In the meantime, while the forces assembled at Guantánamo and everyone was arguing over what naval strength to send, General Miles came to the late conclusion that a landing at Cape Fajardo was no longer operative, even though convoys were already at sea, heading for it from Charleston and Tampa; it would be better to take possession first of the south side of the island, which was, in his words, "strongly disaffected to the Spanish cause," and lightly garrisoned in the bargain. He had come to this conclusion partly through the reports of army Lieutenant Henry Whitney, who, disguised as a British merchant seaman, had made a reconnaissance of the island in June, reporting on conditions and defenses. The tiny port of Guánica and the city of Ponce on the south coast were now the first objectives of the invasion. As Miles later explained to Russell Alger, "[M]arching across the country [over the mountains to San Juan], rather than under the guns of the fleet [along the north coast], will have in every way a desirable effect on the inhabitants of this country." (Whether Miles would have obtained more by surprise than he lost by choosing a long, easily defended, and potentially difficult route to the center of Spanish resistance around San Juan is impossible to say because the campaign ended in a cease-fire.) Further, Miles dissembled, Cape

Fajardo had been selected by the navy as the landing site and was really more of an open roadstead than a safe harbor. Also, it was well known on the island that the invasion was heading there, "the Spaniards being thus able to concentrate their forces in that vicinity before our arrival"—which, as it happens, they did not. Lastly, Miles said, the change was because the Cape Fajardo–San Juan road was not suitable for wagons or artillery.[19]

On the afternoon of July 21, the expedition sailed with orders from the Navy Department (which, along with the War Department, was ignorant of the switch in objective) to rendezvous off Cape Fajardo and disembark troops at such points indicated by General Miles. Over the next two days, Miles further outlined his change of plans to Captain Francis Higgenson, skipper of the battleship *Massachusetts,* appointed to command the naval escort of the operation. "As it is always advisable not to do what your enemy expects you to do," Miles thought it might be advisable to make a "demonstration," a feint, near Cape Fajardo, in order to draw Spanish forces to the vicinity, then quickly move south, taking Guánica and nearby Ponce before the enemy had time to react. The expedition could sail from Cape Fajardo to Guánica in one night, making it impossible for the Spanish to concentrate their forces before the American beachhead had been well reinforced.[20]

From the naval point of view, Captain Higgenson objected that he could not cover the landings as well on the south coast as from Cape Fajardo along the coastal road to San Juan. The water at Guánica was too shallow to permit the entrance of the *Massachusetts, Columbia,* and *Dixie,* and in case of heavy weather, the vessels might not even be able to lie off the port. Additionally, the south coast of Puerto Rico had been imperfectly surveyed and was lined with dangerous reefs. Cape Fajardo was only thirty miles from St. Thomas in the Virgin Islands, where, in the absence of colliers, the vessels could coal, and both army and navy commanders might keep in touch with Washington through the cable. Higgenson strongly recommended the convoy continue to Cape Fajardo, keeping Guánica "in reserve," should insurmountable obstacles be found.[21]

On July 24, with the convoy to the north of the Mona Passage between Hispañola and Puerto Rico, heading toward Cape Fajardo, Miles signaled to Higgenson to send in advance of landing at Guánica any naval vessels he could spare to take the place by coup de main; then "If secured, hold, and report quickly to us [off Cape Fajardo]," where the general still intended to perform his feinting demonstration. He ended this communication with yet another justification for altering the objective. Guánica was more important than Fajardo because from there the army had enough troops to march on and capture Ponce, giving the fleet a secure port on the south coast. "All right," Higgenson signaled back, "Guánica it is."[22]

As it happened, the deception at Cape Fajardo was given up as well, and after detaching the *Dixie* to redirect the reinforcements from Charleston and Tampa to the south coast, the convoy headed south through the Mona Passage and arrived off Guánica at dawn, July 25. It was a pretty little harbor, protected by very high cliffs. The town consisted of one street running inland for a mile under the shade of crimson trees, along which were pastel-painted houses. Finding no batteries bearing on the entrance, Higgenson sent in the *Gloucester* under Commander Wainwright to reconnoiter. He did this with some apprehension, not knowing what mines or concealed guns might be in the harbor. The *Gloucester* opened fire with a 3-pounder gun on the Spanish flag flying over the local blockhouse and steamed in.

Finding no resistance, Commander Wainwright sent a landing party ashore. The sailors quickly constructed a barricade of stone and barbed wire, "Fort Wainwright," across the single street, set up a Colt machine gun, and sprayed a troop of Spanish cavalry on a nearby hill, killing four men. When the remainder of the enemy fled, along with the civilian population, the *Gloucester* wigwagged for reinforcements. Higgenson immediately hoisted out his boats, ordered the transports into the harbor, and landed Garretson's brigade, with a battery of regular artillery. Within a few hours, the American troops were camped along the street, the civilians who had fled returned, and the town opened for business with a warm welcome to the new arrivals.

At daylight on July 26, Garretson attacked a concentration of Spanish troops at Yauco, six miles north of Guánica, driving them back and giving the Americans quick possession of the railroad and highway to Ponce.

On July 27, the *Wasp* and *Annapolis* convoyed in the leading elements of Major General James Harrison Wilson's command, the 1st Division, First Army Corps, consisting of the bulk of Brigadier Oswald

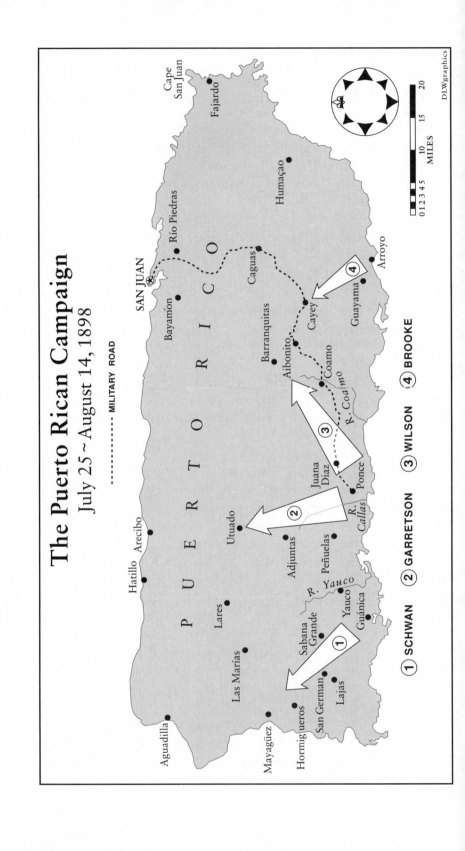

The Puerto Rican Campaign
July 25 ~ August 14, 1898

----------- MILITARY ROAD

(1) SCHWAN   (2) GARRETSON   (3) WILSON   (4) BROOKE

DLWgraphics

Ernst's brigade of two infantry regiments, with detachments from the Signal and Hospital corps'. These troops were not landed, being directed instead by General Miles directly to Ponce along with the bulk of the naval force. The cruiser *Columbia,* stationed off Cape Fajardo, dispatched arriving transports to the new destination on the south coast. Unloading at a good harbor, in three days Miles had about twelve thousand troops deployed on the southern rim of the island.

The city of Ponce, which lies two miles inland from the port, capitulated without a fight, although the Spanish commander, with about three hundred men, had orders to resist. On the evening of July 27, Commander Charles Davis of the *Dixie,* the senior officer present, sent ashore his executive officer, Lieutenant Greenlief Merriam, under a flag of truce to demand surrender. The *Wasp* maneuvered and anchored so that her guns commanded the main street of the port; the other vessels trained their batteries on the beach area. At the port captain's office, Merriam demanded the unconditional surrender of both the harbor and the city. The Spanish officer replied with a shrug, according to Merriam, "that as far as he was concerned we held the port and it was ours." As for Ponce, that was the responsibility of the colonel commanding the garrison, and though Merriam tried to communicate with him, the effort failed.[23]

After Merriam returned to his ship, the British and German consuls, along with, as Commander Davis reported, "several gentlemen" representing commercial interests of the city, boarded the *Dixie* and announced their authority from the Spanish garrison commander to negotiate Ponce's surrender. After some discussion in which Davis refused to accede to their request for more time to communicate with the government in San Juan, they left the ship to confer with the garrison commander. Shortly after midnight, July 28, they returned to the *Dixie* and agreed to surrender. The terms included withdrawal of the Spanish garrison without pursuit for forty-eight hours, the municipal government of Ponce to remain in place, the police and fire brigade to be maintained to preserve order until its occupation by U.S. troops, and the harbormaster not to be arrested as a prisoner of war. Subject to the approval of the American senior officers, Miles and Higgenson, who had yet to arrive, Davis agreed.

At daylight, Davis landed two officers and a squad of nine marines, who hoisted the American flag over the port captain's office. Guards with a Colt machine gun were posted at the customs and cable houses. Two hours later, the first of the boats from the arriving army transports came ashore, bearing General Wilson. Shortly thereafter General Miles landed with his headquarters staff and the colors. A naval reconnaissance party entered Ponce, going a mile beyond the city. They reported everything tranquil, "the natives," said Commander Davis, "almost overpowering them with their demonstrations of welcome." Political prisoners were released from the city hall jail, over which the American flag was hoisted, and the mayor formally turned his municipality over to Naval Cadet George Lodge.[24]

The Spanish troops, about five hundred, retreated precipitately, leaving a fair cache of arms and ammunition behind them. They set fire to the rolling stock, knocked down telegraph poles, destroyed the cable station, and planted land mines along the road to Yauco just to the north.

In full dress, Miles and Wilson entered the city, receiving its homage from the balcony of the mayor's palace, such as it was. Five companies of the municipal fire brigade paraded before them in their honor. The flags of numerous foreign nations flew all over the city; as Richard Harding Davis observed, "one would have thought the population was composed entirely of English, Germans, French, and Swiss and members of the Red Cross Society." It seems the Spanish had been warned the Americans would loot their houses and possessions, and to prevent this, they invited foreign friends into their homes, telling them first to bring their flags.

In short order, the railroad was back in operation and signs reading "English Spoken Here" hung outside most of the shops. On the bandstand of the plaza, where the Spanish military band had played every Thursday and Sunday, the U.S. Army's provost guards slept, cooked, and banged away on a "rheumatic piano," replacing the martial strains of the "March of Isabella" with "Rosy O'Grady."[25]

On the same day General Miles issued a proclamation to the people of Puerto Rico that gained considerable local support, as the great majority of the island's citizens either actively collaborated with the Americans, or at the very least did nothing to impede the invaders' advance. The United States, Miles proclaimed, was engaged in a war "in the cause of liberty, justice, and humanity," and in that light had come to occupy the island of Puerto Rico. "They come," he continued, "bearing the banner of freedom inspired by a noble purpose to seek the enemies of our country and yours, and to destroy or capture all who are in armed resistance." The first effect of this occupation, he told them, was the release of the island from its former political ties to Spain, "and it is hoped a cheerful acceptance of the government of the United States."[26]

The occupation of the southern littoral of Puerto Rico was now complete, involving virtually nothing beyond landing and taking possession. "This is a beautiful and prosperous country," Miles informed Secretary Alger. "The army will soon be in mountain region; weather delightful; troops in best of health and spirits; anticipate no insurmountable obstacles in future results." Correspondent Richard Harding Davis waxed equally bright. "The people of Ponce," he wrote after the war, "were certainly the most friendly in the world. Nothing could shake their enthusiasm. . . . The natives gave our men freely of everything." The "richer and better class" of Puerto Ricans in Ponce even opened a Red Cross hospital for the army at their own expense.[27]

On July 29 Miles established martial law in those areas occupied by United States forces. Municipal ordinances were retained insofar as they affected the rights of private property and individuals and the punishment of petty crime. Major civilian crimes came under the jurisdiction of army provost courts. The local police constabulary was preserved; schools and churches were protected. All public funds and property belonging to the Spanish government were seized. The ports in American possession were reopened to trade with customs duties collected at the going rate.

Once established at Guánica and Ponce, Miles developed an elaborate campaign to end all Spanish resistance on the island. In order to advance against the strength of Spanish military concentrations around San Juan, he decided to send four columns north, three from the Ponce region and one from Arroyo on the southeast coast, forty miles east of Ponce, where a landing by Major General John R. Brooke was accomplished on August 2. On the left flank, commanded by Brigadier General Theodore Schwan, was the smallest of the four, a sort of "flying column," composed strictly of regulars: the 11th Infantry, a troop of the 5th Cavalry, two batteries of light artillery, plus Signal and Hospital corps' units, totaling 1,464 men. These would advance to Mayagüez on the west coast, and from there move inland through Lares to the north coast town of Arecibo, which maintained rail connections to San Juan.

Garretson's brigade, the 6th Massachusetts, 6th Illinois, plus four companies of the 19th Infantry, a troop of the 2nd Cavalry, a troop of the New York Volunteer Cavalry, and Signal and Hospital detachments—in all, 3,060 men—set off on the direct route north from Ponce, through Adjuntas and Utuado, for a linkup with Schwan at Arecibo. Once united, the combined forces would constitute a provisional division for the assault on San Juan.

Major General Wilson led the third column, Ernst's brigade of two Wisconsin regiments, the 16th Pennsylvania, three batteries of light artillery, including two dynamite guns and one Gatling, a troop of New York Cavalry, a company of the U.S. Volunteer Signal Corps, and a Hospital detachment—3,417 men—northeast from Ponce through Coamo to the Spanish strongpoint of Aibonito, a position of great natural strength on the crest of the mountains, north of Arroyo.

On the right flank, from Arroyo, General Brooke commanded the heaviest of the columns, comprising the 3rd Illinois, 4th Ohio, and 4th Pennsylvania infantry, one company of the 8th U.S. Infantry, three batteries of light artillery, the Pennsylvania City Troop of cavalry, and Signal and Hospital units, in all totaling 4,790 men. This column would move inland through Guayama to Cayey, getting behind Aibonito. Wilson and Brooke would then unite, driving together up the good military road that bisected the island, linking up near San Juan with the troops coming from Arecibo. The operational plan, a complicated one, stressed maneuver over frontal assaults to isolate and outflank the enemy positions. By August 5, the columns were ready to advance.

The navy, too, had a plan for taking San Juan, and one, moreover, that excluded the army from any participation. On August 2, Commander Davis of the *Dixie* wrote to Admiral Sampson proposing an alternate means of capturing San Juan. "I am strongly of the opinion," he noted, "that San Juan . . . could be taken by a fleet under your command and by a coup de main, without the assistance of the army and in advance of its approach from the South and the complete conquest of the island . . . accomplished by this means." He would first send in a flag of truce with the notice of a bombardment and a demand for surrender. If this were refused, the battleships and monitors would open fire on the Morro defenses and the city, coupled with a landing by the fleet's marines. This, he thought, would ensure "an immediate surrender of the city and with it the possession of the whole island, or would entirely destroy the place."[28]

Sampson thought the proposition had merit and two days later broached the subject in a cable to Secretary Long, recommending that the movement of the Eastern Squadron be delayed and the ships used against San Juan instead. The capital city, he postulated, "can be destroyed from the water and may yield without much resistance to a proper show of naval strength." The antiarmy bias in this communication attracted the notice of Captain Mahan and the Naval War Board. Mahan, writing to Long on August 5, argued that the navy's armored ships had been entirely responsible for the present and highly favorable military situation. Noting that disease had decimated General Shafter's command, he ridiculed Miles's overland campaign in Puerto Rico, concluding, "[His] line of operations . . . I have viewed from the first with great distrust, and the news is not calculated to justify his course in choosing the farthest point, almost, we could find from San Juan to land [his forces]."[29]

The navy may well have wished to execute Davis's plan, but all prospects for its execution collapsed when Miles learned of it. After hearing that naval vessels had been ordered to steam from Ponce to San Juan, he cabled the War Department, "In order that there may be no conflict of authority I request that no aggressive action be taken against that place; that no landings be made or communication held with Spanish officials or forces on this island by the Navy. . . . The control of all military affairs on the land of this island can be safely left to the army." As one historian noted, "[T]he suspicious commander feared the navy trying to cut the army out of what minor glory remained to be accumulated in the war." Secretary Alger naturally supported his field general's position, wiring back that he had been assured by the president and Navy Department that "there is no cause for your apprehension, but, for a certainty, positive orders have been issued preventing the move you suggest."[30]

Miles now had every reason for optimism. His forces were growing by the day, whereas those of the enemy were static. Indeed, he even turned down an offer by the War Department for additional reinforcements, saying, "I think enough troops have been ordered to Puerto Rico."[31]

At his end, Captain General Macías clearly understood the desperate straits. In total contradiction to his pronouncement of the previous March, he cabled War Minister Correa, "[T]he majority of this country [does not] wish to call itself Spanish, preferring American domination. This the enemy knows, and it is proved to him today by greetings and adhesions in towns that are going to be occupied." His own forces were scarce and there was no hope of reinforcements. What units remained along the coasts "at most can make an honorable retreat." Consciously or not, Macías maintained a clear grasp of Mahanian principles. The Americans, he continued, were "master of the sea and . . . could move [their] forces with ease and rapidity, displaying superiority everywhere." There was nothing to prevent the foe from "easy and short" occupation of the whole coast of Puerto Rico, "with the exception of this place [San Juan]." The report was devastating to the Spanish government, who were offering feelers for an armistice. The worse the situation became in Puerto Rico, the less likely it was that they could retain it at the peace table.[32]

General Miles's offensive began on August 5, and it came none too soon. "The rumors of peace are thick," wrote one of Wilson's staff officers, "and everyone is more disgusted than ever. I am not bloodthirsty; but I should like to see a little real fighting after all this farce." At 8:00 A.M., two units of Brooke's command, the 4th Ohio and 3rd Illinois, advanced west along the coastal road on Guayama. About 300 Spanish troops occupied the place but offered hardly any resistance. They were driven back and pursued along the road to Cayey with a loss of four Americans wounded, one Spaniard killed and two injured. By evening, the American infantry held strong positions on the outskirts of the town. Brooke then sent two companies of the 4th Ohio to reconnoiter along the main road to Cayey "for the purpose of developing the enemy's position and to clear the way for the engineers to map the country correctly." They were met with a sharp fire from the Spanish in position along the hilltops. When part of the recon force fell back on Guayama, bringing reports of a repulse, Brooke sent the rest of the regiment forward, whereupon the Spanish retired to stronger points further along the road. American losses amounted to five wounded and two prostrated by heat.[33]

On account of grounded transports, Brooke was deprived of his cavalry, artillery, and rations, and forced to wait until August 13 to renew his advance. He planned a general attack against a Spanish force variously estimated at anywhere from 600 to 1,500 infantry; unmolested for a week, they had entrenched along the crests and passes of the hills north of Guayama, a natural defensive position that could prove exceedingly difficult to take, and that according to one observer, "lent itself most admirably to the genius of the Spanish engineer." The trenches were cleverly hidden among the palms and banana groves and covered at least five miles of the defiles between three ranges of heights, reaching forward into a convex arc aimed at the American front, with advance outposts on the sharp spurs that jutted out from the main divide. The Spanish position centered on Guamani Pass, 2,100 feet high, through which the main road to Cayey led. The trenches, with barbed-wire barricades, covered about four miles of the main road south of the pass and every important trail that could be used to flank the position.[34]

Brooke intended an artillery barrage on the Spanish center, simultaneous with a flank attack by the 4th Ohio on the Spanish right anchored on the crest of the Sierra de Jajome, a 2,400-foot outcropping thrust up from the main line of hills. Brooke's artillery was about to open fire on the Spanish trenches, and the Ohio volunteers were just south of their objective, when a telegram arrived at his headquarters announcing an armistice, dated August 12: "The President directs that all military operations against the enemy be suspended. Peace negotiations are nearing completion, a protocol having just been signed by representatives of the two countries."[35]

On August 7, Wilson's outposts occupied a line across the narrow valley of the Descalabrado River, about three-quarters of the way from Ponce to Coamo and halfway to Aibonito. The Coamo garrison, at least 250 men, barred the way to the main objective, Aibonito, and could not be taken by direct assault without great losses. Wilson decided to flank it by turning the Spanish right. He ordered the 16th Pennsylvania along difficult mountain trails, forward into the valley of the Coamo River, a stream that flowed behind the village; the troops thereby came onto the main road in the rear of the town. At sunup on the morning of August 9, Wilson's artillery shelled and destroyed the blockhouse commanding the road to Coamo, while

General Ernst, with the bulk of his brigade, advanced in a direct attack on the town. As soon as Ernst moved forward, the Spanish began to retreat, coming under the fire of the 16th Pennsylvania in their rear. The Spanish lost 16 killed and wounded; 170 men were taken prisoner. Those of the enemy who managed to escape the net were pursued along the road by the troop of New York cavalry attached to Ernst's brigade, which was halted by enemy artillery fire just in front of Aibonito.

On the slopes below the batteries and the town lay the infantry trenches. They were practically impregnable against a direct assault, and Wilson, after a careful reconnaissance of all approaches, opted to turn it by a flanking movement with Ernst's brigade around the Spanish right as he had done at Coamo. To divert the enemy's attention from the movement, Wilson ordered a battery of the 3rd Artillery to advance from Coamo and open fire from the reverse slope of a low ridge on the Spanish batteries 2,250 yards in front and below them. The Spanish replied with counterfire, which was suppressed, and the American guns then trained on the infantry trenches, whose defenders were put to rout at the first direct shot. At this point a regiment might have been ordered forward and would certainly have captured the Spanish position. But, as with Brooke, the armistice telegram arrived, putting an end to Wilson's flank march on Aibonito.

On August 6, Schwan's column began moving westward toward Mayagüez. On the afternoon of the tenth, the cavalry came up against the enemy's forward positions at Hormigueros. Here the entire Mayagüez garrison, some 1,300 men, of whom about 900 were regulars, had selected a position of great natural strength on hills commanding Schwan's line of march. In the engagement, the Spanish were completely routed, with the American infantry pushing along the main road and the cavalry executing a right-flanking maneuver. It was the only time in the war that U.S. Cavalry fought a mounted engagement. The Spanish suffered about fifty casualties, and the Americans one dead and sixteen wounded.

Schwan camped on the battlefield and early the next morning resumed the march. In midmorning, August 11, with the band playing and the colors uncased and flying, the column entered Mayagüez. Schwan promptly resumed the pursuit of the enemy fleeing toward Lares. On the thirteenth, his advance guard overtook the Spaniards crossing the Rio Prieto, inflicting heavy losses on the enemy. Anticipating constant pursuit, the portion of the Spanish force that did eventually reach Lares on the evening of the thirteenth evacuated it the next day. The task set for Schwan's column had been nearly accomplished when early on the fourteenth, word came of the suspension of hostilities. As it happened, the engagement on the Prieto had the distinction of being the last skirmish of the war.

At the conclusion of the campaign, Miles cabled Russell Alger, "Please notice on a map our troops occupy best part of Puerto Rico. They are moving in such strong column[s] that nothing could check their progress." He was sure that if the war had gone on, he could have overrun the whole island in four more days. He was probably right, basing his assessment on the fact that the Spanish would prove as easy to deal with in the latter stages of the campaign as in the earlier. Macías had no means of conducting a lengthy defense. The military and naval events at Santiago had deprived his army of the will to resist.[36]

Many of the difficulties that afflicted the campaign against Santiago did not accompany the Puerto Rico expedition. The landings at Guánica, Ponce, and Arroyo went much more smoothly than those at Daiquirí and Siboney. The presence of an effective contingent of engineers greatly assisted with the landings. Medical problems posed no serious difficulties. Casualties were very light in the six engagements fought, resulting in seven killed and thirty-six wounded; Spanish losses were about ten times as great.

Miles properly ensured that his men did not alienate the locals. When Brigadier General Roy Stone discovered a soldier had defrauded a restaurant with Confederate money, he wrote, "It seems to me that nothing but a drum-head court-martial and a little cold lead will serve in a case of this kind if the guilty party can be found." The offender, a member of the 6th Illinois, was subjected to a general court-martial and received a sentence of thirteen months in solitary confinement in a federal penitentiary.[37] This type of swift action, coupled with Miles's attempts to free Puerto Rican political prisoners held in Spain, went far to assure the eventual loyalty of the population.

During the last phases of the campaign, all manner of political pressure had been exerted in Washington to send certain volunteer regiments into action. Typical was the plea from U.S. senator Thomas H. Carter of Montana to the adjutant general: "If possible, send

Grigsby's cavalry to Porto Rico or Cuba. They want to get into or near a fight." The War Department tried to accommodate these by a policy of representing each state with at least one unit per expedition. General Corbin pointed out to Senator Lodge, who wanted additional units sent from Massachusetts, that his state was already well represented in the Caribbean, whereas other states had no troops there at all. "The pressure for this representation is of such character," Corbin wrote, "as to force the Secretary to equalize the assignments among several states." Some protests were honored when it was judged that complainants had "good" reason to bray. Corbin decided to send an Indiana regiment from Chickamauga to Puerto Rico when Senator Charles W. Fairbanks pointed out that troops from all neighboring states had been dispatched, but none from Indiana.[38]

Yet when the fighting stopped, the political demands to bring the volunteers home without delay were even more strident and frequent. A complainer from Vermont wrote Russell Alger protesting the sending of his state's troops to Puerto Rico "unless their services are actually needed there. . . . An excursion to Porto Rico after the war is over will not add to their honor nor to the honor of Vermont."[39]

The views of the home folk and of the volunteer troops themselves forced General Miles into an early decision. On August 23 he proposed to send a third of his force back to the United States, not by whole units, but by thirds of units. The War Department had a different plan in mind, releasing entire regiments, mustering out one hundred thousand volunteers, service-wide, as soon as possible. Miles was authorized to send home the New York and Pennsylvania cavalries immediately.

The campaign to conquer Puerto Rico, conceived in part to force Spain to the peace table before it became necessary to conduct extensive operations against Havana, ended successfully. Its most important consequence was the eventual American annexation of the island, something not officially thought of until well into the war. From a strategic point of view, it was within the realm of the large-policy advocates to absorb Puerto Rico into the American polity as an important buttress along the Atlantic approaches to the as yet unbuilt isthmian canal, which assured American hegemony over the entire Western Hemisphere.

CHAPTER 16

THE MANILA CAMPAIGN

We all await anxiously [Cámara's] squadron and reinforcements; it is very urgent that they come before it is too late.
—*Admiral Patricio Montojo, June 8, 1898*

The situation is most critical at Manila. The Spanish may surrender at any moment.
—*Rear Admiral George Dewey, July 26, 1898*

The resounding Battle of Manila Bay left little rest for Commodore Dewey or the officers and men of the Asiatic Squadron. A blockade of Manila had to be established and enforced, and immunity from surprise attack by the Spanish insured. The Cavite arsenal and navy yard needed to be occupied, its stores protected, and its precincts policed. Among the commodore's diverse cares were 250 Spanish sick and wounded in the Cavite naval hospital. Although controlling the bay and, like as not, able to force a surrender of the city by threatening a bombardment, he had informed Secretary Long that he hadn't the manpower to hold it. He also desperately needed ammunition, a good portion of which had been used up during the battle. As for Manila, the city was running short of food "on account of not having economized stores."[1]

In response to Dewey's cabled needs, Secretary Long told him the cruiser *Charleston* was fast loading ammunition at San Francisco, to be followed by several steamers with additional stores and a number of troops. "How many will you require?" Long needed to know. He also informed Dewey of his promotion to "acting" rear admiral—the "acting" part of his new rank was negated later in the day with a second cable making it a permanent rank: "You will hoist the flag of a rear admiral, and will wear the uniform, and will affix that title to your official signature."[2]

Dewey responded on May 13, asking for 5,000 troops, who "should make provision for extremely hot, moist climate." He estimated Spanish forces in the Manila area at around 10,000 men, an extremely close calculation, being less than 500 over the actual figure. Taking that into account, Dewey's request for only 5,000 men clearly indicates that at the moment he had nothing more in mind than the capture of the city and gave no thought to a military campaign to conquer the entire archipelago.[3]

In Washington, even before Dewey's telegrams announcing victory in the Battle of Manila Bay, a conflict had been brewing among the War Department and senior army commanders as to what actually constituted America's role in the Philippines; was it merely to hold Manila Bay as a naval base, or to acquire the whole archipelago? Now, in response to Dewey's cable, General Miles suggested that Brigadier General Thomas M. Anderson be appointed to command an expedition of regulars and northwestern state volunteers consisting of something less than the 5,000 men Dewey had requested, for what nonetheless seemed to be a much expanded mission, "to occupy the Philippine Islands," not merely Manila, the bay, and its environs. Whether Miles really meant this is unclear. In any event, he changed his mind soon enough.[4]

With Dewey's first Hong Kong cables in hand, the War Department detached Major General Wesley Merritt, the second-ranking officer in the U.S. Army, from the Department of the East to command a newly organized Department of the Pacific and its striking arm, the Eighth Army Corps, now forming in San Francisco, for duty in the Philippines. Unlike General Shafter, or Miles for that matter, Merritt had graduated from West Point and, as a young commander of a cavalry division at the end of the Civil War, had experience in handling large formations of troops.

On May 13, Merritt was asked by the president for his estimate of the number of men necessary to constitute an expedition to the Philippines, with, as Merritt put it, "a fair chance of success after arriving there." Merritt considered Miles's numbers dangerously low in both regulars and total numbers. He wanted to point out to the president "in very emphatic terms" that the volunteers from the northwestern states were neither as efficiently drilled nor as disciplined as those from the East or Midwest. For that reason, he urgently requested the number of regulars be increased. "I feel," he said, "that I would be doing the country, the force in Manila harbor, and myself a great injustice to attempt to carry out your wishes with a small force or one differently constituted."[5]

Merritt indicated that, although an immense volunteer reserve could indeed be advanced "to perfection" as soldiers in the United States, they were within supporting distance of any operations in Cuba or Puerto Rico. Not so the Philippines, seven thousand miles from the American mainland. An operation there "must depend upon itself" in case of casualties from sickness or battle, and could not be readily reinforced. Instead of the fewer than 5,000 men Miles had proposed, Merritt recommended an expedition of 14,000, of whom nearly half would be regulars.[6]

After reading Merritt's objections, Miles upgraded his own estimate in a letter to Russell Alger. He now proposed two regiments of regular infantry, two squadrons of regular cavalry, and one heavy and two light batteries of artillery. Added to these he recommended 12,975 volunteers from western and midwestern states, bringing the total to about 15,000 men. Nor was this all. With an eye to the somewhat distant future, Miles also advocated sending a substantial amount of heavy coast artillery, "there to be mounted as speedily as possible for the defense of that [Manila] harbor."[7]

The letter was passed on to Merritt, who "Respectfully returned" it as "unsuited to the ends to be accomplished and insufficient in efficiency for the expedition to the Philippines." The contingent of regulars, he noted, was "but a small proportion" of the forty-two regiments constituting the regular army, especially when the work to be done "consists of conquering a territory 7,000 miles from our base," defended by a trained and acclimated Spanish force of perhaps 25,000 men, and "inhabited by 14,000,000 of people [actually, around 8 million to 10 million], the majority of whom will regard us with the intense hatred born of race and religion."[8]

In his turn, Miles rejected Merritt's arguments. He believed the estimates of both Spanish troop strength and the Filipino population were highly exaggerated. Also, while Miles had perhaps intimated previously an archipelago-wide campaign, the expedition now building in San Francisco was "not expected to carry on a war to conquer an extensive territory, and the chief object" was to quickly establish a "strong garrison to command the harbor of Manila" and relieve Dewey's squadron "with the least possible delay."[9]

Assembling the first contingents of the Philippine expeditionary force went much better than the mess at Tampa Bay, not least because San Francisco had the port facilities to manage it. On May 25, commanded by Brigadier General Thomas Anderson, the first units—the band and one battalion of the 14th Infantry, the 1st California, 2nd Oregon, a detachment of California heavy artillery, plus 76 replacements—and four hundred tons of ammunition for Admiral Dewey, sailed aboard the *City of Pekin, City of Sydney,* and *Australia*. In all, the force numbered 2,500 men.

The convoy, stopping at Honolulu for coal, linked up with the cruiser *Charleston* for the remainder of the journey. The cruiser's commanding officer, Captain Henry Glass, had received orders three weeks before to capture the Spanish outpost of Guam, a convenient, if distant, linking point between the navy's new coaling station at Pearl Harbor and the Philippine Islands. Using whatever force necessary, Glass was to seize the island, make prisoners of the governor and any armed forces, and destroy its fortifications and all enemy naval vessels encountered.

At daylight, June 20, the expedition hove off the north end of the island. At the capital, Agaña, there were no vessels of any kind. Further down the coast, at the harbor of San Luis D'Apra, Glass expected to find a Spanish gunboat and whatever military force the island possessed. Instead he found the main fortifications, forts Santiago and Santa Cruz, abandoned and in ruins. The *Charleston* steamed directly into the harbor, fired a few shots from her secondary battery, and received no response.

A boat flying the Spanish flag put out from the shore and approached the ship. Up the *Charleston*'s accommodation ladder came the captain of the port and the island's health officer, a surgeon of the Spanish army; they hadn't the slightest idea that war existed between the United States and Spain, their last news being from Manila in mid-April. Glass informed the men they were now prisoners of war. When they replied that no resistance could be made by the force of Spanish troops on the island, Glass released them on parole with instructions to bring the governor, Lieutenant Colonel Juan Marina, on board. In the early evening, the governor's secretary arrived to tell Glass that by Spanish law, the governor was prohibited from entering a foreign vessel and to request the captain come ashore for a conference. In the words of the governor as conveyed by his secretary, "I await you to accede to your wishes as far as possible, and to agree as to our mutual situations." Because it was too late in the day to send a landing force ashore, Glass informed the secretary he would send an officer with a communication in the morning.[10]

At 8:30 A.M. the following day, the *Charleston*'s marine detachment of thirty men, along with two companies of the 2nd Oregon, landed under the command of the cruiser's executive officer, Lieutenant William Braunersreuther. They carried a flag of truce and a written demand for the immediate surrender of the island, along with all officials and persons in the military service of Spain. The lieutenant was ordered to wait no more than half an hour for a reply. Shortly after noon, Braunersreuther returned to the *Charleston* with the governor and three officers of his staff. Colonel Marina handed Glass a letter asserting that, since the island was without defenses of any kind, he was unable to make the slightest resistance, and had "regretfully to accede to your demands." At the same time, he protested "against this act of violence," as he had received no information from his government that Spain and the United States were at war. He ended with "God be with you!"[11]

In midafternoon, formal possession of Guam was accomplished with the raising of the American flag over Fort Santa Cruz and was saluted with twenty-one guns from the *Charleston*. The prisoners, who included fifty-six Spanish marines, were sent to the *City of Sydney*. The harbor forts were entirely useless for defense, and Glass did not find it necessary to blow them up. There were only four cast-iron saluting guns at Agaña, and these were inoperable even for that purpose. The few native troops on the island were overjoyed at being relieved of their arms and in grateful appreciation bestowed their buttons and badges on the landing force. All were allowed to return

to their homes. With that, the *Charleston* and the transports continued the voyage to Manila.

At Manila Bay, Admiral Dewey had not only the Spanish to deal with
but also the very complicated issue of the insurgency. In the long run,
this was to have as much importance for the future of the Philippine
Islands as the naval battle of Manila Bay. Dewey, after his overwhelming victory, received as great a degree of public adulation as
any American since the Civil War. Americans, both in and out of government, considered that he, better than any other, understood the
complex developments in the archipelago that were reported in the
press during the spring and summer of 1898. As the *Washington Post*
noted, "It is by no means certain that history will not glorify Dewey
quite as much for his management of the stormy elements on the
island[s] as for his splendid naval achievements."[12]

In fact, Dewey was nearly as uninformed about the explosive state
of affairs in the Philippines as his admirers in the United States. Having
little direct contact with the Filipino people, he relied on hearsay, rumors, and the advice of non-Filipino consular officials who frequently
served to reinforce his own misconceptions of facts and events. Most of
Dewey's information regarding the political situation came from the
former U.S. consul at Manila, Oscar Williams, a well-meaning official
who had accompanied the squadron from Hong Kong. He had already
assured Dewey that the Filipinos then in revolt against Spain would
welcome an American attack on the city proper and a subsequent annexation of the islands to the United States. As Williams cabled the
State Department, the insurgent leadership "all hope the Philippines
will be held as a colony of the United States." It was fatal advice.[13]

Dewey received much the same counsel from Edouard André, the
Belgian consul general, who held large economic interests in Manila.
As a businessman, he was naturally anxious to have law and order restored in the islands by a "civilized" power, rather than face the un-
certainties of an insurgent-led government. André's advice regarding
annexation was much the same as Williams's. "The Indians," he told
Dewey, "do not desire independence. They know they are not strong
enough; they trust the United States government, and they know that
they will be treated rightly."[14]

Similar assurances came from American consul Rounseville Wild-man in Hong Kong, who reported that "in spite of all statements to the contrary, I know [the insurgents] are fighting for annexation to the U.S. first and for independence second if the U.S. decides to de-cline." On the basis of this advice, Dewey could only conclude that the insurgents were fighting not for independence, but merely to throw off Spanish domination, and that if the United States should choose to annex the islands, the Filipinos would accept it. As Dewey, still somewhat naive about the whole situation, told a reporter in 1901, "At the beginning I don't believe Aguinaldo had any idea of in-dependence at all. I think it was simply a case of success turning a man's head."[15]

By mid-May, Emilio Aguinaldo, cooling his heels in Hong Kong, was reluctant to return to the Philippines. Even considering the vic-tory of the Americans at Manila Bay, he believed the journey ill ad-vised without first making solid arrangements with the Americans as to their intentions for the future of the islands. However, he eventu-ally yielded to the urgings of members of his junta in exile and agreed to return to the islands. He arrived at Cavite on May 19, a passenger aboard the *McCulloch*.

Before a Senate committee in 1902, during which time a protracted rebellion by the Filipinos against the United States was in full force, Dewey was asked why he had permitted Aguinaldo's return. Dewey, who was actually grateful for the rebel support against a common enemy at the time, was somewhat flip in his response to the question. "God knows," he replied. "I don't know. They were taking my time about frivolous things. I let [him] come over as an act of courtesy, just as you sometimes give money to a man to get rid of him; not that I expected anything from them. . . . I was told that at my first gun there would be 25,000 or 30,000 Filipinos [rising]. But they did not rise. There was not one under arms, and when Aguinaldo came, the first information he received that they were beginning to assemble I gave him."[16]

Aguinaldo and Dewey conferred aboard the *Olympia*. According to the admiral, he told the insurgent leader, "Well, now, go ashore there; we have got our forces at the arsenal of Cavite, go ashore and start your army." According to Aguinaldo, Dewey virtually promised the future independence of the islands. "America," Dewey is alleged to have said, though there is no record of it save Aguinaldo's later account, was "exceedingly well off as regards territory, revenue and resources and, therefore needs no colonies." Dewey, as Aguinaldo wrote, assured him there was absolutely no reason to entertain doubts "about the recognition of the independence of the Philippines by the United States."[17]

Whether or not Dewey actually made the statement to Aguinaldo, there was no reason for the admiral to think otherwise, if he was so inclined, and at times it seems he was. Congress had recently passed the Teller Amendment disavowing any intention to annex Cuba, and it was only logical to assume that if the American people did not desire an island ninety miles from Key West, they would have little interest in an archipelago seven thousand miles further away. Dewey, though he owed his position to the intercession of Theodore Roosevelt, held no imperialist notions; the attack on the Philippines, he told his son, was not to acquire territory for the United States, but only because "they belong to Spain," and she "derives large revenues" from them. He told his autobiographical ghostwriter, Frederick Palmer, "Our government is not fitted for colonies. There will be resistance in Congress. . . . We have ample room for development at home. The colonies of European nations are vital to their economic life; ours could not be."[18]

On May 24, Aguinaldo issued the first of a series of independence proclamations addressed to the Filipino people. He began by thanking "[t]he great North American Nation, the cradle of genuine liberty," and thus a friend to the oppressed, for coming to the "disinterested" aid of the Philippine rebellion. The articles of the initial manifesto, which was crafted in the form of rules of warfare against Spain, protected the lives and property of all foreigners, "Chinese being included," as well as all Spaniards who did not aid in suppressing the rebellion. Those Spaniards directly involved, i.e., the Spanish army, would receive humane treatment if they laid down their arms. Hospitals and ambulances would be respected. Any insurgent who disobeyed the prescription would be tried by court-martial and "put to death if the said disobedience has resulted in murder, robbery, or rape."[19]

The second edict dealt with the late Treaty of Biyak-na-Bató, entered into with the Spanish in 1897, wherein the rebels agreed to lay down their arms in return for their self-exile, a cash payment, and the amelioration of the worst of the Spanish colonial excesses. But no reforms had taken place, "reforms," said Aguinaldo, "which we demand to advance our country to the rank of a civilized nation, like our neighbor, Japan." The Spanish government, he continued, remained powerless to act against Spain's most conservative interests, the army and church, "which constantly arrest the progress" of any settlement of Filipino grievances, to say nothing of autonomy or independence. Now that the United States had entered the equation, Aguinaldo announced his assumption of military and political command of all insurgent forces "for the attainment of our lofty aspirations, establishing a dictatorial government" until the islands were conquered and a representational government could be established. "That was the first intimation; the first I had ever heard of the independence of the Philippines," Dewey later told the Senate committee. Actually Dewey attached so little importance to the decrees that he did not even cable their contents to Washington, relying instead on the regular mails. "I never dreamed they wanted independence," he said.[20]

Aguinaldo's activities soon began to stimulate interest within the McKinley administration, and Dewey found himself responding to inquiries. On May 26 Secretary Long requested detailed information regarding any conferences, relations, and cooperation, military or otherwise, maintained with the insurgent leadership. From the time of the coming of Aguinaldo and for the next several weeks, Dewey treated the rebels as associates in a joint cause, telling the Senate committee, "We had a common enemy, and of course I wanted his help." They shared intelligence information, and Dewey turned over the captured Spanish arms and ammunition at the Cavite arsenal. He also permitted the rebels more or less free use of the bay to transport munitions, supplies, and recruits to their lines around the city of Manila. As Dewey reported to the Navy Department, "Have advised frequently to conduct the war humanely, which he [Aguinaldo] has done invariably." Relations remained, for the time, "cordial, but I am not in his confidence." Aguinaldo expected to capture Manila on his own, but as Dewey informed the department, he doubted the rebels' ability to do so without artillery. As for the overarching question of the future of the islands, "In my opinion," Dewey noted, "these people are far superior in their intelligence and more capable of self-government than the natives of Cuba, and I am familiar with both races." Regarding promises, Dewey had not bound the United States in any way. The request by Long represented a significant awareness of the rebels as a major component in the military equation of the Philippines, and it became highly probable that their presence would influence any postwar settlement.[21]

In actuality, the Americans never offered much more than encouragement and a few arms to the rebels. When the Senate investigating committee asked Admiral Dewey why he had even gone this far, given his belief that Manila would surrender to American forces without much resistance, he replied that his actions constituted "a good military act, a proper military act. The Filipinos were our friends, assisting us; they were doing our work. I believed then that they would accept us with open arms."[22]

In fact, it was a prudent action, for while waiting for the American expeditions to arrive, as Dewey said, "the closer [the rebels] invested the city the easier it would be when our troops arrived to march in." When Dewey was pressed further to explain his dealings with the insurgents, he drew upon an analogy with his service in the Civil War. "The only friends we had in the South were the negroes," he said, "and we made use of them; they assisted us on many occasions. I said these people [the Filipinos] are our friends, and 'we have come here and they will help us' exactly as the negroes helped us in the Civil War."[23]

Dewey, however, failed to weigh the political consequences of his actions, innocent and well-meaning as they might have been. If Aguinaldo thought the admiral had the power to negotiate, he was certainly in error. Aguinaldo read far too much into Dewey's actions in aiding him. The later controversy and Philippine insurrection against the United States were in large part due to the fact that neither the authorities in Washington nor the insurgent leadership were aware of the real intentions of the other—indeed, the McKinley administration was not aware yet of its own design regarding the Philippines—until each side was committed to policies about which there was no compromise: annexation of the archipelago by the United States, and full independence by the rebels.

Active rebel military operations began in late May with a shipment of 2,282 Remington rifles and 175,000 rounds of ammunition from China. This purchase was made by Consul Wildman with Mexican gold pesos provided by Aguinaldo. Arms hidden following the Treaty of Biyak-na-Bató suddenly appeared from where they had been hidden, other weapons came from deserting Filipinos in the Spanish army—eventually, something like fourteen thousand native troops deserted to Aguinaldo's lines, forming the backbone of his forces. "He whipped the Spaniards battle after battle," Dewey told the Senate committee. Rebel success in the field stemmed from both their own activities and the weakness of the Spanish garrison. The most important actions occurred under Aguinaldo's direct command in the immediate vicinity of Manila. His initial objective was to seize the province of Cavite, the first step toward conquest of Manila. With surpassing speed, the rebels broke the Spanish line south of the city and moved into the capital's outer suburbs. According to a contemporary historian, Spanish officers "seem [ed] to have felt that surrender was inevitable; that as they were doomed to pass as prisoners to the insurgents it would be well to pass without unnecessary loss of blood." Had the Spanish detached garrisons chosen to fight their way back to Manila, they might well have succeeded, but the will to make the effort simply did not exist. After the outlying posts had been captured, the insurgents dominated all areas north, east, and south of the capital, capturing the water pumping stations and several main roads leading nearly up to the walled city, while to the west, the seaward flank, lay the American squadron.[24]

While these events transpired in the Philippines, in Spain, efforts were being made to send to sea a naval "Squadron of Reserve." Its highly conflicting orders at times bordered on the ludicrous. This was the force under Rear Admiral Manuel Cámara, which began a half-hearted step to Manila to break the American blockade. His original mission was stipulated on May 27, with delusional instructions from Navy Minister Auñón: Cámara would complete coaling and provisioning at Cádiz and proceed to Las Palmas in the Canaries. There, the squadron would divide into three divisions; the first, initially under Cámara's personal command, consisted of the armored cruiser *Carlos V* and three armed liners; the second consisted of the battleship *Pelayo*, the ancient ironclad *Vitoria*, and three destroyers; the third division was formed of three auxiliary cruisers.[25]

The squadron would take care to conceal its final destination by cruising the regular shipping lanes, ostensibly for the West Indies; but Cámara's division would head instead for Bermuda and ascertain the disposition of American naval forces along the Atlantic coast. From there, Cámara would select an American city, "as you may deem best adapted—Charleston, if possible—to carry out from south to north a series of hostile acts." Once, as the Spanish thought, the Americans determined an enemy force on their coast, units would be detached from Key West, leaving that place naked to the attack by the second and third divisions of the squadron. The Americans might even weaken the blockade of Santiago, enabling the escape of Cervera's ships.[26]

Having accomplished on the Atlantic coast whatever it could, Cámara's cruiser division was then to head for the Bahamas to collect intelligence, and from there, at his discretion, to steam around the eastern point of Cuba, enter Santiago, and join Cervera, or follow the north coast for Havana; barring that, it was to head for San Juan, Puerto Rico. The second division, built around the *Pelayo*, would cruise well to the east, drawing American forces away from the scene of the action. Then, leaving Cámara in the Western Hemisphere, they would return to Spain for further orders. The third division of auxiliary cruisers had orders to steam for Cape San Roque, the bulge of Brazil, and cut into American merchant traffic plying the South Atlantic. Cámara's orders ended with hopes his operations would "serve as a brilliant example of what may be accomplished in spite of the scarcity of resources, by energy, intelligence, and good will placed at the service of king and country."[27]

None of this happened. Sometime in the middle of June, while Cámara was fitting-out in Cádiz, War Minister Correa alerted Admiral Auñón to the grave situation in the Philippines. He suggested that Cámara's mission to the West Indies be canceled and all or part of the squadron leave immediately for the Far East to "calm [the] anxiety of public opinion and raise [the] spirit of [our] fighting forces through knowledge that reinforcements are coming."[28]

On June 15 came the new orders for Cámara. The main object of his expedition now was to reassert Spanish sovereignty in the Philippines, giving the United States no grounds to claim conquest when the question of peace should come. He was to arrange for the immediate departure of the squadron from Cádiz and head for the Suez Canal,

leaving his colliers to catch up. Once he was at Port Said, the Mediterranean entrance to the canal, new orders would arrive. The ships—
the *Pelayo* and *Carlos V*, the armed liners *Rápido* and *Patriota*, two
loaded troop transports with two regiments of infantry and a battalion of marines, and four colliers—were to pass through the canal and
coal in the Red Sea.[29]

East of the Gulf of Aden, Cámara had several options. He could
detach the troop transports to various widely scattered islands in the
Philippine archipelago, or he might, if he chose, keep the squadron intact. In any event, he ought, "if possible, enter into communication
with the authorities at Manila for the purpose of cooperating in the
future." As it was impossible to foretell conditions there at the "comparatively remote" date of his arrival, he was permitted from the time
he touched land at Mindanao, the southern big island of the group, to
make his own plans and "take such steps as will lead to the attainment of the total or partial success of this enterprise." It was suggested he could operate in the Visayas, the central islands of the
archipelago, land on the east coast of Luzon, or pass around the north
end of that island to operate against Subic Bay or Manila. In regard
to the latter, he was only to engage American forces if he met them
"without signal inferiority on your side." Given that he had a battleship, and Dewey did not, Cámara, had he reached Manila Bay before
Dewey received reinforcements, might indeed have done some considerable damage.[30]

The new orders concluded with instructions that if Cámara succeeded in communicating with Manila, he was to consult the captain
general and "do anything that may lead to the defense or reconquest
of the archipelago." If he found it necessary to enter neutral ports on
account of battle damage or other reasons, French colonies or Siam
was preferable. That these orders were given with any earnest intent
for their realistic completion is hardly possible.[31]

On June 18, Secretary Long informed Dewey via the cable to
Hong Kong that Cámara's force had been spotted by the U.S. consul
at Gibraltar, sailing east. As reinforcements, the monitor *Monterey*
had sailed from San Diego on the eleventh, and the monitor *Monadnock* and collier *Brutus* would steam for Manila in a week's time.
Further, the second element of the army's expedition, 3,500 men, had
left San Francisco on the fifteenth. Dewey's response, dated June 25,

contained the pressing question of whether the monitors would arrive in time to meet Cámara, and a suggestion: "In my judgment, if the coast of Spain was threatened, the squadron of the enemy would have to return."[32]

On June 26, Cámara arrived off Port Said, but as a result of feverish American diplomatic activity was refused permission to buy coal or to transship it from his colliers into his warships while in Egyptian waters; the grounds in international law were that the Spanish already had coal enough to return to a home port. To make doubly sure of hobbling the Spanish, the U.S. consul secured a lien on all coal at Suez city at the other end of the canal. On July 1, Cámara sent two of his transports into the waterway, while with the rest of the squadron he attempted to partially coal in the Mediterranean's international waters. On the fifth, he reentered the canal, but was directed by the Anglo-Egyptian authorities to leave Suez in twenty-four hours as stipulated under international law. Cámara tried to continue the voyage into the Red Sea and attempted to coal. On July 8 he reversed course back into the canal, where he received orders to return to Spain.

In all, Spain reaped nothing whatever from the Cámara fiasco, expending £64,000 in toll fees for the useless steaming back and forth. In a pathetic postscript, Cámara's new orders, dated July 23, directed him to steam along the Spanish coast, keeping close to shore so as to be seen and prominently showing the national flag. At night the flag was to be illuminated by searchlights, reassuring all that the Spanish navy was on guard against the feared American incursion into their coasts, which never came.

In the meantime, the first American expeditionary force had arrived at Cavite on June 30 and disembarked. One of General Anderson's first tasks was dealing with Aguinaldo. In an interview held the next day at the arsenal, Anderson got the impression that his coming did not wholly gladden the insurgent chief, who hoped to take Manila with only the assistance of Dewey's squadron. "He did not seem pleased at the incoming of our land forces, hoping as I believe, that he could take the city with his own army, with the cooperation of the American fleet." Anderson did not think the rebels could do it; and more attuned to the insurgent attitude than Admiral Dewey, he indicated that if given the opportunity, Aguinaldo, would "antagonize any effort on our part to establish a provisional government."[33]

The second expedition, commanded by Brigadier General Francis Vinton Greene, West Point graduate, Civil War veteran, and late commander of the 71st New York, had sailed from San Francisco on the morning of June 15. Consisting of about 3,500 men, it was formed of one battalion each of the 18th and 23rd Infantry regiments, the 1st Colorado, 1st Nebraska, 10th Pennsylvania, two batteries of the Utah Light Artillery, and a detachment of regular engineers. On the fifteenth of July, the convoy was met off Cape Engaño, the northern tip of Luzon, by the Boston for the final leg to Manila Bay. "We had been thirty days without news from the outer world," General Greene later wrote. The Boston brought the latest information from Hong Kong, dated two weeks back, consisting of a few brief telegrams regarding Cámara's squadron passing through the Suez Canal and coaling in the Red Sea, and also that General Merritt had sailed with the third component of the expedition on June 28. "These telegrams," Greene mused, "showed that a most interesting race was in progress on two sides of the globe, each of the contestants with about seven thousand nautical miles to go. . . . I figured that Cámara would reach Manila July 26, Merritt July 28, and the [monitor] Monterey August 4. Would he [Cámara] sail to intercept Merritt? Would his arrival be delayed beyond August 4? Would he come at all?"[34]

Dewey himself was convinced that if Cámara continued his voyage he would reach Manila before the Monterey. Dewey, having no battleships, was entirely outclassed by the Pelayo. Outdated and slow as she was, the ship still carried two 12-inch and two 11-inch guns, against which Dewey's ships, all unarmored, would stand little chance. To Dewey's mind, the safety of the army, both Anderson's men and the as yet to arrive expeditions, depended entirely on keeping his fleet intact. Dewey therefore concluded that if news did not come in a week that Cámara had turned back, he would take the squadron and Anderson's empty transports to the north of Luzon and cruise east until he came up with the monitors, then return and destroy Cámara in Manila Bay. He asked Anderson what his plans were should this happen. Anderson replied that he would take thirty days' rations, march into the hills about twenty miles east of Cavite, entrench, and await the return of the fleet. As it happened, Dewey received word around July 15 that Cámara had turned back, as Greene said, "just as it was becoming necessary to take steps to carry the [evacuation] plan into operation."[35]

Every bit as important as Cámara's aborted voyage, on June 12, Dewey informed the Navy Department of the arrival in the bay of Vice Admiral Otto von Diederichs in the protected cruiser *Kaiserin Augusta*. This brought the number of German warships to three, with the British having two, the French and Japanese one each; more German warships were expected. Japan was careful to assure the United States that her ships were present in Philippine waters only to protect Japanese subjects and to observe naval operations. If pressed, she was prepared, even willing, to assume imperial responsibilities in the Philippines, but she avoided, for the time, any steps that might provoke the United States.

The presence in Manila Bay of the foreign warships highlighted the delicate situation in which Dewey found himself in regard to neutral nations, especially Great Britain and Germany. Britain's desire for American support in Asia and her need to prevent Spanish possessions from falling to Germany certainly accounted in large part for her generous attitude toward the United States, so different from what she had manifested approaching the Union during the first half of the American Civil War. From the onset, British officials in London and the Far East cordially encouraged American naval officers and diplomats concerned with the Pacific situation. Dewey's squadron was supplied in large part from British territories, and but for British goodwill, he would not have been able to communicate by cable with Washington through Hong Kong. Though the British government had ruled that belligerents could not send telegrams regarding operations through British ports, Dewey experienced no interruption of cable service.

Dewey used the *McCulloch* or the steamer *Zafiro*. He had purchased the *Zafiro* early on and placed a naval officer in command. Use of the merchantman also greatly mitigated the monotonous diet of ship's fare for the mess decks and wardrooms. In Manila Bay only a little fruit or a few eggs might occasionally be bought from the natives. In Hong Kong, on the other hand, most anything in any quantity could be bought, save for fresh beef, and the *Zafiro* could accommodate these loads.

A fair amount of discretion, however, had to be employed in the purchasing, loading, and shipment, as the Americans needed to be most careful to commit no act that might constitute a breach of British neutrality. Fresh provisions were invariably bought through Chinese compradors from Chinese merchants and sent off, usually at night, to the *Zafiro* coaling at anchor in the Chinese zone of Hong Kong harbor.

It was the Germans, however, that gave Dewey the most headaches, and to such an extent that he cabled the Department on July 4, "Hope *Monterey* will be here before [Spanish] surrender to prevent possible interference by the Germans." This telegram, the first to suggest that the Germans might clog themselves into the situation, caused a degree of excitement in Washington and became yet another impetus to dispatching the Eastern Squadron from Caribbean waters to reinforce Dewey. The German foreign ministry, in fact, was fishing among the powers for diplomatic support for a scheme to acquire part of the Philippines, or to neutralize them under some sort of international protection. The British were openly opposed and informed the American ambassador, John Hay, that they would prefer that the United States take the islands.

From the remnants of the Spanish and Portuguese empires, Germany, in its quest for overseas colonies, hoped to secure coaling stations and bases commanding a sea lane from Europe to the Far East around the southern tip of Africa. In the western Pacific, the German navy had its eye on the Sulu Archipelago, the southern Philippine island of Mindanao, the Carolines, and all of the Samoan group. To varying degrees, the United States also had an interest in these very same places. Early in May, following the Battle of Manila Bay, Berlin deduced that Spanish rule in the Philippines was fast crumbling. The kaiser's government, advised by the foreign ministry that command of Far Eastern waters would pass to the power controlling the Philippines, determined that the islands should not be transferred by Spain to a third power unless Germany received some compensation. On June 2, Vice Admiral Otto von Diederichs, commanding Germany's Far Eastern Squadron, was ordered to the Philippines to investigate the state of Spanish rule, the attitudes of the natives, and foreign intentions toward the islands.

If the McKinley administration needed firsthand intelligence regarding German intentions, it got it from the U.S. naval attaché in Berlin, Commander Francis Barber. He warned that only an overwhelming superiority of force and an evident will to use it would compel German respect for American intentions in the Philippines. Barber's alarm was provoked by two interviews U.S. Ambassador Andrew D. White had with the acting chief of the German foreign ministry, Baron Oswald von Richthofen. Von Richthofen appeared offended that the United States had been thoughtless enough to annex Hawaii without, in the words of one historian, "graciously stepping aside for Germany in Samoa." Von Richthofen was visibly interested in the fate of the Philippines and the Spanish islands of the Ladrones (Marianas), and he left no doubt that Germany badly wanted the Carolines and Palaus as well. Impressed, White advised the State Department that the United States should be "friendly to German aspirations" in order to assure Germany's "friendly cooperation" in both Asia and other spheres.[36]

Though there was much anxiety in Dewey's mind regarding the Germans and their intentions and actions in the Philippines, he did not, save for a few brief telegrams, notify Washington of the potential seriousness of the situation. After the war, Dewey declared in his autobiography that he had decided to deal with the Germans himself, without adding to the problems of the administration. At a White House dinner, President McKinley mentioned repeated press statements regarding the friction between Dewey and von Diederichs, commenting, "There is no record of it at all on the files." Dewey replied, "No, Mr. President. As I was on the spot and familiar with the situation from day to day, it seemed best that I look after it myself, at a time when you had worries enough of your own." But if Dewey's confrontations with the Germans were as serious as he later represented, and they were, his failure to keep the administration fully informed is difficult to defend.[37]

Dewey notwithstanding, the State Department was concerned, and intimated to the German foreign ministry that the size and activities of the German squadron in Manila Bay was raising misgivings. Secretary of State Rufus Day directed Ambassador White to inquire whether Germany intended to keep such a force at Manila for the foreseeable future, to which von Richthofen replied that the German squadron implied no ill will toward the United States. German public opinion, said von Richthofen, demanded an effective demonstration on behalf of Germany's subjects at Manila, few though they were. Von Richthofen later cautioned White that no word of the American inquiry should reach the kaiser, as he might consider it a personal affront.

Unfortunately, at this meeting in late July, White allowed the conversation to turn to possible territorial advantages Germany might obtain from the peace settlement. He even intimated that German and American diplomats might reach a private understanding regarding the prospective peace talks. For this indiscretion, White was admonished by Secretary Day. The secretary admitted himself wholly unprepared for White's willingness to discuss with the Germans questions arising from the war, as these lay "exclusively between the United States and Spain."[38]

Meanwhile, the German naval force that gathered at Manila soon equaled, and to a degree exceeded, Dewey's in power. The cruiser *Irene* came on May 6 and the *Cormoran* on May 9.[39]

Generally, until the arrival of von Diederichs in the cruiser *Kaiserin Augusta* on June 12, the Germans kept only two ships at Manila. A week later, they gained a clear superiority over the Americans with the appearance of the old central battery ironclad *Kaiser* and the cruiser *Princess Wilhelm*. Though von Diederichs maintained that his ships had been assembled to facilitate the exchange of relief crews from Germany, he admitted privately that the concentration of so large a squadron at Manila, out of all proportion to legitimate German interests in the Philippines, was a diplomatic blunder. Insofar as the German presence encouraged the Americans and British to draw closer together, it had an effect directly opposite to that desired by Berlin, which was to strengthen the position of Germany in the Philippines in the event the United States decided not to annex them.

According to Commander Nathan Sargent, who compiled an extensive account of the entire naval facet of the Manila campaign, "The Germans soon acted as if Manila Bay were absolutely in their possession." Their vessels constantly shifted positions, cruised about at will, ran in and out at all hours of the day and night, and finally, without any permission, established a temporary station at Mariveles, on Bataan, across Boca Chica from Corregidor. Here they landed their men, ostensibly for drill, and took possession of the quarantine station, and von Diederichs occupied a large house lately deserted by the local Spanish official. On July 5, Dewey's patience reached its limit, and he went in the *McCulloch* to Mariveles. He passed around the German ships anchored there, and departed without communicating, "allowing them to draw their own conclusions from his visit." As Dewey later put it, heavily downgrading the various incidents, "It was only natural to reason . . . [the Germans] might not be familiar with the customs and laws of blockades. I knew the German naval officers were very self-reliant, keen to take offense about their rights, and most ambitious to learn by observation, which I always liked to think explained their . . . proceedings."[40]

Dewey may have subsequently dismissed German activity, but their constant arrivals and departures were, at the time, great sources of annoyance and concern. General Anderson reported to the adjutant general that the Germans were "showing evident hostility" toward the Americans. As Captain Edward Chichester of HMS *Immortalité* reported to his government, the German "ways are certainly mysterious, but the American officials look on the same as a 'game of Bluff.' "[41]

On July 6 the transport *Darmstadt* sailed into the bay with relief crews for the German ships, and Dewey feared her 1,400 men might be used as a landing force for a more permanent German presence. Lieutenant Ellicott of the *Baltimore* thought there "seemed to be some hook-up between the Germans and Cámara." Rumors also abounded that the Germans were helping the Spanish improvise torpedo boats in the Pasig River. A press correspondent was surprised when he called upon Dewey one morning and found him discussing battle plans, "if we should have to fight the Germans."[42]

According to Commander Sargent, the Germans, feeling "secure in their strength," became more aggressive. Their officers landed in Manila and were soon on the most cordial terms with the Spanish, who openly asserted that the German squadron would intervene on their behalf. Von Diederichs visited Captain General Augustín, and the latter returned the call at night, remaining on board the German flagship for two hours.[43]

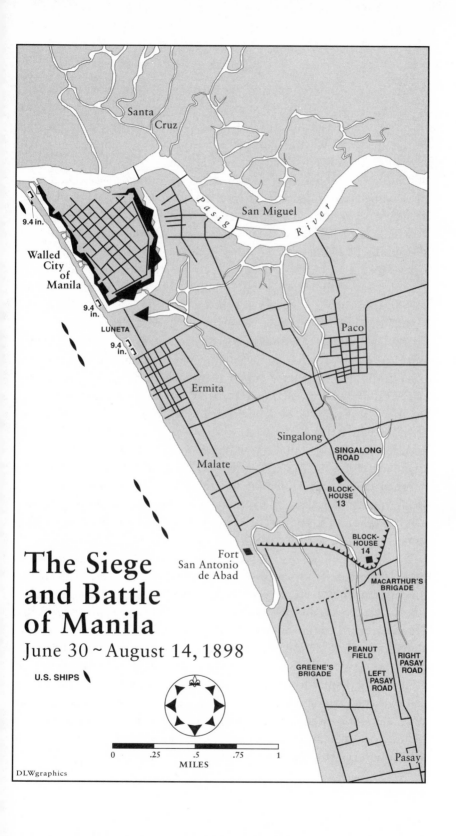

Santa Cruz

San Miguel

Pasig River

9.4 in.

Walled
City
of
Manila

9.4 in.

LUNETA

9.4 in.

Paco

Ermita

Singalong

SINGALONG ROAD

Malate

BLOCK-HOUSE 13

BLOCK-HOUSE 14

The Siege
and Battle
of Manila
June 30 ~ August 14, 1898

Fort
San Antonio
de Abad

MACARTHUR'S BRIGADE

U.S. SHIPS

PEANUT FIELD

RIGHT PASAY ROAD

GREENE'S BRIGADE

LEFT PASAY ROAD

Pasay

0   .25   .5   .75   1
MILES

DLWgraphics

On July 7, Dewey, exasperated, sent his flag lieutenant, Thomas Brumby, to the German flagship to present several grievances to Admiral von Diederichs. Von Diederichs expressed surprise on learning of the incidents, which is not so very remarkable, as there is no mention of them in his detailed reports to his superiors, or in those of his subordinate commanders. As Brumby recounted, von Diederichs "disclaimed any intention of interfering in the least with Admiral Dewey's operations and said he would as far as possible avoid all movements of his ships . . . at night—that Admiral Dewey had conducted the blockade in the mildest possible way and he did not want to embarrass him in the slightest." At the conclusion of his report, Brumby added that the German admiral was "most polite," and did not wish to interfere in any manner with Admiral Dewey's actions, "and I was convinced of his sincerity and personal probity."[44]

That same day, Aguinaldo, or one of his agents, informed Admiral Dewey that a German warship was meddling with insurgent operations in Subic Bay, which the rebels had taken—except for Isla Grande, where a Spanish garrison still held out. The *Irene* had been cruising in the bay when approached by a Spanish launch flying a white flag and carrying a message from the Spanish commander. Fearing the place was about to fall, he implored the German vessel to evacuate his women and children. The German skipper, Commander Obenheimer, hesitated. He was under orders from von Diederichs not to interfere in any way with operations. On the other hand, he felt he could not very well leave noncombatants to the rebels.

Stories had made the rounds in Manila of the treatment of the Spanish who fell into rebel hands; actually they were treated humanely, but the tales said otherwise. Obenheimer had no time to request instructions and with reluctance headed for Isla Grande. When Dewey learned of this he sent the *Raleigh* and *Concord* to investigate the situation. After the war, the rumor had it that Dewey had purposely sent two of his smaller vessels so that, in case the *Irene* wanted to fight, she would have a reasonably fair encounter. But this is nonsense. As the two ships entered the bay, the *Raleigh* at general quarters, the *Concord* not yet at action stations, they passed the *Irene* coming out. The postwar story that fire was opened by the American ships on the German or that the *Irene* slipped her cable in her haste to escape are equally fallacious. Both sides barely acknowledged the presence of the other and there was no incident of any kind between them. Actually, Captain Coghlan of the *Raleigh* believed the Spanish on Isla Grande had adequate force to resist a rebel attack. A few shots with light guns, however, were loosed on the island, at which point the Spanish garrison of 1,300 surrendered to the Americans without resistance.

Three days after the affair at Isla Grande, on July 10, von Diederichs sent his flag lieutenant, Hintze, to the *Olympia* with a verbal response to the complaints expressed by Brumby. Hintze was also instructed to refer to an incident that occurred on June 27, when an officer of the *McCulloch* "improperly" stopped and boarded the *Irene* off Corregidor. According to Hintze's report, Dewey snapped, completely losing his temper. "Why," he said, voice rising, "I shall stop each vessel whatever may be her colors. And if she does not stop, I shall fire at her! And that means war, do you know Sir? And I tell you, if Germany wants war, all right, we are ready."[45]

Commander Sargent relates the story in a slightly different way. According to him, Hintze, "in a particularly precise Prussian manner," recapped the German complaints, giving to each subject the preliminary phrase, "And his Excellency [von Diederichs] protests." When he had reached the matter of the boarding of the *Irene,* repeating the monotonous, "And his Excellency protests," Dewey turned beet red as his indignation boiled over. When Hintze had finished, Dewey "in a suave manner" said, "and does 'His Excellency' know that it is my force and not his which is blockading this port?" Hintze answered in the affirmative. "And," Dewey continued, "is he aware that he has no rights here except such as I chose to allow him, and does he realize that he cannot communicate with that city except by my permission?" Hintze reportedly shrugged. "One would imagine, sir," Dewey seethed, "that you were conducting this blockade." At that Hintze gave a gesture of negation. "Do you want war with us?" Dewey asked. "Certainly not," Hintze replied. "Well, it looks like it," the admiral went on, and you are very near it; and," his voice rising until it could be heard in the wardroom below, "you can have it as soon as you like."[46]

In consternation, Hintze backed away and, in an awed voice, according to Sargent, said to Lieutenant Brumby, "Your admiral seems to be much in earnest." "Yes," replied Brumby, "and you can be certain that he means every word he says." At that point, Hintze took his leave.[47]

Once Dewey had been reinforced by the *Charleston* and Anderson's troops on June 30, which also gave him someone with whom to share the burdens, tensions between the Americans and Germans eased considerably. He and von Diederichs took to exchanging visits, and Dewey allowed the German to buy fresh meat from a steamer whose cargo had been purchased by the Americans in Hong Kong. "The Germans are behaving better," Dewey wrote consul Rounseville Wildman in Hong Kong, "and I don't think there is the slightest intention on their part to interfere at present. What they may do later remains to be seen."[48]

On August 2 von Diederichs informed Berlin that his stay at Manila had caused him to be extremely skeptical of any insurgent inclination toward Germany. The Filipinos repeatedly inquired why such a large squadron had been sent to Manila when during past outbreaks one or two ships had sufficed. It was widely believed among the rebels that the Germans had come to take sides with the Spanish against the insurrection. Under these circumstances, the German government rapidly lost interest in the Philippines and concentrated on acquiring the Ladrones and Carolines. On August 18, Ambassador White in Berlin reported that von Diederichs and the battleship *Kaiser* had been ordered to represent Germany at the celebration of the coronation of the Queen of the Netherlands at Batavia. Dewey had by this time been strengthened by the arrival of the two monitors, *Monterey* and *Monadnock,* and was superior to the German squadron, with or without the *Kaiser.*

After the capture of Manila, the observing foreign warships gradually dispersed. Dewey, in making his last visit to the French admiral, told him he particularly wanted to offer his thanks for the strict French observance of neutrality, adding that he especially appreciated it as he was aware that French sympathies had not been entirely with the United States. "And, Admiral," the Frenchman replied, "you must let me congratulate you that in all your conduct of affairs here you have not made a single mistake." "Oh, yes I have," Dewey replied, "I made one—I should have sunk that squadron over there," pointing to the remaining German ships.[49]

...dent McKinley and his wartime cabinet. From left to right, all ...d: the president; Lyman T. Gage, Treasury; John W. Griggs, ...ney general; John D. Long, Navy; Rufus Day, State; Russell ..., War; Charles Emory Smith, postmaster general. (Harper & ...ers, New York, 1898)

Don Práxedes Mateo Sagasta, Liberal prime minister of Spain during the Cuban War of Independence and the Spanish-American War. His strategy of offering largely empty promises for true Cuban autonomy and his inability to quell the Cuban revolution were major causes of the Spanish-American War. (Harper)

General Don Arsenio Martínez Campos, governor and captain general of Cuba. Named Spain's leading soldier, and a comparative liberal in matters dealing with the Cuban people and rebels, he refused to initiate harsh anti-insurgent measures and was recalled to Spain. (Harper)

General Don Ramón Blanco y Arenas, last Spanish governor and captain general of Cuba. He relieved the highly controversial Weyler, revoked *reconcentración*, declared the island autonomous, and proved a more humane commander and administrator. It was, however, too late to save Spanish fortunes. (Harper)

...ral Don Valeriano Weyler y Nicolau, governor and captain ...al of Cuba, arriving at Havana. Named "the Butcher" by ...merican press, Weyler succeeded Martínez Campos, initi- ...the notorious *reconcentrado* order, forcibly moving the ...nts into fortified zones. By his harsh, and largely success- ...ctions against the Cuban rebels he turned U.S. public opin- ...to an active ally of the revolution. (Harper)

A standard Spanish stone blockhouse and its garrison. The blockhouses dotted the length and breadth of Cuba in an attempt to secure the countryside from the rebels. (Pearson, New York, 1898)

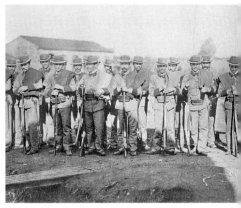

A Spanish infantry platoon in winter uniforms, c. 1897. (Pearson)

Cuban mounted *guerrilleros* in the service of Spain. A fair numb Cubans served as irregular troops in the Spanish army during bot War of Independence and the Spanish-American War. (Harper)

General Arsenio Linares Pomba, commander of the Spanish Fourth Army Corps, wounded at the Battle of San Juan Hill, July 1, 1898. (Felipe González Rojas, Madrid, 1910)

José Martí, *apostól* of Cuba dependence, founder of the ban Revolutionary Party, was killed in action durin, first months of the war for pendence, May 1895. (Gon Rojas)

General Máximo Gómez, the wispy, ruthless commander in chief of the Cuban rebel armies during the War of Independence. (Harper)

The "Bronze Titan," General Antonio Maceo, the brilliant black field commander of the rebels' Liberation Army during the Cuban War of Independence. He was killed in December 1896. (Harper)

al Calixto García (seatommander of the Cuban s in Oriente Province, ing to James Creelman, spondent for the New *World*. (D. Appleton, York, 1898)

Cuban rebels, eastern Oriente Province. (Appleton)

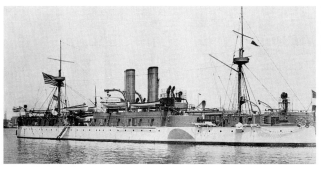

The second-class battleship M[aine] whose explosion and loss at Ha[vana] on February 15, 1898, triggere[d the] Spanish-American War. (U.S. Nav[y)

A Spanish navy diving crew by the wreck of the battleship *Maine*, Havana, February 1898. (Pearson)

The wreck of the *Maine* the day [after] the explosion. (Collier, New [York,] 1898)

Captain William T. Sampson of the battleship *Iowa*, immediately before taking up command of the North Atlantic Squadron, with the rank of rear admiral, April 1898. (Appleton)

Rear Admiral Winfield Scott Schley. As a commodore he commanded the Flying Squadron, executing some highly controversial movements during the hunt for the Spanish fleet and the Battle of Santiago. (W. B. Conkey, Chicago, 1902)

The armored cruiser *New York*, flagship of the U.S. North Atlantic Squadron. (U.S. Navy)

The armored cruiser *Brooklyn*, flagship of the Flying Squadron. The *New York* lies anchored to starboard. (U.S. Navy)

New York signaling at the close of battle. (U.S. Navy)

The first-class battleship *Oregon*, whose monumental voyage around South America made manifest America's strategic need for a Central American isthmian canal. (U.S. Navy)

econd-class battleship
. Smallest of the U.S.
red ships, she none-
s performed well in
e and battle. (U.S.
)

The Spanish cruiser *Alfonso XII*, station ship at Havana. The c[r]uisers *Reina Cristina*, at Manila, and *Reina Mercedes*, at Santiag[o,] Cuba, were of the same, largely obsolete, class. (Collier)

Rear Admiral Don Patricio Montojo y Pasaron, commander of the doomed, outgunned Spanish squadron in the Battle of Manila Bay, May 1, 1898. (Harper)

Church service aboard the cruiser *Reina Cristina*, Spanish flagship sunk in the Battle of Manila Bay. (Harper)

The protected cruiser *Oly[mpia,]* Commodore Dewey's flagsh[ip at] Manila Bay. (U.S. Navy)

Rear Admiral George Dewey aboard his flagship *Olympia*, Manila Bay, summer 1898. (Minnesota Historical Society)

scene, U.S. infantry, summer
A crate of the hated canned
roast beef" can be seen at
(Pearson)

The 1st U.S. Volunteer Cavalry, the "Rough Riders," at drill, Tampa, June 1898. With the exception of one mounted squadron, the Cavalry Division left most of its horses behind when it embarked for the Santiago campaign. (Minnesota Historical Society)

Major General William Rufus Shafter, crusty commander of the U.S. Fifth Army Corps, supervising embarkation at Tampa, June 1898. (Harper)

Major General Joseph ("Fighting Joe") Wheeler, in full dress. A West Point graduate, an ex-Confederate cavalry officer, and a serving congressman in 1898, Wheeler, at age sixty-two, was commissioned by the president for the war and creditably commanded the Cavalry Division during the Santiago campaign. (Drexel, Philadelphia, 1899)

The chaotic loading of the transports at the port of Tampa, Florida, June 1898. (Harper)

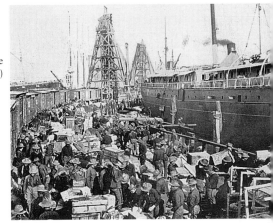

Colonel Theodore Roosevelt, ex–assistant secretary of the navy, here commanding the 1st United States Volunteer Cavalry, nicknamed the Rough Riders, the most famous American unit of the war. (Harper)

Transport life: U.S. troops en route to Santiago de Cuba, 1898. (Harper)

. . .

One day after the arrival of General Greene's contingent on July 17, Dewey furnished a steam launch for the two American generals, to reconnoiter the Spanish positions south of Manila. Greene and Anderson cruised well beyond the Spanish lines, within easy rifle shot, but drew no fire. Having obtained a fair idea of the enemy in the vicinity of the eastern shore of Manila Bay, they searched for a site to land Greene's force and to move Anderson's up from Cavite. They picked out a flat field, planted with peanuts but otherwise entirely open, about a mile and a half long by a quarter mile wide, south of the southern suburb of Malate. It was enclosed on three sides by dense clumps of bamboo and rice paddies, and on the fourth side by the bay. It was sufficiently large to accommodate up to eight thousand men, and its northern edge, facing the Spanish, was just out of rifle range. "The existence of this field," said Greene, "so close to the Spanish lines, was a piece of good fortune for us, as subsequent reconnaissance showed the entire country about Manila to be composed of rice swamps and bamboo thickets and there was not a place between Cavite and Manila where five thousand troops could be encamped in one body." The field was named "Camp Dewey."[50]

The difficulties of getting Greene's men ashore and moving Anderson's over from Cavite were, according to Greene, "not slight." As Camp Dewey was within easy range of the Spanish artillery, and the water was shallow, it was thought best not to bring up the transports from Cavite. To disembark they used the navy's steam launches, two captured Spanish tugs, and a dozen or so *cascos,* native lighters resembling a Chinese junk without sails. Each of these latter craft was capable of carrying about two hundred men with their equipment and ten days' rations. Strings of three or four *cascos* were loaded to capacity and towed to the landing site until they touched ground. The men then jumped into the water and waded ashore. The Spanish did not open fire or interfere in any manner. In three days, four thousand men and eight field guns were over the beaches, into the peanut field, without losing a man.[51]

Neither animals nor wagons had been brought from the United States, and in getting into position on the line, the army was forced to use native *caramattas,* light two-wheeled wagons drawn by ponies and capable of holding not more than five hundred pounds. In addition, there was the carabao, or water buffalo, dragging a heavy two-wheeled cart or sledge through the mud.

The Spanish lines facing the Americans began at the southern edge of Malate, about three-quarters of a mile inland at a blockhouse with the number 14 clearly painted on it. The position stretched westward until it touched the bay at a strong stonework, Fort San Antonio de Abad, which was armed with nine pieces of artillery, ancient and modern. The fort was sited on a small peninsula formed by a stream that flowed out from the city. One hundred feet wide, and reportedly unfordable, the stream was spanned by a stone bridge, fronted with stone parapets backed with sandbags five feet high and eight feet thick. The line was manned throughout by Spanish infantry, with strong reserves behind them.

The portion of the Spanish lines nearest the beach could be clearly made out from the vantage point of a white house, erroneously called by the Americans the "convent." It sat a little less than a thousand yards from the enemy and had proved a good target for Spanish artillery and infantry fire, being completely riddled with bullets and shells. As General Greene said, the "slightest exposure" at either the blockhouse or the "convent" instantly "brought a rain of bullets."[52]

The insurgents lay just outside the Spanish lines, in many places between the Spanish and the Americans. They were positioned in small trenches and numbered about ten thousand men. These rebel forces blockaded the city on its landward side to such an extent that they prevented any food from entering. They had also captured the waterworks, cutting the supply to the city.

Inside Manila, meat was very scarce, with the Spanish living on horses, which were regularly slaughtered, and the Chinese population reportedly eating cats and dogs. During the day, it was mostly quiet along the lines. But at night, the city was brilliantly lit by electric lamps. A sputtering infantry fire, with an occasional shot from a field gun, usually broke out between the Spanish and rebel lines near midnight, lasted for an hour or more, ceased, then reopened just before sunup. "At daylight," said General Greene, "the firing ceased by mutual consent."[53]

The insurgents, Greene noted, "took turns serving in the trenches for a few days and then returning to their homes in the vicinity for a week to rest, their posts and arms being taken by others. . . . They were constantly engaged in desultory fighting with the Spaniards." The Spanish, Greene thought, would have had no trouble in overrunning the rebel positions, but they never tried. "The Spaniard," Greene theorized, "like the Turk, is not given to offensive operations. His plan of warfare is to fight behind entrenchments, barbed wire, and fortifications."[54]

As the days passed, despite the facade of mutual cooperation, Anderson, Greene's immediate superior, became suspicious of the insurgent design. In mid-July he noted to the adjutant general that, despite their outward courtesy toward the Americans, "in many ways [the Filipinos] obstruct our purposes, and are using every effort to take Manila without us." Heeding Dewey's advice, Anderson took no action to impede Aguinaldo's efforts to form a government, seeking to avoid any interference that would limit the actions of Merritt, scheduled to arrive within a week. Also, much like Dewey, Anderson found his regard for the Filipino rebels increasing. "They are not ignorant savage tribes, but have a civilization of their own," he reported, and "though insignificant in appearance are fierce fighters, and for a tropical people they are industrious."[55]

On July 24, General Merritt and his staff arrived in the steamer *Newport,* and one week later came the third echelon of the expedition, commanded by Brigadier General Arthur MacArthur. The 4,847 officers and men mustered one battalion each of the 18th and 23rd Infantry, four batteries of the 3rd Artillery, one company of engineers, the 13th Minnesota Infantry, two battalions each of the 1st Idaho and 1st North Dakota Infantry, the Astor Battery of the New York Volunteer Artillery, a company of the Volunteer Signal Corps, a detachment of the Hospital Corps, 30 civilian clerks, 2 civilian messengers, and 3 press correspondents. On the arrival of this reinforcement, the U.S. Army in the Philippines was designated 2nd Division, Eighth Corps.

Merritt's orders from President McKinley stated that since the destruction of the Spanish squadron at Manila, it had become necessary to send in an army of occupation for the twofold purpose of completing the reduction of Spanish power in the Philippines and giving security and order to the islands while they were in the possession of the United States. The first effect of the military occupation was "the severance of the former political relations of the inhabitants and the establishment of a new political power." Under these circumstances, the populace, "so long as they perform[ed] their duties," were entitled to be secure in their persons and property and in all their private rights and relations. In furtherance of these goals, Merritt immediately published a proclamation declaring that the United States had come not to make war on the Filipino people, but to "protect them in their homes, jobs, and personal and religious rights." The municipal authorities, courts, and native constabulary were to remain in power if they accepted the authority of the United States. Ports occupied by the Americans were to be open to the commerce of all nations at the usual customs rates. These were substantially the same dicta as the orders and proclamations of Shafter in Cuba and Miles in Puerto Rico.[56]

Merritt, deciding to have no contact with Aguinaldo until American forces were in possession of Manila, moved preparations for the siege forward and began conducting operations without reference to the rebels. There was, however, one exception. Greene was ordered, "on my own responsibility" and without reference to any directives by Merritt, to promise one rebel commander some pieces of modern artillery, to move to the right in order to provide the Americans with unobstructed control of the roads to their immediate front. President McKinley later justified Merritt's noncommunications with the rebels thusly: "It was fitting that whatever was to be done in the way of decisive operations in that quarter [Manila] should be accomplished by the strong arm of the United States alone. . . . Divided victory was not possible."[57]

On July 26 almost everyone inside Manila knew that if reinforcements did not come from Spain the garrison could not survive a determined attack, particularly one that involved both the Americans and the insurgents. When Captain General Augustín informed Madrid through the diplomatic pouches of friendly consuls of the latest arrival of American forces, he proposed, on the assumption that peace talks had begun with the United States, that negotiations go forward for a local truce; otherwise he expected an early assault on the city. Morale among the Spanish population was extremely low. The whole situation had become chaotic when the latest American reinforcements had appeared just as the city received word that Cámara had returned to Spain.

One Spanish inhabitant recorded the mood of the city: "A great part of the population, civil as well as military, believed that it [Manila] ought to be capitulated . . . since they considered the defense impossible, that it would occasion thousands of victims needlessly; for another thing, they added, the downright conduct of the homeland relieves us of all obligation to her." As in the case of Santiago de Cuba, the Manila garrison manifested little inclination to fight the Americans any distance outside the gates of the city. Another observer, however, reported that spirits were high among the Spanish troops manning the lines outside the walls and along the line at Malate. "In the trenches," he said, "the soldiers continued singing and firing, and if someone had pronounced the word *surrender* they would have lynched him."[58]

Yet on July 29, Dewey cabled the Navy Department, "From information I consider reliable, Spanish Governor-General would surrender to the United States forces at once, were it not for insurgent complication. In any event they must capitulate very soon." Dewey and Merritt were both working toward this end. Merritt, however, doubted the city could be taken without a fight.[59]

It seemed the chief Spanish interest was in assuring the city would fall to the Americans and not the insurgents. Dewey later claimed that as early as May, Augustín had hinted to the British consul, Robert Rawson-Walker, that he was prepared to surrender Manila to the Americans. But Dewey, who at that time had no troops to garrison the city, declined. By late July, however, a considerable body of American soldiery had come east, and Dewey took up the thread of negotiations through the Belgian consul, Edouard André. Augustín, and his successor, General Fermín Jáudenes y Alvarez, were not averse to a bloodless capitulation of the city, provided the rebels were kept out. Jáudenes told André he "was willing to surrender to white people but never to Niggers." Augustín, prior to his relief as governor and captain general, revealed to André that he might be willing to surrender to the Americans provided they agreed to keep the "Indians" out of the city and take the insurgent leaders into custody. Dewey refused to consider this, but assured André he'd keep the rebels out, and even Aguinaldo would not be permitted to enter if the Spanish desired to keep him out.[60]

This independent approach against Manila mirrored the Cuban policy of icing the insurgents from any meaningful cooperation in military operations and diplomatic interchange. Given McKinley's desire to maintain firm control of future developments and hold open all possible options it was doubtless the logical course.

Other than occasional picket firing, the American forces kept up work on the trenches without interference by the Spanish. Rain, however, was incessant, and the black loam, saturated with water, washed down almost as soon as it was thrown up. No sandbags were yet available, but bamboo poles were cut from the groves and used with success to hold the parapets in place.

Shortly before midnight during the night of July 31 to August 1, with the rain falling very heavily, the Spanish opened a heavy infantry and artillery fire at the Americans in their trenches. Instead of going unanswered, as was usual, by men who were perfectly protected, this fire was answered by the Pennsylvanians, whose bright muzzle flashes from their old Springfield rifles provided the Spanish with innumerable aiming points. The whole American camp was roused and under arms. A battery of the 3rd Artillery moved forward into the trenches, as did a battalion of the 1st California. The remaining California battalion and the whole 1st Colorado advanced to within 1,200 yards of the trenches and were held in reserve. Spanish fire ceased at 2:00 A.M. Ten Americans had been killed and forty-three wounded, most because they stood up in the trench.

In the morning, Greene ordered the 1st Colorado and one battalion of the 1st California to extend the trench eastward to the Pasay road, the easternmost avenue leading into Manila from the south. Though constantly interrupted by enemy fire, this work was continued every day by troops occupying the trenches in turn, until a strong line, about 1,200 yards in length, extended inland from the bay. As finally completed, the work was very strong in profile, being from five to six feet high and eight to ten feet thick at the base. The trenches were occupied by the troops in succession for twenty-four hours' duty, with three battalions in the line and one in reserve along the crossroad to Pasay. Outposts from the latter position guarded against a Spanish surprise from the northeast and east. Service in the trenches, said General Greene, "was of the most arduous character" as the rain was almost incessant and the men had no protection from it. They were wet during their whole twenty-four hours in the line, and the mud was so deep that shoes were ruined and a considerable number of the men were rendered barefoot. Any exposure above or behind the trenches promptly brought down enemy fire, so the men had to sit in the mud under cover and remain awake and prepared to meet an attack during their entire stint. After one particularly heavy rain, a portion of the trench contained two feet of water. "These hardships," Greene said, "were endured by the men of the different regiments . . . with the finest possible spirit and without a murmur of complaint."[61]

On August 4, Captain General Basilio Augustín was replaced in command of the Philippines by his deputy, General Fermín Jáudenes y Alvarez, with orders to hold the city at all costs, especially as peace negotiations had begun. To give Manila up prematurely might have disastrous consequences for Spain. Augustín's summary sacking was due to the message he had sent to Madrid in which he pointed out the critical condition of affairs in Manila, the hopelessness of its defense, the exhausted state of his forces, the increase of the American forces, and the utter despair that had existed since news came of Cámara's return to Spain. In view of these considerations, he declined to accept responsibility for the situation. The Spanish government immediately relieved him of command. For his part, Dewey informed the Navy Department the relief was due to Augustín's predilection to "surrender without a struggle."[62]

The day of the Spanish change of command, Dewey finally received the reinforcement of the monitor *Monterey,* a ship capable of "receiving and giving the hardest knocks of war." The Spanish lines, at right angles to the beach, were completely enfiladed by the fleet's guns. And now that the monitor had arrived, Greene was anxious that a decisive step should be taken toward the reduction of the Spanish positions. He had already lost twelve men, with fifty-two wounded, in nightly harassing fire. To General Merritt at Cavite he sent back a suggestion that the *Monterey,* anchoring at a point opposite Fort San Antonio de Abad, "could demolish this fort the minute it opened fire." Dewey, on the other hand, was convinced that a little delay would cause the city to yield without a fight. As he told Greene, "It was better to have small losses, night by night in the trenches than to run the risk of greater losses by premature attack." Dewey placed the decision in Greene's hands. If he burned a blue light on the beach, the *Raleigh* would immediately open fire on the Spanish positions, assisted by the *Charleston,*

Boston, and *Monterey.* These ships had steam up every night and their captains were instructed to go to the army's aid should the need arise. "But I hope," Dewey said, "you will not burn the light unless you are on the point of being driven out." Greene replied there was little danger of that.[63]

Merritt, too, sought a bombardment that would force the enemy from its positions: the fleet's guns could cover the entire line from Fort San Antonio de Abad to blockhouse No. 14. He urged immediate action, but failed to sway Dewey. Dewey's general tendency to seek a negotiated peace rather than a military solution at Manila might have been influenced to some extent by the siege of Santiago de Cuba. Writing to Rounseville Wildman in early July, he noted, "Manila is ready to fall into our hands, but I doubt very much if any movement is made before the arrival of more [American] troops. We don't want too many 'drawn' battles like that in Santiago."[64]

On the night of August 5, the Spanish again opened fire on the American trenches. "As usual," noted General Greene, "the mistake was made of thinking the Spaniards were advancing and our men fired away nearly 20,000 rounds." American losses amounted to three killed and seven wounded.[65]

With MacArthur's 1st Brigade occupying the right flank of the line and Greene's 2nd Brigade the left, there were, on August 7, about 8,500 Americans ashore, and both Merritt and Dewey thought it time to prepare a joint demand to the Spanish to surrender. The note, addressed to General Jáudenes and delivered in the morning by Captain Edward Chichester of the Royal Navy, informed the Spanish chief that operations by U.S. land and naval forces against the Manila defenses might begin at any time after the expiration of forty-eight hours from the time of receipt, "or sooner if made necessary by an attack on your part." The notice was being given in order for the Spanish to remove all noncombatants from the city.[66]

Jáudenes responded in the afternoon, stating that since his positions were surrounded by insurgent forces, "I am without places of refuge for the increased number of wounded, sick, women, and children who are now lodged within the walls." However, from the time of tendering the surrender demand until the actual battle for the city, firing ceased all along the line; nobody wanted any needless casualties. But Greene noted, "[I]t was with great difficulty, and in some cases not without force, that the insurgents were restrained from opening fire and thus drawing the fire of the Spaniards."[67]

The forty-eight-hour notice for the surrender expired at noon, August 9, the grace period being used by many of the foreign residents of Manila to evacuate themselves and their property to the foreign warships. Red Cross flags began to appear over buildings in many parts of the city, a clear indication of the anticipation of a bombardment. But instead of carrying out the threat, another joint note was sent to Jáudenes by Dewey and Merritt. This time they cited the "inevitable suffering in store for the wounded, sick, women, and children," in the event it became their duty to reduce the defenses of the old part of town, the walled city, where the noncombatants were gathered. This plea, they felt assured, playing to Jáudenes's sense of personal honor, would "appeal successfully to the sympathies of a general capable of making [a] determined and prolonged resistance." They submitted, therefore, that, surrounded on every side by a constantly increasing force, with a "powerful fleet in your front," and deprived of all prospect of reinforcement, "a most useless sacrifice of life would result in the event of an attack"; thus, every consideration of humanity made it imperative that he not subject the city to the "horrors" of a bombardment. Accordingly, they again demanded the surrender of the city and the forces under his command.[68]

Jáudenes replied the same day, telling Dewey and Merritt that naturally he likewise shared their sentiments regarding the noncombatants. In response to the entreaty for surrender, he had assembled the "council of defense," which declared that the American demand could not be granted, "but taking account of the most exceptional circumstances existing in this city," he asked permission and time to consult with his government via the cable at Hong Kong. The reply from Merritt and Dewey was terse: "We respectfully inform your excellency that we decline to grant the time requested."[69]

An attack, therefore, was scheduled for the following morning. Before dawn the ships of Dewey's squadron were cleared for action. All merchant vessels were ordered away from the city, and the foreign warships took up better positions to observe the battle. The *Olympia* was slowly steaming toward the city when a signal was broken out from her halyards: "Attack is postponed." It seemed that MacArthur's brigade was not ready and Merritt needed a spell

to position his men for the assault. In the squadron, the disappointment was intense, and the sailors loudly complained of having to
drag the heavy shells back into the magazines. As Commander Sargent put it, "A further delay had been added to the three wearying
months of blockade."[70]

With the attack postponed, Belgian consul Edouard André continued his tireless work attempting to persuade Jáudenes to capitulate.
He warned him that if a prolonged resistance were made, the Americans would be compelled to permit the insurgents into the city. He
convinced the general to summon another meeting of his defense
council. The committee agreed the situation was hopeless, but they
believed that some sort of attack and resistance needed to be made to
satisfy the Spanish government and the demands of the Spanish military code. However, they promised André that the 9.4-inch coastal
guns on the Luneta would not fire on the American ships unless they
opened fire on the walled city.

For their part, the American ships and the army's field artillery
would open a bombardment in the general vicinity of Fort San Antonio de Abad, following which the *Olympia* was to steam in front of
the walled city flying the international signal "DWHB"—"Do you
surrender?"—upon which Jáudenes would display a white flag over
Fort San Antonio and the city walls. It was expected that the Spanish
troops would fall back into Manila upon the fire of the ships. Then,
on the hoisting of the white flag, American officers of the fleet and
army would enter the city to arrange surrender terms. In other words,
it was to be a battle where everyone avoided inflicting casualties on
their respective enemies. The rebels, however, were neither consulted
nor involved in the agreement. In any case, they would not have been
enthusiastic about a plan that was designed primarily to keep them
out of the capital city.[71]

On August 12, the *Concord* stationed herself a mile off the end of
the Manila breakwater to control entry and exit from the city. The
naval captains repaired to the *Olympia*, where they received their instructions not to fire into the city proper unless they themselves were
fired upon. Merritt issued general orders for an attack on the enemy's
lines the next day, commencing at noon. U.S. forces were to make no
advance during the firing, "but hold the trenches, the infantry covering the artillery." MacArthur's 1st Brigade held the right, opposite

blockhouse No. 14, with eight battalions forward and three in reserve. Greene's 2nd Brigade was positioned on the left, next to the bay fronting Fort San Antonio, having seven battalions in the front and eight in reserve. All men carried a day's cooked rations and 100 rounds of Springfield or 150 of Krag ammunition.[72]

Merritt wrote a second memo to general officers: Anderson commanding the 2nd Division, MacArthur and Greene the two brigades. The troops were to hold themselves in readiness to advance only after the enemy had been so "shaken" by the bombardment as to make the advance practicable without a "serious disadvantage" to U.S. forces. In the event of a white flag being displayed by the enemy on the angle of the walled city, or prominently anywhere in sight, the troops were to advance "in good order and quietly." Merritt intended the surrender of the city to be accomplished without the loss of life. If firing continued from the enemy artillery, or if there was "important" fire from its trenches, the American troops were not to advance unless so ordered from Merritt's headquarters.[73]

The memorandum provided careful instructions to the brigade commanders to prevent the rebels from advancing beyond certain points. Greene's brigade, once past the trenches at the beach, was to move forward through the suburbs of Malate and Ermita as fast as possible, placing guards in the Spanish positions along the way. He was then to turn eastward, behind the walled city, cross a portion of his brigade over the Pasig, and establish headquarters in the Binondo section, protecting the principal business district. Forcible encounters with the rebels were to be carefully avoided, "but pillage, rapine, or violence by the native inhabitants or disorderly insurgents must be prevented at any cost." MacArthur's orders were simpler: to advance on a very narrow front up the Pasay road to the eastern suburb of Paco, driving any of the enemy before them and entering the walled city from the east. Merritt established his headquarters on the *Zafiro,* along with six companies of the 2nd Oregon as a floating reserve and provost guard for the walled city.[74]

At 9:00 A.M., the signal flew out from the *Olympia:* "Ships take their stations." The *Concord* was already off the mouth of the Pasig. The *Boston, Baltimore, Charleston,* and *Monterey* cruised off the front of the walled city. Opposite Fort San Antonio steamed the *Olympia, Raleigh,* and *Petrel,* and the captured gunboat and tug *Callao* and

Barcelo. Half an hour later, the *Olympia* opened fire on the fort, followed by the rest of the ships in her line. In the *Raleigh,* Captain Coghlan, privy to the arrangement with the Spanish, gave the range at 7,000 yards, too far to hit the fort. The gunners who did not know of the deal lowered their sight bars to 2,700 yards and continually struck the target. Coghlan ordered a cease-fire and hauled out of the line.

On the ground, Greene's first line, extending to a rice paddy about 700 yards inland, consisted of the 18th Infantry, 1st Colorado, and the 3rd Artillery. In reserve were the 1st California, 1st Nebraska, and 10th Pennsylvania. A drizzle fell, turning into a heavy thunderstorm, from which the men's ponchos offered little protection. During a pause in the thunder, the boom of rebel guns was heard near the Pasay road to the right of Greene's lines. Greene looked with distaste in that direction, saying to a reporter, "Those idiots of insurgents will spoil the whole game with their foolishness."[75]

With the correspondent writing of "great masses of vapor and heavy showers of rain" sweeping over the bay, making the scene ashore almost invisible, the field artillery joined the *Olympia* in her fire against Fort San Antonio de Abad; the Spanish made no reply. In half an hour, Greene gave the order to advance. There was some time lost due to the difficulty in getting signals to the ships to cease firing. But soon enough, the Colorado infantry streamed up the beach and forded the creek fronting the fort, which they found deserted, save for two dead Spaniards and one wounded. In a few minutes the U.S. flag was hoisted, its appearance accompanied by an exultant yell all along the line. According to the reporter, it "drowned all other sounds with its strident savage note of victory."[76]

Firing now erupted on the right flank of Greene's line, from the vicinity of blockhouse No. 14, and word came that MacArthur's advance had met with "stubborn resistance." But Greene's men moved rapidly up the beach, past the fort, and onto the high bank along the shore, honeycombed with Spanish trenches and zigzags. From here came some desultory shooting from the enemy. Greene called a short halt, and though a spattering of fire continued from the houses of Malate and occasionally a heavier fire from the bamboo thickets to their right, the brigade swarmed up the *camino real* into Malate. It was almost as if they were on an exercise march. No return fire was yet allowed, but shortly a few volleys were loosed in the direction of the most annoying Spanish fire, and from then on, spasms of firing from both sides increased in frequency.

The troops dashed by squads across the second line of Spanish defenses, peppering the retreating enemy whenever they came in sight. Greene halted the brigade and re-formed his men in the Malate plaza, about a mile from the walled city gates. Pushing rapidly up the *camino real*, the troops came on a civilian who shouted, "The Spaniards have raised a white flag!" Greene, followed by a mounted escort of the brigade staff, galloped ahead up to the Luneta, which they found deserted. The gray walls of the citadel loomed directly in front, perhaps four hundred yards off, and on a prominent corner he saw a great white sheet, tied by its corners to a swaying bamboo pole. The parapet was lined with hundreds of Spanish infantry.[77]

Greene and his party continued to the walls, and the closer they got, the more they seemed to become the targets of rifle fire, and they could not tell from where it was coming. The staff party had none of the signs of authority about it, everyone wearing a poncho or raincoat and splashed head to foot with mud. Greene, coming to the southwest angle of the citadel, spoke to an officer who appeared in an embrasure, asking the man if the city had surrendered. Informed that American officers were on their way ashore to receive the surrender, Greene was directed to enter the walled city, where he would probably be met by a Spanish officer. By this time, a company of the 23rd Infantry from MacArthur's command appeared coming up the Paco road near the parapet.

The road was also filled with Spanish troops falling back. A California battalion arrived on the scene with firing still going on close at hand. Greene directed the Spanish officers to march their men into the walled city. Soon after they had disappeared into the covered way beyond the moat bridge, a carriage with two men dressed in livery dashed out and handed Greene a note. It was from Lieutenant Colonel Charles Whittier of Merritt's staff, who along with Lieutenant Brumby, Dewey's flag lieutenant, had come ashore as soon as the white flag had been hoisted. The note was written from the office of the captain general, asking Greene to stop the firing as surrender negotiations were currently in progress.

Greene entered the city with the messenger and was escorted to the *ayuntamiento*, or city hall, and in one of the "beautiful rooms" he found generals Augustín and Jáudenes, Admiral Montojo, and Whittier and Brumby. The Spanish officers were all in "handsome, fresh uniforms and presented a striking contrast to the muddy, bedraggled appearance of myself and the aide I had brought with me." The Spanish had drawn up terms of surrender that, Whittier informed Greene, would most likely be accepted by Merritt, currently on his way ashore. Greene, who had had nothing to eat since before dawn, asked if there was any food nearby, to which Jáudenes, profusely apologizing, stated there was none, but he would send to his house for some. No time for that, Greene said. His aide, however, broke out some hardtack and a flask of good American whiskey. "Politeness," Greene said, "compelled them [the Spanish] to partake of these, although I fear they were not to their taste."[78]

Greene returned to the troops outside the walls and sent a battalion of the 3rd Artillery down the Paco road to prevent any rebels entering the city from that direction. Feeling satisfied there would be no attack from the Spanish troops within the walled city, he put his regiments in motion toward the Pasig River bridges, brushing aside a considerable body of insurgents, perhaps three thousand men who had penetrated the outskirts from Paco and who were now on the main road with their flag, expecting to march into the walled city and plant it on the walls. Greene rode up to their officer in command and requested him to move aside. The man declined, stating his intention to enter the city with the Americans. Greene explained this was impossible, but the insurgent commander stood firm. It would have been very awkward if a fight broke out, for the city walls, only a few feet away, were massed with Spanish troops, and if firing erupted between the rebels and Americans, they would probably take part in it. As Greene said, "[W]ith the insurgents in front, and the Spaniards behind fortifications in our rear, we would have been in a bad box if fighting had begun."[79]

Greene opted to handle the situation in the way "that mobs are handled in large cities." Bringing up his leading regiment, the 1st Nebraska, he formed it in column of companies and at "port arms," wheeled each company in succession to the right and pushed the rebels bodily into the fields and lanes to one side of the road. They were stunned by this unexpected movement, "and by the enormous size of the Nebraska men." Ordering this regiment to prevent the insurgents from entering the city, Greene moved the rest of his command across the iron bridge into the Binondo business district on the far side of the Pasig. The 1st California then marched along the river, crossed the eastern bridge, and occupied the districts of Quiapo, San Miguel, and Malacañan. Greene took the 1st Nebraska downriver to the port captain's office, where he ordered the Spanish flag hauled down and the U.S. colors raised. The Nebraska regiment was then posted in that part of the city containing the customhouse and shipping warehouses. The 3rd Artillery was held to guard the northern and eastern bridges leading to the "new" city across the Pasig. In the districts over the Pasig, the 1st Colorado deployed at San Sebastian and Sampaloc, while the 10th Pennsylvania occupied Santa Cruz. The Utah batteries, the Hotchkiss guns, and the engineer company were stationed in the center of the city, near the Hotel de Oriente, where Greene established his headquarters. In this way, every bridge and principal street leading into the city from the north side of the Pasig was occupied before dark.[80]

MacArthur's 1st Brigade on the right had a more difficult time of it. His front was very narrow, running between impassable rice paddies on either side. Moreover, Merritt's orders not to have any outward rupture with the insurgents and not to build any fresh trenches that might bring on an engagement had prevented him from making proper arrangements for the advance of his troops. He was obliged, therefore, to form them in detachments behind stone walls and houses on either side of the Pasay road to within two hundred yards of blockhouse No. 14.

The men were all in position before 9:00 A.M. The Astor Battery and the 13th Minnesota were on the right side of the road, and one Utah gun and the 23rd Infantry were on the left; the remaining battalions were held in reserve. From his position, MacArthur could see the flag staff on Fort San Antonio, but not the ships in the bay, nor Greene's trenches. He heard the bombardment of the squadron and then Greene's infantry firing, saw the Spanish flag hauled down from the fort, and heard the cheering that followed.

These events happened shortly before 11:00, and not long after, the white flag announcing the Spanish surrender was hoisted from the city walls. This could not be seen by MacArthur's forces. Nor was he aware that Whittier and Brumby were heading ashore to receive the submission. That lack of knowledge and the Americans' own defective arrangements for communicating with the beach brought on a real engagement with loss of life that might have been avoided. The fundamental difficulty, though, was the presence of thousands of insurgent troops on MacArthur's side of the line; the Spanish were determined to oppose their entry into Manila, and they directed the main part of their firing at them.

A company of the 23rd Infantry discovered that the Spanish line to their immediate front was abandoned, and a general advance was immediately ordered. At around 11:20 the U.S. flag was placed atop blockhouse No. 14 without opposition or loss. MacArthur stationed a battalion of the 23rd at this point to prevent armed bodies of rebels from crossing the trenches in the direction of the city. The advance resumed, the 13th Minnesota leading, followed by the Astor Battery, a battalion of the 23rd Infantry, a battalion of the 14th Infantry, and bringing up the rear, the 1st North Dakota.

Just south of the village of Singalong, MacArthur found blockhouse No. 13 abandoned and burning, causing a continuous explosion of small-arms ammunition. Together with a scattering of fire from the retreating Spanish, this slowed the advance for a time. In Singalong, the advance again came under "loose" fire, whose intensity increased as the forward movement pressed onward, and very soon MacArthur's brigade was committed to a fierce firefight. The strong opposition was coming from blockhouse No. 20, a detached work with emplacements for six guns. Fortunately, the embrasures were empty, but the place was occupied by a strong rear guard of Spanish infantry. An advance party of the 13th Minnesota, reinforced by volunteers from the Astor Battery, rushed forward, taking losses but reaching a point less than eighty yards from the blockhouse.

According to a correspondent on the scene, "There was plenty of shelter in the houses and behind the walls and, as the retreat of the enemy was a foregone conclusion, there was no necessity for reckless exposure. . . . A line of Minnesota men lay across the open road so crowded together that they could scarcely handle their rifles, and, exposed to the severe fire at close range, lost heavily and to no purpose." A reconnaissance discovered the fire coming from a heavily barricaded house and sandbag breastwork across the road, about two hundred yards from the village. A dash across was made by volunteers, but on reaching the position they found it deserted. The advance continued. Many large bodies of rebels were pushing forward on the flanks of MacArthur's brigade, sometimes crowding with the American troops in such a way that they had to be elbowed aside. The rebels soon increased to several thousand men who swarmed over the rice paddies between Ermita and Paco, finding themselves intermingled with the retreating Spanish, who opened a heavy fire on them.[81]

At 1:30, all firing ceased and two scouting parties reported the retreat of the Spanish. MacArthur's men entered the city without incident through the Paco suburb. General Merritt soon followed Colonel Whittier and Lieutenant Brumby ashore, going at once to the *ayuntamiento,* where, after a conversation with the Spanish authorities, a preliminary agreement of capitulation was drawn up and signed. Immediately after, the Spanish colors were hauled down from the walls and Brumby hoisted the large U.S. flag he had brought ashore for the purpose; on sighting it, a salute was fired from the squadron. The 2nd Oregon landed from the *Zafiro* and was posted as a provost guard within the walled city. Its colonel was directed to receive the Spanish arms and deposit them securely. The city was filled with Spanish troops, regiments forming and standing in line in the streets. The work of disarming them went quickly and no untoward incident occurred.

On August 14, an American and Spanish commission drew up the final terms of surrender. The city and defenses of Manila, its suburbs, and all Spanish troops therein had surrendered, with the honors of war, to the Americans. All Spanish troops were to remain in their barracks under orders of their own officers, subject to American control until the conclusion of a peace treaty. Officers were to retain their side arms, horses, and private property, with public horses and property of all kinds to be turned over to American staff officers. A full roster of Spanish personnel and equipment was to be supplied. Spanish families might leave Manila at any time, the costs of their repatriation to be referred to the American government. As with the capitulation at Santiago, the retention of Spanish small arms was a major issue, but it was worked out between the parties without reference to Washington. "[T]he return of arms surrendered by the Spanish forces," read the clause, "shall take place when they evacuate the city or when the American army evacuates." Spanish officers and enlisted men were to be supplied from American sources according to their rank with rations and "necessary aid." The remainder of the agreement was very similar to that of Santiago. All funds in the Spanish treasury and other public moneys were to be transferred to U.S. authority. The city, inhabitants, churches, religious worship, educational establishments, and private property were "placed under the special safeguard of the faith and honor of the American army."[82]

Late on the day of battle, the special circumstances regarding relations with the insurgents prompted a joint cable from Merritt and Dewey to their respective departments. The rebels had demanded a "joint occupation" of Manila, and the Americans needed to know "how far [we] shall proceed in forcing obedience of the insurgents in this matter and others that may arise. Is the government willing to use all means to make the natives submit to the authority of the United States?"[83]

On August 15, Merritt appointed General Anderson to command the district and environs of Cavite, and MacArthur as military commandant of the walled city and provost marshal of Manila. General Greene was placed in charge of fiscal affairs. A little over a week later, Major General Elwell S. Otis arrived from San Francisco to assume command of the Eighth Corps, while Merritt took on the mantle of military governor of the Philippines.

The political situation regarding Manila, indeed the entire archipelago, was extremely complicated. On August 12, a day *before* the attack on Manila, Secretary of State Rufus Day and Jules Cambon, the French ambassador representing Spain, had signed the protocol of peace in Washington ending hostilities, putting in question the validity of the American capture of Manila. A telegram informing of the armistice had been sent to the American commanders late in the afternoon of the same day, but did not arrive in Manila until August 16, three days after the battle. Addressed to Merritt, it read: "The president directs all military operations against the enemy be suspended. Peace negotiations are nearing completion, a protocol having just been signed by representatives of the two countries. You will inform the commander of the Spanish forces in the Philippines of these instructions."[84]

Dewey got a similar cable from the Navy Department, with the addition that the United States was to occupy and hold the city, bay, and harbor of Manila pending the conclusion of a peace treaty, "which shall determine the control, disposition and government of the Philippines." Dewey also received instructions from the president requesting any important information he could provide, especially regarding "the desirability of the several islands; the character of the population; coal and other mineral deposits; their harbor and commercial advantages, and in a naval and commercial sense, which would be the most advantageous." It was more than a hint at imperial expansion into the furthest reaches of the western Pacific.[85]

Merritt and Dewey received the president's reply to their cable on August 17. In clear directions, McKinley stated, "There must be no joint occupation with the insurgents." The United States, in its possession of the city, bay, and harbor of Manila, "must preserve peace." The rebels and all other parties must recognize the military occupation and authority of the United States and the cessation of hostilities proclaimed by the president. It ended with instructions to use "any means in your judgment necessary to this end." Some weeks later, Merritt sent a message to the adjutant general that though the rebels appeared anxious to be friendly, they were "far otherwise," making "unfortunate and exaggerated demands such as could come only from persons who, if their words were sincere, supposed themselves in control of the situation."[86]

Dewey responded to the president's request for data on the Philippines on August 20. He listed the most important islands, stating "Luzon is in all respects the most desirable to retain." It held the premier commercial port and produced all the good tobacco. "Friendly natives. Civilization somewhat advanced." For coaling and naval purposes, he recommended Subic Bay, with its deep water, landlocked geography, "easily defended." Strategically, command of the bay and city of Manila, with the navy yard and arsenal of Cavite, he considered "most valuable."[87]

The entire operation in the Philippines, from the Battle of Manila Bay to the nearly bloodless capture of the city, had been a resounding naval and military success. But with the fate of the islands still uncertain, the tension and suspicion between the Americans and the rebels steadily increased. Primary responsibility for dealing with the insurgents lay with the army. They refused to provide the rebel leadership any assurance regarding the political future of the islands—not that they knew themselves. The rebels, in their turn, began quietly planning for an uprising against the Americans should that prove necessary. They accumulated arms and consolidated their hold on Luzon outside Manila and the outer islands. By mid-October, Dewey reported the rebels in control of most of the archipelago, "which is in a state of anarchy."[88]

The American command seemed to agree. "Now that the Spanish power has been overthrown," wrote General Greene to the State Department, "he [Aguinaldo] cannot maintain independence without the help of some strong nation. Admiral Dewey fully concurs in these views."[89]

In November, Dewey received contrary counsel from two of his own officers, Paymaster Willis Wilcox and Naval Cadet Leonard Sargent, who had undertaken an extended reconnaissance of northern Luzon during October and November. They visited seven provinces, traveled hundreds of miles, and spoke with hundreds of people. Sargent noted, "It is a tribute to the efficiency of Aguinaldo's government and to the law-abiding character of his subjects that Mr. Wilcox and I pursued our journey . . . with only the most pleasing recollections of the quiet and orderly life we found the natives to be leading under the new regime." They discerned the Filipino people desired the protection of the United States at sea, but feared any interference otherwise. "On one point they seem united, that whatever our government may have done for them, it has not gained the right to annex them."[90]

Dewey sent this report to the Navy Department, and in his addendum noted that "it contained the most complete and reliable information obtainable" in regard to the situation in Luzon. It also significantly altered Dewey's view on the aims of the insurgent movement. Consul Oscar Williams, too, was beginning to have second thoughts about the desire of the locals to hinge themselves to the United States, writing to Dewey in late November, "I shudder at the thought of local war. Neither of us will live to see it end if by shot and shell we attempt to conquer these natives."[91]

With the Wilcox-Sargent reconnaissance and Williams's letter in mind, Dewey responded to a request from the Navy Department for "suggestions as to the government of the islands." He urged the U.S. government to promise the Filipino people "a large and gradually increasing degree of autonomy under American rule." In early January 1899, he cabled the department that the natives had become "excited and frightened, being misled by false reports [of Spanish reoccupation] spread by the Spaniards." He strongly urged the president to send a small civilian commission to "adjust differences." On the same day, in a letter to his mentor, Senator Proctor, Dewey expressed fears that the United States might become involved in war with the natives, who were "little more than children." To his son, George junior, he wrote, "[A]ffairs are in a very critical state and we may be fighting the insurgents at any moment. We don't want a war with them if we can help it and perhaps it would be better to give up the islands rather than have one."[92]

CHAPTER 17

PEACE

[T]hose poor dear Quixotes act more foolishly than ever. They want to force us, after killing them, to disfigure the corpse.
—*John Hay, U.S. Ambassador to Great Britain,*
July 6, 1898

I consider . . . that the intention of the Americans is to annex everything of value in the colonial empire of Spain with the least sacrifice possible.
—*the Duke of Almodóvar, Spanish Foreign Minister,*
November 3, 1898

On May, 8, 1898, one week following Dewey's annihilation of the Spanish squadron at Manila Bay, word came to Washington via Ambassador Hay in London of unofficial peace feelers from a senior member of the British government. Joseph Chamberlain, the colonial secretary, wanted to know if the United States would end the war if Spain agreed to evacuate Cuba. This query stoked the first real consideration of peace terms in the McKinley administration. After discussing Hay's message with the president, Secretary of State Day cabled the ambassador asking whether Spain had initiated the inquiry.

Actually, they had not; the feeler had come purely on Chamberlain's own account and reflected, Hay said, Britain's "willingness to take a prominent part, if needed, in the work of pacification."[1]

Though Britain would have no role in any forthcoming negotiations, the Hay-Chamberlain conversation brought forth from the administration the essence of peace terms. On June 3, accenting new realities that had not obtained a month earlier—namely, the blockading of Admiral Cervera in Santiago—the president reasoned that Spain might now submit to terms. Accordingly, Day laid out four provisions to be communicated to Spain unofficially through third parties: first, Spain must evacuate Cuba and deliver title to the island to the United States, enabling America to "restore and establish order . . . until a stable government [is] established"; second, because the United States did not intend to exact a monetary indemnity from Spain for the cost of the war, it required instead the cession of Puerto Rico, a solution that would satisfy the "just and lawful" claims of the United States stemming from the war; third, the Philippines would remain Spanish, except for "a port and necessary appurtenances, to be selected by the United States"; and finally, Spain must cede a port in the Ladrone (Marianas) Islands possessing a harbor and coaling station.[2]

Day concluded with a warning that these were the absolute minimum the United States would accept if the war were to end immediately; continued Spanish resistance would lead to material alterations in the American position very much to Spain's disadvantage. Premier Sagasta must also understand that the United States was definitely not proposing peace; anything of that sort must emanate from Spain herself. The Spanish did not respond.

Just over a week later, events in the Philippines superseded the initial American demands. Rufus Day now informed John Hay that "the insurgents . . . have become an important factor . . . and must have consideration in any terms of settlement." This view reflected the renewal of the Philippine rebellion around Manila. Led by Emilio Aguinaldo with the encouragement, not to say material aid, of Admiral Dewey, it began the process that over the next several months completely overturned the administration's policy on the Philippines.[3]

On July 6, in the wake of the smashing American victory at the naval Battle of Santiago, Hay penned a note to President McKinley: The battle, he thought, "ought to end the war, but those poor Quixotes act more foolishly than ever. They want to force us, after killing them, to disfigure the corpse." Hay also sensed a certain irritation among the European powers with Spain for obstinately refusing to ask for peace now that there was absolutely no hope of success in Cuba.[4]

By mid-July, Spanish attitudes shifted as the military situation deteriorated. Guam fell without a shot, American arms were about to secure their second triumph in Cuba, the Eighth U.S. Army Corps was camped on the outskirts of Manila, and eighteen thousand troops were poised to descend on Puerto Rico. At sea, Admiral Cámara had turned back from Suez, thereby freeing the U.S. Navy for operations against the Canaries or off the Spanish coast itself, something the Sagasta ministry dreaded. On July 14, with the fall of Santiago imminent, Sagasta suspended constitutional guarantees in Spain, hoping to muzzle domestic criticism in the face of a peace initiative.

On July 18, the Duke of Almodóvar, who had replaced Pío Gullón in the foreign ministry, asked his ambassador in Paris, Fernando León y Castillo, to propose to the French government that its envoy in Washington, Jules Cambon, present a communication to the Americans. Spain, said Almodóvar, would settle the war on the basis of Cuban independence. "Our principal argument is the suffering imposed by the war upon the inhabitants of that Antille, now so totally blockaded that it is impossible for us to send food there." He hoped Cambon could get from the McKinley administration a suspension of hostilities, an armistice, preliminary to final, definite negotiations. The matter to be discussed would be limited to the Cuban question alone; Spain was adamant about not extending talks beyond that. Cuba could go absolutely free, become an American protectorate, or better yet, be annexed to the United States. Spain would reasonably indemnify the United States for any territory other than Cuba held by American forces. And finally, she wanted a quick agreement, with negotiators meeting in a neutral place, Paris for instance.[5]

The Spanish venture, roundabout through Paris to Washington, took eight days. Almodóvar was informed that France could not act on the matter immediately because the French president was on vacation and the foreign minister lay ill. Speed, though, was of the essence, Almodóvar told León y Castillo. Manila might capitulate at any time, and he expected an attack on Puerto Rico momentarily. These were all "contingencies which compel haste."[6]

The queen regent now stepped in with a letter to be handed by Ambassador Cambon to the president. The note, sent in cipher, was not delivered until July 26. (The key to the cipher lay with the Spanish archives in the Austro-Hungarian embassy in Washington, and the Austrian minister being absent, another key had to be obtained from the Spanish consul in Montreal.)

Cambon was received by President McKinley and Secretary Day in the White House library and the letter was tendered. Spain, wrote the queen regent, faced the uneven contest with "resignation," endeavoring to defend her possessions and "to protect her honor," with no hope other than to oppose to the utmost extent of her strength the war foisted upon her by the United States. To put an end to the calamities, "already so great," and to avert further evils, the two countries might mutually attempt to arrive at conditions to end the war other than by force of arms. In this Spanish-American war, Spain had but one object, the same one she maintained in the struggle against the Cuban rebels, namely, "the vindication of her prestige, her honor, her name." She was prepared to spare Cuba the continuation of the horrors of war if the United States was likewise disposed. From the president, she wished to learn upon what basis the political status of Cuba might be established and what the United States proposed to end the war.[7]

Cambon, whose function at this point was merely that of an intermediary, expressed his personal hope that McKinley would feel inclined "to be humanely Christian and generous." He alluded to the fact that pacification of Cuba had been the original cause of the war, commenting that if this were done, the war would cease to have any reason for continuation. Day answered that if he understood the letter and Cambon correctly, Spain, while limiting herself to an inquiry on Cuba, desired to know on what condition hostilities might be terminated "in all the points where they now exist." That was something the administration could not answer immediately, and Cambon was bowed out with polite evasions. He knew Spain had lost the first round; the United States, he was sure, would not confine itself exclusively to Cuba.[8]

Cabinet meetings were held to develop terms for ending what Ambassador Hay had called "the Splendid little war." They were almost exactly in accord with the previous note sent to Hay in response to the aborted British peace feeler. According to Navy Secretary Long, he was sure President McKinley would meet the Spanish "in a liberal spirit." He had no doubt provisions could be arranged, but thought there would be a lengthy delay in negotiations. The United States would insist upon Cuban independence, and he was sure Spain would accede to that. The United States would seek no monetary indemnity, demanding instead the cession of Puerto Rico, "which I think she will yield." The question of the Philippines, Long thought, was "more difficult and complicated." The cabinet had been polled and had put forth various options, including annexing the entire archipelago, as Agriculture Secretary Wilson wished, seeing the islands as prime ground for evangelizing, perhaps forgetting they were already predominantly Roman Catholic. Cornelius Bliss of Interior saw great commercial advantages and wanted annexation also. Secretaries Long, Day, and Lyman Gage of Treasury wanted only a naval base and a cable station, or at most, the island of Luzon. Secretary of War Russell Alger and Postmaster General Charles Smith took no positions. It was significant that neither the right to keep Manila nor the advantage of a permanent naval base was disputed by even the most antiexpansionist members, such as Long and Day. The point at issue was whether to require of Spain the abdication of larger territory in the islands.[9]

Initially McKinley professed a "natural revulsion" against the acquisition of vast unknown territories thousands of miles away. Revisionist historians to the contrary, he really did not want the islands, seeking only, as Secretary Day wished, a "hitching post" for the navy and increased commerce with the Far East. But domestic politics intruded. Every thinking person and journal in the United States, from the most vocal jingoist to diehard antiexpansionists, believed that Spanish rule of the Philippines had ended with Dewey's victory in Manila Bay. The question was, what of the islands' future? Were they to be independent, acquired, partitioned, sold, or transferred to another empire? Public opinion was unquestionably swinging toward American ownership. Seeking to stay ahead of the popular curve, McKinley now moved forward in incremental steps on the road to complete American dominance of the archipelago. As Senator Lodge correctly judged, "[The president] means to go much farther than anyone I think guesses."[10]

The second reason for the evolution of the president's Philippine policy was uneasiness about the insurgents, Aguinaldo in particular, whom the administration did not trust. He had repeatedly claimed the United States, in the persons of U.S. Consul E. Spencer Pratt in Singapore and Admiral Dewey in Manila Bay, had offered the Filipinos freedom in return for their alliance against Spain. This was definitely not so, and neither man had the authority to promise it in any case. But military reports from the Philippines confirmed that an American occupation must inevitably crash up against the independence plans of the rebel leadership.

Letters and telegrams regarding imperial acquisitions poured into the White House, and the president paid close attention. Beyond anything, he wished to avoid the kind of split between himself and the great majority of the nation that had occurred in the months immediately preceding the war.

In due course, the president would describe his transit as a choice between lesser evils. As he saw it, "When the Philippines dropped into our laps I confess I did not know what to do with them." In fact, he likely didn't even know where they were: "When we received the cable from Admiral Dewey . . . I looked up their location on the globe. I could not have told where those darned islands were within 2,000 miles!" He had wanted only Manila, then expanded his reach to retain the main island of Luzon. But for the rest, to return the islands to Spain would be nothing less than "cowardly and dishonorable"; they would merely continue their centuries of misrule. Nor could the United States broker a deal whereby the islands would be transferred to another colonial power—"that would be bad business and discreditable." As for independence, as was planned for Cuba, the president thought the Philippines "unfit for self government—and they would soon have anarchy and misrule over there worse than Spain's was." There was but one option remaining—"there was nothing left for us to do but to take them all, and to educate the Filipinos, and uplift and civilize and Christianize them."[11]

While the administration deliberated, the Spanish leadership expressed great concern over strong indications that the Americans were planning an early conquest of Puerto Rico. On July 27, Foreign Minister Almodóvar alerted Ambassador León y Castillo in Paris of Miles's landing in Puerto Rico, insisting that "the United States is unwarrantably attempting military aggression without doubt the object of making more onerous the conditions of peace." The landing at Guánica,

Almodóvar said, had surprised the Spanish government, coming as it did after the American president had received the first note from Spain offering to end the war "outside the employment of arms."[12]

The next day Almodóvar, through the French foreign ministry, sent Jules Cambon a statement of Spain's position. Spain would accept the independence of Cuba without "reserve," though they hoped the United States would take it outright, "preferring definite annexation" as a way to protect the lives of Spaniards and Cuban loyalists in the island. But Puerto Rico and the Philippines needed to be dealt with separately; they were wholly different issues. Spain accepted the "principle of indemnification [to the victor] in reasonable proportion and measure." Almodóvar stressed that Spain did not provoke the war, and though "fortune has been adverse to us," the Spanish government stood on the opinion that the "conqueror should not be the arbiter of territories" that had been attacked by the United States.[13]

The president replied with a lengthy résumé of the events that had precipitated the war and made Spanish surrender of Cuba a necessity. But, he went on, the United States was inclined to offer "a brave adversary generous terms of peace." In terms almost identical to those put forward in June, McKinley said that though the government did not share Spanish apprehension of the dangers of premature independence for Cuba, it recognized the fact that in the "distracted and prostrate condition" of the island, "aid and guidance will be necessary," and these America was prepared to give: Cuba would become an American protectorate for a period to be determined by the United States. Given that, the United States required certain Spanish forfeitures as preliminaries to a formal peace treaty. First, Spain must relinquish all claim to sovereignty over Cuba and immediately evacuate the island. Second, "desirous of exhibiting signal generosity," the president eschewed a demand for a cash indemnity for the prosecution of the war. Instead, to compensate for the losses and expenses to the United States, he required the cession of Puerto Rico and also an island in the Ladrones, probably Guam. Third, on similar grounds, the United States was "entitled to occupy" and would hold the city, bay, and harbor of Manila pending conclusion of a peace treaty that would determine the control, disposition, and government of the archipelago. If Spain accepted these terms in their entirety, the United States was

ready to name commissioners to meet with their Spanish counterparts
for settling the final particulars and drafting a treaty of peace.[14]

Notified that the president's reply was ready, Jules Cambon hastened to the White House. He was no longer merely a messenger, but
had received credentials from the Spanish government authorizing
him to act on Spain's behalf, with full powers to negotiate. He had
also been informed by Madrid that it was anxious to conclude an
armistice without delay and was very reluctant to part with any territory other than Cuba, the ostensible cause of the war. When Cambon
read the American demands he was nothing less than appalled, and
pleaded for easier terms. "With regard to Cuba," he said, Spain was
disposed to go further than the American demand for relinquishment
of sovereignty—she was willing to permit a full American annexation. But the claim for Puerto Rico and Guam was unacceptable.
Merely because "the fortune of arms has permitted an American soldier to put his foot" to certain ground did not make that ipso facto
conquered territory. The American invasion of Mexico in 1847 was
brought up as an example. The United States had not taken all the
land it had "conquered" in that war, and it certainly at this point had
not occupied all of Puerto Rico, or taken Manila.[15]

Secretary Day responded by reminding Cambon that it would be
very difficult to find another example where a victor, after a costly
war, did not demand a cash indemnity. "This is true," Cambon
agreed, "but is not the cession of Cuba the richest of indemnification?" However great the cost of the war to the United States, to demand the rest of the Antilles and Guam far exceeded Spanish
responsibilities as a vanquished power. McKinley now stepped in: the
first points, he said—Cuba, Puerto Rico, and Guam—"do not admit
of discussion." As for the future of the Philippines, "its control, possession, and government" would be resolved by the peace negotiators, though he was determined not to modify the basic particular of
holding Manila, the bay, and the port.[16]

After a pressing appeal to McKinley's generosity, Cambon was
able to winkle a slight easement from the president; in reference to
the Philippines, despite Day's opposition, the word "possession" was
changed to "disposition." Cambon would later inform the Spanish
government that when Day left the room to make the correction on the
document, McKinley dropped his official pose and "talked familiarly

with me," expressing sorrow that Spain had not sought peace immediately after the Battle of Manila Bay. Had she done so, McKinley said,
"the conditions which we would have demanded would have been
less rigorous than those of the present." If these stipulations were
now refused, McKinley went on, Spain would necessarily be exposed
to "greater sacrifices." He begged Cambon to make this known to
Madrid in no uncertain terms. When Day returned to the room, it remained only to raise the matter of where the peace negotiations should
take place; McKinley desired Washington, "[W]here the Spanish
plenipotentiaries would be courteously received." The question would
be transmitted to Madrid.[17]

After two and a half hours, Cambon took his leave. In a cable to the
French foreign minister pointing out the intransigence of the American
position, he stated his belief that Spain would gain nothing by any
delay: "If the Madrid Cabinet procrastinates in its reply and does not
resign itself at once to certain necessary sacrifices, such as Porto Rico,
the conditions that will be imposed on it later will be harder."[18]

Almodóvar nonetheless sent back instructions for the ambassador
to seek modifications. He desperately wanted to substitute something
for Puerto Rico, again contending that Spain had not started the war
and that responsibility for indemnification should instead fall to Cuba.
Almodóvar cited the example of the Schleswig-Holstein War of 1864,
when Prussia had seized the two provinces from Denmark; it was out
of the two duchies that the indemnity to Prussia had been forced, and
not out of Denmark itself. Almodóvar also held that the provision concerning the Philippines lacked precision, arguing that Spain should
continue to exercise sovereignty in the archipelago at the conclusion of
hostilities and that the "temporary occupation of Manila, its port,
[and] the bay" by the United States was to continue only for the time
necessary for an understanding between the two countries regarding
administrative reforms. Further, any discussions concerning the future
of the Philippines were to be held between the Spanish and Americans
only; the insurgents must be completely excluded.[19]

Cambon returned to the White House on August 4 to discuss the
points raised by Almodóvar. Spain, he said, considered the American
conditions "excessively rigorous" and the ceding of Puerto Rico as
"particularly severe." Cambon argued that Puerto Rico "has not for
a moment been an element of conflict" between Spain and the United

States, that its people remained loyal to Spain, and that Spain desired in consequence that the Americans accept other territory instead. But McKinley showed himself, according to Cambon, "inflexible," reiterating that the only question not definitely resolved was that of the Philippines; Puerto Rico was not a matter open to discussion.[20]

Seeking any balm, no matter how minor, Cambon asked if the negotiations for the final treaty might be held in Paris. To this McKinley was willing to bend, stipulating that each negotiating team consist of five commissioners. In his account of the conversations, Cambon again pressed upon Almodóvar his belief that any vacillation would further aggravate the severity of the American conditions.

At this point in the indirect American-Spanish talks, an unforeseen incident erupted that might have given Spain some much needed leverage. The round-robin letter citing the deplorable condition of the Fifth Corps in Cuba was leaked to the press. McKinley was furious when he read the accounts in the evening papers, realizing they constituted public notice of America's possible inability to hold the only territory thus far actually surrendered by Spain—eastern Oriente Province. He was, according to Russell Alger, "very much excited and indignant." The public clamor for the return of the troops made a shaky platform on which to make sweeping demands. Cambon wrote that had he known of the military situation earlier, he "might have been able to make use of it with Mr. McKinley to obtain better conditions for Spain." In fact, though the round-robin did cause some acute embarrassment to the administration, the imminent conquest of Puerto Rico and the capture of Manila undercut any purchase Spain might gain by using the plight of the army at Santiago to soften the American terms. Indeed, if Sagasta and Almodóvar had seized upon this to delay matters, the American conditions would certainly have become more galling and exacting.[21]

In an effort to modify the American provisos, Cambon informed the McKinley administration that constitutional restraints precluded Spain from evacuating any territory before the signing of a peace treaty, and further, the Cortes needed to authorize any such settlement. More significant was Almodóvar's other tack. In a formal note to Secretary Day, the Spanish government reluctantly swallowed the dicta regarding Cuba, Puerto Rico, and Guam, but hedged on the Philippines. Though Sagasta and his cabinet agreed to discuss the question at a formal peace conference, they did not renounce the sovereignty of Spain over the archipelago, leaving it to the negotiators to arrive at the proper solution, agreeing "to such reforms which the conditions of these possessions and the level of culture of their natives may render desirable." Subject to this, Spain would accept the still unformed Philippine article in the American demands.[22]

Cambon presented the Spanish note on August 9, and reported back that during its translated reading both McKinley and Day became "visibly annoyed." After a prolonged silence, McKinley spoke: "I demand of Spain the cession and consequently the immediate evacuation of the islands of Cuba and Puerto Rico." Instead of the "categorical" acceptance the administration had expected, the Spanish government instead offered a response "in which it invokes the necessity of obtaining the approbation of the Cortes. I can not," McKinley said, "lend myself to entering into these considerations of domestic government." Sensing that McKinley was on the verge of terminating the conversation, Cambon begged the president to state what "pledges of sincerity" Spain could offer. McKinley answered immediately, "There is a means of putting an end to all quibbles. We can draft a . . . protocol which will set forth the conditions proposed to Spain," on the terms already formulated. The two governments could simply sign a contract stating the premises and arranging a peace conference to hammer them out. This executive agreement would not require legislative confirmation, it would merely bring to a halt hostilities; it would be, in effect, an armistice, on the basis of certain preliminary agreements.[23]

The following day, August 10, Secretary Day forwarded the draft protocol to Cambon. It was a document McKinley would later describe as a "virtual ultimatum." Cambon immediately recommended to Madrid that it acquiesce; if not, "Spain will have nothing more to expect from a conqueror resolved to procure all the profit possible from the advantages it has obtained." The terms of the protocol differed from those offered on July 30 only in the mention of commissions to supervise the evacuation of the Antilles and of commissioners of peace to meet in Paris not later than October 1. Cambon added one very significant point. Article VI now included specific notice that hostilities would cease with the signing of the document and all forces were to remain in their present positions.[24]

The Sagasta government accepted the inevitable. After a cabinet meeting in which Almodóvar reviewed the protocol, they authorized Cambon to sign in the name of Spain. This, finally, reflected Spain's realization that the United States intended to force even more drastic outcomes if she continued to procrastinate. The large garrisons at Havana, Manila, and San Juan, all as yet undefeated in the field, would eventually be forced to ignominious capitulation because they could not be reinforced or provisioned by sea, and further hostilities might well entail a naval attack on the Spanish coast.

The protocol was signed in the White House on August 12. There were two copies, parallel versions in French and English. On McKinley's instructions, reporters and photographers were excluded. Day, the only cabinet member present, brought in his three assistant secretaries. McKinley arrived with four members of the White House staff. Cambon and his first secretary of legation were ushered into the Cabinet Room. "Mr. Ambassador," said Day, "the papers are ready." Cambon and Day took seats and signed the statement of terms, and with only one exception, the war was over. Assistant Navy Secretary Charles Allen and a photographer were let into the room. The president shook Cambon's hand and warmly thanked the ambassador and France for their good offices in bringing about the armistice. McKinley invited Cambon to stay for the signing of the proclamation to American forces ending hostilities.[25]

Rufus Day turned to the big globe in the room and said to the president's secretary, George Cortelyou, "Let's see what we get by this." Though the elation of colonialism would pass, the decision to demand colonies was of enormous importance, signaling the entrance of the United States on the world stage as a principal player. Though it would rear its head again, notably in the years between World Wars I and II, the era of continuous policy American isolationism had drawn to a close. The placid, insular America was gone. Horace Porter, the American ambassador to France, summed it up in a letter to Mark Hannah: "No war in history has accomplished so much in so short a time with so little loss." Senator Redfield Proctor agreed: "The nation has at a bound gone forward in the estimation of the world more than we would have done in fifty years of peace. It is almost a creation or new birth." Finley Peter Dunne's fictional satirist, "Mr. Dooley," perhaps put the national mood best: "We ar-re a gr-reat people," said his friend, Mr. Hennessey. "We ar-re that," Dooley replied. "We ar-re that. An' th' best iv it is, we know we ar-re."[26]

Eugenio Montero Ríos, leader of the Spanish Liberal Party and soon to head Spain's peace commission, signaled Madrid's view of the protocol. It made "the catastrophe [of the war] definitive and irreparable," and left only one large question to be decided at Paris, the future of the Philippines. But the outcome of the war and the signing of the protocol ensured the United States held the "whip hand" during the final peace negotiations. The state of the Philippines, Montero Ríos knew, would be decided in Washington, not Paris; Spain would lose everything.[27]

Along the wires and submarine cables, the news of the armistice flashed to the American military commanders in Cuba and Puerto Rico, where operations immediately ceased. But there was the unavoidable delay in reaching the Philippines. At the time of the signing, 4:35 P.M. Washington time, it was the morning of August 13 on the other side of the world and U.S. troops were closing in on Manila. It would be three days before a steamer from Hong Kong arrived with the news, by which time, the city had fallen to the Americans.

McKinley quickly selected the American team of peace commissioners. Rufus Day, who held moderate views on the Philippines, was designated chairman. To take his place as secretary of state, John Hay was recalled from his post in London. The selection of the experienced, internationalist Hay, highly intelligent, widely traveled, with a host of influential friends, was yet another indicator of America's entrance into world politics. Knowing that the U.S. Senate had the final word on all treaties, McKinley shrewdly chose three members of the Foreign Relations Committee for the commission: Chairman Cushman K. Davis of Minnesota and William P. Frye of Maine were both fire-eating Republican jingoes as regards large-policy expansionism. Senator George Gray, a conservative Democrat from Delaware who had deplored the acquisition of Hawaii, represented the antiexpansionists. Whitelaw Reid, former ambassador to France, expansionist, and Republican Party stalwart, publisher of the *New York Tribune*, rounded out the team. With Day having moderate views on expansion, and only Gray opposed, the large-policy advocates held sway, just as McKinley intended.

Premier Sagasta faced a far more difficult task in choosing his plenipotentiaries. Just days after the signing of the protocol, Francisco Silvela, one of the leading Conservative critics, inaugurated a soul-searing examination of the disastrous war, maintaining that Spain was now "*sin pulso,*" without pulse, devoid of life, and that only a massive effort to reconstruct and dignify the action of the nation over the next months and, indeed, years, could restore the nation to vigor. Speaking again some weeks later, Silvela placed the blame for the utter defeat of Spain squarely on the Liberal ministry of Sagasta. Given that, the Conservatives refused to serve on the peace commission, forcing Sagasta to rely on members of his own party. To head the delegation, he chose party leader and Senate President Eugenio Montero Ríos. For associates, Sagasta appointed Senator Buenaventura Abarzuza (author of the ill-fated Cuban reform laws that bore his name); Associate Justice of the Supreme Court José de Garnica y Díaz; Wenceslas Ramírez de Villa-Urrutia, minister to Belgium; and to provide the commission military advice, Major General Rafael Cerero y Sáenz, chief engineer of the First Army Corps. Rufus Day, when he sat down at the negotiating table, considered the Spaniards "men of ability and dignity."[28]

Spain revealed her negotiating position in early September, when Almodóvar noted that the surrender of Manila had taken place one day *after* the signing of the protocol ending hostilities on August 12. He instructed Cambon to assert that Manila and its environs should be considered as ceded temporarily by Spain without renunciation of her sovereignty and "not as conquered . . . by a belligerent army." The distinction, he maintained, was "essential and the consequences are radically different." The American reply defied most historical precedents and the language of the pact itself, claiming that the suspension of hostilities began not with the signing of the armistice, but when notification reached the commanders in the field. For the United States, Day claimed, it did not matter whether the basis of American authority at Manila was the protocol or the Spanish surrender of the city because, "in any case, the powers of the military occupant are the same."[29]

To say the Philippines were on President McKinley's mind is an understatement; he had been thinking of their future since receiving Dewey's telegram of the victory in Manila Bay. But it was still far from certain how much of the archipelago the United States would take. The European powers and Japan were actively carving up China, Korea,

Southeast Asia; if America was to gain a trade advantage in the region, it needed a secure foothold. McKinley had first regarded the city of Manila as sufficient for the purpose; extensive territory in the rest of the islands was not critical to commercial aims. There were also political risks, colonial administration headaches, and international involvements that large landgrabs brought with them. Taking it all was also really anathema to McKinley's conscience. He had already denounced forced annexation as "criminal aggression," had disavowed "greed of conquest," and had insisted that justice and humanity were the grounds for entering the war against Spain. In allegiance to America's traditional principles and heritage of keeping expansion to continental limits, he naturally shied from committing the nation to a path of colonization in the Philippines.[30]

Night after night the president walked the floors of the White House, often falling to his knees to pray. Yet he was simply not able to bring himself to renounce a demand for the islands. He could find no course other than annexation that promised peace in the Pacific and protection of American interests, strategic and commercial. Commander Royal B. Bradford, chief of the navy's Bureau of Equipment, was brought in as an adviser. He had been to the Philippines three times, making a study of coaling stations and naval bases. He argued that in wartime, occupation of Manila and the bay without the rest of Luzon was a source of weakness rather than strength. But taking just Luzon posed its own problems. So crowded together were the islands that any one of them needed a large defensive garrison if others were in an enemy's possession. Economic interdependence was another deterrent to sharing the archipelago with a commercial rival. Separation of the islands from their commercial and political hub at Manila was impractical.[31]

The "powers" had to be considered. German imperialism was creeping ever forward, and the State Department was frankly aghast at encouragement of Germany in that direction by the American ambassador in Berlin, Andrew White. Hay warned the president that if Germany succeeded in her ambitions for a substantial Pacific empire, there was "grave danger of complication with other European powers."[32]

Japan had already officially offered to oversee the Philippines should the Americans decline, but Japanese domination meant grave complications with Russia, a conflict already festering in East Asia.

Great Britain hoped from the outset that the United States would claim the whole archipelago, and had become so alarmed for the security of her nearby Malayan colonies at America's vacillation that she insisted on an option to buy the Philippines should the United States force Spain to sell them. Eventually McKinley narrowed his options to two: permitting Spain to keep the whole thing, except for a cable and naval base at Manila; or the United States taking it all. He was loath to abandon the islands to Spanish misrule, and at least in this, the American public was united.

If Spain were enabled to retain the Philippines, less Manila, the question arose of whether she could afford them. Even with Manila's revenues, the colony had been a drain on Spanish resources. The indications were that if the islands were restored to Spain, she would eventually be forced to sell. Secretary of State John Hay advised adding a stipulation that if the islands were restored to Spain, she must secure the approval of the United States before "alienating" any part of the territory to a foreign power.

But the more the administration thought of allowing Spain to keep the Philippines, the more difficult that option seemed. The machinery of Spanish colonial government had collapsed. Isolated Spanish garrisons were helpless as the insurgent rebellion spread across Luzon and to neighboring islands. What held the Philippines together now was a consuming hatred of Spain, and continued Spanish proprietorship would merely stimulate the rebellion—a sure invitation to foreign intervention. Independence was never seriously considered. For a brief moment McKinley examined, then rejected a proposal of Philippine self-government under an American protectorate. But from the president's viewpoint that was the worst possible scenario: responsibility without authority.

Given the administration's perspective, a native, independent government was impossible. In the Philippines, as in Cuba, the administration had refused to ally itself officially with the rebels. On the grounds of justice to all Filipino people, McKinley could not consent to support rule by an arbitrary faction—Aguinaldo's. On grounds of national security, the United States could not associate itself with a weak sovereignty that was inexperienced in resisting foreign intrigues and unable to prevent foreign interference in the archipelago's affairs. In Cuba, the Monroe Doctrine and the proximity to the United States obviated concerns about foreign intervention. This was not the case with the Philippines.

Anything but outright annexation by the United States would lead to partition of the Philippines on the international auction block. McKinley's choice seemed inescapable, but he had not yet pronounced it when, in consultation with the cabinet, he drew up instructions for the peace commissioners. The notion of keeping only the city, port, and bay of Manila was now expanded to include American jurisdiction over Luzon as necessary protection for the naval base. But the picture was still not complete. They awaited advice from Merritt and Dewey. General Greene was summoned home to give his counsel. Doubts began to creep into the president's mind. In his confidential instructions to the peace commissioners, while remaining firm on all points of the protocol, he waffled on the Philippines, trying to balance the case for "moderation, restraint, and reason in victory."[33]

Assuming the lofty ground, something the president was very adept at, he told the commissioners the nation had taken up arms only in sublime obedience to humanitarian dictates and to fulfill high public and moral obligations. Loud jingoes aside, America had "no design of aggrandizement and no ambition of conquest." Yet the imperial obligations imposed by the presence of American forces in Manila could not be ignored. As McKinley ponderously told the commissioners, "The march of events rules and overrules human action." The war had fortuitously brought to the United States "new duties and responsibilities" to be discharged "as becomes a great nation on whose growth and career from the beginning the Ruler of Nations has plainly written the high command and pledge of civilization."[34]

Nearly everyone who visited the White House that late summer offered a solution to the Philippine problem. Missionaries wanted the islands to save souls for Christianity. Sentiment in the business community was mixed, though most of its spokesmen argued for acquisition of the islands as a stepping-stone to the lucrative Asian trade. *Bradstreet's* magazine thought that in time Manila might rival Hong Kong as a "distributive trade center."[35]

Navy Secretary John D. Long received much correspondence regarding the Philippines. One writer compared Dewey's battle in Manila Bay with Robert Clive's victory at the Battle of Plassey in

1757, which cemented Britain's preeminent position in India. The writer argued the popular view that Pacific expansion was justified on the grounds that the United States required new markets for its exploding industrial production. "Even now," he said, "our domestic consumption cannot take more than seventy-five percent of our manufactured products. . . . Hence the necessity of great foreign markets for such surplus."[36]

The ethical argument for an expansionist policy was provided Long by the Reverend Jesse H. Jones. Though he had originally opposed the war, the cleric was now ready to harvest its benefits. The United States must retain the Philippines: "We have taken them by our might; we can not give them up except in utter weakness." Otherwise, said Jones, "we will be false to our duty to that people and to the whole human race to lead the way to freedom and progress, hope and prosperity." This was an appealing argument, associating overseas expansion with the civilizing mission that America claimed for itself throughout its history.[37]

There was also a growing group of antiexpansionists that corresponded with Long. Perhaps most notable was William Endicott Jr., son of a Massachusetts jurist and former secretary of war. He argued two cogent points against expansion in general: the war had been waged to free Cuba, a humanitarian motive that precluded territorial expansion; and absorption of overseas colonies dictated a total change in the nature of America's government, in particular a much larger military and naval establishment. In Endicott's opinion, "the perils now confronting the republic are greater than at any time in its history, save only during the Civil War." He thought it "wise statesmanship" to escape the dangers of the larger policy "by returning to the traditions of the fathers," concluding, "it may be old fogeyism but I think George Washington is a safer counselor to tie to than [Senator] Lodge."[38]

Long thought so, too, but he knew what the people were demanding. To a friend in Hingham, Massachusetts, he wrote, "You and I don't want the Philippines, but it's no use disguising the fact that an overwhelming majority of the people do."[39]

McKinley, in leaving the Philippine question open to later settlement at the peace conference, actually committed his administration to retaining the territory. Whatever else he might say in his few guarded statements, he knew that postponing the ultimate question would develop and focus public opinion in support of his decision to retain the islands. There was only the briefest time at which he could have rejected keeping the Philippines, and that was immediately after receiving the telegram of Dewey's victory. Now that hostilities had ended, he could bide his time and delay any proceedings while he gauged the public temper and maneuvered factions of support. As one historian said, "In the end, he adroitly appeared to capitulate and accept the islands, just as he had capitulated to the demand to free Cuba."[40]

On September 16, as the peace commission prepared to depart for Paris, McKinley held a farewell dinner at the White House. There were final instructions, and the president spoke informally, asking for views. Day still shrank from a full annexation commitment and believed that the United States held only a slender claim to the islands either by right of conquest or as a war indemnity. At most, he would take Luzon. Territorial expansion, Day thought, should be limited to the Caribbean. Cushman K. Davis somewhat moderated his stand on getting the whole thing and now wanted only Manila and Luzon, suggesting that perhaps the Netherlands could be persuaded to buy the predominantly Muslim islands of Mindanao and the Sulu group. Senator William Frye noted New England's general objections to annexation, but nevertheless favored absorbing the whole archipelago. Gray, who was not there, would have sided with Day. Whitelaw Reid wanted it all and assumed McKinley agreed with him. "He [McKinley] believed," Reid noted in his diary, "the acquisition of territory was naturally attractive to the American mind . . . but thought it would probably be more attractive [now rather] than later on, when the difficulties, expense and loss of life which it entailed, became manifest." What was the president prepared to do? "He thought," Reid wrote, "we could not possibly give up Manila, and doubted the wisdom of attempting to hold it without the entire island to which it belonged. Beyond this he did not seem inclined to go."[41]

As McKinley read the formal instructions, lofty sentences in which he rationalized his course of action, the path became clearer: the acquisition of an empire, for which he had previously shown no personal inclination. "The plain teachings of history," he intoned, justified the independence of Cuba, under American guidance, and the annexation of Puerto Rico. In the Pacific, the United States could not accept less than "the cession in full right and sovereignty of the island of Luzon"; the U.S. Navy had won the Battle of Manila Bay, and the U.S. Army had captured the capital city. He said a few words regarding commercial opportunities that American diplomacy could not ignore, but observed that this depended less on large territorial possession than on the concept of free trade in the Pacific: "Asking only for the open door for ourselves, we are ready to accord the open door to others." Finally, McKinley stressed the need for quick action in the negotiations; he wanted the treaty ready to submit to the Senate at the start of the new legislative season in January 1899.[42]

On arriving in Paris, the commissioners gained a general impression that the European powers would pose no obstacle to the American position and, indeed, nothing was to occur to encourage the forlorn Spanish hope of a European diplomatic intervention on their behalf. French Foreign Minister Theophilé Delcassé invited the U.S. and Spanish delegations to an informal breakfast. At the meal, Reid wrote to McKinley that Fernando de León y Castillo, the Spanish ambassador to France, "struck at once what I believe is to be their permanent tone—one of rather proud supplication. . . . 'You have had a great victory,' " León y Castillo had commented, "the first you have really had over a foreign foe, for Mexico didn't count. Now you must prove your greatness by your magnanimity." Later in the smoking room, he again had Reid's ear. "Do not forget that we are poor," he said, "do not forget that we have been defeated; do not forget that it was Spain that opened the New World; do not forget that the greatness of your victory will be dimmed by any lack of magnanimity to a fallen foe." This statement to Reid indicated at the outset that Spain recognized its lack of bargaining power. In the absence of diplomatic support from the European powers, it had been forced to depend for mercy on the goodwill of the conqueror.[43]

On October 1, just as the Paris talks were getting under way, Aguinaldo sent one of his trusted advisers, Felipe Agoncillo, to Washington to ask President McKinley personally what the administration planned to do with the Philippines and, according to Aguinaldo, to avert a future Philippine-American war. McKinley listened to a long recital of grievances against Spain, slowly and painstakingly delivered through an interpreter. Agoncillo mentioned that the Philippines had been pledged independence in return for their help to the Americans, the Pratt "promise" allegedly made in Singapore prior to Dewey's sailing for Manila. The president made no response to Agoncillo's talk of independence, asking only for a copy of the statement to study later. Hardly mollified, Agoncillo told McKinley that he would journey to Paris to inform the commissioners that "never under any circumstances [would the Filipinos] consent again to be placed in any manner in any degree under the rule of Spain." The president sent Agoncillo's statement to Paris, with the admonition that he be given no official recognition. He was barred from the conference room, and the Filipino position was never brought forward in the negotiations.[44]

The basic strategies of the two sides became evident at the very beginning of the talks. Before sitting down with the Spanish, Reid convinced his colleagues that they ought to seek agreement on the issues already settled in principle by the armistice protocol of August 12, especially the question of the independence of Cuba and the cession of Puerto Rico, before dealing with the sticky matter of the Philippines. The Spanish opted to maneuver differently. Seeking to retain control of the Philippines, they hoped to carry the legal argument that Spain still retained sovereignty over the archipelago. At the first session, Eugenio Montero Ríos advanced the claim that the capitulation of Manila, which took place after the signing of the protocol, could not serve as a legal basis for negotiations concerning the disposition of the Philippines. Though Reid thought the Spaniard had merit in his argument, Day quashed it, insisting the question lay outside the purview of the negotiators. The Americans were in possession of the city and that put an end to all argument. As Day hammered home the point, Reid observed that Montero Ríos "looked as if he was losing his last friend on earth, and the others obviously experienced considerable emotion also at being thus brought face to face with the results of the war."[45]

Mirroring the Spanish diplomacy before the war, Montero Ríos took refuge in delay. Reid wrote McKinley that the Spanish delegation leader was "so long-winded in Spanish that if he had equal command of one or two other languages he would be intolerable." But Reid clearly understood the Spanish method, jotting in his diary, "Since they have to consent to the dismemberment of their . . . [empire], they wish to make the process as slow as possible, and to be able to show to their countrymen that they protested and struggled at every turn, using every resource to avert their unhappy fate."[46]

Lacking an alternative course of action, Spain strove to place the United States in an indefensible position before international opinion by presenting the claim, a plausible one, that the Americans could not take the Philippines by right of conquest, as truly, they had won only Manila, Cavite, and their immediate environs. Likewise, the post-armistice capture of Manila was open to serious question. If the Spaniards could prolong the negotiations they might generate sympathy among the powers and conceivably open the way to international arbitration, a procedure from which Spain could actually benefit: certainly, they could do no worse than in the present bilateral dealing with the Americans. The Spanish also sought to delay a decision at least until the American congressional elections, hoping that an upset Democratic victory might force moderate terms on the McKinley administration. Sensing the intent of the Spanish commissioners, the American delegation attempted to force the proceedings forward. When Day learned the Spanish wished to discuss certain minor questions concerning the evacuation of Cuba and Puerto Rico, he immediately squelched it as a delaying maneuver.

At the October 5 session, the Spanish moved from the trivial to the momentous as Montero Ríos shocked the American delegation by attempting to saddle the United States with the Cuban debt—the monetary obligation of Cuba incurred by Spain during the late War of Independence, a sum of around $400 million. Montero Ríos understood that Spanish creditors, both private and governmental, were extremely unlikely to recover any claims made on Cuba. Given the financial crisis in Spain, this matter took on major significance. It was an essential reason Spain wished to transfer Cuban sovereignty to the United States rather than merely relinquishing ownership to an independent, and bankrupt, Cuba. John Bassett Moore of the State Department, counsel and secretary of the American delegation, judged that the Spanish considered "these financial burdens . . . more important, from the pecuniary standpoint, than . . . the relinquishment of territory." Montero Ríos realized that in renouncing sovereignty over Cuba, the United States would have "excellent ground for not accepting, or . . . even discussing anything relative to the transmission of the Cuban debts . . . which are now pressing upon Spain."[47]

Almodóvar supported Montero Ríos in this ploy, instructing him to advocate strongly the transfer of Cuban sovereignty to the United

States and have the treaty specify "mutual rights and obligations," with precise wording regarding the payment of the Cuban debt. The linking of Cuban sovereignty and the debt questions provoked an angry rebuttal from the American side of the table. Day quickly informed Hay in Washington: Unless otherwise instructed, he cabled, "we expect to take position . . . that the Spanish proposals as to so-called Cuban charges and obligations . . . for the service of the island"—rebellion costs, capital expenses, civil and ecclesiastical salaries, military and civilian pensions—"are excluded from discussion." The Puerto Rico debt, should Spain introduce that, would be likewise dismissed by the United States as beyond the pale of the negotiations.[48]

The American delegation, having the full support of the McKinley administration, stood firm on the language of the armistice protocol concerning the question of Spain's relinquishment of Cuban title: independent, not annexed. Oddly, Gray, the antiexpansionist, favored U.S. sovereignty because it would minimize complications when the United States began "pacifying [the] island and restoring order in accordance with our own ideas."[49]

On October 14, after fruitless discussions with the Spanish, Day proposed to resolve the deadlock by drafting a clause providing for Cuban independence in language closely resembling that of the protocol; Spain, having already signed that document, might find this one acceptable. It did not. Montero Ríos cabled Almodóvar that "after four hours of discussion I saw that it was necessary to declare that it was an absolute condition of Spain that the treaty contain the acceptance on the part of the United States of the sovereignty that the Crown of Spain renounces."[50]

To resolve the issue their way, the Spanish commissioners attempted personal diplomacy. At a dinner in the U.S. embassy, Montero Ríos explained to Reid, who spoke French and was thus the only member of the American delegation who could converse with the Spanish without an interpreter, that Spain wished to accumulate sufficient funds for economic development at home out of moneys gained from the disposition of her colonies. "The whole tone of his talk," Reid noted of Montero Ríos, "indicated a readiness to be rid of the colonies, but a feeling that they ought to get money enough for them to be able to prosecute internal improvements and develop their own country." Ambassador León y Castillo joined them, advancing the argument that American acceptance of the Cuban debt would demonstrate magnanimity to a fallen nation by a victorious one. Reid was unmoved, insisting the Spanish could not expect the United States to pay for Spain's war against the Cuban rebels.[51]

Realizing the Americans meant to hold firm on the debt issue and that it might cause the peace negotiations to collapse, bringing a resumption of hostilities, Montero Ríos proposed a tactic to Almodóvar that could keep the talks going and cause minimal damage to Spanish pride in the process. Given its inability to offer further armed resistance, Spain could announce that it had succumbed to the American demands regarding Cuban independence and debt, but with extreme objection and a refusal to insert the matter into any final treaty. Spain would "accede to what is demanded" without acknowledging the right of such demands. It meant the possible rupture of the talks, but at the same time offered "the advantage of saving our unfortunate country from new disasters." It would be peace without a treaty.[52]

This truly reflected the feebleness of the Spanish position. Almodóvar favored a different approach, using the diplomatic surrender suggested by Montero Ríos only as a last resort. Believing the United States could not submit to a sudden end to the conference, "which would merit before the world the qualification of brutal," Almodóvar wanted to propose arbitration to end the impasse. If the Americans refused, their actions would "serve to augment the justice of Spain in this contention." It was hardly less humiliating than the plan pushed by Montero Ríos. Spain, the diplomats would come to realize, had to adopt highly undesirable policies because it lacked the power to do anything else.[53]

Putting the Almodóvar plan into operation, León y Castillo cornered Reid at a small dinner in the Spanish embassy and explained the inauspicious consequences of a deadlock. Making an attempt at flattery, he told the American, "You are the only diplomat there. It is the duty of a diplomat to find some middle way, to avoid the absolute failure of negotiations, to accomplish something." When Reid proved unreceptive, León y Castillo suggested the negotiators approve a mixed commission to apportion the Cuban debt. Reid, to their great and naive surprise, remained adamantly opposed.[54]

At the October 24 plenary session, Day became visibly impatient at continued Spanish efforts to transfer Cuban sovereignty and the debt to the United States. He sought authority from the State Department "to repeat that our position on the Cuban debt is final," and if the Spanish rejected that, nothing else was left than to give notice of one more meeting to withdraw the armistice protocol. The war might actually be renewed. Hay made no objection, and it appeared the conference had reached deadlock.[55]

Day, however, decided to go the extra mile to keep the talks from collapsing. He suggested that a clause might be inserted into the treaty obligating the United States to use its good offices with Cuba in arranging compensation to Spain for the costs of certain insular improvements. A mixed commission could be created to determine any Cuban obligations under this clause. If such an arrangement were made for Cuba, it would also have to be adopted at least in part for the Philippines, Puerto Rico, and Guam. Day believed Spain had some merit in its argument that certain local debts could be passed on with sovereignty. But the McKinley administration totally rejected this, Hay cabling back that "under no circumstances will the Government of the United States assume any part of what is known as the Cuban debt"; nor would it use its "good offices" to induce any Cuban government to assume it.[56]

Sensing that the Americans had called their bluff on the debt issue, Montero Ríos conceived the idea of exchanging the debt for some American monetary compensation for whatever they wished to retain of the Philippines. To explore this, he once again made informal inquiries among the Americans. León y Castillo spoke to the U.S. ambassador to France, Horace Porter, who agreed to pass on the Spanish suggestions to Rufus Day. León y Castillo also urged the necessity of Philippine compensation on Whitelaw Reid, saying, "Montero Ríos would be hooted through the streets of Madrid if he obtained no abatement of . . . some terms." Reid replied that he and his colleagues could not expect a rousing welcome home if they made concessions contrary to American interests, but he hinted at the possibility of some type of arrangement aimed at loosening the terms. He warned, though, that the American people were determined to get a sizable chunk of the archipelago.[57]

The Spanish now opted to push ahead with their plan to raise the Philippine issue despite Reid's warning. Montero Ríos offered acceptance of the American clauses for Cuba, Puerto Rico, and Guam, but subject to the outcome of future discussions, meaning, in fact, that his acceptance could be withdrawn later. Emilio de Ojeda, secretary of the Spanish delegation, explained to Day after a formal negotiating session that Spain "accepted [the] articles in the hope of liberal treatment in the Philippine islands," adding that "no government in Spain could sign [a] treaty giving up everything and live, and that such surrender without some relief would mean national bankruptcy."[58]

Montero Ríos reported to Almodóvar that if the Americans made no promise of compensation for what they wished to grab in the Philippines, he would ask for a suspension of the conference. In that event, again emphasizing Spain's weakness in confronting the American terms, he proposed submitting a document stating that though Spain did not accept the American demands, it must bow to *force majeure.*" This posture, he said, constituted "the only road which prudence, combined with dignity, leaves Spain in facing a conqueror who would overthrow . . . the most elementary and sacred principles of justice." He had, however, serious doubts that Spain would receive any compromise from the Americans, who were obviously not in a generous mood.[59]

While the conference was deadlocked on the matter of the Cuban debt, and before taking up the the Philippines, the American delegation consulted various observers in preparation for the coming discussion. General Merritt arrived in Paris with the reports of a number of officers from his late command. He assured the American commissioners that the insurgents would fight to the very bitter end against Spain, and that Spain had not the strength to quell them. "I think," he said, "there is no danger of conflict as long as these people think the United States is going to take possession there. If they imagine . . . that the Spaniards are to be reinstated . . . I think they will be very violent."[60]

Merritt also brought Admiral Dewey's noncommittal views to Paris. Dewey did not take a definite position concerning the disposition of the islands, more or less advocating the retention of Luzon only, and irritating the expansionists on the commission. When Reid questioned Merritt about this in private, the general hazarded a guess that Dewey might be considering a presidential candidacy in 1900,

and indeed there was a short-lived boomlet in that direction. It was
evident to Merritt that Dewey had his eye on the future and wished to
avoid statements that could make him "unavailable as a candidate."
The commission considered Merritt's briefing and Dewey's views,
such as they were, highly disappointing. They had hoped for competent military advice on the matter of annexation, and thus far had not
gotten it.[61]

If the expansionists were disappointed with Admiral Dewey, they
received a heady briefing from Commander Royal Bradford, the
naval attaché to the commission. He was in favor of annexing Cuba,
was not averse to taking a slice of China, and had little patience with
the argument of overextension, saying, "If we were to enclose ourselves within a shell, like a turtle, and defend ourselves after the manner of a turtle, then any possession outside of our own country may
be said to be a source of weakness." Bradford not only wanted to acquire all of the Philippines, but also the Carolines in the central Pacific and all of the Ladrones, not just Guam.[62]

After two weeks of discussion with Bradford, commissioners
Davis, Frye, and Reid were confirmed in their belief that the United
States should annex the whole of the Philippines. The reasons were
many: there was no logical way to partition the islands; the whole
group could be defended as easily as part of it; there was the probability that partition would cause disturbances among the Filipino
population; negative influences to commerce would flow from partition; the United States had a moral obligation not to return the islands to a repressive Spain; and the material and moral benefits that
would accrue to the Filipinos as a result of America taking over were
manifest. In opposition, Senator Gray would have no part of them:
the islands were not contiguous with the United States; their possession would require an enlarged navy; American labor would suffer
from annexation; and divisions might develop in the United States
over what he referred to as the "church question"—Protestant mis-
sionary societies in conflict with the Catholic Church. Further, the
United States had no obligation to the Filipinos even if it had conducted military operations in the islands, and the American system of
government had no provision for the colonial administration of a
subject people. Lastly, annexation of the Philippines would sully the
good moral object of the war.

On October 25, Day cabled Secretary of State Hay the opinions of the commissioners, pro and con. He himself did not agree that the United States needed to demand the whole archipelago. The danger of the rest of it passing to a European power could be obviated in a treaty prohibiting "alienation" without the agreement of the United States. "This gives us practical control of the situation," he noted, "with a base for the navy and commerce in the East, and responsibility for the people to whom we owe obligation and those most likely fit for self government." In light of the disagreement in the commission—Davis, Frye, and Reid for all; Gray for none; himself for some—Day asked for immediate instructions.[63]

Hay wired back within twenty-four hours: having spoken to the president, he was unequivocal as to the American position setting the nation on the course of empire. The retention of Manila, or the cession of Luzon, leaving the rest of the islands to Spanish rule or to future contention as a weakly independent state, "cannot be justified on political, commercial, or humanitarian grounds. The cession must be of the whole archipelago or none. The latter is wholly inadmissible, and the former must therefore be required." The president, Hay explained, after the most thorough consideration, was "deeply sensitive" to the grave responsibilities this direction entailed, yet it offered fewer problems than any other path, best serving the interests of the Filipino people, "for whose welfare we cannot escape responsibility."[64]

William McKinley, on whom the final decision lay, had come to this conclusion through two main conduits: a report and briefing by General Francis Vinton Greene and the reception the president received to his speeches during a campaign swing through the Midwest. Greene's memo, which was also presented to the American commissioners in Paris by General Merritt, emphasized that only full annexation would provide peace and prosperity to the Philippines. To return all or part of them to Spain meant continued rebellion, leading inevitably to foreign intervention. Independence, Greene thought, was not an intelligent option. Aguinaldo's insurgent government was a "pure despotism, a dictatorship of the South American type." Independence, according to Greene, did not claim the unstinting loyalty of the Filipino "intelligent classes," who mostly preferred the guiding hand of a strong nation. Their ideal was a Philippine republic under American protection. But it was difficult to see how protection could be offered without leading inevitably to possession. The president had already considered and rejected this course as responsibility without authority, and was glad Greene agreed.[65]

Greene devoted a large part of his briefing and memo to the potential wealth of the islands and the commercial advantages resulting if the archipelago were "explored with American energy." Greene could speak with some authority on the thriving trade at Manila, having been appointed by General Merritt as the chief of the various bureaus of collection, with complete access to fiscal information. He fully believed that trade might be enormously extended under American auspices, but only on condition the country not be divided.[66]

The Philippines aside, the peace talks were in serious danger of foundering on the Cuban debt and sovereignty issues when President McKinley decided to take a midwestern trip to campaign for Republican congressional seats and to measure the mood for Philippine annexation. If the midwestern bulwark of the party favored this huge step, then he could safely ignore opposition in other parts of the country. This tack strongly suggested that the president painfully remembered his near political disaster just before the war, when he had desperately sought an alternative to conflict despite the nearly unanimous public clamor for intervention. If the president hoped the quick military victory or the annexation of Puerto Rico might satisfy the national desire for overseas territory, he soon learned he was wrong. By August, a poll published in the magazine *Public Opinion* showed that 43 percent of the respondents favored retention of the Philippines, while less than 25 percent were opposed; something over 32 percent were "wavering" in favor of keeping the islands. This was something the president could not ignore. Uncle Joe Cannon, chairman of the House Ways and Means Committee, said the "President's ear was so close to the ground it was full of grasshoppers."[67]

William McKinley had not been west of the Mississippi since taking office, and loyal Republicans turned out by the thousands in Iowa, Omaha, St. Louis, and Chicago. From October 11 to October 21, the whole region—and via press accounts, the whole country— resonated with the inspiring generalizations of which the president was a master. On the first day, at Tama, Iowa, the president posed the issue of responsibility "that has been put upon us by the results of the war." At Boone, Iowa, he raised the flag of national unity: "We are all together in this fight; we must be all together in the conclusion." To rousing cheers, the president warmed to his mission.[68]

He spoke of justice and humanity and the "courage of destiny." He trusted that the war would bring "blessings that are now beyond calculation." At Hastings, Iowa, the president voiced a direct allusion to territorial expansion: "We have good money," went the oration, "we have ample revenues, we have unquestioned national credit, but what we want is new markets, and as trade follows the flag it looks very much as if we are going to have new markets."[69]

The heroes of Manila Bay, Santiago, and Puerto Rico were lauded in the speeches. They had made immortal history, and who could diminish the splendor of their deeds? Making barely masked references to expansion, the president said, "Shall we deny ourselves what the rest of the world so freely and so justly accords to us?" The American people would do their duty, he told a cheering crowd in Omaha, and the genius of the nation would make it the equal to every labor. At Springfield, Illinois, he appealed to the nation's humanitarian instincts: "We went to war, not because we wanted to, but because humanity demanded it . . . [and] having gone to war for humanity's sake, we must accept no settlement that will not take into account the interests of humanity." The comment received sustained applause.[70]

Penultimately, the president touched on the theme of destiny, which he clearly developed in Chicago on October 18. "My countrymen," he began, "the currents of destiny flow through the hearts of the people. Who will check them? Who will divert them? And the movements of men, planned and designed by the Master of men, will never be interrupted by the American people"; who were they to stand in the way?[71]

Finally, in the last major speech, given in Chicago the following day, the president combined the themes of humanity, duty, and destiny as they intimated territorial expansion, without ever actually advocating such a path. The war with Spain had been fought to halt "oppression at our very doors," not for territorial gain. That noble sentiment must continue to guide the nation, and the nation must show the world the "full demonstration of the sincerity" of its purpose. He then easily segued into duty, and from there, destiny: "Destiny which results from the duty performed may bring anxiety and perils," the president waxed richly, "but never failure and dishonor."

There was deafening applause. With these sentiments, William McKinley completed his interview with the national heartland and returned to Washington ready to make public his decision concerning the Philippines.[72]

The president had learned what he set out to discover: that the great mass of his supporters approved the annexation of the Philippines, at least in the veiled way he had presented the issue. Had he followed his own private instincts, it is possible he would not have ordered the commissioners to demand all or even part of the islands. Some months later, when he asked President Jacob Gould Schurman of Cornell University to visit the Philippines as head of a commission of inquiry, the academician refused, saying he opposed overseas expansion. To that McKinley replied, "Oh, that need not trouble you. I don't want the Philippines either . . . but . . . [there] was no alternative." Was the president sincere, or was he saying what his listener wanted to hear? We do not know.[73]

On October 28, Hay sent further guidance to the commissioners. The Philippines, he noted, could probably be claimed by right of conquest, even though American forces had taken only Cavite and the peanut fields south of Manila prior to the signing of the armistice protocol. Hay also emphasized certain points that the president had developed during the midwestern trip, namely, that the United States in its demand for the Philippines "should be governed only by motives which will exalt our nation. . . . Territorial expansion should be our least concern." The United States desired the Philippines out of the moral obligations of "duty and humanity."[74]

The American delegation now held its final instructions concerning the one area of policy in the original September 16 directive from the president that had undergone substantial alteration during the peace negotiations. On October 31, Rufus Day announced the American aspiration to annex all of the Philippines, noting that the United States would provide Spain with compensation for "necessary [public] works and improvements of a pacific character." This confirmed the worst fears of the Spanish. Montero Ríos expressed "amazement" at the magnitude of the demand, observing that England, Germany, and Russia would not find this direction by the United States "very much in harmony with the interest of each in the extreme Orient." But in fact, England was in complete favor of the United States taking the

Philippines, while Germany and Spain were making their own secret deals for the purchase of the remnants of the Spanish empire in the Pacific. As for Russia, she was far more concerned with territorial grabbings by Japan on the Asian mainland than with America in the Philippines.[75]

The Spanish delegates wired Almodóvar asking for instructions in the face of the ultimate American demand. First, the duke replied, the Spanish were to insist on retaining the islands; then they were to retreat to a second line of defense, indicating a Spanish willingness to rent "these colonies to development companies under conditions which safeguard all interests." If the United States rejected this stratagem, Spain could then demand a temporary suspension of the talks, giving time for her delegates to consult the government in Madrid on further maneuvers. Almodóvar had an eye on American domestic politics: "Meanwhile," he said, "we shall see if the American elections . . . [bring] conditions [that] change the aspect of negotiations." Outlining this point to León y Castillo, Almodóvar summarized his motives: "By means of these alternative positions we shall be able to continue [negotiations] during the month [of November] until we see if the horizon improves." But these were the actions of a drowning man, and Almodóvar knew it, telling León y Castillo, "I consider . . . that the intention of the Americans is to annex everything of value in the colonial empire of Spain with the least sacrifice possible, and we should exert ourselves to prevent this."[76]

The Spanish position led to some uneasiness among the American delegation. Gray thought Spain might break off the talks entirely. Reid and Frye were somewhat more optimistic, basing their assumptions for a successful conclusion on the American promise to compensate Spain for the cession of the Philippines, but neither was truly confident about a favorable outcome. On October 30, Frye informed President McKinley of his fears that negotiations might fail and proposed to offer $10 million to $20 million as compensation for the islands. "If no treaty, then war," he cabled, "a continued disturbance of business, and expenditure of a million dollars a day, and further loss of life." But if the war should resume, he suggested that the United States militarily occupy the whole of the Philippines.[77]

Through the conduit of John Hay, Frye received McKinley's response to his concerns. On the question of compensation, the commissioners were to be generous in all matters that did not disregard a "principle of duty." Whatever the delegates deemed wise and best in the matter of Spanish debts for internal improvements in the Philippines and public works "of a pacific character" would receive the president's "favorable consideration." But he did not wish the American delegation to disregard "well-established precedents," or to propose any conditions "that will not be worthy of ourselves and merit the approval of the best judgments of mankind." The president was willing to offer a "reasonable sum of money" to compensate Spain for certain civil improvements to the islands, which were fairly chargeable to the United States under established international law. This calmed the fears of the commissioners to a considerable degree, providing as it did some measure of face-saving for Spain.[78]

Yet, at the same time, a majority of the American delegation threw a wrench into the administration's position. On November 3, Day noted to the State Department that captures of territory, namely Manila, after the signing of the armistice protocol must be disregarded and the status quo "restored as far as practicable." The United States, he said, could annex the Philippines not by right of conquest, but only as indemnity for losses and the expenses of the war. For his precedent, Day cited the Pan-American Congress of 1889–90 in which Secretary of State James G. Blaine committed the United States to oppose any territorial acquisitions by conquest. Day maintained, Reid noted in his diary, "that this was the tendency of civilization. . . . [He thought] it would never do for the United States government to take Luzon or any other territory by [right of] conquest."[79]

Reid had pointed out this position to Day some weeks before, but the judge had taken the opposite position at that time. Now he changed his mind and frankly admitted it. McKinley, however, remained adamant. Perhaps to get the commission back on track, John Hay offered the view that Dewey's destruction of the Spanish squadron on May 1 in fact "was the conquest of Manila, the capital of the Philippines," and not the later campaign. To stiffen the resolve of the commissioners, Hay reported that the president was confident they would negotiate a settlement on "just and honorable grounds."[80]

On Friday, November 4, Day informed the State Department that the American delegation had not actually yielded the claim to the Philippines by right of conquest, but that a majority of the commissioners did not believe its use in the negotiations would result in a favorable outcome. He noted the flaw in Hay's argument that Dewey's victory constituted capture of Manila, since subsequent military operations, its actual capitulation, and the acceptance of the armistice protocol precluded making "demands upon that ground." In an addendum, Cushman Davis agreed that the United States could demand cession of the entire archipelago on "other and more valid grounds than a perfected territorial conquest," for example, indemnity, general military success, or the future security and welfare of the islands.[81]

During these exchanges, William McKinley remained steady in his convictions that battlefield victory provided a conclusive basis for annexation, and he stubbornly stuck to that view. To abandon it meant certain embarrassment for the United States and nothing in the situation required the president to modify his position. This resolution now also buttressed his intention to reject unreasonable Spanish claims for compensation.

Meanwhile, the Spanish commission practiced the diplomacy at which it was most adept, the delaying tactics indicated by Almodóvar. On November 4, the Americans received a Spanish note objecting to the cession of the Philippines and arguing that Spain retained sovereignty and the United States could not raise a point not mentioned in the armistice protocol—only Manila, the bay, and the port had been referred to. Nothing had occurred to justify the expanded American demands.

Montero Ríos worried this might cause the Americans to break off negotiations and renew the war. He also opposed Almodóvar's suggestion about offering leases to development companies since it implied that Spain lacked the wherewithal to administer her own colonies, and in any case, the Americans would reject it because it offered them no advantages. Almodóvar shrugged his diplomatic shoulders and directed Montero Ríos to respond to the American demand for the Philippines with a request for a suspension in the negotiations. He hinted that help might come from "the interference of European interests in the questions under debate," something "not impossible." This was wishful thinking.[82]

On November 9, following instructions from Washington, the American delegation absolutely rejected the Spanish contentions and reiterated the arguments it had put forth earlier against them. When Montero Ríos asked Almodóvar for direction, the duke repeated the views that Spain had presented all along: the cession of Cuba relieved Spain of the Cuban debt and the United States had never acquired sovereignty over the Philippines. In regard to the Philippines, Almodóvar declared that "force, alone, which we can not resist, would oblige us to submit to the loss," but not until exhausting all other means "to guard our rights." The statement indicated that when pushed to the precipice, the Spanish government knew it must concede the issue. Montero Ríos, however, concerned that the conference might soon dissolve over Spanish intransigence, wanted to place the onus for such a development squarely on the Americans. He would do this by proposing arbitration of the Philippine question, something he knew the Americans would reject. Almodóvar gave his assent to this tactic; should the Americans refuse, Montero Ríos was to suspend further negotiations. Clearly Madrid was at a loss to think of anything other than ways to stall, gain time, and hope for a miracle.[83]

Faced with this position, and not wanting to break up the conference, the Americans requested guidance from Washington, at the same time sending their individual positions on the correct course of action. Rufus Day, still believing that the whole archipelago was likely to prove more a burden than a benefit to the United States, urged only commercial and naval advantages and would not take more than Luzon and any essential nearby islands. He suggested a lump sum of $15 million, "recognizing that we are dealing with a bankrupt people." Rather than failing to secure a peace treaty, he would permit Spain to keep Mindanao and the Sulu Islands, which he considered, along with the money payment for Luzon, "a substantial concession." The United States might also take an island in the Carolines for a naval base.[84]

Senator Frye remained firm for getting all of the Philippines, proposing a payment of $10 million "in gold," which he considered a fair estimate of the debt chargeable to the islands. But if necessary to secure a treaty, he would settle for Luzon and the islands of Mindoro and Palawan, along with Ponape in the Carolines. As a consequence of American generosity in allowing her to keep certain colonies, Spain must free all political prisoners and ensure freedom of religion in all of its remaining Pacific possessions. She must also grant cable landing rights wherever the United States wished in the Pacific, as well as in the Canaries, in Spanish African and Mediterranean chattels, and in Spain itself.[85]

George Gray remained opposed on principle to territorial expansion. But if the United States did acquire new lands, he favored "such reasonable concessions as would comport with the magnanimity of a great nation dealing with a weak and prostrate foe," rather than a policy of "forcible seizure." He thought it would be most unfortunate if the United States abandoned the lofty position it had assumed at the beginning of the war, and instead of crowning her triumphs "by setting an example of moderation, restraint, and reason in victory, act[ed] the part of a ruthless conqueror."[86]

Whitelaw Reid wanted to take all the Philippines, basing his argument on the principle of indemnity. But if a compromise was necessary, he proposed leaving Mindanao and the Sulus to Spain in return for all of the Ladrones and the Carolines. He also wished Spain to guarantee religious freedom and free trade in the Philippines left to her. If neither of these suggestions was accepted, he proposed that the United States take both the Philippines and the Carolines, offering $12 to $15 million for the lot.

Senator Cushman K. Davis, the most hard-line of the American team, demanded the entirety of the Philippines, Puerto Rico, and Guam, along with Cuban independence, all without compensation to Spain. He was convinced Spain was delaying the negotiations in order "to entangle the United States with some of the European powers." In his opinion, the situation required that the United States present an ultimatum insisting on a treaty that would encompass all of his demands, adding, "[W]e shall never get a treaty except as a result of such an unyielding ultimatum."[87]

Secretary Hay considered the opinions and on November 13, cabled the instructions that guided the American delegation throughout the rest of the peace conference. The United States, as the victor, was clearly entitled to an indemnity for the cost of the war, and Spain had to pay up. Naturally, the United States could not hope to be fully indemnified and did not expect to be; the war, after all, had cost a million dollars a day, and "it would probably be difficult for Spain to pay money." All she had left were the Philippines, the Ladrones, and the Carolines. Surely, Spain did not expect the United States to turn the

Philippines back to her ownership and bear the cost of the war without any indemnity except Puerto Rico, "which we have, and which is wholly inadequate."[88]

From the standpoint of indemnity, both the Philippines and the Carolines were insufficient to pay the American expenses for the war. "But aside from this," Hay added, "do we not owe an obligation to the people of the Philippines which will not permit us to return them to the sovereignty of Spain?" Could the United States justify such a course, "or could we permit their barter to some other power?" Willing or not, the United States had the responsibility of duty, which "we can not escape." He thereby instructed Day to insist on the complete cession of the Philippines and, if necessary, to pay Spain $10 to $20 million, and more if commercial advantages and naval and cable stations in the Carolines were thrown in. The president did not believe that division of the Philippines "can bring us anything but embarrassment in the future." The United States could yield on trade and commercial questions, "but the questions of duty and humanity appeal to the President so strongly" that he could not offer any solution other than the one contained herein.[89]

On November 21, Day handed the Spanish commissioners an ultimatum, giving Spain one week to respond. Montero Ríos had already made his request for arbitration, and in this light, it was not really known how Madrid would answer. Reid was optimistic. From his own diplomatic sources, he surmised that the queen regent was ready to accept; it was Premier Sagasta who was the stumbling block. Writing to McKinley, he said, "I think from inside news from Madrid, from the Court, that the queen regent is now convinced that nothing can be gained" by arguing the Cuban debt question or the retention of the Philippines, "and that she is anxious to accept the inevitable and end the agony." Sagasta, though, "shrinks from a decision, which however inevitable, means for him permanent exile from power; and the politicians on the Commission here feel as if they were being asked to sign their own death warrants."[90]

The American ultimatum demanded that Spain accept $20 million for the Philippines, with both sides relinquishing all further claims, and the Spanish to have free commercial access to the islands for ten years. When this was accepted and final agreement was reached on the clauses relating to Cuba, Puerto Rico, and Guam, the Americans wanted to discuss several minor matters: the guarantee of religious freedom in the Carolines, the liberation of political prisoners in the Philippines and Cuba, annexation of Kusaie in the Carolines, along with cable landing rights elsewhere in those islands, and the renewal of American-Spanish treaties in effect prior to the war.

Reid made a special visit to Ambassador León y Castillo to inform him of the ultimatum and to emphasize its significance. These, noted León y Castillo to Almodóvar, "were their final words . . . all discussion being now unprofitable and useless."[91]

The chief innovation of the ultimatum was the insertion of Kusaie, a result of purely naval considerations. Commander Bradford had impressed upon the American commissioners the strategic significance of the Carolines and the Ladrones. These island groups commanded the line of communications from Hawaii to the Philippines. Bradford also indicated that Germany would likely take whatever the Americans left to the Spanish in the Pacific. This argument led Reid, Davis, and Frye to demand the inclusion of Kusaie in the American annexation list.

Bradford was correct in his prediction of German intentions in the Pacific. After learning of the August 12 armistice protocol, Berlin had concentrated on acquiring the Carolines and the Ladrones. Their efforts led to a secret understanding between Spain and Germany on September 10, providing for the cession of Kusaie, Yap, and Ponape, all in the Carolines, conditional on the outcome of Spanish negotiations with the United States. It was held so secret by the Spanish government that it is likely that Montero Ríos did not even know.

German diplomats reacted immediately to the American demand for Kusaie. Count Münster, the German ambassador in Paris, went out of his way several times to assure Reid that Germany had no designs on the Philippines, nor on the Carolines. Quite possibly Münster did not know of the secret agreements either. Day and the American team would have been outraged had they known that Germany was actively contending for the Carolines and had already made a clandestine preliminary arrangement to buy them from Spain.

Spain carefully considered its response to the American ultimatum. The Spanish delegation was divided, with Abarzuza and Villa-Urrutia arguing for acceptance, knowing the Americans would budge no further, and Montero Ríos leading those who insisted on the possibility of additional negotiations. Montero Ríos proposed either to offer both the Antilles and the Philippines to the United States with the proviso that all debts be passed along with them, or to make the cessions with the understanding that the United States would underwrite the amount to discharge the debts. If the United States refused these offers, he preferred, given Spain's lack of wherewithal to defend them, to leave everything to the United States and walk away from the negotiations without signing a formal treaty.

The ultimatum itself placed the duke of Almodóvar in a predicament. In a cable to Montero Ríos, he explained the difficulty: "If it were possible to investigate the real temper of the American Government in case we retire without signing, we could decide with more certainty such a grave matter." What concerned him was the possibility that should the Spanish walk out, the United States might immediately resume hostilities, possibly against the Canary Islands, or the Spanish coast.[92]

By this time, the United States had voted in its midterm elections, which the Spanish hoped would return the Democrats to power in Congress, bringing with them a generally antiexpansionist mood. That didn't happen. The election returns in the East showed the familiar tendency to vote against the incumbent president's party, the narrow victory of Theodore Roosevelt for governor of New York being the big success. But in the Midwest, the Republicans rallied to save the House and chose state legislators to support their candidates for the U.S. Senate when their legislatures voted in January 1899. (The Senate was still elected by indirect vote, i.e., of the state legislatures.) The elections assured McKinley of a good working majority for deliberating what would be a frankly expansionist peace treaty.

On November 24, Montero Ríos suggested counteroffers to the United States, all in pursuit of his general plan of making a cession contingent on the American assumption of the colonial debt. First, cession of the entire Philippine archipelago for $100 million in compensation for public works in the Philippines and the Antilles; second, cession of the Philippines, with the exception of Mindanao and Jolo, for $50 million, plus the cession of Kusaie, and the right to land cables in the Carolines or Ladrones; third, the free cession of the Philippines with the submission of the debt question placed before an international arbitration panel. He concluded that if all three met with refusal by the United States, it provided "one more proof of the abnegation of Spain to the limit consonant with her dignity and of the arbitrary and uncompromising attitude of the United States."[93]

The Americans forwarded the new Spanish proposals to Washington. President McKinley remained adamant and yielded nothing. As Hay noted to Day, the president "finds no reason for departing from his last instruction." The Americans were ordered to "decline" the latest Spanish offer.[94]

While the cable traffic went back and forth, the Sagasta ministry in Madrid finally faced the fact that it could do nothing in the face of the American ultimatum. On November 25, Almodóvar ordered the Spanish delegation to sign a treaty of peace and take the $20 million offered for the Philippines, as "further resistance will be useless and the rupture of the negotiations which is threatened will be dangerous." Simultaneous with the signing, the Spanish commissioners were to craft "a severe protest as a final demonstration against the violence practiced" by the United States."[95]

At the November 28 plenary session, Montero Ríos, after delivering his pro forma protest, unveiled the Spanish decision to sign a peace treaty embodying the American terms. As Reid relayed to McKinley, the scene "when they presented their answer to our ultimatum was dignified and mournful. They looked and no doubt felt as if they were at a funeral of some dear one in the family."[96]

The commissions wrangled for two more weeks over minor additions to the treaty. Spain sought commercial concessions in the Antilles in exchange for Kusaie, but nothing came of this. Arrangements were made to recover all Spanish prisoners of war held by the Cuban and Filipino rebels in return for the Spanish release of all Cuban and Filipino political prisoners. Madrid successfully resisted American efforts to specify, de jure, that the United States maintain the right to preserve public order in the Philippines in the time period between the signing of the treaty and its ratification, something that might take a couple of months. But this was only a legality. In their turn, the Americans managed to block a Spanish effort to begin a new inquiry into the sinking of the *Maine*. That could prove a great political embarrassment should new facts counter the results reported by the U.S. Navy's board of inquiry.

Over these two weeks, Montero Ríos led his delegation in obfuscating every issue except the cash payments. When he demanded that Spain get to keep all her heavy coast artillery presently in the

Philippines, whatever their worth, Day cabled for instructions. General Merritt, who was still in Paris, volunteered that their removal would leave Manila helpless, forcing the United States to provide replacements immediately. The Americans opposed the Spanish on this point, though they permitted a removal of the Spanish heavy mobile artillery. These minor issues became quite vexing to the Americans, who showed their displeasure, much to Spanish surprise. Cushman Davis, for one, was unwilling to submit "further to what [I consider] an irrational dictatorial tone and persistent bullying." In any case, President McKinley scotched any more deal making; it would be the signing of the treaty or a resumption of the war.[97]

On December 10, the two delegations formally affixed their signatures to the treaty. Its seventeen articles thoroughly reflected the one-sided outcome of the negotiations. Though far harsher terms might have been demanded, on the two most contentious issues—the attempt to foist the colonial debt onto the United States and the American demand for all of the Philippines—the United States forced the settlement to its complete advantage.

The treaty's articles as submitted to the respective governments for ratification were:

1. Spain to relinquish sovereignty in Cuba, with the United States to discharge obligations under international law for the protection of life and property so long as it occupied the island.
2. Spain to cede Puerto Rico and Guam to the United States.
3. Spain to cede the Philippine Islands to the United States for a payment of $20 million, to be tendered within three months of ratification.
4. Spain to receive ten years of commercial treatment in the Philippines equal to the United States.
5. The United States to return at its own expense all Spanish troops in the Philippines, together with their arms.
6. Spain to release all political prisoners and prisoners of war in the theaters of conflict, with the United States using its power to persuade the Filipino rebels to do likewise.
7. Each nation to renounce reciprocal indemnity claims.
8. Spain to receive the public records and archives of its former colonies.

9. Spanish citizens to have the freedom to remain in ceded or relinquished territories with the provision of declaring permanent citizenship within one year.
10. Freedom of religion guaranteed in all ceded or relinquished territories.
11. Spanish citizens in ceded or relinquished territories to be subject to local laws.
12. Court proceedings pending at the time of ratification to be completed.
13. Spanish copyrights and patents to be protected.
14. Spain to have consular offices in the lost territories.
15. Each country to assess the same amounts of customs duties subject to six months notice of termination.
16. The United States to assume all financial obligations for Cuba during its period of occupation.
17. A seventeenth clause spelled out the ratification procedure.[98]

The most notable omission in the treaty was any mention of Kusaie or any part of the Carolines. Spain might conceivably have ceded all or part of the island group had the Americans granted to her trading concessions in the Antilles, but the administration was unwilling to confer this. In the end, Spain and Germany completed negotiations for her remaining Pacific colonies on December 21, expanding the secret agreement of the previous September. Germany received the Ladrones, less Guam, the Carolines, and the Palaus. She had already bought the Marshalls in 1895, and with these new holdings completed a chain of islands in the Pacific that stretched from the Bismarck Archipelago northeast of New Guinea to the Ladrones. The United States compensated itself for Kusaie: on January 17, 1899, the gunboat *Bennington* landed and took possession of Wake Island, a dot of an atoll two thousand miles west of Pearl Harbor, a logical station for landing the transpacific cable between Honolulu and Manila.[99]

At the onset of the U.S. Senate debate, it appeared—rightly—that the American public strongly endorsed approval of the treaty. The New York *Herald* polled 498 newspapers and found 305 favored territorial expansion and thus the treaty. New England and the middle Atlantic states all showed inclinations toward territorial acquisition, and the West, overwhelmingly so. Only in the Democratic South did a bare majority voice itself against ratification. But the legislative debate in the Senate would transcend sectional lines.

Soon after the treaty was introduced into the Senate on December 10, George Vest, antiexpansionist Democrat of Missouri, produced a resolution claiming constitutional impediments. Nowhere in the Constitution, he argued, was there a grant of power authorizing the president to secure territory to be held permanently as a colony; all land held by the United States, he claimed, must be prepared for eventual statehood. Another antiexpansionist constitutional view was put forward by William E. Mason, Democrat of Illinois. He maintained that the principle of self-determination ruled out annexation of territory. The government of the United States, he said, "will not attempt to govern the people of any country in the world without the consent of the people themselves, or subject them by force to our domination against their will."[100]

Early in the new year of 1899, Georgia Democratic senator Augustus O. Bacon proposed the United States announce that it intended to grant the Philippines independence "when a stable and independent government should have been duly elected." This approach, offered earlier in the Teller Amendment relating to Cuban independence, gave the administration, and expansionists generally, some concern, as both realized that the humanitarian motive in declaring the late war would surface in arguments against ratifying the treaty. Arthur P. Gorman, Democrat of Maryland, who had his eye on the presidential nomination of 1900 on an antiexpansion platform, managed to unite some conservative Republicans and all but half a dozen Democrats to oppose the treaty, thus denying the two-thirds majority necessary for ratification. The Republican majority, however, were not worried, knowing they could wait until the new and even more partisan Republican Congress convened in March.

On February 4, just days before the Senate voted, word came that an exchange of shots between American and Filipino outposts had widened into a general engagement in the Philippines. It was the beginning of what became the two-year Philippine insurrection, as bloody a colonial fight as was ever fought. The antiexpansionists were acutely embarrassed, for in the uncertainty over who had fired the first shot, they felt bound to support the president's policy. Even William Jennings Bryan, out of office but the leader of the antis, was constrained to defend the national interest until the general course on the Philippines was determined. Though an antiexpansionist to the core, he was willing to support the treaty in order to grant the Philippines independence should the Democrats win the White House in the 1900 elections. And William McKinley immediately grasped the import of the fighting. "How foolish these people [the Filipino insurgents] are. This means ratification of the treaty; the people will insist on ratification."[101]

When the vote was cast on February 6, it was 57 yeas to 27 nays, two votes over the needed two-thirds majority. Bryan's maneuvers likely helped bring it over the edge, as had Henry Cabot Lodge, who cajoled four reluctant Republicans to vote in favor of the national leadership. The president, too, can be credited, shrewdly having appointed three senators to the peace commission as well as developing the lofty annexationist arguments of humanity, duty, and destiny.

In Spain, the treaty was considered a national humiliation and attacked severely by the opposition. In the Cortes, it passed by only two votes, a division too narrow for legislative approval. The queen regent was forced to use her constitutional powers to override the legislature, and Spain ratified the document on March 19. Shortly after, Sagasta fell from power and the Conservatives formed the new ministry. The Liberals, though, had accomplished the very important wartime goal of preserving, at least for a time and in the face of overwhelming defeat, the constitutional monarchy and parliamentary government.

The acceptance of the treaty committed the United States, for better or worse, to an imperial presence in the Pacific; as such, it became a buffer to Japanese designs on the entire region. But McKinley, speaking in Boston, depicted himself not as a conqueror or colonizer but as an emancipator of a conquered people. The United States would establish justice and order in the Philippines so that a "reign of reason" would begin. He was less specific about the long term, but he denied selfish motives. "No imperial designs lurk in the American mind," he told the Home Market Club. "They are alien to American sentiment, thought and purpose. Our principles undergo no change under a tropical sun. They go with the flag."[102]

Whitelaw Reid echoed the same sentiments to the Lotus Club in New York. Speaking of the Philippine insurrection against the United States, something he characterized as "that irritation of a Malay half-breed's [Aguinaldo's] folly," he was completely prepared to argue that "nobody ever doubted that they would give us trouble. That is the price nations must pay for going to war, even in a just cause."[103]

CHAPTER 18

SCANDAL

I am very much afraid that with Alger the trouble is congeni-
tal. He simply can't do better; he *can not* learn by experience.
—*Acting Brigadier General Theodore Roosevelt*
to Senator Henry Cabot Lodge, September 4, 1898

The Major-General Commanding the Army had no sufficient
justification for alleging that the refrigerated beef was embalmed or was unfit for issue to troops.
—*Report of the U.S. Army "Beef Court,"*
April 1899

George Cortelyou, the president's secretary, was always intensely annoyed at Russell Alger's habit of heading down to the White House
lobby after a conference with the chief executive to give his own view
of events to reporters. At the beginning of August, when the appalling
conditions in the first returning transports from Santiago had made
the news and greatly angered the president, McKinley, quite out of
character, had chewed Alger out for two days, pointedly asking the
secretary detailed questions about the ship contracts and Shafter's
arrangements for the return of troops from the front. McKinley ordered immediate boards of inspection at both New York and Santiago. They, however, accomplished nothing of value before peace
passed them by.

Cortelyou observed that Alger did not share the president's anguish. To the contrary, he exhibited "watchful solicitude" to shield

631

General Shafter "and other personal friends" in the shipping companies from any official reprimand. In conversations with the press,
Alger omitted "every sharp criticism, every word of reproof dictated
by the President."[1]

This glimpse of Russell Alger is enlightening. "The President is
long-suffering," wrote his private secretary, "and slow to suspect his
advisers of self-seeking." With false modesty, Cortelyou admitted to
his diary that he was no judge of human nature, and there was "not
much of it" anyway in the person of Russell Alger. But unless "drastic measures" were resorted to, War Department management during the war "will be one of the few blots on the record of this
administration."[2]

Cortelyou wasn't alone. William McKinley's closest associates were
beginning to draw distance between themselves and Russell Alger, dis-
trusting his egotistical character and the doubtful conduct of his cabinet department. The scapegoating had begun, and Alger, often rightly,
sometimes not, was to bear a large part of the onus for the failure of the
department's bureaus to meet the demands of a sudden foreign war.
There had been no thought of reorganizing the dilapidated Indian-
fighting establishment he oversaw, and there was no time to do it during the mobilization and fighting anyway. Granted huge appropriations
of money and gigantic increases in personnel, it nevertheless maintained a "general store" mentality, incapable of responding to the new
situation. The errors of delay, omission, and commission of senior bureau functionaries hewing to archaic practices became the price paid
for decades of national neglect in applying lessons of modern efficiency
to the management of the War Department.

Given these not insubstantial shortcomings, the press abandoned
all restraint, demanding an investigation of the conduct of the war
and the instant dismissal of Russell Alger from the cabinet. The word
"Algerism"—meaning a cynical dereliction in office, coupled with im-
putations of corruption and venality—entered the popular lexicon.
It was futile to speak in his defense. And along with Russell Alger,
the bureau chiefs—Commissary General Eagan and Surgeon General
Sternberg—were "consigned . . . to the blackest pit of obloquy."[3]

That the staff bureaus, to say nothing of army command and operations, needed finer scrutiny than was provided by the press and innuendo was readily apparent. On September 8, likely by direction of
the president, Russell Alger asked for the appointment of a special

commission "of the most distinguished soldiers and civilians that can be selected" to investigate every aspect of the War Department's administration of the conflict.[4]

McKinley first offered the chairmanship to General John Schofield, ex–commanding general of the army, who turned it down, suspecting that the commission was a political maneuver rather than an initial step toward badly needed military reform. Eventually the president selected retired General Grenville M. Dodge, a railroad millionaire, experienced Civil War officer, active Iowa Republican, and friend of Russell Alger, to head the investigation, immediately dubbed the "Dodge Commission." Of the eight additional members, six were active or retired soldiers; the two civilians were a retired governor of Vermont and a prominent Ohio physician.

Schofield was basically correct when he assumed the inquiry was not intended as an instrument of progressive action. Dodge himself dismissed most criticism of the War Department as unwarranted and instead blamed field and camp commanders for the errors in carrying out what was otherwise a generally sensible policy.

From the time of its formation, the executive purpose of the Dodge Commission remained ambiguous. In his instructions to its members, President McKinley pointedly did not ask them to propose army reforms. Instead, the president considered it a sort of grand jury, called upon to seek out the guilty and enjoined to probe every War Department bureau and office. "The people of the country," the president declared, "are entitled to know whether or not the citizens who so promptly responded to the call of duty have been neglected or maltreated by the Government. . . . If there have been wrongs committed, the wrongdoers must not escape conviction and punishment."[5]

If this was indeed the commission's charge, said General Schofield, then the investigation would amount to little more than a witch-hunt, where men could be tried and condemned without the legal safeguards provided in a military or civilian court.

Schofield was right. For McKinley, the commission was a political stroke. Uninterested in proposing an agenda for true military reform, he hoped the investigation would stifle public commotion, at least until after the November 1898 congressional elections.

Though the Democrats derided the commission as a whitewash, and a number of army officers avoided the sessions in fear controversy would damage their careers, the investigation did achieve a bit more than the narrow results the president sought. From October through December, the committee delved into every detail of the War Department's administration. They closely questioned Secretary Alger and the bureau chiefs and visited a dozen cities, taking testimony from officers of every rank, from enlisted men, nurses, welfare workers, and concerned citizens; they inspected the volunteer army camps where a great deal of the abuses had occurred.

The administration took heart that the parade of witnesses failed to reveal any instance of notable idiocy or corruption in high places. In many cases, quite the opposite was found. Officers of the stature of Leonard Wood and Henry Lawton, heroes of the Santiago campaign, asserted that the army had done its honest best in very trying circumstances. Partly as a result of the Dodge Commission's work, Republican politicians in the weeks immediately prior to the November elections reported promising alterations of public opinion in favor of the government, and even of Russell Alger.

But on December 21, General Miles appeared before the panel in Washington. His testimony brought forth for the first time what seemed like an explicit instance of malfeasance in the War Department. It wasn't surprising that Miles should attack the administration. A feud between the commanding general on one hand and the secretary of war, the bureau chiefs, and the McKinley administration on the other had been simmering for some time. Ever since becoming commanding general, Nelson Miles had been spoiling for a fight. The germ of the conflict lay in the outmoded system of authority in the War Department, which was essentially divided into two parts: the field army of the infantry, artillery, and cavalry, plus the adjutant general and inspector general on the one hand, and the staff bureaus on the other. The commanding general held no brief over the bureaus. If he wished some action of the Quartermaster's Department, for example, he had to make his request through the secretary of war. This led to a degree of factionalism that waxed or waned depending on the personalities of the major general commanding the army and the civilian cabinet secretary. In the case of Miles and Alger, both exceedingly egotistical men, it led to outright hatred of each other over who would have the president's ear in matters of strategy and military policy. But until the convening of the Dodge Commission, the internecine battle was kept largely within the confines of the army itself and was not aired in public. Miles, politically ambitious but also politically naive, hoped to ride army scandals uncovered by the Dodge Commission into a run for the presidency.

Miles found his issue in the quality of the army's refrigerated and canned beef. Refrigerated beef—fresh dressed carcass—as soon as the army learned how to store and transport it, became the favorite component of the ration in all theaters and camps. Canned "fresh roast beef," on the other hand, used by all units at one time or another, was universally loathed. Often forced by field conditions to eat it as it came from the can, the soldiers quickly learned to hate it. In the damp heat of Santiago, the meat nearly liquefied into sludge. Roosevelt thought it "nauseating." At times, the meatpackers foisted on the army several bad lots containing scraps of gristle, pieces of rope, and sometimes dead maggots.

The man responsible for the army's food was the chief of the Subsistence Department, Commissary General Charles Patrick Eagan, an Irish immigrant who had joined the army as a volunteer in 1862. An infantryman, highly respected for his courage against both Confederates and Indians, he transferred to the Subsistence Department and rose by slow promotion to commissary general in May 1898. The office's principal responsibility lay in feeding the enlisted men of the army, purchasing and issuing the components of a ration set by act of Congress to protect the troops from food faddish commanders and the War Department from contractor pressures.[6]

To Eagan, the meatpacking industry's new technologies of refrigeration and canning offered healthful, economic fare. Where he could not use refrigerated beef, he substituted the canned fresh roast beef, part of the "travel" ration since the 1870s but little used until 1898 and meant as the principal ingredient for stew. The navy bought half a million pounds of it annually, and the British and French armies imported huge amounts.

Regarding the product, Colonel John Weston of the Subsistence Department, reported to Eagan in March 1898: "I have made hash, also stew, from it that was fit for the immortal gods and not beneath the notice of a general, using a little bacon, potatoes, onions, flour, and condiments; just what a soldier has. . . . It will not be steak, or choice roast; still it will be fresh beef."[7]

Colonel Weston was assigned to the Fifth Corps as General Shafter's commissary general. He chose the supplies for the expedition and he selected plenty of canned beef, as well as large quantities of bacon. In Cuba, according to Weston, the troops had complete freedom of choice. There was sometimes a shortage of bacon, but no man was ever refused it when available. Yet the hated canned roast beef, not improved by the heat of the transport holds, was regularly delivered to the trenches, and some units got no other meat ration until after the fall of Santiago.

There was no use in supplying potatoes and onions since the Fifth Corps had left its cooking gear afloat. The beef became a torture to the men who had to eat it. Famished soldiers became nauseated by the very sight of the contents in the can. Eventually they could not gag the slimy mess down, or keep it down if they could.

Miles heard his first complaints about army canned beef during his inspection trip to Tampa in June. In late September, upon his return to the United States following the Puerto Rico campaign, he ordered every regimental commander who had served in the Caribbean to forward to the War Department an evaluation of canned roast beef. The reports, often in harsh language, thoroughly condemned the product. At the same time, Miles received an alarming report on the refrigerated beef. This emanated from a volunteer surgeon on his staff, Dr. William Daly, in civilian life a Pittsburgh physician and long a trusted friend of the commanding general.

Daly had accompanied Miles to both Tampa and Puerto Rico. There he had eaten refrigerated beef that tasted to him of boric and salicylic acid, poisonous chemicals sometimes injected into beef as a preservative. Daly had eaten such meat previously, on a western hunting trip, and remembered the taste. In Puerto Rico, he later claimed, he had performed a chemical analysis of a sample of suspect beef and found acid traces. On his return to the United States, Daly put his findings in a letter to the commanding general. Although many officers complained about the canned roast beef, Daly was the only one to voice suspicion of the refrigerated beef. On his allegations rested what was to become the army's great "embalmed beef" scandal.

By the end of October, Miles had accumulated what looked like patently strong evidence against both canned and refrigerated beef, each still being issued to the troops in quantity. Miles's obligations to his men might seem to have required that he relate the alarming facts immediately to the secretary of war, or even to the president, and to demand quick investigation and corrective action. But he made no report.

Until Miles testified before the Dodge Commission, he kept this information close, while the troops, presumably, were eating poisoned meat. The issue remained hidden until December 21. On that day, appearing before the Dodge Commission, Miles was asked a question regarding the quality of his supplies during the Puerto Rico campaign. Poor food, he replied, had been "one of the serious causes of so much sickness and distress on the part of the troops." He went on to criticize Commissary General Eagan for abandoning the army's traditional beef on the hoof in favor of the new processed meats and avowed there "was some serious defect in that refrigerator beef, and also the canned beef that was furnished." In answer to further questions, Miles bolstered his charges by introducing the adverse regimental reports on the canned beef and Dr. Daly's letter, claiming "the [refrigerated] beef to be allegedly preserved with secret chemicals."[8]

While Miles did not directly assign corrupt motives to Alger and Eagan, he nonetheless implied them, even erroneously arguing that the canned "fresh beef" was not legally part of the army ration, but introduced as a "pretense of experiment." Immediately after his testimony, Miles elaborated his charges to the press. The next day, the *New York Journal* headlined, "Miles Makes Grave Charges Against the Administration—Poisons Used in Beef Made the Soldiers Ill— Tons of Bad Meat Sent to Troops in Porto Rico."[9]

Commissary General Eagan was enraged, claiming, "General Miles has crucified me upon a cross of falsehood and misrepresentation." According to Russell Alger, the charges of bad beef struck Eagan "with the suddenness and sharpness of a blow from an assassin's knife out of the dark." Miles further infuriated Eagan by ignoring the commissary general's request for clarification of the *Journal* interview. Eagan actually considered challenging Miles to a duel, but settled instead for a public rebuttal before the Dodge Commission.[10]

Consulting no one, he prepared a lengthy statement, which he read to the body. It wrecked his career. He began by declaring the ration beef, both refrigerated and canned, to be sound, nutritious food, untainted, he insisted, by any poisonous chemicals. Becoming increasingly agitated as he read, at times coming close to tears, Eagan charged that Miles had deeply maligned him and his bureau by implying corruption in office and neglect of duty. On this point, he labeled Miles's remarks "a scandalous libel, reflecting upon the honor of every officer . . . who has purchased meat, and especially and particularly on the Commissary General—myself."[11]

Miles's accusations had inflicted deep personal wounds, and Eagan minced no words. "I wish to force the lie back into his throat," Eagan seethed, "covered with the contents of a camp latrine. I wish to brand it as a falsehood of whole cloth, without a particle of truth to sustain it, and unless he can prove his statement he should be denounced by every honest man, barred from the clubs, barred from the society of decent people, and so ostracized that the street bootblacks would not condescend to speak to him, for he fouled his own nest, he has aspersed the honor of a brother officer without a particle of evidence or fact to sustain in any degree his scandalous, libelous, malicious falsehood." Further on in the testimony, Eagan squarely branded Miles a "liar, with as black a heart as the man who blew up the *Maine*."[12]

The commissioners were truly stunned by the outburst and forced Eagan to expunge the most vituperative passages from his statement before accepting it into the record. Eagan's thirty-six-year army career was finished. His abusive language on Miles—his superior in rank—transformed the entire issue to one of insubordination. Russell Alger had no choice but to order Eagan's court-martial for conduct unbecoming an officer and prejudicial to good order and discipline.

The court-martial, presided over by General Merritt, convened at the Ebbitt House hotel, where Eagan swore under oath that he had received "before God, not one cent" from the meatpackers. The court, however, found Eagan guilty of the insubordination charges, sentencing him to dismissal from the army; privately, it recommended clemency to the president. McKinley confirmed the court's verdict. At the same time, in recognition of Eagan's long and loyal service and the extreme circumstances that had provoked his outburst, the president commuted the sentence to suspension from rank and duty, with full pay, for six years, until his retirement.[13]

Eagan's protestations were discredited by the public, now in full whoop over what they saw as the beef scandal. There was much disapproval when McKinley commuted the court-martial sentence. It was even hinted that the president's action in the matter was the result of executive sympathy with the packers of "embalmed beef."

In addition to attacking a branch of the army, Miles had also clawed a major American industry. The meatpackers took great offense at the aspersions cast on their products (in the case of refrigerated beef, they were not true, at least in the product supplied to the military) and the damage done thereby to domestic and foreign markets. With their enthusiastic cooperation, the Dodge Commission temporarily transformed itself into a beef investigating board, conducting a painstaking inquiry into the quality of the army's ration beef. It listened to protracted testimony from officers who had served in all theaters of the war, and confirmed the army's hatred for canned roast beef, but its unanimous approval of the refrigerated product. Miles's charges against the Subsistence Department for contracting "embalmed beef" with the connivance of the meatpackers were dismissed and his conduct in bringing them was censured.[14]

The public, though, considered the Dodge Commission's findings a cover-up. The press began calling for a special tribunal to investigate the beef controversy, a demand that was exacerbated in a widely circulated interview in which General Miles was quoted as declaring he possessed "overwhelming evidence" of the use of chemical preservatives in army beef.[15]

On February 10, 1899, William McKinley formed a board of officers, the "Beef Court," to investigate Miles's latest allegations "in respect to the unfitness" of food furnished by the Subsistence Department to the troops in the field. Miles was the court's first witness. He produced none of the promised evidence and actually distanced himself from his own earlier comments, even repudiating the press interviews he had given and denying any implication of fraud in his remarks about Alger and Eagan conniving with the meat packing industry.

Actually, Miles disavowed so many of his statements that the court found it difficult to establish just what his charges contained. The beef court rehashed all the material previously covered by the Dodge Commission. It interrogated witnesses, visited packing plants, tasted the canned and refrigerated beef, and had it analyzed by government chemists. As had the Dodge Commission, the court dismissed as groundless Miles's accusation that the refrigerated beef contained chemical preservatives. It also claimed that canned roast beef was a wholesome food, but condemned its issue to troops in the tropics without first conducting experiments. Commissary General Eagan came in for criticism here, the court severely calling into question his purchase of 7 million canned roast beef rations as "a colossal error for which there is no palliation."[16]

The beef court reserved strong approbation for General Miles, finding he had no justification for alleging that refrigerated beef was "embalmed or was unfit" for issue to the troops. It also found that Miles committed a serious error when, if he believed—or knew, as he claimed—that the beef was bad, he did not immediately report it to the secretary of war so that proper remedies might be applied. So concluded the beef scandal, with the characters of the Subsistence Department, of Eagan, Miles, and Russell Alger, even the president, tarnished in the public mind.

By the time John Hay penned his "splendid little war" comment to Theodore Roosevelt in the late summer of 1898, the army's role in the conflict had begun to appear something less than splendid. The war, at least in Cuba, the main theater, had ended in sickness and confusion. Epidemics of malaria and other diseases drove the Fifth Corps from Santiago in unqualified panic. On the home front, the great assembly camps of the volunteers were ravaged by sickness. Public complaints concerned with the supposed neglect of the troops increased markedly during the weeks immediately following the armistice. The deficiencies that came to light in July and August were, in the main, the inevitable consequences of rapid overmobilization, outdated procedures, and the rigors of tropical campaigning. Those realities, however, did little to spare reputations.

The breakdown centered on the Army Medical Department and in the masses of volunteers mustered in the first weeks of the war for no sound military reason and quartered in large, often inefficiently managed camps throughout the hot months of summer.

Though it was headed by one of the nation's most eminent scientific physicians, Surgeon General George Sternberg, and contained one of the best-educated groups of surgeons in the country, the Medical Department operated in the face of paralyzing political and administrative impediments. It had little authority or prestige within the army; line and staff alike belittled medical officers as "nobody but doctors." As a result of its bottom ranking on the War Department totem pole, secretaries of war and commanding generals normally assigned low priorities to its requisitions for modernizing legislation, personnel, and funds. Surgeons in camp and field had no authority to enforce their hygienic and sanitary recommendations, and commanders often dismissed their warnings and suggestions, disparaging the doctors as "stuffy old women who tried to coddle the soldiers."[17]

But even had the Medical Department maintained the full confidence and cooperation of the army, the medical science on which it depended was relatively undeveloped. Physicians needed to learn far more about yellow fever, malaria, and typhoid, the maladies that struck the army in the summer of 1898, and their understanding of how the diseases spread contained wide gaps and misconceptions. Army surgeons, much like their civilian colleagues, usually misdiagnosed malaria, confusing it with the early phases of yellow fever, or confused typhoid with malaria. Inasmuch as they failed to recognize the initial cases of disease among the soldiery, they acted too late to check the spread of epidemics. And when they did intervene, mistaken concepts of how the diseases spread led the army doctors to adopt improper measures to prevent infection and contagion.

The mosquito was not yet recognized as the carrier of yellow fever and malaria, physicians attributing outbreaks of these tropical diseases to a variety of conditions, including impure water, infected buildings, and trench digging (which supposedly freed a "miasma" in the soil). Doctors who fought typhoid understood that polluted water and filthy camp conditions fostered the spread of the disease. But they had yet to comprehend that typhoid was contagious and that the virus remained lethal for protracted periods in places once occupied by its victims.

During the opening months of the war, the Medical Department encountered a slew of obstacles, a number of its own making, such as the faulty distribution of medicines, hospital equipment, and surgical supplies to the training camps. Mirroring the other bureaus of the War Department, it began hostilities with supplies barely sufficient for the maintenance of the peacetime army. In accord with the other bureaus and arms of the War Department, the surgeon general placed immense orders for every sort of material immediately upon the declaration of war. Sternberg, though, plagued by delays in manufacturing and delivery in the early weeks, was forced to borrow medical supplies from state National Guard stocks, meager as they usually were. Adhering to the general mobilization policy, Sternberg established a priority system to assure full medical outfits for units slated for active campaigning overseas—necessary, but a dangerous deletion for those not chosen. At Chickamauga Battlefield Park's Camp Thomas, Camp Alger in Falls Church, Virginia, and Jacksonville, Florida, regimental and division surgeons were forced to turn to the Red Cross and other private agencies because, as an army doctor said, "they honored requisitions at once and the United States government did not."[18]

The Medical Department was also hobbled by a severe shortage of physicians and enlisted hospital corpsmen. Though it received a large wartime contingent of volunteer commissioned surgeons, the bureau began the war with hardly enough officers to tend to the standing regular army. Congress authorized the surgeon general to supplement his uniformed medical officers with an unlimited number of civilian contract physicians. For lack of time and not enough regular officers to staff examining boards, Sternberg appointed these men after only the most superficial assessment of their professional qualities.

Surgeon General Sternberg ordered his few regular army physicians into the highest-ranking and most responsible billets in the field formations, camps, and base hospitals. Yet, as was the situation in all the War Department bureaus, a qualified staff sufficient for the volunteer-bloated army did not begin to take shape until the effects of its absence became dreadfully plain.

To provide nurses, stretcher bearers, and ambulance drivers, the Medical Department was forced to enlarge its small Hospital Corps of enlisted men. Major efforts to attract civilian recruits and to persuade medically qualified volunteers to transfer from line regiments generally met with failure; although by late August the Hospital Corps had grown from its peacetime strength of 791 to almost 6,000 men, this was still barely half the number required for an army of 275,000. Most of these new medical recruits lacked any training or experience. In their search for hospital ward attendants, camp and unit commanders temporarily detailed squads of infantrymen for the duty. These soldiers, usually the dregs of their regiments, were worse than useless in caring for patients, and their neglect of basic sanitary precautions notably abetted the spread of typhoid in the training camps.

Driven by urgency, Sternberg (for the first time since the Civil War) employed large numbers of female nurses in the army's hospitals. By war's end, over 1,100 of these professionally qualified women were working in wards in the United States and in the campaign theaters. Sternberg also recruited Dr. Anita Newcomb McGee as the Medical Department's chief of nurses. Though her appointment initiated the arrival of the female nurse as a permanent addition to the army, the full benefits of this innovation were not accomplished until many military hospitals came close to collapse for want of trained attendants.

Hospital organization in the field and camp was, from the first, a constantly disruptive problem. Each regiment, regular or volunteer, arrived at the training camps with its own organic, self-contained hospital. In early May, as divisions and corps formed, the Medical Department, adhering to a plan perfected in the Civil War, consolidated the regimental medical establishments in each division into a single two-hundred-bed field hospital. These divisional hospitals theoretically moved with the troops, collecting the sick and wounded for treatment and sending the worst cases to large base or general hospitals for intensive care. This system left the fighting regiments unimpeded by casualties and assured efficient medical treatment near to the encampment or battlefield. The operation had worked well during the Civil War; Sternberg and the Army Medical Department expected the same results now.

It did not happen. From the outset in the camps, the division hospitals collapsed in dissension and disorder. Shortages of equipment and trained personnel delayed organization, and the removal of surgeons from their regiments left too few physicians close to the troops for proper supervision of sanitary measures.

Once organized, the divisional hospitals in the volunteer camps operated in a state of constant administrative turmoil. The lack of regular medical officers forced Surgeon General Sternberg to assign volunteer physicians to command a number of these hospitals, where the intricacies of requesting supplies, keeping records for hundreds of patients, and training green hospital corpsmen were beyond their ability. The epidemics of late summer caught the hospitals at the volunteer camps with many of their deficiencies still uncorrected. A more aggressive surgeon general, wise in the craft of politics and administration, might have overcome at least a portion of his bureau's defects. But Sternberg was a research scientist, not an organizer or administrator; he assumed his duty accomplished on the issuance of an order. He disseminated excellent instructions for camp sanitation, but had no method of enforcement. His office called for no regular supply reports, and Sternberg admitted to the Dodge Commission that he knew nothing of the shortages of medical stores in the camps until he read of them in the newspapers.

From the beginning of mobilization, unit commanders and medical officers had kept an apprehensively keen eye for the outbreak of typhoid fever among the large concentrations of troops in the camps. They remembered well its ravages in the armies of the Civil War, and from past experience expected the volunteers to deal laxly with sanitation, making themselves especially vulnerable to the disease. Until the middle of the summer, however, the volunteer army, in spite of camp abuses, seemed healthy enough. Sick rates remained low and hardly any typhoid cases appeared.

Typhoid epidemics maintain a seasonal cycle, however: uncommon in spring, but more abundant in the middle and late summer. Actually, in the first months of the war, more cases existed in the camps than the surgeons knew of, and they committed the error, common in the medical practice of the era, of diagnosing the initial cases as malaria or other ailments. Many of the soldiers were infected by the disease in its incubatory phases, when no symptoms were manifest. Before falling sick themselves, they spread the bacteria through kitchens, tents, and latrines. The abundance of flies, bad sanitation, and the paucity of disinfectants completed the cycle. When camp physicians finally understood the disease was upon them, there was no longer any prospect of halting its spread.

At camps Thomas and Alger, the division hospitals—subject to medical shortages of all kinds—broke down under the crowd of fever-ridden patients. As the epidemic spread, divisional surgeons evacuated many of their typhoid cases to army base or civilian hospitals. But by late July, with the base hospitals already overcrowded, Surgeon General Sternberg directed that the sick be ministered to in the camps. In many of their hospitals, this order resulted in jammed wards, insufficient patient care, and shortages of every imaginable supply, from medicines to cots, bedding, and bedpans. At Camp Thomas, men stricken with typhoid sometimes lay in their own filth for as long as a full day because of the lack of clean linen to change their beds.

Once aware of the crisis, however, the Medical Department acted vigorously, albeit late, to stem it. Sternberg dispatched additional supplies, dozens of contract physicians, and hundreds of female nurses to the divisional hospitals. Chief surgeons were granted wide latitude to purchase locally, without having to rely on the army's ponderous supply mechanisms. To relieve camp congestion and to receive casualties from the Caribbean, Sternberg, in late July, established a thousand-bed hospital at Fort Monroe, Virginia, and one of 750 beds at Camp Thomas.

Early in August, on the recommendation of surgeons and troop commanders, and responding to political pressure from citizens who demanded their men be removed from what the press had labeled death traps, Russell Alger ordered a massive troop redeployment to healthier sites. Those still at Tampa, which had its share of rain, typhoid, and malaria, moved to Fernandina, Florida. Then, to escape heat and mosquitoes, they shifted again to Huntsville, Alabama. With the exception of the Seventh Corps at Jacksonville, all formations were transferred to new camps in high, rolling country, with cool, dry, healthful climates.

The health of the army at home gradually improved. The disease mortality rate, which topped off at nearly six per thousand in late summer, dropped to barely over one and a half per thousand in November. But nothing could gloss the fact that the army had suffered a medical disaster. Further, few, if any, of the measures taken against typhoid had been effective in halting its fury. The sickness had simply expended itself. Almost 21,000 men contracted the disease, mostly in the volunteer regiments, and about 1,500 men died. Adding the casualties of other illnesses, about 2,500 officers and men died of sickness in the war, ten times the number killed in action. The country demanded justifications the administration could not provide and brusquely cast aside the offered excuses.

Of the more than 200,000 volunteers mustered in April and May, no more than 35,000 left the country or were even assigned to expeditions before the signing of the armistice protocol. The rest sat out the war in the camps. The volunteers endured in these camps many of the shortages and hardships of a field campaign. The War Department deliberately withheld certain items—such as floorboards for their tents—on the assumption that the soldiers needed toughening for field service. Slow manufacture and delivery, added to the priority given to outfitting the First, Fifth, and Eighth Corps, left the volunteer camps short of uniforms, arms, tents, camp equipment, and cooking gear well into July. At camps Thomas and Alger, the quartermasters lacked wagons to haul stores from the railroad depots. Tent shortages forced six or eight men to sleep under canvas designed for four. For weeks at Jacksonville, the men ate with their fingers, using shingles and pieces of bread for plates because of delays in the arrival of mess gear.

Chickamauga and Camp Alger were also particularly filthy, providing a great breeding ground for disease. As a result of supply shortages, the soldiers lacked shovels to dig latrines and garbage pits. They had no disinfectants, and no kettles in which to boil drinking water. In both camps, the commanding officers, senior regulars, disregarded the well-established practice of widely dispersing troops for proper sanitation, and packed far too many men into too few acres of ground. Men often dug latrines and refuse pits within yards of their field kitchens, hospitals, and tents. At Camp Thomas, a stratum of limestone less than two feet beneath the surface of the soil prevented the digging of pits deep enough for the absorption of latrine contents. In rainy weather, the shallow holes flooded and overflowed, spreading sewage. Despite the spading of numerous wells, camps Thomas and Alger suffered from water shortages. The soldiers, with barely sufficient quantities for drinking and cooking, were denied enough for frequent washing. At Camp Alger, the troops had to march seven miles to the Potomac River for weekly baths.

Through carelessness and indiscipline, the volunteers polluted the camps. Officers, both volunteer and regular, failed to enforce regulations controlling the use and maintenance of latrines and paid little attention to the disposal of refuse. In many a new regiment, the men threw garbage on the ground near their tents and defecated in the surrounding woods. Near the camp of the 3rd U.S. Volunteer Cavalry at Chickamauga, a board of inspection reported, "It was quite impossible to walk through the woods . . . without soiling one's feet with fecal matter." Unfortunately, the senior commanders in the camps, mostly regular officers chafing at home-front inaction, made little attempt to put an end to such indifference.[19]

With the signing of the armistice protocol in August, discipline and morale among the volunteers began to fall apart. Men who had keenly awaited the call to action felt betrayed by the sudden end to the war. A regular officer on the staff at Camp Thomas wrote to his wife: "Everybody is disgusted after working in the most enthusiastic way . . . to have it all go for nothing. . . . The enthusiasm has gone out of this army and they all want to go home." Bored, homesick soldiers declined to obey orders, insulted their officers, and on occasion even struck them. An Illinois regiment mutinied at Camp Thomas, and large-scale fights broke out everywhere. Drunken soldiers off base rioted in the town streets. Volunteers circulated petitions and wrote letters to congressmen and hometown papers demanding the disbandment of their regiments.

Following the Spanish surrender at Santiago, Russell Alger, acting under the fantasy that all was in hand on that front, began unhurried preparations for the return of the Fifth Corps to the United States. On July 23, he informed General Shafter that as soon as it was medically safe to move them, troops would begin shipping north to rest, recuperate, and prepare for another campaign. In reply, Shafter expressed his wholehearted approval of an early evacuation, but transmitted no sense of the crisis enveloping his command, reporting only that units were shifting their bivouacs to escape the fever.

Inside of a week, Alger, acting on Surgeon General Sternberg's recommendation, leased from the Long Island Railroad five thousand acres of rolling land at Montauk Point, the easternmost tip of Long Island, for the Fifth Corps' convalescent area. Army officers from New York City had inspected the site as early as June, finding it well watered, breezy, and remote enough from population centers for effective quarantine. Troops arriving from Santiago could disembark without having to pass through any port cities. Initially, the War Department intended a modest-sized camp through which the Fifth Corps' regiments, a few at a time, could progress on their way to new ports of embarkation or demobilization. The site consisted of a detention camp at which the newly arrived regiments would be quarantined until proved free of infectious disease, and a general encampment where the men would rest and regain their strength. Each camp contained a large hospital. The army received use of the railroad's docks, buildings, and other facilities on the site. The railroad agreed to install sidings, warehouses, and terminals at its own expense, in return for which the army agreed to employ no other carrier than the Long Island Railroad for travel between New York and Montauk. The Quartermaster's, Medical, and Subsistence departments sent officers to contract for building materials and food, and for the digging of wells. The place was named Camp Wikoff, in honor of the officer killed at the Battle of San Juan Hill.

On August 1, the War Department ordered a portion of Wheeler's Cavalry Division north to Montauk. If these relatively healthy formations kept free of yellow fever on arriving, others could regularly follow on. The next day conditions around Santiago speeded up the pace. General Shafter reported the likelihood that an epidemic of yellow fever would break out; to avoid it, he urged that the whole corps be sent north "as rapidly as possible while the sickness is of a mild type." In a long telegram, Shafter truthfully detailed the disintegration of his command; it had become "really an army of convalescents." There was no time to rotate a few regiments, or even a division at a time; the whole corps had to move "immediately," and he was "sustained" in that view "by every medical officer present."[20]

Shafter's alarming messages, combined with the publication of the round-robin letter from his subordinate commanders, stampeded the president and War Department into ordering a precipitate withdrawal of the Fifth Corps from Santiago. A major problem with this movement was the condition of Camp Wikoff. Work had not proceeded well. There was congestion at the wholly inadequate railroad terminal, and the tardy arrival of building supplies and civilian workers, coupled with labor strikes, slowed construction, notably of tent floors.

The first transports carrying the Fifth Corps left Santiago on August 7, followed by others as quickly as the troops could embark. The seriously ill shipped out on specially fitted transports at the end of the month. The regiments began to arrive at Camp Wikoff on August 14, following a voyage home that was agreeable on some vessels and awful on others. "[W]e did not have good food on our transport coming back here," wrote Theodore Roosevelt to Senator Lodge, "we did not have good water; and we were so crowded that if an epidemic had broken out, we should have had literally no place in which to isolate a single patient."[21]

Some units had a truly terrible time settling into camp. Private Charles Post of the 71st New York recalled landing at Montauk: "Not a man was fit to walk to his regiment—and some regiments were farther off, and no one knew where. . . . [A] hospital sergeant came around with some milk; it was enough for only half the men lying there. . . . A little later another hospital sergeant came among us with some beef extract, about a wineglass full to a man. . . . Then a few stretcher bearers came and began moving us to the tents. . . . The tent was shelter from the wind, and there were blankets. The grass of the plateau was its floor." Some hours later, a volunteer nurse brought some food in an iron bucket. "It was a pailful of greasy water, lukewarm, and filled with ragged morsels of gristle and sinew, with potatoes here and there. It had the flavor of tallow, slightly moldy or rancid. We ladled it out by the light of his lantern, and I drank what I could in the dark."[22]

In spite of situations such as these, the War Department strove mightily to put Camp Wikoff in order. Wheeler, landing on August 15, was placed in command, with allowance to order whatever he thought necessary to make the troops comfortable. He made full use of his authority, buying tons of special foods for sick men, hiring additional doctors and nurses, and building a steam laundry and bakery. Dramatizing the administration's concern, Secretary Alger visited the camp twice and ordered extra issues of clothing and supplies. Speeding up work, steamers were chartered to move stores more quickly from New York. Water pipes were laid to each regiment's area, and further quantities of supplies of every kind were sent.

Conditions at Camp Wikoff slowly improved. Units that arrived from Santiago after the middle of August found floored tents ready to receive them and water piped to each company street. The Medical Department enlarged its hospitals and brought in large numbers of contract physicians and something like three hundred female nurses. Soldiers satiated themselves on the rich foods provided by private relief agencies; many did not even bother to draw their regular army rations.

Certain problems, however, continued to plague Camp Wikoff throughout its existence. Traffic on the Long Island Railroad, operating twice its usual number of trains per day, continued slow and congested. There were never enough wagons at the camp sidings, so that supplies piled up at the depot for want of vehicles. Quarantine regulations collapsed. In the camp and its hospitals, everyone—officers and enlisted men, sick and healthy—visited freely, in complete disregard of the spread of infection. The camp hospitals, which treated over ten thousand patients in one month, could not entirely overcome the early confusion. A War Department order that permitted surgeons to send convalescents home on leave caused a good many problems. In attempting to ameliorate their overcrowded wards, Camp Wikoff doctors sent hundreds of men off prematurely. As a result, sick and sometimes dying soldiers collapsed in passenger cars and stations across the length of Long Island. An ambience of noise, confusion, and indiscipline from first to last permeated the camp.

In late August and early September, the volunteer regiments of the Fifth Corps left for their home states on leave, at the end of which they were mustered out of the army. Regular units also began to return to the posts they had left when mobilization was declared in April. To prevent the dreadful scenes of sick soldiers dropping in streets and on station platforms, medical examining boards were established, with leave granted only to those men deemed fit enough to travel. At the same time, over a thousand of Camp Wikoff's sick were transferred to civilian hospitals from Boston to Philadelphia, which markedly improved the care of those who remained.

By the last week of September, only seven regular regiments remained in camp, and the hospitals quickly emptied. On October 3, General Shafter announced the formal disbanding of the Fifth Army Corps. Of the 21,000 men who had passed through Camp Wikoff, 257 died, mostly victims of disease.

During the time of the $50 million defense appropriation, and for the first weeks of mobilization, the War Department received a fair amount of praise for its vigorous and seemingly proficient response to the war crisis. In early June, the *Army and Navy Journal* commended "the rapidity with which the emergencies have been met by the staff departments and other authorities." But by autumn opinion had changed. Ordinary soldiers and their relatives, politicians, war correspondents, and editors now focused on the discomfort and shortages of equipment in the training camps.

Coming hard on the change in home-front attitudes, the correspondents at Santiago, led by Richard Harding Davis, wired back scathing denunciations of Shafter's tactics, supply management, and personal conduct. The round-robin affair, the mess at Montauk, and the typhoid epidemic lengthened the list of complaints against the War Department. It had starved the troops, and raised to command incompetents who wasted the lives of their men in mishandled battles or left the survivors to die miserably of disease in flyblown, barren hospitals. Critics pointed to the stark contrast between the clean efficiency of the navy's conduct of the war and the bloody, disease-ridden methods of the army.

Russell Alger became the symbol of all that had gone wrong. He was hardly the man to head the War Department in a time of crisis; he was vain, irritable, self-righteous, and at best a mediocrity. As early as May, before the army suffered its battlefield and camp miseries, the *New York Times* called for his replacement with a "serious" secretary of war. By September, Alger had become so unpopular throughout the country that Republican candidates, fearing defeat in the fall elections, pleaded with McKinley to remove the Michigan albatross from the party's collective neck. "How I wish you could be Secretary of War," wrote Senator Lodge to New York gubernatorial candidate Theodore Roosevelt; "your appointment would be the most popular thing the President could do. . . . It is too bad to make the party responsible for Alger."[23]

Specific charges against Alger were usually vague; his enemies simply blamed him for every tactical mistake, every logistic shortage, every corrupt contractor or supplier. "Algerism," however, did not in strict truth fit the man. Indeed, no evidence of enrichment or venality ever surfaced. The Reverend Teunis Hamlin, of Washington's Church of the Covenant, probably best expressed the national mood against Alger and the War Department; speaking in September 1898, he told his congregation, "Whether there have been deliberate crimes against the lives of our soldiers or the blunders of ignorance and incompetence that are as bad as crimes, the public does not yet know. But it does know that in Cuba they were but half clothed, half fed, half sheltered, half doctored."[24]

Alger exacerbated the issue by disparaging sickness and hardship as inevitable companions of war, and to the end he insisted that no important decisions made by himself, the department bureaucracy, or the field commanders had been anything but correct. He was contemptuous of his critics and made no distinction between politically motivated defamation and objective criticism of the War Department at home and military operations abroad. "What do you want me to do?" he asked a reporter. "To get down into the sewer with these people?" Sustained by commiserating friends, he insisted he would never resign under a cloud and would continue in office until the facts exonerated him.[25]

Alger's problem—indeed, that of the army and War Department as a whole—was that it was unfit, as constituted, to fight an overseas war on short notice. It was still struggling out of its Indian-fighting history, and so far as global, or even hemispheric, thinking was concerned, was very much in a coast-defense mind-set. Expeditions overseas were near the bottom of the list of priorities when the *Maine* exploded. "The underlying fact of all," commented Senator Lodge truthfully, "is that we never have a sufficient army and are always unprepared when we go to war."[26]

The astonishing fact, however, remained that the War Department, burdened with tens of thousands of volunteers it neither wanted nor needed, who were overwhelming an archaic bureaucratic machinery, was still able to mobilize an army from civilian life, concentrate it in training camps, and arm, equip, clothe, and feed at least that part which engaged in active operations. It fought battles on each side of the globe, from Puerto Rico to Manila, and, with the large strategic contribution of the navy, closed the whole matter in three months. The Dodge Commission, whose findings were published in February 1899, found no corruption or intentional neglect of duty, noting rightly instead that "there was lacking in the general administration of the War Department . . . that complete grasp of the situation which was essential to the highest efficiency and discipline of the Army." It was a direct rebuke to Alger's competency, and by extension, the whole War Department and army bureaucracy and field commands.[27]

Russell Alger had to go, the scapegoat for everything muddled by the War Department in the fight against Spain. "Sweep Alger out of the way," wrote one editor. "Remove the polluting influence of Michigan politics and the rest will follow as a matter of course. Algerism is at the bottom of the war scandals. Remove Alger and you administer to Algerism its death blow." But would he go quietly with grace, or hang on to a pathetic end?[28]

In mid-February 1899, accompanying the president and Navy Secretary Long to Boston, Alger had the satisfaction of loyal applause from the Civil War veterans of the Grand Army of the Republic, then holding its convention in the city. But the country was mired in the scandals of the beef contracts, and Alger was also subjected to outbursts of hissing and yells of "Three cheers for General Miles!" and "Yah, yah, yah! Beef! Beef!" Alger came away deeply wounded.[29]

But he still clung to his statement that he would never resign office "under fire." During the height of the beef court hearings, Alger met with the president, later declaring that he had tendered his resignation and that McKinley had refused it. After the meeting, he told waiting reporters that unless some unforeseen situation arose, he intended to head the War Department for the remainder of the president's term.

When fighting erupted in the Philippines between American forces and the rebels under Aguinaldo, Democratic and antiexpansionist papers denounced the conflict as "the President's war." Naturally, every casualty, every misstep became charged against the "corrupt" and incompetent War Department. William McKinley needed to inspire the nation to confidence in the management of the Philippine insurrection, and that was impossible with his secretary of war still very much in evidence. Everyone understood that Russell Alger had to disappear, except Russell Alger, oblivious of the political mess he was creating. Yet no hint came from the president that he no longer wished him in the cabinet, and he treated the secretary with every courtesy. It was clear to all of McKinley's close friends and associates, however, that he was now waiting for Alger's resignation, and finally, despite his demeanor of breezy ingenuousness, Alger realized it too.

Still, he publicly claimed there was "nothing but air" in the rumor of his departure. He would certainly not resign that year. Secretary of State Hay sent the president a clipping of the interview in which Alger had made that statement, Hay noting, "This is deplorable—after all the trouble we have taken to save his dignity."[30]

There were also new events abroad that warranted giving Alger the boot. A Manila version of the round-robin was about to explode in the press, this time over military censorship of newspaper correspondents. The official reports from the military commander, Major General El-well Otis, had presented an optimistic view not shared by senior officers in the field, battling Aguinaldo's guerrillas. Otis had censored the bloody facts of the Philippine insurrection on the grounds that "they would alarm the people at home." The Manila correspondents combined to send their scoop reflecting the field officers' attitudes, not through Otis's headquarters, as required, but direct via Hong Kong to their papers. It hit the streets on July 17 and created a sensation.

McKinley now had two political millstones from the War Department around his neck, Alger and Otis. He tried to get Hay to deliver the blow to Alger. But when Hay declined the honor, McKinley shoved the problem to his ailing vice president, Garret Hobart, a man close to Alger and who could not turn the president down. Still, no resignation came. To George Cortelyou, McKinley, at last exasperated, said, "I think something will happen tomorrow; something will come to a head tomorrow."[31]

The White House offices had hardly opened for business the following morning when McKinley summoned Cortelyou for a walk. "Well," said the president, "he was over and left it with me." The early-morning interview with Russell Alger, ending with the tendering of his resignation, was short and devoid of embarrassment. It was also unconditional—it would take place at the president's pleasure, August 1. In Alger's place, McKinley appointed the progressive New York Republican lawyer Elihu Root to begin the long-needed modernization of the U.S. Army. General Miles would hang on as commanding general until 1903, when the man and the position were replaced by the army's first chief of staff, General Samuel Young, late of the Cavalry Division at Santiago.[32]

EMPIRE

I took the [Panama] Canal Zone, and let Congress debate.
—*President Theodore Roosevelt*

In the congressional fight over the Treaty of Paris, the Republican Senate leadership agreed to follow the presidential path. In effect, William McKinley was the floor manager for the treaty. In the Teller Ammendment granting Cuban independence, and in the summer annexation of Hawaii, he had played a well-nigh invisible role. But the taking of Puerto Rico, Guam, and the Philippines was the result of the instrumental involvement of the president. The White House, not Congress, emerged from the war as the fount of decision and action in foreign affairs.

Had President McKinley and the Senate acted differently, eschewing an American empire, acquired almost by default, the European powers and Japan would have been mightily confused. The United States had now joined the imperial club, comporting itself as a confident great power was expected to, taking, as a historian said, "what it could and keeping it."[1]

In dealing with the Cuban crisis prior to the war, both Grover Cleveland and William McKinley initially held a single purpose uppermost: to avert any international tangles that could upset the flow of the nation's business, still emerging from the depression of 1893. When the Cuban problem, by now afflicting American politics and institutions, did not go away, McKinley found himself holding a bad hand. He could initiate a war with Spain or resist public opinion and risk losing Republican control of Congress. Though he was morally revolted by the cruelties of the Cuban revolution, it was domestic politics that forced McKinley ultimately to initiate hostilities with Spain. When American public emotion climbed to hysterical heights following the *Maine* disaster, McKinley caved to the popular will for war. At that point, neither the president nor the public at large—save large-policy expansionists—had any design beyond Cuban independence. War with monarchical, Catholic Spain had no original aim but to kick the withered Spaniard, after four hundred years, out of the Western Hemisphere.

But as the summer moved on and American success assumed geostrategic proportions around the globe, presidential and public aspirations underwent a sea change. The absorption of Puerto Rico, Guam, and the Philippines, along with the annexation of Hawaii, was an attempt to construct an empire, but one that differed from the colonial chattels of the European powers—an altruistic export of American politics, ideals, and morality. This, however, stood side by side with one of the standard excuses for empire, markets, especially in Asia, for a surplus of manufactured goods pouring out of highly mechanized factories and bountiful farms.

Until 1898, Americans believed that their political institutions were adapted only for contiguous North America. Imperial holdings, most believed, would destroy the American republic just as surely as they had subverted the Roman republic. It was such attitudes that led to the scuttling of the Hawaiian annexation treaty during Cleveland's term in 1893. Five years later, however, the United States easily annexed Hawaii.

The islands had been an indivisible element of the American economy since the first third of the nineteenth century, when Protestant missionaries fashioned strong religious and temporal ties between the islands and the United States. A commercial reciprocity treaty with the Kingdom of Hawaii in 1875 provided the United States with a virtual veto over Hawaii's foreign relations. American capital developed vast sugar plantations whose continued prosperity was completely dependent on American markets. In the strategic sphere, Alfred Thayer Mahan had termed the islands the great Pacific "central station." They were the closest, indeed the only, Pacific rampart to any future Central American isthmian canal. Facing in the other direction, Hawaii sat athwart the sea routes from the Western Hemisphere to the Philippines, China, and Japan. "To have a central position such as this,"

Mahan said, "at once fix[es] the attention of the strategist [and] of the statesmen of commerce."[2]

When, in the spring of 1898, the Senate Foreign Relations Committee issued its report advocating the acquisition of Hawaii, it argued in Mahanian terms that the strategic nature of the islands was "the main argument in favor of the annexation." The report quashed one of the principal antiexpansionist arguments, that of confining the United States to the North American landmass, by raising the specter of Japanese encroachment as a prime reason for annexation. "The issue in Hawaii," the senators noted, "is not between monarchy and the Republic. . . . The issue is whether, in that inevitable struggle, Asia [i.e., Japan] or America shall have the vantage ground of the control of the naval 'Key of the Pacific,' the commercial 'Cross-roads of the Pacific.' "[3]

In the July summer of the war, the large-policy advocates in the administration and Senate achieved their objective; Hawaii was annexed to the United States. Dewey's operations in the Philippines had taught America that possession of Hawaii, if the United States hoped to become a commanding presence in the Far East, was absolutely essential, serving as it would as a naval base projecting power to the Orient.

The Philippines were the logical next step westward, a gateway to chimerical riches in China and the Far East. From the strategic viewpoint, American control of the Philippines offered an instant check to Japanese and German expansionist goals in the area. For the United States, the danger of an American military presence here lurked in the fact that it was too distant to support from the navy's new Hawaiian bases, something that became excruciatingly manifest in the early weeks of World War II. Guam (with the rest of the Ladrones/Marianas), in strategic reality the eastern defense wall of the Philippines, was supposed to alleviate the pressure on extensive American supply lines in the western Pacific, serving as a way station between Pearl Harbor and Manila. But Congress refused to fortify it, and when the Japanese came in December 1941, it fell in a day, cutting the Philippines off from Hawaii and the West Coast of the United States.

But in 1898, the political impossibility of permitting Spain to keep the Philippines, and the unpalatable option of granting independence, naturally drew the American business community and the McKinley administration to the potential of the region as prime territory for financial and commercial expansion. Senator Mark Hannah, mega-industrialist and close adviser to the president, declared for "a strong foothold in the Philippine Islands," for then "we can and will take a strong slice of the commerce of Asia. That is what we want . . . and it is better to strike for it while the iron is hot."[4]

On the Caribbean side of the new American empire, gaining Puerto Rico from Spain and Guantánamo Bay from an "independent" Cuba (as well as the purchase of the Virgin Islands from Denmark) had a singular purpose, the defense of the Atlantic approaches to the yet to be built Central American isthmian canal. The voyage of the *Oregon* around Cape Horn had made it manifestly apparent that if the United States was to become a significant participant in commercial or colonial imperialism, it had to be able to protect its holdings by moving strong elements of its rapidly growing navy quickly from ocean to ocean. A canal would also immeasurably ease commerce between the east and west coasts of the Western Hemisphere. The Spanish-American War guaranteed not only that the canal would be built, but that the United States would build, control, and defend it. It would be the linchpin of America's hemispheric hegemony and national defense priorities for nearly half a century.

By 1899, the United States had forged a new empire. American politicians, naval officers, and businessmen had created it amid much debate and with conscious purpose. The empire expanded from the continental frontier, as defined by Frederick Jackson Turner, to pre-eminence in the Western Hemisphere, and, for good or ill, into the farthest reaches of the Pacific. America, as Alfred Thayer Mahan had predicted, now looked outward.

NOTES

CHAPTER 1: STATE OF THE UNION

1. William Roscoe Thayer, *The Life of John Hay*, vol. 2, p. 94; Henry Adams, *The Education of Henry Adams*, pp. 340–341.
2. Wilbur R. Jacobs, ed., *The Historical World of Frederick Jackson Turner*, p. 4.
3. James D. Bennett, *Frederick Jackson Turner*, p. 42.
4. Frederick Jackson Turner, *The Frontier in American History*, p. 30.
5. In January 1893, a revolutionary party of white planters, mostly descendants of American missionaries, overthrew, with the help of a landing party from the U.S. cruiser *Boston*, the theatrical monarchy of Queen Liliuokalani, proclaiming a republic. A treaty of annexation to the United States was hastily drawn and was submitted by the lame-duck President Benjamin Harrison for ratification to the Senate. When Grover Cleveland became president in March 1893, he withdrew the treaty.
6. Turner, *The Frontier in American History*, p. 38.
7. Virtually every regular army officer, Union and Confederate, in the Civil War learned his trade from Dennis Mahan while a cadet at West Point.
8. Allan Westcott, ed., *American Sea Power Since 1775*, p. 211.
9. Albert Gleaves, *The Life and Letters of Stephen Bleecker Luce*, p. 179.
10. W. D. Puleston, *Mahan*, pp. 68–69, italics added.
11. William E. Livezey, *Mahan on Sea Power*, p. 12. Luce's fears for the school's existence were not ill-founded. Congress made no appropriation for the college in 1887 and it closed its doors for a year. Mahan spent that time as part of a commission selecting the site of a naval base on the northwest coast. For several years thereafter, there was no certainty of the college's permanence.
12. Robert Seager II, *Alfred Thayer Mahan*, p. 205.
13. Mahan soon realized this as false doctrine. A nation no longer needed to ship products under her own flag to become commercially prosperous; she only needed to have a navy capable of protecting the goods and vessels.

14. Seager, *Mahan,* pp. 25–77 passim.
15. Ibid., p. 25.
16. Ibid., pp. 57, 416.
17. Alfred Thayer Mahan, "The United States Looking Outward," *The Interest of America in Sea Power,* pp. 21–22.
18. Puleston, *Alfred Thayer Mahan,* p. 115. Mahan was president of the War College at the time, 1893, and he used all his by then considerable political influence to keep from going to sea, to no avail. The *Chicago,* flagship of the European Squadron, flew the flag of Rear Admiral Henry Erben, a decidedly unintellectual companion who had to be uncomfortably included in the receptions given Mahan in what turned into, at no authorial instigation, a triumphant two-year book tour.
19. Theodore Roosevelt, "The Influence of Sea Power Upon History," *Atlantic Monthly,* October 1890, pp. 563–567; Seager, *Alfred Thayer Mahan,* p. 210.
20. William A. Robinson, *Thomas B. Reed,* p. 251.
21. The *Maine,* authorized as Armored Cruiser No. 1, was reclassified as a second-class battleship during her fitting out.
22. Walter LaFeber, *The New Empire,* pp. 102–103; Roger Butterfield, *The American Past,* p. 253.
23. Seager, *Alfred Thayer Mahan,* p. 138.
24. Robley D. Evans, *A Sailor's Log,* p. 171.
25. Cruisers of the era came in several guises. The largest in size, tonnage, and guns were the "armored" cruisers, named for the vertical side armor along their hulls. Internal protection of engines, boilers, magazines, etc., was given by a horizontal protective deck running the length of the hull below the waterline. "Protected" cruisers had the protective deck only. "Unprotected" and lesser types dispensed with virtually all armor, save local shielding around the main guns. Except for the earliest types, all armor was of specially hardened steel alloy.
26. *New York Herald,* March 31, 1889; Navy Department, *Annual Report of the Secretary of the Navy,* 1889, p. 36.
27. Navy Department, *Annual Report, 1889,* pp. 3–11.
28. 64th Congress, 2nd Session, Senate Document No. 555, *Navy Yearbook, 1916,* p. 64; Harold and Margaret Sprout, *The Rise of American Naval Power 1775–1918,* p. 211.
29. Sprout, *Rise of American Naval Power,* pp. 212–213.
30. Walter Millis, *The Martial Spirit,* p. 7; Butterfield, *The American Past,* p. 254.
31. Grover Cleveland was the only Democratic president (1885–1889, 1893–1897) between the disgraced James Buchanan who left office in March 1861 and Woodrow Wilson's election in 1912.
32. H. Wayne Morgan, *From Hayes to McKinley,* pp. 454–455.
33. Thayer, *The Life of John Hay,* vol. 2, pp. 101–102.
34. Morgan, *From Hayes to McKinley,* p. 465.
35. Ibid., p. 468.

36. Allan Nevins, *Grover Cleveland*, pp. 649–650.
37. Morgan, *From Hayes to McKinley*, pp. 468–469; Thomas Beer, *Hanna*, pp. 132–133. Hanna undoubtedly used the words "shit house"; his biographer, however, was too delicate to repeat it, indicating instead, a "Primordial American noun, compound, meaning latrine."
38. Nevins, *Grover Cleveland*, p. 612.
39. Beer, *Hanna*, pp. 132–133.
40. Butterfield, *The American Past*, p. 266.
41. Nevins, *Grover Cleveland*, p. 613.
42. Ibid., pp. 614–615. Altgeld, a reforming, regular Democrat, was no stranger to social strife, having pardoned in the past year the anarchist Haymarket Riot bombers of 1886 on the grounds of their receiving unfair, prejudiced trials.
43. Richard Olney could be as pigheaded a man as any who ever lived, a trait best symbolized when he forever shut his door to a beloved daughter when she married a dentist, someone Olney considered beneath her social station.
44. Nevins, *Grover Cleveland*, pp. 618–619; *New York Times*, July 3, 1894.
45. Henry James, *Richard Olney*, p. 49.
46. Ibid., p. 50.
47. Nelson Miles becomes a considerable figure in this work. He had an excellent Civil War record, being appointed major general of volunteers and a corps commander at age twenty-six. He married well, Mary Sherman, sister of Senator John Sherman (he of the "Sherman" Anti-trust Act) of Ohio and General William Tecumseh Sherman. Miles was an Indian fighter of no mean prowess; he beat Crazy Horse at Wolf Mountain, Montana, and was instrumental in obtaining the surrenders of both Chief Joseph and Geronimo. He commanded the expedition that put down the Ghost Dance cult rebellion in 1890, culminating in the massacre at Wounded Knee. In 1895 he succeeded Schofield as commanding general of the U.S. Army.
48. War Department, *Annual Report*, vol. 1, 1894, pp. 108–109.
49. Robert Wooster, *Nelson A. Miles*, p. 199–201.
50. Nevins, *Grover Cleveland*, pp. 623–624.
51. Ibid., p. 626.
52. Robinson, *Thomas B. Reed*, p. 321.
53. Morgan, *From Hayes to McKinley*, p. 476; Nevins, *Grover Cleveland*, pp. 650, 675.
54. *New York Times*, February 28, 1895.
55. Nevins, *Grover Cleveland*, p. 629.
56. *Washington Post*, May 11, 1895.
57. Nevins, *Grover Cleveland*, p. 634.
58. State Department, *Foreign Relations*, 1895, vol. 1, p. 545.
59. Ibid.
60. From Thomas Jefferson's presidency until Woodrow Wilson's, the president's "annual message," now popularly called "the state of the union"

message, was delivered by messenger to Congress and read aloud by a relay of clerks in the well of the House of Representatives, with none of the stagy theater now attendant. It was presented before the "old" Congress adjourned in December, rather than to the "new" Congress convening in January.

61. Nevins, *Grover Cleveland*, p. 637.
62. *Foreign Relations*, 1895, vol. 1, pp. 563–576 ff.
63. Nevins, *Grover Cleveland*, pp. 640–641; James, *Richard Olney*, p. 140.
64. Nevins, *Grover Cleveland*, p. 641–642; Henry Pringle, *Theodore Roosevelt*, p. 167. Pringle's views of Theodore Roosevelt are generally negative, ascribing to TR the political mind of an eight-year-old with a toy gun. This is sometimes correct, but hardly to the extent the biographer conjures.
65. Joseph E. Wisan, *The Cuban Crisis as Reflected in the New York Press*, p. 23n; Pringle, *Theodore Roosevelt*, p. 168.
66. Richard E. Welch Jr., *The Presidencies of Grover Cleveland*, p. 209.
67. Ibid.
68. Butterfield, *The American Past*, p. 271; Morgan, *From Hayes to McKinley*, p. 506.
69. Ibid., p. 272.
70. Edmund Morris, *The Rise of Theodore Roosevelt*, p. 554.

CHAPTER 2: EVER FAITHFUL ISLE

1. Earl R. Beck, "The Martínez Campos Government of 1879: Spain's Last Chance in Cuba," *Hispanic American Historical Review* (hereinafter cited as *HAHR*), May 1976, pp. 270–271. The office of governor general was the overall authority; the captain general was the military commander. The positions were invariably held by the same individual, a senior general of the Spanish army.
2. *Foreign Relations*, 1879, pp. 944–951, passim.
3. Beck, "The Martínez Campos Government of 1879," pp. 276–278.
4. Ibid., p. 280.
5. Jorge Mañach, *Martí*, p. 28.
6. Ibid., p. 20.
7. Ibid., pp. 36–40, passim.
8. Ibid., p. 60.
9. Philip S. Foner, *The Spanish-Cuban-American War* (hereinafter cited as *SCAW*), vol. 1, p. xx. Tomás Estrada Palma later became the first president of independent Cuba in 1902.
10. Ibid., p. xxii.
11. Ibid., p. xxv.
12. Ibid., pp. xxx–1; Detroit *Free Press*, May 16, 1891.
13. Foner, *SCAW*, vol. 1, p. 2.
14. Filibustering, the illegal running of guns and fighters, from the Spanish *filibustero*, "freebooter."

15. Foner, *SCAW,* vol 1, p. 4.
16. Ibid., p. 8.
17. Ibid., pp. 8–9; see *The America of José Martí: Selected Writings,* trans. Juan de Onis, N.Y.: 1953, pp. 247–249.
18. Foner, *SCAW,* vol. 1, p. 14; Ernest R. May, *Imperial Democracy,* p. 96; French Ensor Chadwick, *Relations of the United States and Spain—Diplomacy* (hereinafter cited as *Diplomacy*), p. 406.
19. Chadwick, *Diplomacy,* p. 406.
20. David F. Trask, *The War with Spain in 1898,* p. 7.
21. New York *World,* April 12, 1895; Valeriano Weyler, *Mi Mando en Cuba,* vol. 1, p. 23; Murat Halstead, *The Story of Cuba,* pp. 138–139; Foner, *SCAW,* vol. 1, p. 16; Chadwick, *Diplomacy,* p. 407; Herbert H. Sargent, *The Campaign of Santiago de Cuba,* vol. 1, p. 30. Numbers for the Spanish army during the Cuban Liberation War and Spanish-American War are imprecise. For the Spanish forces in Cuba at the outset, estimates run from 13,000 men of the *Ejército de España,* the regular army (Chadwick), to 20,000 (Foner), added to whom are 60,000-plus *voluntarios, guerrilleros,* marines, and *Guardia Civil* rural constabulary. I have chosen Chadwick's figure as the more realistic for the Cuban War of Independence and Sargent's for the Spanish-American War.
22. Hugh Thomas, *Cuba,* pp. 320–321.
23. Ibid.
24. Richard Harding Davis, *Cuba in War Time,* pp. 78–79, 91–96.
25. Ibid., p. 37.
26. Ibid., pp. 82–83.
27. Bashkina, "A Page from the Cuban People's Heroic History," *International Affairs* [Moscow], March 1964, p. 118; Foner, *SCAW,* vol. 1, p. 20; Graham A. Cosmas, *An Army for Empire,* p. 76.
28. Foner, *SCAW,* vol. 1, p. 35.
29. Ibid., p. 20.
30. Halstead, *The Story of Cuba,* p. 139.
31. Foner, *SCAW,* vol. 1, pp. 21–22; Clarence King, "Fire and Sword in Cuba," *Forum,* September 1896, p. 37.
32. Charles E. Chapman, *History of the Cuban Republic,* pp. 81–82.
33. Foner, *SCAW,* vol. 1, pp. 21–22.
34. Bashkina, "A Page from the Cuban People's Heroic History," p. 119.
35. May, *Imperial Democracy,* pp. 99–100.
36. Trask, *The War with Spain in 1898,* p. 5.
37. Foner, *SCAW,* vol. 1, p. 49.
38. Ibid., pp. 50–51; Foner, *Antonio Maceo,* p. 199.
39. Winston Churchill, *My Early Life,* pp. 78–87, passim.
40. King, "Fire and Sword in Cuba," pp. 44–45.
41. Ibid., p. 48.
42. Foner, *SCAW,* vol. 1, pp. 59–60.

43. Ibid., p. 61.
44. Ibid.,
45. Bashkina, "A Page from the Cuban People's Heroic History," pp. 119–120.
46. Foner, *SCAW*, vol. 1, p. 63
47. Foner, *Antonio Maceo*, p. 215.
48. Wisan, *The Cuban Crisis as Reflected in the New York Press*, p. 66n.
49. May, *Imperial Democracy*, pp. 100–101; Marcus M. Wilkerson, *Public Opinion and the Spanish-American War*; Trumbull White, *Pictorial History of Our War with Spain*, pp. 228–229.
50. Sargent, *The Campaign of Santiago de Cuba*, vol. 1, p. 27.
51. Davis, *Cuba in War Time*, p. 20.
52. Foner, *SCAW*, vol. 1, p. 113.
53. Frederick Funston, *Memories of Two Wars*, p. 100; Chapman, *History of the Cuban Republic*, p. 81; Wilkerson, *Public Opinion and the Spanish-American War*, p. 40; Foner, *SCAW*, vol. 1, p. 117; Weyler, *Mi Mando en Cuba*, vol. 1, pp. 165–166.
54. Foner, *Antonio Maceo*, p. 230; Bashkina, "A Page from the Cuban People's Heroic History," p. 121.
55. Foner, *Antonio Maceo*, p. 231.
56. Bashkina, "A Page from the Cuban People's Heroic History," p. 121.
57. Foner, *Antonio Maceo*, pp. 234–235; Foner, *SCAW*, vol. 1, p. 84.
58. May, *Imperial Democracy*, p. 103.
59. Ibid., p. 104.
60. Foner, *SCAW*, vol. 1, p. 93.
61. Hugh Thomas, *Cuba*, p. 331; Bashkina, "A Page from the Cuban People's Heroic History," p. 122.
62. Leonard Williams, "The Army of Spain: Its Present Qualities and Modern Value," *Journal of the Military Service Institution of the United States*, September 1897, p. 351.
63. May, *Imperial Democracy*, pp. 106–107.
64. Ibid., pp. 110–111.

CHAPTER 3: *MAINE* TO HAVANA

1. Francis W. Hirst, *Life and Letters of Thomas Jefferson*, pp. 539–541. John A. S. Grenville and George Berkeley Young, *Politics, Strategy, and American Diplomacy* (hereinafter cited as *PSAD*), p. 179. In 1819, a year after the First Seminole War, Adams, secretary of state to President James Monroe, negotiated the surrender of all Spanish claims to west Florida, ceded east Florida to the United States, and canceled all Spanish claims to the Pacific Northwest. These significant diplomatic defeats to Spain were the result of her inability to keep the peace in her North American colonies.
2. Chadwick, *Diplomacy*, pp. 256–260.
3. Ibid., pp. 262–267; May, *Imperial Democracy*, p. 91.
4. May, *Imperial Democracy*, p. 68.

5. Chadwick, *Diplomacy*, pp. 422–423.

6. Wilkerson, *Public Opinion and the Spanish-American War*, pp. 18–20; Wisan, *The Cuban Crisis as Reflected in the New York Press*, pp. 71–72.

7. Chadwick, *Diplomacy*, pp. 422–423. Captain Moreu would later command the armored cruiser *Cristóbal Colón* at the Battle of Santiago.

8. Grenville and Young, *PSAD*, p. 185.

9. Ibid., pp. 187–188.

10. Chadwick, *Diplomacy*, pp. 425–426; Grenville and Young, *PSAD*, p. 183.

11. An insurgent navy is not a ludicrous thought, as shown by the Continental navy in the American Revolution and the Confederate navy in the American Civil War. At the outset of that conflict, Abraham Lincoln recognized the Southern Confederacy as a belligerent power, thus providing the United States the rights of blockade and search and seizure on the high seas, something that would not have obtained otherwise. On the other hand, the insurgent navies maintained the identical rights of search and seizure on the high seas.

12. Festus P. Summers, ed., *The Cabinet Diary of William L. Wilson*, pp. 35–36.

13. *New York Tribune*, March 2, 12, 1896.

14. Grenville and Young, *PSAD*, p. 190; *Foreign Relations*, 1897, pp. 540–544. Revisionists to the contrary, the vast majority of American *military* interventions in Latin America were for strategic purposes first, humanitarian motives second, and economic salvation a far-distant third.

15. *Foreign Relations*, 1897, pp. 540–544.

16. Ibid.

17. Ibid.

18. Wilkerson, *Public Opinion and the Spanish-American War*, p. 26.

19. Chadwick, *Diplomacy*, pp. 468–469.

20. Wilkerson, *Public Opinion and the Spanish-American War*, pp. 22–25.

21. James, *Richard Olney*, pp. 297–303; Chadwick, *Diplomacy*, pp. 465–467. Chadwick would command the armored cruiser *New York*, flagship of the North Atlantic Squadron, in the Spanish-American War.

22. Chadwick, *Diplomacy*, p. 415.

23. Gerald G. Eggert, "Our Man in Havana: Fitzhugh Lee," *HAHR*, November 1967, pp. 466–467; May, *Imperial Democracy*, p. 89.

24. Eggert, "Our Man in Havana," pp. 466–469. In a geopolitical sense, the Mexican-American War of 1846–1847 established the United States as the preeminent power in North America.

25. Ibid., pp. 466–468.

26. Ibid.

27. Nevins, *Letters of Grover Cleveland*, pp. 448–449.

28. Summers, *Cabinet Diary of William L. Wilson*, pp. 169, 183.

29. Wisan, *The Cuban Crisis*, p. 170.

30. Ibid., p. 173.

31. Summers, *Cabinet Diary of William L. Wilson*, p. 193; Foner, *SCAW*, vol. 1, p. 207.

32. *Foreign Relations,* 1896, pp. xxix–xxxvi.
33. Ibid. Tomás Estrada Palma, general legate of the Junta and the Cuban "Republic," proudly admitted to a clench-jawed Richard Olney that he and his whole delegation were already American citizens.
34. Ibid.
35. James, *Richard Olney,* pp. 168–169. James Cameron was the son of Simon Cameron, Lincoln's corrupt first secretary of war.
36. May, *Imperial Democracy,* p. 118.
37. Ibid.
38. *Literary Digest,* vol. 15, 1897, p. 381.
39. George F. Parker, *Recollections of Grover Cleveland,* pp. 249–250.
40. May, *Imperial Democracy,* p. 114.
41. H. Wayne Morgan, *William McKinley and His America,* pp. 251–253, 255; Margaret Leech, *In the Days of McKinley,* pp. 152–153.
42. Leech, *In the Days of McKinley,* pp. 103–104; Russell Weighley, *History of the United States Army,* p. 305.
43. Morris, *Rise of Theodore Roosevelt,* p. 560; Paolo Coletta, "John Davis Long," in Paolo Coletta, ed., *American Secretaries of the Navy,* vol. 1, pp. 431–432. There was a time before 1881, and the appointment by President Garfield of William H. Hunt, that the Navy Department was also a seat for the time-serving and incompetent. With notable exceptions such as George Bancroft, champion of merit promotions and founder of the U.S. Naval Academy, and the excellent Gideon Welles, Lincoln's iron-willed Civil War chief, who held the longest tenure, 1861–1869, the closest most navy secretaries came to the salt of their department was picking through a barrel of pork.
44. Morris, *Rise of Theodore Roosevelt,* pp. 554–556.
45. Ibid.
46. Morison, *Letters of Theodore Roosevelt,* vol. 1, pp. 568–569.
47. Morris, *Rise of Theodore Roosevelt,* p. 560.
48. Morison, *Letters of Theodore Roosevelt,* vol 1, p. 589.
49. Mayo, *America of Yesterday,* p. 147.
50. Ronald Spector, *Admiral of the New Empire,* p. 34; Grenville and Young, *PSAD,* p. 272.
51. Grenville and Young, *PSAD,* p. 272.
52. John B. Hattendorf, et al., *Sailors and Scholars,* pp. 45–46. Just in case Richard Olney's 20-inch gun really hit its target, Taylor's students also outlined a plan for defending the New England coast in a war against Great Britain over the Venezuelan boundary dispute.
53. John A. S. Grenville, "American Naval Preparations for War with Spain, 1896–1898," *Journal of American Studies,* vol. 2, No. 1, pp. 34–35; Grenville and Young, *PSAD,* pp. 273–274.
54. Grenville and Young, *PSAD,* p. 274.
55. Spector, *Admiral of the New Empire,* pp. 32–33.
56. Grenville, "American Naval Preparations for War with Spain," pp. 36, 40.

57. Ibid., pp. 37, 41–47. The "Sicard plan" is also noteworthy for outlining the United States' first known war plan against Japan, predating the famous, ongoing "Orange Plan" by sixteen years.

58. May, *Imperial Democracy*, p. 117.

59. Sherman's name, as secretary of state, appears on virtually all diplomatic notes, letters, and other official papers. Alvey A. Adee, no matter the administration, drafted the precise language. He is, in every sense, the American version of the fictional Sir Humphrey Applebee, the cynical, all-knowing, permanent bureaucrat in the British television series *Yes, Minister.*

60. Foner, *SCAW,* vol. 1, p. 117.

61. *Foreign Relations, 1897,* pp. 507–508.

62. May, *Imperial Democracy,* p. 125.

63. Louis L. Gould, *The Spanish-American War and President McKinley,* p. 10.

64. Ibid., p. 13; William R. Braisted, *The United States Navy in the Pacific, 1897–1909,* pp. 12–13.

65. Gould, *The Spanish-American War and President McKinley,* pp. 28–29.

66. *Foreign Relations, 1898,* pp. 558–561.

67. Ibid., p. 580; Foner, *SCAW,* vol. 1, p. 217; Grenville and Young, *PSAD,* pp. 249–250. The killer, Angiolillo, claimed the act as retaliation for the execution of anarchists convicted of bombing a religious procession in Barcelona.

68. *Foreign Relations, 1898,* pp. 592–594.

69. *Spanish Diplomatic Correspondence and Documents, 1896–1900,* pp. 29–35.

70. Morgan, *William McKinley and His America,* p. 344.

71. *Foreign Relations.* 1898, pp. 582–589, passim; Foner, *SCAW,* vol. 1, pp. 127–128.

72. Foner, *SCAW,* vol. 1, p. 128. One was actually killed, even though protected as an official emissary.

73. Thomas, *Cuba,* p. 353; Frederick Palmer, *Bliss, Peacemaker,* p. 48; Teodore Agoncillo, *Malolos: The Crisis of the Republic,* p. 11.

74. *Chicago Tribune,* November 20, 1897.

75. Spector, *Admiral of the New Empire,* p. 39.

76. John Barrett, *Admiral George Dewey,* pp. 13–14.

77. Richard S. West Jr., *Admirals of American Empire,* pp. 142–143. The Bureau of Navigation, primus inter pares in the department, also functioned until 1942 as the assignment desk for personnel.

78. George Dewey, *Autobiography of George Dewey,* p. 167. The Naval Academy class of 1858 numbered fifteen acting midshipmen. Howell stood second, Dewey fifth. Of that class, four men achieved admiral's rank.

79. Theodore Roosevelt, *Theodore Roosevelt: An Autobiography,* pp. 210–211.

80. Morris, *Rise of Theodore Roosevelt,* pp. 586–587.

81. Morison, *Letters of Theodore Roosevelt,* vol. 1, p. 691.

82. Lauren Hall Healy and Luis Kutner, *The Admiral,* p. 136; Dewey, *Autobiography,* pp. 148–149; Spector, *Admiral of the New Empire,* p. 38.

83. Healy and Kutner, *The Admiral,* pp. 136–137.
84. Ibid., p. 138; Dewey, *Autobiography,* p. 153.
85. John D. Long, *The New American Navy,* vol. 1, pp. 134–135; Charles Dwight Sigsbee, "Personal Narrative of the *Maine*" (part 1), *Century Magazine,* November 1898, p. 76.
86. Hyman G. Rickover, *How the Battleship* Maine *Was Destroyed,* p. 23.
87. *Foreign Relations,* 1897, pp. xi–xxii, passim.
88. Wisan, *The Cuban Crisis,* pp. 363–364.
89. Gould, *The Spanish-American War and President McKinley,* p. 31; Diane E. Cooper, "Diplomat and Intelligence Officer: The Duties of Lt. George L. Dyer, U.S. Naval Attaché," in James C. Bradford, ed., *Crucible of Empire,* p. 10.
90. *Spanish Diplomatic Correspondence and Documents,* p. 52.
91. Sigsbee, "Personal Narrative of the *Maine*" (part 1), p. 79.
92. *Foreign Relations,* 1898, p. 647–650.
93. Ibid., pp. 598–599.
94. *Spanish Diplomatic Correspondence,* p. 62; *Annual Reports of the Navy Department,* 1898: Appendix to the Report of the Chief of the Bureau of Navigation (hereinafter cited as, Navy Department, *Annual Report,* 1898, BuNav Appendix), p. 21.
95. Thomas, *Cuba,* p. 357; *Foreign Relations,* 1898, pp. 1024–1025.
96. Wisan, *Cuban Crisis,* pp. 374–375; *Foreign Relations,* 1898, p. 1025.
97. Margaret Long, ed., *Journal of John D. Long,* pp. 212–213.
98. Ibid.; Morison, *Letters of Theodore Roosevelt,* pp. 759–763.
99. Wisan, *Cuban Crisis,* p. 375.
100. *Spanish Diplomatic Correspondence,* pp. 64–65; Wisan, *Cuban Crisis,* p. 385n.
101. Chadwick, *Diplomacy,* p. 532.
102. Mayo, *America of Yesterday,* pp. 153–155.
103. *Spanish Diplomatic Correspondence,* p. 68.
104. Mayo, *America of Yesterday,* pp. 154–155.
105. *Spanish Diplomatic Correspondence,* p. 68.
106. *Foreign Relations,* 1898, pp. 1025–1026.
107. *Spanish Diplomatic Correspondence,* p. 69.
108. Charles D. Sigsbee, *The* Maine, pp. 18–21.
109. John D. Long, "The Navy Department in the War," in *The American-Spanish War,* p. 341; Sigsbee, *The* Maine, pp. 22–26.
110. *Foreign Relations,* 1898, p. 1026.

CHAPTER 4: "FOR NATIONAL DEFENSE, FIFTY MILLION DOLLARS"

1. *Spanish Diplomatic Correspondence and Documents,* p. 64.
2. The information in the following paragraphs regarding the *Maine*'s security and routine in Havana, and Captain Sigsbee's impressions are taken from

Charles D. Sigsbee, *The* Maine, pp. 28–57, passim, and Charles D. Sigsbee, "Personal Narrative of the *Maine*," *Century Illustrated Monthly Magazine*, vol. 57, pp. 74–97, passim.

3. 55th Congress, 2nd Session, Senate Document No. 230. *Consular Correspondence Respecting the Condition of the* Reconcentrados *in Cuba* (hereinafter cited as *Consular Correspondence*), p. 32.

4. *Spanish Diplomatic Correspondence and Documents*, p. 71. William McKinley loved smoking a good cigar, though he would never do so in public.

5. Navy Department, *Annual Report*, 1898, BuNav Appendix, pp. 21–22.

6. Chadwick, *Diplomacy*, pp. 535–537; *Foreign Relations*, 1898, pp. 657–664.

7. *Foreign Relations*, 1898, pp. 664–665.

8. *Spanish Diplomatic Correspondence and Documents*, p. 80.

9. Ibid.

10. *Foreign Relations*, 1898, pp. 1007–1008.

11. Ibid.

12. Horatio S. Rubens, *Liberty: The Story of Cuba*, pp. 287–288.

13. Wisan, *The Cuban Crisis as Reflected in the New York Press*, pp. 381–382; *Spanish Diplomatic Correspondence and Documents*, p. 81.

14. Morgan, *William McKinley and His America*, p. 357; Mayo, *America of Yesterday*, pp. 161–162.

15. Morgan, *William McKinley and His America*, p. 358.

16. Wisan, *The Cuban Crisis as Reflected in the New York Press*, pp. 382–385; May, *Imperial Democracy*, p. 138.

17. *Foreign Relations*, 1898, p. 680; *Spanish Diplomatic Correspondence and Documents*, pp. 84–85; Chadwick, *Diplomacy*, pp. 540–541.

18. *Consular Correspondence*, p. 86.

19. Rickover, *How the Battleship* Maine *Was Destroyed*, pp. 39–40.

20. Ibid., pp. 40–41; French Ensor Chadwick, *The Relations of the United States and Spain: The Spanish-American War* (hereinafter cited as *Spanish-American War*), vol. 1, p. 7.

21. Sigsbee, *The* Maine, pp. 59–63; Charles D. Sigsbee, "My Story of the *Maine*," *Cosmopolitan Magazine*, August 1912, pp. 376–377.

22. Sigsbee, *The* Maine, pp. 63–67; Sigsbee, "My Story of the *Maine*," p. 377.

23. Sigsbee, *The* Maine, pp. 63–67.

24. 55th Congress, 2nd Session, Senate Document No. 207, *Report of the Naval Court of Inquiry Upon the Destruction of the United States Battle Ship* Maine (hereinafter cited as *Maine Court of Inquiry*), p. 21; Herbert W. Wilson, *The Downfall of Spain*, p. 16.

25. Wilson, *The Downfall of Spain*, pp. 9–11.

26. Sigsbee, *The* Maine, pp. 67–75; Wat T. Cluverius, "A Midshipman on the *Maine*," United States Naval Institute *Proceedings* (hereinafter cited as, *USNIP*), February 1918, pp. 245–246.

27. 55th Congress, 2nd Session, Senate Document No. 231, *Lives Lost by the Sinking of the U.S. Battle Ship* Maine, p. 2.

28. Sigsbee, *The* Maine, pp. 75–79; Sigsbee, "My Story of the *Maine*," *Cosmopolitan Magazine,* July 1912, p. 150.
29. Sigsbee, "My Story of the *Maine*," pp. 150–151; *Maine* Court of Inquiry, p. 286.
30. Sigsbee, "My Story of the *Maine*," p. 152.
31. Chadwick, *Spanish-American War,* vol. 1, p. 9.
32. Rickover, *How the Battleship* Maine *Was Destroyed,* p. 43; Mayo, *America of Yesterday,* p. 162;
33. John D. Long, "The Navy Department in the War," in [n.a.] *The American-Spanish War: A History by the War Leaders,* pp. 342–343; Margaret Long, ed., *The Journal of John D. Long,* pp. 214–215. Dickens is quoted in Gould, *The Spanish-American War and President McKinley,* p. 85. Walter Millis in *The Martial Spirit,* p. 102, describes Long telephoning the White House, ordering the "watchman" to wake the president immediately and call him to the phone. According to this popular, undocumented account, repeated by H. Wayne Morgan in *William McKinley and His America,* p. 360, and others, the president took his head in both hands and uttered, "The *Maine* blown up! The *Maine* blown up!"
34. *Foreign Relations,* 1898, p. 1029; Sigsbee, *The* Maine, p. 104.
35. *Spanish Diplomatic Correspondence and Documents,* p. 86.
36. Wisan, *The Cuban Crisis as Reflected in the New York Press,* pp. 390–391.
37. Ibid., pp. 391–392.
38. Ibid., p. 395.
39. Ibid., pp. 396–399.
40. May, *Imperial Democracy,* p. 140.
41. Morison, *Letters of Theodore Roosevelt,* vol. 1, p. 775; Mayo, *America of Yesterday,* pp. 163–164.
42. Rickover, *How the Battleship* Maine *Was Destroyed,* pp. 45–46. Lieutenant (later Admiral) Frank Friday Fletcher is the namesake of the *Fletcher* class destroyers, and the father of Vice Admiral Frank Jack Fletcher of World War II.
43. Sigsbee, "My Story of the *Maine*," p. 154.
44. Morison, *Letters of Theodore Roosevelt,* vol. 1, p. 780.
45. *Spanish Diplomatic Correspondence and Documents,* p. 45; Elbert J. Benton, *International Law and Diplomacy of the Spanish-American War,* pp. 77–78.
46. Ibid.
47. 55th Congress, 2nd Session, Senate Document No. 231, Part 7, *Report of the Spanish Naval Court of Inquiry as to the Cause of the Destruction of the U.S.B.S.* Maine (hereinafter cited as *Spanish Naval Court of Inquiry),* p. 913.
48. Ibid., pp. 903–904. The harbor *was* mined, of that there is no doubt. Vice Admiral Don José María Beránger, navy minister in the Cánovas cabinet, informed the *Heraldo de Madrid* on April 16, 1898, of 190 mines arming the ports of Havana, Cienfuegos, Nuevitas, and Santiago de Cuba. There

was nothing untoward or sinister about the practice. The mines would have guarded the harbor entrances, not the inner anchorage. See Navy Department, *Annual Report,* 1898, BuNav Appendix, p. 28. Captain Severo Gómez Núñez, a Spanish artillery officer, indicates twenty-eight "*Defensas submarinas del puerto*"—underwater defenses for the port of Havana. See Severo Gómez Núñes, *La Guerra Hispano-Americana: La Habana—Influencia de las Plazas de Guerra,* pp. 92–93.

49. *Spanish Naval Court of Inquiry,* pp. 965–967.
50. Ibid.
51. Ibid.; Chadwick, *Diplomacy,* p. 562n.
52. By comparison, the wreck of the battleship *Arizona* at Pearl Harbor, struck by eight Japanese bombs, one of which exploded a magazine, blowing her up, was still recognizable. This was not so with the *Maine.*
53. Rickover, *How the Battleship* Maine *Was Destroyed,* p. 57; Maine *Court of Inquiry,* p. 111.
54. Maine *Court of Inquiry,* pp. 113–115.
55. Rickover, *How the Battleship* Maine *Was Destroyed,* p. 61; Wisan, *The Cuban Crisis as Reflected in the New York Press,* pp. 393–394; Navy Department, *Annual Report,* 1898, BuNav Appendix, p. 22; "Admiral Antonio Eulate," *HAHR,* vol. 13, 1933, pp. 371–377. In United States warships, radios first went to sea in 1899, with temporary installations in the battleship *Massachusetts,* armored cruiser *New York,* and torpedo boat *Porter.* The first permanent sets were installed in the armored cruisers *West Virginia* and *Colorado,* laid down in 1901. Holland's submarine, the navy's first, was purchased by the government and commissioned into the fleet in 1900 as the USS *Holland.*
56. Margaret Long, *Journal of John D. Long,* p. 216.
57. *Foreign Relations,* 1898, pp. 664–665.
58. May, *Imperial Democracy,* p. 142; Margaret Long, *Journal of John D. Long,* p. 216.
59. Joseph Bucklin Bishop, *Theodore Roosevelt and His Time,* vol. 1, p. 86.
60. Morris, *The Rise of Theodore Roosevelt,* p. 602; Margaret Long, *Journal of John D. Long,* p. 216.
61. Navy Department, *Annual Report,* 1898, BuNav Appendix, pp. 22–23; Trask, *The War with Spain in 1898,* p. 81; William Henry Harbaugh, *Power and Responsibility: The Life and Times of Theodore Roosevelt,* p. 95.
62. Margaret Long, *Journal of John D. Long,* pp. 216–217; Navy Department, *Annual Report,* 1898, BuNav Appendix, p. 23.
63. Mayo, *America of Yesterday,* p. 171.
64. Maine *Court of Inquiry,* p. 204.
65. Rickover, *How the Battleship* Maine *Was Destroyed,* p. 64; Mayo, *America of Yesterday,* pp. 171–172.
66. Chadwick, *Spanish-American War,* vol. 1, p. 12; Navy Department, *Annual Report,* 1898, BuNav Appendix, p. 24.
67. *Foreign Relations,* 1898, pp. 666–669, 673–676, 680–681.

68. Ibid., p. 693.
69. May, *Imperial Democracy*, pp. 164–165.
70. Margaret Long, *Journal of John D. Long*, p. 220; May, *Imperial Democracy*, p. 142.
71. L. White Busbey, *Uncle Joe Cannon*, p. 186.
72. Ibid., pp. 186, 192.
73. Ibid., p. 186
74. Ibid.; Chadwick, *Diplomacy*, p. 545; Robinson, *Thomas B. Reed*, p. 360. The funds were considered a temporary measure only, to be kept available until January 1, 1899, at which time any unspent dollars would revert to the Treasury.
75. Wisan, *The Cuban Crisis as Reflected in the New York Press*, p. 410; May, *Imperial Democracy*, pp. 145–146; Margaret Long, *Journal of John D. Long*, p. 221.
76. *Foreign Relations*, 1898, p. 684.
77. John D. Long, *The New American Navy*, vol. 1, p. 152.
78. Graham A. Cosmas, *An Army for Empire*, pp. 76–79.
79. Ibid., pp. 80–81.
80. Ibid.
81. Ibid., p. 82; William Addleman Ganoe, *History of the United States Army*, p. 370; Russell A. Alger, *The Spanish-American War*, pp. 8–9; *Army and Navy Journal*, March 12, 1898.
82. Maine *Court of Inquiry*, pp. 242–244, 256–260; Rickover, *How the Battleship* Maine *Was Destroyed*, pp. 67–68.
83. Morison, *Letters of Theodore Roosevelt*, vol. 1, p. 795; Rickover, *How the Battleship* Maine *Was Sunk*, p. 67.
84. Gerald F. Linderman, *The Mirror of War*, pp. 40–41, 44; Morgan, *William McKinley and His America*, p. 365.
85. Linderman, *The Mirror of War*, pp. 44–45; Wisan, *The Cuban Crisis as Reflected in the New York Press*, p. 412 ff.
86. Morgan, *William McKinley and His America*, p. 365.
87. Julius W. Pratt, *Expansionists of 1898*, pp. 246–247, 284–285.
88. Arthur Wallace Dunn, *From Harrison to Harding*, vol. 1, p. 234.
89. Morgan, *William McKinley and His America*, p. 366.
90. *Foreign Relations*, 1898, p. 685.
91. Ibid., pp. 688–689.
92. Ibid.
93. Ibid., pp. 692–693, 695.
94. Arthur Wallace Dunn, *Gridiron Nights*, p. 72.
95. Herman Hagedorn, *Leonard Wood*, vol. 1, p. 141.
96. Chadwick, *Diplomacy*, pp. 561–563n; Maine *Court of Inquiry*, pp. 279–281. The destruction of the *Maine* was due to spontaneous combustion of ill-ventilated bituminous coal, a known phenomenon, in coal bunker A-16, port side, forward. This, in turn, transmitting heat through an adjacent red-hot steel bulkhead, ignited perhaps three hundred pounds of gunpowder of

a 6-inch reserve magazine, which detonated several tons of powder and munitions in the main, forward 10-inch magazines. The portion of the ship between the midships superstructure and the forecastle, including the starboard 10-inch turret and its guns, disappeared in the blast. The ship sank headfirst, the bow and forecastle into the mud, and capsized to starboard. The keel remained intact. The remainder of the ship, from the superstructure, aft, shoving forward and down, bent the keel into the inverted V. See Rickover, *How the Battleship* Maine *Was Destroyed,* pp. 98–103.

97. *Foreign Relations,* 1898, pp. 689–701, passim.

98. Ibid.

99. Ibid., p. 701.

100. May, *Imperial Democracy,* pp. 145–146; Mrs. Garret A. [Jennie] Hobart, *Memories,* p. 61; H. Wayne Morgan, *America's Road to Empire,* p. 55.

101. Louis A. Coolidge, *An Old Fashioned Senator: The Story of Orville H. Platt,* pp. 271–272.

102. *Foreign Relations,* p. 712; Trask, *The War with Spain in 1898,* pp. 39–40.

103. *Foreign Relations,* pp. 711–712.

104. Ibid., pp. 711–713.

105. Frederick Palmer, *Bliss: Peacemaker,* p. 52.

106. Leech, *In the Days of McKinley,* p. 176.

107. Ibid.

108. Maine *Court of Inquiry,* pp. 3–5, 281.

109. Leech, *In the Days of McKinley,* pp. 177–178; Gould, *President McKinley and the Spanish-American War,* p. 43.

110. Leech, *In the Days of McKinley,* pp. 177–178; *New York Times,* March 30, 1898; Charles G. Dawes, *Journal of the McKinley Years,* p. 150; Gould, *The Spanish-American War and President McKinley,* p. 43.

111. Olcott, *The Life of William McKinley,* vol. 2, p. 342.

112. *Foreign Relations,* 1898, p. 712.

113. Ibid., pp. 718, 721.

114. Ibid., pp. 726–727; 55th Congress, 2nd Session, Senate Document No. 230, *Consular Correspondence Reflecting the* Reconcentrados *in Cuba,* p. 28.

115. *Foreign Relations,* 1898, p. 728.

116. Hobart, *Memories,* p. 60; *New York Times,* April 7, 1898.

117. Mayo, *America of Yesterday,* p. 176.

118. *Spanish Diplomatic Correspondence and Documents,* p. 109.

119. *Foreign Relations,* 1898, pp. 732, 735–736.

120. Ibid., pp. 732–733.

121. *Spanish Diplomatic Correspondence and Documents,* p. 111.

122. *Foreign Relations,* 1898, pp. 750–760, passim.

123. Mayo, *America of Yesterday,* p. 176; Navy Department, *Annual Report,* 1898, BuNav Appendix, p. 25.

124. Mayo, *America of Yesterday,* pp. 176–177; *Foreign Relations,* 1898, pp. 571, 734.

125. *Foreign Relations,* 1898, pp. 740–741.
126. Leech, *In the Days of McKinley,* p. 183; Mayo, *America of Yesterday,* pp. 176–177.
127. *Foreign Relations,* 1898, p. 750.
128. Ibid., p. 747.
129. Mayo, *America of Yesterday,* pp. 177–178.
130. *Foreign Relations,* 1898, pp. 750–760, passim.
131. Ibid., pp. 757–759.
132. Ibid., pp. 757–760; Gould, *The Spanish American War and President McKinley,* p. 49.
133. Wisan, *The Cuban Crisis as Reflected in the New York Press,* pp. 441–443; Morison, *Letters of Theodore Roosevelt,* vol. 2, p. 815.
134. Ibid.
135. Gould, *The Spanish-American War and President McKinley,* pp. 50–51; Benton, *International Law and Diplomacy of the Spanish-American War,* p. 98.
136. Leon B. Richardson, *William E. Chandler: Republican,* pp. 581–582.
137. Benton, *International Law and Diplomacy of the Spanish-American War,* pp. 97–98.
138. *Spanish Diplomatic Correspondence and Documents,* p. 136.
139. Margaret Long, *Journal of John D. Long,* p. 223.
140. Benton, *International Law and Diplomacy of the Spanish-American War,* pp. 99–100; *Spanish Diplomatic Correspondence and Documents,* p. 135.
141. Mayo, *America of Yesterday,* pp. 183–184.
142. May, *Imperial Democracy,* p. 177.
143. *Foreign Relations,* 1898, pp. 767–768.
144. Palmer, *Bliss: Peacemaker,* p. 54.
145. *Foreign Relations,* 1898, pp. 769–770.
146. Mayo, *America of Yesterday,* p. 186.
147. Ibid.
148. Chadwick, *Diplomacy,* p. 586.
149. Chadwick, *The Spanish-American War,* vol. 1, p. 157.

CHAPTER 5: MANILA BAY

1. Spector, *Admiral of the New Empire,* p. 42.
2. Ibid., p. 45.
3. Navy Department, *Annual Report,* 1898, BuNav Appendix, pp. 22–23. It should be noted that times and dates given for East Asia are thirteen hours later than occurrences on the American East Coast and the Caribbean.
4. Asa Walker, "The Battle of Manila Bay," *Naval Actions and History 1779–1898,* p. 369.
5. Spector, *Admiral of the New Empire,* pp. 45–46.
6. Ibid., pp. 46–47.

7. Leon Wolff, *Little Brown Brother,* p. 24–25.
8. Henry F. Graff, ed., *American Imperialism and the Philippine Insurrection,* pp. x–xi, 2; Agoncillo, *Malolos,* pp. 121–122.
9. Graff, *American Imperialism and the Philippine Insurrection,* p. xi; Agoncillo, *Malolos,* pp. 123–125.
10. Graff, pp. xi, 2; Agoncillo, *Malolos,* p. 125.
11. Dewey, *Autobiography,* pp. 159; Navy Department, *Annual Report,* 1898, BuNav Appendix, pp. 66–67.
12. Walker, "Battle of Manila Bay," p. 372; Dewey, *Autobiography,* p. 170.
13. Walker, pp. 372–373; Dewey, pp. 171–172.
14. Navy Department, *Annual Report,* 1898, BuNav Appendix, p. 66; John M. Ellicott, "The Naval Battle of Manila," *USNIP,* September 1900, pp. 489–490.
15. Dewey, *Autobiography,* pp. 171–172.
16. Sargent, *Admiral Dewey and the Manila Campaign,* pp. 20, 96; Carlos G. Calkins, "Historical and Professional Notes on the Naval Campaign of Manila Bay" (hereinafter cited as "Naval Campaign of Manila Bay"), *USNIP,* June 1899, p. 268.
17. Carlos G. Calkins, "The Naval Battle of Manila Bay," in *The American-Spanish War: A History by War Leaders,* p. 105.
18. Navy Department, *Annual Report,* 1898, BuNav Appendix, p. 67; Laurin Hall Healy and Luis Kutner, *The Admiral,* p. 168.
19. Calkins, "Naval Battle of Manila Bay," pp. 103–105, 107.
20. Calkins, "Naval Campaign of Manila Bay," pp. 268–269.
21. Dewey, *Autobiography,* pp. 175–176; Healy and Kutner, *The Admiral,* p. 157.
22. Ellicott, "The Naval Battle of Manila," p. 493; Dewey, *Autobiography,* pp. 172–173.
23. War Department, *Correspondence Relating to the War with Spain,* vol. 2, p. 654; Severo Gómez Núñez, *La Guerra Hispano-Americana: Puerto-Rico y Filipinas,* p. 174.
24. Chadwick, *Spanish-American War,* vol. 1, p. 161.
25. Ibid., pp. 161–162.
26. Ibid., p. 167; Trask, *The War with Spain in 1898,* pp. 69–70.
27. Chadwick, *Spanish-American War,* vol. 1, p. 163; John M. Ellicott, "The Defenses of Manila Bay," *USNIP,* June 1900, pp. 279–285, passim. Accounts differ on the placement of the four 9.4-inch coastal guns. Inasmuch as Lieutenant Ellicott observed them in situ, and fought in the battle as well, I have relied generally on his statements and estimates.
28. Adelbert Dewey, *The Life and Letters of Admiral Dewey,* pp. 273–274.
29. Calkins, "Naval Campaign of Manila Bay," pp. 311–313; Sargent, *Admiral Dewey and the Manila Campaign,* pp. 25–26.
30. Calkins, "Naval Campaign of Manila Bay," pp. 311–313.
31. Navy Department, *Annual Report,* 1898, BuNav Appendix, p. 89.

32. Ibid.; Herbert W. Wilson, *The Downfall of Spain*, pp. 130–131; Chadwick, *Spanish-American War*, vol. 1, p. 164. The gunnery factor is computed by taking a given caliber, e.g., 8-inch, squaring it, and multiplying the result by the number of those guns in the ship. Thus, the *Olympia*'s main battery factor: $8 \times 8 \times 4 = 256$. Her secondary battery factor is arrived at the same way, only using ten 5-inch guns: $5 \times 5 \times 10 = 250$, giving a combined factor of 506. By contrast, the *Reina Cristina*, with six 6.2-inch guns and a secondary battery of two 2.7-inch guns, the latter being unable to deliver ship-killing damage, factors to 230.6, and if the smaller guns are computed, 245. Admiral Pascual Cervera y Topete, commander of Spain's fleet in the Battle of Santiago de Cuba, used a similar method of calculation to show Spain had no business in challenging the United States to mortal combat afloat.

33. Navy Department, *Annual Report*, 1898, BuNav Appendix, p. 89.

36. Ibid., pp. 89–90; Chadwick, *Spanish-American War*, vol. 1, pp. 169–171; Wilson, *The Downfall of Spain*, pp. 130–131.

37. Navy Department, *Annual Report*, 1898, BuNav Appendix, p. 90; Wilson, *The Downfall of Spain*, p. 129.

38. Navy Department, *Annual Report*, 1898, BuNav Appendix, p. 90.

39. Ellicott, "The Naval Battle of Manila," pp. 494–495.

41. Walker, "The Battle of Manila Bay," pp. 373–374; Bradley Fiske, *From Midshipman to Rear Admiral*, p. 242; Spector, *Admiral of the New Empire*, p. 56. A "league" equals three miles.

42. Calkins, "The Naval Battle of Manila Bay," p. 109; Walker, "The Battle of Manila Bay," pp. 374–375.

43. Walker, "The Battle of Manila Bay," pp. 374–375; Spector, *Admiral of the New Empire*, p. 56.

44. Healy and Kutner, *The Admiral*, pp. 174–175; Walker, "The Battle of Manila Bay," p. 376.

46. Fiske, *From Midshipman to Rear Admiral*, p. 242.

47. Healy and Kutner, *The Admiral*, p. 177.

48. Ibid., pp. 177–178; Walker, "The Battle of Manila Bay," pp. 377–378; Spector, *Admiral of the New Empire*, pp. 57–58. It was not uncommon, even at this late date, for seamen to fight barefoot. The sanding of the decks provided traction if they became slippery with blood.

49. Joseph L. Stickney, "With Dewey at Manila," *Harper's New Monthly Magazine*, February 1899, p. 479; Walker, "The Battle of Manila Bay," p. 378; Hugh Rodman, *Yarns of a Kentucky Admiral*, pp. 242–243.

50. Fiske, *From Midshipman to Rear Admiral*, p. 245.

51. Calkins, "Naval Campaign of Manila Bay," p. 274; Rodman, *Yarns of a Kentucky Admiral*, pp. 241–242.

52. Calkins, "Naval Campaign of Manila Bay," p. 275; Walker, "The Battle of Manila Bay," p. 379.

53. Dewey, *Autobiography,* p. 191; Sargent, *Admiral Dewey and the Manila Campaign,* pp. 275–276; Rodman, *Yarns of a Kentucky Admiral,* pp. 242–243.

54. Navy Department, *Annual Report,* 1898, BuNav Appendix, pp. 90–92.

55. Ibid.

56. Ibid.; Wilson, *The Downfall of Spain,* pp. 134–135; John M. Ellicott, "Effect of Gun-Fire, Battle of Manila Bay," *USNIP,* June 1899, p. 333.

57. Navy Department, *Annual Report,* 1898, BuNav Appendix, pp. 90–92; Wilson, *The Downfall of Spain,* p. 136; Ellicott, "Effect of Gun-Fire," p. 333.

58. Navy Department, *Annual Report,* 1898, BuNav Appendix, p. 92.

59. Calkins, "Naval Campaign of Manila Bay," pp. 274–276.

60. Chadwick, *The Spanish-American War,* vol. 1, pp. 178–179.

61. Calkins, "Naval Campaign of Manila Bay," p. 276; Navy Department, *Annual Report,* 1898, BuNav Appendix, pp. 70 ff.; Stickney, "With Dewey at Manila," p. 479. Commodore Dewey reported two boats. Captain Gridley reported one boat making two advances. Commander Wood of the *Petrel* reported "a yellow launch, apparently a torpedo boat, attempting to turn our flank." Mr. Stickney derides the claim that it was "an innocent market boat."

62. Rodman, *Yarns of a Kentucky Admiral,* pp. 243–244.

63. Calkins, "Naval Campaign of Manila Bay," pp. 282–283.

64. Ibid.; Fiske, *From Midshipman to Rear Admiral,* p. 249.

65. Dewey, *Autobiography,* pp. 193–194; Stickney, "With Dewey at Manila," p. 475.

66. Stickney, "With Dewey at Manila," p. 477.

67. Chadwick, *Spanish-American War,* vol. 1, pp. 182–183; Calkins, "Naval Campaign of Manila Bay," p. 283; BuNav Appendix, p. 78.

68. Navy Department, *Annual Report,* 1898, BuNav Appendix, p. 92; Chadwick, *Spanish-American War,* vol. 1, p. 188.

69. Navy Department, *Annual Report,* 1898, BuNav Appendix, pp. 80–81.

70. Ibid., pp. 78–81; Chadwick, *Spanish-American War,* vol. 1, p. 188.

71. Navy Department, *Annual Report,* 1898, BuNav Appendix, p. 81.

72. Fiske, *From Midshipman to Rear Admiral,* pp. 254–255.

73. Ibid., pp. 255–256.

74. Sargent, *Admiral Dewey and the Manila Campaign,* pp. 41–42. Dewey could have connected a telegraph key to the severed end aboard the *Zafiro,* but the cable company in Hong Kong refused to accept any messages transmitted this way. According to the British naval historian Herbert W. Wilson, Dewey might have legally taken "severe reprisals" against the company's property in Manila. See Wilson, *The Downfall of Spain,* p. 157.

75. Sargent, *Admiral Dewey and the Manila Campaign,* p. 44.

76. Navy Department, *Annual Report,* 1898, BuNav Appendix, p. 68.

77. Ibid.

78. Chadwick, *Spanish-American War,* vol. 1, pp. 208–210.
79. Mayo, *America of Yesterday,* pp. 189–190.
80. Chadwick, *Spanish-American War,* vol. 1, pp. 207–208.

CHAPTER 6: WHEN JOHNNY WENT MARCHING OFF

1. By contrast, Spain, with around 18 million people, counted a total military establishment at home and her colonies at perhaps 350,000 men. Herbert H. Sargent, *The Campaign of Santiago de Cuba,* vol. 1, p. 79; vol. 3, pp. 194, 197.
2. Henry F. Pringle, *Theodore Roosevelt,* p. 446
3. War Department, *Report of the Secretary of War,* 1898, vol. 1, pp. 254–255.
4. Ibid., pp. 255–256.
5. *New York Tribune,* April 5, 6, 1898.
6. *Army and Navy Journal,* March 26, 1898.
7. Millis, *The Martial Spirit,* p. 155.
8. Graham A. Cosmas, *An Army for Empire,* p. 89.
9. Marvin A. Kreidberg and Merton G. Henry, *History of Military Mobilization in the United States Army 1775–1945,* p. 152.
10. Ibid., pp. 165–166; Russell A. Alger, *The Spanish-American War,* pp. 26–27.
11. Nelson A. Miles, "The War with Spain," part 1, *North American Review,* May 1899, p. 516.
12. Kreidberg and Henry, *History of Military Mobilization,* p. 158.
13. Charles H. Brown, *The Correspondents War,* p. 159.
14. *Army and Navy Journal,* April 30, 1898.
15. Corps are usually designated under Roman numerals, viz., V Corps. In this instance, however, they will be spelled out as there are no numerically designated larger formations involved, e.g., there was no First Army.
16. Leech, *In the Days of McKinley,* p. 217.
17. Kreidberg and Henry, *History of Military Mobilization,* p. 156.
18. War Department, *Correspondence Relating to the War with Spain,* vol. 1, p. 24.
19. John H. Parker, *History of the Gatling Gun Detachment,* p. 18.
20. Alger, *The Spanish-American War,* p. 41.
21. Chadwick, *The Spanish-American War,* vol. 1, p. 75–76.
22. War Department, *Correspondence Relating to the War with Spain,* vol. 1, pp. 8–9.
23. Miles, "The War with Spain," part 1, p. 524; Mayo, *America of Yesterday,* p. 183; Morison, *Letters of Theodore Roosevelt,* vol. 2, p. 818.
24. Alger, *The Spanish-American War,* pp. 44–45; John D. Miley, *In Cuba with Shafter,* p. 2.
25. Mayo, *America of Yesterday,* p. 188.
26. Ibid., p. 189.

27. Morison, *Letters of Theodore Roosevelt,* vol. 2, p. 819.
28. *Army and Navy Journal,* May 28, 1898.
29. Alger, *The Spanish-American War,* p. 46; H. Wayne Morgan, *William McKinley and His America,* p. 390.
30. Miley, *In Cuba with Shafter,* p. 6.
31. Alger, *The Spanish-American War,* p. 47.
32. War Department, *Correspondence Relating to the War with Spain,* vol. 2, p. 646.
33. Ibid., p. 648.
34. Ibid., pp. 648–649.
35. Ibid., pp. 676–678.
36. *Selections from the Correspondence of Theodore Roosevelt and Henry Cabot Lodge,* vol. 1, p. 300.
37. Miles, *Serving the Republic,* p. 272.
38. Ibid., pp. 272–273.
39. Mayo, *America of Yesterday,* pp. 196–197.
40. Cosmas, *An Army for Empire,* p. 181. (See *WIC,* vol. 5, p. 2415)
41. Ibid., p. 183.
42. Frank E. Vandiver, *Black Jack: The Life of General John J. Pershing,* vol. 1, pp. 181–182.
43. Parker, *History of the Gatling Gun Detachment,* p. 16; Alger, *The Spanish-American War,* pp. 67–68.
44. Theodore Roosevelt, *The Rough Riders,* p. 36.
45. Richard Harding Davis, *The Cuban and Puerto Rican Campaigns,* pp. 46, 48–51; Miley, *In Cuba with Shafter,* p. 15.
46. Davis, *The Cuban and Puerto Rican Campaigns,* pp. 66, 73.
47. Ibid., pp. 79–80.
48. Alger, *The Spanish-American War,* p. 63; Miley, *In Cuba with Shafter,* pp. 15–16.
49. Alger, *The Spanish-American War,* pp. 63–64.
50. Ibid., p. 64.
51. Vandiver, *Black Jack,* vol. 1, p. 185.
52. Ibid., p. 186.
53. Charles Post, *The Little War of Private Post,* p. 93.
54. Roosevelt, *The Rough Riders,* pp. 37–38.
55. Ibid., pp. 38–39.
56. Ibid., pp. 40–41.
57. Ibid., p. 42.

CHAPTER 7: VIVA ESPAÑA!

1. Victor M. Concas y Palau, *The Squadron of Admiral Cervera,* p. 15.
2. Severo Gómez Núñez, *La Guerra Hispano-Americana: La Habana,* pp. 29–30.

3. Herbert W. Wilson, *The Downfall of Spain*, p. 68.
4. Pascual Cervera y Topete, *The Spanish-American War: A Collection of Documents Relative to the Squadron Operations in the West Indies* (hereinafter cited as *Documents*), p. 12.
5. Wilson, *The Downfall of Spain*, pp. 98–99. The Battle of Cape Trafalgar, October 21, 1805. Britain's Vice Admiral Nelson with twenty-seven ships singularly defeated a Franco-Spanish fleet of thirty-three, capturing eighteen. Eleven Spanish ships of the line were sunk or taken as prizes.
6. Cervera, *Documents*, p. 22.
7. Ibid., p. 24.
8. Ibid., pp. 24–25.
9. Ibid., p. 25.
10. Ibid., pp. 26–27; Navy Department, *Annual Report*, 1898, BuNav Appendix, pp. 27–29.
11. Cervera, *Documents*, p. 28.
12. Ibid., p. 30.
13. Ibid., p. 32.
14. Ibid., pp. 34–35.
15. Ibid., pp. 42–43; Chadwick, *The Spanish-American War*, vol. 1, p. 109.
16. Cervera, *Documents*, pp. 43–44.
17. Ibid., pp. 46, 49.
18. Ibid., pp. 51–52.
19. Ibid., p. 53.
20. Concas y Palau, *The Squadron of Admiral Cervera*, pp. 26–27.
21. Cervera, *Documents*, p. 54.
22. Concas y Palau, *The Squadron of Admiral Cervera*, p. 33.
23. Cervera, *Documents*, p. 55.
24. Chadwick, *The Spanish-American War*, vol. 1, p. 122.
25. Cervera, *Documents*, p. 65. They were, of course, not battleships, except as falsely listed in the Spanish naval register.
26. Ibid., pp. 55–56; Wilson, *The Downfall of Spain*, p. 101.
27. Concas y Palau, *The Squadron of Admiral Cervera*, p. 33.
28. Cervera, *Documents*, p. 67.
29. Ibid., p. 68.
30. Concas y Palau, *The Squadron of Admiral Cervera*, p. 43.
31. Ibid., pp. 43–44.
32. Ibid., p. 44; Cervera, *Documents*, p. 72
33. Concas y Palau, *The Squadron of Admiral Cervera*, p. 45.
34. Ibid., p. 46.
35. Ibid., p. 47.
36. Ibid.
37. Ibid., p. 49.
38. Ibid., p. 50.
39. Cervera, *Documents*, pp. 72–73.

40. Ibid.; Concas y Palau, *The Squadron of Admiral Cervera*, p. 51.
41. Cervera, *Documents*, p. 78.

CHAPTER 8: HUNTING CERVERA

1. Walter Millis, *The Martial Sprit*, p. 202; Alger, *The Spanish-American War*, p. 38.
2. Richard S. West Jr., *Admirals of American Empire*, p. 224; Millis, *The Martial Sprit*, p. 203.
3. West, *Admirals of American Empire*, p. 224.
4. Winfield Scott Schley, *Forty-five Years under the Flag*, p. 257.
5. West, *Admirals of American Empire*, p. 225.
6. Davis, *The Cuban and Puerto Rican Campaigns*, p. 29.
7. West, *Admirals of American Empire*, p. 227.
8. John D. Long, *The New American Navy*, vol. 1, p. 231.
9. Robley D. Evans, *A Sailor's Log*, p. 410; Chadwick, *The Spanish-American War*, vol. 1, p. 130.
10. West, *Admirals of American Empire*, p. 229; Chadwick, *The Spanish-American War*, vol. 1, p. 133.
11. Davis, *The Cuban and Puerto Rican Campaigns*, pp. 27–28.
12. Ibid., pp. 30–31.
13. Ibid., p. 33.
14. Navy Department, *Annual Report*, 1898, BuNav Appendix, pp. 190–196.
15. Chadwick, *The Spanish-American War*, vol. 1, p. 238.
16. Ibid., pp. 219–220.
17. Ibid.
18. Ibid., pp. 221–223.
19. W. A. M. Goode, *With Sampson through the War*, pp. 63–64.
20. Chadwick, *The Spanish-American War*, vol. 1, pp. 224–225. Already an obsolete type, the three monitors with Admiral Sampson each took two decades of desultory construction to complete. All were finished in 1896, and mounted four heavy guns in two turrets.
21. Ibid.
22. Wilson, *The Downfall of Spain*, p. 194.
23. John R. Spears, "The Chase for Cervera," *Scribner's Magazine*, August 1898, p. 146.
24. Ibid., p. 147.
25. Ibid., p. 148; Chadwick, *The Spanish-American War*, vol. 1, p. 232.
26. Spears, "The Chase for Cervera," p. 149.
27. Chadwick, *The Spanish-American War*, vol. 1, p. 234.
28. Navy Department, *Annual Report*, 1898, BuNav Appendix, pp. 407–410; Chadwick, *The Spanish-American War*, vol. 1, p. 240.
29. Navy Department, *Annual Report*, 1898, BuNav Appendix, pp. 407–410.
30. Ibid., pp. 387–388.

31. Ibid., p. 392.

32. Ibid., pp. 393–394; Chawdick, *The Spanish-American War,* vol. 1, p. 268.

33. Chadwick, *The Spanish-American War,* vol. 1, p. 269.

34. *Record of Proceedings of a Court of Inquiry in the Case of Rear Admiral Winfield S. Schley* (hereinafter cited as *Schley Court of Inquiry*), vol. 1, p. 858.

35. Chadwick, *The Spanish-American War,* vol. 1, pp. 272, 275.

36. Ibid., pp. 286, 288–289.

37. *Schley Court of Inquiry,* vol. 1, p. 278.

38. Ibid., p. 280; Chadwick, *The Spanish-American War,* vol. 1, p. 293.

39. The federal prize court duly condemned the coal as contraband of war, but released the ship as a neutral, a decision that infuriated Admiral Sampson.

40. *Schley Court of Inquiry,* vol. 1, p. 120; Chadwick, *The Spanish-American War,* vol. 1, p. 303; Wilson, *The Downfall of Spain,* p. 227; Evans, *A Sailor's Log,* p. 429.

41. Navy Department, *Annual Report,* 1898, BuNav Appendix, p. 397.

42. Ibid.

43. Cervera, *Documents,* p. 83; Concas y Palau, *The Squadron of Admiral Cervera,* p. 54.

44. Cervera, *Documents,* pp. 84–86.

45. Ibid., pp. 88–89.

46. Ibid.

47. Ibid., pp. 91–92.

48. Ibid., pp. 96–97.

49. Ibid; Chadwick, *The Spanish-American War,* vol. 1, p. 315.

50. Chadwick, *The Spanish-American War,* vol. 1, pp. 327–328.

51. West, *Admirals of American Empire,* pp. 288–289; Edgar Stanton Maclay, *A History of the United States Navy* vol. 3, pp. 296–298. Maclay, a civilian employee of the Brooklyn Navy Yard, received his information from anti-Schley factions from within the service and the press. He was subsequently fired from his navy yard job, and Congress prohibited the use of his history at the Naval Academy. The publisher issued a new volume with the offending passages expunged.

52. Chadwick, *The Spanish-American War,* vol. 1, pp. 295–296.

53. Navy Department, *Annual Report,* 1898, BuNav Appendix, pp. 397–398.

54. Chadwick, *The Spanish-American War,* vol. 1, p. 322–325.

55. Ibid.

56. Ibid., p. 326.

57. Ibid., p. 328; Graham, *Schley and Santiago,* p. 149.

58. Graham, *Schley and Santiago,* p. 161.

59. "Abstract log of the *Cristóbal Colón,*" *Proceedings* of the U.S. Naval Institute, December 1898, following page 492.

60. Graham, *Schley and Santiago,* p. 176.

61. "Abstract log of the *Cristóbal Colón.*" It is not known what is meant by "bowls in the round house," perhaps commodes in the officers' head.
62. Navy Department, *Annual Report,* 1898, BuNav Appendix, p. 400; Chadwick, *The Spanish-American War,* vol. 1, p. 325.
63. Goode, *With Sampson through the War,* p. 143.

CHAPTER 9: EMPIRE BUILDERS

1. Navy Department, *Annual Report,* 1898, BuNav Appendix, pp. 47–48; William H. Allen, "The Voyage of the *Oregon,*" in *The American-Spanish War: A History by the War Leaders,* p. 166.
2. Charles Clark, *My Fifty Years in the Navy,* pp. 141–142.
3. Allen, "The Voyage of the *Oregon,*" p. 167.
4. Navy Department, *Annual Report,* 1898, BuNav Appendix, p. 48; Allen, "The Voyage of the *Oregon,*" p. 168.
5. Clark, *My Fifty Years in the Navy,* p. 142.
6. Ibid., p. 144.
7. Ibid., p. 145.
8. Navy Department, *Annual Report,* 1898, BuNav Appendix, p. 51; Clark, *My Fifty Years in the Navy,* pp. 146–147.
9. Clark, *My Fifty Years in the Navy,* p. 147.
10. Ibid., pp. 147–148.
11. Navy Department, *Annual Report,* 1898, BuNav Appendix, pp. 51–52.
12. Clark, *My Fifty Years in the Navy,* p. 149.
13. Allen, "The Voyage of the *Oregon,*" p. 175.
14. West, *Admirals of American Empire,* p. 212; Morison, *Letters of Theodore Roosevelt,* vol. 1, pp. 793–794.
15. *Army and Navy Journal,* May 7, 1898.
16. West, *Admirals of American Empire,* p. 215.
17. Ibid., p. 216. In 1913 Rear Admiral Bradley Fiske, navigator of the *Petrel* at Manila Bay, was appointed to the chrysalis post of "Aid for Operations." Three years later, Rear Admiral William S. Benson was appointed the first Chief of Naval Operations.
18. *Army and Navy Journal,* May 28, 1898.
19. Seager, *Alfred Thayer Mahan,* p. 373; *Army and Navy Journal,* May 14, 1898.
20. *Army and Navy Journal,* May 21, 1898.
21. Ibid., August 27, 1898.
22. West, *Admirals of American Empire,* p. 221.
23. Ibid.

CHAPTER 10: BLOCKADE

1. Chadwick, *The Spanish-American War,* vol. 1, p. 348.
2. Richmond P. Hobson, *The Sinking of the* Merrimac, p. 24.

3. Graham, *Schley and Santiago*, p. 190.

4. Hobson, *The Sinking of the* Merrimac, p. 21.

5. Ibid., pp. 68–69.

6. Ibid., pp. 90–91.

7. Ibid., pp. 91–92.

8. Ibid., pp. 92, 94–95.

9. Ibid., pp. 96–97.

10. Cervera, *Documents*, p. 100.

11. Ibid.

12. Chadwick, *The Spanish-American War*, vol. 1, pp. 351–352.

13. Navy Department, *Annual Report*, 1898, BuNav Appendix, p. 451.

14. Cervera, *Documents*, pp. 102–103.

15. Ibid., p. 103.

16. Chadwick, *The Spanish-American War*, vol. 1, pp. 368–370.

17. Long, *The New American Navy*, vol. 2, p. 13; Trask, *The War with Spain in 1898*, p. 190.

18. José Müller y Tejeiro, "Battles and Capitulations of Santiago de Cuba," *USNIP*, 1899, p. 151.

CHAPTER 11: THE SANTIAGO CAMPAIGN

1. Herschel V. Cashin, *Under Fire with the Tenth U.S. Cavalry*, p. 68; Miley, *In Cuba with Shafter*, p. 48; Virgil Carrington Jones, *Roosevelt's Rough Riders*, pp. 75–76.

2. Davis, *The Cuban and Porto Rican Campaigns*, p. 86; Jones, *Roosevelt's Rough Riders*, p. 78.

3. *Letters of Theodore Roosevelt*, vol. 2, p. 844.

4. Davis, *The Cuban and Porto Rican Campaigns*, pp. 90–91; Trask, *The War with Spain in 1898*, p. 195.

5. Davis, *The Cuban and Porto Rican Campaigns*, p. 94; Post, *The Little War of Private Post*, p. 88.

6. Jones, *Roosevelt's Rough Riders*, p. 73.

7. Post, *The Little War of Private Post*, p. 87.

8. Ibid., p. 98.

9. Ibid., p. 106; Jones, *Roosevelt's Rough Riders*, p. 81; Davis, *The Cuban and Porto Rican Campaigns*, p. 108.

10. Post, *The Little War of Private Post*, pp. 106–107; Trask, *The War with Spain in 1898*, p. 194.

11. Long, *The New American Navy*, vol. 2, p. 22; William T. Sampson, "The Atlantic Fleet in the Spanish War," *Century Magazine*, April 1899, pp. 904–905.

12. Alger, *The Spanish-American War*, pp. 89–90.

13. Ibid., p. 84.

14. Trask, *The War with Spain in 1898*, p. 204.

15. Herbert H. Sargent, *The Campaign of Santiago de Cuba,* vol. 2, pp. 16–17; Miley, *In Cuba with Shafter,* p. 58.

16. Millis, *The Martial Spirit,* p. 262; Navy Department, *Annual Report,* 1898, BuNav Appendix, pp. 497–498.

17. Navy Department, *Annual Report,* 1898, BuNav Appendix, pp. 689–691.

18. Anastasio Azoy, *Charge!: The Story of the Battle of San Juan Hill,* p. 72.

19. Navy Department, *Annual Report,* 1898, BuNav Appendix, p. 498.

20. Ibid., p. 686.

21. Ibid.

22. Ibid.; Davis, *The Cuban and Porto Rican Campaigns,* p. 116.

23. Navy Department, *Annual Report,* 1898, BuNav Appendix, p. 686.

24. Chadwick, *The Spanish-American War,* vol. 2, p. 33.

25. Brown, *Correspondents War,* pp. 304–305.

26. Post, *The Little War of Private Post,* pp. 109–111; Miley, *In Cuba with Shafter,* p. 70.

27. Morris, *The Rise of Theodore Roosevelt,* p. 638.

28. Freidel, *The Splendid Little War,* p. 89; Navy Department, *Annual Report,* 1898, BuNav Appendix, p. 688.

29. Roosevelt, *Rough Riders,* p. 49.

30. Trask, *The War with Spain in 1898;* Parker, *History of the Gatling Gun Detachment,* p. 78.

31. Freidel, *The Splendid Little War,* p. 91.

32. Chadwick, *The Spanish-American War,* vol. 2, p. 42.

33. Herbert Sargent, *The Campaign of Santiago de Cuba,* vol. 2, p. 48.

34. Müller y Tejeiro, "Battles and Capitulation of Santiago de Cuba," p. 142.

35. Ibid., p. 148; Herbert Sargent, *The Campaign of Santiago de Cuba,* vol. 3, p. 218.

36. Müller y Tejeiro, "Battles and Capitulation of Santiago de Cuba," p. 108.

37. Ibid., p. 142.

38. Ibid., pp. 118–119.

39. Ibid., p. 138.

40. Azoy, *Charge,* p. 31; Morris, *The Rise of Theodore Roosevelt,* p. 639.

41. Roosevelt, *The Rough Riders,* p. 51; Jones, *Roosevelt's Rough Riders,* pp. 111–112.

42. Roosevelt, *The Rough Riders,* p. 51.

43. Herbert Sargent, *The Campaign of Santiago de Cuba,* vol. 3, p. 218.

44. Ibid., vol. 2, pp. 55–57.

45. Miley, *In Cuba with Shafter,* p. 82.

46. Jones, *Roosevelt's Rough Riders,* p. 121.

47. Wheeler, *The Santiago Campaign,* pp. 26–27.

48. Ibid., pp. 28–29.

49. Wheeler, *The Santiago Campaign,* pp. 28–29; Jones, *Roosevelt's Rough Riders,* p. 125; Cashin, *Under Fire with the Tenth U.S. Cavalry,* p. 218; Azoy, *Charge!,* p. 88.

50. Roosevelt, *The Rough Riders*, p. 55.
51. Fish's grandfather served as secretary of state in the Grant administration, and due to his efforts, the United States and Spain averted conflict in 1873 during the Ten Years' War.
52. Wheeler, *The Santiago Campaign*, pp. 32–33.
53. Roosevelt, *The Rough Riders*, p. 57.
54. Morris, *The Rise of Theodore Roosevelt*, pp. 643–644.
55. Jones, *Roosevelt's Rough Riders*, p. 126.
56. Morris, *The Rise of Theodore Roosevelt*, p. 644; Davis, *The Cuban and Porto Rican Campaigns*, p. 149; Roosevelt, *The Rough Riders*, p. 59.
57. Roosevelt, *The Rough Riders*, p. 61.
58. Ibid., pp. 62–63.
59. Ibid., p. 64.
60. Morris, *The Rise of Theodore Roosevelt*, pp. 644–645; Azoy, *Charge!*, p. 95; Wheeler, *The Santiago Campaign*, p. 34.
61. Roosevelt, *The Rough Riders*, p. 65.
62. Azoy, *Charge!*, p. 96.

CHAPTER 12: SAN JUAN HILL

1. Miley, *In Cuba with Shafter*, pp. 88–89.
2. Roosevelt, *The Rough Riders*, p. 71.
3. Chadwick, *The Spanish-American War*, vol. 2, p. 66; Davis, *The Cuban and Porto Rican Campaigns*, pp. 175–176.
4. Miley, *In Cuba with Shafter*, p. 96.
5. Ibid., pp. 90–92.
6. Ibid., p. 93.
7. War Department, *Correspondence Relating to the War with Spain*, p. 60; Wheeler, *The Santiago Campaign*, p. 262.
8. 56th Congress, 1st Session, Senate Document. No. 221, *Report of the Commission Appointed by the President to Investigate the Conduct of the War Department in the War with Spain* (hereinafter cited as, *CWS*), vol. 4, p. 946.
9. Ibid., p. 901.
10. Trask, *The War with Spain in 1898*, p. 231.
11. Davis, *The Cuban and Porto Rican Campaigns*, pp. 182–183.
12. *CWS*, vol. 4, pp. 907–908.
13. Davis, *The Cuban and Porto Rican Campaigns*, p. 188.
14. Ibid., pp. 189–190.
15. Chadwick, *The Spanish-American War*, vol. 2, p. 57.
16. Arthur A. Lee, "The Regulars at El Caney," *Scribner's Magazine*, October 1898, p. 403.
17. Ibid., p. 404.
18. Ibid., p. 405.
19. Freidel, *The Splendid Little War*, pp. 128–129. A year earlier, the French had developed their famous, and deadly, 75mm rapid-fire field gun, firing

fixed ammunition with smokeless powder at a rate that approached fifteen rounds a minute. By contrast, the U.S. artillery, though breech-loading, still fired unfixed ammunition—black powder and shot loaded separately—and having no recoil mechanism, the gun had to be repositioned and reaimed after every round, giving it a firing rate of perhaps two per minute.

20. Lee, "The Regulars at El Caney," p. 405.
21. Ibid.
22. Ibid., pp. 408–409.
23. Theophilus G. Steward, *The Colored Regulars in the United States Army,* p. 158; Joseph Edgar Chamblin, "How the Spaniards Fought at Caney," *Scribner's Magazine,* September 1898, p. 278.
24. Chadwick, *The Spanish-American War,* vol. 2, p. 80; Trask, *The War with Spain in 1898,* p. 237.
25. Freidel, *The Splendid Little War,* pp. 134–135.
26. Lee, "The Regulars at El Caney," pp. 409–410.
27. Ibid., p. 410; Freidel, *The Splendid Little War,* p. 135.
28. Freidel, *The Splendid Little War,* p. 138.
29. Lee, "The Regulars at El Caney," pp. 412–413.
30. Jones, *Roosevelt's Rough Riders,* p. 172.
31. Chadwick, *The Spanish-American War,* vol. 2, p. 86.
32. Roosevelt, *The Rough Riders,* pp. 73–74, 77–78; Hagedorn, *Leonard Wood,* vol. 1, p. 174.
33. War Department, *Annual Report,* 1898, part 2, p. 165.
34. Davis, *The Cuban and Porto Rican Campaigns,* p. 212.
35. Chadwick, *The Spanish-American War,* vol. 2, p. 87.
36. War Department, *Annual Report,* 1898, part 2, pp. 164–165; Alger, *The Spanish-American War,* pp. 158–159.
37. Alger, *The Spanish-American War,* p. 161.
38. Chadwick, *The Spanish-American War,* vol. 2, p. 87; Davis, *The Cuban and Porto Rican Campaigns,* pp. 206–207.
39. Roosevelt, *The Rough Riders,* p. 81.
40. Millis, *The Martial Spirit,* pp. 288–289; Chadwick, *The Spanish-American War,* vol. 2, p. 91; Sargent, *The Campaign of Santiago de Cuba,* vol. 2, p. 117.
41. Roosevelt, *The Rough Riders,* p. 81.
42. Ibid., pp. 82–83.
43. Ibid., p. 83.
44. Ibid., p. 85.
45. Ibid., p. 87.
46. Millis, *The Martial Spirit,* p. 289.
47. Ibid., p. 88.
48. Ibid., p. 89.
49. Ibid., p. 288.
50. Sargent, *The Campaign of Santiago de Cuba,* vol. 2, p. 119; Chadwick, *The Spanish-American War,* vol. 2, p. 93.

51. Davis, *The Cuban and Porto Rican Campaigns,* pp. 220–223.
52. Chadwick, *The Spanish-American War,* vol. 2, p. 94.
53. Ibid.
54. Ibid., p. 95.
55. Davis, *The Cuban and Porto Rican Campaigns,* pp. 220–223.
56. Roosevelt, *The Rough Riders,* p. 90.
57. Alger, *The Spanish-American War,* pp. 166–167.
58. Roosevelt, *The Rough Riders,* p. 94; Müller, "Battles and Capitulation of Santiago de Cuba," pp. 158–160.
59. Alger, *The Spanish-American War,* p. 169; Wheeler, *The Santiago Campaign,* p. 46.
60. Müller, "Battles and Capitulation of Santiago de Cuba," pp. 160–161; Leech, *In the Days of McKinley,* p. 251.
61. War Department, *Correspondence Relating to the War with Spain,* vol. 1, p. 70.
62. Chadwick, *The Spanish-American War,* vol. 2, p. 103.
63. George Kennan, *Campaigning in Cuba,* p. 132.
64. Ibid., pp. 135–136.
65. Davis, *The Cuban and Porto Rican Campaigns,* pp. 249–250.
66. Navy Department, *Annual Report,* 1898, BuNav Appendix, p. 504.
67. Ibid.
68. Alger, *The Spanish-American War,* p. 176.
69. Ibid.
70. War Department, *Correspondence Relating to the War with Spain,* vol. 1, pp. 74–75.
71. Chadwick, *The Spanish-American War,* vol. 2, pp. 110–111.
72. War Department, *Correspondence Relating to the War with Spain,* vol. 1, p. 72; Alger, *The Spanish-American War,* p. 173.
73. Alger, *The Spanish-American War,* p. 174.
74. Ibid., pp. 174, 177; War Department, *Correspondence Relating to the War with Spain,* vol. 1, pp. 75, 78.
75. War Department, *Correspondence Relating to the War with Spain,* pp. 77–78.

CHAPTER 13: FOURTH OF JULY PRESENT

1. Goode, *With Sampson through the War,* p. 194.
2. Chadwick, *The Spanish-American War,* vol. 2, p. 106.
3. Ibid., pp. 107–108.
4. Cervera, *Documents,* p. 106.
5. Ibid.
6. Ibid., pp. 106–107.
7. Ibid., pp. 107–108.
8. Ibid., p. 109.

9. Ibid., pp. 110–111.
10. Ibid., p. 111.
11. Ibid., p. 112.
12. Ibid., p. 113.
13. Ibid.
14. Ibid.
15. Ibid., p. 115.
16. Ibid.
17. Ibid.
18. Ibid., p. 116.
19. Ibid., pp. 116–117.
20. Ibid., pp. 117–118.
21. Ibid., pp. 118–119.
22. Ibid., p. 120.
23. Concas y Palau, *The Squadron of Admiral Cervera*, p. 68.
24. Ibid., pp. 68–69.
25. Ibid.
26. Ibid., p. 79.
27. Ibid., p. 73.
28. Ibid.
29. Müller y Tejeiro, "Battles and Capitulation of Santiago de Cuba," p. 173.
30. Concas y Palau, *The Squadron of Admiral Cervera*, p. 74.
31. Robley Evans, "The *Iowa* at Santiago," in "The Story of the Captains," *Century Magazine*, May 1899, p. 52.
32. Ibid., p. 50.
33. The *New York* and the *Brooklyn* were designed with ingenious twin sets of engines, two forward in the engineering spaces and two aft, connected by a manual coupling. In normal cruising situations, the forward engines were left idle. The coupling (or uncoupling) could only be done if the engines were stopped. Thus in the coming battle, the two ships, the fastest in the blockading fleet, were unable to steam at their optimum twenty-plus knots.
34. Edgar Stanton Maclay, *Life and Adventures of Jack Philip*, pp. 265–267; John W. Philip, "The *Texas* at Santiago," in "The Story of the Captains," *Century Magazine*, May 1899, p. 90.
35. Evans, "The *Iowa* at Santiago," p. 50.
36. Ibid., pp. 51, 53.
37. Chadwick, *The Spanish-American War*, vol. 2, pp. 130–132; Goode, *With Sampson through the War*, pp. 196, 199.
38. Edward W. Eberle, "The *Oregon* at Santiago," in "The Story of the Captains," *Century*, May 1899, pp. 104–105.
39. Henry Clay Taylor, "The *Indiana* at Santiago," in "The Story of the Captains," *Century*, May 1899, pp. 63–65.
40. Ibid., p. 65.
41. Ibid., p. 66.

42. Francis Cook, "The *Brooklyn* at Santiago," in "The Story of the Captains," *Century,* May 1899, pp. 95–96.

43. *Schley Court of Inquiry,* vol. 2, p. 1387. On her after engines alone, the *Brooklyn* could make fifteen knots. On all four engines, her trial speed approached twenty-two knots. However, to connect the forward engines to the propeller shafts required the ship to stop, and Cook was not about to give that order.

44. Ibid., vol. 1, p. 641; vol. 2, p. 1388. The wording of Schley's order itself has led to much confusion and error even among naval historians (for such, see Harold D. Langley's "Winfield Scott Schley" in *Admirals of the New Steel Navy.*) Schley's orders were for the *helm,* the wheel. Inasmuch as the ship's rudder acted opposite to the turning of the helm, an order to put the helm "hard-a-port" meant turning the ship to starboard, and vice versa.

45. Ibid., vol. 1, p. 641; vol. 2, p. 1388. Maclay, *History of the United States Navy,* vol. 3, pp. 364–365; Maclay, *Life and Adventures of Jack Philip,* p. 268.

46. Maclay, *Life and Adventures of Jack Philip,* pp. 268–269.

47. Ibid., pp. 269–270.

48. Ibid., pp. 270–271.

49. Chadwick, *The Spanish-American War,* vol. 2, p. 136.

50. *Schley Court of Inquiry,* vol. 2, p. 1389.

51. Concas y Palau, *The Squadron of Admiral Cervera,* p. 90; Wilson, *The Downfall of Spain,* p. 309.

52. Wilson, *The Downfall of Spain,* p. 310; Concas y Palau, *The Squadron of Admiral Cervera,* p. 76.

53. Cervera, *Documents,* pp. 123–124; Concas y Palau, *The Squadron of Admiral Cervera,* pp. 75–76.

54. Navy Department, *Annual Report,* 1898, BuNav Appendix, p. 524; Cook, "The *Brooklyn* at Santiago," p. 98; *Schley Court of Inquiry,* vol. 2, p. 1389.

55. Cervera, *Documents,* p. 124.

56. Concas y Palau, *The Squadron of Admiral Cervera,* p. 83.

57. Cervera, *Documents,* p. 128.

58. Maclay, *Life and Adventures of Jack Philip,* pp. 272–274.

59. Evans, "The *Iowa* at Santiago," pp. 53–54.

60. Eberle, "The *Oregon* at Santiago," p. 107.

61. Cervera, *Documents,* pp. 128–129.

62. Eberle, "The *Oregon* at Santiago," p. 107; Cook, "The *Brooklyn* at Santiago," p. 99.

63. Richard Wainwright, "The *Gloucester* at Santiago," in "The Story of the Captains," *Century,* p. 77.

64. Cervera, *Documents,* p. 132; Wilson, *The Downfall of Spain,* pp. 306–307.

65. Wainwright, "The *Gloucester* at Santiago," p. 80.

66. Wilson, *The Downfall of Spain,* pp. 305–306; Evans, "The *Iowa* at Santiago," p. 56.

67. Wainwright, "The *Gloucester* at Santiago," pp. 80–81.
68. Ibid., pp. 81–82.
69. Cervera, *Documents*, pp. 125–126; Chadwick, *The Spanish-American War,* vol. 2, pp. 168–169.
70. Cervera, *Documents*, p. 130.
71. Wilson, *The Downfall of Spain*, p. 314.
72. Ibid., pp. 314–315.
73. Concas y Palau, *The Squadron of Admiral Cervera*, p. 78; Cervera, *Documents*, p. 130.
74. Cervera, *Documents*, p. 131.
75. Navy Department, *Annual Report*, 1898, BuNav Appendix, p. 523.
76. Cervera, *Documents*, p. 131; *Schley Court of Inquiry,* vol. 2, p. 1390.
77. Wilson, *The Downfall of Spain*, p. 328.
78. Evans, "The *Iowa* at Santiago," p. 58.
79. Ibid.
80. Ibid., pp. 58, 61.
81. Goode, *With Sampson through the War*, p. 199; Wilson, *The Downfall of Spain*, p. 320.
82. Navy Department, *Annual Report*, 1898, BuNav Appendix, pp. 520–521.
83. Evans, "The *Iowa* at Santiago," p. 54.
84. Maclay, *Life and Adventures of Jack Philip*, pp. 275–277.
85. *Schley Court of Inquiry,* vol. 2, pp. 1389, 1391.
86. Navy Department, *Annual Report*, 1898, BuNav Appendix, p. 523.
87. Wilson, *The Downfall of Spain*, pp. 317–318.
88. Cervera, *Documents*, p. 127; Concas y Palau, *The Squadron of Admiral Cervera*, p. 79.
89. Cervera, *Documents*, p. 127; West, *Admirals of American Empire*, p. 265.
90. Navy Department, *Annual Report*, 1898, BuNav Appendix, pp. 523–524; Cook, "The *Brooklyn* at Santiago," pp. 98–99.
91. West, *Admirals of American Empire*, p. 265; *Schley Court of Inquiry,* vol. 2, pp. 1829–1830. Schley's court of inquiry convened in September 1901, presided over by Admiral Dewey. It found that Schley's conduct immediately prior to his establishment of the blockade of Santiago had been characterized by "vacillation, dilatoriness, and lack of enterprise." As for his actions during the Battle of Santiago, the court considered the *Brooklyn*'s controversial turn to have "caused her to lose distance and position with the Spanish vessels." Schley's personal conduct, however, the court judged to be "self-possessed," and the commodore "encouraged in his own person his subordinate officers and men to fight courageously."
92. Navy Department, *Annual Report*, 1898, BuNav Appendix, p. 521.
93. Ibid., p. 554; Chadwick, *The Spanish-American War,* vol. 2, p. 165.
94. Taylor, "The *Indiana* at Santiago," pp. 71–73.

95. Chadwick, *The Spanish-American War*, vol. 2, p. 176; Evans, "The *Iowa* at Santiago," p. 62.
96. Cervera, *Documents*, p. 123.
97. Chadwick, *The Spanish-American War*, vol. 2, p. 165.

CHAPTER 14: CAPITULATION

1. Davis, *The Cuban and Porto Rican Campaigns*, pp. 224, 227.
2. Ibid., p. 227.
3. Müller y Tejeiro, "Battles and Capitulation of Santiago de Cuba," p. 46.
4. War Department, *Correspondence Relating to the War with Spain*, vol. 1, p. 87; Navy Department, *Annual Report*, 1898, BuNav Appendix, p. 609.
5. Davis, *The Cuban and Porto Rican Campaigns*, pp. 255–257.
6. Ibid., pp. 277–278.
7. War Department, *Correspondence Relating to the War with Spain*, vol. 1, pp. 106–107.
8. Ibid., pp. 106, 113.
9. Davis, *The Cuban and Porto Rican Campaigns*, p. 280.
10. Miley, *In Cuba with Shafter*, p. 130; Leech, *In the Days of McKinley*, p. 252.
11. Chadwick, *The Spanish-American War*, vol. 2, p. 192.
12. Trask, *The War with Spain in 1898*, p. 290; Morison, *Letters of Theodore Roosevelt*, vol. 2, p. 849. In 1809, the British sent an expedition of forty thousand men to capture Antwerp from the French. They failed dismally. In the aftermath, a garrison of fifteen thousand men was left on the Dutch island of Walcherin, nearly half of whom died during an epidemic of malaria.
13. War Department, *Correspondence Relating to the War with Spain*, vol. 1, pp. 90–91; Miley, *In Cuba with Shafter*, p. 133.
14. War Department, *Correspondence Relating to the War with Spain*, vol. 1, pp. 90–91; Miley, *In Cuba with Shafter*, pp. 131–132.
15. Leech, *In the Days of McKinley*, pp. 263–264.
16. Chadwick, *The Spanish-American War*, vol. 2, pp. 112–113.
17. Ibid., pp. 193–194.
18. Miley, *In Cuba with Shafter*, pp. 137–138.
19. Müller y Tejeiro, "Battles and Capitulation of Santiago de Cuba," p. 184. The *Reina Mercedes* was raised by the Americans after the war and refitted at Portsmouth, New Hampshire. From 1905 to 1912 she served as a stationary receiving ship at Newport, Rhode Island. From 1912 until stricken from the Navy List in 1957 she served as station ship at the U.S. Naval Academy, Annapolis.
20. Miley, *In Cuba with Shafter*, p. 133.
21. Müller y Tejeiro, "Battles and Capitulation of Santiago de Cuba," p. 216.
22. Ibid., pp. 216–217; Chadwick, *The Spanish-American War*, vol. 2, p. 199.
23. Müller y Tejeiro, "Battles and Capitulation of Santiago de Cuba," pp. 218–219.

24. War Department, *Correspondence Relating to the War with Spain,* vol. 1, pp. 88–89.
25. Ibid., p. 89.
26. Ibid.
27. Ibid., pp. 89–90.
28. Ibid., p. 91.
29. Chadwick, *The Spanish-American War,* vol. 2, pp. 201, 203.
30. Ibid., p. 202.
31. Davis, *The Cuban and Porto Rican Campaigns,* pp. 265–266.
32. Ibid., pp. 269–270.
33. Chadwick, *The Spanish-American War,* vol. 2, pp. 204–205; Miley, *In Cuba with Shafter,* p. 143.
34. Chadwick, *The Spanish-American War,* vol. 2, p. 207.
35. Ibid., p. 211.
36. Ibid., pp. 211–212.
37. Sargent, *The Campaign of Santiago de Cuba,* vol. 3, pp. 15–16.
38. War Department, *Correspondence Relating to the War with Spain,* vol. 1, pp. 117–118.
39. Ibid.
40. Ibid., pp. 116, 119.
41. Chadwick, *The Spanish-American War,* vol. 2, p. 219.
42. Müller y Tejeiro, "Battles and Capitulation of Santiago de Cuba," pp. 231–232.
43. Ibid., pp. 232–233.
44. Miley, *In Cuba with Shafter,* p. 153; Chadwick, *The Spanish-American War,* vol. 2, p. 219.
45. Alger, *The Spanish-American War,* p. 235; Navy Department, *Annual Report,* 1898, BuNav Appendix, pp. 629–630; Chadwick, *The Spanish-American War,* vol. 2, p. 222.
46. Leech, *In the Days of McKinley,* p. 266; Chadwick, *The Spanish-American War,* vol. 2, pp. 222–223.
47. War Department, *Annual Report,* 1898, Report of the Major General Commanding the Army, p. 19.
48. Miles, *Serving the Republic,* p. 287.
49. Chadwick, *The Spanish-American War,* vol. 2, p. 229.
50. Miles, *Serving the Republic,* p. 287; Miley, *In Cuba with Shafter,* p. 155.
51. Chadwick, *The Spanish-American War,* vol. 2, p. 227.
52. Ibid.
53. Ibid.
54. Ibid.
55. Ibid.
56. Ibid., pp. 226.
57. Miley, *In Cuba with Shafter,* pp. 162–163.
58. Chadwick, *The Spanish-American War,* vol. 2, p. 228.

59. Ibid., p. 227.
60. War Department, *Correspondence Relating to the War with Spain,* vol. 1, p. 134.
61. Ibid., p. 136; Navy Department, *Annual Report,* 1898, BuNav Appendix, p. 624.
62. Navy Department, *Annual Report,* 1898, BuNav Appendix, p. 624.
63. Chadwick, *The Spanish-American War,* vol. 2, p. 233; War Department, *Annual Report,* 1898, Report of the Major General Commanding the Army, p. 20.
64. Ibid., pp. 234–235. Miles's orders specifically precluded his taking command at Santiago. It is assumed that Shafter in this instance simply deferred to his nominal senior in presenting the American position. War Department, *Annual Report,* 1898, Report of the Major General Commanding the Army, p. 20.
65. War Department, *Correspondence Relating to the War with Spain,* vol. 1, p. 134.
66. Ibid., p. 137.
67. Leech, *In the Days of McKinley,* p. 268.
68. Mayo, *America of Yesterday,* p. 203.
69. Ibid., p. 204.
70. War Department, *Correspondence Relating to the War with Spain,* vol. 1, p. 136.
71. Navy Department, *Annual Report,* 1898, BuNav Appendix, p. 625.
72. Chadwick, *The Spanish-American War,* vol. 2, p. 236.
73. War Department, *Correspondence Relating to the War with Spain,* vol. 1, pp. 142–143.
74. Navy Department, *Annual Report,* 1898, BuNav Appendix, p. 626.
75. Ivan Musicant, *The Banana Wars,* p. 34; Chadwick, *The Spanish-American War,* vol. 2, pp. 245–247.
76. Miley, *In Cuba with Shafter,* pp. 169–170; Navy Department, *Annual Report,* 1898, BuNav Appendix, p. 626.
77. Chadwick, *The Spanish-American War,* vol. 2, pp. 241–242.
78. War Department, *Correspondence Relating to the War with Spain,* vol. 1, pp. 145, 147.
79. Ibid., p. 149.
80. Ibid., pp. 148–149.
81. Ibid.
82. Chadwick, *The Spanish-American War,* vol. 2, p. 244.
83. Ibid., pp. 244–245; War Department, *Correspondence Relating to the War with Spain,* vol. 1, p. 150.
84. Chadwick, *The Spanish-American War,* vol. 2, pp. 245, 247.
85. Müller y Tejeiro, "Battles and Capitulation of Santiago de Cuba," pp. 219–220; Miley, *In Cuba with Shafter,* pp. 186–187.
86. Wheeler, *The Santiago Campaign,* pp. 180–181.
87. Ibid., p. 183; Brown, *Correspondents War,* pp. 401–402.

88. Freidel, *The Splendid Little War,* pp. 256–257.
89. Post, *The Little War of Private Post,* p. 248.
90. Edward E. Capehart, "The Mine Defenses of Santiago Harbor," *Proceedings* of the United States Naval Institute, December 1898, p. 603.
91. Miley, *In Cuba with Shafter,* p. 214.
92. War Department, *Correspondence Relating to the War with Spain,* vol. 1, p. 160.
93. Ibid., pp. 160–161.
94. Hermann Hagedorn, *Leonard Wood,* vol. 1, p. 184.
95. Ibid., pp. 184–185.
96. Musicant, *The Banana Wars,* p. 38.
97. Hagedorn, *Leonard Wood,* vol. 1, p. 187.
98. Ibid., pp. 187–188.
99. Ibid., pp. 188–189.
100. Ibid.
101. Ibid., pp. 192, 198.
102. Roosevelt, *The Rough Riders,* p. 137.
103. Miley, *In Cuba with Shafter,* pp. 215–216.
104. Roosevelt, *The Rough Riders,* p. 137.
105. Leech, *In the Days of McKinley,* pp. 271–272.
106. Ibid., p. 275; Chadwick, *The Spanish-American War,* vol. 2, pp. 255–256.
107. War Department, *Correspondence Relating to the War with Spain,* vol. 1, pp. 200–201.
108. Ibid.
109. Roosevelt, *The Rough Riders,* pp. 141–142.
110. Ibid., p. 143; War Department, *Correspondence Relating to the War with Spain,* vol. 1, p. 202; Chadwick, *The Spanish-American War,* vol. 2, p. 258.
111. Leech, *In the Days of McKinley,* pp. 276–277; Roosevelt, *The Rough Riders,* p. 143; Chadwick, *The Spanish-American War,* vol. 2, p. 259.
112. Alger, *The Spanish-American War,* pp. 269–270, 273.
113. Ibid., p. 273.

CHAPTER 15: PUERTO RICO

1. Trask, *The War with Spain in 1898,* p. 338.
2. Mahan, *Lessons of the War with Spain,* pp. 27–28.
3. Long, *The New American Navy,* vol. 1, p. 205.
4. Trask, *The War with Spain in 1898,* p. 340.
5. War Department, *Correspondence Relating to the War with Spain,* vol. 1, p. 263.
6. Ibid.
7. Ibid.
8. Ibid., p. 264.
9. Trask, *The War with Spain in 1898,* p. 341.

10. Chadwick, *The Spanish-American War,* vol. 2, p. 269.
11. Ibid., p. 270.
12. War Department, *Correspondence Relating to the War with Spain,* vol. 1, p. 281.
13. Ibid., p. 283; Chadwick, *The Spanish-American War,* vol. 2, p. 272.
14. Chadwick, *The Spanish-American War,* vol. 2, p. 274.
15. Ibid., pp. 276–277.
16. Ibid., pp. 278–279.
17. Ibid., p. 279.
18. Ibid., pp. 279–280.
19. Ibid., pp. 284–285; War Department, *Correspondence Relating to the War with Spain,* vol. 1, p. 338.
20. Chadwick, *The Spanish-American War,* vol. 2, pp. 285–286.
21. Ibid.
22. Ibid., p. 287.
23. Navy Department, *Annual Report,* 1898, BuNav Appendix, pp. 644–645.
24. Ibid., pp. 643–644.
25. Davis, *The Cuban and Porto Rico Campaigns,* pp. 322, 325.
26. Nelson A. Miles, "The War with Spain," part 3, *North American Review,* July 1899, p. 133.
27. War Department, *Correspondence Relating to the War with Spain,* vol. 1, p. 330; Davis, *The Cuban and Porto Rican Campaigns,* pp. 325–326.
28. Navy Department, *Annual Report,* 1898, BuNav Appendix, pp. 646–647.
29. Trask, *The War with Spain in 1898,* p. 361.
30. War Department, *Correspondence Relating to the War with Spain,* vol. 1, p. 372, 379–380; Trask, *The War with Spain in 1898,* p. 362.
31. War Department, *Correspondence Relating to the War with Spain,* vol. 1, p. 368.
32. Trask, *The War with Spain in 1898,* p. 360.
33. Ibid., p. 362; Henry H. Whitney, "Miles's Campaign in Puerto Rico," in *The American-Spanish War: A History by War Leaders,* p. 206.
34. Whitney, "Miles's Campaign in Puerto Rico," p. 207.
35. War Department, *Correspondence Relating to the War with Spain,* vol. 1, p. 383.
36. Ibid., p. 393.
37. Trask, *The War with Spain in 1898,* p. 365.
38. War Department, *Correspondence Relating to the War with Spain,* vol. 1, p. 308.
39. Ibid., p. 340.

CHAPTER 16: THE MANILA CAMPAIGN

1. Dewey, *Autobiography,* p. 206; Navy Department, *Annual Report,* 1898, BuNav Appendix, p. 68. Dewey's cable was dated May 4 aboard the

Olympia but was not sent until the seventh from Hong Kong, the closest cable connection. It took two to three days for the cutter *McCulloch* or one of the storeships to reach Hong Kong from Manila. Thus nearly a week could pass between the time Dewey communicated with Washington and receiving its reply. Contrast this with Admiral Sampson's cable facilities to Key West, first at St. Nicolas Môle, Haiti, then at Guantánamo Bay, enabling two-way communications with the Navy Department within a matter of hours, or a day at most.

2. Navy Department, *Annual Report,* 1898, BuNav Appendix, p. 69.
3. Ibid., pp. 97–98.
4. War Department, *Correspondence Relating to the War with Spain,* vol. 2, pp. 634–635.
5. Ibid., pp. 643–644.
6. Ibid.
7. Ibid., pp. 647–648.
8. Ibid.
9. Ibid., p. 649.
10. Navy Department, *Annual Report,* 1898, BuNav Appendix, p. 152. The statement of the governor not being permitted to board a foreign vessel cannot be correct. In Manila the Spanish governor general visited the German flagship *Kaiser* on more than one occasion during Dewey's blockade of the port.
11. Ibid., pp. 153, 155.
12. *Washington Post,* June 28, 1898; Spector, *Admiral of the New Empire,* p. 83.
13. Spector, *Admiral of the New Empire,* p. 85.
14. Ibid., p. 85.
15. Ibid., p. 86.
16. Henry R. Graff, ed., *American Imperialism and the Philippine Insurrection,* p. 9.
17. Ibid., p. 3; Agoncillo, *Malolos,* p. 134.
18. Spector, *Admiral of the New Empire,* p. 89.
19. Navy Department, *Annual Report,* 1898, BuNav Appendix, p. 104.
20. Ibid.; Graff, *American Imperialism and the Philippine Insurrection,* p. 3.
21. Graff, *American Imperialism and the Philippine Insurrection,* p. 3; Navy Department, *Annual Report,* 1898, BuNav Appendix, pp. 103–104.
22. Graff, *American Imperialism and the Philippine Insurrection,* p. 12.
23. Ibid., p. 15.
24. Ibid., p. 3; Trask, *The War with Spain in 1898,* p. 407.
25. Indicative of the self-delusion of certain high officers of the Spanish navy, the orders issued by Auñón listed the *Carlos V* and *Rapido* as a battleship and cruiser respectively.
26. Cervera, *Documents,* pp. 147–148.
27. Ibid., pp. 148–150.
28. Ibid., p. 150.

29. Ibid., p. 152.
30. Ibid.
31. Ibid., p. 153.
32. Navy Department, *Annual Report,* 1898, BuNav Appendix, pp. 107, 109.
33. War Department, *Annual Report,* 1898, vol. 1, Report of the Major General Commanding, p. 54; War Department, *Correspondence Relating to the War with Spain,* part 2, pp. 777–779.
34. Francis Vinton Greene, "The Capture of Manila," *Century Magazine,* March 1899, pp. 786–787.
35. Ibid., p. 788.
36. William R. Braisted, *The United States Navy in the Pacific, 1897–1909,* pp. 39–40.
37. Ibid., p. 35; Dewey, *Autobiography,* p. 220.
38. Braisted, *The United States Navy in the Pacific,* p. 42.
39. Dewey in his autobiography claimed the *Raleigh* fired a shot across the bow of the *Cormoran* when the German failed to stop on receiving a visual signal to do so. No record of this is mentioned in the ship's log.
40. Dewey, *Autobiography,* p. 222; Sargent, *Admiral Dewey and the Manila Campaign,* p. 69.
41. Thomas A. Bailey, "Dewey and the Germans at Manila Bay," *American Historical Review,* October 1939, p. 65.
42. Spector, *Admiral of the New Empire,* p. 76.
43. Sargent, *Admiral Dewey and the Manila Campaign,* p. 68.
44. Bailey, "Dewey and the Germans at Manila Bay," p. 67.
45. Ibid., p. 67.
46. Sargent, *Admiral Dewey and the Manila Campaign,* pp. 72–73.
47. Ibid. According to Bailey, "Dewey and the Germans at Manila Bay," p. 68. All of the numerous versions of this incident agree that Dewey threatened war.
48. Spector, *Admiral of the New Empire,* p. 81.
49. Sargent, *Admiral Dewey and the Manila Campaign,* p. 76.
50. Ibid.
51. Greene, "The Capture of Manila," p. 789.
52. Ibid., pp. 789–790.
53. Ibid.
54. Ibid.
55. Trask, *The War with Spain in 1898,* p. 409.
56. Chadwick, *The Spanish-American War,* vol. 2, pp. 395–396.
57. *Foreign Relations,* 1898, p. lix; Greene, "The Capture of Manila," *Century Illustrated Monthly Magazine,* April 1899, p. 915.
58. Trask, *The War with Spain in 1898,* pp. 411, 603n.
59. Navy Department, *Annual Report,* 1898, BuNav Appendix, p. 118.
60. Spector, *Admiral of the New Empire,* pp. 93–94.
61. Chadwick, *The Spanish-American War,* vol. 2, p. 401.

62. Navy Department, *Annual Report*, 1898, BuNav Appendix, p. 126.
63. Greene, "The Capture of Manila," April 1899, pp. 922–923.
64. Trask, *The War with Spain in 1898*, pp. 603–604.
65. Greene, "The Capture of Manila," April 1899, p. 924.
66. Navy Department, *Annual Report*, 1898, BuNav Appendix, p. 121.
67. Ibid.; Greene, "The Capture of Manila," April 1899, p. 924.
68. Navy Department, *Annual Report*, 1898, BuNav Appendix, p. 122.
69. Ibid.
70. Sargent, *Admiral Dewey and the Manila Campaign*, p. 83.
71. Chadwick, *The Spanish-American War*, vol. 2, pp. 404, 408.
72. Ibid., pp. 408–409.
73. Ibid., p. 409.
74. Ibid., p. 410.
75. Ibid., pp. 411–412.
76. Ibid., p. 413.
77. Ibid., pp. 413–414.
78. Greene, "The Capture of Manila," April 1899, p. 929.
79. Ibid., p. 930.
80. Ibid.
81. Chadwick, *The Spanish-American War*, vol 2, pp. 418–420; War Department, *Annual Report*, 1898, Report of the Major General Commanding the Army, pp. 80–81.
82. Chadwick, *The Spanish-American War*, vol. 2, pp. 421–422.
83. Navy Department, *Annual Report*, 1898, BuNav Appendix, p. 123.
84. War Department, *Correspondence Relating to the War with Spain*, vol. 2, p. 750.
85. Navy Department, *Annual Report*, 1898, BuNav Appendix, pp. 118, 122–123.
86. Ibid., p. 124; Chadwick, *The Spanish-American War*, vol. 2, p. 425.
87. Navy Department, *Annual Report*, 1898, BuNav Appendix, p. 123.
88. Spector, *Admiral of the New Empire*, p. 97.
89. Ibid.
90. Ibid., pp. 97–98.
91. Ibid.
92. Ibid., pp. 98–99.

CHAPTER 17: PEACE

1. Trask, *The War with Spain in 1898*, p. 424.
2. Ibid., p. 425.
3. Ibid.
4. Olcott, *Life of William McKinley*, vol. 2, pp. 132–133.
5. *Spanish Diplomatic Correspondence and Documents*, p. 200.
6. Ibid., p. 201.

7. *Foreign Relations*, 1898, pp. 819–820.
8. Chadwick, *The Spanish-American War*, vol. 2, p. 430; Leech, *In the Days of McKinley*, p. 282.
9. Mayo, *America of Yesterday*, pp. 210–211.
10. Olcott, *Life of William McKinley*, vol. 2, p. 63; May, *Imperial Democracy*, p. 250.
11. Ibid., pp. 110–111; H. H. Kohlsaat, *From McKinley to Harding*, p. 68.
12. *Spanish Diplomatic Correspondence and Documents*, p. 206.
13. Ibid., p. 209.
14. *Foreign Relations*, 1898, pp. 820–821.
15. *Spanish Diplomatic Correspondence and Documents*, p. 213.
16. Ibid., pp. 212–214.
17. Ibid., p. 214.
18. Trask, *The War with Spain in 1898*, p. 430.
19. *Spanish Diplomatic Correspondence and Documents*, p. 215.
20. Ibid., p. 216.
21. Trask, *The War with Spain in 1898*, p. 433; Alger, *The Spanish-American War*, p. 271.
22. *Foreign Relations*, 1898, p. 823.
23. *Spanish Diplomatic Correspondence and Documents*, p. 220.
24. Ibid.; *Foreign Relations*, 1898, pp. lix, 834.
25. Leech, *In the Days of McKinley*, pp. 289–290.
26. H. Wayne Morgan, *America's Road to Empire*, p. 83.
27. Trask, *The War with Spain in 1898*, p. 435.
28. Ibid., p. 436; Chadwick, *The Spanish-American War*, vol. 2, p. 450n; H. Wayne Morgan, *America's Road to Empire*, p. 93.
29. *Spanish Diplomatic Correspondence and Documents*, pp. 238, 245.
30. Leech, *In the Days of McKinley*, p. 326.
31. Ibid., pp. 326–327.
32. Ibid., p. 327.
33. Ibid., p. 331.
34. *Foreign Relation*, 1898, pp. 806–807.
35. Julius Pratt, *Expansionists of 1898*, p. 269.
36. Trask, *The War with Spain in 1898*, p. 437.
37. Ibid., p. 438.
38. Ibid.
39. Mayo, *America of Yesterday*, p. 115.
40. Morgan, *America's Road to Empire*, p. 82.
41. Trask, *The War with Spain in 1898*, p. 441.
42. *Foreign Relations*, 1898, pp. 906–908.
43. Olcott, *Life of William McKinley*, vol. 2, pp. 123–124.
44. Paolo Coletta, ed., *Threshold to American Imperialism*, pp. 137–138.
45. H. Wayne Morgan, *Making Peace with Spain: The Diary of Whitelaw Reid*, p. 53.

46. Ibid.; Olcott, *Life of William McKinley*, vol. 2, p. 124; John Bassett Moore, "The Treaty of Peace," in *The American-Spanish War: A History by the War Leaders*, p. 477.

47. *Spanish Diplomatic Correspondence and Documents*, pp. 282–283.

48. *Foreign Relations*, 1898, p. 924.

49. Ibid., p. 927; *Spanish Diplomatic Correspondence and Documents*, p. 291.

50. *Foreign Relations*, 1898, p. 924.

51. Morgan, *Making Peace with Spain: The Diary of Whitelaw Reid*, p. 87.

52. *Spanish Diplomatic Correspondence and Documents*, pp. 293–294.

53. Ibid., p. 293.

54. Morgan, *Making Peace with Spain: The Diary of Whitelaw Reid*, p. 94.

55. *Foreign Relations*, 1898, p. 930.

56. Ibid., pp. 931–932.

57. Morgan, *Making Peace with Spain: The Diary of Whitelaw Reid*, p. 115.

58. *Foreign Relations*, 1898, p. 936.

59. *Spanish Diplomatic Correspondence and Documents*, pp. 303–304.

60. 55th Congress, 3rd Session, Senate Document No. 62, Part 1, *Treaty of Peace between the United States and Spain*, p. 367.

61. Morgan, *Making Peace with Spain: The Diary of Whitelaw Reid*, p. 58.

62. *Treaty of Peace between the United States and Spain*, pp. 472–490, passim.

63. *Foreign Relations*, 1898, p. 934.

64. Ibid., p. 995.

65. *Treaty of Peace between the United States and Spain*, pp. 404–429, passim.

66. Ibid.

67. Trask, *The War with Spain in 1898*, pp. 616–617; Morgan, *Making Peace with Spain: The Diary of Whitelaw Reid*, p. 102n.

68. *Speeches and Addresses of William McKinley*, pp. 90–91, 95.

69. Leech, *In the Days of McKinley*, p. 341.

70. *Speeches and Addresses of William McKinley*, p. 131.

71. Ibid., p. 134.

72. Ibid.

73. Leech, *In the Days of McKinley*, p. 344.

74. *Foreign Relations*, 1898, pp. 937–938.

75. *Spanish Diplomatic Correspondence and Documents*, pp. 310, 311–312.

76. Ibid., pp. 312–313.

77. *Foreign Relations*, 1898, p. 939.

78. Ibid., pp. 939–940.

79. Ibid.: Morgan, *Making Peace with Spain: The Diary of Whitelaw Reid*, p. 129.

80. Morgan, *Making Peace with Spain: The Diary of Whitelaw Reid*, p. 130; *Foreign Relations*, 1898, p. 940.

81. *Foreign Relations*, 1898, p. 941.

82. *Spanish Diplomatic Correspondence and Documents*, p. 316.

83. Ibid.

84. *Foreign Relations,* 1898, p. 945. Japan, after capturing the Carolines from Germany in World War I, transformed its island of Truk into a major naval and air bastion, straddling key routes to East and Southeast Asia. The United States bypassed it in World War II, aiming for the Marianas (formerly the Ladrones) instead.
85. Ibid.
86. Ibid., pp. 945–946.
87. Ibid., pp. 947–948.
88. Ibid., p. 948.
89. Ibid., pp. 948–949.
90. Olcott, *Life of William McKinley,* vol. 2, p. 126.
91. *Spanish Diplomatic Correspondence and Documents,* p. 326.
92. Ibid., p. 327.
93. Ibid., pp. 332–333.
94. *Foreign Relations,* 1898, p. 960.
95. *Spanish Diplomatic Correspondence and Documents,* pp. 333–334.
96. Olcott, *Life of William McKinley,* vol. 2, p. 128.
97. Coletta, *Threshold to American Imperialism,* p. 158.
98. *Foreign Relations,* 1898, pp. 831–840.
99. Japan seized the German empire in the Pacific during the first year of World War I, and retained it under a League of Nations mandate. Most of it became fortified as Japan's Pacific defense perimeter, and was the scene of much hard fighting during World War II.
100. Trask, *The War with Spain in 1898,* pp. 468–469.
101. Leech, *In the Days of McKinley,* p. 358.
102. *Speeches and Addresses of William McKinley,* p. 172.
103. Trask, *The War with Spain in 1898,* p. 472.

CHAPTER 18: SCANDAL

1. Leech, *In the Days of McKinley,* p. 292.
2. Ibid.
3. Ibid., p. 297.
4. Cosmas, *An Army for Empire,* p. 284.
5. Ibid., p. 285.
6. In peacetime officers purchased their own food. When on active campaign they generally partook of the enlisted men's ration and were expected to reimburse the government for its cost.
7. Alger, *The Spanish-American War,* pp. 388–389; Roosevelt, *The Rough Riders,* p. 61.
8. Alger, *The Spanish-American War,* p. 396; WIC, vol. 7, pp. 3256–3263, passim.
9. Alger, *The Spanish-American War,* pp. 380, 383; Cosmas, *An Army for Empire,* p. 291.

10. Alger, *The Spanish-American War*, p. 379.
11. *Army and Navy Journal*, January 14, 1899.
12. Ibid.
13. Leech, *In the Days of McKinley*, p. 319.
14. Alger, *The Spanish-American War*, p. 395; Upton Sinclair's *The Jungle*, depicting the horrors of the meatpacking industry, would not be published until 1906.
15. Leech, *In the Days of McKinley*, p. 319.
16. Cosmas, *An Army for Empire*, p. 294.
17. Ibid., p. 248.
18. *WIC*, vol. 4, pp. 1540–1541.
19. Cosmas, *An Army for Empire*, p. 268.
20. Alger, *The Spanish-American War*, pp. 263–264; War Department, *Correspondence Relating to the War with Spain*, vol. 1, p. 194.
21. *Roosevelt-Lodge Correspondence*, vol. 1, pp. 340–341.
22. Post, *The Little War of Private Post*, pp. 309–310.
23. *Roosevelt-Lodge Correspondence*, vol. 1, p. 338; Cosmas, *An Army for Empire*, p. 282; *New York Times*, May 18, 1898.
24. Alger, *The Spanish-American War*, pp. 432–433.
25. Leech, *In the Days of McKinley*, p. 314.
26. *Roosevelt-Lodge Correspondence*, vol. 1, pp. 319–320, 356–357.
27. *Speeches and Addresses of William McKinley*, p. 83.
28. Cosmas, *An Army for Empire*, p. 282.
29. *New York Times*, February 17–18, 1899.
30. Leech, *In the Days of McKinley*, p. 376.
31. Ibid., p. 377.
32. Ibid., pp. 377–378.

EMPIRE

1. May, *Imperial Democracy*, p. 263.
2. Mahan, *The Interest of America in Sea Power*, p. 43.
3. Walter LaFeber, *The New Empire*, p. 410.
4. Ibid., pp. 410–411.

BIBLIOGRAPHY

GOVERNMENT PUBLICATIONS

54th Congress, 1st Session, Senate Report No. 141. *[Hostilities Existing in Cuba.]* Washington: GPO, 1896.

55th Congress, 2nd Session, Senate Report No. 207. *Report of the Naval Court of Inquiry upon the Destruction of the United States Battleship* Maine *in Havana Harbor, February 15, 1898.* Washington: GPO, 1898.

55th Congress, 2nd Session, Senate Document No. 230. *Consular Correspondence Respecting the Condition of the* Reconcentrados *in Cuba, the State of the War in That Island, and the Prospects of the Projected Autonomy.* Washington: GPO, 1898.

55th Congress, 2nd Session, Senate Report No. 231. *Lives Lost by the Sinking of the U.S. Battle Ship* Maine. Washington: GPO, 1898.

55th Congress, 3rd Session, House Document No. 2. *Annual Reports of the Navy Department for the Year 1898: Appendix to the Report of the Chief of the Bureau of Navigation.* Washington: GPO, 1898. [Plus additional *Annual Reports of the Navy Department,* 1889–1902].

55th Congress, 3rd Session, Senate Document No. 62, part 2. *A Treaty of Peace between the United States and Spain* . . . [plus] *Accompanying Papers.* Washington: GPO, 1899.

56th Congress, 1st Session, Senate Document No. 221. *Report of the Committee Appointed by the President to Investigate the Conduct of the War Department in the War with Spain.* 8 vols. Washington: GPO, 1900.

56th Congress, 2nd Session, Senate Document No. 231, part 7. *Compilation of Reports of Committee on Foreign Relations* . . . : Diplomatic Relations with Foreign Nations—Affairs in Cuba. Washington: GPO, 1901.

Baquer, Miguel Alonso. "The Spanish-American War of 1898 and Its Effects on Spanish Military Institutions." *Proceedings of the 1982 International Military History Symposium.* Washington: U.S. Army Center of Military History, 1984.

Concas y Palau, Víctor M. *The Squadron of Admiral Cervera.* Washington: Navy Department, 1900.

Cummings, Damon. *Admiral Richard Wainwright and the United States Fleet.* Washington: GPO, 1962.

Dastrup, Boyd L. *King of Battle: A Branch History of the U.S. Army's Field Artillery.* Fort Monroe, Va.: Office of the Command Historian, U.S. Army Training and Doctrine Command, 1992.

Kreidberg, Marvin A., and Merton G. Henry. *History of Military Mobilization in the United States Army 1775–1945.* Washington: U.S. Army, 1955.

Ministerio de Estado. *Spanish Diplomatic Correspondence and Documents 1896–1900 Presented to the Cortes by the Minister of State.* Washington: GPO, 1905.

Navy Department. *Dictionary of American Naval Fighting Ships.* 8 vols. Washington: Naval Historical Center, 1970–1981.

————. *Record of Proceedings of a Court of Inquiry in the Case of Rear Admiral Winfield S. Schley, U.S. Navy. . . .* 2 vols. Washington: GPO, 1901.

————. *Register of the Commissioned and Warrant Officers of the Navy of the United States and of the Marine Corps to January 1, 1898 / July 1, 1898.* Washington: GPO, 1898.

Núñez, Severo Gómez. *The Spanish-American War: Blockades and Coast Defense.* Office of Naval Intelligence, War Notes No. 6, Information from Abroad. Washington: GPO, 1899.

Rickover, Hyman G. *How the Battleship* Maine *Was Destroyed.* Washington: Naval History Division, Navy Department, 1976.

Risch, Erna. *Quartermaster Support of the Army: A History of the Corps 1775–1939.* Washington: Quartermaster Historian's Office, Office of the Quartermaster General, 1962.

The Spanish-American War: A Collection of Documents Relative to the Squadron Operations in the West Indies. Arranged by Rear Admiral Pascual Cervera y Topete. Washington: Navy Department, 1899.

State Department. *Papers Relating to the Foreign Relations of the United States. . . .* Washington: GPO, 1894–1899.

Tillman, B. R., Jr., ed. *Navy Yearbook* [1916]: *. . . A Resume of Annual Naval Appropriation Laws from 1883 to 1917, Inclusive. . . .* Washington: GPO, 1916.

War Department, Adjutant General's Office. *Correspondence Relating to the War with Spain: Including the Insurrection in the Philippine Islands. . . .* Washington: GPO, 1902.

————. *Annual Report of the Secretary of War* (various years). Washington: GPO, 1894–1906.

SECONDARY SOURCES

Books

Agoncillo, Teodoro A. *Malolos: The Crisis of the Republic.* Quezon City: University of the Philippines, 1960.

Alger, Russell A. *The Spanish-American War.* New York: Harper, 1901.

The American-Spanish War: A History by the War Leaders. Norwich, Conn.: Haskell, 1899.

Arderius, Francisco. *La Escuadra Española en Santiago de Cuba.* Barcelona: Maucci, 1903.

Azoy, Anastasio. *Charge!: The Story of the Battle of San Juan Hill.* New York: Longmans, 1961.

Barker, Albert. *Everyday Life in the Navy: Autobiography of Rear Admiral Albert S. Barker, USN.* Boston: Badger, 1928.

Barrett, John. *Admiral George Dewey: A Sketch of the Man.* New York: Harper, 1899.

Beer, Thomas. *Hanna.* New York: Knopf, 1929.

Bemis, Samuel Flagg, ed. *American Secretaries of State and Their Diplomacy.* Vol. 9. New York: Pageant, 1958.

Benjamin, Park. *The United States Naval Academy.* New York: Putnam's, 1900.

Bennett, James D. *Frederick Jackson Turner.* Boston: Twayne, 1975.

Benton, Elbert J. *International Law and Diplomacy of the Spanish-American War.* Baltimore: Johns Hopkins Press, 1908.

Bishop, Joseph Bucklin. *Theodore Roosevelt and His Time: Shown in His Own Letters.* New York: Scribner's, 1920.

Bradford, James C., ed. *Admirals of the New Steel Navy: Makers of the American Naval Tradition 1880–1930.* Annapolis, Md.: Naval Institute Press, 1990.

Braisted, William Reynolds. *The United States Navy in the Pacific, 1897–1909.* Austin, Tex.: University of Texas Press, 1958.

Brassey, Thomas A., ed. *Naval Annual, 1897.* Portsmouth, England: Griffin, 1897.

Brown, Charles H. *The Correspondents' War: Journalists in the Spanish-American War.* New York: Scribner's, 1967.

Busbey, L. White. *Uncle Joe Cannon.* New York: Henry Holt, 1927.

Callahan, Edward, ed. *List of Officers of the Navy of the United States and of the Marine Corps from 1775 to 1900. . . .* New York: Haskell House (reprint edition), 1969.

Cashin, Herschel V., et al. *Under Fire with the Tenth U.S. Cavalry. . . .* London: Tennyson, 1899.

Chadwick, French Ensor. *Relations of the United States and Spain: Diplomacy.* New York: Scribner's, 1909.

———. *Relations of the United States and Spain: The Spanish-American War.* 2 vols. New York: Scribner's, 1911.

Chapman, Charles E. *A History of the Cuban Republic: A Study in Hispanic American Politics.* New York: Macmillan, 1927.

Churchill, Winston. *My Early Life: A Roving Commission.* London: Oldhams, 1930.

Cogar, William B. *Dictionary of Admirals of the U.S. Navy.* 2 vols. Annapolis, Md.: Naval Institute Press, 1989.

Coletta, Paolo, ed. *American Secretaries of the Navy.* 2 vols. Annapolis, Md.: Naval Institute Press, 1980.

———. *Bowman Hendry McCalla: A Fighting Sailor.* Washington: University Press of America, 1979.

———. *Threshold to American Internationalism: Essays on the Foreign Policies of William McKinley.* New York: Exposition, 1970.

Coolidge, Louis Arthur. *An Old-Fashioned Senator: the Story of Orville H. Platt of Connecticut.* New York: Putnam's, 1910.

Coontz, Robert E. *From Mississippi to the Sea.* Philadelphia: Dorrance, 1930.

Cooper, Jerry M. *The Army and Civil Disorder: Federal Military Intervention in Labor Disputes, 1877–1900.* Westport, Conn.: Greenwood, 1980.

Cosmas, Graham A. *An Army for Empire: The United States Army in the Spanish-American War.* Columbia, Mo.: University of Missouri Press, 1971.

Cruse, Thomas. *Apache Days and After.* Caldwell, Idaho: Caxton, 1941.

Davis, Richard Harding. *Cuba in War Time.* New York: Russell, 1898.

———. *The Cuban and Porto Rican Campaigns.* New York: Scribner's, 1898.

———. *Notes of a War Correspondent.* New York: Scribner's, 1911.

Dawes, Charles G. *A Journal of the McKinley Years*. Chicago: Lakeside, 1950.

Dewey, Adelbert M. *Life and Letters of Admiral Dewey*. Akron, Ohio: Werner, 1899.

Dewey, George. *Autobiography of George Dewey, Admiral of the Navy*. Annapolis, Md.: Naval Institute Press, 1987.

Dugdale, E. T. S., ed. *German Diplomatic Documents 1871–1914*. Vol. 2. New York: Harper, 1929.

Dunn, Arthur Wallace. *From Harrison to Harding: A Personal Narrative, Covering a Third of a Century 1888–1921*. New York: Putnam's, 1922.

————. *Gridiron Nights: Humorous and Satirical Views of Politics and Statesmen as Presented by the Famous Dining Club*. New York: Stokes, 1915.

Eggert, Gerald G. *Richard Olney: Evolution of a Statesman*. University Park, Pa.: Pennsylvania State University Press, 1974.

Evans, Robley D. *A Sailor's Log*. New York: Appleton, 1901.

Ferrara, Orestes. *The Last Spanish War: Revelations in "Diplomacy."* New York: Paisley, 1937.

Fiske, Bradley A. *From Midshipman to Rear Admiral*. New York: Century, 1919.

Flint, Grover. *Marching with Gómez: A War Correspondent's Field Note-Book Kept during Four Months with the Cuban Army*. Boston: Lamson, Wolffe, 1898.

Foner, Philip S. *Antonio Maceo: The "Bronze Titan" of Cuba's Struggle for Independence*. New York: Monthly Review, 1977.

————. *A History of Cuba and Its Relations with the United States*. 2 vols. New York: International, 1963.

————. *Spanish-Cuban-American War and the Birth of American Imperialism 1895–1902*. 2 vols. New York: Monthly Review, 1972.

Freidel, Frank. *The Splendid Little War*. Boston: Little, Brown, 1958.

Ganoe, William Addleman. *History of the United States Army*. New York: Appleton-Century, 1942.

Gleaves, Albert. *The Life and Letters of Rear-Admiral Stephen B. Luce, U.S. Navy: Founder of the Naval War College*. New York: Putnam's, 1925.

Gómez Núñez, Severo. *La Guerra Hispano-Americana: La Habana—Influencia de las Plazas de Guerra*. Madrid: n.p., 1900.

————. *La Guerra Hispano-Americana: Puerto Rico y Filipinas*. Madrid: n.p., 1902.

————. *La Guerra Hispano-Americana: Santiago de Cuba*. Madrid: n.p., 1901.

Goode, W. A. M. *With Sampson through the War.* New York: Doubleday, 1899.

Gould, Lewis L. *The Spanish-American War and President McKinley.* Lawrence, Kans.: University Press of Kansas, 1982.

Graff, Henry F., ed. *American Imperialism and the Philippine Insurrection: Testimony Taken from Hearings on Affairs in the Philippine Islands before the Senate Committee on the Philippines—1902.* Boston: Little, Brown, 1969.

Graham, George Edward. *Schley and Santiago.* Chicago: Conkey, 1902.

Grenville, John A. S., and George Berkeley Young. *Politics, Strategy, and American Diplomacy: Studies in Foreign Policy, 1873–1917.* New Haven, Conn.: Yale University Press, 1966.

Hagedorn, Hermann. *Leonard Wood.* Vol. 1. New York: Harper, 1931.

Halstead, Murat. *Full Official History of the War with Spain.* . . . Chicago: n.p., 1899.

———. *Story of Cuba: Her Struggles for Liberty.* . . . Boston: Hastings, 1898.

Hattendorf, John B., et al. *Sailors and Scholars: The Centennial History of the U.S. Naval War College.* Newport, R.I.: Naval War College Press, 1984.

Healy, David F. *The United States in Cuba 1898–1902: Generals, Politicians and the Search for Policy.* Madison: University of Wisconsin Press, 1963.

Healy, Laurin Hall, and Luis Kutner. *The Admiral.* Chicago: Ziff-Davis, 1944.

Herrick, Walter R., Jr. *The American Naval Revolution.* Baton Rouge: Louisiana State University Press, 1966.

Hirst, Francis W. *Life and Letters of Thomas Jefferson.* New York: Macmillan, 1926.

Hobart, Mrs. Garret A. [Jennie]. *Memories.* Patterson, N.J.: Privately printed, 1930.

Jacobs, Wilbur R., ed. *The Historical World of Frederick Jackson Turner: With Selections from his Correspondence.* New Haven, Conn.: Yale University Press, 1968.

James, Henry. *Richard Olney and His Public Service.* Boston: Houghton Mifflin, 1923.

Jones, Virgil Carrington. *Roosevelt's Rough Riders.* Garden City, N.Y.: Doubleday, 1971.

Kohlsaat, H. H. *From McKinley to Harding: Personal Recollections of Our Presidents.* New York: Scribner's, 1923.

LaFeber, Walter. *The New Empire: An Interpretation of American Expansion 1860–1898.* Ithaca, N.Y.: Cornell University Press, 1963.

Latimer, Elizabeth Wormeley. *Spain in the Nineteenth Century.* Chicago: McClurg, 1898.

Lee, Fitzhugh. *Cuba's Struggle against Spain.* . . . New York: American Historical Press, 1899.

Leech, Margaret. *In the Days of McKinley.* New York: Harper, 1959.

Linderman, Gerald F. *The Mirror of War: American Society and the Spanish-American War.* Ann Arbor: University of Michigan Press, 1974.

Livezey, William. *Mahan on Sea Power.* Norman, Okla.: University of Oklahoma Press, 1980.

Long, John D. *The New American Navy.* 2 vols. New York: Outlook, 1903.

Long, Margaret, ed. *The Journal of John D. Long.* Ringe, N.H.: Richard R. Smith, 1956.

Maclay, Edgar Stanton. *A History of the United States Navy from 1775 to 1901.* New York: Appleton, 1901.

————. *Life and Adventures of "Jack" Philip, Rear Admiral United States Navy.* New York: Baker & Taylor, 1903.

Madariaga, Salvador de. *Spain: A Modern History.* New York: Praeger, 1958.

Mahan, Alfred Thayer. *From Sail to Steam: Recollections of a Naval Life.* New York: Harper, 1907.

————. *Influence of Sea Power upon History 1670–1783.* Boston: Little, Brown, 1890.

————. *Interest of America in Sea Power, Present and Future.* New York: Houghton Mifflin, 1890.

————. *Lessons of the War with Spain.* . . . Boston: Little, Brown, 1899.

Mañach, Jorge. *Martí: Apostle of Freedom.* New York: Devin-Adair, 1950.

May, Ernest R. *Imperial Democracy: The Emergence of America as a Great Power.* New York: Harcourt Brace, 1961.

Mayo, Lawrence Shaw. *America of Yesterday: As Reflected in the Journal of John Davis Long.* . . . Boston: Atlantic Monthly Press, 1923.

[McKinley, William]. *Speeches and Addresses of William McKinley, 1893–1900.* New York: Doubleday, 1900.

Miles, Nelson A. *Serving the Republic: Memoirs of the Civil and Military Life of General Nelson A. Miles.* . . . New York: Harper, 1911.

Miley, John D. *In Cuba with Shafter.* New York: Scribner's, 1899.

Millett, Allan R. *Semper Fidelis: The History of the United States Marine Corps.* New York: Macmillan, 1980.

Millis, Walter. *The Martial Spirit.* Boston: Literary Guild, 1931.

Morgan, H. Wayne. *America's Road to Empire: The War with Spain and Overseas Expansion.* New York: John Wiley, 1965.

———. *From Hayes to McKinley: National Party Politics, 1877–1896.* Syracuse, N.Y.: Syracuse University Press, 1969.

———, ed. *Making Peace with Spain: The Diary of Whitelaw Reid, September–December, 1898.* Austin: University of Texas Press, 1965.

———. *William McKinley and His America.* Syracuse, N.Y.: Syracuse University Press, 1963.

Morison, Elting E., ed. *The Letters of Theodore Roosevelt.* Vols. 1–2. Cambridge, Mass.: Harvard University Press, 1951.

Morris, Edmund. *The Rise of Theodore Roosevelt.* New York: Coward, McCann, 1979.

Moynihan, James H. *The Life of Archbishop John Ireland.* New York: Harper, 1953.

Musicant, Ivan. *The Banana Wars: A History of United States Military Intervention in Latin America. . . .* New York: Macmillan, 1990.

———. *U.S. Armored Cruisers: A Design and Operational History.* Annapolis, Md.: Naval Institute Press, 1985.

Nevins, Allan. *Grover Cleveland: A Study in Courage.* New York: Dodd, Mead, 1962.

———. ed. *Letters of Grover Cleveland.* Boston: Houghton Mifflin, 1933.

Nofi, Albert A. *The Spanish-American War, 1898.* Conshohocken, Pa.: Combined Books, 1996.

Olcott, Charles S. *The Life of William McKinley.* 2 vols. Boston: Houghton Mifflin, 1916.

Palmer, Frederick. *Bliss, Peacemaker: The Life and Letters of Tasker Howard Bliss.* New York: Dodd, Mead, 1934.

Parker, George F. *Recollections of Grover Cleveland.* New York: Century, 1909.

Parker, John H. *History of the Gatling Gun Detachment. . . .* Kansas City: Hudson-Kimberly, 1898.

Perkins, Dexter. *A History of the Monroe Doctrine.* Boston: Little, Brown, 1955.

Post, Charles Johnson. *The Little War of Private Post.* Boston: Little, Brown, 1960.

Pratt, Julius W. *Expansionists of 1898: The Acquisition of Hawaii and the Spanish Islands.* Baltimore: Johns Hopkins Press, 1936.

Prego, Louis. *The Battles of San Juan and El Caney.* Santiago de Cuba: Beltran, 1911.

Pringle, Henry F. *Theodore Roosevelt.* New York: Harcourt, 1931.

Puleston, W. D. *Mahan: The Life and Work of Captain Alfred Thayer Mahan, USN.* New Haven, Conn.: Yale University Press, 1939.

Reilly, John C., and Robert L. Scheina. *American Battleships 1886–1923: Predreadnought Design and Construction.* Annapolis, Md.: Naval Institute Press, 1980.

Reynolds, Clark G. *Famous American Admirals.* New York: Van Nostrand, 1978.

Rhodes, James Ford. *The McKinley and Roosevelt Administrations 1897–1909.* New York: Macmillan, 1922.

Richardson, Leon B. *William E. Chandler: Republican.* New York: Dodd, Mead, 1940.

Rodman, Hugh. *Yarns of a Kentucky Admiral.* Indianapolis: Bobbs-Merrill, 1928.

Roosevelt, Theodore. *An Autobiography.* New York: Scribner's, 1913.

———. *The Rough Riders.* New York: Scribner's, 1926.

Roseboom, Eugene H. *A History of Presidential Elections.* New York: Macmillan, 1957.

Rubens, Horatio. *Liberty: The Story of Cuba.* New York: Brewer, 1932.

Sargent, Herbert H. *The Campaign of Santiago de Cuba.* 3 vols. New York: Books for Libraries Press, 1970.

Sargent, Nathan. *Admiral Dewey and the Manila Campaign.* Washington: Naval Historical Foundation, 1947.

Schley, Winfield Scott. *Forty-five Years under the Flag.* New York: Appleton, 1904.

Schofield, John M. *Forty-six Years in the Army.* New York: Century, 1897.

Seager, Robert II. *Alfred Thayer Mahan: The Man and His Letters.* Annapolis, Md.: Naval Institute Press, 1977.

Selections from the Correspondence of Theodore Roosevelt and Henry Cabot Lodge 1884–1918. Vol. 1. New York: Scribner's, 1925.

Sigsbee, Charles D. *The* Maine: *An Account of Her Destruction in Havana Harbor.* New York: Century, 1899.

Socolofsky, Homer E., and Allan B. Spetter. *The Presidency of Benjamin Harrison.* Lawrence, Kans.: University Press of Kansas, 1987.

Spector, Ronald. *Admiral of the New Empire: The Life and Career of George Dewey.* Baton Rouge: Louisiana State University Press, 1974.

Sprout, Harold, and Margaret Sprout. *The Rise of American Naval Power 1776–1918.* Princeton: Princeton University Press, 1942.

Steward, Theophilus G. *The Colored Regulars in the United States Army.* New York: Arno, 1969.

Summers, Festus P., ed. *The Cabinet Diary of William L. Wilson 1896–1897.* Chapel Hill, N.C.: University of North Carolina Press, 1957.

Thayer, William Roscoe. *Life and Letters of John Hay.* 2 vols. Boston: Houghton Mifflin, 1915.

Thomas, Hugh. *Cuba: Or the Pursuit of Freedom.* London: Eyre, 1971.

Through the War by Camera. New York: Pearson, 1898.

Turner, Frederick Jackson. *The Frontier in American History.* New York: Henry Holt, 1920.

Vandiver, Frank E. *Black Jack: The Life and Times of John J. Pershing.* Vol. 1. College Station, Tex.: Texas A & M University Press, 1977.

Walker, Asa. "The Battle of Manila Bay." In *Papers of the Military Society of Massachusetts.* Vol. 12, *Naval Actions and History.* Boston: Griffith, 1902.

Weigley, Russell F. *History of the United States Army.* New York: Macmillan, 1984.

Welch, Richard E. *The Presidencies of Grover Cleveland.* Lawrence, Kans.: University Press of Kansas, 1988.

West, Richard S., Jr. *Admirals of American Empire.* Indianapolis: Bobbs-Merrill, 1948.

Westcott, Allan, ed. *American Sea Power since 1775.* Chicago: Lippincott, 1947.

Weyler y Nicolau, Valeriano. *Mi Mando en Cuba.* 5 vols. Madrid: Gonzales Rojas, 1910.

White, Trumbull. *Pictorial History of Our War with Spain. . . .* Chicago: Freedom, 1898.

Wilkerson, Marcus M. *Public Opinion and the Spanish-American War: A Study in War Propaganda.* New York: Russell, 1932.

Wilson, Herbert W. *The Downfall of Spain: Naval History of the Spanish-American War.* New York: Burt Franklin (reprint edition), 1971.

Wisan, Joseph E. *The Cuban Crisis as Reflected in the New York Press (1895–1898).* New York: Octagon, 1965.

Wooster, Robert. *Nelson A. Miles: And the Twilight of the Frontier Army.* Lincoln, Nebr.: University of Nebraska Press, 1993.

Periodicals
"Abstract Log of the *Cristóbal Colón.*" *Proceedings* of the United States Naval Institute, December 1898.

Auxier, George W. "Middle Western Newspapers and the Spanish-American War." *Mississippi Valley Historical Review,* March 1940.

———. "The Propaganda Activities of the Cuban *Junta* in Precipitation of the Spanish-American War, 1895–1898." *Hispanic American Historical Review,* May 1939.

Bailey, Thomas A. "Dewey and the Germans at Manila Bay." *American Historical Review,* October 1939.

Bashkina, N. "A Page from the Cuban People's Heroic History." *International Affairs* (Moscow), March 1964.

Beck, Earl R. "The Martínez Campos Government of 1879: Spain's Last Chance in Cuba." *Hispanic American Historical Review,* May 1976.

Calkins, Carlos Gilman. "Historical and Professional Notes on the Naval Campaign of Manila Bay in 1898." *Proceedings* of the United States Naval Institute, June 1899.

Capehart, Edward E. "The Mine Defense of Santiago Harbor." *Proceedings* of the United States Naval Institute, December 1898.

Chamberlin, Joseph E. "How the Spaniards Fought at Caney." *Scribner's,* September 1898.

Cluverius, W. T. "A Midshipman on the *Maine.*" *Proceedings* of the United States Naval Institute, February 1918.

de Saint Hubert, Christian, and Carlos Alfaro Zaforteza. "The Spanish Navy of 1898." *Warship International,* no. 1, 1980, no. 3, 1981.

Eggert, Gerald G. "Our Man in Havana: Fitzhugh Lee." *Hispanic American Historical Review,* November 1967.

Ellicott, John M. "The Defenses of Manila Bay." *Proceedings* of the United States Naval Institute, June 1900.

———. "Effect of Gun-Fire, Battle of Manila Bay, May 1, 1898." *Proceedings* of the United States Naval Institute, June 1899.

———. "The Naval Battle of Manila." *Proceedings* of the United States Naval Institute, September 1900.

Grenville, John A. S. "American Naval Preparations for War with Spain, 1896–1898." *Journal of American Studies* 2(1968).

Herbert, Hilary A. "A Plea for the Navy." *Forum,* September 1897.

J[acobsen]. "Sketches from the Spanish-American War." *Proceedings* of the United States Naval Institute, 1899.

King, Clarence. "Fire and Sword in Cuba." *Forum,* September 1896.

Lee, Arthur A. "The Regulars at El Caney." *Scribner's,* October 1898.

Mahan, Alfred Thayer. "Naval Education." *Proceedings* of the United States Naval Institute, 1879.

Mendez, Alfred F. "Admiral Antonio Eulate." *Hispanic American Historical Review,* September 1933.

Miles, Nelson A. "The War with Spain." *North American Review,* May, June, July, 1899.

Müller, José. "Battles and Capitulation of Santiago de Cuba." *Proceedings* of the United States Naval Institute, 1899.

Pratt, Julius W. "The 'Large Policy' of 1898." *Mississippi Valley Historical Review,* September 1932.

Roosevelt, Theodore. "The Influence of Sea Power upon History." *Atlantic Monthly,* October 1890.

Sampson, William T. "The Atlantic Fleet in the Spanish War." *Century Magazine,* April 1899.

Shafter, William R. "The Capture of Santiago de Cuba." *Century Illustrated Monthly Magazine,* February 1899.

Sigsbee, Charles D. "My Story of the *Maine.*" *Cosmopolitan Magazine,* July 1912.

———. "Personal Narrative of the *Maine.*" *Century Magazine,* November 1898.

Spears, John R. "The Chase of Cervera." *Scribner's Magazine,* August 1898.

Stickney, Joseph L. "With Dewey at Manila." *Harper's New Monthly Magazine,* February 1899.

"The Story of the Captains: Personal Narratives of the Naval Engagement near Santiago de Cuba . . . by Officers of the American Fleet." *Century Illustrated Monthly Magazine,* May 1899.

Williams, Leonard. "The Army of Spain: Its Present Qualities and Modern Value." *Journal of the Military Service Institution of the United States* 21 (September 1897).

Williams, William Appleman. "The Frontier Thesis and American Foreign Policy." *Pacific Historical Review,* November 1955.

Newspapers
Army and Navy Journal, 1898–1899.

New York Herald, various issues, 1897, 1899.

New York Times, various issues, 1897–1899.

New York *World,* various issues, 1897–1899.

Washington Post, various issues, 1897–1899.

INDEX

Abarzuza, Buenaventura, 599, 623
Abarzuza laws, 50, 51, 52, 73
Adams, Henry, 3
Adams, John Quincy, 78
Adee, Alvey A., 97, 104, 133, 134
Agoncillo, Felipe, 605–6
Aguadores, Battle of, 426–27
Aguinaldo, Emilio, 584, 587, 605, 630, 653
  government formation, 567
  independence following Spanish defeat,
    expectation of, 547–49, 550, 590–91
  Manila campaign, 197–98, 551, 554–55,
    562
  war against Spanish occupation, 197
Aibonito, Battle of, 537–38
Alamo (U.S. steamer), 394
Aldrich, Nelson, 172
Alfonso XII, King, 40
Alfonso XII (Spanish cruiser), 126, 137,
  140, 321, 322, 483
Alfonso XIII, King, 52
Alger, Russell, 113, 177, 188, 250, 595
  appointment to War Department, 98
  Army, U.S.
    mobilization planning, 239, 242
    preparedness shortcomings, 257, 259,
      264
    readiness program, 160, 161, 162
    volunteer army, creation of, 243, 247
  beef scandal, 637, 640, 653
  Camp Wikoff, 649
  Cervera squadron, U.S. fears regarding,
    297
  Cuba campaign
    U.S. strategic planning, 252–53, 254,
      256, 257
    westward march of combined U.S.-
      Cuban forces, proposed, 265
  Dodge Commission, 632–33
  Eagan's court-martial, 638

Manila campaign, 260, 543
  medical scandal, 645
  Miles's relationship with, 237, 634
  personal qualities, 237
  Philippines' annexation by United States,
    590
  Puerto Rico campaign, 519, 520, 523–
    24, 525–26, 527, 535, 539, 540
  resignation of, 652–54
  Santiago campaign, 396
    abandonment of Santiago, Spanish
      offer regarding, 484, 491–92
    attack on Santiago, preparations for,
      478, 484–85
    decision to undertake, 264
    disease problem, 361, 513–14
    dispatches to and from Washington,
      429–31
    "forcing the harbor" issue, 492, 494–95
    Miles's role as de facto commander,
      494, 495
    return of troops to United States, 513–
      14, 647, 649
    San Juan heights, battle for, 412–13, 414
    surrender demands, 487
    surrender negotiations, 493, 496, 500
    transport shipping for, 470
  War Department mismanagement, blame
    for, 631–32, 651–52
Algerism, 632
Alicante (Spanish hospital ship), 293, 295
Allen, U.S. Captain, 316
Allen, Charles, 597
Allen, Captain Leven, 420–22
Allen, Lieutenant William H., 330, 331, 335
Alliança affair, 81–82
Almirante Abreu (Brazilian cruiser), 159
Almirante Oquendo (Spanish cruiser), 127,
  279, 280, 284, 285, 289, 291, 295,
  320, 327, 435

717

volunteer army
 camps for, 645–47
 creation of, 189, 243–49

Wachusett (U.S. screw-sloop), 6, 13, 332
Wagner, Major Arthur, 369, 397
Wainwright, Lieutenant Commander
  Richard, 102, 127–28, 139, 140,
  147, 454, 455–56, 457, 529
Wake Island, 627
Walker, Commander Asa, 194, 199, 214,
  215, 216, 217, 219, 220
Walker, Edwin, 25, 26
Wall Street Journal, 165
War Department, U.S.
 administrative and technical bureaus,
  236–37
 Alger's appointment as secretary, 98
 beef scandal, 634–40
 Camp Wikoff, 647–50
 medical scandal, 640–45
 mismanagement charge against, 631–34,
  651–52
 Subsistence Department, 635
 system of authority, 634
 volunteer camps, 645–47
 see also Army, U.S.
Washington Evening Star, 84, 145
Washington Post, 33–34, 546
Washington Star, 184
Wasp (U.S. armed yacht), 524, 529, 531
Watson, Commodore John, 468, 482, 483
Weaver, General James B., 17, 18
Wells, Private Ogden, 356, 376
Weston, Colonel John, 635–36
Weyler y Nicolau, Captain General Valeri-
  ano, 53, 108
 background of, 67–68
 Cuban insurrection of 1895, 67, 68–72,
  74–75, 77
Wheeler, General Joseph, 269, 395, 396,
  397, 427, 428, 429, 469, 492, 496,
  498, 503, 649
 Daiquirí landing, 362, 368
 Las Guásimas, Battle of, 375–76, 378,
  379, 380, 381, 385, 386, 387
 San Juan heights, battle for, 416, 423–24
White, Andrew D., 558, 559, 564, 600
Whitney, Lieutenant Henry, 527
Whitney, William C., 13
Whittier, Lieutenant Colonel Charles, 577,
  578

Wikoff, Colonel Charles, 413, 414
Wilcox, Willis, 584
Wildes, Captain Frank, 200
Wildman, Rounseville, 233, 547, 550, 564,
  572
Wilhelm, Kaiser, 10
Williams, Oscar, 193, 194–95, 200–201,
  202, 203, 204, 229, 546, 584
Wilmington (U.S. gunboat), 304
Wilson, Agriculture Secretary, 590
Wilson, Herbert, 209
Wilson, Major General James H., 529,
  532, 534, 536, 537
Wilson, William, 86
Winder, Lieutenant William, 216
Windom (U.S. Revenue cutter), 305
Winslow (U.S. torpedo boat), 304
Wompatuck (U.S. tug), 309, 310, 364, 366
Wood, Commander Edward, 197, 219, 228
Wood, Colonel Leonard, 168, 273, 274,
  357, 376, 410, 411, 634
 Las Guásimas, Battle of, 379, 380, 381,
  382, 383, 384, 385, 386, 387
 military governorship of Santiago, 509–
  11
Woodford, Stewart L., 108, 118, 131, 134,
  135–36, 152, 156–57, 159, 166–67,
  170–71, 173, 176–77, 178, 179,
  180, 182, 183, 188, 189, 517
 appointment as ambassador to Spain,
  106–7
World's Columbian Exposition, 3
World War I, 10
World War II, 657
Worth, U.S. Lieutenant Colonel, 414

Yale (U.S. armed liner), 305, 314, 319,
  326, 328, 470, 474, 487, 521, 523,
  524, 525, 526
Yankee (U.S. cruiser), 347, 350
Yauco operation, 529
yellow fever, 56, 258, 484, 488, 511, 512,
  641
Young, Lieutenant Charles, 246
Young, Brigadier General Samuel, 376,
  378, 379, 380, 381–82, 383, 384,
  385, 654
Yucatán (U.S. transport), 274, 353, 354,
  355, 364, 368, 514

Zafiro (U.S. steamer), 198–99, 230, 556–
  57, 575